The Baha Mousa Public Inquiry Report

Chairman: Sir William Gage

Volume III

Presented to Parliament pursuant to Section 26 of the Inquiries Act 2005
Ordered by the House of Commons to be printed on 8 September 2011

HC 1452–III   LONDON: THE STATIONERY OFFICE   £155.00

Three volumes not be sold separately

Volume III – Parts X to XVII and Summary

Part XIV

Part XV

Part XVI

Part XVII

Summary

Part X

Handovers and 1 Black Watch

Chapter 1: Introduction

10.1   Evidence from members of Op Telic 2 Battlegroups including, but not limited to 1 Queen's Lancashire Regiment (1QLR), demonstrated that a practice of hooding detainees continued in the early part of Op Telic 2. This was so despite the oral order from Maj Gen Robin Brims, General Officer Commanding (GOC) 1 (UK) Div during Op Telic 1 which had prohibited hooding, and the further written order FRAGO 152 which had prohibited covering detainees' faces. It will be remembered from Part IX of this Report that FRAGO 152 was issued on 20 May 2003. It included an annex which provided renewed guidance on the detention of civilians, drafted by Lt Col Nicholas Mercer. The FRAGO referred to a number of civilian deaths in custody and reiterated the principles of the use of minimum force, delivery of detainees to the Royal Military Police (RMP) as soon as it was possible to do so, and treating detainees with humanity and dignity. It also included the direction that *"Under no circumstances should their faces be covered as this might impair breathing"*.[1]

10.2   As the evidence set out in this Part of the Report demonstrates, a significant number of leading personnel at Division, Brigade and Battlegroup level during Op Telic 2 were not aware of the ban on hooding and nor, it seems, at handovers did they receive guidance or direction in matters of detail concerning prisoner handling. Most significantly, the Op Telic 1 orders prohibiting hooding were not followed by 1 QLR.

10.3   Some have described this as a loss of "corporate knowledge" within the UK Armed Forces between the Op Telic 1 and Op Telic 2 phases of operations in Iraq. That is, however, in my opinion an oversimplification. There was not a wholesale failure in the prohibition on hooding being handed over between the Op Telic 1 and Op Telic 2 formations, since some soldiers who deployed during Op Telic 2 were aware of the prohibition. Moreover, to describe the shortcomings in the handover as a loss of corporate knowledge assumes that relevant staff officers and Battlegroup postholders in Op Telic 1 knew of the prohibition on hooding. In fact the evidence shows that a significant number of staff officers deployed on Op Telic 1 did not become aware of the prohibition on hooding, and for this reason could not hand it over to their successors.

10.4   The picture that has emerged is that there was only patchy knowledge of the prohibition on hooding resulting from the handover from Op Telic 1 formations to their successors in Op Telic 2. In examining this picture it is convenient to look from the top down at Divisional, Brigade and Battlegroup levels.

---

[1] MOD017063

10.5   The handover between formations was organised in what I understand to be the conventional way, namely that the Battlegroups handed over first, followed by Brigade, and finally Division. This arrangement was obviously designed to avoid the confusion that would result from all formations replacing each other at exactly the same time. It had the advantage that the incoming Battlegroups came under the command, albeit for a brief period, of the existing headquarters in theatre. Similarly, the incoming Brigade came under command of the existing in-theatre Divisional Headquarters. It follows that once the new Division had taken over, it would assume command of Brigades and Battlegroups which were already established and functioning on the ground. For Op Telic 1 and Op Telic 2, the relevant dates of these handovers were as follows.

10.6   At Battlegroup level 1 QLR assumed command from 1 Black Watch (BW) after a handover which took place over 25 to 27 June 2003. The formal flag change occurred on 27 June 2003.[2] 19 Mech Bde assumed responsibility for Basra from 7 Armd Bde on 4 July 2003.[3] At Divisional level the handover occurred between 10 and 12 July 2003.[4]

10.7   There was some inconsistency at Divisional level as to whether officers referred to their posts and branches with the prefix "J" or "G". The "J" denotes a Joint Service Headquarters whereas a "G" denotes a single Service post. Certainly in Op Telic 2, the Divisional Headquarters was technically a Joint Service Headquarters because it was involved in, for example, training the Iraqi navy. Nothing turns on this point. However, purely for ease of comparison, save in direct quotations, I shall refer to the Divisional posts and branches as "J" and those at Brigade as G.

---

[2] MOD011054; MOD030935
[3] MOD011054; MOD030935
[4] Lamb BMI04908, paragraph 2; Wall BMI04509, paragraph 13; MOD015209

Chapter 2: Divisional Level

10.8 At Divisional level between 1 (UK) Div and 3 (UK) Div there is evidence that the prohibition on hooding and/or FRAGO 152 was handed over at least to some of the incoming officers. However, the prohibition on hooding was not by any means universally understood within 1 (UK) Div and nor was the issue of prisoner handling accorded any special priority as a subject for handover.

The Divisional Commanders

10.9 The GOC 1 (UK) Div, at the time of the handover to 3 (UK) Div, was Maj Gen Peter Wall. He had taken over as GOC from Brims on about 12 or 13 May 2003.[5] Before that date Wall had been in regular telephone contact with Brims because he had held the post of Chief of Staff at the National Contingent Command (NCC) Headquarters until April 2003. From his work in that post, Wall was aware of the issues that had been raised at the Joint Field Interrogation Team (JFIT) in relation to the hooding of detainees and that the International Committee of the Red Cross (ICRC) had been involved in these issues.[6] However, Wall was not aware at the time of Brims' oral order banning hooding although he was aware that Air Marshal Brian Burridge had ordered that hooding should cease.[7] Wall remembered that during the handover from Brims, the issue of prisoner handling was not discussed at all.[8] Brims' evidence was consistent with this; he said that to his knowledge he never talked to Wall about prisoner of war handling as "...*it simply was not a major issue at the time*".[9]

10.10 It was, therefore, not surprising that Wall said in evidence that he was unlikely to have included prisoner handling as a topic for discussion during his own handover to Maj Gen Graeme Lamb the GOC of 3 (UK) Div. Prisoner handling was "...*not on the radar*" and he was under the impression that "...*the system was working as it should*".[10] His understanding was that the issue of prisoner handling would have been dealt with during the handover by the provost staff, the legal staff and possibly the J3 (Operations) staff officers.[11]

10.11 Wall also said that he had no knowledge of the practice of hooding being applied by troops on the ground. For this reason he had no direct knowledge of the issue to prompt a handover of information or procedures about the use of hoods.[12]

---

[5] Wall BMI04509, paragraph 13
[6] Wall BMI04508-9, paragraph 11
[7] Wall BMI 97/133/17-135/17
[8] Wall BMI04510, paragraph 16
[9] Brims BMI07403, paragraph 75
[10] Wall BMI04525, paragraph 64
[11] Wall BMI04526, paragraph 65
[12] Wall BMI 97/96/11-97/11

10.12   Lamb agreed. He told the Inquiry that prisoner handling and detainee issues were not raised during the handover he received from Wall. Lamb had not expected those issues to be discussed and would have been surprised if they were. The handover principally concerned matters at a general strategic level, and did not touch on matters such as prisoner handling unless there was a particular problem.[13] Lamb was not made aware of FRAGO 152 during this handover nor was he aware of any other order prohibiting hooding.[14] He told the Inquiry that in fact this was not necessarily the sort of information of which he would have expected his Chief of Staff to make him aware.[15]

10.13   Lamb said that he did not know what arrangements were in place to ensure that the 1 (UK) Div orders were handed over to 3 (UK) Div. Understandably, Lamb stated that he would not have read through all 1 (UK) Div orders himself. He thought that the Chief of Staff of 3 (UK) Div would be better placed to answer how this would occur.[16]

10.14   The 1 (UK) Div Chief of Staff was Col Patrick Marriott. He told the Inquiry that the handover to his counterpart Chief of Staff from 3 (UK) Div, Col Richard Barrons, would only have included a briefing on matters of general concern. He understood that individual staff branches would be responsible for particular FRAGOs. They would therefore have been responsible for handing orders over to the respective incoming staff. He thought that FRAGO 152 would have been dealt with by the J2 branch handover.[17] Marriott was fully aware of the issues surrounding the use of hooding at the JFIT and the oral order issued by Brims to prohibit the practice.[18]

10.15   Barrons' evidence was generally consistent with Marriott's account.   He said that within a Divisional staff handover he would have expected individual staff branches to handover existing orders to their successors, "…*so that everyone was quite clear what the extant set of instructions were and where to find them*".[19] As Chief of Staff he would have expected the heads of various staff branches to provide him with documents as and when he needed them.[20]

10.16   However, although the two Divisional Chiefs of Staff agreed that the individual staff branches would be responsible for orders and matters of detail during handover, Barrons did have a vague recollection of a discussion he had during the handover from Marriott in which he thought it was possible that Marriott discussed prisoner handling with him. Barrons remembered, albeit vaguely, a conversation in which Marriott mentioned that hooding was banned. It arose in the context of a discussion about deaths in custody and the Camp Breadbasket incident.   However, he did not remember Marriott mentioning the differences of opinion between different staff officers and formations during Op Telic 1 as to whether hooding should be banned. Barrons said he did not see the written order, FRAGO 152, itself.[21]

---

[13] Lamb BMI 103/91/7-19; Lamb BMI04916, paragraph 25
[14] Lamb BMI04916, paragraph 27
[15] Lamb BMI 103/91/20-92/14
[16] Lamb BMI04916, paragraph 26
[17] Marriott BMI06138, paragraphs 46-48
[18] Marriott BMI06131-4, paragraphs 20-26
[19] Barrons BMI 99/104/14-105/7
[20] Barrons BMI06224, paragraph 23
[21] Barrons BMI 99/105/12-106/12

10.17 Barrons accepted that he personally did not do anything to make sure that the prohibition on hooding, to which he had been alerted, was brought to the attention of those units and sub-units within 3 (UK) Div being deployed on Op Telic 2. He explained, "… *I don't believe that at the time there was any sense that it was an issue that was in doubt or needed reaffirming*".[22]

10.18 During his evidence Barrons expanded on an analysis suggested by Counsel to the Inquiry that the knowledge of Op Telic 2 soldiers would have been dependent on a number of factors. He said:

> "A…*There are three parts to this particular aspect. The first is that the order should have been conveyed to all members of Op Telic 1, as you say; secondly, that during the handover between the incoming 19 Brigade and the outgoing 7 Brigade, at all levels of the chain of command down to company level there should have been a handover of those instructions; thirdly, key pieces of information like that should have formed part of the pre-deployment training for 19 Brigade in that the in place force, 7 Brigade, should communicate that sort of thing back to the UK training machine to make sure that the appropriate training occurs before deployment.*"[23]

10.19 Barrons' explanation in this regard specified three routes by which an adequate handover of knowledge might have been achieved: pre-deployment training, Brigade level handovers and Battlegroup level handovers. However, it should not be forgotten that a similar horizontal transfer of knowledge should have occurred at Divisional level between 1 (UK) Div and 3 (UK) Div.

10.20 At Deputy Chief of Staff level, the 1 (UK) Div Deputy Chief of Staff was Col Andrew Cowling. He gave an account in his Inquiry witness statement that in general terms the handover would have involved detailed written briefs and discussions. During his oral evidence Cowling confirmed that he had never been aware of an order banning hooding.[24]

10.21 Cowling's own handover focused on logistical issues, not prisoner handling, albeit he could not now remember the specifics of the handover. He was confident that a document such as FRAGO 152 would have been handed over to the incoming units, but he was not aware who was responsible for doing this.[25] He would have expected staff officers at SO2 level to sit down with the future incumbent of the post and hand over the relevant "activities", including FRAGOs.[26]

10.22 Col Barry Le Grys was Cowling's counterpart at 3 (UK) Div. He said in his Inquiry witness statement that although he received a briefing and documents on handover, he did not remember FRAGO 152 or any other order relating to hooding. He said that he would have only read orders to the extent that they were relevant to his sphere of responsibility.[27]

---

[22] Barrons BMI 99/111/19-112/4
[23] Barrons BMI 99/111/6-18
[24] Cowling BMI 70/15/21-16/19; Cowling BMI07167, paragraph 43
[25] Cowling BMI07170, paragraphs 56-57
[26] Cowling BMI 70/19/19-22/1
[27] Le Grys BMI03759-60, paragraphs 19-22

10.23   Since neither Lamb nor Le Grys were made aware of the prohibition on hooding, they can hardly be criticised personally for failing to take action in respect of it. In the case of Barrons, I accept his evidence that he had a vague recollection of a prohibition on hooding. This is consistent with the fact that Marriott, his predecessor, had been involved in the issue during Op Telic 1.

10.24   The question arises as to whether Barrons should have taken further action such as re-issuing an order prohibiting hooding or ensuring by other means that the incoming UK Brigade and its Battlegroups were aware of it. I shall return to more general and corporate criticisms of the way in which prisoner handling was addressed in the handover process. As to Barrons' personal performance and conduct, I conclude that although the prohibition on hooding was mentioned to him there was nothing to suggest to him that this required immediate action. I accept that it was not raised as a particular matter of current concern for him. With the pressure of dealing with a multinational Division and its coordination both internally and with the United States led coalition, Barrons would have had a huge amount on which to focus. It was not unreasonable for him to believe that this prohibition would have been handed over "horizontally" from Brigade to Brigade and Battlegroup to Battlegroup, as well as from relevant 1 (UK) Div staff officers to the staff officers within 3 (UK) Div. Barrons was an impressive witness, measured and convincing in the account that he gave. With the benefit of hindsight, it is apparent that it would have been beneficial for an order prohibiting hooding to have been re-issued for the benefit of the incoming Op Telic 2 forces. However, I do not consider that Barrons was personally at fault for not taking this course. There is insufficient evidence of any concerns about hooding, or wider concerns about prisoner handling coming to Barrons' attention, to justify such a criticism of his personal conduct.

Divisional J3 (Operations) Branch

10.25   Maj Justin Maciejewski was the J3 Operations Staff Officer at 1 (UK) Div. He handed over to Maj Simon Hulme SO2 J3. His handover concerned current operations and problems that the occupation was facing. He did not remember the topic of handling detainees featuring during the handover. He did not personally handover any FRAGOs to Hulme; this would have been done at the level of Captain.[28] Maciejewski did, however, know that hooding had been an issue, and although he was not aware of a specific oral order from Brims, he said that he was aware of FRAGO 152.[29]

Divisional J3 (Training and Plans) Branch

10.26   Maciejewski worked alongside Maj Douglas Chalmers, SO2 and head of J3 Plans, the lead Planning Officer for 1 (UK) Div.[30] Chalmers did not give evidence to the Inquiry. Capt Benedict Ryan was the SO3 J3 Plans within 1 (UK) Div. His Inquiry witness statement explained that the function of J3 Plans was to deal with future operational planning. It worked closely with the J3 Operations Branch, headed by Maciejewski, which was generally responsible for the implementation of the plans.[31] Ryan stated that his handover (to a Canadian officer, whose name he was unable

---

[28] Maciejewski BMI04130, paragraph 58
[29] Maciejewski BMI04125-7, paragraphs 42-46
[30] Maciejewski BMI04114, paragraph 7
[31] Ryan BMI02791, paragraphs 28-29

to remember), would not have covered prisoner handling and treatment, as this was not something for which his post was responsible. He thought that this kind of information would have been covered during the handover between other branches, in particular, the Legal Branch.[32]

10.27   Capt Antony Pearce was the SO3 J3 Training and Plans at 3 (UK) Div. He remembered receiving a handover from Ryan. Pearce described the handover as *"generalist"* in nature and that it did not cover specific operations. He also drew a distinction between plans and operations; the current operations desk would have had responsibility for taking over existing orders, whereas the plans cell worked on future orders. Pearce did not remember FRAGO 152.[33]

10.28   Although Chalmers did not give evidence to the Inquiry, his 3 (UK) Div replacement did. Lt Col James Murray-Playfair held the role of Chief J5 Plans at 3 (UK) Div; but due to the changes associated with Op Telic 2's transition to a multi national headquarters, this was not a precise replication of Chalmers' role.

10.29   Murray-Playfair gave the following explanation of his role and the branch designations applied during Op Telic 2 at Divisional level, describing the difference between the Operations and Training, and Planning Branches:[34]

> 5.   As plans developed for 3 Div HQ's deployment, I was asked by the Chief of Staff ("COS"), Colonel Barrons, to assume the operational role of Chief J5 Plans, a joint appointment responsible for planning of the campaign and specific divisional operations in Iraq. I therefore held specific major responsibilities for planning of the campaign in Iraq and for the reform of the Iraqi security sector (i.e. Army, Navy and Police forces), which were non existent on our arrival. In this post I was not responsible for the conduct of operations, which were managed by J3. I held no specific responsibility for prisoner handling, standards of treatment or tactical questioning. In response to the Inquiry's reference to my working in both J5 and G3, I should point out that the J prefix is used to identify posts in a Joint HQ and G is used to describe single service posts. The service branch naming convention allocates the number 3 to cover Operations and Training while the number 5 is allocated to Plans. In UK I worked in G3 (Training) in a solely Army HQ in peacetime, working on training issues. In Iraq I worked in J5, as a joint planner (we were redesigning the Iraqi Navy as well as the Army). In Iraq I had no responsibility for the conduct of operations since I did not work in the G3 or J3 branch.

10.30   Murray-Playfair told the Inquiry that he met Chalmers during the reconnaissance period in June 2003 and received a handover briefing in relation to recent operations conducted by 1 (UK) Div. During this handover he would have received files containing

---

[32] Ryan BMI02797-8, paragraphs 57-58
[33] Pearce BMI07284-5, paragraph 6
[34] Murray-Playfair BMI05488, paragraph 5

key documents, but he did not remember receiving any briefing on prisoner handling, nor would he have expected one from the Plans branch (J5), as this was an issue that was usually dealt with by J2 or J3.[35]

10.31　During his oral evidence, Murray-Playfair was asked about FRAGO 152. He said he had no recollection of having seen this order. He said he would have expected the important orders to be passed from 1 (UK) Div to 3 (UK) Div and from 7 Armd Bde to 19 Mech Bde to ensure that people were aware of the current standing operational procedures. He stated that as either G3 Training (his role before deployment) or as J5 (once in theatre) the handing over of relevant orders and possible re-issue of them was not any part of his role. He expected that *each individual would take ownership of the continuity of information in their policy lane*", and therefore, in relation to FRAGO 152, the staff branches concerned would be the Legal, J3, RMP and J2 branches.[36]

Divisional J2 (Intelligence) Branch

10.32　The J2 (Intelligence) Branch at 1 (UK) Div was led by Maj George Waters, the SO2 J2, and S002, the SO2 J2X. Waters had overall responsibility for intelligence matters within the division while S002 managed the HUMINT activities. Waters was not present in theatre at the time of the handover to his successor, Lt Col Graham Le Fevre, the SO1 J2 ISTAR at 3 (UK) Div.

10.33　Waters' evidence as to what he knew of the prohibition on hooding was that he remembered the meeting at which Brims the GOC had issued the oral order prohibiting hooding. He had not mentioned this in his Inquiry witness statement, but after reading other witnesses' accounts to this Inquiry he said he was confident it had occurred.[37] Waters was an excellent witness and I accept his evidence as truthful and accurate. Waters was also aware of FRAGO 152. When asked in oral evidence how he would have interpreted the phrase, "*Under no circumstances should their faces be covered as this might impair breathing*", he gave the unequivocal reply, "*Don't hood people*".[38]

10.34　Le Fevre's account was that he in fact had no direct predecessor, as the role in Op Telic 1 had changed from a warfighting footing to one of peace support. In the absence of Waters, who had by then left theatre, he received a handover from an Intelligence Corps officer, Capt Fiona Galbraith.[39] She had been the SO3 to Waters.[40] Le Fevre's evidence was that prisoner handling was not covered as part of this handover.[41] He had no recollection of either FRAGO 152 or any other order prohibiting the hooding of prisoners,[42] nor did he remember FRAGO 29 forming part of the handover.[43]

---

[35] Murray-Playfair BMI 86/220/4-18; Murray-Playfair BMI05489-90, paragraphs 9-13

[36] Murray-Playfair BMI 86/220/19-225/9

[37] Waters BMI 71/109/25-112/22

[38] Waters BMI 71/117/15-118/8

[39] Le Fevre BMI06545, paragraph 28

[40] Waters BMI02667, paragraph 22; Galbraith did not provide a witness statement to the Inquiry but she gave two witness statements to the SIB in September 2006 in connection with the Court Martial (MOD012166, MOD012728). They are not relevant to the Inquiry's purposes.

[41] Le Fevre BMI06545, paragraph 29

[42] Le Fevre BMI06546, paragraph 31

[43] Le Fevre BMI 85/14/1-7

10.35   Capt Andrew Haseldine, the SO3 J2 for 3 (UK) Div also received his handover from Galbraith. He had responsibility for coordinating the G2 branch under Le Fevre.[44] He was informed by Galbraith that he would have the responsibility for advising the 3 (UK) Div Chief of Staff of the ongoing intelligence value of the internees held at the Theatre Internment Facility (TIF). He did not, however, discuss prisoner handling policy, or a prohibition on the use of hoods or the covering of faces. He said his attention was not drawn to FRAGO 152. Galbraith did not mention to him anything concerning the ICRC visit to the JFIT or the debate about hooding.[45]

10.36   Haseldine said that he was not surprised that prisoner handling was not mentioned during his handover, as in his mind it was not within the remit of his post. When asked whether FRAGO 152 should have been mentioned in the handover process between staff officers, Haseldine's view was it certainly should have been mentioned between the senior legal officers, and the J3 Operations officers.[46]

10.37   Without criticising Haseldine, I observe that his evidence is an example of the pattern of staff officers accepting that the prohibition on hooding ought to have been handed over, but stating that the responsibility for doing so rested with a different branch in the headquarters or even with a different formation.

10.38   On the HUMINT side of the J2 branch, S002, the SO2 J2X for 1 (UK) Div conducted a direct handover with S015, the SO2 J2X for 3 (UK) Div. Despite the absence of a firm memory of doing so, S002 told the Inquiry that he believed he would have informed S015 about the issue of hooding at the JFIT; that they would have visited the JFIT together; and that he was sure S015 was informed of the no hooding rule.[47]

10.39   S015's evidence was not wholly consistent with that of S002. S015 said that he did not remember visiting the TIF as part of his handover. Also, he did not remember receiving FRAGO 152 and it was not covered during his handover. S015 already understood through his training that hooding was banned, but he said that this was reinforced on arrival in theatre. He did not remember S002 mentioning the ban on hooding, but stated it was possible that he had done so.[48] He did not remember whether any aspects of prisoner handling were addressed during handover. Moreover, he did not remember the controversy surrounding the ICRC concerns about the JFIT or the debate about the legality of hooding being raised during the handover. He stated that had those issues been canvassed they would "*very much*" have been the sort of thing he would have remembered: it was more likely than not that this was not mentioned.[49]

10.40   Although there were some aspects of both S002's and S015's evidence that I found problematic, on balance I found S015 to be the more reliable witness overall. While I think it is quite possible that S002 did mention the prohibition on hooding to S015, I think it unlikely that S002 detailed the background of the ICRC's concerns or the debate over the legality of hooding. I think it likely that S015 would have remembered this had it been explained. However, since S015 was already of the view from his training that prisoners should not be hooded, I consider that the omission of any explanation of the background to the prohibition on hooding by S002 did not have any real bearing on the issues with which the Inquiry is concerned.

---

[44] Haseldine BMI04599, paragraph 29

[45] Haseldine BMI 83/29/11-32/9; Haseldine BMI04600, paragraphs 36-37

[46] Haseldine BMI 83/30/7-31/17

[47] S002 BMI 82/138/7-22

[48] S015 BMI06523 paragraph 32; S015 BMI06527, paragraph 49

[49] S015 BMI 84/102/2-103/16

Divisional Legal Branch

10.41 It will be remembered that the senior legal officer at 1 (UK) Div was Lt Col Nicholas Mercer. On the handover to 3 (UK) Div, Mercer was replaced by Lt Col Charles Barnett. Mercer addressed the issue of the handover in his Inquiry witness statement, describing how during his handover to Barnett he expressed the view that *"the mistreatment of prisoners was the most serious issue in Theatre"*.[50]

10.42 Mercer wrote a set of handover notes for Barnett.[51] Those notes reflect many aspects of the role being transferred, such as the setting up of the courts, claims policies and the review of internment. But the notes also contained guidance under the heading *"Deaths In Custody"* alerting his successor to the fact that FRAGOs had been issued to Brigades concerning the treatment of civilians, and *"as a result of the further cases, a further FRAGO was issued which set out the procedures which had to be adopted upon the temporary detention of a civilian. This has been reduced into a card and is available for all troops"*.[52] In his supplementary statement, Mercer explained that the FRAGOs he was referring to in this memo were FRAGO 152, FRAGO 163, and FRAGO 29.[53]

10.43 During his oral evidence Mercer said that he understood that the incoming team had read all the FRAGOs issued by 1 (UK) Div. However, this understanding came later and not at the time of the handover itself. He only reached this understanding after being told by Barnett following the Court Martial proceedings, that he had read all FRAGOs written by HQ 1 (UK) Div (including FRAGO 152) before he arrived in theatre.[54]

10.44 Barnett confirmed that Mercer had given him a briefing and a file of documents on handover. He discussed, with Mercer, Brims' oral orders banning hooding and Mercer showed him a draft of a further order banning hooding which had been issued.[55] However, Barnett did not remember the same emphasis being placed on the issue of prisoner handling as described by Mercer, stating:

> *"I don't remember him saying it was the most important matter. It was an important matter but not the most important matter. It certainly was not the focus of our handover".*[56]

10.45 Barnett was already aware of FRAGO 152 and the fact that it reinforced the ban on hooding. He thought that *"therefore there was no requirement on my part to action any aspect in relation to hooding"*. Barnett's understanding of his responsibility on this point was fortified by his view that FRAGOs were regarded as binding on subsequent formations. His expectation was that the ban on hooding would have been part of the pre-deployment training for 19 Mech Bde units since the Brigade had been copied in on FRAGOs before they arrived in theatre. He expected this to have included FRAGO 152.[57]

---

[50] Mercer BMI04081, paragraph 95
[51] MOD052575
[52] MOD052579
[53] Mercer BMI06899, paragraph 13. I have addressed these orders in Part IX of this Report.
[54] Mercer BMI 68/145/2-16; Mercer BMI04081, paragraph 95
[55] Barnett BMI06615, paragraph 94
[56] Barnett BMI 86/41/17-25
[57] Barnett BMI06616, paragraph 95

10.46 Barnett also suggested that he would have expected detention and detainee handling issues to have been discussed in the handover between Provost branch, J2 Intelligence and J1.[58]

10.47 Also relevant to the handover between the legal staffs is the evidence of Capt Sian Ellis-Davies, the 3 (UK) Div SO3 Operational Law. At the time of the handover from 1 (UK) Div to 3 (UK) Div, there were no legal SO3s at 1 (UK) Div HQ. As a result Ellis-Davies did not receive a direct personal handover. However, she was present during some of the handover between Mercer and Barnett, and she also stated that Barnett passed on to her a lot of information that he had acquired from Mercer. In her Inquiry witness statement Ellis-Davies told the Inquiry that she could not remember any discussion of hooding, stress positions, conditioning, or any specific issues regarding prisoner handling.[59] In oral evidence however, she gave a slightly different account, in which she said that at some point in theatre she became aware of the fact that an order had been issued banning hooding. She was not able to pinpoint the time at which this information had become known to her.[60]

10.48 There are, in my view, some understandable differences of emphasis in the evidence of Barnett and Mercer. There is no doubt that Barnett was aware of both the prohibition on hooding, and of FRAGO 152. It is also clear that prisoner handling was raised as an issue, and one of concern, although I think it most likely that it was raised as one of a number of areas of concern rather than as the most important legal issue in theatre.

Summary of the position at Divisional Level

10.49 In summary, therefore, **within 1 (UK) Div** the evidence shows the following:

(1) firstly, Wall the GOC knew that Burridge had ordered that hooding should cease but he did not know at the time of the order given by Brims and this was not mentioned when Brims gave his handover to Wall. Wall in turn did not mention prisoner handling or hooding at his handover to Lamb. At the level of Divisional Commander it is perhaps not surprising that this level of detail was not covered within the actual handovers;

(2) secondly, Marriott as Chief of Staff knew of the ban on hooding and I find that he did at least mention it to his successor, Barrons. Wall's Deputy Chief of Staff, Cowling, did not know of the ban on hooding and thus was not in a position to include it in his handover;

(3) thirdly, the SO2 J3 Ops Maciejewski knew of FRAGO 152 but at the handover he concentrated on current operations and problems. On the plans side, it seems from the evidence of Ryan that the handover did not cover prisoner handling matters;

(4) fourthly, Waters as the SO2 J2 was not in theatre by the time of the handover. S002 the SO2 J2X at the JFIT knew of the prohibition on hooding and while it is possible that he mentioned the prohibition on hooding to S015 I find it unlikely that he gave any detail regarding the background; and

---

[58] Barnett BMI06617, paragraph 97
[59] Ellis-Davies BMI05075, paragraph 8
[60] Ellis-Davies BMI 85/126/17-127/9

(5) fifthly, within the Legal branch the handover undoubtedly did cover prisoner handling and the prohibition on hooding.

10.50 Correspondingly, **within 3 (UK) Division** at the start of Op Telic 2:

(1) firstly, Lamb and his Deputy Chief of Staff, Le Grys, were unaware of the oral order ban on hooding or the content of FRAGO 152;

(2) secondly, the SO1 J2 Le Fevre and the SO3 J2 Haseldine, were also unaware of the oral order ban on hooding or the content of FRAGO 152;

(3) thirdly, SO15, the SO2 J2X (HUMINT) was already aware that hooding was prohibited before his deployment, and while it is possible this fact may have been mentioned again to him during the handover, it is probable that FRAGO 152, the controversy involving the ICRC at the JFIT and the debate about the legality of hooding during Op Telic 1, were not drawn to his attention;

(4) fourthly, on the Plans side, Murray-Playfair did not recall receiving any briefing on prisoner handling, and would not, in his role, have expected one; and

(5) fifthly, Barnett, as the SO1 Legal, was made fully aware of the prohibition on hooding that had been introduced and he was also aware of FRAGO 152.

10.51 Arising out of the above, I make the following comments. The general tenor of the evidence suggested that the topic of prisoner handling was for the most part not given a high priority by senior officers of each Division during the handover. It appears not to have been seen by them as a pressing concern; see for example Brims, Wall and Barrons. Given the wide scope of their responsibilities, I do not find this surprising.

10.52 In the same vein some of the senior officers in both Divisions held the view that their handovers were concerned with general strategic overviews. They felt they would not necessarily expect to brief or be briefed to the level of detail of the correct process for prisoner handling; see for example Lamb, Marriott and Cowling.

10.53 Most of the more senior officers took the view that the responsibility for the handover of FRAGOs was the concern of heads of individual branches and not those at Chief of Staff, Deputy Chief of Staff or GOC level of seniority. This was an opinion advanced by Marriott, Cowling and Barrons.

10.54 Officers within a number of separate branches thought that responsibility for handing over orders such as FRAGO 152 was vested in or shared with a different branch than their own: for example, Murray-Playfair (Ops/Plans), Haseldine (Intelligence) and Barnett (Legal). The problem with this approach was that it ran the risk of the responsibility for handing over a FRAGO falling between two stools.

10.55 I note that it was a recurring feature of the evidence the Inquiry heard concerning the handover between Op Telic 1 and 2 that officers in close hierarchical, and sometimes physical, proximity seem to have emerged from the handover period with inconsistent and sometimes conflicting knowledge in respect of the prohibition on hooding.

10.56 One of the problems which the above description of the Divisional handover highlights is that no one single branch appears to have regarded it as its responsibility to lead in matters of prisoner handling and detention. In my view this was unfortunate and contributed to the patchy knowledge of the ban on hooding in both 1 (UK) Div and 3 (UK) Div. It also points to the good sense of the present practice in Op Herrick in which there is one covering different aspects of prisoner handling and detention (see Part XVI).

Chapter 3: Brigade Level

10.57 As I have addressed in Part IX of this Report, FRAGO 63 of 21 May 2003 was the Brigade level iteration of FRAGO 152. It had attached Mercer's guidance on the detention of civilians, including the prohibition on covering detainees faces, and stating:

> *"At Annex A is a comprehensive guide to the detention of civilians which is to be briefed to all those likely to be in a position of contact with civilians under detention at any stage in the chain. BGs and sub-units are to adhere to this policy."* [61]

10.58 Amongst other units, FRAGO 63 was addressed for "Action" to 1 BW. Significantly, however, it was addressed for "Info" to 19 Mech Bde who were at that time not in theatre but preparing to deploy for Op Telic 2.

10.59 At the time of the handover, 7 Armd Bde was commanded by Brig Adrian Bradshaw, who took over from his predecessor Brig Graham Binns on 11 May 2003.[62] Bradshaw's evidence to the Inquiry was that his handover would have consisted of extensive briefings given to Brig William Moore, the Commander of 19 Mech Bde. According to Bradshaw, all extant FRAGOs would have been handed across and would have been assumed to have been extant until superseded by new 19 Mech Bde orders.[63]

10.60 Although Bradshaw was not in command of 7 Armd Bde at the time of the ICRC concerns about the JFIT, he nevertheless said that given the recent mistreatment allegations, it was *"highly unlikely"* that prisoner handling would not have been discussed. Bradshaw very fairly added the caveat that it was not possible for him to be sure of this as there was no written record.[64] However, Bradshaw explained that the incident at Camp Breadbasket had *"scored quite an impression on all our minds and so, as I say, I find it unlikely that it did not at least get a mention…"*. When asked about Moore's account that prisoner handling was not mentioned at the handover and was not seen as a significant issue on handover, Bradshaw admitted that it was possible that it had not been mentioned, but that he would find that surprising.[65] Bradshaw did not admit to any failing on his own part if the issue had not been communicated between himself and Moore directly, but said that it would have been a failing if the extant orders were not passed over at staff level, but that he was sure they had been.[66] Although Bradshaw was not aware of hooding occurring in Iraq or of Brims' oral order, he had issued FRAGO 63 after 7 Armd Bde received FRAGO 152 from 1 (UK) Div.[67] FRAGO 63 was issued on 21 May 2003,[68] after Bradshaw took over command of 7 Armd Bde on 11 May 2003.[69]

10.61 Bradshaw was asked whether, given other responsibilities, prisoner handling was low on the list of priorities during the handover. He did not agree that it was. He said:

---

[61] MOD031014
[62] Bradshaw BMI05233, paragraph 5
[63] Bradshaw BMI05249, paragraphs 58-59
[64] Bradshaw BMI 96/35/17-36/3; Bradshaw BMI05249, paragraph 58
[65] Bradshaw BMI 96/36/24-38/19
[66] Bradshaw BMI 96/39/1-11
[67] Bradshaw BMI05243, paragraphs 38-39
[68] Bradshaw BMI05243, paragraph 37
[69] Bradshaw BMI05233, paragraph 5

> *"I would actually rather put it that issues of prisoner handling were covered by a written set of rules which were included in orders and FRAGOs, which were part of the operational staff work, which were handed across to 19 Brigade, and one would expect that that sort of material would be poured over by staff and re-issued in the name of the incoming formation. So a lot of very important issues, including prisoner handling, would have effectively been covered in the handover by the handover of operational staff work –*
>
> *Q. By subordinates, as it were?*
>
> *A. By subordinates, but absolutely in my name, and I was confident that that happened."* [70]

10.62   Moore confirmed in his Inquiry witness statement that 19 Mech Bde staff had the benefit of a one week handover period and that he personally had a one day handover from Bradshaw. He described the process as one in which the 19 Mech Bde Chief of Staff and Deputy Chief of Staff would deal with all incoming orders. He said that before deployment the Chief of Staff and Deputy Chief of Staff were already showing him those orders they considered needed his attention. [71]

10.63   It was Moore's account nonetheless that he did not remember seeing FRAGO 152, although it was possible he had seen it as part of the documentation copied to 19 Mech Bde before their deployment. [72] Moore was not aware of any ban on the use of hooding. [73] He was also not aware during his time in Iraq that hooding was a standard practice at ground level. [74] Furthermore, he did not remember prisoner handling being an issue at the time of the handover. He said that he understood that a system for prisoner handling had been established by 1 (UK) Div and appeared to be working. He was not given any information to the contrary. [75] Moore was also unaware of the changes made to the existing system of prisoner handling by FRAGO 29 issued shortly before the handover. [76]

10.64   In summary, therefore, Bradshaw was confident that his staff would have handed over all relevant documents. But he was not able to be sure that FRAGO 152 and FRAGO 63 were definitely transferred. He assumed they had been. Despite his initial confidence that he would have discussed issues of prisoner handling with Moore, he accepted the possibility that this might not have happened. Moore on the other hand, had a positive memory that prisoner handling issues were not included. On balance, in my opinion it is likely that Moore's recollection was the more accurate.

10.65   Maj Christopher Parker was Chief of Staff of 7 Armd Bde. He accepted that he had overall "control" for ensuring that there was an effective handover at Brigade level, but he referred to the fact that the Chief of Staff at 1 (UK) Div, Marriott and the SO2 Operations at 1 (UK) Div, Maciejewski, at a higher level of command, were charged overall with ensuring that there was an effective handover. [77] Parker said that he was extremely keen to ensure that the handover was done well. He said that he had been engaged in physically passing procedures, knowledge and files to his counterpart, Maj Hugh Eaton of 19 Mech Bde. [78] He suggested that Maj Ian Jaggard-Hawkins

---

[70] Bradshaw BMI 96/36/11-23
[71] Moore BMI06953-4, paragraphs 39-42
[72] Moore BMI06955, paragraph 43
[73] Moore BMI 99/24/8-11
[74] Moore BMI 99/22/23-23/9
[75] Moore BMI 99/21/2-22/1
[76] Moore BMI 99/49/9-14
[77] Parker BMI06328, paragraph 106
[78] Parker BMI06327, paragraph 104

was otherwise responsible for ensuring all paperwork was effectively handed over to 19 Mech Bde.[79] In this latter respect I think that Parker's recollection was mistaken. Jaggard-Hawkins provided a witness statement to the Inquiry detailing his role and responsibilities within 7 Armd Bde at this time. It appears that Jaggard-Hawkins did not have general custody of 7 Brigade orders or paperwork.[80]

10.66 Nevertheless, Parker did not remember handing over to 19 Mech Bde any orders or saying anything in relation to prisoner handling, since he believed that:

> "...the treatment of prisoners was simply not an issue at that stage. As far as I was concerned, at that time, we had a good system operating with prisoners processed by the RMP, who knew what they were doing. It was a system that, as far as I was aware, was apparently working well."[81]

10.67 In his Inquiry witness statement, Parker said that did not remember seeing FRAGO 152 or FRAGO 63[82] and was not aware of any order prohibiting hooding before FRAGO 152.[83] It seems likely, however, that Parker was aware of these FRAGOs at the time. That is so because Parker had some recollection of a discussion amongst the Brigade staff concerning the tension between ensuring operational security requirements and the order that hooding was prohibited.[84] He suggested that his staff were reminded to use their common sense in resolving this tension. However, Parker's oral evidence on this aspect was less than clear. Ultimately, he appeared to say that the order that went down to the 19 Mech Bde units, FRAGO 63, did simply ban the use of hooding albeit that Parker regretted that better wording had not been used.[85]

10.68 In his oral evidence, Parker explained that FRAGO 152 would have been handed over in the process as all orders were handed over on paper and electronic copy. However, he did not remember whether his personal handover to Eaton had included any reference to FRAGO 152.[86]

10.69 Eaton said that he had regular pre-handover telephone conversations with Parker. He remembered that the actual handover process did not necessarily involve the physical handing over of documents and in addition, issued orders were stored on the IT system. He expressed the opinion that *"you would expect to be briefed by your counterpart on what the key issues were in theatre and how they were dealt with in the past or being dealt with currently"*. Eaton did not remember being handed a copy of FRAGO 152.[87]

---

[79] Parker BMI06328, paragraph 106
[80] Jaggard-Hawkins BMI07266-7, paragraphs 37-40
[81] Parker BMI06328, paragraph 108
[82] Parker BMI06322, paragraph 88; Parker BMI06325, paragraph 96
[83] Parker BMI06324, paragraph 94
[84] Parker BMI 96/94/4-104; Parker BMI06324-5, paragraph 95
[85] Ibid.
[86] Parker BMI 96/106/19-107/8
[87] Eaton BMI06063, paragraph 32

10.70 Eaton also provided a useful insight into the manner in which handovers were conducted at that time. He explained that it would have been impractical for one individual to review each order that was left behind by the outgoing unit. Each post holder in each of the staff branches received a handover from their predecessor and would have discussed the most important issues and orders therein.[88]

10.71 When asked about his personal handover from Parker, Eaton stated that the issue of prisoner handling was not one of those topics marked out as a priority. The prohibition on prisoners' faces being covered, the relevant content of FRAGO 152 and FRAGO 63, or a prohibition on the use of hoods more generally, were not discussed with him.[89] It is not possible for me to decide whether Parker did or did not merely hand over, along with all other existing orders, copies of FRAGO 152 and FRAGO 63, either electronically or as physical documents. Given the recollection of both parties I find it impossible to determine with certainty whether or not the prohibition on the use of hooding was expressly discussed, although it would appear unlikely that this was the case.

10.72 As regards the handing over of FRAGO 63 at Brigade level, Eaton would have expected this to have involved staff in both G2 and G3 branches. He would have expected FRAGO 63 to have been handed over notwithstanding subsequent FRAGOs relating to the detention and internment process. However, the key factor he stressed was how significant an issue prisoner handling was in the minds of officers at the point of handover. There would have been several extant directives and the incumbent would not have gone through every single one with his counterpart.[90]

10.73 Eaton was an important witness in relation to a further feature of FRAGO 63. As I have referred to above, the Brigade FRAGO was stated to be circulated to 19 Mech Bde for information before their deployment. The prohibition on covering the face of detainees ought therefore to have been communicated to 19 Mech Bde before the handover process even took place.

10.74 Eaton accepted that as the Chief of Staff of 19 Mech Bde he would have been responsible for all the pre-deployment information that came into Brigade headquarters in the form of FRAGOs circulated from theatre. He had no recollection of seeing FRAGO 63 and said that he had doubts as to whether it was in fact received by 19 Mech Bde due to problems with the data links between theatre and 19 Mech Bde headquarters in the UK. He accepted that had such an order been received by 19 Mech Bde it could reasonably have been expected that he should have translated it into a standard operating instruction to inform 19 Mech Bde how they were to conduct prisoner handling once deployed.[91] Had Eaton seen the order, a standard operating instruction would have been generated as he would have deduced that this was a particular issue which needed specific attention.

10.75 Although Eaton's primary position was that there were significant communication difficulties with those in theatre, he accepted the possibility that FRAGO 63 might in fact have been received by 19 Mech Bde but due to the demands of preparing for Op Telic 2, the point might have been missed and no instruction issued.[92]

---

[88] Eaton BMI 98/74/2-22; Eaton BMI06063, paragraph 32
[89] Eaton BMI 98/71/24-72/14
[90] Eaton BMI 98/76/7-78/8
[91] Eaton BMI 98/78/9-83/4
[92] Eaton BMI 98/78/9-83/4

10.76 The Deputy Chief of Staff of 19 Mech Bde, Maj James Landon, gave evidence only in relation to a pre-deployment recce in early May 2003. He was absent at the formal handover.[93] Although Landon thought that the issue of prisoners was discussed on this recce,[94] he was not aware of FRAGO 152 or of its contents.[95]

10.77 Landon told the Inquiry that he would have understood the content of FRAGO 63, the 7 Armd Bde level order circulated to 19 Mech Bde prohibiting the covering of detainees' faces, to be a change to ordinary operational practice in which hooding was permissible. Nonetheless, he too stated that just because the intent was to have transmitted FRAGO 63 to 19 Mech Bde it did not mean that this had occurred in practice. This account supported that of Eaton. On the assumption that it had been received by 19 Mech Bde, it would have gone to Eaton as Chief of Staff. Landon, with some apparent reluctance, said that if he had been Chief of Staff he would have ensured that the section on detention was fed into 19 Mech Bde pre-deployment training.[96]

10.78 If the point about hooding in FRAGO 63 was indeed missed, as was recognised as a possibility by Eaton, that was, in my opinion, highly regrettable. I bear in mind the fact that during preparations for deployment there are myriad pressing demands at all levels of the chain of command. However, I also consider that read as a whole, FRAGO 63 ought to have conveyed to the reader, at the least, concerns in relation to hooding against the background of a number of deaths in UK custody. The successful transmission of the order from theatre to 19 Mech Bde is subject to some plausible doubt. If it was received by 19 Mech Bde, however, FRAGO 63 should have been read and should have been understood as too high a priority to be overlooked notwithstanding other competing demands.

Brigade G3 (Operations) Branch

10.79 Maj Rupert Steptoe was the SO2 G3 (Ops)/G5 (Plans) at 19 Mech Bde. His actual role in theatre requires some clarification. In his statement to the Special Investigation Branch (SIB) he had referred to his role being a G3 plans officer,[97] whereas in his Inquiry witness statement he stated he was the G5 plans for HQ 19 Mech Bde.[98] He explained that his post was technically "a G3/G5 training plans", with the training element falling under G3 and the plans element under G5. He explained the difference in nomenclature as "G3 traditionally is the shorter term current part of an operation or the preparation and G5 is looking beyond 48 hours". He confirmed that when he was in Iraq G5 was essentially his role, and he had a G3 Operations officer working under him.[99]

10.80 Steptoe was responsible for issuing orders and FRAGOs based upon those received from the Divisional headquarters, although I accept, as he clarified in his oral evidence, he was not exclusively responsible for this process.[100]

---

[93] Landon BMI04941, paragraph 62
[94] Landon BMI 80/149/16-22
[95] Landon BMI04941, paragraph 63
[96] Landon BMI 80/159/5-166/6
[97] Steptoe MOD000960
[98] Steptoe BMI03191, paragraph 36
[99] Steptoe BMI 78/19/7-20/17
[100] Steptoe BMI 78/20/18-21/10

10.81 Steptoe was an important witness in this regard. He told the Inquiry that he did not remember anything being mentioned in relation to prisoner handling during his handover process and did not remember reading FRAGOs in relation to prisoner handling,[101] specifically FRAGO 152,[102] nor did he remember seeing FRAGO 63.[103]

10.82 During his handover he spent three to four days with Maciejewski the SO2 G3 Ops 1 UK Div.[104] He then worked alongside his counterpart at 7 Armd Bde for three days. He did not remember this officer's name, but remembered he was a member of the Royal Tank Regiment.[105]

10.83 According to Steptoe, it was not the general practice for 19 Mech Bde to re-issue to the 19 Mech Bde Battlegroups orders that had previously been issued by way of 7 Armd Bde FRAGOs. As Steptoe perceived it, the in-theatre Battlegroups that had already received 7 Armd Bde FRAGOs were responsible for passing on all relevant information to their successor Battlegroups and for ensuring that 19 Mech Bde units were aware of FRAGOs that still had a bearing on future operations.[106]

10.84 Steptoe also highlighted a related issue which explained why the handover between Op Telic 1 and 2 was not optimal. He said it was very difficult to handover corporate knowledge as the pre-deployment training had not yet fed in the lessons from theatre. He said "*Immediately in the aftermath of the war-fighting phase, I think the handover of corporate knowledge was very blurred*". There was a more efficient mechanism, and thus less problematic, by the time Op Telic 2 units conducted their own handover.[107]

10.85 Steptoe's account included detail about how the handover of orders was physically achieved. He did not remember hard copies of existing FRAGOs being handed over by 7 Armd Bde; merely that an electronic folder was handed over with the IT systems. He did not inherit a folder which said "*These FRAGOs are still extant, you must read these FRAGOs*".[108] Steptoe's position was that in order to learn of important issues in theatre he was dependent on what was handed over to him and on what his predecessor thought important.[109] It would not have been practical for him to have gone back over every line of the previous FRAGOs.[110] He would have hoped that "*the important stuff*" was handed over to him orally.[111] Had he been made aware of the change in position, namely that hooding had been banned under 1 (UK) Div/7 Armd Bde, he would have spoken to the SO2 legal to check the position. He would then have reissued the order to Battlegroups.[112]

[101] Steptoe BMI03197, paragraph 65
[102] Steptoe BMI03198, paragraph 70
[103] Steptoe BMI 78/34/4-6
[104] Steptoe BMI03195, paragraph 58
[105] Steptoe BMI03195, paragraph 60
[106] Steptoe BMI 78/23/4-24/1; Steptoe BMI03196, paragraph 63
[107] Steptoe BMI 78/24/9-24
[108] Steptoe BMI 78//26/14-28/4
[109] Steptoe BMI 78/29/6-15
[110] Steptoe BMI 78/30/13-17
[111] Steptoe BMI 78/27/20-21
[112] Steptoe BMI 78/25/4-26/13

10.86 Steptoe openly volunteered that he had failed to pick up and extract from the previous orders, however they were stored, the sentence from FRAGO 152/FRAGO 63 which effectively prohibited hooding. However, he maintained that it was not practical to have expected him in the circumstances to have found that one sentence among the entirety of those orders that had been handed over.[113]

10.87 Steptoe was replaced by Capt Miles Mitchell part way through the tour. Mitchell described his role as SO3 Plans/Training. Nevertheless his description of the actual tasks he undertook once in post was consistent with that given by Steptoe: "*Generally on operations I dealt with helping the Senior Planning Group (SPG) to plan 'future operations' that required coordination at Regimental level*".[114] He confirmed in oral evidence that his operations role in theatre consisted of planning future operations.[115]

10.88 Mitchell, in turn, did not remember Steptoe's handover to him including any reference to prisoner handling, nor did he remember hooding being discussed.[116] In fact, Mitchell's own recollection was that he never saw FRAGO 152 and cannot remember learning that hooding had been banned. It is therefore not surprising that these features were not mentioned in his handover.[117]

10.89 It is relevant also to record that Mitchell in his evidence to the Inquiry said that during the handover difficulties were experienced in accessing orders stored on the IT system. It was frequently difficult to access copies of reference documents which were electronically stored.[118]

10.90 Similarly, Capt Charles Burbridge, the SO3 Operations Officer (Organisation and Deployment) 19 Mech Bde, who had the responsibility for the routine management and coordination of day to day Brigade operations,[119] told the Inquiry that he did not discuss detention on his handover; the ban on hooding did not feature, nor was he shown any specific FRAGOs. He would have expected to have been told of the ban if it represented a change to a standard operating procedure.[120]

10.91 Capt Oliver King was also a member of the 19 Mech Bde G3 Ops team. He said that during the handover only those orders which were still in regular use for G3 Ops work were specifically mentioned.[121] He could not remember whether or not he had seen FRAGO 152, but said that even if he had, he would not have picked up on the reference to the impairment of breathing as relevant to his work. This was because he thought that Brigade staff were not involved in prisoner handling at a practical and day to day level.[122]

---

[113] Steptoe BMI 78/36/24-37/15
[114] Mitchell BMI04954, paragraph 18
[115] Mitchell BMI 79/3/21-4/10
[116] Mitchell BMI 79/3/8-20
[117] Mitchell BMI04957-61, paragraphs 25-29
[118] Mitchell BMI04957, paragraph 25
[119] Burbridge BMI04787, paragraph 29
[120] Burbridge BMI 79/31/25-33/16; Burbridge BMI04787, paragraphs 27-28
[121] Capt Oliver King BMI03578, paragraphs 45-46
[122] Capt Oliver King BMI03580, paragraph 53

10.92 Nevertheless, King also accepted that the distribution of FRAGO 63 to 19 Mech Bde, had it been successfully executed, would have essentially put the Brigade on notice of the prohibition on hooding. King's opinion was that it would then have been a responsibility of the Chief of Staff to reiterate this message in a 19 Mech Bde FRAGO, or standard operating instruction which would have gone down to Battlegroup units.[123]

Brigade Legal Branch

10.93 Capt Christopher Heron, SO3 Legal at 7 Armd Bde, did not remember whether his handover to Maj Russell Clifton included discussions on prisoner handling to any great extent,[124] but he did mention that Clifton spoke to Mercer about prisoner handling. Heron thought that Mercer had specifically mentioned the prohibition on hooding to Clifton.[125] In his Inquiry witness statement, Heron stated that he personally told Clifton that hooding was banned.[126] Heron also said that he handed over a file of documents to Clifton but did not remember specifically handing over FRAGO 152.[127] By the time Heron gave his oral evidence his recollection on the latter aspect was different; he stated that he remembered handing over FRAGO 152 and its Brigade equivalent FRAGO 63.[128]

10.94 Clifton's account did not entirely coincide with that of Heron. Clifton stated that his handover with Heron did not include issues relevant to internee handling, rather it focused on reforms to the justice system.[129] Clifton understood that hooding had been banned by 1 (UK) Div, and he understood this to be a blanket ban, having been informed of this directly by Mercer.[130] Due to the fact that Mercer informed him of the concerns surrounding the handling of prisoners, and that Mercer seemed quite animated on this subject, Clifton decided to review the relevant orders in order to update or reiterate them.[131]

10.95 Ultimately, I am not sure that it matters whether Clifton's knowledge of the ban on hooding came from direct contact with Mercer at Division or from Heron as his Brigade level predecessor, or from both. Whichever was the case, the handover between the legal elements of the formations meant that both the Division and Brigade level senior lawyers for Op Telic 2 were clearly aware of the prohibition on hooding.

---

[123] Capt Oliver King BMI 78/99/2-105/19
[124] Heron BMI06869, paragraph 41
[125] Heron BMI06869, paragraph 42
[126] Heron BMI 64/150/11-151/13; Heron BMI06869, paragraph 42
[127] Heron BMI06869, paragraph 42
[128] Heron BMI 64/153/2-8
[129] Clifton BMI 81/14/4-11; Clifton BMI04567, paragraph 36
[130] Clifton BMI 81/15/1-16/10
[131] Clifton BMI04567, paragraph 36

Brigade G2 (Intelligence) Branch

10.96   Capt Christopher Medhurst-Cocksworth was the G2 Int at 7 Armd Bde. He described delivering a "*rough and ready*" briefing during handover in relation to operations on the ground.[132] He did not remember there being a focus on prisoner handling during the handover he gave, stating that from his perspective there was "*nothing to say*" on the subject. In the absence of any adverse reports he thought "*the process was working normally*".[133] He did not remember saying anything directly to his successor, Maj Mark Robinson, about prisoner handling as it was not a feature of his normal daily business. Nor did he discuss with Robinson the Brigade's role in providing tactical questioners to Battlegroups.[134] He told the Inquiry that he would have expected FRAGO 63 to have been handed to the incoming G2 team, in a hard copy file, but he could not specifically remember FRAGO 63 being contained in this file. He thought the responsibility for the express handover of a FRAGO banning the covering of detainees' faces lay with the operations team.[135]

10.97   Robinson of 19 Mech Bde was under the impression that the handover "*was not as comprehensive as it could have been*", in the sense that 7 Armd Bde were "*...keen to get out*". He did not remember any mention of prisoner handling or of hooding, nor did he remember receiving copies of any orders in relation to prisoner handling or tactical questioning.[136] Robinson went on to explain that during his handover, Medhurst-Cocksworth also did not make him aware of the effect of FRAGO 29, which made G2 Intelligence the lead branch on internment issues.[137]

Summary of the position at Brigade Level

10.98   After the handover between the two Brigades, within 19 Mech Bde, the Brigade Commander Moore, the Chief of Staff Eaton and Deputy Chief of Staff Landon, and staff within the G2, G3 and G5 branches (Robinson, Steptoe, Burbridge and King) did not know of the ban on hooding or the relevant FRAGOs. This was not, on any view, an acceptable state of affairs. That said, others including Clifton clearly were aware of the prohibition, although in my view this was probably because of Clifton's personal contact with Mercer.

10.99   In relation to the Brigade handover there are points to observe which are similar to those at Division:

(1)   the topic of prisoner handling was seemingly a relatively low priority and little more was effected than the physical handing over of hard copies of past orders, or the location of those orders on the computer systems, without going into detail of the contents (see the evidence of Bradshaw, Medhurst-Cocksworth, Moore detailed above);

(2)   those of more senior rank were also of the view that communication of the actual detail in orders would be completed by staff officers lower down the chain of command (see the evidence of Moore, Bradshaw detailed above);

---

[132] Medhurst-Cocksworth BMI01714, paragraph 37
[133] Medhurst-Cocksworth BMI01714, paragraph 38
[134] Medhurst-Cocksworth BMI 68/170/16-171/12
[135] Medhurst-Cocksworth BMI 68/172/1-23
[136] Robinson BMI04312, paragraph 37
[137] Robinson BMI 80/96/4-19

(3)   the incoming Brigade was heavily reliant on the in-post staff to highlight the important parts of existing orders (see the evidence of Steptoe and Burbridge detailed above); and

(4)   there was no re-issue of existing orders by the incoming Brigade, instead there was a reliance placed on the horizontal communication of existing orders at Battlegroup level. This was a further example of staff officers relying on the level of command below them to ensure that the new soldier on the ground understood the orders and protocol already in place (see the evidence of Steptoe detailed above).

10.100 A significant further feature in relation to the Brigade level handover is whether or not 19 Mech Bde had already had the opportunity to digest the importance of FRAGO 63 after it was circulated to them for information in May 2003, some weeks before their deployment. That could, and on some of the evidence, should have led 19 Mech Bde to issue their own standard operating instructions in accordance with FRAGO 152/FRAGO 63. If FRAGO 63 did get through to 19 Mech Bde, Eaton, at a time of considerable pressure, did not take sufficient action in response to it. But I have already expressed the view that it is possible that the order did not reach 19 Mech Bde. Eaton and Landon gave evidence that communication difficulties might have prevented FRAGO 63 from getting through.

Chapter 4: Battlegroup Level

1 Black Watch/1 QLR Background

10.101 As will already be apparent from previous Parts of the Report, there is extensive evidence of the use of hoods and stress positions by 1 QLR on detainees during their tour up to the time of the events of 14 to 16 September 2003. For this reason, in order to trace the origin or reasons for the use on detainees by 1 QLR of these practices, it has been necessary to examine the handover between 1 BW and 1 QLR in rather greater detail than at Divisional and Brigade level. The scope of this Chapter is therefore wider than the previous chapters in this Part and covers not only the handover of orders, but also the handover of relevant practices used by 1 BW in its handling of prisoners.

10.102 1 BW were the predecessor Battlegroup in Basra to 1 QLR. 1 BW had deployed to Iraq as part of 7 Armd Bde at the start of Op Telic 1. It took part in the warfighting phase after which it became responsible for that part of Basra City which on the handover became the responsibility of 1 QLR. Its headquarters and companies occupied the same locations as did 1 QLR on its arrival in Iraq.

10.103 1 QLR conducted a recce to Iraq visiting 1 BW between 7 and 10 May 2003. The handover took place from 24 to 26 June 2003. It is relevant to note that this Battlegroup handover preceded the handovers at Brigade and Divisional level. It follows that what was handed over to 1 QLR by 1 BW were orders and practices which were governed by orders and instructions given by 1 (UK) Div and 7 Armd Bde.

10.104 A number of 1 QLR witnesses stated that they adopted procedures, particularly hooding, which they saw being used by 1 BW both in the recce and during the handover. Col Jorge Mendonça said in his Inquiry witness statement that the 1 QLR ethos at the handover was:

> "... to accept the extant system (unless it was clearly wrong) and make any changes or improvements later (once 1 BW had departed) on the basis of experience or an insistence on higher standards."[138]

The Orders

10.105 As previously explained FRAGO 152 and its Brigade equivalent FRAGO 63 had been issued on 20 to 21 May 2003. They both contained in an enclosure drafted by Mercer, an annex, which read in the material part:

> "Under no circumstances should their (detainees) faces be covered as this might impair breathing. Medical assistance should also be close at hand at all times. The Royal Military Police are specially trained in all these matters and timely delivery to the Military Police is the best way to ensure the correct procedures are adopted at the outset."[139]

This instruction ought to have reached all units including 1 BW. As I have set out in the previous Chapter, FRAGO 63 was also sent to 19 Mech Bde for information in

---

[138] Mendonça BMI01100, paragraph 37
[139] MOD019147

accordance with the practice that all units which were in waiting to take over should be made aware of important orders to units already in theatre.

10.106 The Inquiry attempted to trace through the Watchkeeper and radio logs of 1(UK) Div, 7 Armd Bde and 1 BW the cascading of FRAGOs 152 and 63. After extensive searches, no reference to either order was discovered. Of course, only orders communicated by radio would be disclosed by these logs. Orders cascaded by hand would not appear on the logs. Core Participants were informed of the searches carried out by the Inquiry (see Circulars 266 and 267). While the information communicated to Core Participants referred to searches for oral orders, the searches in fact included searches for references to written orders. None were found. The Inquiry was informed by email on 28 February 2011 that further electronic searches had been undertaken by the MoD but the searches have not retrieved anything which confirmed that 1 BW had received FRAGO 63.

10.107 However, it is certain that at least one copy of FRAGO 63 reached a unit under command of 7 Armd Bde. In searches conducted by the MoD the receipt by the Joint Nuclear Biological Chemical (NBC) Regiment of FRAGO 63 on 23 May 2003 was logged in the Joint NBC Regiment's operational log. There was further evidence corroborating the NBC Regiment's receipt of FRAGO 63.[140] I infer from this that FRAGO 63 was certainly sent out by 7 Armd Bde's Headquarters. That in turn lends some support for FRAGO 63 having reached 1 BW.

10.108 As I shall record, most of the 1 BW witnesses who remembered seeing FRAGO 152 and FRAGO 63 said that they believed that the part of the annex set out above was an order banning hooding.

10.109 What does not appear to have been cascaded down to 7 Armd Bde or its Battlegroups was either the NCC or Brims' earlier oral orders which were promulgated at the end of March and the beginning of April 2003. This lends support to my finding that although these orders were given orally by Burridge and Brims they did not reach Brigades.

The Black Watch Evidence: The Handover, Hooding and Stress Positions

10.110 The Inquiry received evidence from a number of Black Watch officers and three Non-Commissioned Officers (NCOs) who gave evidence on these issues. A further officer, Capt Angus Philp, the adjutant, made an Inquiry witness statement which was read into the evidence.[141] The officers who gave evidence were Lt Col Michael Riddell-Webster, the Commanding Officer, Maj Hugh Channer, the Second in Command, S056, the Officer Commanding Support Company, Maj Anthony Fraser, the Officer Commanding Headquarters Company, Capt Mark Percy, the Operations Officer, Capt Nicholas Ord, who took over from Percy before the end of the tour, Capt Michael Williamson, the Intelligence Officer and Capt Travis Vincent, the Watchkeeper and, for the last three weeks of the tour, the Officer Commanding HQ Company.

---

[140] Mercer's guidance attached to FRAGO 63 was circulated within the NBC Regiment in hard copy on 24 May 2003: MOD041862
[141] Philp BMI03804

10.111 The NCOs who gave evidence were RSM David Bruce, WO1 Thomas Henderson and Sgt John Gallacher.

10.112 I make it clear at the outset that save for Henderson and Gallacher all of the above witnesses denied seeing stress positions being used by 1 BW or any other unit during their tour.

10.113 On the totality of this evidence, there can be little doubt that 1 BW did hood detainees during their tour on Op Telic 1. Riddell-Webster said that when 1 BW took prisoners in the combat phase it was a standard operating procedure that they were to be hooded. His understanding of the origin of this standard operating procedure was from pre-deployment training. Prisoners were to be hooded for the period of transit until they got to the location at which they were to be held.[142] Once they reached a secure location the hoods should be removed.[143] Riddell-Webster said after the fall of Basra hooding generally ceased but he could not remember an order which actually banned hooding.[144] As to the content of the handover, Riddell-Webster remembered that he provided Mendonça with all the orders from Brigade that were currently in operation, but prisoner handling was not dealt with as a specific issue; nor did he and Mendonça discuss hooding.[145] In oral evidence to the Inquiry Riddell-Webster suggested it would be for the Adjutant and Ops officers to take their opposite numbers through the Brigade FRAGOs.[146]

10.114 Riddell-Webster did not remember FRAGO 63 but he was sure it would have been discussed at an Orders Group (O Group). When he was shown FRAGO 63, during his evidence, he said he would have understood it to mean that 1 BW should stop hooding.[147] Further, he accepted that by the time of the handover to 1 QLR there should have been no hooding.[148]

10.115 Channer understood that hooding was permissible only in very specific and limited circumstances where operational security was at risk.[149] He said he only saw prisoners on two separate occasions and on neither occasion were they hooded.[150] He could not remember any order which prohibited hooding.[151] Channer also did not remember reading out FRAGO 152 at an O Group as S056 said he had.[152] He said it was standard practice on handover for extant orders to be handed from the Ops officer to his opposite number. Prisoner handling orders would have been handed on by Williamson as 1 BW's Intelligence officer to his opposite number.[153]

---

[142] Riddell-Webster BMI 63/107/15-110/2
[143] Riddell-Webster BMI03403, paragraph 12
[144] Riddell-Webster BMI03403, paragraph 13
[145] Riddell-Webster BMI03415, paragraph 51
[146] Riddell-Webster BMI 63/130/16-131/17
[147] Riddell-Webster BMI 63/134/1-11
[148] Riddell-Webster BMI 63/132/10-13
[149] Channer BMI 63/4/25-5/7
[150] Channer BMI 63/34/12-35/7
[151] Channer BMI 63/19/8-10; Channer BMI 63/24/3-8
[152] Channer BMI 63/29/7-31/8
[153] Channer BMI01663, paragraphs 85-86

10.116 Philp, in his Inquiry witness statement, said he believed detainees would only have been hooded if this was deemed necessary when they were captured. They were not kept hooded once they reached the Temporary Detention Facility (TDF).[154]

10.117 S056, the Officer Commanding C Company, 1 BW, remembered that in training for Op Telic the use of hooding was discussed. He believed it was permissible but not a standard operating procedure.[155] He remembered directions being given in, he thought, FRAGO 63 or FRAGO 152, which "... to all intents and purposes banned – stopped the use of a hood which would cover the face".[156] He remembered Channer reading this direction out at an O Group. He disseminated the order to his company and he was confident that thereafter all hooding by soldiers in his company ceased. He said at the time of the handover by him to Maj Paul Davis, the Officer Commanding A Company 1 QLR, hoods were not being used.[157]

10.118 Williamson had attended a course at the Joint Services Intelligence Organisation (JSIO), Chicksands, in January 2003. He had no recollection of being taught about hooding or of an instruction authorising hooding.[158] Williamson said the course which he attended was the same as the one attended by Gallacher.[159] He had not seen hoods used before Op Telic 1.[160] However, when deployed to Iraq hoods were used for security purposes.[161] He said that as a matter of course every detainee at Battlegroup Main (BG Main) during Op Telic was hooded.[162] He had a vague recollection of discussions about hooding towards the end of the tour. The discussion was about covering the eyes of detainees in ways other than hooding.[163] However, he had no recollection of seeing FRAGO 63 which, in any event, he would interpret not to ban the use of hoods, but to require that if hoods were used they did not cover the face.[164] He said at the handover he would probably have discussed the prohibition on hooding in passing, but as he had no direct involvement in Ops it would have been no more than a passing comment.[165]

10.119 Percy, 1 BW's Ops officer for much of the tour, was not aware of the use of hoods by 1 BW at any stage during the tour.[166] He did not remember seeing either FRAGO 152 or FRAGO 63[167] but had a recollection that the use of hooding was stopped.[168] He did not take part in the handover as Ops officer because by then he had become a company commander.[169]

---

[154] Philp BMI03817, paragraph 65
[155] S056 BMI 79/87/12-88/14
[156] S056 BMI 79/90/4-24
[157] S056 BMI 79/95/14-96/24
[158] Williamson BMI 62/82/13-83/17
[159] Williamson BMI 62/85/1-3
[160] Williamson BMI 62/71/16-19
[161] Williamson BMI 62/73/18-74/1
[162] Williamson BMI03214, paragraph 34
[163] Williamson BMI 62/127/17-128/2
[164] Williamson BMI 62/128/20-130/25
[165] Williamson BMI 62/133/12-134/22
[166] Percy BMI 61/87/7-13
[167] Percy BMI03799, paragraph 55
[168] Percy BMI03796-7, paragraphs 46-47
[169] Percy BMI03801, paragraph 65

10.120 Ord was Ops Officer of 1 BW from late May 2003. He conducted the handover to Capt Michael Elliott (his opposite number at 1 QLR). He said that he had never personally seen hooding in Iraq.[170] He said that he had copied all relevant orders for Elliott. These would have included FRAGO 63. He did not have an understanding of how prisoner handling was dealt with and would not have gone through the orders in any detail. He said he would have gone through key orders with Elliott but was unable to remember if this included FRAGO 63.[171] In oral evidence to the Inquiry Ord asserted that he was certain FRAGO 63 was handed over as it was a key order.[172]

10.121 Fraser remembered a shemagh being used as a blindfold on some occasions. He did not remember whether sandbags were used.[173] He did not recall a time when hooding ceased and he said 1 BW continued to deprive people of sight when it was necessary to do so. He did not remember seeing a FRAGO banning the use of hoods or the covering of faces.[174] However, he left theatre before the end of the tour.[175]

10.122 Vincent took over from Fraser when the latter left theatre.[176] He is an Australian and fits the description given by Maj Anthony Royce of the officer to whom he spoke during the recce (see below). His evidence was that he had no knowledge of the process of prisoner handling. He denied that he had told Royce that hooding was a standard operating procedure.[177]

10.123 Bruce regarded hooding as a procedure used by the Army for as long as he could remember. He never thought it was inhumane.[178] He recalled hoods being used in training in Canada. There was never any suggestion that it was inappropriate.[179] He attended the Prisoner Handling and Tactical Questioning (PH&TQ) course at Chicksands in 2003. This was a later course than the one attended by Williamson and Gallacher. There, he was told that a detainee should be blindfolded from the point of capture to the TDF and from the TDF to the tactical questioner.[180] However, at Chicksands it was made clear that blindfolding should not be used solely to disorientate a prisoner for questioning.[181] It was also made clear that stress positions were prohibited.[182]

10.124 Bruce said he had a vague memory that at one point in the tour instructions were given that detainees should not be hooded.[183] His recollection was that prisoners were hooded in the early combat phase but he believed this had ceased after the order to stop hooding.[184] He was not present at the handover because he had left theatre a few weeks earlier.[185]

---

[170] Ord BMI07554, paragraph 33
[171] Ord BMI07569-70, paragraphs 103-107
[172] Ord BMI 82/189/21-191/22
[173] Fraser BMI 63/52/6-16
[174] Fraser BMI 63/54/23-55/18
[175] Fraser BMI 63/67/24-68/5
[176] Ibid.
[177] Vincent BMI 98/129/23-130/5; Vincent BMI 98/135/4-16
[178] Bruce BMI 62/38/10-20
[179] Bruce BMI 62/7/10-8/15
[180] Bruce BMI 62/12/25-13/17
[181] Bruce BMI 62/14/13-18
[182] Bruce BMI 62/16/22-17/16
[183] Bruce BMI 62/30/12-17
[184] Bruce BMI 62/37/3-15
[185] Bruce BMI02705, paragraph 46

Gallacher's evidence and his briefing

10.125 Gallacher stood out as a witness whose evidence was somewhat different to the evidence of all the other Black Watch witnesses. He attended the same JSIO course at Chicksands in January 2003 which Williamson attended. In marked contrast to Williamson and Bruce his evidence was that at Chicksands, during a role-playing exercise, he was placed in a stress position and hooded with a sandbag.[186] He described this as a method for conditioning High Value Targets (HVTs).[187] It is, however, not clear from his evidence whether the role-playing exercise took place as a demonstration of how to treat prisoners or during the conduct after capture element of the course.[188] He might also have picked up the use of stress positions from conversation in the margins of the course. Perhaps it does not matter, because I accept that whatever the explanation was for his understanding of these techniques, he genuinely believed it was a method of conditioning detainees before they were questioned. I have addressed these issues in more detail in Part VI of this Report.

10.126 Gallacher said on his return to 1 BW after the course at Chicksands and before they were deployed to Iraq, he briefed the whole Brigade on everything he had been taught about prisoner handling, including the use of hoods and stress positions. Also included in his lecture was a section on conduct after capture.[189] He said that he told his audience that hooding could and should be used at certain times, but stress positions were not to be used.[190] There is some contemporaneous support for the suggestion that Gallacher briefed members of 1 BW on the use of hooding.[191] His belief was that stress positions could only be used if ordered by Intelligence or the Battlegroup chain of command.[192] Later in his oral evidence, Gallacher said that he told the audience that they could be expected to be put in stress positions if captured but it was highly unlikely the audience *"…would do it … because it's quite impossible to put somebody in a stress position when they are in the back of a Warrior vehicle."*[193]

10.127 In his position as Provost Sergeant, Gallacher said he subjected HVTs brought into 1 BW to hooding and stress positions. He would get an indication from either Williamson or Col Sgt John Penman, the second in command (2IC) of the Intelligence Cell, as to which prisoners were HVTs. Penman gave him this indication 99% of the time.[194] Gallacher would then put them in stress positions but *"never, ever"* would he kick or punch them. However, he might have had to manhandle them.[195] He agreed that the prisoner would also be hooded.[196]

---

[186] Gallacher BMI 61/7/16-8/16; Gallacher BMI06879, paragraph 16
[187] Gallacher BMI 61/9/20-24
[188] Gallacher BMI 61/17/7-20; Gallacher BMI06879, paragraph 16
[189] Gallacher BMI06881, paragraph 24
[190] Gallacher BMI 61/20/5-11
[191] MOD055778. In the context of one of the 1 BW deaths in custody (see below, Chapter 5), as SIB interim report of June 2003 records that Gallacher told the SIB that *"... prior to the conflict whilst in Kuwait, he gave refresher training to members of 1 BW, stating this included hooding and restraint".*
[192] Gallacher BMI06880, paragraph 18
[193] Gallacher BMI 61/45/2-11
[194] Gallacher BMI 61/23/20-24/8
[195] Gallacher BMI 61/27/4-23
[196] Gallacher BMI 61/28/20-22

10.128 Gallacher said detainees were usually hooded and in stress positions for no longer than twenty to 30 minutes[197] and that this type of conditioning was only used by him on approximately five to ten detainees.[198]

10.129 Gallacher remembered the handover which involved Payne, whom he knew, and one other 1 QLR soldier whom he thought might have been Provost Sgt Paul Smith.[199] Gallacher did not think he had referred to any orders but he did demonstrate the whole process from the point of arrival of the prisoners at BG Main to the transfer to Um Qasr. He told the two 1 QLR soldiers about HVTs and that hooding and stress positions were permitted for them.[200] He refuted Payne's suggestion that Payne learned nothing of this at the handover.[201]

10.130 Apart from Henderson, no member of 1 BW who gave evidence to the Inquiry admitted seeing Gallacher either put detainees in stress positions or seeing them hooded and in stress positions. Williamson said he never went to the TDF because as the Intelligence officer he did not want to risk being identified.[202] If he had seen detainees in stress positions and hooded in the TDF he would have told the RSM and Gallacher that it should not be happening. Bruce also said, as did other witnesses, that he was unaware of Gallacher carrying out these practices.[203] It is also of note that Payne, who must have had contact with Gallacher during the handover, made no mention of seeing prisoners being hooded or in stress positions in the TDF during the handover.[204]

Henderson's evidence

10.131 Henderson was called to give evidence to the Inquiry largely because of the contents of a book entitled "Warrior" which he co-authored with another person. He described prisoners being brought into the detention area by a company, other than his company, and being made to kneel on the ground with their hands on their heads. At the time they were hooded.[205] His company only hooded prisoners who were dangerous.[206] He did not receive any direction or order prohibiting prisoners' faces being covered but he did not remember any detainee being hooded from about mid-May onwards.[207]

10.132 Henderson explained that he had been taught about the use of stress positions in pre-deployment training "...*by way of a verbal presentation in the cinema in Fallingbostal*".[208] He said that he had been taught to hood and handcuff prisoners upon capture of them in order to maintain control.[209]

---

[197] Gallacher BMI 61/27/24-28/1
[198] Gallacher BMI 61/33/10-13
[199] Gallacher BMI06891, paragraph 80
[200] Gallacher BMI06892, paragraphs 81-3
[201] Gallacher BMI 61/58/23-59/8
[202] Williamson BMI 62/103/16-104/8
[203] Bruce BMI 62/46/17-23
[204] Payne BMI 32/33/11-34/2
[205] Henderson BMI06457, paragraph 93
[206] Henderson BMI 60/15/5-14; Henderson BMI06455, paragraph 85
[207] Henderson BMI 60/66/14-21
[208] Henderson BMI 60/13/21-14/8
[209] Henderson BMI 60/11/6-13

10.133 In his Inquiry witness statement Henderson confirmed that extracts from his book, which were subsequently put to him by Counsel to the Inquiry, were accurate.[210] He remembered the lecturer in Fallingbostal referring to prisoners being made to run between two lines of soldiers with the soldiers "...*shoving the prisoner along at speed while shouting at them ...*". This was referred to as "*running them through screaming gauntlets*".[211]

10.134 Henderson said that prisoners would be made to sit or kneel down at Camp Stephen, but stress positions, as described by the lecturer, were never used.[212] It is suggested by those representing Henderson that the lecturer was probably Gallacher.[213]

Other evidence relating to Gallacher's briefing and Henderson's evidence

10.135 A number of witnesses gave evidence refuting Henderson's allegations. Williamson said he had no recollection of stress positions being referred to in pre-deployment training. He felt confident that if they had been mentioned he would have remembered.[214] He also had no recollection of "screaming gauntlets".[215] He said he was not aware that Gallacher briefed others that stress positions were legitimate. He said if he had been aware of this he would have contradicted Gallacher. He was also unaware of Gallacher's practice when dealing with HVTs.[216]

10.136 Bruce remembered Gallacher providing a briefing on what he had learned on the course.[217] He did not attend the briefing[218] but he said he could not remember Gallacher cascading the information which he had seen in Gallacher's Inquiry witness statement, namely about hooding and stress positions.[219]

10.137 Fraser said he had never heard of the term "screaming gauntlets" before the Inquiry. He denied categorically that it had been taught at Fallingbostal.[220] Percy also did not remember being given any information on stress positions, hooding or "running gauntlets" by Gallacher in a briefing.[221]

10.138 Finally, Henderson in his book alleged that there was a FRAGO that authorised the use of hooding. In the book this is described as a reference to S056, his company commander, digging out a FRAGO clearly authorising the practice of hooding.[222] In oral evidence Henderson admitted that he had not seen the order. He explained that he had heard of its existence and that it was an oral order which would be found in radio logs.[223] S056 had no recollection of such an order and thought it

---

[210] Henderson BMI06448, paragraph 48

[211] Henderson BMI06449, paragraph 51

[212] Henderson BMI 60/34/19-35/8

[213] SUB000932, paragraph 512; SUB000940, paragraph 536

[214] Williamson BMI 62/73/2-17

[215] Williamson BMI 62/83/18-84/4

[216] Williamson BMI 62/96/11-23

[217] Bruce BMI 62/27/17-19

[218] Bruce BMI 62/56/21-57/2

[219] Bruce BMI 62/26/12-25

[220] Fraser BMI 63/50/1-6

[221] Percy BMI 61/71/7-18

[222] Henderson BMI 60/44/5-45/15; BMI02847

[223] Henderson BMI 60/46/18-47/4

improbable that it would have been made orally.[224] As I have explained above, the Inquiry has found no record in the relevant radio operator's logbook relating to any orders referring to hooding.

1 QLR Witnesses: The Recce

10.139 Mendonça led a small party from 1 QLR on a visit to 1 BW from 7 to 10 May 2003 (the recce). The purpose was for each member of the party to meet his or her opposite number in 1 BW in order to obtain a preliminary idea of the nature of the duties 1 QLR would be performing on deployment to Iraq. The recce was aimed at assisting 1 QLR when it came to pre-deployment briefings. Of those 1 QLR officers who went on the recce, Mendonça, Maj John Lighten, Elliott and Royce said that on this visit they saw prisoners who were hooded. None of them saw any prisoner in a stress position.

10.140 Mendonça said that on the recce he saw prisoners hooded either in Camp Stephen or being brought into Camp Stephen. He did not discuss the details of prisoner handling with his opposite number, Riddell-Webster.[225]

10.141 Lighten, the Officer Commanding B Company, saw an arrested man with a hood on his head. He understood the man had been arrested on suspicion of murder.[226] In oral evidence he was uncertain whether he witnessed this on the recce or at the handover.[227]

10.142 Elliott, at the time of Op Telic 1 and the first half of Op Telic 2, the Operations Officer, went on the recce. He said he did not remember any emphasis being put on hooding but he saw this practice when he visited one of the company locations. He understood the use of hooding outside the camp was to protect the identity of the detainees. Inside the camp it was to protect the security of the camp.[228] He could not recall seeing detainee handling during the handover period.[229]

10.143 Royce, later the Battlegroup Internment Review Officer (BGIRO), said that he spent most of his time on the recce with a young Australian who was the Officer Commanding HQ Company, 1 BW. This officer explained to him that when captured, detainees were hooded and handcuffed. He said hooding and handcuffing was a standard operating procedure "*from 7 Armd Bde*". It had continued after the warfighting phase ended.[230] Royce said he assumed that 1 QLR companies had inherited these procedures from 1 BW companies from which they took over.[231]

---

[224] S056 BMI07955, paragraph 8
[225] Riddell-Webster BMI 59/226/18-227/23
[226] Lighten BMI05967, paragraph 50
[227] Lighten BMI 56/85/15-86/11
[228] Elliott BMI06392, paragraph 16
[229] Elliott BMI 58/182/14-15
[230] Royce BMI03147, paragraph 50
[231] Royce BMI03148, paragraph 51

1 QLR Witnesses: The Handover

10.144 The handover by 1 BW to 1 QLR took place from 24 to 26 June 2003. A number of 1 QLR officers and soldiers said that during this period they saw detained civilians either being hooded or brought into camp hooded. Mendonça's evidence about the handover went no further than what he had said about the recce. He left it to the Ops officer, Elliott, to alert him to whatever orders it was relevant for him to see.[232] Major Stephen Bostock, at the time 2IC, remembered seeing 1 BW hooding detainees during that time. He understood it was a local security measure. Those detained were hooded when arrested but had their hoods removed when they were in the TDF. He believed this was a 1 BW standard operating procedure. He thought, as a security procedure, it was reasonable and legitimate. He saw no hooding after 1 BW had left.[233]

10.145 Maj Mark Kenyon, the Officer Commanding C Company 1 QLR, said he saw hooded detainees being brought into camp at C Company's location by 1 BW patrols. He remembered seeing his soldiers being shown the use of sandbags and plasticuffs on detained prisoners.[234]

10.146 Lighten also said he understood from 1 BW that hooding was used for security purposes. He saw some suspected looters with sandbags over their heads during the handover from Maj Douglas Hay, the Officer Commanding B Company, 1 BW. Lighten could not be certain whether this had been on the recce or at the handover.[235] But he understood the hooding was for security to prevent detainees seeing the layout of the camp[236]; and *"As far as I understand it we simply trained our troops to continue operating as the Black Watch had operated"*.[237]

10.147 Royce, who had been told about hooding by the officer commanding HQ Company at the time of the recce, said he raised the matter on handover with one of the 1 BW Battlegroup staff. He did so because in pre-deployment training at Catterick he had been told hooding was not permitted, but he had seen detainees with hoods on at the time of the handover. The Black Watch officer told him that it had been sanctioned by Brigade for security reasons inside the camp.[238]

10.148 Royce's recollection of this conversation, which he described in evidence,[239] is very similar to the description in his Inquiry witness statement of the conversation he said he had with the Australian Black Watch officer during the recce. I have a strong suspicion that unwittingly Royce was confused as to whether there was one or two conversations. It seems to me more likely that there was only one conversation and that was with the Australian officer. This is, in my opinion, not a significant issue, since I accept that whether the conversation occurred on the recce or at the handover, Royce had such a conversation with a Black Watch officer.

---

[232] Mendonça BMI01101, paragraph 38

[233] Bostock BMI 55/139/15-140/14; Bostock BMI04548, paragraph 29

[234] Kenyon BMI 60/100/24-101/11; Kenyon BMI01503, paragraph 11

[235] Lighten BMI 56/84/23-87/17

[236] Lighten BMI05967, paragraphs 52-53

[237] Ibid., paragraph 54

[238] I address this evidence in Parts VI and XIII of this Report

[239] Royce BMI 57/21/20-23/25

10.149 Capt Shaun Cronin, 1 QLR's Intelligence Officer at the time of the handover, did not remember anything relating to prisoner handling being discussed with his opposite number at the handover. He would not have expected to have done so since his role did not include anything to do with prisoner handling.[240] He believed at the time that hooding was permitted.[241]

10.150 Elliott was not specifically asked in evidence to comment on Ord's evidence since what Ord said about the handover only emerged after Elliott had given evidence. But the tenor of his evidence was to the effect that he had no knowledge of any order banning hooding. In a witness statement made by Elliott subsequent to him giving evidence he said he did not think he could have seen FRAGO 63. He believed hooding was current practice and if he had seen FRAGO 63 banning hooding he was certain he would have remembered it and that at the time he would then have alerted others to the issue.[242]

10.151 WO2 Noel Parry, CSM of C Company, accepted that hooding of detainees was carried out by 1 QLR and said he believed it had been part of the process handed over by 1 BW.[243]

10.152 1QLR's RSM, George Briscoe, and three 1 QLR soldiers said that they also saw detainees who had been hooded by 1 BW units at the handover. The three soldiers were Paul Smith, the Provost Sgt, Cpl Kevin Stacey and Pte Anthony Riley.

10.153 Briscoe said that out on a patrol with 1 BW, at the handover, he witnessed the use of hoods and cuffs which he described as "*general policy*". He said 1 QLR continued with this practice as "[n]*o orders had been received to the contrary and no one suggested that it was wrong*".[244]

10.154 Smith remembered that he shadowed Gallacher during the handover, but that it was a rushed and unsatisfactory process.[245] He did not remember receiving any specific instructions or procedural information as to the handling of detainees.[246] He said that he saw 1 BW practising hooding on detainees but was not given any guidelines for the use of hoods on them.[247]

10.155 Stacey said that hooding had been a standard operating procedure of the Black Watch which 1 QLR had taken over. He went out with 1 BW and recalled a prisoner being hooded.[248]

10.156 Riley said that at the handover, they had seen 1 BW bringing prisoners to the camp with hoods on.[249] They adopted their practices.[250]

---

[240] Cronin BMI06376, paragraph 18
[241] Cronin BMI 58/5/1-4
[242] Elliott BMI09033, paragraph 5
[243] Parry BMI 58/96/22-97/6
[244] Briscoe BMI 43/111/17-19; Briscoe BMI00728, paragraph 20
[245] Sgt Paul Smith BMI 44/177/17-178/5
[246] Sgt Paul Smith BMI05000, paragraphs 42-44
[247] Sgt Paul Smith BMI 44/167/13-168/15; Sgt Paul Smith BMI05002 paragraphs 49-50
[248] Stacey BMI 21/131/25-132/5; Stacey BMI01562, paragraph 45
[249] Pte Anthony Riley BMI 19/29/5-14
[250] MOD000620

10.157 Payne did not claim to have learned hooding or the conditioning of prisoners from 1 BW. He described having an *"informal"* discussion with the Provost Sergeant of 1 BW, whom I find was Gallacher, during which he was told that the responsibility for detainees consisted only of taking their names and organising transport to the TIF. He was told that was all that 1 BW did, they did not *"process"* the detainees in any way. Payne said that he had observed and learned nothing about hooding or conditioning from 1 BW which resulted in the way they were later used by 1 QLR.[251]

10.158 None of the 1 QLR personnel saw stress positions in use either during the recce or at the handover.

Findings and Conclusions in relation to 1 BW and 1 QLR

10.159 It was clear and not in dispute that during Op Telic 1, 1 BW did hood prisoners, whether prisoners of war or civilians. That they did so is consistent with my findings in relation to training in Part VI of this Report. There had been no clear doctrine or training policy about the means by which and circumstances in which sight deprivation could be applied. No doubt the use of hoods during the combat phase for transfer of prisoners from point of capture to the capturing units' location was regarded as a reasonable security precaution. It was clear that Brims' oral order prohibiting hooding in early April 2003 did not reach 1 BW.

10.160 The evidence concerning whether FRAGO 63 reached 1 BW was not entirely consistent. I found the 1 BW officers and NCOs who gave evidence to the Inquiry an impressive body of witnesses. Men like S056 gave their evidence with an air of real authority. I have no difficulty in accepting that following an order from S056 the men of C Company, 1 BW, did stop hooding detainees. However, not all the 1 BW witnesses remembered seeing FRAGO 63. Wilkinson and Bruce did not remember seeing FRAGO 63 but each had a vague memory of hooding ending before the end of the tour. Channer and Fraser did not remember any ban on hooding. In Fraser's case he probably had left theatre by the time FRAGO 63 was promulgated. On balance, I accept that FRAGO 63 was cascaded down from 7 Armd Bde to 1 BW.

10.161 There is, in my judgment, no doubt that FRAGO 63 was regarded by most of the officers of 1 BW who saw it, as a ban on hooding. It ought, as Riddell-Webster accepted, to have put a stop to hooding by any sub-unit of 1 BW by the time of the handover. However, for reasons which I will explain, I find that it did not, or at least it did not put a stop to hooding universally throughout the Battlegroup.

10.162 As for 1 QLR witnesses, on this issue, in my opinion, there is no reason to doubt the evidence of those who said they saw hooding occurring at the time of the recce. At the time of the 1 QLR recce, FRAGO 63 had not yet been issued. Since 1 BW had not received the earlier oral ban on hooding, it is not surprising that 1 QLR saw 1 BW hooding prisoners during the recce.

---

[251] Payne BMI 32/30/17-34/4; Payne BMI01724, paragraph 33

10.163 The evidence of members of 1 QLR seeing hooding at the time of the handover is more significant. By then, FRAGO 63 had been issued and so 1 BW ought to have stopped hooding. However, in my judgment, there is no reason to doubt the evidence of those who said they saw hooding by 1 BW on the handover. The evidence of Bostock, Kenyon, Provost Sgt Smith, Stacey and Anthony Riley, is too large a body of evidence to be discounted as inaccurate. I accept their evidence on this issue and I find that some elements of 1 BW were still hooding detainees at the time of the handover. I find, however, that such hooding was only for transfer of detainees from the point of capture to the company location or the TDF at BG Main.

10.164 In my view it is too much of a coincidence that Royce should describe the officer to whom he spoke as an Australian and for Vincent, an Australian, to have been on the strength at 1 BW headquarters. Whether it was Vincent to whom he spoke or another officer to whom, as I believe, he spoke at about the same time, I find that Royce was told that hooding at point of capture was a standard operating procedure. However, I am unable to determine whether this was at the time of the recce or the handover.

10.165 It follows from these findings that, in my judgment, some elements of 1 BW did continue to hood detainees arrested by them after FRAGO 63 had been received by the Battlegroup. This practice should have been stopped by the time of the handover. It is not possible to identify any particular sub-unit of 1 BW which continued to hood. But the overall responsibility for ensuring that the order was carried out must rest with the Commanding Officer and the RSM. Riddell-Webster and Bruce must, in my opinion, bear some responsibility in failing to ensure FRAGO 63 was effectively communicated and enforced across the Battlegroup.

10.166 It also follows from the above that, at least initially on their tour, 1 QLR probably carried out the practice of hooding detainees at point of capture in part because they had seen it operated by 1 BW.

10.167 Gallacher's evidence requires separate consideration. As may be imagined, his evidence has come in for both adverse and favourable comments from Core Participants and the Detainees. I found him to be a straightforward and honest witness. I have no doubt that he was telling the truth as he believed it to be about the events with which his evidence was concerned (see also Part VI, Chapter 4).

10.168 It is surprising that no other 1 BW witness observed his use of these techniques. But I reject the suggestion that others knew what he was doing. The explanation for this discrepancy, in my view, is that Gallacher's use of the techniques on HVTs was limited to a small number of detainees and for short periods of time in respect of each of them.

10.169 Gallacher should not have employed these techniques, and as an experienced NCO he ought to have realised they might be inhumane. However, on the assumption that, as I find, he believed he was permitted to deploy them, he did so only for short periods and he directly and personally supervised the detainees who were subjected to these techniques. His responsibility for doing so was therefore less than it otherwise might have been.

10.170 Bearing in mind none of the 1 QLR personnel say they saw these techniques being used by Gallacher, there is, in my opinion, no reason to find that any member of 1 QLR was influenced by anything which they saw Gallacher doing.

10.171 Nevertheless, the importance of Gallacher's evidence is that he picked up the use of these techniques from what he learned and was taught on his course at the JSIO, Chicksands. While I have found that the techniques were not authorised by the Prisoner Handling and Tactical Questioning (PH&TQ) course, it is a matter of concern that a student could have come away from the course mistakenly understanding them to be permitted.

10.172 As to Gallacher's use of hooding and stress positions, I find that none of the 1 QLR personnel were aware of the use made by Gallacher of hooding and stress positions on HVTs. I have no hesitation in reaching this conclusion in respect of all of the 1 QLR witnesses save for Provost Sgt Smith and Payne. In respect of these two men, not without a certain amount of hesitation, the conclusion I reach is that they did not understand from anything that they saw or were told by Gallacher that stress positions could be used on detainees. Payne, particularly, would have had a strong motive for accepting that he learned of the use of stress positions from Gallacher. For this reason it is difficult to believe that he was not telling the truth when he said he learned nothing of these techniques from Gallacher. I find that it is unlikely that in the relatively brief handover to 1 QLR Gallacher mentioned the use of stress positions on a limited number of HVTs. I reach the same conclusion in respect of Smith.

10.173 As for Henderson's evidence, I accept that he did attend some kind of pre-deployment lecture at which the lecturer spoke about prisoners being hooded and put in stress positions. I do not think it likely that this was from an Operational Training Advisory Group (OPTAG) instructor as Henderson at one stage suggested. I think it more probable that this links to Gallacher's mistaken understanding of hooding and stress positions and that Gallacher was probably the lecturer. I do not accept Henderson's evidence that the lecture included that detainees were made to run "the screaming gauntlet". There is no other evidence to support this allegation. I cannot tell from where this description came; it may have been a mistaken recollection confused with other training or possibly an exaggeration to add colour to his book.

10.174 It follows that I find Gallacher did give a lecture which included references to the use of hooding and stress positions as an aid to tactical questioning. What influence this had on the knowledge of 1 BW personnel on the use of these techniques is very hard to gauge. The Inquiry has not uncovered any witness other than Henderson who knew of these practices. It is also impossible to know whether it influenced other Battlegroups if indeed they were present. Gallacher suggested in his oral evidence that the talk he gave would have included that stress positions should not in fact be used. The only conclusion I can reach is that there may have been others in 1 BW or other Battlegroups who did think that hooding was permissible as an aid to tactical questioning. It is less likely this was conveyed in relation to stress positions. On the evidence received by the Inquiry I am confident that in 1 BW no one other than Gallacher used stress positions.

10.175 One final issue on hooding concerning 1 BW requires consideration. I have already found that FRAGO 63 was cascaded down to 1 BW. What I find difficult to understand is how it could not have come to the attention of 1 QLR on the handover. Ord, the 1 BW Operations Officer at the time of the handover, said that although he had not himself seen hooding, he was aware of FRAGO 63 and disseminated it appropriately throughout the Battlegroup. I have no doubt that he would have sought to do so, though it is less clear whether the order was in fact received by every relevant BW officer. Ord said he also handed all the key extant orders over to his opposite number in 1 QLR at the time of the handover. He said that he remembered going through all the orders one by one with his opposite number, Elliott. He was not, however, able to remember handing over that particular document, namely FRAGO 63 although he could not see how it would have been filtered out.[252]

10.176 As I have recorded above, in a supplementary statement, Elliott took issue with the suggestion that he received FRAGO 63. He believed hooding was current practice and if he had seen FRAGO 63 banning hooding he was certain he would have remembered it and that at the time he would then have alerted others to the issue.

10.177 At the Court Martial all parties proceeded on the basis that FRAGO 152 was not distributed to units at "ground level".[253] Leading Counsel for Mendonça at the Court Martial (and the Inquiry) Timothy Langdale QC asserted without challenge that neither 1 QLR nor any other unit at 19 Mech Bde ever received or saw FRAGO 152, which it must be assumed included FRAGO 63.[254] Further, an SIB Criminal Case Review Report into the Court Martial[255] stated that despite extensive inquiries FRAGO 152 was not recovered from similar documents submitted by Battlegroups on Op Telics 1 and 2. It recorded that "*This tends to suggest that they* [Battlegroups] *never had sight of it or received it.*"[256]

10.178 The Criminal Case Review Report went on to conclude that handover/takeover procedures at the time were poor and that "*There were no standard procedures for taking over extant theatre orders, policies and Standard Operating Procedures and, crucially, no method of checking that all incoming formations and units at every level had a copy of extant theatre instructions and were implementing them.*"[257]

10.179 Despite the concession made by the prosecution at the Court Martial and the conclusion in the Criminal Case Review Report, for the reasons referred to above, I adhere to my finding that the effect of FRAGO 152 was cascaded down to 1 BW in FRAGO 63. I am much less certain that it reached 19 Mech Bde or 1 QLR. The Inquiry has uncovered no evidence to show positively that it did reach 1 QLR. The only evidence that it did is derived from the evidence of Ord that he would have handed over all extant orders to Elliott. Given the paucity of direct evidence, I am unable to resolve this dispute. I think it very unlikely that Ord drew any particular attention to FRAGO 63 at the handover. That is not perhaps surprising given that FRAGO 29 had become the main order relating to the internment process. It is possible that FRAGO 63 was nevertheless in the group of extant orders that Ord handed over to Elliott. If that were the case, I think it likely that Elliott did not alight on the significance of the

---

[252] Ord BMI 82/198/5-25
[253] See Prosecuting Counsel, Julian Bevan QC's opening statement, CM 7/32/6-16
[254] CM 9/98/3-13
[255] MOD020524
[256] MOD020556
[257] Ibid.

prohibition on covering the faces of detainees contained within FRAGO 63. For the reasons I have explored in Part IX of this Report, that part of the guidance had not been given any particular prominence in FRAGO 63.

10.180 However, it is also possible that FRAGO 63 was simply not within the orders handed over by Ord to Elliott. In view of the Criminal Case Review Report, and the suggestion that no copy of the Order was found amongst 1 QLR's documents, this possibility cannot lightly be dismissed.[258] One can only speculate as to the reasons why this might have occurred. Other than administrative error, it may have been because subsequent orders, in particular FRAGO 29 had addressed the internment process. It may also have related to the fact that there appears to have been some issue with not all parts of 1 BW receiving the order that hooding was to cease.

10.181 In these circumstances, neither Ord nor Elliott can fairly be criticised for personal failures in relation to the handover of orders from 1 BW to 1 QLR.

10.182 What is clear, looking at the 1 BW / 1 QLR handover more broadly, is that whether or not the prohibition on covering detainees' faces in FRAGO 63 was part of the handover of written orders, the handover did not succeed in effectively conveying to 1 QLR that hooding had been banned in theatre.

---

[258] The Criminal Case Review Report refers to FRAGO 152 rather than FRAGO 63, its Brigade equivalent (MOD020556). However, no doubt the Report would have made it clear if a copy of FRAGO 63 had been found.

Chapter 5: Deaths in 1 BW Custody

10.183 Although what follows has no relevance to the issues relating to handovers, it is a convenient place in which to deal with evidence of civilian deaths in the custody of 1 BW during Op Telic 1.

10.184 In the course of its investigations the Inquiry touched on some evidence concerning the death in custody of four Iraqi civilians. Three of these deaths were connected with 1 BW. The first death involved C Company 1 BW; the second involved members of 32 Engineer Regiment who at the time were attached to 1 BW. The third died following an attempted arrest by 1 BW soldiers of a suspected looter. The very brief facts of each are as follows.

10.185 The first of these deaths was the subject of an SIB investigation. The SIB's report dated 8 July 2003 recited the evidence it had uncovered consisting principally of statements taken from 1 BW's officers and soldiers, and some medical evidence. [259] In short, the evidence appeared to show that on 8 May 2003, an Iraqi national was arrested by men from C Company following a planned search of a house in Basra. The house was found to have on the premises ammunition and weapon ancillaries. The detainee was hooded and taken to C Company's camp. Evidence from members of the detainee's family described him being beaten and kicked by soldiers. Evidence of the soldiers of 1 BW who detained this man was to the effect that on arrest he had been hooded for transit to C Company's camp. At the camp the hood was removed and he was left alone. Shortly afterwards he was found lying down and immobile. He was removed to the Czech Republic military hospital for examination and treatment but on arrival was pronounced dead. On examination by two Iraqi hospital forensic assistants no visible injuries were found and without performing a post mortem they pronounced him dead, attributing his death to cardiac arrest.

10.186 Heron, the legal officer at 7 Armd Bde, was recorded in the SIB report as having stated that the practice of hooding was "...open to debate".[260] However Heron said in oral evidence that he would have been very surprised if these were the words he had used; he knew of the concerns that Mercer had raised about hooding and was aware of the oral order that it should stop. Heron said that he was not aware that 1 BW were hooding prisoners and would have reported that as a matter of concern had he known.[261]

10.187 Both Henderson and S056 gave some evidence to the Inquiry concerning this first death in 1 BW custody. Henderson confirmed his understanding that the Detainee was not hooded at the time of his death. Henderson said that the RMP were particularly interested in the fact that the detainee had been hooded, but it had never been suggested to Henderson that this had contributed to the death. Henderson suggested in his book that when the RMP were investigating the death, S056 his Officer Commanding, had dug out a FRAGO from battalion headquarters authorising hooding. In fact, Henderson clarified in his oral evidence that he had never seen this order himself and it was only that S056 had intimated to the RMP that an order had been given in relation to hooding.[262] S056 recalled this death in custody and the conclusion of the investigation that the detainee had died of a heart attack. He did

---

259 MOD052221
260 MOD052223
261 Heron BMI 64/108/1-109/18
262 Henderson BMI 60/43/7-48/10

not recall a particular focus on the detainee having been hooded. Nor could S056 remember a FRAGO which had authorised hooding or providing this to the SIB.[263] I do not accept the suggestion that S056 produced a FRAGO that had positively authorised hooding. There is no support for that in the SIB report.

10.188 Richard Johnson, at the time Deputy Head of Policy Operations (POLOps), was asked in evidence to the Inquiry about a document entitled "*Update on the Death of an Iraqi Civilian detainee*" dated 20 May 2003.[264] This related in part to the first 1 BW death in custody but made no mention of the fact that he had been hooded. Johnson said he had some recollection of the case. He said he did not think he would have seen a full copy of the SIB report on the same death. Johnson was unsure that he had the amount of detail to know the deceased had been hooded when he arrived at the company location. "*It is not impossible that I would have known about it*".[265]

10.189 The second death occurred on 13 May 2003. Initially, such evidence as was available to the Inquiry surrounding this death was limited and came from a register of *Iraq Investigations Involving UK Service Personnel*[266] and an appendix dated 14 May 2004 to a letter sent by Amnesty International to the Prime Minister, the Rt. Hon. Tony Blair MP.[267] Subsequently, the MoD also disclosed to the Inquiry the SIB's interim report of June 2003[268], and final report of 16 February 2004.[269] The deceased, Abdul Jabbar Musa Ali, was arrested by 1 BW soldiers at his house. His son was arrested with him. They were both detained by 1 BW soldiers. Ali's son alleged that both of them were beaten by the soldiers and when they were removed from the house they were blindfolded and handcuffed. During his detention Ali became ill and was pronounced dead at 21.58hrs on 13 May 2003. He was examined by a Regimental Medical Officer (RMO) and a medic before being removed to hospital. The RMO gave the cause of death as a suspected heart attack. From the interim report, it would seem that one of the guards accepted that Ali did have a sandbag on his head while held in 1 BW custody.[270] The same report records Capt Neil Wilson of the Military Provost Staff (MPS) as having given briefings that the hooding of prisoners was not to be carried out (see further Part VI, Chapter 7 of this Report).[271] It also records Heron as stating that hooding was not referred to in the two MPS briefings he had attended or in his own briefings, and that hooding by JFIT personnel had been raised but that "*To date, the issue remains unresolved*".[272] Finally, I note that this interim report recorded Gallacher as saying that hooding of detainees had been taught at the PH&TQ course; that he had briefed members of 1 BW on hooding; that he had received no briefing indicating that hooding should not be carried out, and that the decision to hood was for the commander on the ground depending on the threat and situation at the time.[273]

---

[263] S056 BMI07955, paragraphs 7-8
[264] MOD052599
[265] Richard Johnson BMI 92/122/4-123/21
[266] MOD047671
[267] MOD007494; MOD007499. See too the Government response at MOD007522; MOD007542
[268] MOD055775
[269] MOD055770
[270] MOD055777, paragraph 11
[271] MOD055777, paragraph 13
[272] MOD055778, paragraph 15
[273] MOD055778, paragraph 16

10.190 The SIB started an investigation but by that time Ali had been buried and the family would not give permission for the body to be exhumed. Accordingly, the investigation went no further.[274]

10.191 The third death involving 1 BW was the death of Said Shabram on 24 May 2003. Brief details of his death also come from the register of *Iraq Investigations Involving UK Service Personnel*.[275] It appears Shabram was arrested by soldiers of 32 Engineer Regiment, at the time attached to 1 BW, for suspected looting. It was alleged that the soldiers forced Shabram to jump into a dock, causing him to die by drowning. Following an investigation an officer and two soldiers were reported to the Army Prosecuting Authority for consideration of a charge of manslaughter. From the information supplied to the Inquiry, the proceedings were temporarily suspended in 2005 due to difficulties in locating witnesses in Iraq,[276] although a further examination of the case was scheduled for later that year.[277]

10.192 The Inquiry has not attempted to investigate further these deaths nor would it have been within the terms of reference for this Inquiry to do so. I understand that each of these deaths are being considered by the Iraq Historic Allegations Team. The Inquiry's evidence touched on these deaths because they involved 1 BW and in the case of two of the deaths in custody, it appears the detainee was hooded. The SIB investigations into these deaths commented on the fact that the detainee had been hooded. These were missed opportunities to notice that the prohibition on hooding had not been adequately communicated. Beyond that, it is not right that I should comment on the 1 BW deaths in custody.

---

[274] MOD007542
[275] MOD047671; MOD047594
[276] MOD047951
[277] MOD047663

Chapter 6: Other Battlegroups

10.193 The Inquiry heard some evidence from members of other Battlegroups deployed on Op Telic 2 at the same time as 1 QLR. I acknowledge that there was only a limited amount of evidence from these sources.

10.194 For example, Maj George Wilson, was the 2IC of 1 King's Own Scottish Borderers (KOSB). He did not describe his Battlegroup as having seen or adopted the practice of hooding during the handover process from the preceding unit. Wilson said that he did not personally witness hooding but he was aware that it had occurred. He thought this was in the early stages of the tour, to transport detainees into their camp. [278] Capt Brian Aitken, BGIRO of 1 KOSB described hooding with sandbags as being a standard operating procedure throughout his career. It was not introduced to him in Iraq. He added that he did not remember seeing anyone hooded whilst on Op Telic 2 and to his knowledge at least, 1 KOSB prisoners were not hooded.[279]

10.195 Lt Col Ciaran Griffin, the Commanding Officer of 1 Kings Battlegroup did not mention the practice of hooding being inherited from previous units on Op Telic 1. His understanding was that hooding was not the subject of any general prohibition. He said hooding with sandbags was a technique sometimes employed by men from 1 Kings during Op Telic 2 but this was only done for security reasons.[280] Capt David Hunt, the Intelligence Officer for 1 Kings described the use of sandbags as hoods at the start of Op Telic 2 as a practice derived from his training and consistent with standard army practices.[281] Troop Leader Lt Joshua King of the Royal Tank Regiment was attached to 1 Kings and undertook tactical questioning for that Battlegroup. His understanding that the use of hooding was appropriate came through the training he had received during the JSIO PH&TQ course. On the same course he was taught that stress positions were banned.[282] WO2 Marc Bannister, was also of the Royal Tank Regiment attached to 1 Kings and carried out tactical questioning for them. He made the same point as regards sight deprivation.[283]

10.196 Capt Gareth Barber, the Intelligence Officer and BGIRO for 40th Regiment Royal Artillery, said that the hooding of prisoners with sandbags was a standard procedure before Op Telic 2.[284]

10.197 Where these witnesses attended courses at the JSIO, Chicksands, a more detailed description of their evidence relating to training is to be found in Part VI, Chapter 4 of this Report. In Part XII, I consider by reference to these witnesses and others whether Op Telic 2 Battlegroups other than 1 QLR hooded prisoners.

10.198 In relation to handovers, I conclude that none of these witnesses from other Op Telic 2 Battlegroups suggested that the hooding of prisoners was a practice that they adopted because of what had been handed over to them by their predecessor Battlegroups from Op Telic 1. At the same time, however, none of them referred to the prohibition on hoods as having been specifically drawn to their attention during the handovers they received.

---

[278] Maj George Wilson BMI01314, paragraph 29
[279] Aitken BMI01617, paragraph 18(c); Aitken BMI01623, paragraph 39
[280] Griffin BMI06562, paragraphs 17-26
[281] Hunt BMI05472, paragraph 26
[282] Lt Joshua King BMI03977, paragraphs 20-36
[283] Bannister BMI05424, paragraph 34
[284] Barber BMI 58/64/14-65/6

Part XI

Op Telic 2: Orders and Guidance on Prisoner Handling

Chapter 1: 13 July 2003, 19 Mech Bde's FRAGO 85 and the Arrest Procedures Card

11.1 As I have addressed in Part X of this Report, 1 Queen's Lancashire Regiment (1 QLR) assumed command from 1 Black Watch (BW) through a relief in place over 25 to 26 June 2003, with the formal flag change occurring on 27 June; 19 Mech Bde assumed responsibility for Basra from 7 Armd Bde on 4 July 2003 and, at Divisional level, the handover occurred between 10 to 12 July 2003.

11.2 In this Part of the Report, I turn now to look at how the orders for prisoner handling developed during the course of Op Telic 2 after 12 July 2003.

11.3 On 13 July 2003, very close to the start of Op Telic 2, 19 Mech Bde issued a miscellaneous FRAGO, FRAGO 85. The order dealt with several aspects not relevant to the Inquiry. However, the first part of the order annexed a guide to arrest procedures that had been prepared by Maj Russell Clifton. I set out the relevant extracts below:[1]

> *DTG: 131600Jul03*
>
> *FRAGO 85 19 MECH BDE MISC FRAGO*
>
> *Time Zone Used Throughout the Order: Local.*
>
> *Task Chg. No change*
>
> *G1*
>
> *1. Arrest Card. S02 Legal has produced a useful guide outlining the correct arrest procedure and detailing the process for interning a person. The attached guide should be issued to patrol commanders.*

---

[1] MOD023089-93

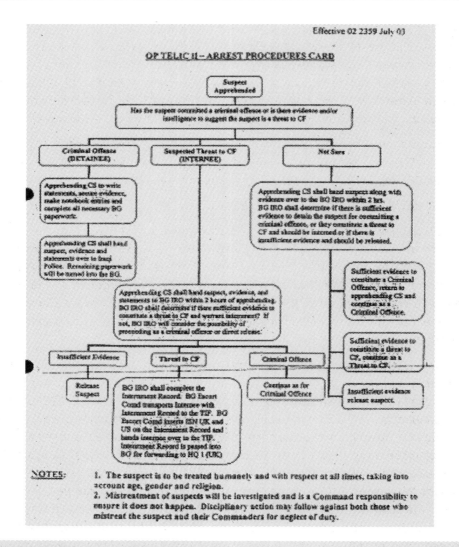

INTERNMENT AND DETENTION

PROCEDURES

1. *HQ 1 (UK) Armd Div FRAGO 29 to OPO 005 03 – Internment procedures dictated that persons assessed as a threat to CF was to be a G2 led G3 Ops responsibility. In accordance with FRAGO 29. Annex A to HQ 19 Mech Bde Misc FRAGO 81 is hereby amended so that the BG Internment Review Officer (BG IRO) replaces the RMP in the decision making process. A revised arrest procedures card for patrol commanders is attached to reflect this change of responsibility. A copy of FRAGO 29 (including Annexes A to D) is attached for Comds. Ops Offrs and BG IROs. Note that FRAGO 29 allows up to 14 hrs from time of capture to transfer to the Theatre Internment Facility.*

DETENTION OF CRIMINALS – EVIDENCE

2. *Further to paragraph 8 of Annex A to FRAGO 81, below is guidance on the type of evidence that it is imperative call signs provide to the Iraqi police when they witness a crime in order to maximise the likelihood of a conviction. Embedded RMP should assist with making the statement wherever possible, as most offences are very similar in law to the UK equivalent. Situation specific advice on evidence is available from the RMP chain of command or SO2 Legal HQ 19 Mech Bde on request.*

3. *At least two statements per incident should be provided, with the date and time of the incident and number, rank, name and unit of the person making the statement clearly shown. Full details of the incident should be given, with an accurate description of the accused and*

his clothing, the time and location of the incident, the actions of the accused before and after discovery, and the details of any complainant/victim if known. Exhibits recovered should be described in detail with any unique identifying marks recorded. If exhibits are retained by the unit for security reasons this should be mentioned in the statement and these exhibits made available to the court if requested and security allows. To help make sure that the statement is taken into consideration by the Investigating Judge it should be translated if possible.

4. CF personnel who provide a statement may be asked to give evidence to the Investigating Judge. CF personnel cannot be compelled to give evidence so it is a command decision whether CF personnel should be made available to give evidence.

INTERNMENT – EVIDENCE AND INTELLIGENCE

5. In all pre-planned operations advice is available from SO2 Legal HQ 19 Mech Bde on the evidence and intelligence required to justify internment. On reactive internment cases the BG IRO must decide whether the security of CF makes it absolutely necessary to intern the suspect concerned. Where an individual has deliberately targeted CF the BG IRO should, taking into consideration the nature of the targeting, decide if there is any way other than internment of guaranteeing the security of CF. If there is not, he may decide that internment is justified.

6. Where a suspect has been engaged in criminal activity assessed as intended to undermine CF security and, or has engaged CF when challenged, the BG IRO should decide if the matter is best dealt with as a criminal act or as an internment case. The BG IRO should first decide if the suspect is likely continue to use criminality to attempt to undermine CF security and/or to engage CF again if caught in a criminal act. If the answer to either question is yes, the BG IRO may make an assessment of the current status of the Iraqi judicial system in the AO to decide what is likely to happen to the suspect if handed over to the Iraqi police. If the BG IRO assesses the suspect is likely to be granted bail, he should consider the effect on the security of CF if the suspect is released. It is open to the BG IRO to decide to pass the suspect over to the Iraqi police with a direction that if the suspect is to be released on bail he should be released back into CF custody. At that stage the decision on internment can be revisited.

7. If the BG IRO feels that the security of CF includes maintaining the goodwill of the community, because losing that goodwill would cause situations that affect the security of CF, he should say so in his justification. There should be evidence or intelligence to back up this assertion – for example information regarding the public view of particular crimes or the issue of bail, and the consequential effect on CF security this may have. The prevalence of the crime involved, and criminal patterns being set in the AO, and the effect of the crime on the community and infrastructure may be relevant here. Evidence or intelligence of intimidation of the Iraqi police or judiciary that leads the BG IRO to believe that the matter cannot be dealt with as a criminal act should also be included, as should an indication of how the criminal process has dealt with such cases in the past.

8. A report from G2 on the AO at the time of the incident should be included if necessary to provide more detail of the environment, threat assessment and intent of the community, and the likely reaction and effect on the security of CF if the suspect is not interned. As much information as possible should be provided on the suspect, including evidence or intelligence of any link to either a pro-regime, terrorist or other organisation that is a threat to CF. Any previous criminal activity or links to organized crime should be detailed, with an assessment of the effect of organized crime on the goodwill of the community and therefore the security of CF. Similarly, any information in relation to tribal feuding (if relevant) and the consequences of releasing the suspect if involved in tribal feuding should be included in the report.

> *9. As much of the justification for internment is likely to be based on generic information about the effectiveness of the local criminal justice system, the incidence of tribal feuding and the effect on the goodwill of the community of continued lawlessness, the BG IRO or G2 may consider keeping a running file on such issues which could assist in deciding whether or not to intern suspects.*
>
> *10. It must be remembered that internment is a draconian process, which effectively amounts to indefinite imprisonment without the protections of the criminal justice system. It should only be used as a last resort when it is absolutely necessary and there is no other way to ensure CF security. Any BG decision to deal with the matter by internment rather than by use of the Iraqi criminal process should be justified. If the justification does not stand up to the review process at the 48 hr point, or at anytime thereafter, the suspect will be released. If any situation specific guidance is required whilst the BG IRO is making the decision whether to intern or not, SO2 Legal HQ 19 Mech Bde can be contacted on Mobile [redacted] or PATRON [redacted]."*

11.4   The following points about this order and the accompanying guidance and arrest card should be noted:

(1)   the arrest procedures card, which was to be issued down to the level of patrol commanders, contained the requirement that suspects be treated "*humanely and with respect at all times, taking into account age, gender and religion*" coupled with a warning about disciplinary action directed at both perpetrators of abuse and their commanders;

(2)   the guidance required call signs who apprehended suspects to hand over the suspects, evidence and statements to the Battlegroup Internment Review Officer (BGIRO) within two hours of apprehension;

(3)   within the guidance, Clifton offered himself to BGIROs as a point of contact in cases where they might require further guidance. He reminded recipients that internment was a draconian process;[2]

(4)   save for the advice to treat prisoners humanely and with respect, the guidance did not address physical aspects of prisoner handling;

(5)   the guidance did not refer to the prohibition on hooding; and

(6)   the fourteen hour time limit derived from FRAGO 29 was referred to in the two pages of guidance that followed the arrest procedures card.[3]

11.5   Clifton told the Inquiry that he had caused the arrest procedures card to be issued earlier than FRAGO 85 itself and he pointed to the date on the card of 2 July 2003. The card was probably issued with an earlier FRAGO, FRAGO 81, on 2 July 2003. Clifton said that he amended the previous card to give a slightly different emphasis, including the express requirement for humane treatment. Clifton said that this was in part because he had learned from Lt Col Nicholas Mercer of investigations into whether there had been mistreatment of prisoners.[4]

11.6   Clifton also said that he envisaged that tactical questioning would be completed within the two hour time frame set for apprehending call signs to get the suspects, together with supporting evidence and statements, to the BGIRO. In that respect, Clifton said

---

[2] Ibid, paragraphs 5 and 10
[3] Ibid, paragraph 1
[4] Clifton BMI 81/26/24-28/17; Clifton BMI04574, paragraph 53

that he would have drafted the order with input from the relevant people. Nobody had alerted him to the possibility that this two hour time frame for tactical questioning would not work. He suggested that for pre-planned arrest operations, much of the intelligence ought to have been in the intelligence pack prepared beforehand. Clifton accepted, however, that the card could have been clearer in conveying that the two hour time limit was also meant to include tactical questioning.[5]

11.7   Clifton was asked why the prohibition on hooding was not referred to in this card. Clifton's answers reveal the confidence he had at the time that the hooding ban had already been communicated to the units who had deployed on Op Telic 2:

> "Q. Given the underlining that Colonel Mercer had given, as you tell us, to the question of the ban on hooding, why didn't the ban on hooding appear in this card?
>
> A. I had understood, from what Colonel Mercer had told me and because the brief had been given before troops arrived in theatre, that that was the standard operating procedure for hooding not to be used. The card, as you can see, is quite detailed as it is. It needed to be small enough that it could be carried on patrol. I didn't stop to consider, I don't think, listing all of the things that were banned and that soldiers should have known were banned.
>
> Q. But we do understand it correctly, do we? One of the things that you remember is the vehemence with which Colonel Mercer, at the very early stage, was at pains to indicate to you the instruction that hooding was banned?
>
> A. Yes.
>
> Q. It didn't occur to you in this card that perhaps reinforcing that by placing it on the card clearly would be of assistance?
>
> A. I did not think about it at the time because I understood that order to be sufficiently understood in theatre and a blanket over-arching "treat suspects humanely" should have sufficed.
>
> Q. Would you have regarded hooding with a hessian sack as being humane treatment?
>
> A. I think it's a question of degree. If you put a hessian sack on somebody's head for 30 seconds, it's probably not inhumane. If you leave it for three hours in the sun, then it gets to the end of the spectrum where it is. I think the purpose of the order was to take away that question of judgment from soldiers on the ground."[6]

11.8   Clifton's diary shows that he followed up FRAGO 85 by mentioning evidence gathering and internment at the Chief of Staff's regular "prayers" meeting, and with a visit to the King's Own Scottish Borders (KOSB) Battlegroup where Clifton had previously advised in favour of the release of some 40 internees when there was insufficient evidence to justify their internment.[7] From his diary, there is no doubt that Clifton frequently raised issues about the internment process, evidence gathering and an increasing desire that he be contacted in cases of doubt regarding internment decisions.[8]

11.9   Lt Col Charles Barnett's evidence was that he remembered 19 Mech Bde's FRAGO 85, even though it was a Brigade rather than a Divisional order. He told the Inquiry that Clifton had drafted it and sent a hard copy of what he was issuing for Barnett's

---

[5] Clifton BMI 81/23/8-26/23
[6] Clifton BMI 81/28/18-29/14
[7] MOD005553; MOD049524
[8] Chief of Staff prayers on 7 Aug 2003 ("*Call re internment before decision made and shit hits the fan*" (MOD005596)) and FRAGO 104 of 22 August 2003 (MOD030393, below at paragraphs 11.27-11.29)

approval. Barnett remembered some discussion about the FRAGO with Clifton and the adding of the guidance card as an extra reminder of the treatment principles and command responsibility.[9]

11.10 Maj Hugh Eaton was the Chief of Staff for 19 Mech Bde until he was succeeded by Maj Edward Fenton. He confirmed that while the main order contained in FRAGO 85 was drafted by Maj Rupert Steptoe, the annex on arrest procedures was drafted by Clifton. Eaton told the Inquiry that he did not at the time notice that the order did not specifically refer to a prohibition on hooding, and he thought that the notes at the bottom of the soldiers' arrest procedures card were both appropriate and necessary guidance.[10]

[9] Barnett BMI07937, paragraph 151; MOD000884
[10] Eaton BMI 98/94/8-95/13

Chapter 2: A Further Soldiers' Card Not Issued

11.11 In Part IX of this Report, I have already addressed how Mercer had prepared a draft soldiers' card for issue by 1 (UK) Div, but that it appears that a decision was taken that it would not be issued before 3 (UK) Div took over for Op Telic 2. The issuing of a soldiers' card was therefore still a live issue by the time of the Divisional handover. Indeed, Mercer referred to the soldiers' card in the section of his handover notes that referred to deaths in custody:

> *"**Deaths in Custody** – This is also an operational matter and there are currently five investigations being conducted by the SIB with regard to death or serious injury whilst in custody. FRAGO's have already been issued to the Brigades on the treatment of civilians and, as a result of the further cases, a further FRAGO was issued which set out the procedures which had to be adopted upon the temporary detention of a civilian. This has been reduced into a card and is available for all troops ..."* [11]

11.12 Mercer's initial drafting of the soldiers' card had been taken forward and at one stage the draft card was put into the form set out below. It will be noted that it included specific guidance against the use of both hooding and the use of stress positions:[12]

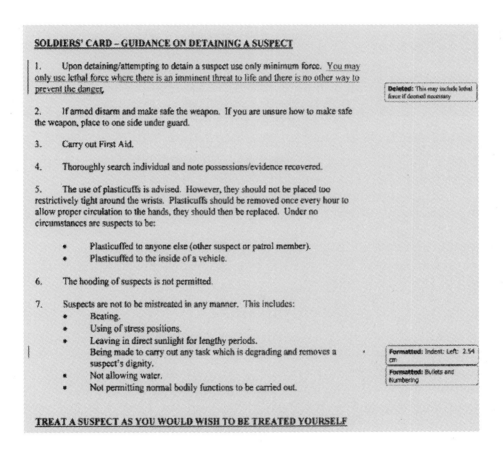

11.13 The surviving documentary record shows that 3 (UK) Div's legal branch noted early in Op Telic 2 that the issuing of a soldiers' card along the lines of Mercer's draft was an outstanding task that would need to be actioned. An unsigned, apparently draft,

---

[11] MOD052579, paragraph 6

[12] MOD049507 (Mercer said that he had input into the wording of the card but that this particular version was not his as he would not have used track changes: Mercer BMI06898, paragraph 11)

note to Barnett dated 11 July 2003 referred to Mercer's production of a soldiers' card stating *"I doubt this has gone any further but will need looking at in due course"*.[13] On 14 July 2003, Capt Sian Ellis-Davies, one of Barnett's SO2s, sent Barnett a *"very rough note"* on internee issues which she had started to address.[14] Ellis-Davies stated that she intended to turn this into a consolidated brief. One of the twelve items included in Ellis-Davies's note was:[15]

> 4.   Paperwork   Maj Clifton's memo includes an arrest card. Soldiers' cards referred to in Comd Legal 1(UK) Armd Div's memo to the GOC of 28 Jun 03 has not been actioned.

11.14   The reference here to Clifton's arrest card is obviously a reference to the card that was attached to FRAGO 85 and which had very recently been issued. Barnett responded to this email, but not for a little over a week. At this stage Barnett's response was positive about issuing a further soldiers' card, although he suggested that it should follow more detailed guidance that was to be issued by way of a FRAGO:[16]

> **From:** Barnett Lt Col CMJ GBR (INET)
> **Sent:** 22 July 2003 11:36
> **To:** Ellis-Davies Capt S GBR (INET)
> **Cc:** Hamnett Capt GBR (INET)
> **Subject:** RE: INTERNEES BRIEFING POINTS- SED
>
> Sian,
>
> Thank you for this. You have done some very good work on this whole subject – well done. I think that we have catered for all your recommendations. We need to do a little work on the soldiers card etc (I tend to the view that they should have one – it can probably follow the FRAGO/Guidance etc – we can discuss Lt Col Mercer's proposals and ideas etc). We also need to finalise the guidance on penal code and procedure

11.15   As I examine later in this Part, the more detailed guidance on prisoner handling was issued as FRAGO 005 but this was not provided until 3 September 2003. While Clifton's arrest procedures card had been issued, it is apparent that no more detailed soldiers' card along the lines envisaged by Mercer was issued before FRAGO 005, or at any time before Baha Mousa's death.

11.16   As a result, the guidance contained in Mercer's draft soldiers' card, including the express prohibitions on hooding and the use of stress positions, was never issued in that form to Op Telic 2 soldiers.

11.17   Ellis-Davies addressed the further soldiers' card in both her Inquiry witness statement and her oral evidence. In her supplementary Inquiry witness statement, Ellis-Davies stated that she remembered there was some uncertainty about whether or not Mercer had issued cards to individual soldiers; she could not remember whether this was established in relation to Op Telic 1 nor whether cards were issued on Op Telic 2. She could not remember seeing the draft of the soldiers' card that had been disclosed to the Inquiry, although she thought, from the contemporaneous documents, that she must have seen it at the time.[17]

---

[13] MOD049464, paragraph 5: the note was probably an early draft from Ellis-Davies
[14] MOD049525-7
[15] MOD049525
[16] MOD049528
[17] Ellis-Davies BMI07867-8, paragraphs 17-21

11.18 In her oral evidence, Ellis-Davies repeated that there had been a stage where the legal branch was not sure whether or not the card had been issued. However, she thought in due course she had reached a point when she concluded that a further soldiers' card had not been issued. Ellis-Davies said that arguably such a card should have been issued but the effect of her evidence was that it was for Barnett to make the decision whether to do so. She said he decided that it did not need to go into the policy that became FRAGO 005 and he took the decision not to advance it.[18] Ellis-Davies was referred to Barnett's email of 22 July 2003. She did not disagree with the suggestion put to her by Counsel for Barnett that the intention had been to look at the issuing of the soldiers' card after FRAGO 005 had been disseminated, and that this had then become overtaken by the events of mid-September (i.e. Baha Mousa's death).[19]

11.19 Although in general an impressive witness, it was apparent that Ellis-Davies' recollection on this aspect of the events was, understandably, relatively vague.

11.20 Barnett's account was that Mercer had told him that the soldiers' card had been sent to the General Officer Commanding (GOC) 1 (UK) Div (Maj Gen Wall) but had not been issued. He said:

> "I remember at the early stages of drafting FRAGO 005 that we took steps to find out whether this further order and the proposed soldier's card had been issued and it was then that we clarified that the soldiers' card had not been actioned. It did not seem crucial in any event as FRAGO 152 had been issued in May 2003 and this made clear that hooding had been banned."[20]

11.21 In his supplementary witness statement, Barnett said that Mercer had told him at the handover that neither the card nor a proposed accompanying draft memorandum had been issued during Op Telic 1. Barnett did not remember Mercer discussing the detail of the card with him at the handover. Barnett referred to the exchange of emails which he had with Ellis-Davies on 14 and 22 July 2003 as well as the draft soldiers' card, which I have set out above at paragraph 12. Barnett suggested that the track changes on the version of the soldiers' card disclosed to the Inquiry were made by Ellis-Davies. Barnett said that he was in favour of issuing a further soldiers' card because it would serve as a reminder to soldiers of their obligations, it could be carried easily for ready reference, and he was aware that the use of such cards for other issues was viewed favourably by the Directorate General Development and Doctrine. However, Barnett indicated that his comment in his email of 22 July to the effect that the card would follow the further FRAGO/guidance reflected his contemporaneous view that the card needed further work. Barnett did not view the issuing of a soldiers' card as being a particularly urgent matter. This was in part because Clifton had already arranged for the issue of his arrest procedures card which included the obligation to treat detainees humanely. In addition, other troop contributing nations had similar guidance in place. Barnett said he also relied upon the fact that guidance had been issued in the legal annexes to Concept of Operation Orders (CONOPS), in the Soldier's Guide to the Law of Armed Conflict (LOAC), the aide memoires on LOAC, in FRAGO 152, the annual LOAC training, and OPTAG and in RSOI (Reception, Staging, Onward Movement and Integration) training.[21]

---

[18] Ellis-Davies BMI 85/156/9-157/10
[19] Ellis-Davies BMI 85/175/10-25
[20] Barnett BMI07915, paragraph 94
[21] Barnett BMI07602-5, paragraphs 3-11

11.22 In oral evidence, Barnett sought to explain why it was that on the one hand he agreed with the concept of issuing a further soldiers' card on detention, and on the other he had preferred to defer the issue of such a card until after promulgation of FRAGO 005, which was to set out the detail of internment procedures. Counsel to the Inquiry pointed out to him that the draft card prepared by Mercer[22] contained references to the prohibition on hooding, mistreatment, beating, using stress positions and leaving prisoners in direct sunlight. Barnett was then asked why the card had not been attached to FRAGO 005. His response was:

> "A. There was some confusion as to which card was being referred to by Colonel Mercer. One of the steps that we immediately took was to try and identify what it may be, and we located this card on one of the computer systems – a stand-alone computer – and I believe this may have been the one that he was referring to in his note. When I tasked Sian Ellis-Davies to look through it, she ascertained that she didn't believe – and we weren't absolutely sure, we didn't believe, so we erred on the side of caution – that it had been issued, so we worked on the basis that it hadn't, and she recommended that perhaps we ought to and I agreed. There were a number of reasons why I didn't issue it with the FRAGO. Firstly that FRAGO I decided – not least because we weren't going to put in the custodial and tactical questioning matters – was going to focus on procedural matters. Secondly, we believed that the requirement to treat people humanely had been adequately provided for and trained already.
>
> I also wasn't content with the content of this card for a number of reasons, and I wanted to issue perhaps separately – in my mind I had the view that there were a number of areas I needed to continue to improve, including things like family visits, but also to do a properly staffed and fuller one. I didn't believe it was important because I thought we had got sufficient in place already. That was my thinking at the time. I wanted to really get that FRAGO out as soon as I could."[23]

11.23 Counsel for the Detainees pressed Barnett as to whether it would not have been desirable for the soldiers' card to have been issued:

> "MR SINGH: ... As I understand it, from paragraph 94 of your witness statement to this Inquiry, this draft soldier's card was not issued to soldiers on the ground, even while Lieutenant Colonel Mercer was in post, your predecessor. Is that your understanding?
>
> A. That was my understanding, yes.
>
> Q. Clearly it is an obvious fact, Colonel, isn't it, that by the time you were deployed in Iraq, not only you but lots of other people, including squaddies on the ground, would be new soldiers in Iraq?
>
> A. Correct, yes.
>
> Q. So would it not have been a good idea at least for those new soldiers to let them have something short and straightforward by way of a card of this sort?
>
> A. They had two cards already.
>
> Q. Did they say the same thing as this?
>
> A. They didn't say the same as this, but they emphasised the requirement, which I have outlined already, of humane treatment of all persons, and those matters were matters which were emphasised significantly in training, ordinary annual training, let alone the pre-deployment training they would have received.

---

[22] MOD049507
[23] Barnett BMI 86/79/16-80/21

> Q. Yes?
>
> A. For example, I know that one of the other commanding officers took me to one side in Catterick, asked me to come to his officers' mess and asked me to expand on certain areas to help inform his in-unit training, which I did. And that was the other battlegroup in Basra.
>
> Q. Forgive me, have you finished?
>
> A. Yes.
>
> Q. Forgive me. But the regular training that you are referring to, to the squaddy on the ground, that didn't tell them specifically in terms, did it, that the hooding of suspects is not permitted?
>
> A. No. It didn't say – the card that they had – the cards that they had, did not say that. But the situation was that when individuals were captured, they were to be handed immediately to the unit's provost staff, which is those trained in custodial matters, and they were to be TQ'd by those trained at JSIO, both of which had significant guidance and I had assured myself that hooding didn't form part of any of that training. So far as I was concerned it didn't need to be reiterated. It was clear as a bell already."[24]

11.24   As will be apparent there is some overlap with the reasons Barnett gave for his decision not to attach the soldiers' card to FRAGO 005 and the reasons for his decision not to include a reference to the ban on hooding in the body of FRAGO 005 itself.

---

[24] Barnett BMI 86/99/10-101/5

Chapter 3: Relevant Orders in August and September

11.25   It appears that 19 Mech Bde's FRAGO 85 (which in turn referred back to 1 (UK) Div's earlier FRAGO 29) remained as the main prisoner handling guidance document throughout July and August of 2003. It was not until 3 September that composite further guidance was issued in the form of 3 (UK) Div's FRAGO 005.

11.26   For completeness, I should however, refer to two orders that were issued in August 2003. It is important to remember that these were being issued against a very much worsening security situation in July to August 2003 to which I have referred in Part I, the Introduction to this Report.

22 August 2003 – 19 Mech Bde FRAGO 104

11.27   The first of these orders was 19 Mech Bde's FRAGO 104 dated 22 August 2003.[25] I deal with it relatively briefly because, as will be seen below, it did not change any of the processes for internees. Rather this order sought to give further guidance on evidence handling and decision making to minimise the risk of inappropriate release of criminal suspects from the Iraqi criminal system.

11.28   The only comment which I need make is that within the guidance it is notable that Clifton had amended his offer of guidance on internment decisions, to a firmer direction that BGIROs *"...must seek legal advice before any decision to intern".*[26]

11.29   In the context of this order, Clifton suggested in his Inquiry witness statement that:

> *"The lawyers did not have tactical oversight of the techniques and practices used during the process to physically handle the prisoners, though would have provided advice if asked, or if we felt any was required. The lawyer's role was to be satisfied that properly trained personnel were competently carrying out their role in the process and that those in command of those personnel were clear on their obligations in law. The lawyer also advised on which process should be followed (either the detention process for criminals or the internment process for those considered a threat to security) and Annex A to 19 Brigade FRAGO 104 specifically ordered that legal advice must be sought on the decision to intern."* [27]

In oral evidence, Clifton explained this paragraph of his witness statement saying that he would have intervened if he became aware of practices which either broke existing orders or which were contrary to law.[28]

30 August 2003 Multinational (South East) CONOPS 03/03

11.30   On 30 August 2003, the Multinational Division (South East) (MND(SE)) headquarters issued a further iteration of the 'Concept of Operations' order, headed *"Multinational*

---

[25] MOD030393-7
[26] MOD030395, paragraph 2
[27] Clifton BMI04568, paragraph 38
[28] Clifton BMI 81/20/12-21/6

Division (South East) CONOPS 03/03".[29] This included a legal annex addressing the Rules of Engagement and legal issues, Annex M.[30] The legal annex was approved by Barnett, having most probably been drafted by Clifton in conjunction with Permanent Joint Headquarters (PJHQ).[31]

11.31 Within the main body of the order, the intent of the Divisional Commander, Maj Gen Graeme Lamb, was described as follows:[32]

a.   Concept of Operations.

(1)   Intent. Comd MND(SE) intends to create the conditions that will enable Iraq to make a swift and successful recovery in all aspects. This will begin with the provision of security from external military threats and the defeat or neutralization of internal threats to the new Iraqi state, its government and its people. MND(SE) operations across the AOR must be seen as a substantial contribution to the security and well-being of all Iraqi people, with no accompanying sense of a renewed or prolonged occupation. As CPA and other international civil agencies become established, MND(SE) will continue to pass to them the civil responsibilities assumed in the immediate aftermath of conflict, commensurate with accelerating the vital momentum required in improving the fabric and quality of life in Iraq. The principle of achieving adequate rather than European standards is paramount, dependency on an enduring Coalition presence is not to be created. As quickly as possible, MND(SE) will enable the reconstitution of viable civil police, border forces, infrastructure security and civil defence forces, so that Coalition Forces are able to drop back from a high profile military presence as Iraqi forces of law and order reassume their tasks. This will expedite a real and perceived return of normality to Iraq combined with adroit, intelligence-led, and well-focused operations to deter or defeat such threats to security as may occur. Throughout, a coordinated ops support campaign across the MND(SE) AOR, coordinated with the international community will secure the continuing trust and support of the Iraqi people and leadership. It is important that unity of purpose and common effect is achieved so that all provinces move ahead in step and differences in progress are not created that could be exploited against us. The Comd's priorities are: the provision of security to the critical infrastructure and the Iraqi people; building a thorough understanding of the needs of each province and the wider Iraqi and regional context; reducing organised crime and large-scale criminality; and creating the conditions for a return to normality.

11.32 Much of the legal annex M which accompanied this order addressed the legal basis of the mission and the Rules of Engagement. However, more relevantly to the Inquiry, there was also a law and order section which reiterated that occupying powers had a legal obligation to ensure public safety, and law and order within the occupied territory in so far as the local population and authorities were not able to do so. It was stated that this was the background against which the Rules of Engagement for Phase 4 of the operation permitted policing activities such as search, seizure and detention.[33] The section addressing detainees and internees indicated that guidance on the handling of detainees and internees was to be promulgated separately. This was a reference to FRAGO 005, which it will be seen, had been in preparation for some time, and was issued on 3 September 2003.

---

[29] MOD023094-103
[30] MOD019748-51
[31] Barnett BMI07938, paragraph 153
[32] MOD023096-7
[33] MOD019750, paragraph 8

> 10. Detainees and Internees 'Guidance on the apprehension and handling of detainees and internees is to be promulgated separately by HQ MND(SE). A copy of the policy is at Appendix 2.
>
> a. Detainees. Coalition Forces may detain individuals who are suspected of committing or having committed a criminal offence. This may include those suspected of committing crimes during the former regime, war crimes and crimes against humanity.
>
> b. Internees Individuals may be interned if it is considered necessary for imperative reasons of security. This may be based on the internees previous associations, activities or membership of an organisation or group.
>
> c. Apprehension. Once an individual is apprehended by Coalition Forces, he will be disarmed if necessary. At the discretion of the on-scene commander in accordance with his orders, they will either be released classified as an internee or a detainee in accordance with MND(SE) policy. In accordance with MND(SE) policy individuals apprehended solely on suspicion of criminal activity will be handed to the Iraqi authorities for dealing under the Iraqi Criminal Justice system. Internees are to be transferred to the Theatre Internment Facility (TIF). All persons apprehended by Coalition forces shall be treated as a minimum in accordance with the standards laid down under LOAC for PWs regardless of their classification.
>
> d. Prisoners of War. ('PWs') Despite the fact that the general warfighting part of the campaign is over, it is possible that some apprehended persons may qualify for status as PWs (for example members of organised armed groups resisting the occupation).
>
> Should the status of an apprehended person be unclear then he should be treated as a PW until such time as his status is clearly established. The detention and onward movement of PWs is a national responsibility and national contingencies should publish guidance on their processing and treatment. UK guidance is contained in JWP 1-10. General guidance on the processing and treatment standards of PWs is as follows:
>
> (1) Treat humanely at all times.
> (2) Provide food (same standards as Coalition forces) taking into account religious or ethnic practices.
> (3) If necessary provide medical care.
> (4) If necessary provide clothes.
> (5) Provide adequate safe facilities (clean, dry etc.).
> (6) Issue a receipt for seized property.
> (7) Protect from physical and mental harm.
>
> e. Criminals. Where possible, persons detained as criminals are to be handed over to the Iraqi authorities for investigation as soon as reasonably practicable. Guidance from MPs should be sought in relation to preserving evidence for eventual prosecution of such criminals.
>
> f. War Criminals/Terrorists. Guidance should immediately be sought from HQ MND(SE) if any person apprehended by Coalition Forces is suspected of being a war criminal or terrorist. Guidance from MPs should be sought in relation to preserving evidence for eventual prosecution of such persons.

11.33 The guidance on detainees and internees within the legal annex was at a fairly high level of generality. However, it is noteworthy that it included reference to treating prisoners of war humanely and protecting them from physical and mental harm:[34]

11.34 Lamb told the Inquiry that although he was not personally involved in issuing prisoner handling orders before Baha Mousa's death, this was the kind of order that set the requisite tone. The detail had to be filled in, consistent with the approach of mission command. He thought it obvious from the general guidance given that the five techniques (excluding hooding for security purposes) would be prohibited.[35]

11.35 Similarly, Col Richard Barrons the Divisional Chief of Staff, accepted that he would have had a part in drafting the main order as it was the core CONOPS for MND(SE).[36] He told the Inquiry that the legal annex set out the overall standards that were expected for prisoner handling.[37]

11.36 I do find it unsurprising that more detail on prisoner handling was not to be found within this particular legal annex or within the main body of the order describing the CONOPS. Both the order itself and the evidence of Lamb and Barrons show that there was an expectation that further guidance was about to be provided on prisoner handling. The key order in that regard was FRAGO 005, to which I now turn.

---

[34] MOD019751
[35] Lamb BMI 103/96/11-99/16; Lamb BMI04912-3, paragraphs 15-16
[36] Barrons BMI06234, paragraph 52
[37] Barrons BMI 99/115/6-116/18

Chapter 4: 3 September 2003: 3 (UK) Div's FRAGO 005, Policy for Apprehending, Handling and Processing of Detainees and Internees

11.37   On 3 September 2003, FRAGO 005 was issued by the Headquarters of MND(SE) under the names of Barrons and Maj Hulme, one of the SO2s in the J3 (Operations) branch. FRAGO 005 was entitled *"Policy for Apprehending, Handling and Processing of Detainees and Internees"* and its stated aim was to ensure a common approach to internee and detainee handling across the Division's area of operations. Importantly, it replaced 1 (UK) Div's FRAGO 29 of 26 June 2003 as the main order on internment procedures, although it was wider in its ambit as it also addressed more closely the procedures for criminal detainees. As such, it was the policy for apprehending, handling and processing detainees and internees that was operative at the time of the detention and abuse of Baha Mousa and the other Detainees.

11.38   Barnett told the Inquiry that FRAGO 005 was intended to consolidate the previous orders and lessons learned relating to detainees and internees. This was to be achieved by creating just one comprehensive document that would serve as an enduring standard operating procedure in place of the variety of different orders which were already in place, but which were to some extent confusing and muddled.[38]

11.39   I need not set out FRAGO 005 in full.[39] However, the following main points about the FRAGO should be noted.

(1)   On any view, FRAGO 005 took a significant time to produce. Emails from Ellis-Davies to Barnett indicate that work on it started some time shortly after 13 July and that it was in its second draft by 23 July 2003.[40] But FRAGO 005 was not sent in its final form to the GOC and Chief of Staff until 30 August and was not issued until 3 September. There are a number of reasons why the order took so long to produce to which I shall briefly return below.

(2)   FRAGO 005 retained the system first adopted in FRAGO 29, by which it was for the BGIROs of each Battlegroup to make an assessment of whether those apprehended should be categorised as detainees or internees and whether they should be handed over to the Iraqi authorities or taken to the Theatre Internment Facility (TIF).

(3)   The time limit specified in FRAGO 29 *"Internees are to be delivered to the TIF within 14hrs of capture"*[41] was amended so as to provide that the fourteen hour deadline was not absolute and inflexible *"Apprehended persons are to be transferred to the TIF within 14 hours of capture, or as soon as possible thereafter"*.[42]

(4)   FRAGO 29 had put the G2, intelligence, staff branch in the lead of the internment process *"This FRAGO announces the intention for G2 Branch to*

---

[38] Barnett BMI07929, paragraph 127
[39] The full version can be found at MOD022623-48
[40] MOD049524; MOD049531
[41] MOD016189
[42] MOD022625-6, paragraph 15

assume overall control of the Internment Process in MND(SE)...Internees are assessed to be a threat to CF and their processing is now a G2 led G3 Ops responsibility".[43] FRAGO 005 reverted to J3 as the lead, at least at Divisional level. *"The handling of internees and detainees is a J3 led operation".*[44]

(5) The guidance in FRAGO 005 did not include any reference to the prohibition on hooding, nor to other aspects of the physical handling of prisoners. Nor did it include any guidance in respect of tactical questioning. FRAGO 005 did not include guidance to be issued down to frontline soldier level in the form of a soldiers' card.

Barnett's Evidence in relation to FRAGO 005

11.40 Barnett was the central witness on the drafting of FRAGO 005. While it is clear that in the drafting of FRAGO 005 he had help from his legal branch, in particular Ellis-Davies, Barnett was the commander of the branch and it was he who forwarded the final draft for approval to Lamb, the GOC, through Barrons.[45]

11.41 As to the time taken to draft FRAGO 005, in his Inquiry witness statement Barnett indicated a number of reasons why it took so long for the order to be produced. Barnett said that the issue of the FRAGO was not considered very urgent as the previous orders were already in place and were:

> *"... felt to be just about satisfactory while a fully considered, staffed, careful and comprehensive review took place. I wanted to ensure that we did not issue instructions piecemeal"* [46]

Barnett explained that once a first draft was in place, this required wide circulation. It was considered not just by other staff branches but also by PJHQ. In respect of FRAGO 005's approach to criminal detainees, Barnett explained that they had to ensure that the senior Iraqi judge of Basra province, Judge Laith, was content with the approach being taken. In addition, Barnett told the Inquiry that the other troop contributing nations and their lawyers had to be consulted to ensure that the order did not contravene the national obligations of the other coalition nations.

11.42 Despite this explanation, I am left with some degree of concern over the time it took for FRAGO 005 to be produced. As I examine in Part XVI of this Report, it is now accepted by the MoD that there should be an enduring document for operations that encapsulates the standard operating procedures for prisoner handling. In July and August 2003, those procedures remained scattered over a number of different orders, as Barnett had himself recognised. However, I accept that FRAGO 005 had to be widely staffed including amongst coalition partners and I can understand that at the time the need for a single composite order detailing detention matters did not have the priority that would hopefully now be given to the production of such an order.

11.43 Ultimately, Baha Mousa's death and the abuse of those detained with him occurred after FRAGO 005 was issued. I do not consider that the delay in producing FRAGO 005 was a contributory factor in the events.

---

[43] MOD016186
[44] MOD022645, paragraph 5
[45] See memorandum of 28 Aug 2003 at MOD049695-6
[46] Barnett BMI07929, paragraph 127

11.44 As to the fact that FRAGO 005 relaxed the previously absolute fourteen hour deadline to deliver prisoners to the TIF, Barnett said in his 13 July 2006 Special Investigation Branch (SIB) statement that units within the Brigade had expressed the view that the size of the area of operations and the high summer temperatures (which affected helicopter day time flying) meant that it was proving difficult to comply with the deadline. He said that he had sought advice from J3, which considered that fourteen hours remained realistic for most situations but that the qualification "*or as soon as possible thereafter*" should be added so as to take into account Battlegroups which were furthest away from the TIF and the operational constraints. In the same statement, Barnett said that he made clear in all his dealings with units that this was to cater for those situations where delivery within fourteen hours was impossible. It was not a carte blanche for Battlegroups to hold detained people for longer periods.[47]

11.45 I heard evidence which supported the concerns which had been raised by Barnett about the practical difficulties that were on some occasions encountered in meeting the fourteen hour time limit to get prisoners to the TIF.[48] In Part IX of this report I have already concluded that, while the disadvantages of FRAGO 29 are far more easily identified with the benefit of hindsight, more consideration could and should have been given at the time to the potential disadvantages of the changes introduced by FRAGO 29. Lessening the requirement that prisoners be moved on from the detaining unit as soon as possible, even if unavoidable given the increased Divisional area of operations and logistical difficulties, should have been accorded higher priority as a risk factor. However, having regard to the evidence about practical difficulties on the ground I do not consider that there was anything wrong with the decision taken by Barnett to relax the absolute fourteen hour time limit to the extent of adding the words "*or as soon as possible thereafter*".

11.46 In my opinion, the more significant issues relating to FRAGO 005 are why, as a consolidating order, FRAGO 005 did not include the prohibition on hooding, did not address the physical aspects of prisoner handling and gave no guidance on tactical questioning.

11.47 On these issues, Barnett said in his evidence firstly that FRAGO 005 was designed to be a "*procedural document*".[49] By this I understood him to mean that it dealt principally with the procedures to be followed in theatre, rather than the nuts and bolts of the physical handling of prisoners during detention and transfers; or how prisoners should be questioned during tactical questioning.

11.48 Secondly, Barnett consistently stated that he had originally intended to include more detail on tactical questioning and custodial procedures in FRAGO 005 but decided not to following consultation with the relevant staff branches. It seems that his original intention was to have short paragraphs on these subjects within the guidance and to signpost the relevant detailed guidance which should be applied. Barnett referred to this in his first SIB statement:

---

[47] MOD000886
[48] Eaton BMI 98/99/20-100/13; S017 BMI 84/40/12-41/2
[49] Barnett BMI07932, paragraph 135

"The policy covered a number of areas including the legal basis for internment, different categories of captured individuals, juvenile and sensitive individuals, evidentiary requirements, documentary requirements, rights of captured individuals, review of detention procedures, transfer procedures and responsibilities for detainees and internees. Initially I envisaged including guidance on arrest, search, questioning and custody procedures. The staffing process, however, demonstrated that these procedures were specifically trained on specialist courses run by the RE (search), MPS (custody), APTC (arrest) and Int Corps (questioning). In addition I had ascertained that these procedures were taught in this manner when I had conducted the OPTAG training as I had wished to ensure that units had appropriate training in these areas. When I again addressed this with the relevant staff branches in theatre it was confirmed to me that LAND mandated training standards required all major units to ensure that they had sufficient personnel trained in those skills in theatre. In addition during my discussions with staff within Provost Branch, in response to my request for a paragraph on custody procedures, I recall them advising that they could not produce a single paragraph to deal with this as the procedures were extensive, there was a specific manual on them and each unit had personnel trained on the specific courses. This aspect was also complicated by the multi national nature of MND (SE) as UK training on these matters would not have been applicable to the other T[roop] C[ontributing] N[ation]s. It was therefore decided not to include these aspects in the Divisional policy as detailed guidance and training was already provided to units." [50]

11.49   At the Court Martial, the thrust of Barnett's evidence on this aspect was that: before deployment, he had been concerned about matters such as arrest, search, tactical questioning and custody training but had been given assurances that these were part of collective training. Barnett said that when he raised the same issue in theatre in the context of drafting FRAGO 005, he received the same response to the effect that each unit had on their strength individuals trained in these specialist areas and therefore it was not appropriate to put further guidance into FRAGO 005 when there were *"extensive procedures already governing those aspects"*. As a result, he did not put anything into FRAGO 005 on these aspects. [51]

11.50   Barnett said that he remembered there were representatives from Provost branch, J2, J3 and J1 at the meeting on FRAGO 005, but that there were many discussions on the formulation of policy. He added there were a number of previous documents which covered the policy which appeared to be working satisfactorily. [52] Barnett said he was aware that there would be some questioning immediately on capture but his understanding was that most of the questioning wherever possible would take place at the TIF. [53]

11.51   In his Inquiry witness statement, Barnett said that he did not include details of hooding in FRAGO 005 because he did not think that at that time it was an issue. He believed that it was clear and that all were aware that it had been prohibited. He repeated his earlier account that he had wanted to insert sections on tactical questioning, arrest and custodial procedures, and had requested paragraphs on those aspects, but that the staff officers were not keen to do so. The reasoning was that these areas had already been trained to specialist personnel and were too complex to summarise in brief. Such summaries would render the document either inaccurate if too short or

---

[50] MOD000885
[51] Barnett CM 62/119/20-124/15; Barnett CM 62/129/14-131/15; Barnett CM 62/138/4-139/1
[52] Barnett CM 62/119/20-120/23
[53] Barnett CM 62/123/23-124/15

unwieldy if too long. He named Lt Col Graham Le Fevre as one of the J2 staff and Lt Col Robert Warren as one of the Provost staff to whom he had spoken.[54]

11.52 Barnett went on to explain in his oral evidence that he considered that the previous orders were "*workable*". Good work had been done but that it was "*scattered*" in different orders.[55] He said that Le Fevre's explanation was balanced and reasonable; it was not a rushed view. He thought the same about the Provost advice he received, although he could not remember if this was from Warren personally, or whether it was one of Warren's majors who had explained that custodial and arrest procedures were all encapsulated in Joint Services Publication (JSP) 469 amongst other guidance. Barnett repeated that the multinational aspect had an effect on what could be said in the order.[56]

11.53 However, Barnett accepted that following Baha Mousa's death, officers did then provide the sort of guidance which he had originally envisaged might be contained in FRAGO 005:

> "Q...after the death of Baha Mousa, and the assaults on some of the other detainees who were present with him, it does seem, doesn't it that a number of people did jump to produce the sort of information that you were asking for here –
>
> A. Absolutely.
>
> Q. The question I put to you – you say "absolutely" – is whether that is an indication both from you and from others that the priority wasn't really being given to the problems and that that priority wasn't given until the tragedy occurred?
>
> A. We had no reason to believe that including it was necessary and we felt that the training given was satisfactory. It didn't appear to be a priority. You are absolutely right that when this incident occurred, it was very clear to me that my initial, if you like, gut reaction was correct and I wanted more training and I gave – not more training, more guidance, to correct things which I, quite frankly, was extremely surprised had been occurring. I was shocked had been occurring".[57]

11.54 Barnett accepted that, had he known at the time what he learned about the use of hoods, he would have provided further guidance (whether in FRAGO 005 or separately). But to the extent that this was a concession, it was one made only with the benefit of hindsight. When asked about his confidence that the prohibition on hooding had been communicated and that prisoner handling principles were clearly understood, Barnett said:

> "A. Well, I knew that all soldiers received their annual training in the Law of Armed Conflict. It was considered of such importance by the British Army that it was a mandatory annual training directive. Not everything is a mandatory annual training directive. LOAC is one. I also knew what I had said in Catterick and I recall saying at the outset, as I was an augmentee, that I wanted to deliver the presentation because I wanted to be satisfied with what I had told people, and I knew that I had had made very clear that no individual captured was to be harmed or humiliated, because I gave that presentation myself.

---

[54] Barnett BMI07932-3, paragraphs 134-135
[55] Barnett BMI 86/49/20-50/11
[56] Barnett BMI 86/55/13-56/24
[57] Barnett BMI 86/57/4-23

> *Q. Did you think that that was a sufficient message to cover, as it were, all the practicalities of prisoner handling?*
>
> *A. Yes. In American parlance it would be described as a bumper sticker headline, if you like. And that's what I said, "Do not harm or humiliate anybody". And if the soldiers recalled what I termed the bumper sticker issue, then that would be very beneficial and they would not be bogged down in the detail. But it wasn't the only area where there was training. As I mentioned before, the concept of operation document – the high level order issued by 3 Div subsequently amended – included a legal annex, a very important document as an annex for every area, and that legal annex contained direction. The purpose of that is to inform the units for their in-unit training and that directed them to comply with JWP 1-10, in itself a comprehensive document with detailed detainee treatment principles and the requirements for medical checks and a range of other matters. The OPTAG presentation is a reminder. We are specifically not meant to duplicate LOAC training. It is –*
>
> *Q. You were giving the headlines as it were?*
>
> *A. Giving the headlines and specific to that mission. So – and there are other areas. There is the soldiers' guide. I also knew that every individual soldier had been issued with the Law of Armed Conflict aide-memoire, which, albeit having been printed for the first phase, the principles in relation to treatment of people were still current and relevant. So, yes, I did take this view and I discussed it on arrival with Russell Clifton, hence one of the amendments to one of his – well, more than one of his orders but one which you have got – and we reiterated it. And we felt that we had more than adequately catered for this".*[58]

Other Evidence Regarding FRAGO 005

11.55 Ellis-Davies did much of the actual drafting of FRAGO 005 with direction from Barnett. She told the Inquiry, again with hindsight, that the order should have contained the prohibition on hooding. However, to do so would have been to pick out hooding as a particular issue which at the time she did not think that it was.[59]

11.56 Le Fevre was the SO1 J2 for MND(SE). While he had no recollection of the advice which Barnett suggested was given to him by Le Fevre, he frankly accepted that he had no reason to believe that Barnett's account was incorrect. Indeed, Le Fevre told the Inquiry that he would have been involved in the staffing process of FRAGO 005 and that Barnett's account of the advice which he said Le Fevre gave was likely to be true.[60] I was impressed that Le Fevre was prepared to accept, in this unequivocal way, a matter on which he had no personal recollection.

11.57 Le Fevre gave the following explanation as to why he may have advised Barnett against the inclusion of further guidance on tactical questioning in FRAGO 005:

> *"Q... He says here, as we can see, you were not keen to do so, to provide suitable paragraphs to assist with the tactical questioning section, as it were, and to set out in writing and in a comprehensive document what might be required?*
>
> *A. That's what he says, yes.*
>
> *Q. If that's right, why would you have been unwilling to provide such material?*

---

[58] Barnett BMI 86/60/9-62/7
[59] Ellis-Davies BMI 85/151/16-152/12
[60] Le Fevre BMI 85/31/16-33/7; Le Fevre BMI07530, paragraphs 4-5

A. As I said, I can't remember specifics but I would refer to the point that this relates to a fragmentary order, and a fragmentary order is just that; it is meant to be a short concise document covering specific points; and I think the point there, when I said it was more complex and required a longer document.

Q. It might be said that something might be better than nothing, if in fact there was the, as it were, deficiency in the written doctrine for tactical questioners. Here was an invitation to add to the sum of knowledge, to give guidance and instruction –

A. Yes, that could be said.

Q. And you apparently declined to do so?

A. It would appear, based on that statement, that that is correct.

Q. Wasn't that, if you like, a missed opportunity?

A. As I said, I believe that the people who had been trained on prisoner handling and tactical questioning knew what they were meant to be doing. And without remembering fully all of the discussions going on at the time, all the other staff work that was underway, I can't remember whether we were working on any separate documentation relating to tactical questioning, this refers only to a specific fragmentary order and, as I said, a fragmentary order is meant to be fragmentary. It is merely a small piece. The point that he raises there is that it would not be sufficient for what was a complex area.

Q. As I think you may know, the fragmentary order in effect became SOI 390.

A. I couldn't refer to the particular number, but yes, quite possibly.

Q. So was it really simply a question, as you put it, of with hindsight you might have done more? Here you were being asked to do more and it seems, if this account be right, that you declined to do so?

A. If the account is right, then, yes, I did decline to do so, but I would have weighed up the factors as to why I made that decision. It would not have been an arbitrary decision.

Q. If indeed, as you have agreed there was, there was a deficiency in the existing doctrine – a deficiency the Inquiry has been told that may have pertained for some years – this was an opportunity lost, wasn't it?

A. Again, in hindsight, one could say that.

Q. If it were, might it be that it was because of the lack of priority, if you like, that was given to this issue?

A. Indeed, it may relate to that. Again, the statement here, I am not sure when that particular discussion took place. Within the context of it, you know, there were other factors that may have been important. I can't remember, I am afraid." [61]

11.58 Le Fevre had earlier in his evidence accepted that there was a lack of adequate and sufficient guidance in relation to the tactical questioning process. But again, he emphasised this was something that was recognised only in hindsight, and he pointed to the significant pressures at the time and the breadth and depth of the J2 responsibilities:

"Q. Could we look, please, at paragraph 46 of your statement to this Inquiry, where you there set out the doctrine or guidance of which you were aware, as I understand it, in 2003. Is that right?

---

[61] Le Fevre BMI 85/33/2-35/11

A. Yes.

Q. JWP 1-10 and the other materials that you there set out at (b), (c) and (d). The Inquiry has heard now quite a bit of evidence that there was not, at this time in Iraq, policy in place that gave at least adequate or sufficient guidance in relation to the TQ'ing process. Would you agree with that proposition?

A. Looking back in hindsight, yes.

Q. If there ought to have been written policy guidance, did you have any responsibility for that at the time?

A. For the tactical questioning piece, yes, that would have been a J2 responsibility which I oversaw.

Q. Ought you not, therefore, Colonel, at the time have sought to rectify that defect?

A. I would make the point that this was but one part of the whole ISTAR effort that we were trying to run in MND(SE) at the time and you had to prioritise what was needed to be done. Inevitably there is an issue comes up, you deal with it, but prisoner handling – sorry, tactical questioning – was not an issue that was high on my agenda until this case came.

Q. So would it be fair to say, from your perspective anyway, that prisoner handling and tactical questioning would have had a low priority in the scheme of things operated by you in Iraq in 2003?

A. Prisoner handling I didn't have responsibility for. That is not a J2 responsibility, as I think you are aware. For the tactical questioning piece, yes, I had responsibility for – to the general for trying to give him an understanding of intelligence across the whole of southern Iraq, an area that is larger than the whole of the island of Ireland with a very large population, a small force available and a relatively small intelligence capability to give him the intelligence he needed. I had many priorities, many requirements and insufficient resources to provide all of those to him.

Q. Tactical questioning is obviously an element of the process of prisoner handling, isn't it?

A. No, tactical questioning is not part of prisoner handling. Tactical questioning is tactical questioning; prisoner handling is a separate issue.

Q. Forgive me. I am not talking in terms of responsibility but tactical questioning forms part of the process, if you like, of the movement of a prisoner from point of capture through to final detention or release?

A. If you believe that that particular prisoner has information of value; you may determine that you don't think they have and therefore tactical questioning is not required.

Q. Yes. If it does take place, it is part of that process obviously?

A. It would take place during that process, yes.

Q. The Inquiry has heard evidence that, if you like, the process involving prisoners from point of capture through to detention or release was something of a low priority in Iraq.

A. Yes.

Q. Is that how you would have viewed it too?

A. It will have depended at the particular point in time. But as I said earlier in my statement here, that the requirement to provide the intelligence picture across the piece to the commander – be it at division or brigade level – this was but one small part of that total effort.

> *Q. Because it was one small part, as you put it, might it be the case that it didn't actually get the attention from you at the time – I am talking about TQ'ing – which it ought to have done?*
>
> *A. As I think you will understand, when you are in an environment where you have many demands against you, there are any number of things that perhaps don't get sufficient attention. You have to prioritise your effort and you have to prioritise the resources, as I have said before. I can look back in hindsight and say clearly I would have liked to have done more, but the circumstances at the time, where we were extraordinarily busy, we had a situation that had deteriorated since we had taken over command and become Multinational Division South East. We had a number of considered threats ranging from the Iranians through to insurgent groups. We were trying to protect our own forces as well as protect the population. We had an infrastructure that was failing. All of that required intelligence support to help the commander make decisions on how to use his resources."* [62]

11.59   S015 was the SO2 J2X responsible to Le Fevre for the human intelligence side of J2 work within the Divisional headquarters. S015's evidence was that he was aware that FRAGO 005 was being drafted but was not aware of a requirement for J2 to produce any guidance on tactical questioning for insertion into the order.

11.60   Warren was the Commanding Officer of 3 Regiment Royal Military Police (RMP) and the Provost Marshal of MND(SE) for Op Telic 2. Warren accepted that Barnett would have involved him in the discussions on FRAGO 005 if he had been in theatre at the time.[63] Warren returned from Op Telic 2 in early September 2003,[64] but he would have been in theatre while the content of FRAGO 005 was being considered. Indeed an email of 8 August 2003 shows that both Warren and one of his majors, Stephen Fielder, were consulted about the content of this policy.[65]

11.61   Warren told the Inquiry that he could not recall giving the advice which Barnett ascribed to him:

> *"Q... Do you recall giving such advice to –*
>
> *A. No I don't, and I am not clear if he is referring to TQ'ing or to whatever the provost role might have been. The only thing I can think of is in all of the instructions and advice I gave, I kept in mind the international aspects of any instruction that we had to write, and that at divisional level our instructions had to apply across our various multinational components. Certainly my experience was each of the military police components that were deployed had different practices and different experiences from the different nations.*
>
> *Q. From the different nations, yes. I follow. Coming back to what he says in paragraph 134, he suggests that he asked for help with tactical questioning, arrest and custodial procedures. Do you have any recollection of that –*
>
> *A. I don't have any recollection of that specific conversation.*
>
> *Q. – or being asked to help with such a document?*
>
> *A. I do recall having had sight of a draft document on such matters and the FRAGO."* [66]

---

[62] Le Fevre BMI 85/28/2-31/15
[63] Warren BMI 83/104/15-25
[64] Warren BMI03453, paragraph 12
[65] MOD051362
[66] Warren BMI 83/105/11-106/6

11.62 Warren went on to explain that his advice would have been that he was comfortable with the level of resource available to the military police, given the pressures and their focus on other activity. He referred in this context to the much more limited provost deployment on Op Telic 2 as compared to Op Telic 1.[67] As I have already referred to in Part IX of this Report, RMP numbers were much reduced for Op Telic 2.

11.63 Warren explained that the military police role in detention matters was in fact quite limited. His understanding was that arrest and detention, whether of internees, detainees or prisoners of war, was a general J3 staff matter.[68]

11.64 Barrons told the Inquiry that he could remember being engaged in the work of FRAGO 005 but he could not remember the extent to which he contributed.[69] Barrons' evidence was that he was not aware that Barnett had initially wanted to include more detail in the order relating to tactical questioning, arrest and custodial procedures. Barrons said that he was not consulted about these matters.[70]

11.65 Barrons could not remember whether or not he had noticed that the prohibition on hooding was not referred to within FRAGO 005. Like a number of others, he did not remember hooding being an issue of prominence at the time. When asked about the omission from FRAGO 005 of the prohibition on hooding, Barrons referred in that regard to the particular difficulty of the multinational constituent of those who would have received the order:

> "Q. Given the breadth of the policy and that it was stated to set out the procedure for handling internees and detainees from the point of apprehension to the authorisation of continued detention and its policy of ensuring a common approach to handling of prisoners, would you agree that it would have been desirable if the prohibition on hooding had been restated somewhere within this policy?
>
> A. Not necessarily, because the document had to service the needs of all the constituent troop-contributing nations in MND(SE). But if the issue of hooding was of particular interest to the UK, which I think is the case, then it would in general terms have been undesirable for it to appear in a document that went to all the contributing nations because it would confuse them in some cases and antagonise them in others and it would possibly be dealt with another way therefore.
>
> Q. Perhaps without going into details about individual nations, was there ever an awareness that other troop-contributing nations within the division were using hessian sandbags as hoods?
>
> A. No.
>
> Q. So that doesn't really provide a reason, does it, for not addressing the prohibition within an order such as this?
>
> A. I think the point I am making is that if the UK has a prohibition – which it did in my understanding – then putting it in an instruction that applied to the whole of the multinational division – bearing in mind that much of the division was not operating in its first language when it was using English with us – there is a risk firstly of confusion, and I simply don't know the other nations' policies on this, so I can shed no further light on that. Secondly, it may be something that would be better dealt with on strictly UK channels.

---

[67] Warren BMI 83/107/17-110/11
[68] Warren BMI 83/110/13-111/23
[69] Barrons BMI 99/125/4-127/10
[70] Barrons BMI 99/129/24-130/7

> Q. *Help us with the UK channels then. If it was not appropriate to go into this individual FRAGO, how might it have found its way into the procedures for the UK?*
>
> A. *If it was felt to be of sufficient prominence then it would have been appropriate for the GOC or indeed myself, on his behalf, to issue a UK-specific instruction.*
>
> Q. *And that would have gone down specifically to presumably 19 Mech Brigade, rather than to the brigades from the other troop-contributing nations?*
>
> A. *It would only have gone to 19 Mech Brigade if it was a UK-only instruction.*[71]

Later in his evidence, Barrons indicated that in order for the prohibition on hooding to be inserted in the multinational FRAGO 005, there would have had to have been checks at MoD level with the other troop contributing nations that such a prohibition was agreed by them.[72]

11.66 With hindsight, Barrons was prepared to accept that it would have been desirable for the prohibition on hooding to have found its way into the guidance that was issued, but he stressed that hooding did not at that stage have the prominence that it later assumed:

> "Q. *Whether in the FRAGO going to all of the troop-contributing nations or, as you have suggested might have been done, in something specific to the UK element, would it not have been desirable at this time, given that there was this statement of procedures, somehow for the prohibition on hooding to have found its way into the guidance?*
>
> A. *With the benefit of hindsight it would clearly have been appropriate, but the fact is at the time the issue of hooding had not assumed its current prominence and therefore there was no particular reason for I or the staff to single it out, either for specific additional guidance or for some clever inclusion in a divisional-wide instruction.*
>
> Q. *You were not, yourself, aware, should I take it, at the time, of any general lack of guidance on the procedures that should be used at the point of capture and from the point of capture to battlegroup detention facilities and so on?*
>
> A. *I was not aware or I would have done something about it.*"[73]

11.67 Clearly, since Barrons could not remember the details of what considerations went into FRAGO 005, his reasoning as to why the prohibition on hooding was not contained within the guidance was to an extent speculative.

11.68 I do not doubt that Barrons was right in indicating that the prohibition on hooding, if it was to be repeated in MND(SE) guidance, would have needed either to be cleared with the other troop contributing nations, or to have been given by way of a UK-specific instruction. I accept, too, that hooding did not have a particular prominence at Divisional level at this stage of the operations.

11.69 I have given careful consideration to Barrons' evidence. He was in every respect a very impressive witness whom I judge both from his evidence and rapid promotion must be a highly capable officer. Nevertheless Barrons' evidence in my judgment did not completely justify or explain the absence of any reference to the prohibition on hooding in the consolidating guidance on detention and internment procedures.

---

[71] Barrons BMI 99/127/11-129/7
[72] Barrons BMI 99/142/15-143/6
[73] Barrons BMI 99/130/8-131/2

The oral bans on hooding by Maj Gen Robin Brims and Air Marshal Brian Burridge were novel in the sense that guidance on hooding was completely absent from Joint Warfare Publication (JWP) 1-10. In written guidance, the prohibition had featured only in FRAGO 152 (and the equivalent Brigade order), which was one of what Barnett described as "*scattered*" orders that addressed detention and internment matters. I do not believe that either the multinational nature of the MND(SE) or the fact that hooding was not of particular prominence justified the omission of the hooding prohibition from the consolidating guidance that was being prepared.

11.70 Lamb told the Inquiry that he was not personally involved in the drafting of FRAGO 005. He commented that the fact that the order did not make any mention of the specifics of prisoner handling suggested that such detail was not considered to be a problem at the time. Lamb suggested that this interpretation was consistent with his own recollection of that stage of the operation.[74] Lamb was not aware at the time of the flow of advice from other staff branches to Barnett that further detail should not be included in the FRAGO. Lamb's own involvement on receipt of the final draft would have been to check with Barrons that he was content with it, and that Barnett was comfortable with the legal side, before himself rapidly going through the order to get a feel for its substance. Lamb himself was not in fact aware of the hooding prohibition and so would not have been able to spot its absence from the order.[75]

---

[74] Lamb BMI04919, paragraph 31(g)
[75] Lamb BMI 103/104/19-109/9

Chapter 5: Enforcement of the Fourteen Hour Rule

11.71 It is convenient in this Part of the Report to say a little more about the fourteen hour rule, its enforcement and occasions when it had been breached. The Inquiry heard evidence from a number of witnesses on this issue. This evidence was not entirely consistent. For instance, Barnett said that he was unaware of breaches of the fourteen hour rule and was confident that Ellis-Davies would have brought it to his attention had there been any requests for an extension of the time for detention.[76] Clifton, on the other hand, accepted that during Op Telic 2 he was aware that there had been breaches of the fourteen hour rule which he attributed initially to the misunderstanding in relation to the opening hours of the TIF to which I have referred in Part IX of this Report. He said it was necessary for him constantly to remind Battlegroups of the need to deliver prisoners within the time limit.[77]

11.72 S017, the Officer Commanding the Joint Forward Interrogation Team (JFIT), stated in her SIB statement and repeated in her Inquiry witness statement that it was a regular occurrence for prisoners to be brought to the TIF later than fourteen hours from their arrest.[78] However, in oral evidence to the Inquiry she put the number of occasions on which this occurred as approximately six.[79] She stated that when units delivered prisoners late, they would be reminded of the policy that they ought to be following. According to S017, the TIF were informed that:

> "...delays were often caused because of security issues surrounding the transportation of detainees and internees to the TIF or because the arresting unit's administration had been too slow, which resulted in a unit holding on to detainees and internees for a longer period of time than expected"[80]

11.73 S017 remembered that generally the delay had been caused by reasons beyond the Battlegroup's control and due to the circumstances of lack of manpower or transport delays. S017 accepted that she was reasonably sympathetic to there being delays:

> "...it was very dependent on the reason. I appreciated that it was very difficult for soldiers to actually get enough manpower together and the transport, especially from places like Al Amarah"[81]

However, S017 did speak to the Divisional HQ when the Battlegroup did not seem to have a good enough reason for the delay.[82] She apparently reported the non-compliance with the fourteen hour rule on two or three occasions to Ellis-Davies and S015, when the delivery time had been at about 24 hours with no reasonable explanation. S017 left it in the hands of Ellis-Davies and S015 and did not herself ascertain what was done in respect of the non-compliance.[83]

---

[76] Barnett BMI 86/83/8-84/6; Barnett BMI07926, paragraph 121; Barnett MOD000886
[77] Clifton BMI 81/80/21-82/2
[78] S017 BMI06813, paragraph 59; S017 MOD000595
[79] S017 BMI 84/40/12-20
[80] S017 BMI06813, paragraph 59
[81] S017 BMI 84/40/21-42/1
[82] S017 BMI 84/41/1-4
[83] S017 BMI 84/42/2-43/5

11.74 Ellis-Davies accepted that she had been aware that there were breaches of the fourteen hour rule. In relation to the frequency of such breaches she said it was not so often that she was concerned about it.[84] In her Inquiry witness statement she said that there was an element of flexibility to the rule, "*...there was also no penalty for not complying with the rule. It was something to which we took a common sense approach.*"[85] I note that in her SIB statement, Ellis-Davies referred to a "*common theme*" of units seeking to extend the time for detention beyond fourteen hours but that she had always advised them that prisoners were to be delivered as soon as possible.[86] As to the reasons for delay, Ellis-Davis suggested that they were due to logistical/transport difficulties. In terms of the length of delay, she could not recall specific time periods, but stated that she would have been surprised if they had run into a second day.[87] She accepted that one of the main reasons for having a fourteen hour rule in the first place was that it was recognised that there was a risk inherent in leaving detainees with the soldiers who had captured them.[88]

11.75 S015 agreed that he had been informed by S017 of the late reception of prisoners to the TIF and told the Inquiry that he had subsequently spoken to Le Fevre on the subject. He thought that the consequence of this discussion was that "*...timings were reinforced with the battlegroup*". He was not however aware of precisely how this was done or any other action that was taken to underline the rule.[89] I note, however, that S015 had previously stated in his Inquiry witness statement that he positively did not remember any action being taken after he had raised the issue of delay with Le Fevre. He stated:

> "*I expect that this was because it was thought that everything was being done by individual units to comply with the deadline when possible and because the operational restraints were unavoidable in the early stages of the operation*"[90]

11.76 Le Fevre remembered discussing with Barnett the difficulties in complying with the fourteen hour rule. He was unsure whether specific concerns had been raised with him in relation to breaches but he described this issue as a "*...discussion item that I remember having input to at various points during my time in theatre*".[91]

11.77 The evidence of Capt Andrew Haseldine, SO3 J2, supported the suggestion that breaches in complying with the fourteen hour rule were generally due to logistical and safety issues:

---

[84] Ellis-Davies BMI 85/135/3-12
[85] Ellis-Davies BMI05094-5, paragraph 62
[86] Ellis-Davies MOD000584
[87] Ellis-Davies BMI 85/135/13-136/15. The evidence of those accepting that breaches did occur was that they did not recall delays running over the 24 hour mark. A further point arose in relation to the Minutes of a Legal Conference held on 3 September 2003. The meeting was attended by Barnett, Clifton and Ellis-Davies and the minutes referred to "*...delays over 48 hours from apprehension to delivery to the TIF and conditions at the TIF*" (MOD049705). While this might naturally have been thought to relate to delay in detainees arriving at the TIF, these witnesses were consistent in explaining during evidence that it was only the delay in related paperwork arriving at the TIF which was being referred to. See Barnett BMI07606, paragraphs 13-14; Clifton BMI 81/79/14-80/19; Ellis-Davies BMI 85/173/23-174/21.
[88] Ellis-Davies BMI 85/185/14-186/6
[89] S015 BMI 84/111/14-113/1; S015 BMI06526-7, paragraph 45
[90] S015 BMI06527, paragraph 45
[91] Le Fevre BMI 85/26/18-28/1

"Q. One aspect that you say you did have some experience of or knowledge of in theatre is issues arising out of the 14-hour time period that existed to get prisoners to the TIF. Can you help us with that? What's your recollection about soldiers meeting or not being able to meet the 14-hour time limit?

A. It was just the fact that it was in the internee case reviews that we used to do, where we used – myself and the SO3 legal used to check the requirements, as we knew them, had been met. Sometimes an internee had not been delivered to the TIF within 14 hours, but that was accepted because of the logistical problems of moving somebody from Basra to the TIF at, say, 3 o'clock in the morning.

Q. Yes.

A. On top of that logistical problem, obviously, there is also the threat of attack by Iraqi insurgents. So what seems like it should be a relatively simple task isn't and sometimes it was generally accepted that if it took longer than 14 hours, then it took longer than 14 hours." [92]

11.78　The Brigade level review immediately after the death of Baha Mousa resulted in Fenton, the Chief of Staff of 19 Mech Bde, recording that the fourteen hour limit appeared rarely to be met.[93] Fenton accepted that he had been aware of the fourteen hour rule breaches before the death.[94] In his oral evidence he went further and accepted that this did not cause enough concern to prompt anyone to intervene; and, as I have already found, that this was illustrative of the less than diligent approach to ensuring the fourteen hour deadline was met:

"I would say I don't think it was taken seriously enough and taken seriously at this time at all, given what I've said in a number of statements, the nature of the operations on the ground at the time that – and the resources therefore required to move and protect a convoy down to Umm Qasr were substantial and therefore there was, I think, an acceptance that if you weren't going to make the 14-hour timeline, well that's just an acceptable breaking of the rules given the nature of the situation." [95]

11.79　Fenton added in relation to the fourteen hour rule that *"...we tried to observe the rule, but if we couldn't make the rule and if it was going to put people's lives at risk to make the rule, then I think it seemed perfectly sensible at that time to allow an extension"*.[96] There were of course competing demands, at times perhaps irreconcilable, faced by soldiers attempting to deliver prisoners to the TIF within set timescales but with limited resources. In oral evidence, Fenton accepted, however, that this was not a matter he chased in order to ensure that the timeline was met.[97] He agreed that a laxity in failing to pick up on breaches of the fourteen hour rule was indicative of the fact that prisoner handling was given a low priority, saying:

"Yes, it was given a low priority in terms of my responsibilities and what I had to deal with at the time

...

I trusted the people that were responsible to do it to be doing it correctly". [98]

---

[92] Haseldine BMI 83/41/17-42/5
[93] MOD030851
[94] Fenton BMI 101/107/16-108/2
[95] Fenton BMI 101/106/22-107/8
[96] Fenton BMI 101/107/12-15
[97] Fenton BMI 101/151/22-152/4
[98] Fenton BMI 101/152/15-20

Fenton accepted that because time was not devoted to this issue, certain practices were allowed to carry on when they ought not to have been.[99]

11.80 It seems clear from this evidence that there were a number of breaches of the fourteen hour rule or at least cases where extensions were sought. I am satisfied from the evidence of witnesses such as S017 and Ellis-Davies that the explanation for delay was normally logistical, transport and safety issues. I have no doubt that, for the most part, the explanations given for the delay by Battlegroups were genuine. It is also apparent from these witnesses that Battlegroups did receive reminders of the fourteen hour rule.

[99] Fenton BMI 101/152/9-153/1

Chapter 6: Conclusions

11.81 I have summarised above the most significant evidence in relation to the development of orders during Op Telic 2 up to the time of the detention of Baha Mousa and the other Detainees. Having regard to all the evidence in relation to these aspects of the Inquiry and to the submissions of the various Core Participants, I make the following findings of fact and reach the following conclusions.

19 Mech Bde FRAGO 85 and the Arrest Procedures Card

11.82 On 13 July 2003, 19 Mech Bde issued FRAGO 85 which had annexed to it guidance on internment and detention, and an arrest procedures card (circulated somewhat earlier) both of which were drafted by Clifton. The annex required suspects to be treated "*humanely and with respect at all times, taking into account age, gender and religion*". Coupled with it was a warning about disciplinary action against both perpetrators and commanders of those who mistreated suspects.

11.83 Brigade FRAGO 85 did not specifically refer to the prohibition on hooding. Because of his connection with Mercer, Clifton was aware from an early stage of the prohibition on hooding. I accept that he understood that the prohibition had already been communicated and that this was the reason why the prohibition was not referred to in FRAGO 85.

11.84 In my view it would have been better if the arrest procedures card had included the prohibition on hooding, but I do not think it would be fair to criticise Clifton for this omission. The card did refer to the need to treat prisoners humanely and warned of disciplinary action. FRAGO 85 was issued very early in Op Telic 2 and did not follow the same detailed staffing process as the later Divisional FRAGO 005 in respect of which fuller and further guidance was being contemplated.

A further soldiers' card not issued

11.85 In the later stages of Op Telic 1, Mercer recommended and drafted a further soldiers' card which specifically referred to the prohibition on hooding and made it clear that stress positions were one of a number of forms of mistreatment which were forbidden. Issuing of this card was deferred to Op Telic 2. I find that the card was mentioned, although not the detail, at the handover between Mercer and Barnett.

11.86 There appears to have been some confusion at the start of Op Telic 2 as to whether or not Mercer's soldiers' card had been issued. I find that after some investigation, Ellis-Davies correctly concluded that it had not. She drew attention to the fact that this was a topic which needed further consideration.

11.87 I accept that Barnett was also, in principle, in favour of issuing a further soldiers' card but deferred its issue for a variety of reasons. Those reasons were that he wanted amendments to the card; he thought it should follow the issue of a further comprehensive FRAGO; he believed that the prohibition on hooding and the need for all prisoners to be treated humanely was already clear; and he was concerned about too many pieces of guidance going to soldiers on the ground. Two related cards had already been issued. In the end, the further soldiers' card was not issued at any time before FRAGO 005 was promulgated on 3 September 2003.

11.88   I find that the decision to defer issuing a further soldiers' card until the issue of FRAGO 005 was, in the circumstances, not unreasonable. However, since the issuing of FRAGO 005 was itself delayed, the soldiers' card should have been issued promptly after FRAGO 005. In fact, no such card was issued.

11.89   I find Barnett and his legal branch at MND(SE) were responsible for the failure to issue a further soldiers' card. It ought to have been issued but I bear in mind that the general duty of soldiers to treat prisoners humanely had been clearly emphasised in a number of orders.

Further orders issued in August 2003

11.90   19 Mech Bde's FRAGO 104 was issued on 22 August 2003 and contained further guidance. However, the guidance was largely confined to evidence handling and decision making relating to detainees and internees.

11.91   MND(SE) issued a further version of the "Concept of Operations" order, headed "Multinational Division (South East) CONOPS 03/03" and dated 30 August 2003. The legal annex included requirements that prisoners of war be treated humanely and protected from physical and mental harm. In my view this was not an order in which it was to be expected that detail on prisoner handling would be found.

FRAGO 005

11.92   It is clear that FRAGO 005 was intended to provide consolidating guidance for Op Telic 2 on detention and internment procedures, and to replace existing guidance which was scattered throughout a number of different orders.

11.93   FRAGO 005 took quite a long time to be drafted. Work on it started in mid-July 2003 but it was not issued until 3 September 2003, nearly two months after 3 (UK) Div took over from 1 (UK) Div. The cause of the length of time which it took to draft this order was largely due to the extent to which it needed to be staffed through the Divisional staff branches as well as through PJHQ. There was also a need to consult the other national troops and the Iraqi judiciary. It seems its production was not considered to be particularly urgent. Although I am left with a degree of concern that it took so long for FRAGO 005 to be produced I do not consider that this delay was a contributory factor in the events surrounding Baha Mousa's death. It was issued ten days before the death.

11.94   FRAGO 005 relaxed the previous absolute time limit of fourteen hours for delivery of internees to the TIF. It provided "*Apprehended persons are to be transferred to the TIF within 14 hours of capture, or as soon as possible thereafter*". As already stated, having regard to the evidence on the practical difficulties on the ground in physically transporting prisoners to the TIF within the fourteen hour time limit, I do not consider that there was anything wrong with the decision taken by Barnett to relax the time limit in this way.

11.95   As the Division's legal adviser and commander of the legal branch, Barnett was a central figure in the production of FRAGO 005. It was his staff who were responsible for leading the drafting process. Barnett was an impressive witness, intelligent, articulate and an officer of sound judgment. I have no hesitation in accepting his evidence as truthful and accurate. He paid tribute to the hard work and skill of his staff. In particular, he spoke well of the industry and talent of Ellis-Davies and Clifton.

11.96 I have considered whether Barnett can be criticised for the failure of FRAGO 005 to make any reference to the prohibition on hooding. Viewed from the perspective of some years later with the knowledge of all the circumstances leading up to and surrounding Baha Mousa's death, it seems obvious that FRAGO 005 should have referred to the ban on hooding. It was designed to be an order consolidating the guidance on prisoner handling. Up to that time the only previous written order at Divisional level that had referred to the prohibition on hooding was FRAGO 152. In my view, the process of consolidating guidance should have led to the prohibition being included in FRAGO 005. This was an unfortunate omission and an error of judgment for which Barnett must take responsibility.

11.97 However, it is only fair that this error of judgment should be seen in the context of the circumstances known to Barnett at the time. I accept that he believed, with some justification, that the prohibition on hooding had already been communicated throughout the Division. It was not, in my view, his duty to check whether and how far it had been disseminated throughout the Division and its sub-units. I also accept that it was a difficult, but not insuperable problem, to give guidance to a Division comprised of troops from different nations. I further accept that in the summer of 2003 prisoner handling had not achieved the prominence it was to have following Baha Mousa's death. Nevertheless, although these and other factors provide considerable mitigation for this error, they do not wholly excuse Barnett's responsibility for it.

11.98 I think it is also right to emphasise that this was an omission and misjudgement by Barnett who was an otherwise obviously capable officer dealing with an array of challenging issues. His misjudgment in relation to FRAGO 005 and the failure of his branch to issue a further soldiers' card should be considered alongside the clear and appropriate lead that Barnett gave in legal advice immediately following Baha Mousa's death.[100]

11.99 As to whether FRAGO 005 ought to have contained further guidance on broader detention and tactical questioning principles, with hindsight it is plain that this would have been desirable. It would, therefore, have been better if Barnett had stuck to his initial instincts in this regard, but I do not think he can be blamed for the omission of such guidance. I accept that he was to a significant extent relying upon assurances that he had been given by other staff officers about the training and guidance which had been given to soldiers.

11.100 I find that Warren and Le Fevre did advise Barnett against the inclusion in FRAGO 005 of further guidance on detention and tactical questioning issues respectively. While I have sympathy with the views they expressed that guidance might be either misleading if too short or unwieldy if too long, I find aspects of their advice to have been inappropriately reassuring.

11.101 In relation to Le Fevre, I accept that he gave what seemed like a careful and measured view. However, having been invited to provide paragraphs by way of guidance on tactical questioning, Le Fevre missed the opportunity to notice that there was in fact

---

[100] See MOD016122 and Part XIV of this Report

extremely limited guidance available in theatre on tactical questioning. Le Fevre's advice to Barnett was, to that extent, more reassuring than it ought to have been.

11.102 After the death of Baha Mousa, the lack of guidance in relation to tactical questioning was noted and commented upon, including at Minister of State level.[101]

11.103 To a somewhat lesser extent, I find that the advice given by Warren (or his SO2 for whom Warren was responsible) was also a little too reassuring. The Provost input suggested it was not appropriate to put guidance on custodial matters into FRAGO 005. They relied upon the fact that each Battlegroup had members specially trained in custody matters. This overlooked the fact that the Regimental Provost staff did not at this time have specific training in operational custody matters in their custody course. The apparent confidence and expectation from the provost staff that the domestic standards of JSP 469 would be applied to operational custody was misplaced, as is evident not just from Payne's conduct but also from the evidence of Gallacher, the Provost Corporal of 1 BW.

11.104 In the sequence of orders during Op Telic 2, from the Divisional handover right through to Baha Mousa's death, it is striking that not one of the orders or guidance documents issued by MND (SE) or 19 Mech Bde referred in any way to the prohibition on hooding or stress positions. Had they done so it is doubtful that the 1 QLR process of conditioning would have developed or continued in the way that it did.

11.105 This reinforces the need for the MoD to avoid in future the situation in which prisoner handling becomes governed by scattered fragmentary orders. As well as improved training and doctrine, prisoner handling calls for a clear and appropriately detailed written standard operating procedure that is maintained through the handover between formations and units in enduring operations.

Enforcement of the Fourteen Hour Rule

11.106 Under FRAGO 005, detainees were to be delivered to the TIF within fourteen hours or as soon as possible thereafter. There was evidence that from time to time the deadline was breached. As I have already said I am satisfied that the explanation for delay was normally logistical, transport and safety issues. I have no doubt that, for the most part, the explanations given for the delay by Battlegroups were genuine. It is also apparent from these witnesses that Battlegroups did receive reminders of the fourteen hour rule.

11.107 In Part II Chapter 20 of the Report I have considered the delay by 1 QLR in transferring the Detainees to the TIF and the reasons for it. The delay in that instance was very substantial and well beyond what could properly be justified. I explained that Fenton accepted 1 QLR's explanation for the delay, but stated that my impression from the evidence was that Brigade was not sufficiently assiduous in ensuring that the fourteen hour deadline was met. In my judgment the same can be said about Division.

11.108 In Part IX of the Report I have suggested that with hindsight more consideration should have been given at the time to the potential disadvantages of the changes introduced by FRAGO 29, including the extension of time for delivery of prisoners to

---

[101] MOD055929, paragraph 2

fourteen hours. Having extended this time limit and then relaxed it further in FRAGO 005 by providing the qualification *"or as soon as possible thereafter"*, in my opinion it was incumbent on Brigade and Division to ensure that so far as possible the time limit was complied with. I recognise that circumstances in which breach of the time limit occurred may have been many and varied, but given the reason lying behind the time limit it would have been desirable had more priority and attention been given to enforcing the need to move prisoners to the TIF as soon as possible and within the period specified.

Part XII

Knowledge of Hooding In Op Telic 2

Chapter 1: Introduction

12.1   In this Part of the Report, I assess:

    (1)   the extent of the knowledge of the prohibition on hooding within the formations and units once deployed on Op Telic 2; and

    (2)   the extent to which witnesses within these units and formations were aware of the use of hooding during Op Telic 2 operations, whether at the point of capture, during transit, or during detention, and whether as an operational security measure, or as a method of conditioning.

12.2   In earlier Parts of the Report I have addressed how training as regards sight deprivation of prisoners was not the subject of consistent training policy (Part VI). I also considered how to some extent hooding continued in Op Telic 1 despite Gen Robin Brims' oral ban on hooding (Part VIII), and the shortcomings in how this prohibition was handed over to the incoming Op Telic 2 forces (Part X). Against that background, it is not surprising that, amongst Op Telic 2 witnesses, there was considerable variation as to their knowledge and understanding of the use of hooding, and the prohibition on hooding in theatre.

12.3   I make clear at the outset that the evidence which emerged undermined any suggestion that there was a widespread practice of hooding deliberately being employed during Op Telic 2 by those who knew that hooding was against orders. On the contrary, the overwhelming majority of witnesses fell into one of three categories:

    (1)   firstly, a relatively small number of witnesses neither knew of the ban on hooding nor that hooding was occurring on operations;

    (2)   secondly, some witnesses clearly knew hooding was the subject of a ban, yet did not know that it was a practice occurring in theatre; and

    (3)   thirdly, some witnesses did not know that there was a ban on hooding in place and were aware to varying degrees that hooding was occurring on operations.

12.4   The category into which each individual witness might fall was tested during oral evidence. The Inquiry has only identified a very few individuals who might fall into a fourth category of those who knew of a ban, became aware of hooding and therefore had a particularly obvious duty to intervene and report the practice.

12.5   The fact that there is very little evidence of witnesses using or endorsing the use of hoods knowing that hooding was prohibited still leaves some important issues for consideration. For instance, I have considered whether those who were aware of the hooding ban, but not aware that hooding was occurring, ought to have been aware of this practice and taken steps to stop it.

12.6   I have also considered whether those who knew that hooding was occurring but were unaware of the ban, ought nevertheless to have taken steps to discover why the practice was being used, for instance whether it was being used for security or disorientation/conditioning; and whether or not they ought to have been aware of the ban.

Chapter 2: Divisional Level

The Senior Officers at Divisional Headquarters

12.7 The General Officer Commanding (GOC), Maj Gen Graeme Lamb, was aware of the Heath Statement, but at the time of Op Telic 2 believed that depriving an individual of sight for a short period of time, necessitated by operational security concerns or for the safety of the detainee or others was acceptable. He understood that ideally hoods would not be used to achieve this. However, in the absence of other resources and providing that care was taken to ensure that the prisoner was able to breathe, Lamb understood that hooding could be used for a short period of time.[1]

12.8 As I have considered in Part X of this Report, prisoner handling issues were not discussed as part of the handover to Lamb, nor was he made aware of FRAGO 152 or any other order prohibiting hooding.[2] In general terms Lamb said that he received no indication that there was any major problem in relation to the processing and handling of prisoners until the death of Baha Mousa. In his Inquiry witness statement, Lamb said that he had visited the Theatre Internment Facility (TIF) on a number of occasions and he had never seen any mistreatment of detainees there or elsewhere during Op Telic 2.[3]

12.9 Lamb also told the Inquiry that he had no direct knowledge of the practice of hooding at all on Op Telic 2. He had only seen prisoners at the TIF, not prisoners being captured or being held at Battlegroup detention facilities. These prisoners at the TIF were not blindfolded or hooded. Lamb also stated that he had not been told that there was any issue that prisoners were still arriving at the TIF wearing hoods.[4]

12.10 During his oral evidence Lamb conceded that blacked-out goggles, an alternative to hoods as a method of sight deprivation, were not readily available to the troops on the ground. He accepted that in those circumstances and given the justifiable security concerns it would have effectively become a standard operating procedure to use a sandbag as a hood. As the matter was not raised with him, Lamb did not give consideration to whether, in the particular context of summertime temperatures in Iraq, hoods could still be properly used.[5]

12.11 As to whether sight deprivation could legitimately be used for puposes of security but might also have the side benefit of prolonging the shock of capture, Lamb said that this was a consequence of, but not the reason for, hooding. He said it had always been self-evident to him that isolation through sight deprivation would prolong the shock of capture. This was not a matter that was talked about or current before Op Telic 2, rather it was something he had always known.[6]

12.12 It follows that Lamb would not necessarily have thought hooding for security purposes was inappropriate had he come across it during Op Telic 2. I accept that he did not in fact see it occur.

---

[1] Lamb BMI 103/74/4-77/24; Lamb BMI04915 paragraphs 22-23
[2] Lamb BMI 103/91/7-19; Lamb BMI04916, paragraph 27
[3] Lamb BMI04920-3, paragraphs 32 and 41
[4] Lamb BMI 103/112/5-113/17
[5] Lamb BMI 103/82/11-83/22
[6] Lamb BMI 103/78/4-17

12.13 Similarly, before the death of Baha Mousa, Col Barry Le Grys, Deputy Chief of Staff (DCOS) of 3 (UK) Div was not aware of FRAGO 152, the written order prohibiting the covering of prisoners' faces, or any other order relating to hooding.[7] He said in his Inquiry witness statement that he did not see and was not aware of any detainees being hooded during his tour.[8]

12.14 In contrast to the GOC and Le Grys, Col Richard Barrons, the Chief of Staff (COS) of the Division was aware that hooding had been banned, as a result of a conversation he had during the handover he received from Col Patrick Marriott, the COS of 1 (UK) Div.[9] But Barrons said that, before Baha Mousa's death, he was not aware of the use of hooding or blindfolding by 19 Mech Bde Battlegroups, or at the TIF.[10]

12.15 As I have addressed in Part X of this Report, Barrons did not personally do anything to make sure that the prohibition on hooding, to which he had been alerted, was brought to the attention of those units and sub-units within 3 (UK) Div being deployed on Op Telic 2. I have commented that with the benefit of hindsight it would have been better for an order prohibiting hooding to have been re-issued to the incoming Op Telic 2 forces. However, I have found that Barrons was not personally at fault for not taking this course. There is insufficient evidence of any concerns about hooding, or wider concerns about prisoner handling coming to Barrons' attention, to justify such a criticism of him.

12.16 When Barrons gave evidence he was asked whether he had checked what the lower formation and Op Telic 2 troops on the gound knew about the hooding ban, he responded *"No, I don't believe I did and I don't believe at the time that there was any sense that it was an issue that was in doubt or needed re-affirming"*.[11] While I have no reason to doubt that Barrons genuinely held this belief, this confidence in the extent to which the ban on hooding was understood can be seen now to have been misplaced, not least because his own GOC and the DCOS were both unaware of it.

12.17 Barrons was pressed on whether the Divisional and Brigade level of command knew, or ought to have known, that hooding was occurring at ground level:

> *"Q. If, as the Inquiry has heard, at least on some evidence, that was a standard operating procedure when 1 QLR arrested suspected insurgents and that it was something that was used by a number of the 19 Mech Brigade battlegroups, at least in the early stages of Op Telic 2, is that something which should have filtered up one way or the other to MND(SE) level?*
>
> *A. If that was the case, it is something that, had it been made known to the divisional headquarters, the divisional headquarters would absolutely have acted on it.*
>
> *Q. That doesn't quite answer my question though; that's to say, "If we had known, we would have done something". Should it have been something that filtered up and was something that should have been within the awareness of the divisional headquarters if it was happening on the ground?*

[7] Le Grys BMI03760, paragraph 22
[8] Le Grys BMI03760, paragraph 24
[9] Barrons BMI06225, paragraph 25
[10] Barrons BMI06234-5, paragraph 55
[11] Barrons BMI 99/112/2-4

> *A. The divisional headquarters will depend on that information being provided by its subordinate chain of command or by some other third party.*
>
> *Q. Again, if it is something that was happening on a fairly routine basis, if the system had been working properly, would you have expected people at divisional level to be aware of it?*
>
> *A. You would have to define what you mean by "the system working properly".*
>
> *Q. The system whereby those at brigade would understand what was happening on operations and that would be passed up in various forms of assess reps and meetings and so on to divisional headquarters?*
>
> *A. I would expect that if the chain of command was in any doubt about the procedures that it was applying or was detecting things that it felt was inappropriate, I would have expected them – indeed required them – to report it."*[12]

12.18 I accept that at the highest level of command within 3 (UK) Div neither Lamb nor Le Grys knew that hooding was occurring. Neither did Barrons, who given his knowledge of a ban would have been expected to intervene had he known.

Plans and Operations Branches

12.19 Within the Divisional Plans branch, Lt Col James Murray-Playfair (the Chief J5 Plans) did not remember seeing FRAGO 152 and was not otherwise aware of a prohibition on hooding.[13]

12.20 Murray-Playfair understood that it was legitimate to deprive a prisoner of sight for security reasons provided that the method used did not impair the prisoner's ability to breathe.[14] In his Inquiry witness statement he said that he did not know what was used by Battlegroups during Op Telic 2 in instances where sight deprivation was necessary, "*...other than local material that was immediately available*",[15] and that "*I did not witness nor do I recall hearing about hooding being used on tour during Op TELIC 2 before Baha Mousa's death*".[16]

12.21 During his oral evidence, Murray-Playfair was asked about aspects of evidence before the Inquiry, including the following: that the use of hoods within 1 Queen's Lancashire Regiment (QLR) might have been standard practice; that hoods were also used by other Battlegroups at least during the early part of Op Telic 2; that hoods may have been used by a RAF Regiment at Basra Airport where the Divisional headquarters were located; and that there may have been concerns about hooded prisoners arriving at the JFIT. He said he would be surprised if this was the case but would not routinely have taken an interest in the issues as his focus was elsewhere.[17]

12.22 Murray-Playfair gave the following explanation of how, if hooding was practised by soldiers on the ground, this might not have been known to staff at Divisional level:

---

[12] Barrons BMI 99/112/9-113/18
[13] Murray-Playfair BMI05493, paragraph 21
[14] Murray-Playfair BMI05492-3, paragraph 19
[15] Murray-Playfair BMI05493, paragraph 20
[16] Murray-Playfair BMI05494-5, paragraph 24
[17] Murray-Playfair BMI 86/225/15-226/3

> *"Q. At divisional level, if that was going on on the ground, who in division ought to have known about it, and by what means?*
>
> *A. Well, if that was going on on the ground and was known in the battlegroups, one would expect the brigade maybe to be aware of it, because they had access to the battlegroups.*
>
> *Q. Yes.*
>
> *A. The difficulty at division is that we are two steps removed from the battlegroups and by August, movement is being severely curtailed, and therefore for a divisional staff officer to get out of his airport lounge, which is where the headquarters was, and to go to the battlegroups was a very difficult thing to achieve. So I wouldn't be surprised if there was – if that knowledge had not made its way to divisional headquarters.*
>
> *Q. It may be that those at divisional headquarters, as you indicate, would be reliant upon information coming from 19 Mech Brigade headquarters, and that much, put it this way, the Inquiry might well understand. But if the system had been working properly at brigade level, who within division – which staff officers, which branches – ought to have been made aware that this was going on?*
>
> *A. That is a subset of current operations and therefore one would expect that that would be – if the information had come up – would be turning in the J3 circle."[18]*

12.23 Murray-Playfair described himself as being a J5 (Plans) and not J3 (Operations) staff officer at the relevant time.[19] In addition the Inquiry received a statement from Capt Antony Pearce, SO3 J3 Training and Plans, who said that he was not aware of or privy to information on the treatment of prisoners.[20]

Provost Staff

12.24 There was also a lack of knowledge of the ban on hooding and the use of hoods on operations, amongst the staff in command of the Royal Military Police (RMP). Senior RMP officers were located at Multi national Division (South East) (MND (SE)) headquarters while the RMP ground level forces were placed under the tactical command of 19 Mech Bde and had elements deployed with each Battlegroup.[21]

12.25 Lt Col Robert Warren was the Commanding Officer of 3 RMP Regiment and the Provost Marshal of MND (SE) during Op Telic 2.[22] He thought that sight deprivation for the purposes of security might be justified, but only through the use of a blindfold or blacked-out goggles rather than hooding, which he thought unacceptable. This was based on his understanding of the Geneva Conventions and the principle of humane treatment rather than any training or instruction he had received.[23] In his Inquiry witness statement Warren said that he did not see any detainees either hooded or blindfolded in Iraq. Further, had he been made aware that such practices were occurring he would have been extremely concerned and would have taken

---

[18] Murray-Playfair BMI 86/226/4-227/6
[19] Murray-Playfair BMI05488, paragraph 5
[20] Pearce BMI07284, paragraph 7
[21] Warren BMI03460-1, paragraphs 41-43; West BMI03821-2, paragraphs 2-4
[22] Warren BMI03453, paragraph 12
[23] Warren BMI03455, paragraphs 22-24

steps to investigate.[24] While in Iraq, Warren was nevertheless unaware of the fact that there had been an order prohibiting the use of hooding.[25]

12.26 Maj Richard West was the Second in Command (2IC) of 3 RMP.[26] He did not see hoods being used during Op Telic 2, and he had not been aware of any ban on the use of hoods until after the death of Baha Mousa in September.[27]

Legal Branch

12.27 The evidence suggests that senior legal officers at Division were aware of a ban on the practice of hooding (for whatever purpose).

12.28 Lt Col Charles Barnett was the Commander Legal, the senior legal adviser to the GOC MND (SE).[28] Before his deployment in theatre, Barnett understood that hooding was not permitted. He knew of the Op Telic 1 prohibition on hooding and of the effect of 1 (UK) Div FRAGO 152 in this regard.[29] Barnett said that he thought that FRAGO 152 had been effectively cascaded down the chain of command.[30]

12.29 Barnett's understanding was that hooding was not to be used in any circumstances.[31] He informed the Inquiry that he had not seen any conditioning techniques used at any stage of the tour.[32] He had visited the JFIT on "*Quite a number*" of occasions, and did not remember seeing there any hooded prisoners.[33]

12.30 Barnett's account, that he knew hooding to be completely banned in theatre, was tested during his oral evidence. While he did not remember including the ban on hooding during the Op Telic 2 pre-deployment Law of Armed Conflict (LOAC) lectures he gave, he was adamant that this did not reflect any degree of uncertainty about the permissibility of hooding or knowledge of its use.[34]

12.31 Barnett drew a distinction between the in-theatre prohibition on hooding and the legal position. He said:

> "*I understood, when I deployed, that hoods were not permitted and were not being used. That's slightly different to my understanding of an interpretation of the law, which would be that I can and could envisage exceptional circumstances where the use of a hood may be permitted but it was not a matter I provided advice to British forces on, with the exception of providing it internally to the divisional headquarters by an email early in my tour.*"[35]

12.32 This email advice arose in the context of a draft US Corp order, FRAGO 455, concerning the categorisation of detainees. It is not necessary for me to address

---

[24] Warren BMI03464, paragraph 52
[25] Warren BMI 83/111/24-113/13
[26] West BMI03821, paragraph 2
[27] West BMI03831-2, paragraph 40(a)
[28] Barnett BMI07905, paragraph 71
[29] Barnett BMI 86/10/18-11/18; Barnett BMI07915-6, paragraph 95
[30] Barnett BMI07946, paragraph 188
[31] Barnett BMI 86/34/11-18
[32] Barnett BMI07948, paragraph 191
[33] Barnett BMI 86/75/24-76/6
[34] Barnett BMI 86/28/11-34/18
[35] Barnett BMI 86/15/8-16

the contents of that draft order, only the comments Barnett made about it, namely the following part of his advice circulated within 3 (UK) Div on 20 July 2003:[36]

> b. There is a direction to handcuff, ankle shackle and hood CAT A & B immediately, during the interrogation process and during transportation. It is also directed that these measures be applied to all the other categories during transportation. Whilst it may be necessary to restrain by handcuffs etc the highest categories and hooding may be necessary and lawful in certain circumstances for good reasons (eg so they cannot id security force personnel, for their own safety etc) we must remember the Geneva Convention obligations that make it clear that individuals must be treated humanely, must be accorded respect and honour, and must be protected from intimidation and acts of curiosity etc. This is open to interpretation but for presentational reasons the UK stopped hooding towards the end of the conflict phase and so it is most certainly politically unacceptable for all but the most exceptional cases to be hooded now.

12.33 In his oral evidence, Barnett sought to clarify what he had meant by referring to certain cases where hooding may be necessary and lawful. He explained, to put the email in context that he had to be careful not to provide advice which would be confrontational toward the US superior headquarters. More substantively, Barnett said that there were no exceptional circumstances which he understood actually permitted hooding to take place. But he said he could envisage two situations that might amount to an exceptional circumstance where hooding would comply with the Geneva Conventions. Firstly, when an individual prisoner was fearful of being identified and requested to be hooded for their own safety. Secondly, for security reasons, if absolutely necessary, and if nothing else was available to effect the deprivation of sight. Regarding the second set of circumstances, Barnett said that even at the time he had effectively discounted this because where there was material with which to hood, it should always be possible to tear that material up to use as a blindfold.[37]

12.34 Barnett denied there was an element of flexibility in the rules of hooding:

> "Q. It wasn't the case, was it, in 2003, both in your time and perhaps before, that, as it were, some escape clause would always be left to cover those occasions when prisoners might be hooded?
>
> A. No. I would emphasise quite clearly, though, that my view of the direction that you must give to soldiers is that you should teach the principles – there are some absolutely forbidden areas – and principles must be applied to the factual circumstances people find themselves in. It is very difficult to write a definitive list of what is not permitted and what is permitted. In doing so you may be in danger of inadvertently suggesting something is permitted when you don't want to.[38]

12.35 As I have addressed in Part XI of this Report, Barnett was mainly responsible for drafting FRAGO 005 the "Policy for Apprehending, Handling and Processing of Detainees and Internees" dated 3 September 2003.[39] Barnett said that had he known that hooding was occurring during operations on Op Telic 2, he would have included the prohibition in FRAGO 005 or issued other directions to meet the issue.[40]

---

[36] MOD052219
[37] Barnett BMI 86/16/4-20/11
[38] Barnett BMI 86/20/22-21/10
[39] MOD022623
[40] Barnett BMI 86/58/10-59/8

12.36 Barnett's account was, therefore, that at all material times he knew hooding to be prohibited and, up until the death of Baha Mousa, there was no requirement for him to take further action because he did not know hooding was occurring.

12.37 Two aspects of the evidence before me might be thought to undermine his account. Firstly, the possibility that Barnett was informed by others that hooding was occurring. Secondly, that operational orders issued during Op Telic 2 contained language either expressly stating that hooding was being used, or using language that should have prompted inquiry.

12.38 In relation to the first issue, Barnett denied ever having it brought to his attention the fact that prisoners were being delivered to the Joint Forward Interrogation Team (JFIT) wearing hoods. He specifically denied that S017, the Officer Commanding the JFIT, had so informed him. S017 said that she informed Barnett, Capt Sian Ellis-Davies, Lt Col Graham Le Fevre and S015 that some prisoners were being delivered to the TIF wearing hoods. I deal with the conflict between the evidence of S017 and Barnett and others on this point below at paragraphs 12.52 to 12.66. I have found that S017 did not alert Barnett to prisoners arriving hooded at the JFIT.

12.39 In respect of the second issue, there were a number of Battlegroup operational orders, which contained language which arguably ought to have caused those aware of the ban on hooding to intervene:

(1) 1 Queen's Lancashire Regiment (QLR)'s Op Quebec order of 13 August 2003 referred to prisoners being *"bagged and tagged"*;[41]

(2) 1 QLR's Op Lightning order of 25 August 2003[42] and Op Quintessential order of 7 September 2003[43] referred to the conditioning of prisoners; and

(3) Op Comiston 2 of 9 September 2003[44] (an order from the 1 King's Own Scottish Borderers (KOSB) Battlegroup) included *"Bag out of sight once in vans"*.

12.40 Barnett told the Inquiry that he would not have seen these orders given the level at which they had been issued. He said that, had he seen them, these types of references would have concerned him and he would have intervened to discover what they meant.[45] He was surprised that these expressions were not brought to his attention as being of concern.[46]

12.41 As I find elsewhere in the Report I found Barnett to be an impressive witness and I accept that he knew hooding was banned. I also accept that he did not see these Battlegroup level orders or the terms within them which might have caused him to intervene.

12.42 Under Barnett's command was Ellis-Davies (the 3 (UK) Div SO3 Operational Law).[47] She explained in her Inquiry witness statement that early in her tour, when collating the materials previously issued in relation to internees and detainees, she became aware of FRAGO 152. She said this merely reinforced the understanding which

---

[41] MOD030899
[42] MOD043232
[43] MOD011741
[44] MOD017034
[45] Barnett BMI07942-4, paragraphs 171-177
[46] Barnett BMI 86/88/2-14
[47] Ellis-Davies BMI 85/116/16-117/3

she already had that hooding was not permitted.[48] She was, however, unable to remember when she first came to this understanding.[49]

12.43 When she gave her oral evidence Ellis-Davies was able to give a little more detail. Although she could no longer remember precisely when, or by what means, she had come to understand before her deployment on Op Telic 2 that hooding was not a permitted practice, while sight deprivation by other methods if necessary for security reasons might be permitted.[50] She regarded hooding as being inhumane but was not aware of the Heath Statement or the 1972 Directive.[51] When she first arrived in theatre, Ellis-Davies did not know that the practice of hooding had been subject to a specific ban during Op Telic 1, but it was something of which she did subsequently become aware.[52] Ellis-Davies also said that she had not been aware of the use of hoods in theatre before the death of Baha Mousa.[53]

12.44 S017 asserted that she had informed Ellis-Davies that prisoners were arriving at the JFIT wearing hoods. Again, I deal with the conflict of evidence on this point below at paragraphs 12.52 to 12.66 and for the reasons given there, on the balance of probabilities I find it unlikely that S017 raised the arrival of hooded prisoners with Ellis-Davies.

Intelligence Branch

12.45 The picture within 3 (UK) Div's intelligence branch was notably different to the legal branch. Some staff officers within the intelligence branch knew that sight deprivation was being effected through the use of hoods, and some of them also understood that hoods were used to maintain the shock of capture and not merely for security purposes.

12.46 Le Fevre was the SO1 J2 ISTAR. As a result of his training on the PH&TQ course in 1984, Le Fevre understood that hooding for security purposes was appropriate.[54] He knew hooding was expressly prohibited for use during tactical questioning and for any conditioning purposes. But his understanding from the course was that depriving a prisoner's sight in this manner might have the incidental effect of maintaining the shock of capture.[55] He had no recollection of seeing FRAGO 152 or any other order prohibiting the use of hooding on prisoners.[56] It would not therefore have been a surprise to him to learn that hooding was taking place.

12.47 Le Fevre's evidence about when he became aware of hooding by British Forces in Iraq was somewhat vague. He stated that it may have been as a result of the Baha Mousa incident but it might have been before that. He had no recollection of how he gained the knowledge or who made him aware of it. Because of his training, Le Fevre did not regard the use of hooding as wrong or a matter of any great importance. He accepted that he did not discover whether or not the hooding was in fact only applied

---

[48] Ellis-Davies BMI05078-9, paragraphs 15-16
[49] Ellis-Davies BMI05083, paragraphs 29 and 32
[50] Ellis-Davies BMI 85/119/8-121/22
[51] Ellis-Davies BMI 85/123/18-124/7
[52] Ellis-Davies BMI 85/125/19-127/9
[53] Ellis-Davies BMI 85/130/4-18
[54] Le Fevre BMI 85/3/16-17; Le Fevre BMI 85/7/14-23
[55] Le Fevre BMI06542, paragraphs 13-14
[56] Le Fevre BMI06456, paragraph 31

for security purposes.[57] Le Fevre was another officer to whom S017 suggested she had reported the fact that prisoners were arriving hooded at the JFIT. This aspect of the evidence is dealt with at paragraphs 12.57 and 12.61 below. In essence, although he did not recall it, Le Fevre said that had this been reported to him he would have assumed it was for security purposes and for this reason it would not have caused him concern.[58]

12.48   S015 was the SO2 J2X for 3 (UK) Div during Op Telic 2.[59]   He was based at HQ MND(SE) and reported to Le Fevre.[60]   Before deployment, S015's understanding was that hooding was not permitted.   He had arrived at this understanding from his training on the PH&TQ course in 1994 and Interrogation course in 1996.   Sight deprivation for security purposes was permitted, but he was confident that it was made very clear on his training courses that the nose and mouth had to be left clear so as not to impede breathing.   In oral evidence, S015 clarified that the use of sandbags as hoods had not expressly been ruled out, but it followed from his training that the bags could not be pulled down over the nose and mouth.[61]   S015 did not remember FRAGO 152 or any other order prohibiting hooding.[62]   In contrast to his immediate superior, Le Fevre, S015 said he would have been surprised had he learned of hooding in theatre:

> "Q [...] can I just ask you in general terms about your understanding about the use of hoods during Op Telic 2 prior to Baha Mousa's death?   What would your understanding have been about whether hoods could be used in theatre?
>
> A. Going back to my training, that hoods should not be used because they may impede the nose and the mouth, but blindfolding could be used for security purposes.
>
> Q. So if you had received a report of the use of hoods, even if it was the use of hoods outside of the immediate interrogation context, that would have struck you, would it, as being concerning?
>
> A. Yes."[63]

12.49   S015 visited the JFIT three or four times a month and did not remember seeing any detainees hooded there.[64]

12.50   Maj Jerry Hartley was an SO2 in 3 (UK) Div J2 branch during Op Telic 2.[65]   He was not certain whether he had been taught that hooding was an impermissible technique;[66] although he would have considered it clearly not permissible as an aid to interrogation, because of his interpretation of general LOAC training.[67]   He did not remember ever seeing FRAGO 152, nor was he aware of any other order which

[57] Le Fevre BMI 85/14/20-18/23
[58] Le Fevre BMI 85/18/24-20/22
[59] S015 BMI 84/84/17-21
[60] S015 BMI06522-3, paragraphs 29 and 33
[61] S015 BMI 84/87/14-90/6; S015 BMI06518-9, paragraph 15
[62] S015 BMI06527-8, paragraphs 47-49
[63] S015 BMI 84/103/19-104/6
[64] S015 BMI06525, paragraph 40
[65] Maj Jerry Hartley BMI03053, paragraph 4
[66] Maj Jerry Hartley BMI03056, paragraph 21
[67] Maj Jerry Hartley BMI03067, paragraph 72

prohibited the hooding of prisoners.[68] He was not aware of hooding being used by 19 Mech Bde or at the TIF.[69]

12.51 Capt Andrew Haseldine was an SO3 J2 in 3 (UK) Div working in MND (SE) headquarters during Op Telic 2.[70] He had completed the Interrogation course at Chicksands.[71] He was instructed on that course to use hoods for security reasons when moving prisoners, but also that hoods helped to maintain the shock of capture. He recalled that *"it was generally accepted that POWs arriving at the POW cage would have been hooded and cuffed from point of capture"*.[72] Thus it would seem that if Haseldine learned of the use of hooding during Op Telic 2 this would not have struck him as surprising. In fact, however, Haseldine did not visit any Battlegroup HQ or detention centres and was not aware of the general practices that were adopted by them.[73] He did see hooding used on one occasion by the RAF squadron who guarded Basra airport (the location of the Multinational Divisional headquarters) and he did not raise any concerns about it.[74]

Reports of Prisoners Arriving Hooded at the JFIT

12.52 Capt S017, the Officer Commanding the JFIT from July to December 2003, told the Inquiry that she had been taught on the PH&TQ course that hooding was prohibited and never acceptable in the prisoner handling chain.[75] However, during her deployment she was not aware of FRAGO 152 or any other order banning hooding.[76]

12.53 S017's evidence was that on some occasions during Op Telic 2, detainees did arrive at the TIF with sandbags covering their heads. S017 stated that she had the sandbags removed immediately and instructed the escorting soldiers to fashion blindfolds by tearing the sandbag material into strips.[77]

12.54 S017 further stated that she had raised the issue of seeing prisoners hooded with both Ellis-Davies and with Barnett. This account was in marked conflict with the accounts of both Barnett and Ellis-Davies, both of whom said that they had no knowledge of hooding occurring on Op Telic 2 before the death of Baha Mousa. S017 said in her Inquiry witness statement that:

> *"The issue of hooding was something that I raised orally during my visits to Div HQ. I did not think it appropriate to raise it at the Detainee and Internee Review Committee Board meetings (detailed below at paragraphs 69 and 70) because the purpose of all discussions there surrounded the release of individuals from the JFIT. However, I did I raise these concerns on a semi-regular basis with Capt Ellis-Davies (approximately six times whilst on tour), on a couple of occasions with Major S015 and Lt Col Barnett and on one occasion with Col Le Fevre, also on an informal basis. Other than Capt Ellis-Davies informing me, on the occasions that I raised it with her, that she would speak to those units adopting the use of hoods to*

---

[68] Maj Jerry Hartley BMI03067, paragraph 74
[69] Maj Jerry Hartley BMI03067, paragraph 72
[70] Haseldine BMI04595, paragraph 4
[71] Haseldine BMI04595, paragraph 7
[72] Haseldine BMI04597, paragraphs 16-17
[73] Haseldine BMI04599-600, paragraph 32
[74] Haseldine BMI 83/36/19-38/25
[75] S017 BMI06798, paragraph 10
[76] S017 BMI06810, paragraph 49
[77] S017 BMI06808-10, paragraphs 45-48

tell them to stop, I am unsure about what, if any, action was taken to resolve the issue. In response to a question from the Inquiry, following the lapse of time I cannot now remember in detail the reactions of Maj S015, Lt Col Barnett or Col Le Fevre when I notified them of prisoners arriving hooded at the TIF but I remember that I was left with the impression that the issue was not regarded as being of particular importance".[78]

12.55 In her oral evidence, S017's account was much less certain in answering questions from Counsel to the Inquiry; in places I thought her answers were, to an extent, inconsistent with her written statement. She was markedly less sure about having raised hooding with Barnett and S015:

Q. *Do you remember, from time to time, detainees or internees arriving hooded?*

A. *Very rarely, but yes.*

Q. *Hooded with sandbags?*

A. *Yes.*

Q. *Was that a process – detainees arriving hooded – which went on throughout the period of your time in Iraq?*

A. *I would say that it occasionally occurred throughout the whole period that I was there.*

Q. *From July through to December?*

A. *Yes.*

Q. *What would happen to detainees who arrived hooded?*

A. *I would immediately remove the hoods and remind the arresting units not to hood them.*

Q. *It must have been apparent, S017, that your reminding the arresting soldiers or the arresting unit was having little effect if indeed this practice was continuing.*

A. *It happened so rarely that I would say it would, and they were all different units, except one, that did it. Some were foreign troops. So only on about two or three occasions were they Brit troops.*

Q. *What, on two or three occasions over the whole period?*

A. *Yes.*

Q. *It wasn't something that you thought you ought to take up with higher authority?*

A. *I did speak to other people about it, but I didn't see it as a huge issue because it was only two or three occasions in the entire time I was there.*

Q. *You say it wasn't a huge issue and you relate the number of occasions as being why it wasn't a huge issue – is that what I understand?*

A. *Yes.*

Q. *– but did you regard hooding of prisoners as inhumane?*

A. *Yes.*

Q. *Wasn't that an important issue?*

A. *Of course it was.*

Q. *And who did you take it up with?*

---

[78] S017 BMI06809-10, paragraph 48

A. I spoke to Captain Ellis-Davies about it initially.

Q. And what was her reaction?

A. She said that she would speak to the particular unit.

Q. So you were able to tell her which unit it was or units it was which were bringing the hooded prisoners in?

A. On two occasions it was the same unit, yes.

Q. And did you, as it were, report this matter to her on each occasion that it happened?

A. No.

Q. Did you report it to someone else?

A. I recall reporting it also to Colonel Le Fevre and I may -- I cannot recall 100 per cent whether I reported it to S015 and also Colonel Barnett.

Q. I don't want you to guess at this -- if you don't know, please tell us -- but are you saying that all those now that you have named would have been told by you, at some time or another, that prisoners were being brought hooded to the TIF?

A. I definitely told Captain Ellis-Davies and Colonel Le Fevre.

Q. But as to S015 and Barnett --

A. I can't recall.

Q. You can't recall. I follow. In paragraph 48 of your statement to this Inquiry –

    […BMI06810 paragraph 48 was read…]

Q. So should we understand that all of those that you name in that paragraph were informed of your concern about prisoners being brought hooded?

A. S015 and Colonel Barnett, I think I'm assuming that I would have told them. However I can be sure about Captain Ellis-Davies and Colonel Le Fevre.

Q. You go on to say:

    "Other than Captain Ellis-Davies informing me, on the occasions that I raised it with her, that she would speak to those units adopting the use of hoods to tell them to stop, I am unsure about what, if any, action was taken to resolve the issue."

    Wasn't it a matter of, if you like, greater importance that you ought to have ensured that further steps were being taken to stop this practice?

A. I had very little access to divisional headquarters, so I didn't get many opportunities to follow up many of the things that I had ongoing at divisional headquarters.

Q. It wasn't the case, S017, was it, that hooding was, if you like, such a regular matter that it received very low priority, indeed from you and others?

A. I would say on the contrary. It is because it happened so infrequently that -- that is why, as opposed to the seriousness of it.

Q. But you didn't follow through to ensure that it was stopped, as it were, sooner rather than later?

A. Again, because it happened so infrequently, I didn't see a trend of it continue to occur.

> *Q. When you did raise the issue of detainees arriving hooded, did anyone raise with you the fact that an order banning hooding existed --*
>
> *A. No.*
>
> *Q. -- or indeed that a FRAGO -- FRAGO 152, which I think you will now be familiar with -- had been brought into operation preventing the covering of the face?*
>
> *A. No.*
>
> *Q. Nobody raised those issues with you?*
>
> *A. No".*[79]

12.56 In further questioning on behalf of Counsel for Ellis-Davies, S017 said that on three occasions when she recalled prisoners arriving hooded, they had in fact been captured by non-UK forces, and it was only as a matter of courtesy that S017 had mentioned to Ellis-Davies that she was going to approach the foreign legal representatives to raise the issue.[80] On the two further occasions involving UK Forces S017 said:

> *"At no time did I formally raise it with her [Ellis-Davies]. It was something that I spoke to her within a context of a wider conversation –*
>
> *Q. I see.*
>
> *A. – and, as I say, on the occasion that it was two of the same units, she said she would speak to them.*
>
> *Q. But you never followed that up?*
>
> *A. No".*[81]

12.57 It follows that S017 knew hooding was prohibited and later witnessed it occurring. In those circumstances she ought to have intervened to prevent it and reported the matter to her superiors. S017's evidence was that she did both intervene and report the matter, at least on an informal basis to Ellis-Davies, and to Le Fevre.

12.58 During her oral evidence Ellis-Davies firmly and without equivocation denied this had occurred. She gave reasons why the conversation would not have occurred in the manner in which S017 said. Firstly, Ellis-Davies said that any matter which involved a need to approach the legal advisers from different nations about a difference in practice would have been of extreme importance. It would have taken place on the basis of legal adviser to legal adviser rather than through the Officer Commanding the JFIT. Secondly, Ellis-Davies disputed S017's account that the soldiers mostly responsible for bringing hooded prisoners to the JFIT were from the RAF. Ellis-Davies said that she had no legal point of contact within the RAF (meaning that she would not have agreed then to go and speak to that unit). In addition, given the role of the RAF Regiment she would not have expected them, regularly or at all to be capturing prisoners, and that as an Army Captain she would have had to mention this to the Commander Legal rather than approach another arm of the Armed Services on her own.[82] Taken together these are, in my view, persuasive reasons tending to support Ellis-Davies' account. Indeed I find Ellis-Davies' evidence rejecting the assertion that she had been told that prisoners were arriving at the JFIT hooded, compelling.

---

[79] S017 BMI 84/21/6-26/1
[80] S017 BMI 84/74/10-25
[81] S017 BMI 84/75/7-15
[82] Ellis-Davies 85/152/14-155/7

12.59 Barnett also denied being made aware of this issue.[83] The highest that S017 was finally able to put this issue in relation to Barnett was that she had assumed she would have told him, not that she positively remembered doing so.[84] I have no reason to doubt S017's honesty as a witness. However, in some cases her recollections, while honestly given, I find were not entirely reliable. As I have recorded in Chapter 4 of Part VI of this Report, this was illustrated by S017 adamantly, but incorrectly, insisting that she had received a training aide memoire before deployment on Op Telic 2 which referred to the ban on hooding, when the document must, I find, have been a later document.

12.60 I accept and prefer Barnett's account that the issue was not raised with him by S017.

12.61 Le Fevre told the Inquiry that he did not remember whether S017 had raised the matter with him, but that it was possible she had. He accepted that he became aware at some point that prisoners had arrived at the JFIT hooded.[85] He further stated that if S017 had raised concerns about hooding with him he would have assumed that it was being done for security purposes, and so it would not have been a matter of importance to him since he thought this was permissible.[86]

12.62 S015's account is more problematic. As detailed above, he knew hooding to be prohibited and would have been concerned to learn it had occurred (see paragraph 48 above).

12.63 S015 made no mention in his Inquiry statement of learning that prisoners were arriving hooded at the JFIT. However, in his oral evidence, S015 said that he had heard about prisoners arriving at the JFIT hooded when they were being delivered by capturing units. According to S015, this had been communicated to him by S017, as she had herself said in evidence. S015 agreed that this was a matter which caused him concern, and he said he had raised it up his chain of command, through Le Fevre to the COS, in order to find out why the capturing unit had employed hooding. S015 said that he did not receive any response to the effect that this was a worrying issue since there had previously been a specific order prohibiting the use of hoods in theatre. S015 also told the Inquiry that he raised this concern with Barnett.[87]

12.64 S015 was asked why he had not mentioned this issue in his Inquiry statement, given that on his own account it had concerned him at the time. S015's explanation was that he had only remembered the matter after becoming aware of S017's evidence given to the Inquiry.[88] I appreciate that S017's evidence may have jogged S015's memory. Nevertheless, I find it surprising that S015 should have gone so far as to state in his Inquiry witness statement that "*I do not recall being made aware of any concerns about the mistreatment of any detainees or of their being hooded*"[89] if in fact S017 had not only raised the hooding of prisoners with him, but S015 had then passed this up the chain of command and he had remembered that he received no response. I regret that on this aspect I found S015 was not an impressive witness. He was the

[83] Barnett BMI 86/76/25-78/12
[84] S017 BMI 84/73/21-74/11
[85] Le Fevre BMI 85/19/4-14
[86] Le Fevre BMI 85/20/4-24
[87] S015 BMI 84/104/24-109/10
[88] S015 BMI 84/106/25-107/17
[89] S015 BMI06526, paragraph 44

direct superior of S017 during Op Telic 2 and he gave oral evidence immediately after S017. Although, of course, I make no criticism of him for listening to S017's evidence, as he was perfectly entitled to do, but I find that S015 was too inclined to give evidence that was consistent with the evidence he had by that time read and heard from S017. I do not take issue with the suggestion that S017 raised the arrival of hooded prisoners with S015 as her immediate superior. But given S015's failure to mention this in his own Inquiry statement, and his original assertion that he could not remember being made aware of any concerns about hooded prisoners, I can place little weight on his account.

12.65   In the final analysis, S017's evidence on this issue was far less certain than, and partly inconsistent with, her Inquiry statement. Also I can place little weight on the relevant aspects of S015's oral evidence for the reasons I have explained above. Both Barnett and Ellis-Davies reject the assertion that they were informed of hooding, and Ellis-Davies in particular gave cogent reasons why the version of events given by S017 was unlikely to have occurred in the manner stated.

12.66   This is an area of the evidence in respect of which I find it difficult to determine the true facts. On balance I find it unlikely that S017 raised the arrival of hooded prisoners with Ellis-Davies. And I find it very unlikely that she raised this with Barnett. I accept that S017 probably did raise this matter with S015 who knew that hooding was the subject of a ban. If S015 raised that matter higher up the chain of command, I do not accept that he did so with Barnett, or that he treated it as a matter of any significant priority. I make clear that S017 was not in my judgment dishonest in any of the evidence she gave, but at times she tended towards over-confidence about the reliability of her own recollection. To her credit, I accept that S017 did intervene directly on the few occasions when she saw hooding at the TIF. Having already indicated that I accept she raised this with her own superior officer S015, I do not find any grounds to criticise her conduct, although aspects of her recollection I find to have been unreliable. I cannot rule out the possibility that S015 raised the matter higher up the chain of command. Even if he did so, I do not consider that he raised it with the level of concern and priority that it deserved. Had he done so, I consider that senior members of the Divisional Headquarters, including Barnett in particular, would have both remembered it and taken action at the time. I accept that S015 gave his evidence honestly but I find that he could and should have done more in respect of S017's concerns.

Chapter 3: Brigade Level

The Senior Officers at Brigade Headquarters

12.67   In his Inquiry witness statement Brig William Moore described his belief and understanding at the time that hooding was only acceptable for security reasons. He was not aware of the Heath Statement.[90] He was also not aware of a ban on the use of hooding and did not remember seeing FRAGO 152. He said "*I think it was probably only some time after Baha Mousa's death that I became aware that 1 Div had banned hooding*".[91]

12.68   During his oral evidence, Moore said his understanding that hooding was acceptable for security reasons was something which he had deduced for himself rather than the result of any specific training.[92] Moore accepted that even if the purpose of sight deprivation was to preserve security, hooding as a means of achieving it should have been a last resort, and even then it might be inhumane:

> *Q. In making that deduction, then, for yourself, did you give consideration as to whether hooding in itself is or was humane?*
>
> *A. I would have said that -- subject to what I said in my statement about the security aspects, I would have said that hooding would have been inhumane.*
>
> *Q. So what is the position, that if there are operational security aspects which overcome the need for acting humanely, you think hooding could be employed?*
>
> *A. I think hooding is one technique that could be employed, but as a last resort. If you were trying to preserve the security of your base or for other reasons, there are other things you could do as opposed to hooding.*
>
> *Q. The Inquiry has heard about some of them, blacked-out goggles or blindfolds, matters and things of that kind. You would have regarded those as being preferable, would you?*
>
> *A. Yes.*
>
> *Q. But would you agree -- and I don't invite you to simply accept it from me -- that, whether there were operational security reasons or no [sic] for hooding, hooding in extremis even, hooding from the beginning must be inhumane?*
>
> *A. I think that if there are no other ways of preventing -- of ensuring security, then -- for example, if you were taking somebody out of the back of a vehicle in your camp and you were moving him to a place where the person was going to be held, if there were no other ways of doing it, then I would accept that hooding might be -- if hooding was the only way of doing it, that might be acceptable, but as a very last resort. I would prefer to do -- prefer to have used other means.*
>
> *Q. Understanding that and accepting it, if I may say so, General, would you nonetheless accept that, even doing it in those circumstances, hooding would be inhumane?*
>
> *A. Yes, I would.*[93]

---

[90] Moore BMI06947, paragraph 21
[91] Moore BMI06964, paragraph 88
[92] Moore BMI 99/9/7-17
[93] Moore BMI 99/9/18-11/3

12.69 Moore's evidence was that he was not aware of any of the Battlegroups within the Brigade area of operations using hoods, and stated that he did not support or sanction its use during Op Telic 2.[94] Expanding on this in oral evidence, he said that he was not aware that hooding was regarded by at least some soldiers on the ground as a standard operating procedure at the point of capture.[95] This was despite the fact that Moore had described in a statement to the Special Investigation Branch (SIB) that, "*I also spent a lot of time on the ground, to ensure I was abreast of events in the AOR* [area of responsibility]. *In addition to the more routine business, about 4 nights a week I would go out with a patrol from one of the Battlegroups*".[96]

12.70 Moore conceded that he should have been aware of hooding if it was a standard practice and that it should have been brought to his attention through his COS or through company commanders with whom he was in regular contact.[97]

12.71 Moore accepted that he was present during the raid on the Ibn Haitham Hotel during Op Salerno. His patrol group entered the hotel and went straight to the roof. They were able to hear the radio traffic for the operation. They descended from the roof and departed the hotel after the arrests had been made. Moore did not remember seeing any of the Detainees, and believed that they had already been removed by the time he came off the roof.[98]

12.72 Moore was asked whether he might have heard the following exchange over the radio. Firstly, on the 1 QLR main radio net at 09:50 on 14 September 2003, serial 105 from A Company J10A to Battlegroup headquarters, "*REQUEST DIRECTION ON METHOD OF MOVE TO BG MAIN*" and the response, "*PLASTICUFFS BUT NO SANDBAGS*".[99] Moore explained that this was the company headquarters communicating to the Battlegroup headquarters and was a separate radio net from the "*personal role radio*" which he was monitoring.[100]

12.73 Secondly, there was an additional message, which appeared to be from A Company forces on the operation to the A Company headquarters at Camp Stephen on the 1 QLR A Company net at 09:48 (or possibly 09:47, it is not possible better to decipher the manuscript entry), serial 732 from J10, "*our normal methods bar sandbagging*". In relation to this radio traffic, Moore's evidence was that, even on the assumption that this was the radio net he was listening into on the day, he would not have heard it because he had left the operation at about 07:30 and was back in his Brigade headquarters at 08:00.[101]

12.74 I entirely accept Moore's evidence that he did not hear these exchanges of radio traffic. Nor do I have any reason to doubt his evidence that he left the Hotel between 07:30 and 08:00. It is on the face of things a little more surprising that Moore did not see the Op Salerno Detainees at any time, since they would not have been taken from the Hotel by the time Moore said he left. All the evidence suggests they were predominantly held in and around the foyer. However, I found Moore an impressive

[94] Moore BMI06963, paragraph 87
[95] Moore BMI 99/22/23-23/6
[96] Moore MOD000603
[97] Moore BMI 99/23/2-17
[98] Moore BMI06968-9, paragraphs 105-113
[99] MOD016020
[100] Moore BMI 99/69/4-24
[101] Moore BMI 99/70/6-71/5

witness whose evidence I accept. I find that he did not see the Op Salerno Detainees at any stage.

12.75   The COS of 19 Mech Bde until 19 August 2003 was Maj Eaton.[102] He had received no guidance in relation to hooding during his training.[103] He did not remember his LOAC or pre-deployment training descending into detail as to the methods to achieve sight deprivation for the purposes of security, and although he had been trained to use blindfolds created by using strips of hessian material before the first Gulf War, he could not remember ever having received any specific instruction that hooding was prohibited before his deployment on Op Telic 2.[104] However, notwithstanding the fact that he had never received training specifically prohibiting hooding, Eaton understood from his general training that the use of hoods would be inhumane.[105]

12.76   Eaton was not aware during Op Telic 2 of FRAGO 152 or its Brigade equivalent FRAGO 63.[106] The position so far as he was concerned was therefore that if he had learned of the use of hooding, despite being unaware of formal prohibition of it, he might have been expected to intervene and prevent it. In Part X of this Report, I have already addressed Eaton's evidence about FRAGO 63 as to whether it was received by 19 Mech Bde.

12.77   Eaton told the Inquiry that he did not know hooding was occurring. He denied that as the COS of the Brigade he would have become aware of the use of hooding as the tour progressed:

> "Q. …. May I turn, then, to the practice in theatre as to what was going on at battlegroup level? Were you aware at any time that hooding was actually going on in theatre?
>
> A. No.
>
> Q. There has been evidence to the Inquiry that within 1 QLR it was a standard operating procedure, at least so far as suspected insurgents were concerned, and some evidence of its use at least in the early stage of Op Telic 2 by other battlegroups as well, again taking it shortly. If that is what was happening on the ground, should that have come to your attention one way or another?
>
> A. Well, if it was happening on the ground, it didn't come to my attention. I mean, I certainly didn't see it. It was certainly not raised to me as an SOP. I mean, the individual battlegroup SOPs would not be, you know, individually referred to me in any case, but I was not aware of it.
>
> Q. Forgive me, I didn't mean to imply that it was a written SOP so much as on the ground it was standard practice that that was what was going on certainly within 1 QLR.
>
> A. No, I understand that. But still the facts remain that if that was the case, I was not aware of it and, if it was the case, it was not referred to me.
>
> Q. And that is the case, is it, despite what you set out in your statement about all of the frequent contact that you as chief of staff would have had with those at battlegroup level where there were daily meetings where liaison officers would be attending, whether in person or by radio?

---

[102] Eaton BMI06058, paragraph 8
[103] Eaton BMI06059, paragraph 13
[104] Eaton BMI 98/57/24-61/11
[105] Eaton BMI 98/61/25-62/6
[106] Eaton BMI 98/79/12-81/9

> *A. Yes, that's correct.*
>
> *Q. Simply not raised, you say?*
>
> *A. No, it wasn't."*[107]

12.78 Eaton's account on this point was tested by reference to 1 QLR orders that he might have seen. The operational order for "Op Quebec" of 13 August 2003 was sent to 19 Mech Bde G3 Ops.[108] Eaton said he would not have expected to have seen this level of order. His understanding of the phrase *"bagging and tagging"* was that it related to tying and bagging the hands of a prisoner to secure forensic evidence.[109]

12.79 I found Eaton to be a straightforward and honest witness. I accept that, at his level in the Brigade, it was quite plausible that he did not see most, if any, individual Battlegroup level operational orders. There is no other evidence to show that he did in fact become aware of hooding occurring during the period of his deployment on Op Telic 2, and I accept that he did not do so.

12.80 Maj Edward Fenton arrived in theatre on 13 August 2003 in order to take over from Eaton as the 19 Mech Bde COS.[110] In his Inquiry statement, Fenton stated he too was not aware of the use of hooding on detainees during Op Telic 2 before the death of Baha Mousa.[111] In oral evidence he expanded on this, explaining that he understood sight deprivation at the point of capture to be a standard operating procedure, but he thought that hooding would be inappropriate for all but the most exceptional circumstances and then only for security reasons. He accepted that the use of hooding was inhumane even when it was used for an operational security reason for a short period of time.[112] He never saw soldiers hooding prisoners in Iraq,[113] nor was he aware of there being any specific ban on the use of hoods during Op Telic 1.[114] Fenton said that he was surprised that no one brought conditioning or the use of hoods to his attention and that no one else in the chain of command who had witnessed it brought it to the attention of the Brigade or Brigade commander.[115]

12.81 In oral evidence, Fenton also addressed two emails which, although generated after the events of 14 to 16 September 2003, potentially cast a different light on his knowledge of hooding and the purposes for which it was applied. By an email to Maj Mark Robinson (including as copy addressees Maj James Landon, Maj Russell Clifton and Capt Charles Burbridge) at 20:49 on 16 September 2003, Fenton had directed a review of tactical questioning procedures, and wrote:

> *"Are we still, under phase 4 ROE and status, allowed to keep detainees handcuffed and hooded? I understand the need to maintain the 'pressure' in order to get a better product, but I feel we are going to have to work hard to justify this in the future".*[116]

---

[107] Eaton BMI 98/95/14-96/22
[108] MOD030899
[109] Eaton BMI 98/96/23-98/11
[110] Fenton BMI05671, paragraph 11
[111] Fenton BMI05691, paragraph 95
[112] Fenton BMI 101/75/16-78/6
[113] Fenton BMI 101/82/10-16
[114] Fenton BMI 101/85/2-18
[115] Fenton BMI 101/81/15-82/9
[116] MOD016114

12.82   This raised two questions. Firstly, as to whether Fenton really did believe at that time that hooding was reserved to exceptional circumstances rather than being commonplace. Secondly, whether the practice of hooding, exceptional or otherwise, was truly confined to use for security purposes, rather than to condition prisoners before questioning. Fenton's answers suggested that maintaining the shock of capture was discussed at least by this stage, and hooding was perhaps one part of this:

> "Q. Can I ask you to the help the Inquiry, please? Your words, your email: "I understand the need to maintain the 'pressure' in order to get a better product..." What does that mean?
>
> A. It means the piece of -- for the shock of capture, as we referred to it, and at initial stages, ensuring that while the prisoner from capture to then being TQ'd is not allowed to collude with other prisoners, to get his story straight and then to prepare himself in such a way that he is not going to provide information.
>
> Q. It has nothing to do with what appears in the previous sentence, "handcuffing and hooding"?
>
> A. Not directly, no. It is just the overall understanding of the process.
>
> Q. Forgive me, what does "not directly" mean?
>
> A. It is not specifically about handcuff and hooding. "Are we allowed to keep the detainees handcuffed and hooded? I understand the need to maintain 'pressure' ..." So, yes, it is related to that, but it is across the piece on a wider thing. What are the procedures in place? What we have we been told to do that I am not aware of that would maintain this pressure on detainees?
>
> Q. It would not be right to interpret the email as saying, in effect, "Are we allowed to keep detainees handcuffed and hooded? I understand that we may need to in order to keep the pressure on them to get better results from questioning and we are going to have to work hard to justify that stance if we are going to maintain it"? Would that be a fair interpretation of what you are writing?
>
> A. It could be a fair interpretation of what I am writing. I am trying to -- as I say to you, I am trying to understand what has happened and what has been developing in the brigade in my absence that I am now trying to sort out and fix."[117]

In stating in this part of his evidence that there were things that soldiers had been told to do that he was not aware of, I understood Fenton to maintain that he had not himself been aware of the use of hooding, let alone hooding for the purposes of disorientation/pressurising the prisoner, prior to Baha Mousa's death.

12.83   Fenton was also asked about an email of 17 September 2003,[118] from Maj Ben Richards setting out questions arising out of the death of Baha Mousa which had been answered by Burbridge. The answers had then been forwarded to Fenton. It included the following question and response:[119]

---

[117] Fenton BMI 101/148/18-150/4
[118] MOD016120
[119] MOD016121

> 9. How long held and bagged? Did he need to be?
> Subject was held for 36 hours in total, of which he was hooded for 23 hours and 40 minutes.
> There was a requirement for the hood as a part of TQ conditioning and disorientation process.

12.84 On its face, this would seem to have been a clear indication that elements of the Brigade chain of command seemingly thought that hooding for the purposes of conditioning and disorientation was appropriate. Fenton, however, stated that he did not agree with the requirement as it was expressed in this email. Fenton suggested that this was contrary to what he understood had been taught. He accepted however, that if such things as hooding for tactical questioning, conditioning and disorientation were going on, he should have known about them.[120]

12.85 Some aspects of Fenton's contribution to the emails following Baha Mousa's death are not without difficulty, as I address later in Part XIV of this Report. However, Fenton was a good witness who I accept was doing his best to give accurate evidence. On balance, I accept that he was not aware of the use of hoods before Baha Mousa's death.

12.86 Landon, the Brigade DCOS,[121] had a different understanding in relation to the permissibility of hooding. His training, throughout the various stages of his career, did not cover the prohibition of hooding, and indeed he remembered that hoods were used on many exercises throughout his Army career.[122]

12.87 Landon initially told the Inquiry that he thought the purpose of hooding was for security reasons.[123] However, in his Inquiry statement he had indicated a different view, stating that maintaining the shock of capture and disorientation were purposes of the practice of hooding, alongside security, even if they were not the predominant purposes.[124] Landon was very reluctant to agree with this interpretation in the face of what he had plainly expressed in his statement, but ultimately agreed that his understanding immediately before Op Telic 2 would have been that hooding, as well as having an operational security purpose, maintained the shock of capture as an additional "*by-product*". His role during Op Telic had nothing to do with the taking of prisoners. He said that he had not thought about the issue of whether or not hooding could be used to maintain the shock of capture if there was no operational security requirement.[125]

12.88 Landon was not aware that there had been a ban on hooding or a prohibition on the covering of prisoners faces during Op Telic 1. He had not seen FRAGO 152 or FRAGO 63. Landon was asked about the fact that, on its face, FRAGO 63, had been distributed for information to 19 Mech Bde. Landon described the difficulties there had been in receiving communications from theatre in the pre-deployment phase to explain the likely reason why he was not aware of FRAGO 63.[126]

12.89 Landon told the Inquiry that he did not see hooding in Iraq, and said that he was not aware that it was going on. He said that if he had seen the practice being applied on

[120] Fenton BMI 101/150/5-151/11
[121] Landon BMI 80/124/16-18
[122] Landon BMI 80/127/1-128/13
[123] Landon BMI 80/131/2-131/7
[124] Landon BMI04933-5, paragraphs 38 and 40
[125] Landon BMI 80/131/8-137/3
[126] Landon BMI 80/158/23-166/7

the ground he would not have been surprised. Had he been a company commander, he would have weighed up the pragmatic necessity of using hoods versus the effect of using hoods, and might have applied the practice himself.[127]

12.90 Landon also told the Inquiry that from discussions with fellow Brigade staff officers following Baha Mousa's death, his impression was that none of his colleagues were aware of the Heath Statement, and no one said that they were aware of a specific prohibition on hooding from Op Telic 1 either.[128]

19 Mech Bde Operations and Plans Branches

12.91 Burbridge, the SO3 Ops at 19 Mech Bde, had not received any training on hooding, but his general understanding was that it was a practice which was used on warfighting operations.[129] He saw hooding once on Op Telic 2, at Basra Palace: a detainee in the back of a vehicle with a sandbag over his head. It made him feel "*slightly uncomfortable*" but he did not question the practice.[130] He maintained, however, that he was not aware that hooding was being used more extensively[131] and he only became aware of a ban on hooding after the death of Baha Mousa.[132]

12.92 During his oral evidence Burbridge said that he understood that hooding was used for purposes of security.[133] However, it will be recalled that he sent email answers on 17 September 2003 stating that hoods were required as part of the disorientation and conditioning process (see paragraph 83 above). Burbridge's account was that the information contained in his reply would have come from the 1 QLR Ops officer. He said that this was simply information he had been told, not what his opinion or own knowledge was:

> "*Q. But there's this, Major, which is what you have said, it seems, in answer to the question: "There was a requirement for the hood as part of TQ conditioning and disorientation process."*
>
> *A. That's not my opinion.*
>
> *Q. That's the answer that you are providing.*
>
> *A. It's the answer I provided based on the information given to me by the battlegroup.*
>
> *Q. So the battlegroup would have given you the information and the battlegroup would have been the battlegroup responsible for the detainee who had died in this case, is that right, Baha Mousa?*
>
> *A. That's correct.*
>
> *Q. So should the Inquiry understand that what you would have been told was that there was a requirement for the hood as part of tactical questioning, conditioning and disorientation process?*
>
> *A. That's the information I would have passed on.*

---

[127] Landon BMI 80/166/19-168/23
[128] Landon BMI 80/181/19-183/10
[129] Burbridge BMI 79/28/15-30/1
[130] Burbridge BMI 79/34/6-35/21
[131] Burbridge BMI 79/35/19-21
[132] Burbridge BMI 79/63/8-15
[133] Burbridge BMI 79/35/22-36/6

Q. In order to pass on that information, presumably you had to understand what it was that you were passing on.

A. Not necessarily, no.

Q. Did you in this case?

A. I understood what he had told me, yes.

Q. What did you understand was meant by the "requirement for the hood as part of TQ, conditioning and disorientation"?

A. I didn't understand because I don't understand the TQ'ing process.

Q. I understand that you may not understand all the ramifications and implications of the TQ'ing process, but you surely understood what the term "conditioning" meant.

A. No, I don't. I had not been trained in conditioning.

Q. When you were told by battlegroup that he was hooded – presumably this is what you were told – as part of the tactical questioning and conditioning process, did you say "What does that mean?"

A. No, I don't think I did. I simply asked the question, I was provided with the answer, I put the answer on email and sent it.

Q. You didn't ask "What does that mean?"

A. I don't think I would have done, no.

Q. "What does that involve, conditioning?"

A. There was very little time.

Q. If you will forgive me for saying so, it is hardly worth providing the answer if it is meaningless, isn't it?

A. I do not think so. That's not meaningless to other people.

Q. So you understand that other people would understand "conditioning" where you didn't; is that what you are telling us?

A. I know there were other people that did understand "conditioning".

Q. What did you understand was meant by "disorientation"?

A. I understood that to mean the shock of capture.

Q. So what did the shock of capture mean to you?

A. To ensure that a prisoner of war is – or maintains a disorientated perspective.

Q. So when – we are now, in September, of course – you were told, as you tell us you were, that apparently there was a requirement to hood for TQ purposes, part of conditioning and disorientation, what was your reaction to that?

A. My reaction to the answer I gave there was one of abhorrence.

Q. Even though you didn't really understand it?

A. I don't think hooding someone for 36 hours is acceptable.

Q. Well, that's part of it. Hooding for 36 hours, not acceptable. What about the conditioning and the disorientation?

> *A. Well, I don't understand what the conditioning process is, but I accepted that disorientation is part of that."*[134]

12.93 Additionally, Burbridge was questioned about the relevant Battlegroup orders issued before the death of Baha Mousa. He confirmed he would have seen 1 QLRs FRAGOs for Op Quebec, Op Quintessential and Op Lightning but by the time of giving his written evidence to the Inquiry he said that he could no longer remember them. He was asked about the phrase *"bagged and tagged"* which appeared in the Op Quebec FRAGO. Although he was initially reluctant to accept it, he could not really avoid the interpretation that *"bagged"* was likely to mean *"hooded"*. He stated that this would not have concerned him unless it related to hooding other than for security purposes.[135]

12.94 When taken to the FRAGO for Op Quintessential, Burbridge said he did not and would not have questioned the term "conditioning", because *"conditioning was the responsibility of G2 ops, it is something I have not been trained in and therefore I didn't – it is not something I would have overanalysed"*.[136]

12.95 Burbridge was, in my opinion, not a very good witness. He was not convincing in his denial of knowledge of these terms being used in the QLR FRAGOs. I have also considered his role in Part XIV of this Report addressing events immediately after Baha Mousa's death. When speaking of his knowledge of conditioning and hooding I consider that Burbridge's evidence was a little disingenuous. I suspect that despite saying that he was not aware before Baha Mousa's death that hooding was used as part of the conditioning process, he may have had some such knowledge. But I accept he had no knowledge of the use of stress positions as an aid to tactical questioning and I recognise that tactical questioning was not a subject of which he had any real knowledge or experience.

12.96 Capt Oliver King was the SO3 G3 Ops (as deputy and night time cover for Burbridge)[137] and through his training he understood that it was acceptable to impede a prisoner's vision for security purposes. He was aware through general conversations during Op Telic 2 that sandbags were routinely used for this purpose, *"...presumably because they are widely available"*.[138] Capt King said in his oral evidence that he was aware of prisoners being hooded with hessian sandbags before the death of Baha Mousa. It was, Capt King said, generally expected for operational security that prisoners would have their sight covered. The discussions had been with his peers rather than with the chain of command, specifically not Burbridge.[139] Capt King thought that hooding was applied for security reasons, but did not actually see it occur.[140]

12.97 Capt King could not remember whether he had seen FRAGO 152, which was issued before his arrival in theatre. Somewhat surprisingly, he said that if he had seen it he would not have picked out the reference to avoiding covering the face of a prisoner and the impairment of breathing, as being relevant to his work. He explained that Brigade staff were not involved in prisoner handling on a practical or day to day

[134] Burbridge BMI 79/38/8-41/5
[135] Burbridge BMI 79/48/1-51/6; MOD030899
[136] Burbridge BMI 79/51/7-52/15; MOD011741
[137] Capt Oliver King BMI 78/72/24-73/23
[138] Capt Oliver King BMI03572, paragraph 21
[139] Capt Oliver King BMI 78/76/17-80/11
[140] Capt Oliver King BMI03576, paragraph 36

level.[141] He nevertheless accepted during oral evidence that such an instruction would have represented a change in policy as far as he understood the position relating to hooding.[142] He did not remember any order in relation to hooding[143] and in fact his view of hooding may well have been the same when he left theatre as it was when he arrived, namely that it was still permissible for security reasons.[144]

12.98 Capt King was also questioned about Operational FRAGOs mentioning hooding or conditioning. He said he would be looking at the "Concept of Operations" and "Coordinating Instructions" section of such orders, rather than looking in detail at all the steps that were necessary to complete the order.[145] He did not accept that as a staff officer dealing with operations he ought to have questioned what appeared in Battlegroup level operation orders:

> "Q. Bearing in mind what your focus was and what your responsibilities were and all the matters relating to tempo of operations, about which the Inquiry has heard quite a lot of evidence, would you accept that you personally ought to have asked some questions about what "conditioned" meant in this order and other orders that may have referred to it?
>
> A. Trying to put myself back then, no, I don't think so, because my attention had to be drawn elsewhere, and there was more than enough for me to be getting on with at that time.
>
> Q. Can you help us, then, with where that responsibility did lie? Who should have been asking the questions at 19 Mech Brigade about it?
>
> A. Perhaps G2 or the – or legal – the chief of staff maybe.
>
> Q. Is this too simplistic? It may be thought that as the staff officer that was dealing with operations, that soldiers who were actually going out on ops needed to know about how prisoners could be treated, and it may be thought from that – again you must tell us if it's too simplistic – that the operations officer at brigade ought to have been involved in that sort of thing. Is that to misunderstand the position? Can you help us?
>
> A. I think there were many strands of activity that would go into, say, the standard operating procedure of the brigade and me, as the ops officer, would not have had intimate knowledge of all of those. So there were certainly a lot of procedural matters that I wasn't 100 per cent au fait with."[146]

12.99 He also gave interesting evidence in relation to the way in which the phrase "*bag and tag*" in this particular order would be interpreted:

> "61. With regards to the particular references to conditioning, the Op Quebec FRAGO states that "Prisoners should arrive for TQ bagged and tagged unless they are over 45 yrs of age". Since joining the Army I have heard the phrase 'bag and tag' used to refer to hooding and plasti-cuffing detainees, although I cannot remember where I heard this. I have been asked by my solicitor whether I have heard the expression being used to mean anything else. I have not. In particular, I have not heard it used to describe the process of affixing an identifying tag to a prisoner.

---

[141] Capt Oliver King BMI03580, paragraph 53
[142] Capt Oliver King BMI 78/100/2-102/5
[143] Capt Oliver King BMI03580, paragraph 54
[144] Capt Oliver King BMI03582-3, paragraph 65
[145] Capt Oliver King BMI03581, paragraph 59
[146] Capt Oliver King BMI 78/90/4-91/9

> *62. In general I would be surprised that an operational order referred to "bag and tag", because I would assume that restraining somebody and hooding them for security purposes would be implicit in the instruction to detain. I therefore presume the reason for including this is not because bagging and tagging was out of the ordinary, but to ensure that in this instance soldiers knew that detainees over 45 were not to be bagged and tagged. I do not know why there was such an age limit in this case, but I presume it was for medical reasons, maybe because of the heat."[147]*

12.100 Capt King's evidence graphically illustrated the significant variation in knowledge of the ban on hooding even in relation to staff officers working directly alongside one another. Despite working in close physical proximity to Clifton, the Brigade legal adviser, King was not aware of the hooding ban. King did not think it too surprising that Clifton knew of the ban and he himself did not, although he did accept that the operations team would have expected to have been alerted to the prohibition:

> *"Q. Physically whereabouts would he have been in Basra Palace relative to you? Did you share an office? Were you close by?*
>
> *A. The brigade headquarters at the time was in one large room. In relation to me, he was probably maybe 15 feet to my left.*
>
> *Q. Major Clifton is yet to give evidence, but in his written evidence to the Inquiry, he tells us that he was well aware that the use of hoods had been prohibited during Op Telic 1 and he understood them to be banned for use in Iraq. Were you aware of that prohibition?*
>
> *A. No.*
>
> *Q. Do you ever recall discussing these matters with Major Clifton at all?*
>
> *A. No.*
>
> *Q. Given the proximity within which you worked, does it surprise you to know that the legal adviser at brigade knew that there was a prohibition on hooding, but you were simply unaware of that?*
>
> *A. There were many strands of activities and that was just one of many. It doesn't surprise me too much that I didn't know everything that he knew.*
>
> *Q. But on this particular matter of hooding, would you have expected to be alerted one way or another if there had been a previous prohibition on hooding that that was in fact the case?*
>
> *A. If stated in policy terms then, yes, we should have known."[148]*

12.101 Maj Rupert Steptoe, the SO2 G5 plans 19 Mech Bde, was deployed on Op Telic 2 up to 21 August 2003.[149] His area of responsibility was principally G5, the longer term planning section, although he did have some input in G3 matters, dealing with day to day issues.[150]

12.102 Steptoe had not had any specific training on the use of hooding, but had seen it used on exercises. He was not given any instruction as to the rights or wrongs of the use of hoods on prisoners, and would have thought that hooding was appropriate if he had seen it occurring for security purposes in Iraq.[151]

---

[147] Capt Oliver King BMI03581-2, paragraphs 61-62
[148] Capt Oliver King BMI 78/81/13-82/15
[149] Steptoe BMI 78/4/1-8
[150] Steptoe BMI 78/18/6-21/6
[151] Steptoe BMI 78/5/3-8/18

12.103 Steptoe was shown two of the Op Telic 2 Battlegroup level FRAGOs, for Op Quebec of 13 August 2003[152] and Op Lightning of 25 August 2003.[153] When asked about those FRAGOs, Steptoe said that if he had read the phrase *"bagging and tagging"* (which appears in the Op Quebec FRAGO) at the time in Iraq, he would have taken it to mean a sandbag over the head of an arrested prisoner and plasticuffs applied to him. However, he did not remember having seen the FRAGO from which this phrase derived.[154] Steptoe was also prepared to concede that even if he had read references to conditioning in these orders (as appeared in the Op Lightning FRAGO) he would not necessarily have been concerned, notwithstanding the fact that he would have understood the meaning of conditioning at that time to have comprised *"physically intimidating a prisoner for interrogation"*.[155]

> *"Q. Let me put the question to you again. Conditioning techniques, as we see from the FRAGO on the screen – at the foot of the middle paragraph – "Prisoners are not to be conditioned [in this situation] unless TQ is authorised ...", and so on, did you understand or did you believe that conditioning could be, in any sense, employed for the purposes of questioning, interrogation or TQ'ing?*
>
> *A. At the time I wasn't in a position or in an environment where it was something I needed to do or even was particularly close to, so it wasn't something that I would have given a great deal of thought to. Had I seen this FRAGO – which I don't believe I did – I don't think it would have raised specific alarm bells to me.*
>
> *Q. So you wouldn't immediately – and this isn't a criticism of you – reading that, have said, "That needs to be looked at"?*
>
> *A. I would agree with you. I would not have gone, "That is illegal, that should be stopped."*[156]

12.104 I accept Steptoe's evidence that he did not see these Battlegroup FRAGOs, as copies of Battlegroup orders would normally have gone to the G3 Operations side rather than to his own post.[157]

12.105 Steptoe was not aware of a ban on hooding while he was in theatre. He admitted that it was surprising that he did not know of the ban and agreed that it might be said that it was vital as a person responsible for disseminating orders which might include orders on prisoner handling that he knew of this. But the fact was that he had not been made aware of it, and he did not remember issuing any FRAGOs in which he dealt with the issue of hooding.[158]

12.106 Steptoe said that he had never seen prisoners being handled in Iraq, and could not therefore speak as to whether prisoners were hooded or not. He did not remember seeing FRAGO 63 and the instruction not to cover detainees' faces as it might impair breathing.[159]

---

[152] MOD030899
[153] MOD043232
[154] Steptoe BMI 78/11/4-13/12
[155] Steptoe BMI 78/10/10-11
[156] Steptoe BMI 78/17/5-24
[157] Steptoe BMI 78/14/5-16
[158] Steptoe BMI 78/31/9-32/11
[159] Steptoe BMI 78/32/12-34/6

12.107 In my opinion, Steptoe was a very good witness, intelligent, clear-headed and sensible. He was another witness in respect of whom, even if he had seen hooding, it would not have prompted a response because he was not aware that the practice was prohibited.

12.108 Capt Miles Mitchell took over from Steptoe as the SO3 G3 Plans/Training in mid August 2003.[160] He did not remember having seen FRAGO 152 or any other order about the hooding of prisoners. He also stated that he did not remember being aware of the Op Telic 1 ban on hooding, FRAGO 152, nor, even after the death of Baha Mousa, there being a prohibition on the use of hooding.[161] Mitchell also confirmed in his oral evidence that he had not been aware of the fact that hooding had been a practice used on operations.[162]

19 Mech Bde Legal

12.109 Clifton was a legal officer for 3 (UK) Division, but deployed to Iraq as the Legal Adviser for its subordinate formation, 19 Mech Bde.[163]

12.110 Clifton's account is that his clear understanding when arriving in Iraq was that hooding was banned. Clifton described being involved with Barnett in the process of drawing up training briefings before deployment of Op Telic 2 troops which specified the ban on hooding, and therefore he concluded that he must have been aware of the ban on hooding before arriving in Iraq. Moreover, he recollected that he had been informed of the ban on hooding in unequivocal terms by Lt Col Nicholas Mercer during his handover.[164]

> Clifton understood from Mercer that the ban on hooding was a blanket ban with no distinction between the use of hooding for security as opposed to shock of capture purposes. Clifton himself had never seen anyone hooded in Iraq, and if he had done, he said, he would have done something about it.[165]

12.111 Clifton was asked about a puzzling feature of the emerging evidence. He was asked how it was that he understood hooding to have been banned and yet he was working closely, at least on tactical questioning issues, with Maj Mark Robinson of the Intelligence branch, who said he did not know of the ban on hooding. Clifton said that he found it incomprehensible that Robinson and Maj Bruce Radbourne were not aware of the ban contained in FRAGO 152/FRAGO 63 and the oral order from Brims.[166]

12.112 Clifton's recollection was inconsistent with the account given by Maj Michael Royce of 1 QLR in relation to the issue of a Brigade sanction for the use by 1 QLR of conditioning techniques. I address this important conflict of evidence in Part XIII of the Report. For present purposes it suffices to record Clifton was fully aware of the prohibition on hooding. He understood it to be entirely ruled out. I accept that, before Baha Mousa's death, Clifton was not aware that hooding was occurring.

---

[160] Mitchell BMI 79/3/2-14
[161] Mitchell BMI 79/15/13-16/23
[162] Mitchell BMI 79/19/1-5
[163] Clifton BMI04559-60, paragraphs 8-11
[164] Clifton BMI 81/14/12-16/2
[165] Clifton BMI 81/16/3-25
[166] Clifton BMI 81/48/22-51/5

19 Mech Bde Intelligence Branch

12.113 Robinson was the 19 Mech Bde SO3 G2,[167] in essence the head of intelligence for the Brigade, reporting to the COS, Eaton (and later Fenton) and the Brigade Commander, Moore.[168] He had been hooded on a survival exercise and had not been told that hooding was prohibited during this exercise, or in any other training that he had undertaken.[169] Robinson's evidence was that before Baha Mousa's death, he was not aware of there being a ban on the use of hoods in place.[170]

12.114 At the outset of his oral evidence, Robinson told the Inquiry that his understanding at the time of deployment was that hooding was permissible for the purposes of security and that he took hooding for security purposes to have a conditioning effect as a *"by-product"*, which he did not think was inhumane.[171]

12.115 Robinson's evidence provided an illustration of the, all too easy, elision of the use of hoods for security purposes with their use as part of a conditioning process. As Robinson explained in his Inquiry witness statement:

> *"In relation to hooding, as already mentioned, at the time I was of the view that hooding was permissible. I knew that it was used for security purposes and I had never heard anyone suggest that it was prohibited. Prisoners would have been hooded for security purposes to prevent them seeing their surroundings and being able to communicate with other prisoners. As for the shock of capture, as I have said I was not trained in tactical questioning or on the shock of capture, but I do not think that I would have considered hooding for the shock of capture as being separate from hooding for security. Arrest, detention and questioning were all part of one process to me and if hooding was required to provide security during this process, then I can see why it may also have a knock on effect of maintaining the shock of capture. Therefore as I said at the Court Martial, if asked, I think that I would have said that hooding prior to interrogation was acceptable. I do not know what I would have said if I was asked about the appropriateness of hooding for shock of capture alone, when there were no security considerations, because to be honest, I never thought about it to that level of detail".[172]*

12.116 During his oral evidence however, Robinson eventually admitted to a more certain understanding of the dual purposes of the practice of hooding in Iraq in 2003. He agreed that in 2003 he would have said that hooding to maintain the shock of capture, absent any security issues, would have been appropriate.[173]

12.117 In contrast to his Inquiry witness statement, Robinson said in his statement to the SIB of 10 May 2005 that one of the methods used to prolong the shock of capture was *"...obscuring surroundings to the individual"*, that is, hooding or blindfolding.[174]

---

[167] Robinson was deployed as a Captain but promoted to Major around two thirds of the way through the tour. Thus his role as described to the Inquiry was SO3 G2; SO3 normally being a post filled by an officer of the rank of Captain (Robinson BMI04305, paragraph 5).

[168] Robinson BMI04312, paragraph 38

[169] Robinson BMI04310, paragraph 26

[170] Robinson BMI 80/35/1-11

[171] Robinson BMI 80/4/8-8/1

[172] Robinson BMI04322, paragraph 63

[173] Robinson BMI 80/27/2-29/22

[174] Robinson MOD000938

Eventually Robinson conceded in oral evidence that this earlier account given in his SIB statement accurately reflected his true understanding.[175]

12.118 Robinson also knew that hooding was being used by units as a method of maintaining the shock of capture. His statement to the SIB in December 2005 specified that *"The Shock of Capture was a Standard Operating Procedure (SOP) adopted within the Brigade area by Battle Groups"*.[176] He did not raise this issue with anyone else, apparently because he had assumed that there was nothing wrong with the practice. Robinson said that although he did not give any instruction as to what was or was not appropriate to be employed by Battlegroups in maintaining the shock of capture, *"Hooding would have been seen as perfectly proper and acceptable, yes"*.[177]

12.119 Robinson was reluctant to concede during his oral evidence that he knew that the methods for maintaining the shock of capture, which on his account would have included hooding, was an established practice being carried out by Battlegroups during Op Telic 2. He only admitted to having assumed that this might be the case.

12.120 Conversely, Robinson was keen to reiterate that the use of hooding was for security purposes only and that the effect of disorientation would be a mere by-product. I do not consider either of those positions accurately reflects Robinson's knowledge and understanding at the time. As I have indicated, Robinson's previous evidence given to the SIB undermined both the account that he had no actual knowledge that Battlegroups were routinely maintaining the shock of capture up to the point of tactical questioning, and the account that hooding was only used if required by security considerations. Yet Robinson was very reluctant to accept the plain meaning of evidence that he had given at earlier stages.

12.121 Robinson was asked about the email written by Fenton on 16 September 2003, which had stated *"Are we still, under phase 4 ROE and status, allowed to keep detainees handcuffed and hooded? I understand the need to maintain the 'pressure' in order to get a better product, but I feel we are going to have to work hard to justify this in future"*.[178] Robinson accepted that he would have agreed with the view that there was a necessity to maintain pressure on a prisoner in order to get a good intelligence product.[179]

12.122 I find that Robinson knew of the practice of hooding on Op Telic 2, and that he knew that it was applied in part in order to maintain the shock of capture. I further find that, although he believed hooding was also for security reasons, he thought maintaining the shock of capture including by hooding was desirable for gaining better intelligence.

12.123 Insofar as Robinson sought to avoid, as I find, the clear meaning and significance of his earlier statements about the purpose of hooding, I found him to be an unimpressive witness. I have considered these aspects of his evidence in further detail in relation to the Brigade sanction in Part XIII of the Report. I conclude in that Part that this evidence was given in an effort to distance himself from the use of hooding as a conditioning technique. However, I have no hesitation in accepting that, like many

---

[175] Robinson BMI 80/30/5-34/24
[176] Robinson MOD000643
[177] Robinson BMI 80/35/17-40/14
[178] MOD016114
[179] Robinson BMI 80/70/10-72/12

others deployed on Op Telic 2, Robinson did not know about the oral order from Brims, had not seen FRAGO 152 or FRAGO 63, and more generally was simply unaware that hooding had been banned.

12.124 The Inquiry also obtained evidence from the following members of the Intelligence branch at 19 Mech Bde: Radbourne, Acting Sgt Andrew French, and WO2 Roderick Paterson. As is the case at Divisional level, those in the Intelligence branch at Brigade were more likely to have encountered the use of hoods due to their involvement in, or proximity to, the tactical questioning process and otherwise dealing with detainees and internees.

12.125 Radbourne was a 19 Mech Bde staff officer who moved between different roles during his deployment on Op Telic 2. When based at 19 Mech Bde HQ he worked for G2 Intelligence and also G3 Operations and G5 Plans.[180] However, he also operated peripatetically within the Brigade area of operation as a tactical questioner for various Battlegroups.[181]

12.126 Radbourne had attended the PH&TQ course in 1995, which had taught him that sight deprivation was appropriate and had demonstrated achieving this with the use of a sandbag. He was told that this was for the purposes of security. He had no subsequent training on the issue, and therefore on deployment in 2003 hooding with a sandbag was something that he considered legitimate. He also understood at that time that hooding could be used to maintain the shock of capture, albeit he stated that this was as a secondary spin-off effect to the security purpose and not the primary purpose for using hoods. This was discussed on the PH&TQ course in 1995, and he subsequently had had no training to gainsay it.[182]

12.127 Furthermore, Radbourne saw hoods applied to prisoners in theatre, and himself used hoods on prisoners before and after tactical questioning sessions. Notwithstanding the climate during Op Telic 2, it appeared to be the case that Radbourne thought it was standard practice to use more than one sandbag as a hood. He had told the Court Martial that this was the case, even though he initially denied it in his evidence to the Inquiry.[183]

12.128 Radbourne was questioned on the statement he had made in 2006 to the SIB which suggested that he appreciated that hooding could be actively used to maintain the shock of capture and not that it was only an ancillary effect. Radbourne accepted that was the way his previous statement read, but said that was not his understanding then or now:

> "Q. Could we have a look, please, at a statement that you made on 6 January 2006 at MOD000980, where you say, towards the foot of page -- you see the date of that, 6 January 2006 -- the penultimate paragraph, Major: "I have been asked to explain my understanding of the purpose of 'hooding'." You said this: "My understanding is that hooding a prisoner ensures the 'shock of capture'." Do you see that?
>
> A. I do, sir.

---

[180] Radbourne BMI04139, paragraphs 13-14
[181] Radbourne BMI04140-1, paragraphs 19-23
[182] Radbourne BMI 78/120/3-123/17
[183] Radbourne BMI 78/141/4-144/24

> *Q. You went on to say: "A second element is security in that when a prisoner is hooded he is not able to view any sensitive locations or equipment."*
>
> *A. I can see I have placed that -- I would -- my personal opinion is that hooding is primarily for security and the secondary aspect is shock of capture. I can see how that is written and how it looks and I would actually disagree with what I have written there.*
>
> *Q. But in 2006 that is what you were saying quite clearly, isn't it?*
>
> *A. It is, sir. I had come back from R&R on Op Telic 7 when this statement was taken and it was an interview carried out in transit through Basra Air Station and I have not nailed down the detail. I disagree with what I have actually written there and I realise I am now in a court of law and this is an official document.*
>
> *Q. It wasn't, was it, that then, in 2006 and perhaps before, your appreciation of the situation was that hooding was permissible to maintain shock of capture?*
>
> *A. Well it's a spin-off, sir.*
>
> *Q. It is a spin-off, as you tell us today, but that isn't really what you were saying in this statement, was it?*
>
> *A. It doesn't look like that in the way it reads, sir, no, I agree."*[184]

12.129 Radbourne was not an impressive witness. He displayed great reluctance to accept that what he had previously said to the SIB revealed the true position rather than being a mistake or a question of differing interpretation. In some instances I regret that I had the impression that he was simply not telling the whole truth until confronted with previous statements he had made.

12.130 I do, however, accept that Radbourne was not aware of the ban on the use of hoods in theatre until after Baha Mousa's death. He stated that he would not have used hoods had he known they were banned and I accept that he would not have done so.[185]

12.131 Paterson was a Section Sgt Maj of 21 Military Intelligence (MI) Section, a unit in support of 19 Mech Bde based at 19 Mech Bde HQ at Basra Palace. He was involved in the collation of intelligence reports for the Brigade.[186] SSgt Mark Davies was the 2IC of this section under Paterson.[187]

12.132 Paterson told the Inquiry that he had received no formal training on prisoner handling or the use of hoods.[188] He said in his Inquiry witness statement that at the time of deployment on Op Telic 2 he understood that hooding with sandbags was "...*permitted practice for the purpose of disorientating a prisoner...*", but he further described this as "...*in order to make it more difficult for him to escape once captured*".[189] In oral evidence to the Inquiry, Paterson stated that the only permissible circumstances for using a hood was when a prisoner was being moved through a sensitive area, i.e. a security reason. He clarified the meaning of his witness statement explaining that

[184] Radbourne BMI 78/124/13-125/23
[185] Radbourne BMI 78/143/4-21
[186] Paterson BMI02613, paragraphs 2-3
[187] Paterson BMI 76/96/11-96/15
[188] Paterson BMI 76/86/8-87/19
[189] Paterson BMI02616, paragraph 12

the disorientation of a prisoner was a security precaution in case of escape rather than to benefit questioning.[190]

12.133 Paterson was not informed during his handover that hooding was prohibited,[191] and although he was aware that hooding had been prohibited in Northern Ireland, he understood that the ban there was only related to using hoods for purposes other than security.[192] He told the Inquiry that he was not aware during Op Telic 2 of hoods being used to maintain the shock of capture.[193] Before the death of Baha Mousa he could not remember ever being instructed or otherwise made aware that the use of hoods on prisoners was not permitted.[194]

12.134 Although Paterson stated that he could not definitely remember seeing hoods being used on prisoners during Op Telic 2, he said that he may have seen hoods being used on one occasion by 1 QLR, during the unloading of prisoners from the back of a vehicle at Basra Palace. He was not aware of the use of hoods by other Battlegroups on the ground during Op Telic 2. He told the Inquiry that in any event he spent 90% of his time in his office and had only a limited opportunity to see what was happening on the ground.

12.135 In summary, Paterson's evidence was that he considered hooding to be a legitimate security measure, so that even if he had seen hooded prisoners, he would not have intervened or referred the issue up the chain of command. There is no evidence on which I could conclude that he knew of hooding being employed for other purposes.

12.136 Paterson's evidence did, however, illustrate that opportunities were missed at Brigade level to become aware of practices at Battlegroup level, including hooding for purposes other than security. He said that the order for Op Quintessential FRAGO 2 would have gone to Robinson at 19 Mech Bde, and to his own team. Although Paterson could not remember seeing it, he accepted that it *"probably would have crossed my desk at some stage"*. The order contained the instruction that *"Detainees are not to be conditioned but must be handcuffed"*.[195] Paterson accepted that in this context he would have taken *"conditioned"* to have indicated the use of stress positions or sleep deprivation.[196] Similarly, the order for Op Lightning, which Paterson said he probably, would have seen, provided that prisoners were not to be conditioned unless tactical questioning was authorised.[197] Paterson could not recall reading these parts of the orders and maintained that they did not indicate that the G2 branch at 19 Mech Bde knew that prohibited practices were occurring:

> *"Q. Yes. Are you able to help the Inquiry with why it was that an order was having specifically to state that detainees should not be conditioned?*
>
> *A. No, sir. I can make assumptions, but I can't give you any details as to why that would be on there.*

[190] Paterson BMI 76/87/20-89/23
[191] Paterson BMI 76/101/21-102/2
[192] Paterson BMI 76/90/20-91/14
[193] Paterson BMI 76/88/11-17
[194] Paterson BMI02621, paragraph 33
[195] Paterson BMI 76/110/13-16
[196] Paterson BMI 76/107/24-110/23
[197] Paterson BMI 76/111/15-112/7

> Q. Because your understanding, you tell us, is that stress positions, for example, were simply unlawful and against the Geneva Conventions.
>
> A. That's correct, sir, yes.
>
> Q. Did these sort of orders coming in to, if I can put it, the G2 side at 19 Mech Brigade not raise questions as to what was going on if, in some orders, there was a specific requirement not to condition prisoners?
>
> A. To be honest, sir, I didn't read every single order or every single part of every order. It should have alerted us at the time, I would agree with you on that."[198]
>
> [...]
>
> "Q...So in this order, 25 August 2003, one seems to have the suggestion that conditioning should not take place unless there was substantial evidence found during the searches which were to be part of the operation. Now, it may be a very difficult question, but do you remember seeing this order?
>
> A. No, I don't remember specifically seeing it, but I probably did see it. But again I don't necessarily read ever [sic] single part of a battlegroup scheme and manoeuvre.
>
> Q. Looking at it now again, would you accept that this ought, at least, to have been raising question marks at 19 Mech Brigade?
>
> A. Yes, sir.
>
> Q. It is not the true position, is it, that a process of conditioning was known about within the G2 side of 19 Mech Brigade?
>
> A. No, sir, I wasn't aware of conditioning."[199]

12.137 French deployed on Op Telic 2 with 19 Mech Bde's Military Intelligence section.[200] His understanding, contrary to that of his colleague Paterson, was that both hooding and blindfolding were impermissible. He had not had any specific training on the issue, but would have deduced this from his knowledge of the Geneva Conventions.[201] He was not made aware of FRAGO 152 nor any other specific prohibition on hooding or covering detainees' faces.[202]

12.138 Although French said in evidence that he occasionally went out on patrols with 1 QLR he stated that he had never seen or become aware of detainees being hooded. French also said that he was not informed of the use of hoods by people working in his section, even those involved in the tactical questioning process. He said that he would have raised it with the chain of command as an issue if he had become aware of the use of hooding.[203] Given the area of work and the understanding of his immediate colleagues I find it is somewhat surprising that French did not know of hooding, but I accept having heard his evidence, that he was telling the truth about this.

---

[198] Paterson BMI 76/110/24-111/14
[199] Paterson BMI 76/112/8-25
[200] A/Sgt Andrew French BMI 77/5/19-6/4
[201] A/Sgt Andrew French BMI 77/9/11-10/11
[202] A/Sgt Andrew French BMI 77/19/19-20/6
[203] A/Sgt Andrew French BMI 77/26/5-27/1

12.139 Sgt Michael Porter was part of the Field Security Team based at Basra Palace during Op Telic 2, and worked alongside Sgt Smulski and SSgt Mark Davies as a tactical questioner.[204]

12.140 Porter had attended the five day PH&TQ course at Chicksands in December 2002. He remembered being taught that sight deprivation was permitted in order to ensure security, when transferring prisoners through sensitive areas and was taught that hooding was a permissible method in order to achieve this.[205]

12.141 Porter acted as a tactical questioner for 1 QLR approximately four to six times during Op Telic 2.[206] When tactically questioning at Battlegroup Main (BG Main) (1 QLR) he would see prisoners hooded when they were brought to the tactical questioning room, in order to stop them seeing the layout of the base.[207] This evidence was in accordance with the pattern of the evidence the Inquiry heard in relation to the practice at 1 QLR's BG Main. However, Porter suggested that on the few occasions he went into the Temporary Detention Facility (TDF) he did not see prisoners who were hooded.[208] Moreover, his Inquiry witness statement indicated that he was only aware of hooding for security reasons and he was not aware of hooding for other purposes, or conditioning techniques being used by 19 Mech Bde Battlegroups.[209]

---

[204] Porter BMI04984-5, paragraphs 22 and 25
[205] Porter BMI 77/65/21-67/14
[206] Porter BMI04986, paragraph 31
[207] Porter BMI04986, paragraph 33
[208] Porter BMI04987, paragraph 37
[209] Porter BMI04988, paragraph 44

Chapter 4: Battlegroups other than 1 QLR

12.142 I consider in this Chapter evidence the Inquiry obtained about the practice in Battlegroups other than 1 QLR. I do so because this may cast some light on what was known about hooding by those at Brigade level. This evidence included witnesses who were operating in the tactical questioning field, either witnessing the practice of troops on operations at ground level or utilising hooding themselves. However, as I point out in the following Part of the Report (Part XIII) it was not appropriate nor proportionate for the Inquiry to fully investigate as these issues do not fall directly within my terms of reference.

First Battalion King's Own Scottish Borderers (1 KOSB)

12.143 Cpl Andrew Bowman operated as an interrogator at Um Qasr, for 3 Military Intelligence Battalion, between July and August 2003. Between August and September 2003 he acted as a tactical questioner for 1 KOSB.[210] Bowman was another soldier who attended Chicksands shortly before deployment on operations in Iraq, in January 2003. In his case he did the longer course qualifying as an interrogator and tactical questioner. He was taught that sight deprivation for security purposes was appropriate, and blindfolds were used for this. He told the Inquiry that sandbags were not used for this purpose although he could not remember whether he was expressly told they could not be used.[211]

12.144 Bowman did not remember that there was any mention of the ban on hooding during his time as an interrogator at the JFIT. He suggested that this was due to the fact that the JFIT itself did not directly receive prisoners; those brought to the JFIT were already prisoners at the TIF. During the early part of the tour (July to August) he said that he never saw anyone hooded or blindfolded. Later during his tour (September to December) when he returned to the JFIT, blindfolds were used. He said that although prisoners were not blindfolded, he had no concerns at all about prisoners being able to see.[212]

12.145 When Bowman was operating as part of 1 KOSB and their Field HUMINT team, he performed a secondary role as the tactical questioner since 1 KOSB did not have any of their own.[213] Prisoners at 1 KOSB were deprived of sight through blindfolds, but only on entering the camp. They were then removed. Bowman remembered that this blindfolding was often effected by using personal clothing such as shemaghs and similar. He did not, however, see sandbags being used.[214] Bowman was a straightforward witness whose evidence was, I believe, truthful and accurate and I accept that he did not witness the use of hoods.

12.146 Capt Brian Aitken, the BGIRO of 1 KOSB,[215] was another witness who did not remember seeing any prisoner hooded during Op Telic 2. He said that to his knowledge those persons detained by 1 KOSB were not hooded. On one occasion he saw blacked-

[210] Bowman BMI 79/115/3-22
[211] Bowman BMI 79/118/1-119/3
[212] Bowman BMI 79/130/10-132/24
[213] Bowman BMI 79/133/6-22
[214] Bowman BMI 79/134/6-15
[215] Aitken BMI01619, paragraph 22

out goggles being used by 1 KOSB on two detainees.[216] However, Aitken also said that the sandbagging of prisoners was standard practice during his Army career and that at no time was he told this was not permitted.[217]

12.147 The evidence of Maj George Wilson, 2IC of 1 KOSB, differed from that of Aitken and Bowman. Wilson said that he gave guidance to his men in 1 KOSB instructing them to use blacked-out ski goggles in order to deprive detainees of their sight.[218] However, he also said that:

> *"It is probable that hoods (sandbags) were used in Iraq to transport detainees into the Camp in the early stages. I did not witness hooding at any time, but I understood that it occurred. In my position as second in command, the only time I came into contact with prisoners was once they were in the detention facility, where in my experience, they were not hooded. In the early stages of the tour, I understand that hoods were used to transport detainees into the Camp and I assume that sandbags or pillowcases would have been employed [...] Somebody (I cannot recall who) came up with the idea of using blacked-out ski goggles to deny vision to detainees entering the Camp [...] Sandbags are not, in my view, very effective in depriving a person of vision, because it is possible to see through the bag".*[219]

12.148 Wilson explained that he had been informed that hoods had been used by 1 KOSB at the start of their Op Telic 2 tour, when moving detainees from the camp gate to the detention facility. He recalled a discussion had taken place within 1 KOSB resulting in blacked-out goggles being placed at the camp front gate for this purpose.[220]

12.149 There was therefore some difference between the evidence of Bowman and Aitken on the one hand, and Wilson on the other, in relation to the use of hoods by 1 KOSB, at least during the early part of Op Telic 2. I do not doubt the honesty of any of their recollections. Aitken and Wilson agreed that blacked-out goggles were used at some point by 1 KOSB to deprive detainees of their sight, and neither they nor Bowman personally saw prisoners hooded by 1 KOSB. I bear in mind Wilson's evidence, as the second in command of the Battlegroup, that he had been informed that hooding had been used by 1 KOSB in the early stages of the tour. I find it probable that this is accurate. It seems most likely that at some point during Op Telic 2, quite possibly earlier than Baha Mousa's death, the practice in relation to detainees at the 1 KOSB camp was altered to the use of blacked-out goggles instead of hoods (as recalled by Aitken and Wilson), or other means of blindfolding such as clothing (as remembered by Bowman).

First Battalion The King's Regiment (1 Kings)

12.150 Lt Joshua King deployed on Op Telic 1 and 2 as a member of 2nd Royal Tank Regiment (2RTR). During Op Telic 2 he led a troop that was attached to 1st Battalion, The King's Regiment (1 Kings).[221]

---

[216] Aitken BMI01617, paragraph 18 c); BMI01623, paragraph 37
[217] Aitken BMI01617, paragraph 18 c)
[218] Maj George Wilson BMI01314, paragraph 28
[219] Maj George Wilson BMI01314-5, paragraphs 29-30
[220] Maj George Wilson, BMI01316, paragraph 32
[221] Lt Joshua King BMI 61/127/17-128/16

12.151 Lt King undertook the PH&TQ course at Chicksands in February 2003. He said that he was taught that detainees should be blindfolded or be deprived of their sight by other means from the point of arrest, and to and from the questioning room. But they were not to be deprived of their sight during the questioning and not otherwise during detention unless there was a security threat or risk of coercion from other prisoners. Furthermore, although blindfolds were used on the course for sight deprivation, it was taught that other material, including sandbags could also be used.[222]

12.152 Although Lt King stated that the "*main*" purpose of the deprivation of sight was for security, he accepted during his oral evidence that an ancillary purpose of maintaining the shock of capture was discussed on the course. He could not remember for certain whether the instructors were involved in these discussions, although he had mentioned the involvement of instructors when describing this in his witness statement.[223]

12.153 His direct experience on the ground was as a tactical questioner predominantly for 1 Kings, and once for 40 Regiment Royal Artillery. He said that he carried out tactical questioning on behalf of 1 QLR. When he was performing the role he informed the Battlegroup staff that the detainees were to be deprived of their sight in transit from the TDF to the tactical questioning room, but they did not have to be deprived of their sight in the detention facility. He thought that, at the start of the tour at least, Battlegroups used hoods rather than blindfolds for sight deprivation.[224]

12.154 Lt King remembered an order to stop hooding early on in his tour and that later on, in September 2003, there was a further instruction that prisoners should no longer be deprived of sight at all (although eventually a compromise was later reached by using blacked-out goggles).[225]

12.155 During his oral evidence Lt King was asked specifically about the purposes of sight deprivation during the tactical questioning processes that he operated. He suggested that it could be argued that preserving the shock of capture was a relevant purpose of sight deprivation, even after the warfighting phase of operations:

> "Q. What was the purpose of sight deprivation of prisoners during that tour?
>
> A. To prevent them from seeing the internal layout of our camp.
>
> Q. Was preservation of the shock of capture a secondary purpose?
>
> A. I don't think that that really came into it during that -- those operations as we were no longer in war fighting. The majority of detainees were probably being brought in for more common criminal causes, as opposed to insurgency.
>
> Q. The shock of capture was something which only applied in the war phase, was it?
>
> A. I think that it probably would be more prevalent during the war phase and something that you may have given more consideration to.
>
> Q. Was the shock of capture not a useful way of extracting information even after the war phase had finished?
>
> A. You could argue the case, yes."[226]

---

[222] Lt Joshua King BMI 61/136/10-138/3
[223] Lt Joshua King BMI 61/138/4-139/11
[224] Lt Joshua King BMI 61/145/5-147/18
[225] Lt Joshua King BMI 61/147/19-149/6
[226] Lt Joshua King BMI 61/149/7-25

12.156 In summary, Lt King's evidence was that if sight deprivation was used (whether by hoods or otherwise) for security purposes, but also in part to maintain the shock of capture, he would have had no reason to question the practice.

12.157 The Intelligence Officer for 1 Kings during Op Telic 2 was Capt David Hunt.[227] His understanding, derived from training on exercises at Sandhurst, included the concept of "*bagging and tagging*" prisoners of war. He believed this expression incorporated hooding for the purposes of security and also for maintaining the shock of capture; this was part of accepted Army practice. In oral evidence Capt Hunt said that he could not remember when he learned that hooding was used for these purposes but that it was an idea "*picked up subsequently*" rather than at Sandhurst.[228] He had had no training on how long a prisoner should be hooded, what material should be used as a hood, or the health implications of hooding.[229]

12.158 The practice adopted by 1 Kings during the beginning of Op Telic 2 was consistent with Capt Hunt's training as he remembered it. Prisoners who were to be tactically questioned were hooded using sandbags.[230] He believed this to be standard Army practice and did not receive any training, orders or instructions to the contrary on deployment to Op Telic 2.[231]

12.159 Capt Hunt also understood, from a briefing held at 19 Mech Bde (and from SSgt Mark Davies), that the shock of capture was to be maintained partly through the use of blindfolding, although the method of blindfolding was not specified.[232] He appeared reluctant to confirm this when it came to his oral evidence, although eventually he did do so.[233] Thus, prisoners waiting to be tactically questioned by 1 Kings would be kept blindfolded (whether by hooding or otherwise) for security, and also to maintain the shock of capture.[234]

12.160 Capt Hunt had told the Court Martial that Robinson at 19 Mech Bde knew of the use of hooding for the purposes of maintaining the shock of capture and had spoken to him about this. Capt Hunt no longer remembered this when he gave evidence to the Inquiry.[235]

12.161 It follows from the above that there was a conflict of evidence between Lt King and Capt Hunt about the practices operated by 1 Kings. This was put directly to Lt King:

> "Q. The intelligence officer for 1 King's – I told you his name is David Hunt. You said you can't remember the name – has said that prisoners at 1 King's remained blindfolded from arrival at 1 King's HQ until they were tactically questioned, even inside the detention facility. Do you not remember that happening?

[227] Capt David Hunt BMI 64/2/14-24
[228] Capt David Hunt BMI 64/9/10-2
[229] Capt David Hunt BMI05465, paragraph 4
[230] Capt David Hunt BMI 64/28/2-22
[231] Capt David Hunt BMI05472, paragraph 26
[232] Capt David Hunt BMI05470-1, paragraphs 20-23
[233] Capt David Hunt BMI 64/21/12-23/6
[234] Capt David Hunt BMI 64/25/10-27/10
[235] Capt David Hunt BMI 64/23/15-25/9

> *A. No.*
>
> *Q. He also says that 1 King's used sight deprivation both for security and in order to maintain the shock of capture. Were you not aware of that?*
>
> *A. I would take that as his opinion.*
>
> *Q. Did you never discuss using sight deprivation to maintain the shock of capture with him or anyone else?*
>
> *A. No.*
>
> *Q. You are quite sure about that?*
>
> *A. Yes."* [236]

12.162 In my view both Capt Hunt and Lt King were honest witnesses. The conduct of operations undertaken by 1 Kings during Op Telic 2 was not the subject of the detailed investigation by the Inquiry and it is unnecessary for me to resolve whether the practice was to deprive prisoners of their sight within their detention facility.

12.163 The evidence of both Capt Hunt and Lt King suggested that there was an order during the early part of Op Telic 2, at least within the 1 Kings Battlegroup, concerning the use of hoods. In his Inquiry statement Capt Hunt said that the Commanding Officer of 1 Kings, Lt Col Ciaran Griffin, ordered that sight deprivation through hooding should be changed to blindfolds. Capt Hunt recalled that this was disseminated orally throughout the Battlegroup and he did not know of any written order banning hooding before this. His recollection was that this occurred during the early part of his tour in June or July 2003 when the heat was so intense that it was wrong to hood prisoners. He became aware of a letter from 19 Mech Bde specifying a ban on hooding which was read at a 1 Kings morning meeting, but this was after 1 Kings had decided to end hooding of its own volition. [237]

12.164 In his witness statement to the Inquiry, Griffin confirmed that his men in 1 Kings had used hoods on prisoners. Griffin thought this was appropriate for security purposes, but not for other reasons such as to frighten or punish. He stated that he did not have any reason to think that any of his men used hoods for such purposes during Op Telic 2. [238] Griffin had no memory of discussing or making a decision about ceasing hooding. He stated that he did not dispute Capt Hunt's recollection in this respect, as it was feasible he would have ceased hooding if he had a concern about it. [239]

40 Regiment Royal Artillery (40 Regt RA)

12.165 I also heard evidence from Capt Gareth Barber who was the BGIRO for 40 Regiment Royal Artillery during Op Telic 2. [240] Barber said that he had received no specific training in relation to hooding, but his general understanding on deployment on Op Telic 2 was that it was a standard operating procedure that the restriction of sight of a detainee was to take place, and that a sandbag was *"the most readily available means of doing so"*. [241]

---

[236] Lt Joshua King BMI 61/150/1-16
[237] Capt David Hunt BMI 64/28/18-29/24; Capt David Hunt BMI05472-3, paragraphs 27-29
[238] Griffin BMI06563, paragraphs 20-21
[239] Griffin BMI06567-8, paragraphs 37-41
[240] Barber BMI 58/44/15-45/1
[241] Barber BMI 58/64/18-65/6

12.166 Barber said that he was only aware of his Battlegroup using hoods on one occasion which occurred during an operation called Op Ferret on 10 July 2003, when up to 40 detainees were hooded by 40 Regt RA. He ordered that hoods were applied for the purposes of both security and in order to maintain the shock of capture. On this occasion, as Barber remembered it, the advice to hood for shock of capture purposes had come from a discussion with SSgt Davies.[242] During his oral evidence, SSgt Davies said he remembered an occasion when he had tactically questioned 25 to 30 individuals with 40 Regt RA. All of those prisoners had been hooded with sandbags for the duration of their captivity, a period of approximately five to six hours. However, SSgt Davies told the Inquiry that on the six or seven occasions he had been called upon to tactically question before Op Salerno (of which, this incident with 40 Regt RA was one such occasion), he had not raised the issue of hoods with anyone. This was because he did not feel the need to as the practice was the norm, and an accepted practice known to every soldier.[243] Although SSgt Davies maintained that the primary reason for hooding was operational security, he also accepted that a "*by-product*" of hooding was disorientation, in respect of which an interrogator would take advantage.[244] I accept that if Barber did discuss hooding with SSgt Davies on this occasion, which in precise terms SSgt Davies did not deny, (he stated only that he had not himself raised the issue of hooding with other Battlegroups) it is possible that Barber came away from that discussion understanding that hoods were applied for the purposes of both security and in order to maintain the shock of capture.

12.167 It was suggested to Barber in evidence that the Inquiry had heard evidence tending to suggest that hooding was much more of a commonplace practice within other Battlegroups. He was referred to the evidence of SSgt Davies that Battlegroups used hoods more or less routinely before Baha Mousa's death, and that Radbourne had told the Inquiry that he routinely briefed Battlegroups that they should hood prisoners on arrest. However, Barber was adamant this was not the position for 40 Regt RA.[245]

12.168 Barber said that he was sure about this because he remembered that after that operation Brigade ordered hooding to cease. Initially he stated that this order had been issued early on during Op Telic 2, in late July or early August. However, in oral evidence he accepted that the Brigade direction banning hooding came possibly later on between August and the end of September 2003.[246] This later timing would accord with the 19 Mech Bde ban on hooding as a response to Baha Mousa's death.

12.169 Barber was in my opinion an honest and largely reliable witness. I accept that his account that 40 Regt RA only used hoods on one occasion, albeit on a significant number of prisoners, was his honest recollection. It may be that 40 Regt RA used hoods less than other Battlegroups. Nevertheless, as is the case with the 1 Kings Battlegroup above, I am not able to reach a definitive conclusion in this regard as I deliberately did not seek to investigate in detail the precise extent of hooding by other Battlegroups.

12.170 I refer to the issue of the use by Battlegroups other than 1 QLR of hoods and stress positions again in the following Part of the Report, Part XIII.

[242] Barber BMI 58/65/7-66/10
[243] SSgt Mark Davies BMI 42/24/16-26/13
[244] SSgt Mark Davies BMI 42/108/5-110/10
[245] Barber BMI 58/66/11-67/23
[246] Barber BMI 58/67/1-71/24

Chapter 5: Conclusions

12.171 At Divisional level, I find that the majority of senior officers did not know of any prohibition on hooding. This state of affairs arose in part because of the nature of the handover (addressed in Part X of this Report), but also an absence of knowledge in relation to the effect of the Heath Statement, the 1972 Directive, the oral order from the GOC of 1 (UK) Div and FRAGO 152 during Op Telic 1. This applied to Lamb (the GOC), Le Grys (the DCOS), Murray-Playfair (the Chief J5 Plans), Warren (PM), West (2IC 3 RMP), Le Fevre (SO1 J2 ISTAR), Hartley (SO2 J2), and Haseldine (SO3 J2).

12.172 Barrons (the COS) and Barnett (the Commander Legal), together with Barnett's subordinate, Ellis-Davies (SO3 Operational Law), were exceptions to this general position. They understood hooding to be impermissible whatever its purpose. S015, who did not know of any formal ban, understood from his training that hoods should not be used as they might impede the function of the nose and mouth.

12.173 In respect of knowledge at Divisional level of hooding on operations, a similar picture emerged. The majority of Inquiry witnesses at this level of the chain of command during Op Telic 2 were not aware that hoods were applied to prisoners. Lamb, Le Grys, Murray-Playfair, Warren, West, Barrons, Barnett and Ellis-Davies all fall into this category.

12.174 The exceptions to this general trend were Le Fevre, S015, Haseldine and Hartley. This in turn reflects a pattern of those in the legal branches of the headquarter formations on Op Telic 2 who tended to be aware of the ban on hooding but did not know that it was a practice being applied on operations. Conversely, most of the evidence was that in the Intelligence branches, officers had no knowledge of a ban on hooding, but in many cases they directly witnessed or were aware of hoods being used at ground level.

12.175 There was, I find, a misplaced confidence among those who knew of a ban on hooding, that this knowledge was widely shared among their colleagues. This was starkly inaccurate given the inconsistent views held across different branches, and sometimes even within the same branch. I do not, however, subject any particular individual to criticism in this regard.

12.176 In considering whether officers at Divisional level should have inquired more into the possibility that hoods were being used on operations, I take into account the following aspects of the evidence I heard. Firstly, as for every soldier on Op Telic 2, the operational environment presented many and varied pressing tasks placing very heavy responsibilities on those in the more senior ranks. The process of prisoner handling was quite rightly viewed as one of those important responsibilities; yet it was but one of the many competing demands. Secondly, a feature of the evidence in relation to the functions of 3 (UK) Div was that a physical isolation existed from the operational level tasks being undertaken by Battlegroups. Broadly speaking, officers at Divisional level were more likely to spend the majority of their time in a desk role rather than being in a position to witness ground level operations.

12.177 Moreover, I accept that for the most part it would have been unlikely for officers at Divisional level to have read the individual Battlegroup level orders which might have alerted them to the use of hooding, or the existence of any type of conditioning process.

12.178 Apart the difficult issue of S017's reporting of hooding to S015, which I have found probably occurred but which was not adequately progressed by S015, I find that there is no other evidence that the issue of hooding was raised to Divisional level by 19 Mech Bde before the death of Baha Mousa.

12.179 At Brigade level, the majority of officers from 19 Mech Bde who have given evidence, apart from Clifton (the Legal Adviser), did not know of a prohibition on the use of hooding. Moore (the Brigade Commander), Eaton (COS until mid August 2003), Fenton (COS from mid August 2003 onwards), Landon (DCOS), Burbridge (SO3 G3 Ops) Capt King (SO3 G3 Ops), Steptoe (SO2 Plans mid August 2003), Mitchell (SO3 Plans mid August 2003 onwards), and those in the Intelligence branch, Robinson (SO3 G2), Radbourne (SO3 G2) and Paterson (Section Sgt Maj 21 (MI) Section), were all unaware of the prohibition on hooding.

12.180 I heard evidence that at Brigade level there was extensive knowledge of the actual practice of hooding during Op Telic 2. As noted above, those in the Intelligence branch, or involved in the tactical questioning process, in this instance, Robinson, Radbourne, Paterson and Porter, knew that hoods were being used as a method of sight deprivation. In the G3 branch Capt King was aware that sandbags were used to hood, and Burbridge saw prisoners wearing hoods on one occasion.

12.181 Those Brigade level witnesses who were aware of the use of hooding included a number who appreciated that it was being used in part to maintain the shock of capture.

12.182 I find that Robinson thought that it was appropriate for prisoners to be hooded solely to maintain the shock of capture and was aware during Op Telic 2 of hoods being used by Battlegroups to maintain the shock of capture (see also Part XIII).

12.183 Similarly, I find Radbourne, who himself used hoods on prisoners, understood that hoods were used expressly to maintain the shock of capture and not merely for security reasons.

12.184 Burbridge was not convincing in his denial of knowledge of the terms used in the QLR FRAGOs. I suspect that despite saying that he was not aware before Baha Mousa's death that hooding was used as part of the conditioning process, he may have had some such knowledge. However, I accept he had no knowledge of the use of stress positions as an aid to tactical questioning and I recognise that tactical questioning was not a subject of which he had any real knowledge or experience.

12.185 The Battlegroup FRAGOs contained language which might have put the reader on notice of the practice of hooding or a level of conditioning by the language, I accept that these orders may not necessarily have been seen widely within the Brigade. However, although some in the Operations branch of 19 Mech Bde were either more likely to have seen, or did in fact see, these orders, I find that there was a reluctance to accept a responsibility to be fully alert to the procedures adopted by the Battlegroups under 19 Mech Bde command.

12.186 Burbridge, who accepted he would have read the FRAGOs in question, gave evidence that he would not have analysed or questioned references to conditioning. Steptoe, who I accept did not see these orders, stated that had he seen a reference to conditioning, it would not have been something to which he would have given a great deal of thought or raised alarm bells. Capt King, who stated that it was very likely he saw the orders, though he could not remember doing so,[247] said that he would not have asked what was meant by conditioning, because as a staff officer he would not expect to have had knowledge of all the many strands of Battlegroup activity. Paterson, who accepted that orders referring to hooding would have "*crossed* [his] *desk*", and agreed that the content of these orders ought to have alerted 19 Mech Bde to practices that needed to be questioned, stated that he would not have read every part of a Battlegroup order.

12.187 Moore said that the practice of hooding should have been brought to his attention through, amongst others, the company commanders with whom he was in regular contact. Whilst I accept Moore's evidence on this point, the same applies to elements of his own Brigade staff. It is extremely unfortunate that none of those within Moore's own headquarters who knew hooding was occurring raised it as a concern for consideration, and that individual orders referring to hooding and conditioning did not lead to more questions being asked. For the most part, the reason for the former appears to have been that those who were aware of the use of hooding were not aware that it had been subject to a prohibition in theatre, nor did their training lead them to question the practice. References to hooding and conditioning in individual Battlegroup operation orders copied to Brigade were badly missed opportunities to notice, and put a stop, to inappropriate use of hooding and conditioning. I accept, however, that the ambiguous nature of the term conditioning, which was sometimes used to denote the lawful use of post-capture pressures on prisoners, is some mitigation for this omission.

12.188 Although the Inquiry has not investigated in detail the use of hooding by other Op Telic 2 Battlegroups, the evidence suggests that 1 Kings and probably to a slightly lesser extent 1 KOSB and 40 Regt RA did use hooding in the early part of Op Telic 2. In the case of 1 Kings, it is likely that hooding was stopped before Baha Mousa's death, following an internal Battlegroup decision. The timing in relation to this is, however, uncertain.

---

[247] Capt Oliver King BMI03580, paragraph 56

Part XIII

The Brigade Sanction

Chapter 1: Introduction

13.1 It is clear that by September 2003, the "*conditioning*" of detainees had become a standard operating procedure within 1 Queens Lancashire Regiment (1 QLR). Conditioning consisted of hooding and placing them in stress positions before tactical questioning. This Part of my Report concerns the origin of this practice in 1 QLR. Specifically, it addresses the question of whether conditioning had been sanctioned by 19 Mech Bde Headquarters.

13.2 On 26 June 2003 FRAGO 29 was promulgated by 1 (UK) Div. It established the Battlegroup Internment Review Officer (BGIRO) regime and was cascaded down to Brigades and Battlegroups (see Part IX of the Report). Maj Anthony Royce said he did not become aware of FRAGO 29 until a morning conference at Brigade Headquarters on 7 July 2003. At the time he was the 1 QLR Battlegroup ISTAR (Intelligence, Surveillance, Target Acquisition and Reconnaissance) Officer. Very shortly after he became aware of FRAGO 29 he was asked by Col Jorge Mendonça to take on the BGIRO responsibility.[1]

13.3 On his appointment to that responsibility Royce drafted the 1 QLR Internment Procedure which was signed by Mendonça on 9 July 2003.[2]

13.4 This is not the place in the Report for a discussion of the BGIRO system. I considered its merits, its defects and the reason for it in Part IX of the Report. For the purposes of this Part it is relevant to note that the time limit within which detainees had to be moved on from capturing units was extended from two to fourteen hours. This meant that Battlegroups could be holding detainees for a longer period of time than hitherto and that there was more scope for tactical questioning.

13.5 Royce was aware of the process of hooding detainees. He said he had learnt of this process on the recce by 1 QLR officers and Non-Commissioned Officers (NCOs) to 1 Black Watch (BW) before the handover at the end of June (see Part X of the Report). He said he had seen a prisoner hooded and handcuffed, which I find occurred either in the recce or the handover. Having spoken to an Australian officer serving with 1 BW, he understood hooding and handcuffing on capture to be a standard operating procedure. At that stage he was told that hooding was for security; there was no discussion about hooding being used to maintain the shock of capture or as an aid to tactical questioning.[3] He had believed that hooding was prohibited for detainees. He said he gained this belief from attendance at a lecture given at Catterick, as I find, by Lt Col Charles Barnett, 3 (UK) Div's legal adviser. This lecture was part of 1 QLR's pre-deployment training (PDT).[4] Barnett thought that he had not mentioned that hooding was banned during his lecture,[5] although that was his view. I have discussed this issue in Part VI of the Report.

---

[1] Royce BMI 57/6/2-7/5; Royce BMI03162, paragraph 79
[2] MOD016356
[3] Royce BMI03147, paragraph 50
[4] Royce BMI03135, paragraphs 17-18
[5] Barnett BMI 86/30/2-15

13.6　As I point out in Part VI, it would seem curious if Barnett did mention the ban on hooding, given the number of people present at the lecture, because the Inquiry has been unable to unearth any evidence to support this assertion. Furthermore, there is no reference to a ban on hooding in Barnett's lecture notes. On the other hand, if Royce had not learnt of the ban at the Catterick training his actions on arrival in theatre would seem to be equally odd. Royce said that as a result of knowing of the ban he decided to speak to officers at Brigade Headquarters about hooding.[6] In my view, if Royce did not in some way learn of the ban on hooding at the Catterick training, it would undermine the whole edifice of his version of the events which resulted from knowledge of this ban. The explanation for this conflict of evidence in my opinion is probably that Royce either gleaned it from something Barnett said (not necessarily in the lecture itself) or he learnt of it from another source during the same training. I shall come below to the conversations which he said he had with Maj Mark Robinson, the officer in charge of the G2 cell at 19 Mech Bde, and Maj Russell Clifton, 19 Mech Bde's legal adviser, on this topic and on the topic of conditioning. Neither of these two officers remembered any such conversation as Royce described having with each of them. It follows that much depends on my assessment of Royce, Robinson and Clifton as witnesses and their credibility.

13.7　Royce's evidence in summary was that early in the tour, he queried the use of hooding with Robinson, the Head of G2 at 19 Mech Bde, and was told that it was permissible. About a fortnight later he spoke first to Robinson and secondly to Clifton, 19 Mech Bde's legal adviser. As a result of both these conversations on the morning of the first "*lifts*" (planned arrests), he was satisfied that the chain of command had sanctioned the use of hooding and stress positions in order to condition detainees before the tactical questioners started their work.[7]

13.8　Before coming to the evidence on the crucial issues arising out of the Royce, Robinson and Clifton conversations, I must mention other evidence which bears on the issue of how hooding and stress positions came to be employed on detainees by 1 QLR.

13.9　In addition to Royce, Provost Sgt Paul Smith and Cpl Donald Payne gave their versions of how these techniques came to be used. Sgt Smith said it was usually the tactical questioner who decided how he wanted the prisoners to be treated. He said the tactical questioner and BGIRO would tell the guards how to treat the detainees.[8] In his Inquiry statement Payne said that a tactical questioner in theatre told Royce, Sgt Smith and himself that he wanted the shock of capture to be maintained before tactical questioning, with detainees kept hooded and in stress positions, and not allowed to sleep. Payne said Royce told him the next day that these practices had been cleared by Brigade.[9] Neither Sgt Smith nor Payne was able to name or otherwise identify the tactical questioner or tactical questioners concerned.[10]

13.10　I have commented in Part II of the Report on the credibility of Sgt Smith and Payne. Suffice it at this stage for me to state that I do not regard their evidence on this issue as necessarily sufficient to support the proposition that hooding and stress positions arose at 1 QLR because they were required by individual tactical questioners. On this issue, I also have regard to the evidence of those witnesses who were trained

---

[6] Royce BMI 57/67/11-69/15

[7] Royce BMI 57/76/16-78/4; Royce BMI03171-2, paragraph 105; Royce BMI03173, paragraph 108

[8] Smith BMI 44/83/21-84/13; Smith BMI05004, paragraph 57

[9] Payne BMI 32/35/24-36/8; Payne BMI01729, paragraphs 45-47

[10] Payne BMI 32/35/10-23; Smith BMI 44/174/22-175/12; Smith BMI 44/176/20-177/2

in tactical questioning and whose evidence on their training and knowledge of conditioning is detailed in Parts VI and XII of the Report.

13.11 Returning to Royce's conversation with Robinson and Clifton, Robinson had no recollection of any such conversation as Royce described, although he did not rule out the possibility that it had taken place.[11] He said he would never have given any sanction for stress positions.[12] Clifton also denied having any conversation with Royce as described by Royce on the topic of hooding detainees and putting them in stress positions.[13] He emphatically denied advising that hooding might take place, or that he had sanctioned conditioning.[14]

13.12 The conflict in the evidence between each of these three officers is sharp. The task of determining where the truth lies has not been an easy one. It has been made no easier by some inconsistencies in various witness statements made by each to the SIB and when giving evidence at the Court Martial. In my opinion all three in their evidence to the Inquiry were doing their best to give truthful and accurate evidence. I do not believe that any of them have deliberately sought to mislead the Inquiry. However, when endeavouring to explain inconsistencies in previous statements, in my opinion each has understandably sought to rationalise what he has said on previous occasions. I also take into account that the crucial time during which the relevant conversations took place was six years before they gave evidence to the Inquiry; and the workload of each at that time must have been very substantial. With this introduction I shall summarise in more detail the evidence of each officer and refer to other evidence which bears on the evidence of one or other of them.

---

[11] Robinson BMI 80/24/7-20
[12] Robinson BMI 80/59/3-19
[13] Clifton BMI 81/44/14-45/5
[14] Clifton BMI04577, paragraph 61

Chapter 2: Royce's Evidence

13.13 Royce made three SIB witness statements dated 6 February 2004,[15] 31 March 2005[16] and 6 December 2005.[17] He gave evidence to the Court Martial on 16 November 2006. His Inquiry witness statement is dated 21 July 2009[18] and he gave evidence to the Inquiry on 10 February 2010. In his oral evidence to the Inquiry he said that at the planning stage of the first lift operation it became apparent that a tactical questioner was not going to be attached to the Battlegroup either at the point of capture or immediately on arrival of detainees at Battlegroup Main Headquarters (BG Main).[19]

13.14 This led to his conversation with Robinson[20] about how conditioning was to be maintained in the intervening time between the detainees arriving at BG Main and the arrival of the tactical questioner:

> "... And it was at that discussion that I clarified what was meant or what they required for maintaining the shock of capture and it was agreed that that would be hooding and stress positions."[21]

13.15 Royce said the issue of what to do with detainees before the tactical questioner arrived generated this discussion and led to him being instructed on what to do.[22] He said:

> "... as far as I was concerned, it was direction from the chain of command, from Major Robinson, who was the relevant brigade staff officer, and I cleared it with the brigade legal officer".[23]

13.16 Royce said in his Inquiry witness statement that the discussion was a three-way discussion between him, Robinson and a member of the Field HUMINT Team. He also said that at some point a tactical questioner may have joined the conversation.[24] He said he was "*pretty sure*" that the tactical questioner was involved in the conversation. He added that the member of the Field HUMINT Team may have been trained in tactical questioning.[25]

13.17 Royce agreed that he had not mentioned the presence of the member of the Field HUMINT Team during this conversation either in his statements to the SIB or in evidence at the Court Martial. In oral evidence to the Inquiry he said he thought that the man was the Officer Commanding the Field HUMINT Team. It is suggested on behalf of those Core Participants represented by the Treasury Solicitor, that Royce's failure to mention the presence of the member of the Field HUMINT Team before making his Inquiry statement severely damaged his credibility.[26]

---

[15] Royce MOD000245
[16] Royce MOD000247
[17] Royce MOD000636
[18] Royce BMI03128
[19] Royce BMI 57/42/4-13
[20] Royce BMI 57/42/14-19
[21] Royce BMI 57/42/19-23
[22] Royce BMI 57/43/21-44/18
[23] Royce BMI 57/44/21-24
[24] Royce BMI03173-4, paragraph 109
[25] Royce BMI 57/74/15-19
[26] Royce BMI 57/122/11-125/16

13.18 The Inquiry has made strenuous efforts to trace the Field HUMINT team member referred to by Royce. Royce could not himself recall the officer's name. His impression that the officer was the Officer Commanding the Field HUMINT Team appeared to be based mainly on the fact that the person was in charge of the particular operation under discussion. Royce indicated three names on an Inquiry list of ciphered witnesses who might have been the officer concerned, but this identification, based as it was mainly on the rank of ciphered witnesses, provided no real assistance.[27] The Officer Commanding the Field HUMINT Team was S016. I am entirely confident that he did not have the conversation with Royce. With S016's assistance, four people were identified as members of the team who could have been present at about that time or who might be able to identify the person concerned. The Inquiry has taken statements from two of the four, and contacted a third. All of these three denied that they had spoken to Royce. The Inquiry was unable to trace the fourth. The results of the Inquiry's efforts to trace these people were disclosed in a statement made by leading Counsel to the Inquiry concluding that *"… if the account of Major Royce is accurate, it has not proved possible to trace the Field HUMINT officer to whom he was referring"*.[28]

13.19 Following his conversation with Robinson, Royce went over to speak to Clifton, the Brigade legal adviser. He said he explained that the Intelligence Cell wanted detainees to be kept in hoods and stress positions pending the arrival of the tactical questioner in order to preserve the shock of capture. He asked Clifton if he was content with conditioning, including stress positions and hooding, being imposed pending the arrival of the tactical questioner. He had absolutely no doubt that approval was given by Clifton.[29] Royce said he was aware at the back of his mind that there might be a Geneva Convention issue, which was why he went to ask a lawyer.[30]

13.20 Royce explained that he believed that he did speak to Mendonça about stress positions, hooding and conditioning but not before he wrote an internment procedure document.[31] Mendonça confirmed that he had some conversation with Royce about conditioning[32] and that he knew about stress positions in general terms.[33] Mendonça also said that he remembered Royce at an O Group meeting clarifying that hooding was sanctioned by Brigade.[34]

13.21 In his first SIB statement dated 6 February 2004 Royce made no mention of the Brigade sanction, nor was there a reference to conditioning, hooding or stress positions.[35] It would appear that the scope of the questions put to him at that stage was narrow.

13.22 In his SIB statement of 31 March 2005, Royce referred to the sanction from Brigade in the following terms:

---

[27] Royce BMI 57/122/11-125/16
[28] Counsel to the Inquiry, Gerard Elias QC BMI 114/138/12-140/9
[29] Royce BMI 57/63/21-65/7
[30] Royce BMI 57/66/21-24
[31] Royce BMI 57/94/6-11
[32] Mendonça BMI 59/130/11-15
[33] Mendonça BMI 59/132/17-22
[34] Mendonça BMI 59/138/2-12
[35] Royce MOD000245

> *"I should clarify that once the Battle Group had assumed control from 1 BW, the practice of hooding and restraining by 1 QLR continued. I sought thereafter, for clarification of whether this was accepted practice by 19 Bde HQ. It should be understood that restraining and hooding was not only to maintain the 'Shock of Capture' for Tactical Questioning but also to prevent escape. I received confirmation at Bde level, from Maj Robinson DWR, in which he indicated to me the practice of hooding was necessary to maintain the 'Shock of Capture'. This practice was only necessary upon individuals who were likely to be Tactically Questioned by the G2 Int Staff and not upon individuals arrested for minor criminal offences.*
>
> *This matter was not a subject we discussed at length otherwise I would have recalled the conversation in greater detail. I recall only that the conversation was in passing in which I asked if we were still hooding, and he agreed giving the 'Shock of Capture' as a reason for doing so. It was not necessary for me to ask of him to explain this term as I was previously aware that the term 'Shock of Capture' referred to maintaining disorientation and insecurity in the mind of the detained individual, for the purpose of Tactical Questioning, which could only be conducted by Bde TQ qualified staff."[36]*

Royce, in the same statement, continued by explaining that he provided this information at an O Group chaired by Mendonça. In this way the Commanding Officer and company commanders were all made aware of the practice and that it would become a standard operating procedure.[37]

13.23 In the same statement Royce referred to his conversation with Clifton in the following terms:

> *"In response to a question raised by WO2 Spence, RMP (SIB), whether I consulted Bde Legal regarding the issue of hooding, I can comment only that at the time the Legal was Maj Clifton, ALS, and I most certainly would have raised the issue with him. The reason I would have done so was that I was concerned that we were conducting a necessary and approved practice for both securing of prisoners and where necessary maintaining the 'Shock of Capture'.*
>
> *I do not recall when or where I raised this issue with Maj Clifton but again it would have been a passing comment to him asking if he was aware of the G2 practices and seeking confirmation from him that he had knowledge of it and had approved it. I would most certainly not have instigated the practice without having first sought his approval."[38]*

13.24 Although there is mention in this statement of the "*shock of capture*" and hooding, there is no reference to stress positions unless "*restraining*" is construed as a reference to stress positions. In addition, Royce did not say that the Clifton conversation had taken place on the same day as his conversation with Robinson.

13.25 In his SIB statement of 6 December 2005, Royce specifically referred to stress positions:

---

[36] MOD000248
[37] MOD000248
[38] MOD000249

"I have today been asked by WO2 Spence to detail whether stress positions were ever used on detainees, when I was in the appointment of BGIRO. Firstly, I understand a stress position to be a position designed to be uncomfortable without inflicting any physical harm upon an individual. I can confirm that stress positions were used on detainees at our unit. This would involve their being placed in the standing position facing a wall with their hands outstretched before them parallel to the ground or where they would be seated on the ground with their hands on their heads".[39]

13.26 This statement also included the following paragraph:

"When asked by WO2 Spence whether I discussed the methods of treatment, 'conditioning', the use of stress positions or the term 'shock of capture' with the CO, Lt Col Mendonça, prior to formulating the Battle Group document I can state that I do not recall discussing these terms with the CO. We definitely discussed the process for dealing with the prisoners prior to my drawing up the Battle Group document in Jul 03, but I do not recall the exact content of this conversation."[40]

13.27 Royce was regarded by the prosecution at the Court Martial as a witness upon whom it could not safely rely. However, the Judge Advocate insisted that he was called as a witness. Accordingly he gave evidence and was cross-examined by all parties, including the prosecution. In fact, save for Royce's evidence in respect of the member of the Field HUMINT Team his evidence on this issue was consistent with his evidence to the Inquiry.

13.28 Royce said that he had a conversation with Robinson about hooding for security purposes before he was appointed BGIRO but spoke to him and Clifton about conditioning only after he had been appointed.[41]

---

[39] MOD000638
[40] MOD000639
[41] Royce CM 43/9/4-25

Chapter 3: Robinson's Evidence

13.29 Robinson made six SIB statements of which only the second, dated 10 May 2005[42] and the third, dated 8 December 2005[43] have any relevance to the issues surrounding the Brigade sanction. He gave evidence at the Court Martial on day 44. His Inquiry statement was signed on 14 September 2009.[44] He gave evidence to the Inquiry on 20 April 2010. In addition to what follows I have summarised Robinson's evidence about his knowledge of hooding in Part XII Chapter 3.

13.30 The substance of Robinson's evidence on this issue was that he was unable to remember a conversation of the sort described by Royce and in any event he would not have given Royce an indication as to what conditioning techniques could properly be used. He was not a subject matter expert (SME).[45] However, he confirmed what he said in his Inquiry witness statement, which was that he could not be certain such a discussion did not take place.[46]

13.31 Robinson conceded that in 2003, before Baha Mousa's death, he would have said that hooding for security reasons was permissible and that as a by-product it would assist the shock of capture.[47] He went on to concede that if Royce had asked him in 2003 if hooding for security reasons and hooding for aiding conditioning were permitted, he would have answered yes to both questions.[48]

13.32 Robinson also confirmed the accuracy of a number of passages which appeared in his SIB statement of 10 May 2005. Firstly he confirmed that there was a pool of tactical questioners at Brigade and that there was a great deal of work for them.[49] Secondly, he made an assumption that the procedures of the tactical questioners were laid down in a qualifying course.[50]

13.33 He agreed that if he had been asked if conditioning prisoners for tactical questioning could take place, he would have answered yes, meaning so as to prolong the shock of capture.[51] However, he explained that if he had been asked about stress positions he would have said they were prohibited.[52]

13.34 In evidence at the Court Martial, Robinson agreed that he had no idea what tactical questioners did.[53]

13.35 Finally, in his SIB statement of 10 May 2005 Robinson stated that no specific direction was given to Battlegroups about how detainees were to be treated:

---

[42] Robinson MOD000936
[43] Robinson MOD000642
[44] Robinson BMI04304
[45] Robinson BMI 80/22/11-23/13
[46] Robinson BMI 80/24/13-20
[47] Robinson BMI 80/28/2-4
[48] Robinson BMI 80/29/23-30/4
[49] Robinson BMI 80/30/5-31/6
[50] Robinson BMI 80/31/12-17
[51] Robinson BMI 80/53/20-54/1
[52] Robinson BMI 80/59/16-19
[53] Robinson CM 44/76/14-22

> *"Up until Sep 03, to the best of my knowledge there were no discussions between Div and Bde on the matter of hooding arrested Iraqi Nationals. I do not believe that any instruction emanated from PJHQ or Div on the use of hoods, as distinct from blindfolds."*[54]

13.36 In his SIB statement of 8 December 2005 he described the shock of capture as a standard operating procedure adopted within the Brigade area. Of the standard operating procedure he said:

> *"This is an established method to maintain disorientation of the individual and inhibit clear thought to prevent him concocting a story prior to Tactical Questioning commencing. I can only offer that I understood this was an SOP as I understand this terminology was part of the training taught to Tactical Questioners at Chicksands and taught briefly to soldiers on the OPTAG packages."*[55]

In the statement he also said, when addressing the shock of capture, that restraints were used.[56] The statement went on to confirm that Brigade Intelligence Cell provided training touching on the tactical questioning process.[57]

13.37 It is quite clear from all his statements and his evidence at the Court Martial and to the Inquiry, that Robinson was not aware of any order or instruction from Division which prohibited, or might be taken to prohibit, hooding.[58]

---

[54] Robinson MOD000939
[55] Robinson MOD000643
[56] Robinson MOD000644
[57] Robinson MOD000643
[58] Robinson BMI 80/57/22-25; Robinson BMI04322, paragraph 63; Robinson CM 44/26/8-13; Robinson MOD000939; Robinson MOD000644

Chapter 4: Clifton's Evidence

13.38   Clifton qualified as a barrister and was called to the Bar in 1996. He joined the Army Legal Service in 1998.[59] He was posted to 3 (UK) Div HQ as an operational lawyer in 2002.[60] On 23 June 2003 he was deployed to Iraq as the SO2 legal in 19 Mech Bde.[61]

13.39   He provided five witness statements to the SIB. They were dated 25 April 2005,[62] 1 August 2005,[63] 15 August 2005,[64] 1 November 2006[65] and 16 November 2006.[66] The last statement was made by Clifton on the day he gave evidence at the Court Martial. His Inquiry witness statement was signed on 28 September 2009.[67] He gave evidence to the Inquiry on 21 April 2010. As with Robinson, I have referred to Clifton's knowledge of the permissibility or otherwise of hooding in Part XII above.

13.40   Clifton clearly recollected having a discussion with Lt Col Nicholas Mercer on the handover between 1 (UK) Div and 3 (UK) Div. He remembered being told by Mercer that hooding had been banned. He said Mercer was quite animated on the topic.[68] He spoke to Robinson about conditioning designed to maintain the shock of capture. Robinson explained to him that conditioning was the use of certain techniques to maintain the shock of capture until tactical questioning had taken place, although he did not remember him mentioning specific techniques. His conversation with Robinson reassured him that conditioning would not cause injury as the detainees would be medically examined and trained G2 staff at Brigade would control the procedure.[69]

13.41   As to stress positions, Clifton said that before Baha Mousa died he did not know that this technique was being used and had not considered it.[70] He believed that tactical questioners were used for the purpose of obtaining time critical intelligence. They had been trained at Intelligence Headquarters. He did not question what techniques were used because he believed, as Robinson had told him, that at Chicksands there would have been a legal adviser.[71] On the critical issue of the disputed conversation with Royce, Clifton's evidence was that Royce did not raise with him issues about the treatment of prisoners.[72]

13.42   He categorically denied that he had the conversation which Royce described having with him.[73] He said that because of his knowledge of the ban on hooding he would not have sanctioned the use of hoods.[74] In addition, he would not have told Royce

---

[59] Clifton BMI04562, paragraph 17
[60] Clifton BMI 81/3/25-4/2; Clifton BMI04562, paragraph 19
[61] Clifton BMI04560, paragraph 11
[62] Clifton MOD000243
[63] Clifton MOD000577
[64] Clifton MOD000580
[65] Clifton MOD000969
[66] Clifton MOD000979
[67] Clifton BMI04557
[68] Clifton BMI 81/8/13-16; Clifton BMI04567, paragraph 36
[69] Clifton BMI04569-71, paragraphs 40-44
[70] Clifton BMI 81/10/1-8
[71] Clifton BMI 81/30/14-31/10
[72] Clifton BMI 81/42/18-20
[73] Clifton BMI 81/44/14-45/3
[74] Clifton BMI 81/47/12-48/21

that putting detainees into stress positions was permitted. In any event he would have sought clarification of what was involved in conditioning before making any comment.[75]

13.43 There is some difficulty with Clifton's insistence to the Inquiry that he would not have told Royce that putting detainees into stress positions was permitted. This was not entirely consistent with his final SIB statement dated 16 November 2006. His evidence given at the Court Martial on the same day might be interpreted as going further and indicating some knowledge of the use of stress positions.[76] In the statement of 16 November 2006 Clifton said:

> *"Further to my previous statements, I have today been asked by WO2 Ritchie G, RMP (SIB), if during my tour in Iraq in 2003, if I was approached by Maj Royce, 1 QLR, in person or by any other means, to explain that he (Maj Royce) intended to use 'stress positions' and to clarify if they were acceptable to maintain the shock of capture prior to tactical questioning.*
>
> *In response, I can say that, due to the amount of time that has passed, I do not recall being asked such a question by Maj Royce, but that it is possible he did ask me that question. If he had I believe I would have answered that there were certain situations when the use of stress positions to maintain the shock of capture prior to tactical questioning would be acceptable, but without knowing the details of the situation it would not be possible to advise. I would also have stated that the Bde had experts who were trained in tactical questioning and that it would be a G2 and G3 decision whether the use of stress positions was appropriate, taking into account any operational imperative to gain information and any legal advice received (if requested). The Bde experts were the only people who should have controlled the conditioning or tactical questioning of detainees and were available for use on specific operations where required."*[77]

Clifton signed the statement as well as the usual preface to all witness statements used in criminal proceedings, namely that the contents were true to the best of his knowledge and belief and he made it knowing that it was to be tendered in evidence.

13.44 In evidence at the Court Martial he said:

> *"Q. What was the position about soldiers, battalions, using stress positions? What was the position as far as you in the Legal department were concerned?*
>
> *A. As far as I was concerned, the stress positions are one of the methods by which detainees can be put in a position whereby they are more likely to answer tactical questions, and there were people engaged in theatre who were experts in that area and they were the people who controlled that kind of situation. I – I was there to advise on legal maters but I was not there to dictate policy in relation to when stress positions could be used or could not be used.*
>
> *Q. I will press you to this extent: was the use of stress positions acceptable in certain situations?*
>
> *A. As far as I was aware, if there was an imperative – an operational imperative to gain – relevance in time sensitive information then there were people who were trained in tactical questioning who were able to use the training that they had been given to obtain that information in the ways that they had been trained to do so.*

---

[75] Clifton BMI 81/45/17-46/5
[76] Clifton BMI 81/66/2-13
[77] Clifton MOD000979

> *Q. Do you recall having any conversations in particular with Major Royce about either hooding or stress positions?*
>
> *A. I do not recall having any conversations about either. I would recall a conversation about hooding mainly because although there are different legal answers as to whether or not hooding might be appropriate, the operational answer had been given: higher formation had said it was not to be used so it was really not a question for me to question that. In relation to stress positions it is quite possible I would or could have had a conversation with him about that, but I do not recall it specifically."*[78]

13.45 Clifton's explanation for these inconsistencies was that the witness statement was purely hypothetical; and that the transcript of his evidence at the Court Martial was incorrect, or that he simply adopted the questioner's tense due to his nervousness giving evidence.[79]

13.46 There is abundant evidence to support Clifton's assertion that he knew of the ban on the use of hoods.[80] The Inquiry has also heard evidence from more senior officers as to Clifton's competency and conscientiousness.[81]

13.47 Further, it is submitted on Clifton's behalf that if he had given the advice which Royce said he did, others would have become aware of this and mentioned it both before and after Baha Mousa's death.[82]

---

[78] Clifton CM 43/167/21-169/4
[79] Clifton BMI 81/63/9-21; Clifton BMI 67/18-70/15
[80] Barnett BMI 86/119/8-11; Heron BMI 64/150/11-151/13; Heron BMI06869-70, paragraph 42
[81] Barnett BMI 86/117/13-118/20; Moore BMI 99/78/2-11. Ellis-Davies although junior to Clifton, agreed with a suggestion put to her that Clifton was on the cautious, careful and methodical end of the spectrum: Ellis-Davies BMI 85/180/19-181/2
[82] SUB000263

Chapter 5: Other Evidence from Members of 1 QLR

13.48   There is other evidence which may be regarded as some support for the Brigade sanction.

13.49   Mendonça knew that detainees were hooded in the Temporary Detention Facility (TDF) but did not know for how long they were hooded and being kept awake by being made to stand up or kneel.[83]   He knew conditioning of detainees was being carried out from what Royce had told him and that it was sanctioned by Brigade.[84]

13.50   Maj Paul Davis, the Officer Commanding Company during the first half of Op Telic 2, remembered a particular O Group meeting when Royce raised the question of hooding, stating that the issue of whether hooding was permitted was under discussion.[85]

13.51   Capt Alan Sweeney, the Signals Officer during Op Telic 2, said that as far as he was aware Royce had questioned Brigade about the use of both sandbags as hoods and stress positions, when the Battlegroup first arrived in theatre. He understood it was recognised as approved Brigade policy.[86]

13.52   Capt Mark Moutarde, the Adjutant, understood that hooding of detainees and placing them in stress positions was part of the process of preparing detainees for tactical questioning. He understood this from his attendance at O Group meetings.[87] Further, he understood there was a specific direction from Brigade approving hooding.[88] His belief was that Mendonça and Royce had been told this in response to a specific question by them to Brigade.[89]

13.53   Capt Richard Osborne, the Operations Officer for the first half of the tour, saw detainees in the TDF in hoods and stress positions and assumed that these practices were authorised.[90] He understood that the authorisation for hooding came from Royce and this had in turn come from Brigade to Royce as BGIRO.[91]

13.54   Sgt Ian Topping, the Mortar Platoon Commander in S Company, remembered detainees being hooded when detained and held at Basra Palace, the location of S Company and Brigade Headquarters. His evidence was that at the beginning of the tour they were given training in this procedure by members of the Intelligence Corps at Basra Palace. Subsequently detainees were taken to the TDF at BG Main.[92] His evidence was supported to a limited extent by Pte Mark Andrew, a member of Topping's platoon. Andrew remembered being told by Topping to hood detainees

---

[83] Mendonca BMI 59/127/3-18
[84] Mendonca BMI 59/146/20-154/21
[85] Davis BMI 56/20/16-23/7
[86] Sweeney BMI 73/18/17-23
[87] Moutarde BMI03998, paragraphs 30-32; Moutarde BMI04000, paragraphs 42-43
[88] Moutarde BMI03998, paragraph 31
[89] Moutarde BMI03999, paragraph 33
[90] Osborne BMI 53/104/5-106/19
[91] Osborne BMI 53/108/3-109/25
[92] Topping BMI 47/46/22-47/15; Topping BMI 47/49/21-51/9

and subsequently a Captain from another unit instructed him to put detainees in stress positions.[93]

13.55 Sgt Smith and Payne both explained that tactical questioners gave orders as to how the detainees were to be treated.[94] Payne believed the practice of hooding and stress positions had been cleared by Brigade.[95]

13.56 While not evidence to support the existence of a Brigade sanction, evidence which came from Sgt David Brown, a member of 1 QLR's Intelligence Cell, underlined the extent to which the conditioning of detainees had become an established and open practice at BG Main. Sgt Brown kept a personal diary during the tour. His entry for 15 August 2003 records a large number of detainees being sandbagged, placed in stress positions and made to stay in the no doubt baking hot sun. It reads:

> *"FRI 15TH*
>
> *UP 0630 – ROUTINE. 23 INTERNEES IN THIS MORNING, ALL NEATLY ARRANGED IN STRESS POSITIONS WITH SAND BAGGED HEADS. SORRY LOOKING BUNCH. OUT ALL DAY IN SUN SOME OF THEM, SOME TRIPLE BAGGED. POOR SODS."*[96]

13.57 Sgt Brown took some photographs of these men which show what he described in his diary.[97] Notably, the scene they depict was in the open air at BG Main and therefore visible to anyone passing through that part of the Camp.

13.58 A young officer known to the Inquiry as S047, who was a platoon commander within S Company 1 QLR, witnessed what appears to have been this incident. He described what he saw in very similar terms to Sgt Brown. He said that he was shocked by this, so questioned it with Smith. He said that Sgt Smith told him that such treatment of detainees had been directed by Brigade Headquarters. He said he was subsequently also told by the S Company Commander (Major Edward Hemesley) that this sort of treatment had been directed by Brigade Headquarters.[98] Neither Sgt Smith nor Hemesley[99] corroborated S047's account. I can therefore place very little weight on this hearsay evidence from S047 in deciding whether there was a Brigade sanction.

---

[93] Andrew BMI 47/10/10-21; Andrew BMI 47/26/16-27/12
[94] Payne BMI 32/47/22-48/10; Smith BMI 44/176/5-19
[95] Payne BMI01729, paragraphs 45-47
[96] BMI00466: see also his witness statement at Brown BMI00454, paragraph 40, which addresses this incident.
[97] BMI00470-2
[98] S047 BMI03375, paragraphs 49-50
[99] Hemesley BMI 57/214/22-216/4

Chapter 6: Evidence from other Battlegroups

13.59 In Part XII I have described the evidence of witnesses concerned with other Battlegroups deployed on Op Telic 2 who were aware of hooding and specified their understanding of its purpose. I shall not repeat in this Part the whole of that evidence. I summarise the portions of their evidence which are relevant to my conclusions in this Part of the Report; and add any evidence which deals with stress positions.

First Battalion King's Own Scottish Borderers (1 KOSB)

13.60 LCpl Andrew Bowman acted as a tactical questioner from time to time for First Battalion King's Own Scottish Borderers (1 KOSB). He said he believed that sight deprivation by blindfolding was only permitted for security reasons.[100] He told the Inquiry that sandbags were not used for this purpose although he could not recall whether it was expressly stated that sandbags could not be used.[101]

13.61 Maj George Wilson, the Second in Command (2IC), said in evidence that his guidance to his men was that blacked-out goggles could be used for security purposes. He said it was probable that in the early stages in Iraq hoods were used when prisoners were brought into camp.[102]

13.62 Capt Brian Aitken's evidence was a little different from that of Wilson. Aitken said that although he did not see any prisoners hooded during Op Telic 2, hooding was standard practice throughout his time in the Army.[103]

13.63 I have found that it is probable that in the early stages of 1 KOSB's deployment detainees were brought into camp hooded. But there was no evidence that prisoners were either hooded or placed in stress positions by 1 KOSB before or as an aid to tactical questioning (see Part XII Chapter 4).

First Battalion the King's Regiment (1 Kings)

13.64 Lt Joshua King carried out tactical questioning for First Battalion the King's Regiment (1 Kings) and other Battlegroups, including once for 1 QLR. He agreed that it could be argued that preserving the shock of capture was a relevant purpose of sight deprivation.[104] He thought, before an order to prohibit hooding was issued, hoods could have been used as a method of sight deprivation rather than goggles or any other method.[105]

13.65 Capt David Hunt, the Intelligence Officer of 1 Kings, said that during the early part of the tour in June or July 2003 hooding of prisoners ceased, not as the result of an order banning the practice, but when the heat became so intense it was obvious that it was wrong to hood prisoners. Capt Hunt said that, following a consultation

---

[100] Bowman BMI 79/118/1-19
[101] Bowman BMI 79/130/10-132/24; Bowman BMI 79/134/6-15
[102] Maj George Wilson BMI01314-5, paragraphs 28-30
[103] Aitken BMI01617, paragraph 18(c)
[104] Lt Joshua King BMI 61/149/7-25
[105] Lt Joshua King BMI 61/147/7-21; Lt Joshua King BMI03988-9, paragraph 54

with the Commanding Officer and the Medical Officer, the practice of hooding was stopped.[106]

13.66 Capt Hunt had stated very clearly in his Inquiry statement that SSgt Mark Davies had briefed him that sight deprivation had two purposes: both security and disorientation of detainees in order to maintain the shock of capture until they were tactically questioned.[107] When he gave oral evidence to the Inquiry Capt Hunt was initially reluctant to say that SSgt Davies had briefed him that disorientation was one of the purposes of sight deprivation; but he eventually accepted that his witness statement was accurate.[108]

13.67 At the Court Martial, Capt Hunt was asked about stress positions. In evidence to the Inquiry he agreed that at the Court Martial he had said that he had been told that stress positions were not permitted, but at that time he was unable to say who had informed him they were prohibited. By the time he gave evidence at the Inquiry he remembered it was SSgt Davies who had told him.[109]

---

[106] Capt Hunt BMI 64/28/2-29/12
[107] Capt Hunt BMI05470-4, paragraphs 22 and 31
[108] Capt Hunt BMI 64/19/11-23/6
[109] Capt Hunt BMI 64/23/7-24/8

Chapter 7: Evidence of Tactical Questioners

13.68 In Part VI of the Report I have set out the evidence of witnesses who had attended courses for tactical questioning. For a full summary of that evidence reference should be made to Chapter 4 of Part VI. In this Part of the Report I refer so far as it is relevant to some of that evidence in order to indicate how it impacts upon my conclusions on this Part of the Report.

13.69 SSgt Davies, the tactical questioner, who with Sgt Ray Smulski (see below) questioned the Detainees (see Part II, Chapter 15) said that on the course he attended at Chicksands in January 2003, blacked out goggles[110] were used but there was no specific instruction on how visual impairment could or should be achieved. He said that at no stage was the use of sandbags ruled out as a means of achieving it.[111] He saw hooding as being for security purposes and for preventing communication though it had a by-product of disorientation.[112] He said that it was made clear that stress positions should not be used.[113] I have found in Part II that SSgt Davies considered one of the purposes of hooding was to cause disorientation and thereby to aid the tactical questioning process, but that he may not have been aware of the use of stress positions.

13.70 Lt Joshua King, on the other hand, instructed guards not to blindfold detainees save when transferring them from the TDF to the room where they were questioned. He told the guards that they must provide water and food. He did not brief the guards to do anything that was intended to deprive the detainees of sleep.[114]

13.71 Smulski said he believed hooding was justified for security reasons but had no idea whether it could be used as part of the process of tactical questioning.[115] However, I have found in Part II that he was in fact aware that hooding was being used as part of the conditioning process. He also commented that keeping detainees awake and exercising them was part of maintaining the shock of capture.[116] I found in Part II that, contrary to his denial, he was aware that the Op Salerno Detainees were being kept in stress positions.

13.72 Maj Bruce Radbourne, a Parachute Regiment officer, was attached to Brigade from 13 August 2003 to October 2003. He had attended a Prisoner Handling and Tactical Questioning (PH&TQ) course in 1995 and volunteered to take on tactical questioning during this tour. He said that he understood that stress positions were prohibited.[117] In an SIB statement he had said that his understanding of the purpose of hooding was that it preserved the shock of capture and security issues were secondary.[118] He reversed this evidence when giving evidence to the Inquiry, saying that security was the primary purpose of hooding and that maintaining the shock of capture was a secondary purpose.[119] In any event, it is clear that he thought that maintaining the shock of capture was at least one of the purposes of hooding. He did not

---

[110] He suggested it was blindfolds in his oral evidence: SSgt Mark Davies BMI 42/8/11-15
[111] SSgt Mark Davies BMI04206, paragraph 10(a)
[112] SSgt Mark Davies BMI04208, paragraph 11(a)
[113] SSgt Mark Davies BMI 42/12/9-19
[114] Lt Joshua King BMI03986-8, paragraphs 47-53
[115] Smulski BMI 40/217/1-21
[116] Smulski BMI 40/228/20-230/2
[117] Radbourne BMI 78/125/24-126/17
[118] Radbourne MOD000980
[119] Radbourne BMI 78/124/13-125/23

condone sleep, food and water deprivation or the use of white noise (see also Part XII Chapter 3).[120]

13.73 SSgt Marc Bannister was at the time of Op Telic 2 a member of Badger Squadron, 2 Royal Tank Regiment; the squadron was attached to 1 Kings. He had qualified as a tactical questioner in January 2003, having attended a PH&TQ course. He agreed that the purpose of using conditioning techniques was to keep the detainee unsettled, disorientated and under his control.[121] He explained that there was a need to place prisoners "*in positions*" before tactical questioning but not afterwards.[122] The need was to maintain the shock of capture.[123] By keeping prisoners in "positions", in my opinion, Bannister was referring to stress positions. He said he routinely told guards to put detainees in "*controlling positions*" for ten to fifteen minutes if they were being difficult.[124] He did not believe that he had ever tactically questioned at 1 QLR's BG Main.[125]

13.74 Sgt Michael Porter, who was at the time of Op Telic 2 a sergeant trained in tactical questioning attached to 19 Mech Bde Headquarters, said he was taught on his tactical questioning course that hooding or blindfolds for security were permitted, but he was taught nothing about stress positions. He was taught that deprivation of sleep was not permitted.[126]

13.75 I have already referred to the evidence on this matter given by Lt Joshua King.

13.76 Finally, following Baha Mousa's death, Major Edward Fenton, the 19 Mech Bde, Chief of Staff, prepared a report on the circumstances surrounding the death. It contained the following passage:

> "6. *Procedures*. …
>
> a. *TQ* … *It is on his* [SSgt Davies] *advice that we hood and hand cuff detainees, in order to enhance the shock of capture and improve the level of information extracted from the suspect.*"[127]

I address SSgt Davies' evidence about this in Part II, Chapter 15 and in Part XIV, Chapter 1. In short he disputed that Fenton's document was an accurate record of his views, but I accept this information must have been given to Fenton by someone.

---

[120] Radbourne BMI04149, paragraph 65
[121] Bannister BMI 71/167/16-21
[122] Bannister BMI05425, paragraph 36
[123] Bannister BMI 71/172/9-14
[124] Bannister BMI 71/181/22-182/9
[125] Bannister BMI 71/180/10-16
[126] Porter BMI 77/66/16-69/8
[127] MOD030850

Chapter 8: Discussion and Conclusions

13.77 I have recited the evidence of 1 QLR witnesses and other witnesses where their evidence bears on the issue of the Brigade sanction. Except where I have specifically ruled out making a finding, this evidence in my view provides the context and background against which to consider the conflict of evidence between Royce, Robinson and Clifton. The following factors are, in my opinion, significant.

13.78 Firstly, Gen Robin Brims' instruction banning hooding, which I accept he gave, was not mentioned by any of the above witnesses save Clifton. Further, none save Clifton and Lt Joshua King appeared to believe that hooding was prohibited as an aid to questioning. I find it particularly surprising that those at 19 Mech Bde appeared to be unaware of the ban on hooding. This issue is more fully discussed in Part X of the Report.

13.79 Secondly, it is clear on the totality of the evidence, and I find, that some tactical questioners did advise guards to keep detainees hooded and in isolation in order to condition them before they were questioned. But apart from Bannister's oblique reference to stress positions as control positions and Smulski's awareness of stress positions being used on the Op Salerno Detainees there is little evidence that stress positions were either used or permitted by tactical questioners. This is supported by some witnesses from other Battlegroups.

13.80 Thirdly, there is a body of evidence from 1 QLR personnel which supports the finding that at some stage, probably early in the tour, the question of hooding detainees was raised at one of the Commanding Officer's daily O Groups. This evidence is associated with evidence of a belief that Royce had obtained an approval or sanction for hooding prisoners. Some believed the sanction included stress positions.

13.81 Fourthly, experience shows that witnesses to conversations can often genuinely misunderstand or be at cross-purposes with those to whom they are speaking. Where opinions or advice are sought memories can be tempered or shaped by what one or other party believed he or she had heard or said. This factor, together with the passage of time, in my view goes some way to explain why Royce, Robinson and Clifton have different recollections of the conversations which they had with each other.

13.82 I approach my findings in respect of the Royce, Robinson and Clifton conflict of evidence with the above in mind. I have already stated that in my judgment none of these three witnesses deliberately intended to mislead the Inquiry. So far as Royce is concerned, I found him an articulate, if rather long-winded, witness. For understandable reasons, he was at pains to explain at some length the reasons for his actions. Much is made by those who submit that he did not give truthful or accurate evidence of the differences in his accounts of these conversations in his SIB statements and evidence at the Court Martial from the accounts which he gave to the Inquiry. In this regard emphasis is placed on the failure by Royce to mention the presence of the Field HUMINT officer at the conversation between Royce and Robinson, until his Inquiry statement. Royce attributed these differences to the fact that he did not have access to his diary when he made his SIB statements.[128]

---

[128] Royce BMI 57/88/15-89/16

13.83 In my judgment Royce may have been mistaken about the content of his conversations with Robinson and Clifton, as to which see my conclusions below, but he cannot have been mistaken in his assertion that they had taken place. If they did not occur the whole edifice of his version of obtaining some sanction for hooding and stress positions must have been fabricated. My view of Royce as a witness is that whatever may be said of him, it would be grossly unfair and wrong to find that he had lied about these conversations which he said he had with Robinson and Clifton. In my judgment the only credible explanation for the evidence of other 1 QLR personnel that Brigade had authorised hooding and stress positions, is that Royce, believing such authority had been given to him by Robinson and Clifton, communicated this to Mendonça and Company Commanders. It is inconceivable that he would have done so if he had not spoken to Clifton and Robinson.

13.84 Despite the inconsistencies in some parts of his evidence, I find that Royce did speak to both Robinson and Clifton about the topic of conditioning detainees in the interval between their arrival at BG Main and the availability of a tactical questioner to start the questioning process.

13.85 Robinson, in my opinion, was not an impressive witness. At the outset of his evidence to the Inquiry, in an effort, in my opinion, to distance himself from the concept of hooding as a conditioning technique, he asserted that hooding was for security and conditioning was a by-product of it.[129] This evidence was rather different from the recognition by him in his SIB statement of 8 December 2005 that hooding was a standard operating procedure to assist the shock of capture.[130] As his oral evidence progressed he more readily accepted that in 2003 he would have agreed that hooding for the purpose of assisting tactical questioning was acceptable.[131]

13.86 But to his credit, Robinson candidly accepted that he may have spoken to Royce about conditioning. I find that he did. If, as I find, the purpose of Royce speaking to Robinson was to discover how the shock of capture was to be maintained whilst detainees were awaiting the arrival of tactical questioners, I have no difficulty in finding that Robinson told him that detainees should be hooded. Accepting, as I do, that at the time Robinson believed hooding to be a standard operating procedure for conditioning before questioning, it seems to me logical and probable that he would have said so to Royce. Again, I find that he did.

13.87 I am less confident about making a finding in respect of stress positions. Robinson has always denied that he believed stress positions to be permissible. Nevertheless, having concluded that Robinson did approve hooding I am inclined to accept Royce's evidence that he also approved stress positions. In my judgment, the likely explanation for him doing so is that at that time he believed conditioning as an aid to tactical questioning was permissible and that it included some form of restraint procedure. His conversation with Royce, as with the conversation between Royce and Clifton, was described by Royce as a passing conversation.[132] It may very well not have seemed significant to Robinson at the time.

13.88 I accept and find that Royce also had a conversation with Clifton. I see no reason for him to imagine or concoct evidence that after seeing Robinson he went to speak

___

129 Robinson BMI 80/7/15-8/20
130 Robinson BMI 80/51/2-11; Robinson MOD000643-4
131 Robinson BMI 80/53/20-54/1; Robinson BMI 80/59/8-15
132 Royce BMI 57/56/14-19

to Clifton. His reasons for doing so were, in my opinion, sensible and credible. However, the content of the conversation is more difficult. Clifton was adamant that he knew hooding was banned by a Divisional order. I accept his evidence that he did know of the ban, having learned about it from Mercer. His description of Mercer being animated about the order fits my impression of Mercer's attitude to hooding. In those circumstances I find it very difficult to believe that Clifton told Royce hooding was permissible.

13.89   On the other hand, Clifton's evidence concerning stress positions was much less convincing. His SIB statement of 16 November 2006, while expressing the answer to a hypothetical question, gave the clear indication that had he been asked about stress positions at the time, he would have answered that there were situations when the use of stress positions to maintain the shock of capture prior to tactical questioning would be permissible. Clifton's evidence to the Court Martial went further because he described stress positions as being one of the methods by which detainees can be put in a position where there are more likely to answer questions. His evidence to the Inquiry was much firmer in seeking to suggest that he would not have told Royce that it was acceptable to put detainees into stress positions.

13.90   I accept that Royce did have some conversation with Clifton, probably just after speaking to Robinson, or within a comparatively short time of his conversation with Robinson. I find that the conversation concerned the legality of conditioning. I find that Clifton did not say or give the impression in terms that hooding was permissible. Bearing in mind his contemporaneous understanding of the permissibility of the use of stress positions, I think it likely that if he did give any advice on stress positions it would have been that they were permissible in some circumstances, if approved by a SME.

13.91   Generally, so far as the conversation between Royce and Clifton is concerned, in my view the explanation for the differences in their recollections stems probably from the "*passing conversation*" being of short duration, concentrating more upon the term "conditioning" rather than the specifics of hooding and stress positions.

13.92   In summary, I find that Royce genuinely believed that he had received some assurance from Brigade through Robinson and Clifton that the practices of hooding and stress positions for the purpose of conditioning detainees before they were questioned was lawful and permissible, but I do not rule out that this was the result of a genuine misunderstanding between all three officers.

Was there a Brigade Sanction?

13.93   Having made the above findings I must add that I do not find that what Robinson and Clifton told Royce amounted to a formal sanction by Brigade for the use on detainees of hoods and stress positions. In my view, at best, it was an expression of opinion as to how to treat detainees so as to assist the tactical questioning process. It did not absolve 1 QLR from ensuring detainees in their care should be treated humanely and in accordance with the Geneva Conventions.

13.94   The question of hooding and stress positions was a matter which Royce rightly regarded as important, hence his inquiry of Clifton after speaking to Robinson. Although I understand his assertion that he trusted Robinson and Clifton as brother officers, in my opinion he would have been well-advised to have obtained written confirmation of the views which he regarded as a Brigade sanction.

13.95 If Royce had sought written confirmation of what he had been told by Robinson and Clifton it would have clarified the authorisation and ruled out any misunderstandings. It might also have concentrated the minds of Robinson and Clifton on whether these techniques could properly be permitted. Had either or both Robinson and Clifton investigated what hooding and stress positions entailed it may very well have been that raising these practices up the chain of command would have put a stop to them there and then. It should certainly have put a stop to hooding, which at that time had already been banned.

13.96 These findings do not absolve Royce from all further responsibility for what happened in the TDF between 14 and 16 September 2003. I accept that he did carefully supervise the use of hoods and stress positions during his time as BGIRO. There is no evidence that in his time detainees were treated in the way the Op Salerno Detainees were. But, in my view, the whole process of hooding detainees and placing them in stress positions was unacceptable. Hooding prisoners in the intense heat experienced at that time of year, as Capt Hunt appreciated, ought not to have occurred. Placing detainees in stress positions, as well as hooding them, obviously exacerbated the distress which the detainees would suffer. There was also a risk that keeping detainees in stress positions might well lead young soldiers to use violence to enforce the stress positions. This was something which, in my opinion, Royce should have appreciated and should have then communicated to Mendonça and those, such as Sgt Smith and Payne, who were involved in supervising the welfare of detainees when they were in the TDF. In my view, at the very least Royce should also have alerted his successor, Maj Michael Peebles, to the dangers involved in conditioning detainees in this way.

13.97 As to the wider question of whether Brigade sanctioned such processes in other Battlegroups, this issue is beyond the scope of the Inquiry's terms of reference and has not been fully investigated. I have recorded evidence of the instances of such processes occurring in other Battlegroups. I have also recorded the views on these practices of tactical questioners in the pool attached to or available to Brigade. In this evidence there is more than a hint that hooding, if not other conditioning practices, was more widespread than in just 1 QLR. However, to have investigated thoroughly whether and to what extent any of the five techniques were used by other Battlegroups would have extended the scope of this Inquiry disproportionately.

Part XIV

Events Immediately After Baha Mousa's Death

Chapter 1: Reporting of the events and of conditioning in theatre

14.1 In the aftermath of the death of Baha Mousa it was immediately understood by the Battlegroup chain of command that the incident would have to be investigated by the Special Investigation Branch (SIB). The SIB was contacted at about 22:30hrs on Monday 15 September by the 1 Queen's Lancashire Regiment (1 QLR) Adjutant, Capt Mark Moutarde.[1] The SIB did not attend Battlegroup Main (BG Main) that evening[2], but first arrived at around 10:00hrs on Tuesday 16 September.[3]

14.2 There is no doubt that the SIB was soon informed of the death. However, the adequacy of the reporting by those in 1 QLR, at 19 Mech Bde, and even further up the chain of command in theatre, concerning the circumstances surrounding Baha Mousa's death has been the focus of some of the Inquiry's investigations.

14.3 In this Part of the Report, I have sought to identify at each level of command in turn, the information provided to the higher formations, so as to assess whether these reports were accurate, sufficiently full and timely. It is also important to consider what such reports revealed about officers' knowledge of the circumstances of Baha Mousa's death, the tactical questioning process, and conditioning of Detainees. This was evidenced both in the information provided by the units on the ground and the questions being asked at Brigade and Divisional level.

The Information immediately provided by 1 QLR

14.4 At Battlegroup level there were three instances of the immediate communication to higher formations or other units independent of 1 QLR of the events surrounding the death of Baha Mousa and the detention of the other Op Salerno Detainees.

14.5 Firstly, a serious incident report (or SINCREP) was sent to 19 Mech Brigade:[4]

---

[1] Moutarde BMI 54/122/9-24; Mendonça BMI 59/188/5-7; MOD005670; MOD005672
[2] This is recorded as being due to the security risks of travelling at night (MOD005671)
[3] SSgt Sherrie Cooper BMI00045, paragraphs 24-25
[4] MOD030957

PROVISIONAL SINCREP

FROM: On behalf of 1 QLR
TO: HQ 19 Bde
COPY TO:

SINCREP NO 5 AT 152340EP03

PRECEDENCE: IMMEDIATE

ALL TIMINGS DELTA.

SER	SUBJECT	DETAIL
1.	TYPE OF INCIDENT	Death in CF Custody
2.	DTG OF INCIDENT	152140DSEP03
3.	LOCATION OF INCIDENT	QU7077 8045
4.	DESCRIPTION	Cas was one of the detainees from OP SALERNO. He had been consistently struggling with his cuffs and hood during the day and lashing out at tps. At 2140 he again slipped his hood and cuffs. 2 members of the gd restrained him, re-cuffed and hooded him and checked pulse. 3 mins later they noticed that he might not be breathing. Gave CPR and EAR and called RMO. CPR and EAR continued for 25 mins.
5.	FRIENDLY FORCES INVOLVED	Pte Reader (Gd), Capt Keilloh, Sgt Golding, Cpl Winstanley, LCpl Baxter, Pte Armstrong, Pte Winstanley
6.	UNIT/SERVICE/PERSONNEL INVOLVED	BG HQ 1 QLR
7.	CASUALTIES/EVACUEES/ DETAINEES	1 x IZ detainee , BAHA NASHEM MOHAMMED, DOB 1978
8.	CIVILIANS INVOLVED	As ser 7
9.	MILITARY HARDWARE	Nil
10.	ENEMY FORCES INVOLVED	Nil
11.	EN UNIT/SERVICE/PERSONNEL INVOLVED	Nil
12.	EN CASUALTIES/EVACUEES/ DETAINEES	Nil
13.	CIVILIAN INVOLVEMENT	As above
14.	EN MILITARY HARDWARE	Nil
15.	ALLIED/FOREIGN INVOLVEMENT	Nil
16.	CIVPOL/PROVOST INVOLVEMENT	Nil
17.	MEDIA INVOLVEMENT/INFORMED	Media Ops Info'd
18.	ACTION TO DATE	Detainee declared dead at 2205D
19.	INTENTIONS	SIB informed.

14.6 I have discussed earlier in the Report the difference between information provided in this SINCREP to Brigade and the immediate report made to Lt Col Jorge Mendonça in the memo "*Brief on Sudden Death of Internee*[5]". In particular, missing from the latter report was any description of a graphic struggle having occurred and the names of some of those soldiers who played a part in the struggle with Baha Mousa: Cpl Donald Payne, Pte Aaron Cooper, LCpl Adrian Redfearn (see Part II, Chapter 16).[6]

14.7 Moutarde admitted that he may have had some input into this SINCREP, but said that it was completed by Ops room staff. He accepted, however, that the Ops room would not have had any knowledge of what had occurred other than through those making the sort of inquiries he made. Moutarde had to accept that there were differences between the memo he prepared for Mendonça and the SINCREP, but he said the SINCREP demonstrated that the necessary people at Brigade Headquarters were informed of the incident, and that the SIB had been informed.[7] Moutarde believed

[5] MOD052586
[6] Moutarde BMI 54/133/25-143/22
[7] Moutarde BMI 54/143/23-146/17

that he would have handed the SIB a copy of the memo on 16 September 2003.[8] I have stated my conclusions in relation to the adequacy of the extent of detail provided to Brigade and the SIB by Moutarde in Part II Chapter 17 of this Report. Though the differences in information between the brief sent to Mendonça and the SINCREP are odd and a little suspicious, there is insufficient evidence to support a finding that Moutarde intended to provide misleading information to Brigade.

14.8   Secondly, Maj Michael Peebles was responsible for the documents which were sent to the Theatre Internment Facility (TIF) with the Op Salerno Detainees. Within these documents there was an opportunity to detail the medical condition and treatment that each Detainee had received.[9]

14.9   Peebles admitted that he was aware that at least one Detainee had been in a frail condition and that an older Detainee had been seen by the medical staff before Baha Mousa's death.[10] He was also aware that two Detainees had been seen in the Regimental Aid Post (RAP) after the death.[11] However, no information in relation to the Detainees' medical condition or treatment was provided to the TIF in the pro-forma space for such information. "Physical injury/marks on suspect" and "Medical Complaints" were each marked "*NONE*".[12] Peebles sought to explain this by saying that this was because he had not been told of any specific injury or ailment, and that the question in essence was were the Detainees fit for detention.[13] If that was a conscious decision made by Peebles at the time it is, in my opinion, open to criticism. It was not true to state that there were no injuries or marks on the Detainees or that there were no medical complaints. Injuries and marks to Detainees were identified almost immediately on their arrival at the Joint Forward Interrogation Team (JFIT). I find that Peebles failed in his duty to ensure that the internment records for the Detainees properly reflected the complaints made and injuries suffered by the Detainees during the period in which they were in 1 QLR custody.

14.10   Thirdly, the Inquiry also heard evidence about a memorandum from Maj Christopher Suss-Francksen to the Chief of Staff at Brigade (Maj Edward Fenton). I have addressed this report briefly in Chapter 18 of Part II of the Report. It related to the Rodgers Multiple[14] delivering the Detainees to the TIF and the approach of what was described as the JFIT Commander's towards Lt Craig Rodgers.[15] Suss-Francksen's evidence was that this memo was prepared on the basis of the information given to him by Rodgers.[16]

---

[8] Moutarde BMI 54/173/6-22

[9] Peebles BMI 40/146/1-13

[10] Peebles BMI 40/145/2-25

[11] Peebles BMI 40/125/3-10

[12] MOD016667; MOD016655; MOD016663; MOD016657; MOD016665; MOD016651; MOD016653; MOD015802; MOD016659; MOD016661

[13] Peebles BMI 40/146/1-20

[14] This expression has been used as convenient shorthand for the Inquiry to describe G10A; and findings relating to individuals within the "Rodgers Multiple" do not imply findings relating to Craig Rodgers unless that is explicitly stated.

[15] MOD017121; MOD017122; the officer concerned was in fact S018 the 2IC of the JFIT rather than the JFIT Commander.

[16] Suss-Francksen BMI01588, paragraph 56

1 QLR/G3319

17 Sep 03

HQ 19 Mech Bde (for COS)

Copy to:

CO

ALLEGATIONS BY JFIT COMMANDER

1. The death of an internee whilst in the custody of 1 QLR is now a matter under investigation by SIB. The investigation should, at the very least, include a post mortem of the deceased and a full examination of the facts revealed by the RMP. It is to everyone's benefit that the investigation includes complete disclosure and scrutiny of the events surrounding the death of the internee from the point of arrest to his death and 1 QLR continue to co-operate fully with the enquiry.

2. Anything other than a full discussion of fact could jeopardise the RMP investigation and allow judgment to be passed by those who would further seek to damage the reputation of the Battalion and the Brigade. To that end the attitude and actions of the JFIT Commander towards the Officer who accompanied the internees to the JFIT, and his subsequent allegations, are most unhelpful. A copy of a statement by the Officer, who accompanied the internees to the JFIT, regarding the allegations and manner of the JFIT Commander is attached.

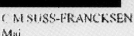

C M SUSS-FRANCKSEN
Maj

952

STATEMENT OF ████████ LT CG RODGERS, 1 PLATOON, ANZIO, 1QLR

I am the above named officer currently serving on Op TELIC II at Camp Stephen in Basra. On 16th September 2003 I was tasked to escort 9 x prisoners from 1QLR Main to Umm Qasr for further questioning at JFIT. Upon arrival at JFIT 1 the prisoners were handed over to Int Corps NCO's under the supervision of Sgt Smith Provost Sergeant 1QLR. Myself and my multiple were waiting in the rest room when Sgt Smith informed me that the prisoners had made allegations of being beaten up at the Hotel Haitham where they were arrested. I made my way with Sgt Smith to the detention camp and was present during the medical examinations of all prisoners. 2 of the prisoners were put on IV Drips due to being 'slightly' dehydrated. I was instructed to wait until the drips had been removed before I returned to Basra. After approximately 7 hours a doctor arrived to inspect the two patients with drips in. He found some injuries on the males including severe bruising and a cracked rib on one male and abdominal pains on another. At this point a Lt Cmdr arrived and introduced himself as the 'man running the JFIT'. He spoke to the doctor about the injuries and asked when they were sustained. I recall clearly the doctor saying 'probably within the last week'. At this point the Lt Cmdr got on his phone and started making phone calls to someone he called 'legal'. He then turned to me in front of a full medical tent and accused 1QLR of keeping the prisoners an illegal length of time, under the incorrect conditions, and then asked if I was the arresting Officer. When I told him I was he took an aggressive stance and tone using his size to try and intimidate me and said, "I have heard about the fight in the hotel what happened?" I responded "There was no fight in the hotel sir" and went on to describe how the men came to be arrested the way they were detained, and who witnessed the condition they were in upon

1058

leaving my custody, including being filmed by associated press walking to the Bedford for transport. He then said "don't lie to me this is very serious you will be dealt with by the highest authority when legal get hold of this". I then responded that I had no problems coming to speak to me and that if he saw the TV footage and got the statements of those present before accusing myself and my soldiers he would realise that there was no fight or heavy handling of prisoners in the hotel. I then went on to tell him that the men were not even plasti-cuffed until they were leaving the building and that they were given water and the two older men were sat up instead of lying face down. He then said that he had seen the baton on the back of my Bedford. To which I responded 'that is because there are 9 prisoners who have already tried to escape twice and only two soldiers guarding them and that the baton would be a much better method of trying to control a prisoner than shooting them. The Lt Cmdr then walked away and made another phone call before returning and telling me my multiple could leave and that the Americans would take over guarding the prisoners. Throughout the duration of the accusations by the commander JFIT the Int Corps NCO's and a police officer from Scotland Yard were present all of whom told me to report the Lt Cmdr for the accusations he had just made.
The above statement is a true and correct recollection of all facts.

CG RODGERS
Lt
ANZIO. 1QLR

14.11   In his oral evidence to the Inquiry, Suss-Franksen accepted that he was in possession of information that indicated that a doctor at the JFIT had said that the Detainees had arrived there with various injuries.[17]   Other than copy this note to the Commanding Officer, Mendonça, Suss-Francksen did not do anything else to ensure that this matter was taken up by the chain of command.[18] Suss-Francksen was also reluctant to accept that the purpose of his memo was to support Rodgers in the face of allegations from the JFIT about the apparent injuries to the Detainees.[19] In Part II, Chapter 17, of this Report, I have already commented that Suss-Francksen substantially understated the seriousness of the conditions in the Temporary Detention Facility (TDF) and of the Detainees when he visited the TDF. It seems to me that on any fair reading of the memo and Rodgers' note, the purpose of Suss-Francksen's memo was to counter any emerging criticism of 1 QLR. However, the memo rightly stresses the importance of a full investigation of the facts by the SIB. On balance, therefore, I find that the memo was an attempt to manage, and limit the damage to, the reputation of 1 QLR, which in hindsight appears ill-judged, rather than having been an attempt to mislead the proper investigations.

14.12   The apparent shortcomings of the documents to which I have referred above might be said to give rise to a suspicion that at the higher level of command in 1 QLR there was a concerted effort to conceal or cover up some of the more unwelcome facts surrounding Baha Mousa's death and injuries to other Detainees. I reject this interpretation of the documents. The SIB had been informed and was making its investigations. As in all such situations, once the SIB was involved all investigation had to be left to its officers. However, it should have been obvious that events in the TDF had gone very wrong with Baha Mousa and other Detainees. I detect in the documents an element of defensiveness in the information passed up from 1 QLR. This is not in itself surprising, but the defensiveness led to a certain playing down of the seriousness of what had occurred. I find that individually Suss-Francksen, Peebles and Moutarde could have done more to make the seriousness of the position clearer.

---

[17] Suss-Francksen BMI 56/203/10-206/20
[18] Suss-Francksen BMI 56/206/13-207/18
[19] Suss-Francksen BMI 56/204/13-205/9

The response at 19 Mech Brigade and 3 (UK) Division level

14.13   At Brigade and Divisional level the gathering of information about the details of the incident started promptly after the receipt of the initial reports from the Battlegroup. From the outset questions were raised in relation to the conduct of the tactical questioning process at Battlegroup level and the length of time this process had taken to occur.

14.14   The email correspondence within 19 Mech Bde and 3 (UK) Div in the days following the death of Baha Mousa, is relevant to the knowledge and awareness of the conditioning processes to which 1 QLR had been subjecting detainees.

14.15   Mendonça gave evidence that he called Brig William Moore of 19 Mech Bde on the evening of 15 September 2003 to inform him of the death.[20] Moore agreed that he had been informed without delay by Mendonça, initially recalling that this had indeed occurred during the night of 15 September 2003.[21] Moore said that the seriousness of the incident was clear to him, and in turn, he had immediately telephoned Maj Gen Graeme Lamb, the General Officer Commanding (GOC).[22] Moore's account changed slightly when he gave oral evidence to the Inquiry: he could no longer remember exactly when he had taken the call from Mendonça.[23] The evidence from Lamb was that he was not informed on the night of the death but was first contacted before a morning meeting held at around 07.00hrs on 16 September 2003.[24]

14.16   It is clear, however, that even on Lamb's recollection, the report of Baha Mousa's death had reached the highest levels of the Brigade and Division within a period of eight to nine hours.

14.17   At 12.00hrs on 16 September 2003 Maj Ben Richards (SO2 J3 Ops, HQ MND SE) sent Fenton (the Chief of Staff of 19 Mech Bde) an email, copied to Capt Charles Burbridge (SO3 Ops at 19 Mech Bde) and Lt Col Graham Le Fevre (SO1 J2 Branch 3 (UK) Div), headed "*Follow up to Incidents 15 Sep*". The email explained that "*GOC has VTC* [a video telephone conference] *with CJO this afternoon. He requires more detail on the incidents last night as follows*": firstly a request in relation to a shooting incident involving the 1 King's Own Scottish Borderers (1 KOSB) ND unit which is not relevant to this Inquiry, and secondly, questions in relation to the "*Death in Custody*". Richards permitted his questions to "*jump ahead*" of the Royal Military Police (RMP) investigation and the post mortem of Baha Mousa. But he said that the GOC (Gen Lamb) needed to be able to answer the questions of the Chief of Joint Operations (Gen Reith).[25]

14.18   At 14.09hrs the same day, in response to the questions posed by Richards, Fenton replied by inserting answers as comments after each question in the body of the original email. (In order to distinguish the question and the answer, Maj Richards' questions are set out in bold below although they do not appear in bold in the original email.) The relevant passages are as follows:

---

[20] Mendonça BMI01135, paragraph 124
[21] Moore BMI06969, paragraph 114; Moore MOD000606
[22] Moore BMI06970, paragraph 115
[23] Moore BMI 99/60/8-15
[24] Lamb BMI 103/114/1-15; Lamb BMI04920, paragraph 33
[25] MOD016115

"Can we confirm that the correct procedures were followed for TQ. As far as we are aware.

Some concern here that prisoner had been in too long – 24 hrs Max? A breakdown of timings please showing how long he had been held. [Fenton explained that the delay in commencing TQ was due to time taken to establish veracity of the identity cards found during Op Salerno, and went on to state] ...TQ then began on late Sun pm. In addition, we have a lack of TQ assets in Bde. As there is only 1 qual TQ rep avail from Bde HQ, the process was taking some time. On the morning of the 15th, BG requested additional sp from Bde, which we then in turn passed to Div J2. The answer from Div was no additional assets were avail, thus detainees were to go to the TIF. At 151030, Bde informed QLR to take detainees to the TIF.

Why the detainees were not transported to the TIF once the additional resources request was denied, we are not yet clear. This will come out of the investigation, but likely it will be due to lack of available resources to conduct the escorts as QLR on BG surge ops."[26]

14.19   It will be seen that at least some of the initial questions from the highest level in 3 (UK) Div focused on the tactical questioning process. The question of the tactical questioning resources available to the Brigade and consequently Battlegroups was readily identified as a cause of the length of detention. This email is also relevant to a point to which I turn below at 14.88 in relation to Fenton's failure to mention in his "Death in Detention" report[27] his own part in the 1 QLR decision not to take Detainees to the TIF on Monday 15 September 2003.

14.20   While Fenton had told Richards that as far as Brigade was aware the correct tactical questioning procedures had been followed (see above), it was apparent to Fenton very soon after the death that the existing policy in relation to tactical questioning needed to be evaluated. Later that same day, at 20.49hrs on the evening of 16 September 2003, Fenton sent an email entitled *"TQ and detention"* to Maj Mark Robinson (SO3 G2 at 19 Mech Bde), copying in Maj James Landon (DCOS, 19 Mech Bde), Maj Russell Clifton (SO2 Legal, 19 Mech Bde) and Burbridge. In it he stated that *"Regardless of where the current investigation goes into the death at 1QLR, we need to review TQ procedures and responsibilities".*[28]

14.21   Fenton went on to ask a series of questions in relation to the tactical questioning process:

"We need to define who is responsible for the welfare of the detainee; is it the CO of the Bn, or the person conducting TQ? Are we currently conducting a hand over between guards and TQ? Does the TQ sign them back over to the guards, both parties ensuring the detainee is fit and well at the end of questioning?

You may reassure me that all this happens, but if not, I'll need convinced that it is something we need not do. This is as much to protect those involved in the system, as the individuals themselves.

What are the laid down timelines for how long the BGs can hold people for?"[29]

---

[26] MOD016115
[27] MOD031229
[28] MOD016114
[29] MOD016114

14.22 He also issued directions to the various addressees, progressing the Brigade's response to the death and ordering that the Ops team be prepared to issue a standard operating procedure:

> "Legal; comment on our obligations
>
> Int: comment on the TQ procedure, the risk we run of losing continuity; identify if we can get the TIF to turn info around faster, thus encouraging BGs to get detainees there sooner. When/ how do we get Bde pers on the TQ cse? Have we told 20 Bde to get people qualified?
>
> Ops: BPT issue an SOP that will be enforced by Bde
>
> DCOS: any thoughts?" [30]

14.23 Notably, Fenton also posed the following question in relation to the handling and treatment of those apprehended:

> "Are we still, under phase 4 ROE and status, allowed to keep detainees handcuffed and hooded? I understand the need to maintain the 'pressure' in order to get a better product, but I feel we are going to have to work hard to justify this in future. Is there an alternative – i.e. if we do not want them to communicate, should they not be kept in separate rooms: if not enough rooms at one locn, why do we not use multiple locns? Do we need to build/adapt a Bde TQ holding facility?
>
> Make no mistake, we may consider ourselves at the 'front line of the war on terror', but I guarantee UK will not see it that way, and we cannot get away with treating people in this manner. So let's tighten up what we do:" [31]

14.24 During his oral evidence, Fenton was asked about this part of the queries that he raised. His evidence was to the effect that these were practices that had been allowed to evolve before his arrival in theatre in August of 2003, of which he had not himself been aware.[32] The fact that Fenton was making this kind of inquiry tends to reveal that such conduct was taking place; that the purpose of hooding and handcuffing was not confined to security reasons; and that at least to some degree this situation was recognised by some at Brigade level. I have addressed this aspect of Fenton's email in Chapter 3 of Part XII of the Report. I accept, however, that Fenton had not himself been aware of the use of hoods or stress positions before Baha Mousa's death.

14.25 Fenton also accepted that his gathering of information after the death had clearly revealed that there was a lack of policy and procedure to provide guidance on how the tactical questioning process worked and where responsibility for the process lay.[33]

14.26 This deficiency in policy and procedure is apparent from the tenor of other responses from the higher ranks in the Brigade. The Deputy Chief of Staff, Landon responded to Fenton's email ten minutes later at 20.49hrs, 16 September 2003. Landon asked:

> "What is the "bible" that sets the rules for the handling of detainees? Is there something set out by JFIT or MPS? Is there a medical examination requirement – fit for detention equivalent that warns when extra care might be required?" [34]

[30] MOD016114
[31] MOD016114
[32] Fenton BMI 101/147/14-150/4
[33] Fenton BMI 101/153/2-154/2
[34] MOD016117

14.27 Burbridge also supplied answers to the initial email questions from Richards.[35] Burbridge replied directly to Richards at 16.19hrs on 16 September 2003 and later forwarded his answers to Fenton at 12.54hrs on 17 September 2003.[36] The most relevant parts of the information supplied by Burbridge in this email were as follows:

> *"Can we confirm that the correct procedures were followed for TQ. Yes, TQ conducted by Bde G2 qualified TQ...*
>
> *Was he injured on arrival; if so, had a medic seen him? Subject was examined by a doctor within 4 hours of his arrival at battlegroup main, with no injuries detected. He was further examined on at least 1 more occasion during his detention*
>
> *How long held and bagged? Did he need to be? Subject was held for 36 hours in total, of which he was hooded for 23 hours and 40 minutes. There was a requirement for the hood as a part of TQ conditioning and disorientation process. Note subject attempted escape repeatedly throughout detention, on average every 10 minutes..."* [37]

14.28 It will be noted that Burbridge was giving quite specific information in relation to the medical examinations and the hooding of the Detainees. It is also relevant that Burbridge stated that there was a "*... requirement for the hood as a part of* [the] *TQ conditioning and disorientation process*".[38]

14.29 Burbridge said that he had obtained this information directly from 1 QLR.[39] Burbridge was also asked about the answer he gave to the question of how long Baha Mousa had been hooded; "*Subject was held for 36 hours in total, of which he was hooded for 23 hours and 40 minutes.*"[40] He said that he would have been told all this by the Battlegroup Operations officer. He simply faithfully recorded it without understanding or questioning what conditioning was or might involve.[41] Burbridge had previously stated in his Inquiry witness statement that he had telephoned Capt Gareth Seeds to ask him the questions, and written down the response. He did not remember the details of that conversation or questioning what Seeds had told him.[42]

14.30 This was Burbridge's account notwithstanding that he said that his reaction to learning that Baha Mousa had been hooded for 23 hours was one of abhorrence. He maintained that before this point in time his understanding of conditioning was that it consisted of no more than the shock of capture, the swift processing and keeping in isolation a detainee, and the modulating of the tone of voice and possible use of shouting during questioning. The latter feature Burbridge learned during in-theatre discussions with Maj Bruce Radbourne, after he, Burbridge, had raised concerns about the tactical questioning process. Burbridge maintained that he had not previously known that conditioning might also comprise hooding or stress positions.[43]

[35] MOD016115
[36] MOD016120
[37] MOD016121
[38] MOD016121
[39] Burbridge BMI 79/38/1-20
[40] MOD016122
[41] Burbridge BMI 79/37/15-41/5
[42] Burbridge BMI04801, paragraph 83
[43] Burbridge BMI 79/41/23-47/25

14.31 My impression of Burbridge was that when speaking of his knowledge of conditioning and hooding his evidence was a little disingenuous. I suspect that despite saying that he was not aware before Baha Mousa's death that hooding was used as part of the conditioning process, he may have had some such knowledge. But I accept he had no knowledge of the use of stress positions as an aid to tactical questioning and I recognise that tactical questioning was not a subject of which he had any real knowledge or experience.

PJHQ and Submissions to Ministers

14.32 There is no doubt that Ministers were promptly informed of Baha Mousa's death and of some of the circumstances in relation to it. The first notification to Ministers appears to have been on 16 September 2003 by way of a submission entitled "*Op TELIC: Death of One Detainee While in UK Custody and One Iraqi Child Seriously Injured after a Negligent Discharge*"[44] This was a submission from the PJHQ J9 Pol/ Ops, Bettina Jordan-Barber, addressed to the Private Secretary to the Secretary of State, and copied to the Private Secretary to the Minister for Armed Forces, the Private Secretary to the Minister for Defence Procurement, the office of the Chief of the Defence Staff and the office of the DCDS(C) (Deputy Chief of Defence Staff (Commitments)), and Head of the Iraq Secretariat. The Secretary of State was invited to note the circumstances of the incident, defensive press lines, and the fact that there was to be SIB investigation. The circumstances of Baha Mousa's death were summarised as follows:[45]

> 4. At 0600HRS on 14 September the First Battalion the Queen's Lancashire Regiment (1 QLR) carried out an anti terrorist and anti criminal arrest operation (Op SALERNO) in the hotel district of Basrah. This was a brigade level operation. During the operation 15 individuals were apprehended and small caches of rocket propelled grenades (RPG) and small arms were confiscated. One of the individuals who had been detained died last night whilst still in the custody of 1 QLR. There were 4 Iraqi witnesses to the arrest.
>
> 5. Although the individual did not need to be forcibly restrained on arrest, advice from theatre suggests that he consistently struggled with his cuffs and hood during the day, repeatedly tried to escape and also allegedly lashed out at guards. At 1840Z the individual slipped his hood. Two members of the guard restrained him and replaced his hood. His pulse was also apparently checked at this time. Three minutes later the guard suspected that he might not be breathing. Cardio pulmonary resuscitation and exhaled air resuscitation were immediately administered and the Regimental Medical Officer was called. This treatment continued for 20 minutes. The detainee was declared dead at 1905 hrs. At this point the individual had been in custody for a total of 36 hours. He had spent 23 hours and 40 minutes of this hooded, albeit not continually. We are continuing to investigate the circumstances surrounding the incident and will provide further information when we have it.

14.33 It is now very apparent that paragraph 5 of this submission was in many respects not an accurate summary of what had in fact occurred, although I should stress that this cannot be seen as a criticism either of the author of the submission nor of those Ministers and senior officers and officials who received it.

14.34 After the close of oral evidence the MoD disclosed to the Inquiry a further copy of this submission. The copy was identical save that it bore manuscript annotations.

---

[44] MOD048699
[45] MOD048700

The further copy of the submission appears to show a comment from the Private Secretary to the Minister of State for the Armed Forces, the Rt. Hon. Adam Ingram and Ingram's own immediate response. The manuscript note to the Minister from his Private Secretary stated:

> *"Minister – to be aware. Tho' hooding can be permitted to protect the identity of our informants during an arrest, we do not usually do so for the protracted periods mentioned."* [46]

14.35 In response Ingram appears to have asked to see the guidelines in place for the use of hoods and the restraint of prisoners. [47]

14.36 The following day at 16.32hrs on 17 September 2003, Lt Col Paul Harkness sent an email to Fenton, entitled *"Follow up on Op Salerno"* asking for answers to a number of questions in order further to assist Jordan-Barber, J9 POLOPS at PJHQ, to provide information for Ministers. Harkness ended his email with an apology that there were a lot of questions, and stated *"Those who are prone to being excitable are doing exactly that – the longer term ramifications of this incident will emerge in due course (i.e. the use of hoods etc)"*. [48]

14.37 At 17.53hrs on 17 September 2003, Fenton replied, supplying brief answers to the questions posed by Harkness, prefacing the information with the words: *"Remember these are second hand (from 2IC 1QLR), may not be accurate"* but also stating:

> *"QLR very much onside with providing info. There is no attempt to 'protect' or hide anyone. They are being as helpful as they can, and are passing on what they have from their own enquiries, conscious of not interfering with the SIB."* [49]

14.38 Fenton supplied his answers in the same manner as previously, by inserting them after the corresponding questions in the original email. The relevant information provided by Fenton was as follows:

> *"**Were the detainees examined (medically) upon arrival?** Within 4 hours after they arrived in QLR locn. No injuries/illness of note that required further investigation".*
>
> ...
>
> *"**How often subsequently?** Not known."* [50]

14.39 In relation to Baha Mousa:

> *"**Did he resist arrest?** Once detained back in the QLR, he apparently tried on numerous occasions to slip his handcuffs and hood. He needed to be restrained for them to be put back on".* [51]

14.40 I note here the information being provided to be passed up to Ministerial level to the effect that repeated attempts were made by Baha Mousa to release himself from his handcuffs and hoods. Fenton in his evidence said that he was dependent on the information given to him by members of 1 QLR, and that the source of this

---

[46] MOD055923
[47] MOD055923
[48] MOD016125
[49] MOD016125
[50] MOD016125
[51] MOD016125

information about Baha Mousa's behaviour was the "Brief on Sudden Death of Internee" provided to Mendonça[52] and the SINCREP to 19 Mech Brigade,[53] both written before this email.

14.41 As I have explained in Chapter 16 of Part II of this Report, it was in fact unsurprising that Baha Mousa might have sought to remove his handcuffs and hood so as to protect himself from assault. Further, I am not satisfied that this represented attempts to escape.

14.42 At this stage of the chronology, there was also an email exchange at Permanent Joint Headquarters (PJHQ) between Lt Col Nick Clapham (SO1 Legal, PJHQ) and Lt Col Ewan Duncan (who was by this time no longer in theatre but was J2 DACOS Plans at PJHQ). Clapham and Duncan were, it will be remembered, individuals who had been involved in the discussions concerning hooding at Divisional and PJHQ level during Op Telic 1, after such concerns had been raised about practices used in the handling of detainees at the JFIT, Um Qasr.

14.43 At 09.21hrs on 17 September 2003 Clapham sent an email, copied amongst others to Duncan, with the subject heading "*Hooding of Persons Detained*", in which he referred to various discussions taking place in PJHQ the previous day about hooding. In it Clapham stated:

> *"Potentially hooding may give rise to various difficulties from discomfort to possible risk of asphyxiation.*
>
> *As I understand it hoods are used as a means of blindfolding either to prevent the detainee seeing persons (including other detainees) or restricted areas, or alternatively as a means of disorientating (by sensory deprivation) a detainee before and during breaks in questioning."* [54]

14.44 On the face of it, this email, could well be interpreted as suggesting that Clapham knew before the death of Baha Mousa, even during Op Telic 1, that hooding was used other than merely for security purposes. However, in his oral evidence, Clapham was careful to make clear that this was in fact information that he had received only later and in light of what had happened to Baha Mousa.[55]

14.45 With regard to hoods being used as a method of preventing detainees seeing other people or restricted areas, Clapham advised:

> *"The use of blindfolds for the first reason outlined above should be legally sustainable so long as this is necessary (i.e. there is [no] other way to achieve the result) and the blindfold is worn for no longer than is required. Steps should also be taken to mitigate any resulting discomfort. During the planning of ops consideration should be given to creating conditions which reduce/ eliminate the need for blindfolding"* [56]

14.46 In respect of his understanding of the use of hoods as a method of disorientation, Clapham went on in the email to say that:

---

[52] MOD052586
[53] MOD030957
[54] MOD022183-4
[55] Clapham BMI 91/85/19-86/20
[56] MOD022184

> *"As far as disorientation is concerned this is difficult to justify… In fact ICRC were critical of our practice of hooding detainees at the TIF during phase 3 and the practice was changed to use blacked-out goggles where it was necessary".* [57]

14.47 Clapham's conclusion was as follows:

> *"…it is unlikely that blindfolding can be justified on grounds of disorientation – I realise that this may prove contr[o]versial and contrary to standard practice and it may be that this requires further consideration/discussion. As far as the protection of persons or info is concerned blindfolding may be justifiable if the means used is suitable or designed for the purpose. Hoods do not fit this requirement. The actual requirement is to mask the eyes and there is no need for the means used to impair breathing. I recommend that steps be taken to ensure that the practice of hooding is ceased and alternative means be considered where blindfolding is necessary for sustainable reasons."* [58]

14.48 In his oral evidence, Clapham explained that he had suggested that his advice on hooding was *"controversial"* because practice varied from nation to nation, hooding had been standard practice until March 2003, and he had to try to appreciate legitimate concerns which *"the operator"* (by this I take Clapham to have been referring to those conducting an interrogation) might hold about military necessity.[59]

14.49 At 13.58hrs on 17 September 2003, Duncan responded to Clapham's email. He replied that he recalled *"…the 'controversy' in the TIF and went there in May to see the conditions and discuss the (then) conflicting legal advice…".*[60]

14.50 Duncan went on to state:

> *"…the ending of hooding has far reaching implications – a growing diversion of opinion with the US and the adverse impact upon interrogations; UK involvement in US ops where blindfolding is the milder end of the spectrum; current doctrine and teaching at DISC: there are more."* [61]

14.51 In answer to Counsel to the Inquiry, Duncan said that it was not in fact his understanding that hoods might be used as a means of disorientating a detainee, as Clapham had stated in his email.[62] When pressed on whether he had ever thought that disorientation was an aspect of hooding, or whether that would be wrong or irrelevant, he stated *"Yes. It's not a purpose of hooding or blindfolding"*. He did not know why Clapham may have made such a mistake, and he said that he saw no purpose in correcting Clapham's understanding.[63]

14.52 However, in his email, Duncan had agreed with what he called the implication in Clapham's email that the ending of hooding had far reaching implications, including on the current teaching at the Defence Intelligence and Security Centre (DISC).[64] Duncan understood when he wrote this in 2003 that current doctrine and teaching at DISC was that the deprivation of sight by hooding was permitted. It was also

---

[57] MOD022184

[58] MOD022184

[59] Clapham BMI 91/84/16-90/24

[60] MOD022183

[61] MOD022183

[62] Duncan BMI 76/49/20-50/22

[63] Duncan BMI 76/77/4-78/4

[64] MOD022183

Duncan's view both when he wrote the email and when he gave evidence to the Inquiry, that depriving prisoners of their sight by hooding should be permitted. Duncan's view was that in some circumstances hooding would contribute to the effectiveness of interrogation because it was quicker and more effective than goggles or other blindfolds and it gave security for coalition forces and security to a detainee from others. I understood him to mean that some prisoners would be more willing to cooperate if their identity had been protected by the use of hoods.[65]

14.53 I accept that the exchange of emails between Clapham and Duncan, to which I have just referred, might be interpreted that, at least Clapham was aware before Baha Mousa's death of hooding being used as an adjunct to tactical questioning and not just for security purposes. It is, however, in my judgment in the face of Clapham's denial, insufficient evidence upon which to base a finding that Clapham did have this knowledge before Baha Mousa died. As for Duncan, as I have said earlier in the Report (see Chapter 5 of Part VIII 8.243 to 8.245), I found him to be a straightforward, articulate and entirely honest witness, who was robust and tough in his approach to his duties. I do not find that he knew that hooding was being used for the purposes of disorientation in the absence of a real security justification. Further, I have found that Duncan was not endeavouring to cover up some hidden motive for supporting hooding. In my view these findings are not inconsistent with a finding that Duncan was, as he explained, a supporter of hooding. In my view it is not inconsistent with his belief that banning hooding might have, as he said in his email, wider repercussions.

The Response of the Divisional Legal and Intelligence Staff Branches

14.54 At approximately the same time as Brigade was gathering information from 1 QLR in relation to Baha Mousa's death, members of the Legal and Intelligence chain of command at 3 (UK) Div were issuing directions in response to the concerns which had arisen from the circumstances of the death.

14.55 Capt Sian Ellis-Davies (SO3 Ops (Operational) Law) emailed Lt Col Charles Barnett setting out information relating to the health of the surviving Op Salerno Detainees. By this stage it was thought that one of the Detainees "*required dialysis*", and it was reported that five others were at the TIF "*...being seen by medics as bruising is appearing*".[66]

14.56 In reply, at 16.10hrs on 17 September 2003, Barnett sent an email entitled "Death in custody – Follow up action".[67] The addressees included Lt Col James Murray-Playfair, Col Richard Barrons, and Le Fevre, and it was copied to Fenton, Landon, Clifton, and Ellis-Davies.

14.57 Barnett set out his intention in the first line: "*This note is intended to ensure that all addressees are fully informed of the legal advice given so far*". The email then dealt with the possibility of treatment in the UK for one of the Detainees, the use of Iraqi medical facilities and the available pathologist. Barnett also commented that:

---

[65] Duncan BMI 76/56/5-58/17; Duncan BMI06052, paragraph 71
[66] MOD016123
[67] MOD016122

"On a more general note we have a duty to ensure that whilst any immediate action that is deemed necessary is taken following the lessons learned procedure (which I understand is being conducted by 19Bde), we do not rush to pre-judge enquiries or make precipitous decisions about actions to be taken (eg referring individual cases to PJHQ or the UK) that have not taken into account all the staff views. In particular there have been some rather excitable and unhelpful comments which may have pushed decisions in a certain direction which was not necessary in law or may have an impact on legal procedures".[68]

14.58 Paragraphs 6 to 8 of Barnett's email focused on issues directly relevant to the Inquiry and I set these passages out in full:[69]

6. On the HQ MND(SE) J3 (with J2 input) front we must do the following to fulfil our legal obligations:

- immediately conduct lessons learned procedure and record the findings. This must involve the necessary staff branches. It should cover TQ, guarding and application of procedures (methods, timelines, hooding etc) as a minimum. 19Bde are conducting? – please confirm. Does it require Div input - probably? If it is found that procedures are not being followed they must be immediately re-enforced. **My strong advice has been that all hooding be immediately stopped** – please confirm that this has happened. This does not pre-judge the requirement for, in the appropriate circumstances, preventing sight (eg when absolutely necessary for security reasons) but we should ensure that this is only when absolutely necessary and it should be done by use of blindfolds and not hoods. In the meantime, pending the lessons learned procedure, we should suspend the prevention of sight by any means. It was stopped under 1 Div at the TIF and I had understood that this was Div wide and so that it was not occurring anywhere within the MND (SE) AO. What did the order by 1 Div say? Has corporate knowledge been lost? Again I know that

the TIF are not hooding. I had believed that TQ did not teach hooding, only blindfolds and so there should not have been an issue at BG/Bde level. Is this correct?
- TIF opening hours require clarification. There have been erroneous comments made during the tour stating that the TIF is not open at night. This is not correct. The UK MPS are available 24hrs a day ███████████████████████████ but it has been made quite clear that the UK regards 24hr availability as necessary to abide by our obligations for both in-processing and also out-processing. All that is required from BGs is as much notice as possible, rather than simply turning up in a helicopter unannounced.
- Ensure the SIB investigation takes place – this is clearly ongoing.
- Subsequent to the SIB investigation there is likely to be a requirement for a board of enquiry.

7. On the HQ MND(SE) J2 front (probably should be J3 lead but as long as it is done) to abide by our legal obligations we must:

- prepare a Div SOI for both TQ and guarding at BG/Bde level. I understand that this is ongoing.
- Ascertain what the policy of the other TCNs is regarding TQ and guarding at Bde/BG level. We must ensure that we are satisfied that they have in place sufficient procedures to abide by legal obligations. We do not need to tell them how, merely ensure that they have a suitable procedure/policy which ensures compliance with the GOC's legal obligations. We must issue a policy letter requiring them to have such procedures in place and requiring them to provide us with their policies. This may more properly form part of a wider letter that requires policies on a number of areas (ie shooting incidents and the recording and investigation thereof are an example).

8. In summary we are responsible in law for the well being of any individual in our custody. This means that we have to be especially careful in the way that we look after them and use the appropriately trained individuals to carry out their particular tasks and do it within our laid down procedures. I am sure that this is the case but we must ensure that the requirement is fully understood and the importance does not get lost with the passage of time, change over of personnel or when there are perceived capability gaps which it is tempting to fill. We are also responsible for the medical condition of internees and also for the welfare of their families if it becomes an issue. When an incident occurs we are obliged to investigate fully and take the appropriate action as described above. We must ensure that all the necessary staff functions provide the required input to arrive at the best decisions. I have therefore copied this lengthy advice to all with an interest so that the legal position is clear in one note and all can see where actions are required so that we are legally sound in our response now that a situation has been identified. I have copied to 19Bde for information as various e-mails have come to me. I have discussed with Russell Clifton (SO2 Legal 19Bde) and there is no point duplicating effort on this one. An amount of work is required but my advice is that it is all necessary. As ever it will be for COS/J3 to co-ordinate the required actions.

---

[68] MOD016122
[69] MOD016122-3

14.59 Barnett had described his surprise, after becoming aware of the death of Baha Mousa, at learning that hooding was being used at all.[70] In oral evidence, he said that his understanding that the order banning hooding had previously been issued to the lowest levels had come to him from Lt Col Nicholas Mercer.[71]

14.60 Barnett had advised, and made expressly clear by this email, that hooding must stop forthwith. Pending a "lessons-learned" procedure, the prevention of sight by any means was suspended.[72] Barnett later accepted that it would be permissible to use blacked-out goggles where absolutely necessary for reasons of security, but with the proviso that they were to be removed as soon as they were no longer required and that the detainee had been advised that their use was temporary.[73] Barnett also wanted to question what was taught in relation to hooding as part of the tactical questioning process, as he had been assured that hooding was not occurring at the TIF. He had previously been told that tactical questioning teaching did not include such methods. But the understanding that hooding could be used had obviously come from somewhere.[74]

14.61 During his oral evidence, Barnett was asked whether his direction to HQ Multinational Division (South East) (MND (SE)) J2/J3 that they must "*prepare a Div SOI for both TQ and guarding at BG/Bde level*",[75] was rather too late at that stage. He replied that before the death of Baha Mousa he did not believe that he needed to press harder to make enquiries to ensure the correct training and policy, as he had been given credible explanations that training on these issues was in place.[76]

14.62 It had nevertheless been recognised by this stage that a Divisional level policy and guidance document in relation to tactical questioning was required.[77]

14.63 In Part XI of this Report I have concluded that there was an error of judgment on Barnett's part in not including the prohibition on hooding in FRAGO 005. It is right, however, that I should note here the clear and appropriate lead that Barnett gave in this email. This is reflected in his emphasis on the need for all hooding to be immediately stopped and for additional guidance to be issued to cover both tactical questioning and guarding procedures.

14.64 At 18.43hrs on the same day, 17 September 2003, Fenton replied to Barnett's email.[78] He stated that the Brigade's action thus far had been:

(1) a review of tactical questioning would be conducted;

(2) an order at the 18.00hrs conference call to cease hooding/blindfolding forthwith;

(3) wherever possible, detainees were to move to the TIF within fourteen hours;

---

[70] Barnett BMI07948, paragraph 192
[71] Barnett BMI 86/70/1-71/8
[72] MOD016122
[73] Barnett BMI07951, paragraph 201
[74] Barnett BMI 86/71/9-72/1; Barnett BMI07950-1, paragraph 201
[75] MOD016123
[76] Barnett BMI 86/72/2-73/10
[77] Barnett BMI 86/75/15-23
[78] MOD049438

(4)   the myth that the TIF was only open to take detainees between 09.00 to 17.00 was to be dispelled; and

(5)   *"A detention timeline highlighting the need for medical inspections, water, food etc will be sent out as* [an] *interim measure pending receipt of the Div policy"*.

14.65   Fenton also stated that *"We await the Div SOI on TQ. In the meantime, the above will be promulgated by G3 Ops tonight"*, he directed *"For G3 Ops, pse draft as per my bullets. Pass to me for comment"*.[79]

14.66   Fenton confirmed that there had been a Brigade conference call held at 18.00hrs on 17 September 2003 at which he issued the order to cease hooding and blindfolding forthwith.[80] In his oral evidence, Fenton explained that this had been intended to mean that hooding was not permitted for any purposes whatsoever.[81]

14.67   In addition to the Divisional lawyers, the intelligence branch of 3 (UK) Div was closely involved in responding to the death. At 10.21hrs on 18 September 2003, Le Fevre (SO1 J2) sent an email to Fenton under the heading "Detainee Handling and Tactical Questioning", copying in Barnett, Murray-Playfair, Robinson, and Richards.[82] It concerned the production of a standard operating instruction to cover the subject.

14.68   In this email Le Fevre informed Fenton that:

> *"...There have been extensive discussions here about the picking up of persons for whatever reason, the management process, the tactical questioning that may then occur...In order to resolve what is clearly a thorny issue a Div SOI is now being produced which will cover the whole process. J2 is starting the process, because someone has to, and all of the other appropriate branches here will provide the necessary input. Once it is completed it will be issued by J3. A few J2 points to start off which I hope will be useful in the short term and tide you over until the SOI is complete..."*[83]

14.69   Le Fevre went on to set out some advice, including that tactical questioning:

> *"...should only take place after an individual has been medically examined. The TQ can only be carried out by personnel who have passed the PH&TQ course run by JSIO. The TQ is the only part of the process of dealing with detainees that is a J2 responsibility...G3 at each level is responsible for the detainee from the perspective of controlling the process from the lift point until the detainee arrives at the TIF, this includes where they are held, how they are controlled and treated, feeding etc etc."*[84]

14.70   Le Fevre accepted that it was a matter of concern that there was not already a Divisional standard operating instruction covering the process of detention and tactical questioning.[85]

14.71   Fenton replied at 11.01hrs on 18 September 2003, confirming that *"We will ensure your points are included in the guidance we are issuing BGs as an interim measure pending receipt of the Div SOI"*. Fenton also explained that:

---

[79] MOD049438
[80] MOD049438
[81] Fenton BMI 101/142/4-21
[82] MOD016127
[83] MOD016127
[84] MOD016127
[85] Le Fevre BMI 85/40/18-25

> *"My review indicates BGs are using Bn Provo Staff, and UK procedures as for our own soldiers in detention as a guide. Hence while it does no harm to review/remind/sharpen up, detention is on the whole handled with professionalism. It is clearly the TQ process which needs refined [sic] and explained to the BGs, such that it can be correctly built-in to the prisoner handling process."* [86]

He raised the need to dispel the *"myth perpetuated by the TIF"* that its opening hours were limited. He also referred to the intelligence relationship between the TIF and BGs:

> *"To encourage BGs to get detainees there more expediently, it would help if we saw some feedback from TIF interviews. I'm told by G2 that we do not get a copy of reports produced by the TIF. There is also a perception that these reports are rarely timely anyway. Is there anything we can do to improve this process?"* [87]

14.72 When asked about these comments by Fenton to the effect that the tactical questioning process needed to be refined, Le Fevre accepted that it was clear at that time that more needed to be done. He said this was why a standard operating instruction was being drafted, of which the tactical questioning process was a part. He pointed out that it was not solely the tactical questioning process that needed to be worked on.[88]

14.73 Le Fevre, in an email reply at 11.44hrs on 18 September 2003 referred to the various resource difficulties at the TIF, and continued:

> *"I can understand your frustration that more info doesn't seem to come out of interro, it is an issue that I am working on. This part of UK military capability is only held in the reserves and it has frankly languished for many years. We need more and we need it now – currently I don't know if the personnel can be replaced."* [89]

14.74 In relation to his comment that interrogation capability had *"languished"*, Le Fevre stated that what he meant was that interrogation capability was delivered by reservists only, with no formed capability in the regular Army.[90]

14.75 By 18 September 2003, therefore, there was a clear recognition that a Divisional level standard operating instruction in tactical questioning and in guarding at Battlegroup level was required. The intention to produce it had been expressed, and the J2 branch had taken the lead in creating new instructions.

The Death in Detention Report

14.76 By the same date, 18 September 2003, as a result of the information gathered by 19 Mech Bde, Fenton had produced a report for his Commander, Moore. The report was headed *"Death in Detention"*[91] with information including a chronology in relation to Baha Mousa's death.

---

[86] MOD016126
[87] MOD016127
[88] Le Fevre BMI 85/42/19-43/7; MOD016126
[89] MOD016126
[90] Le Fevre BMI 85/44/3-11
[91] MOD030849

14.77   The chronology of events in this report contained some inaccuracies, including the names and time of arrival of the tactical questioning staff, and information relating to the feeding and watering of the Detainees, which other evidence might not support.[92]

14.78   The chronology also included, in respect of conditioning, the information that, as regards Sunday 14 September 2003, *"1030 Hoods placed on detainees"* and *"Hoods were removed periodically throughout the day by Provo staff"*. As regards later on the Sunday, *"2130 – 2200 Bn Provo Sgt ordered hoods and cuffs to be taken off"* with the remark *"TQ team then required that they were put back on"*. As to the Monday morning, the following was recorded, *"0730 – 1200 Final 3 detainees undergo TQ"* with the remark *"Hooded again after TQ, and remained that way until detainee died"*.[93]

14.79   There were a number of other passages of interest to the Inquiry in this report in relation to the responsibility for detainees during the tactical questioning process, the use of hooding for conditioning purposes, and incorrect assumptions that the TIF/JFIT was closed at certain times of the day.

14.80   The report set out the contemporaneous understanding of the responsibility for detainees:

> *"There is no clear answer whether it is BG staff or Int Corps reps that are responsible for TQ and prisoner handling in theatre. It is clear however from this incident that an ad hoc arrangement has developed across the Bde AO. BGs are encouraged to conduct TQ by the JFIT as part of the interrogation process a suspect is put through from capture to internment... Responsibility throughout however must be assumed to lie with the CO, delegated to the BG Internment Officer, (Major Peebles in this case) and the Bn Provo staff that run the detention centre. Major Peebles has received no formal training in this role, and assumed the post midway through the tour from another QLR officer. The Bn Provo Staff are trained in line with current UK legislation for the handling of servicemen in detention. They are not trained in TQ...I have not been able to identify the authority for the handling of detainees during TQ, nor can Div. The detail of how to categorise detainees, and the subsequent procedure to determine whether they should go to the TIF or IZ police is well documented. Reference A covers this in detail and was distr to BGs on 05 Sep 03. There is no available documentation covering TQ procedures in theatre that we in Bde can identify. MND(SE) is now attempting to codify a TQ SOP."* [94]

14.81   The report also described the tactical questioning process which had been conducted in relation to the Op Salerno Detainees:

> *"...TQ was conducted by Sgt Swarovski (FST) [I find that Sgt Smulski must have been the intended name] and SSgt Davies, Int Corps. Both are properly trained and in date in TQ procedures. Reference B was produced by SSgt Davies as a brief on TQ for COS. It is on his advice that we hood and hand cuff detainees, in order to enhance the shock of capture and improve the level of information extracted from the suspect."* [95]

---

[92] MOD030849-50
[93] MOD030849-50
[94] MOD030850
[95] MOD030850

14.82 The report addressed the delays in moving detainees to the TIF, citing the following points: lack of trained tactical questioning personnel in the Brigade, the closed TIF "*myth*", and the fact that Brigade and Battlegroups received little feedback or actionable intelligence from the TIF thus encouraging them to obtain information before the detainees were sent to the TIF.[96]

14.83 The report detailed subsequent Brigade action as follows:

> "An order was issued at the 171800hrs Bde Conf Call to cease all hooding and blindfolding forthwith. G3 Ops has been tasked to issue an order detailing the salient points of detainee handling, while we await Div direction…Only TQ qualified pers to conduct TQ."[97]

14.84 In summary, Fenton wrote:

> "The BG detention staffs are treating detainees within the guidelines for unit detention centres in the UK, and understand their duty of care. It is clear however an ad hoc process of TQ has evolved, without clear guidance on BG responsibility. This has been left to qualified TQ in theatre, FHT, and SF. A review of procedures is underway."[98]

14.85 Fenton told the Inquiry that he had become aware during the process of gathering information about the death that Baha Mousa had been hooded and he knew at a relatively early stage that there were allegations of serious assaults having been committed on other Detainees. He had become aware of the latter point by the communication to him of S018's complaints in the memo drafted by Suss-Francksen and the statement provided by Rodgers (see above, paragraphs 14.10 to 14.11). He was also aware that an SIB investigation had been initiated and he was anxious not to interfere in that process.[99]

14.86 Fenton wrote this report on the assumption and understanding that Baha Mousa had died of a heart attack. Fenton believes he was informed of this either by 1 QLR or by seeing the death certificate.[100] Fenton had also assumed that hooding had contributed to this condition. He accepted that this assumption was an indication of awareness at the time of the potential dangers of hooding to the health of a prisoner.[101]

14.87 Fenton said that 1 QLR had supplied him and Burbridge with the information set out in the chronology of events which appeared in his report. He could not remember whom exactly it was who provided specific information relating to the watering and feeding of detainees, but suggested either he or Burbridge would have obtained these times and details from the 1 QLR Ops Officer or the Second in Command (2IC). He did not doublecheck the information provided.[102] Fenton said that he was told by SSgt Mark Davies that hooding and handcuffing were used to enhance the shock of capture.[103]

---

[96] MOD030851

[97] MOD030851

[98] MOD030852

[99] Fenton BMI 101/124/13-125/18; Fenton BMI05690, paragraph 94

[100] The latter appears very unlikely since Fenton's report pre-dates the post mortem report

[101] Fenton BMI 101/125/22-127/20

[102] Fenton BMI 101/127/21-132/13

[103] Fenton BMI 101/137/8-138/23

14.88 Fenton's report contained a notable omission. It did not include any mention of the conversation he maintained he had with Suss-Francksen on Monday evening, discussing the reasons why 1 QLR had not complied with the fourteen hour transfer to the TIF deadline. The delay was justified at that time by lack of Battlegroup resources, the dangers of travelling at night and the (erroneous) understanding that the TIF was closed after 17.00hrs. This conversation resulted in an effective Brigade sanction for the continued holding of the Op Salerno Detainees at BG Main until Tuesday morning.[104] Suss-Francksen said he could not remember the details of this conversation but did not deny that it occurred.[105] I deal with this in Chapter 20 of Part II.

14.89 In his oral evidence, Fenton, after some initial reluctance, accepted that this was a relevant fact which should have appeared in the chronology of his report. He rejected the suggestion that the conversation may have occurred earlier during the Monday morning, and that he subsequently felt some of the responsibility might fall on him for sanctioning a longer period of detention.[106] He also stated that he did not make the connection at the time that one effect of the extension of the time limit was that Battlegroups might carry on the tactical questioning process for longer.[107]

14.90 I reiterate in my view this is a singular omission. Naturally, Fenton was to a considerable extent dependent on information passed to him by those soldiers in 1 QLR closer to the events in question. When providing a statement for the Court Martial proceedings on behalf of Mendonça, Suss-Francksen said that he had considered Fenton's report and that he did not believe he had provided the information contained in Fenton's report.[108] In his Inquiry witness statement, in contrast, Suss-Francksen admitted the possibility that he provided information to Fenton for his report to Moore, although at the time he made his statement he did not remember the conversation or any details.[109]

14.91 In his oral evidence to the Inquiry, Suss-Francksen initially said that he had not seen the "Death in Detention" report and that he did not believe he had any input into it. His account was that Fenton had spoken to the 1 QLR Ops room to obtain the information and then had telephoned Suss-Francksen to clarify points of detail, but without telling Suss-Francksen what was in the report. He told the Inquiry that he was able to provide clarification probably by asking Peebles for the details. He denied that there was any sort of cover-up being put forward in the information he provided.[110]

14.92 Peebles' evidence was consistent with Suss-Francksen on this aspect. He said that he provided some of the information included in Fenton's report, having received questions from Brigade via Suss-Francksen. He said that he had provided the information that hoods had been removed periodically and that the Detainees had been given water every 30 minutes, and that they had been given an evening meal. He had done so after being given this information by Payne.[111] When questioned

[104] Fenton BMI 101/111/5-113/19
[105] Suss-Francksen BMI01586, paragraph 50
[106] Fenton BMI 101/132/23-134/18
[107] Fenton BMI 101/140/1-141/15
[108] MOD048652
[109] Suss-Francksen BMI01588, paragraph 55
[110] Suss-Francksen BMI 56/210/2-211/20
[111] Peebles BMI 40/142/6-143/25

about events which are absent from the timeline, such as the two Detainees who presented medical complaints after the death, Peebles said that he only passed on information which he was asked about, via the 2IC at Battlegroup Headquarters. He stated that he had not been asked about stress positions or conditioning and that was why they were not mentioned in the report.[112]

14.93 There was a significant dispute between Fenton and SSgt Davies in relation to whether or not Davies had provided the information that *"… we hood and hand cuff detainees, in order to enhance the shock of capture and improve the level of information extracted from the suspect"*.[113] SSgt Davies' evidence was that he spoke to Fenton about his report, but that his dealings with Fenton and his own input into documents was by way of assisting Brigade in creating a new tactical questioning policy with Radbourne. SSgt Davies stated that he was not responsible for providing any of the timings in the Fenton report; this information had come from 1 QLR.[114] In his oral evidence SSgt Davies said that he would not have regarded hooding as an appropriate part of the conditioning process, although he refined this by stating that he thought hooding was acceptable in the *"operational context"* for the purposes of isolation, a state which was itself a proper part of conditioning.[115]

14.94 The factual issues between Fenton and Suss-Francksen and Fenton and SSgt Davies are the sort of mismatches in recollections which, given the passage of time and the tempo of operations, are to be expected. My assessment of Fenton as a witness was that he was a good witness who was doing his best to give accurate evidence. I do not think it is strictly necessary for me to resolve these factual issues, but if it was, I would prefer Fenton's evidence on these issues to the evidence of both Suss-Francksen and SSgt Davies. What is of significance is firstly, that for whatever reason, the fourteen hour time limit was exceeded by a considerable margin and secondly, it was not mentioned in Fenton's report to the Brigade Commander. In my opinion it ought to have been. There were also some inaccuracies in the report which arose out of the information supplied by 1 QLR personnel to Brigade. It is also clear that Baha Mousa's death spurred Brigade into deriving new policy and practice in respect of the tactical questioning process.

14.95 The more detailed information that had now been gathered was forwarded to Ministers. On 18 September 2003 a follow-up brief was sent to the Secretary of State with same copy addressees within the MoD as the previous submission circulated by Jordan-Barber.[116] One copy of this submission provided to the Inquiry appears to be the copy from the Private Office of the Secretary of State. It shows in manuscript on the first page the message *"SofS – This could be very messy – 2 soldiers have been arrested – Min (AF) will deal as lead Minister"*. The Rt. Hon. Geoff Hoon MP, Secretary of State for Defence, confirmed during his oral evidence that the handwriting was almost certainly that of his military assistant, Mr Martin Williams.[117]

---

[112] Peebles BMI 40/144/1-22
[113] MOD030850
[114] Davies BMI 42/91/21-92/13
[115] Davies BMI 42/142/9-145/16
[116] MOD048704
[117] Hoon BMI 103/207/2-20

14.96 The submission was not one seeking any particular decision but rather providing information to note. It included an update of information in relation to the death of Baha Mousa and injury to two other Detainees. In summary:[118]

(1) the Secretary of State was invited to note the new information available including about the Op Salerno raid and the fact that one of the Detainees was being treated for renal failure;

(2) it was made explicit that the fourteen hour timeframe had not been complied with;

(3) in respect of tactical questioning, paragraph 7 of the submission read: "*In this instance the Tactical Questioning (TQ) of the suspects was conducted by two Intelligence Corps Staff Sergeants, both fully trained in TQ. It would appear that the hooding of the suspects took place on the advice of one of the Staff Sergeants. However, there is currently no documentation in theatre covering TQ procedures. MND(SE) are reviewing this urgently*";

(4) the action being taken by the Brigade was set out including a reinforcement of the fourteen hour deadline; and details of the instruction that "*There is to be no hooding or blindfolding although temporary blindfolding will be allowed to deny the detainee ability to see inside the CF bases*", "*Medical inspections, by Doctors, to be conducted on arrival, periodically as required and at the end of the detention period*", "*TQ is to be conducted by fully qualified personnel only*"; and

(5) the Secretary of State was also invited to note that procedures in theatre were being reviewed.

14.97 When this submission was forwarded to Ingram his Private Secretary added the comment in manuscript:

> "*Minister – This looks very murky. In addition to advice on SOPs for detainee handling (and I find para 7 difficult to believe), we should ask for clear advice on the timelines for investigation*".[119]

14.98 Back in theatre, Barrons (Chief of Staff 3 (UK) Div) sent an email reply to Fenton at 15.28hrs on 18 September 2003, probably after being provided with the Death in Detention report produced by Fenton.[120] It summarised the action taken since the death and the information known by 18 September 2003, the third day after Baha Mousa's death. It also addressed what policy and practice had hitherto been in place:

---

[118] MOD048704

[119] MOD055918; for the content of paragraph 7 of the submission that was being referred to by Ingram's Private Secretary, see paragraph 14.96(3) above)

[120] MOD030849

> *"Div policies and procedures break down as follows:*
>
> *Apprehension, handling, processing – Div policy as issued in Sep*
>
> *TQ – no policy visible and practise is based on trg on TQ course. SOP required and in hand with J2 lead*
>
> *Detention procedures based on normal unit drills for detaining own soldiers. Addtl guidance (no hooding or stress positions) believed to have been issued by 1xx in Jul, but corporate loss of memory (and lack of e connectivity or e handover of docs) may account for this having been lost*
>
> *A considered follow up will ident any gaps in policy over the weekend*
>
> *Immediate Lessons Learned Process has ident following:*
>
> *Instructions issued to cease practise of hooding if it is happening. Comd Legal will draft letter to Bde articulating circumstances in which eye covers can be used on detainees*
>
> *Procedures are being refreshed at all levels*
>
> *Div SOI on TQ required...*"[121]

14.99 In respect of this email Le Fevre accepted in his oral evidence that there was no tactical questioning policy in theatre, and that the doctrine in relation to tactical questioning was as trained on the tactical questioning course. He was pressed as to whether the reality of the situation which had been exposed was that there was a deficiency that ought to have been identified and addressed at an earlier stage.[122] He responded that this was:

> *"...one factor of many that we were trying to deal with. Clearly policy is put in place as and when you can have the resources available to do it. If there isn't a perceived issue, something will not necessarily get a high priority to be dealt with."*[123]

14.100 The 19 Mech Bde staff also met to discuss the need for further guidance and direction. This is evidenced in a letter sent on 20 September 2003 by Paul Driver, the Aide De Camp to Moore, entitled *"COMMAND GROUP 19 SEPT 03"*.[124] The addressees included the Brigade Commander (Moore), Chief of Staff (Fenton), Deputy Chief of Staff (Landon) and all Commanding Officers, with a copy to the policy adviser (POLAD) (Robert Harkins). It confirmed the outcome of the 19 Mech Bde Command Group meeting held on 19 September 2003. Such meetings reviewed the events of the past week within the Brigade Area of Operations and provided guidance and direction for the forthcoming week. Attached at Annex A was a list of the action points from the meeting, including the following:[125]

(1) under the heading "Discussion": *"The tactical questioning (TQ) system is working well and must remain robust. The hooding/blindfolding of suspects should have ceased after the warfighting phase of OP TELIC"*;

(2) under the heading "Agreement": *"Blindfolding of suspects is to cease until otherwise instructed by Bde"*;

---

[121] MOD016128
[122] Le Fevre BMI 85/44/12-45/10
[123] Le Fevre BMI 85/45/11-16
[124] MOD016702
[125] MOD016703

(3) under the heading "Discussion": "*Div are to issue a TQ SOI. There will be greater scrutiny of timelines. BGs will have 14 hours before suspects must be in the TIF*", and in response to this under "Agreement", "*If BGs require more time they are to inform Bde who will in turn inform Div*".

Correspondence related to the drafting of new tactical questioning policy

14.101 From 19 or 20 September 2003 up to 30 September 2003 the new Divisional order SOI 390 was being drafted.

14.102 On 21 September 2003, Barnett replied to Murray-Playfair's email "DETENTION DEATH AND FOLLOW UP" in which Murray-Playfair had sought to identify the remaining follow-up points for action arising out of the death of Baha Mousa.[126] Barnett informed Murray-Playfair that the tactical questioning and detention procedures standard operating instruction was intended to be in two parts; one dealing with the tactical questioning and the other dealing with detention. The part on detention was to be based on the training given to Regimental Provost (RP) staff on the Military Corrective Training Centre (MCTC) courses. Barnett indicated that the standard operating instruction was to be completed shortly and would include "*...a para confirming the order which banned hooding and providing guidance on the parameters re blindfolds/blacked out goggles*".

14.103 The need to ensure that standard operating instructions relating to tactical questioning and detention were in place in theatre appears to have been a concern at Ministerial level, at least to some degree, from soon after the death.

14.104 On 22 September 2003 Ingram's Private Secretary recorded that the Minister had taken note of the key points from the submissions of 16 and 18 September 2003. Notably, he continued:

> "*Minister (AF) was surprised that there seems to be no extant policy governing the use of hoods/restraints and similarly that Tactical Questioning procedures are unavailable in Theatre. He notes that both these shortcomings are being addressed. He has asked for a forecast of how long the SIB investigation is likely to take. It would be useful to have this by the end of the week.*" [127]

14.105 This Loose Minute from Ingram's Private Secretary was only disclosed after the close of oral evidence. Ingram was asked during his oral evidence whether, given the information he received in the submissions, he thought that the practice of the use of hoods, or the circumstances in which they could be used, ought to have been investigated or reviewed under his auspices.[128]

14.106 Ingram answered this by referring to the contemporaneous knowledge he would have possessed from the submissions, that MND(SE) were already reviewing the matter and a further review would have been otiose. Ingram was also asked whether he, as the responsible Minister, ought to have kept this matter in his domain. He

---

[126] MOD049733
[127] MOD055928-9
[128] Ingram BMI 97/34/11-35/18

answered that there was no evidence that he did not do so.[129] With the benefit of the 22 September 2003 Loose Minute it is in my opinion clear that Ingram did raise some concern about the lack of extant tactical questioning and hooding policies. He noted that these were shortcomings, but that they were being addressed. In my opinion, there is no sufficient basis to criticise Ingram for his immediate response to Baha Mousa's death as revealed in this sequence of submissions.

14.107 On 23 September 2003 Barnett sent an email to his legal staff including Ellis-Davies, Capt Toby Hamnett and Clifton, in relation to the Internment Record. It included the following phrase, which it might be thought, cast a certain light on the potential lack of relevant doctrine and guidance before the death of Baha Mousa:[130]

> Pse note that there will be amendments to the occasional document with the development of the TQ and detention SOI. Everyone is waking up and providing the input that they didn't when we circulated for comments/input previously. This is partly to do with the fact ha there are new, more pro active staff in some areas and also as it is now absolutely clear that the house has to be in order with intense scrutiny on these issues.
>
> I will see how many changes/amendments become necessary and then consider whether to re-issues the whole policy. If I do it will contain a specific para on treatment of detainees and refer to the TQ and detention SOI etc. It will also be issued with the proper co-ordinating instructions that Sian is finalising. Please let me have sight. I am afraid I am being a bit of a slave driver until the very end – although it doesn't look as if it can wipe the smile off your face!

14.108 Barnett was asked in evidence about what might be thought to be a rather barbed comment in this email that *"Everyone is waking up and providing the input that they didn't when we circulated for comments/input previously"*,[131] Barnett accepted that, albeit amongst others, this was a reference to Le Fevre and to Lt Col Robert Warren (the CO of 3 RMP (PM)) who Barnett had approached in the drafting process for FRAGO 005.[132] I have considered the drafting of FRAGO 005, and the absence of any reference to tactical questioning guidance and the prohibition on hooding, in Part XI of this Report.

14.109 Barnett explained during his oral evidence that he was in no doubt about the crucial point. There ought to have been a standard operating instruction on tactical questioning for use at Brigade level:

> *"I was in no doubt because it became clear from this instance that there wasn't one. I think some of the enquiries that had been made by the acting chief of staff had identified that there wasn't one. That didn't mean to say there was no -- there were people that were doing it that were trained, but there was no policy document in place there."*[133]

14.110 Finally, in this chain of reports to Ministers, on the 26 September 2003 a further submission, again from Jordan-Barber, was sent to the same addressees, in reply to a request for a forecast on how long the SIB investigation into the death might take.[134]

---

[129] Ingram BMI 97/34/24-36/1
[130] MOD049738
[131] MOD049738
[132] Barnett BMI 86/73/11-75/14
[133] Barnett BMI 86/75/17-23
[134] MOD054822

14.111 The material passage is the final paragraph, in which Jordan-Barber stated that:

> *"The use of hooding has already been stopped in theatre, but PJHQ is working on additional guidance and direction that will be provided to theatre in the very near future. In addition PJHQ will be asking CDI to review his current teaching and doctrine polic[i]es on the use of restraints and on tactical questioning."*[135]

14.112 What is evident, as illustrated at various times and by various officers in the above emails, is that there was a lack of policy and guidance, particularly in relation to the physical aspects of prisoner handling and the tactical questioning process.

14.113 Once this was recognised after Baha Mousa's death, officers at each level of command in theatre moved to fill the gap. At 1 QLR, Peebles reviewed the Battlegroup's practices. At Brigade level a new standard operating procedure was directed to be drawn up; and at Divisional level it was recognised that a standard operating instruction was needed. I now turn briefly to each of these documents all of which were promulgated after Baha Mousa's death.

---

[135] MOD054823

Chapter 2: Changes in Procedure in Theatre

Battlegroup Level

14.114 Peebles drafted a document called *"Recommendations on Battlegroup Internment Procedures"*, dated 18 September 2003.[136] It was addressed to the senior ranks of 1 QLR and the Provost side: the Commanding Officer, the 2IC, the Quartermaster, Adjutant, Operations Officer, Regimental Sergeant Major (RSM), the attached Royal Military Police (RMP) and the Provost Sergeant.

14.115 Peebles introduced the document with the statement that *"The death of a detainee in custody has highlighted a number of areas where improvements should be made in order* [to] *prevent a reoccurrence of such an event"*. Amongst the recommendations and changes, and information about what was described as "current" procedures in place, were the following. Firstly, a lockable cell facility was to be requested as a statement of requirement. Secondly, a request was to be made to Brigade for *"...the use of blacked out ski masks should be made as a counter intelligence measure for use in transit and when moving out of the holding facility"*. Thirdly, in relation to the medics: *"Currently all prisoners are inspected on arrival by the RMO..."* and *"Medical staff have paid regular visits to the holding centre at the request of the RP Staff. A more regular routine of visits, one on the hour every hour should be developed in order to provide a constant monitor of the health of prisoners..."*[137] In relation to this matter Peebles was assisted by input from Dr Derek Keilloh.[138]

14.116 Fourthly, in relation to tactical questioning:

> *"Comd Legal will be requested to allow the use of questioning by qualified personnel as we now have the time to be deliberate in our follow up. Questioning should does not have to be* [sic] *conducted in the manner of TQ and should be recorded as evidence. Once they go to the TIF this valuable opportunity is lost. My recommendation on TQ is that it is suspended until a clearly defined policy directive is issued by the chain of command."* [139]

14.117 Fifthly, as for responsibility for the handling of detainees: *"The responsibility for the handling and welfare of prisoners will go to the sub-units who made the arrest and who are to provide the guard. The guard force will come under the command of the RP staff and the normal chain of command adopted in a UK military establishment...On each occasion the Guard will be formally briefed on the treatment of prisoners using a set format provided by the RP staff"*. Guards were required to sign an occurrence book and a log to record visitors and movements of the detainees was to be kept. It was recommended that the Adjutant inspect the detainees and the guard twice during detainees' stay.[140]

---

[136] MOD016200
[137] MOD016200-201
[138] Peebles BMI 40/125/25-126/7; Peebles BMI 40/188/15-22
[139] MOD016201
[140] MOD016201

14.118 In his summary paragraph, Peebles wrote:

> *"The instructions on internment procedure currently focus on the completion of documentary evidence in order to secure internment within 14 hours. There have been detailed forms issued but nothing has been written by either Legal or the Provo Chain to provide exacting guidance or best practice on the matter of Tactical Questioning and prisoner handling in this theatre and in this phase of operations. Indeed the facilities and resources at BG level are scarce and the pressures of operational commitments coupled with the myth of opening times of the TIF mean that timelines have been difficult to meet. However the rules on the treatment of detainees are understood under the Law of Armed Conflict on which all soldiers are trained and the RP staff are well versed on the treatment of prisoners. Tactical Questioning is known to be a grey area and should now be reviewed. There is an operational necessity for this to take place in order to gain immediate intelligence for follow up operations to be organised."* [141]

14.119 Peebles recommended the following immediate action: a request for permission to use blacked-out goggles, the suspension of tactical questioning, and a request for a direction from Brigade on the use of formal questioning.[142]

14.120 On 18 September 2003, Peebles drafted guidance, revising the 1 QLR Internment Procedure previously introduced by May Antony Royce, entitled *"1 QLR Internment Procedure (Revised)"*.[143] It set out the procedures to be in place to deal with internees. The most relevant aspects were that internees were to be brought to BG Main as soon as possible and in any event within two hours of arrest. They were to be seen by the BGIRO and Regimental Medical Officer (RMO), and had to be delivered to the TIF within fourteen hours. There must be a medical inspection on arrival and at least three times within the fourteen hours of detention. The Provost Sergeant was to brief guards on their responsibilities and prisoner handling. *"The Provo Sgt is responsible for prisoner handling and their welfare whilst in custody just as he does in a UK military establishment".*[144]

14.121 As to tactical questioning, only a qualified tactical questioner was to question a detainee. The Company Ops Officer had to ensure that potential internees were reported to the Battlegroup Internment Review Officer (BGIRO). The Company was not to conduct tactical questioning but should question the arrestee to the extent necessary to determine the status as a potential internee. Finally, blindfolds and sandbags were prohibited and internment was to be a G2 led function.[145]

14.122 Attached as *"to follow"*[146] was a Prisoner Handling Brief.[147] It was to be given by the Provost staff to the guards. It included the following instructions in respect of the treatment of detainees:

> *"Every 15 minutes they are to be stood up and conduct limited limb movements in order to avoid deep vein thrombosis and prevent stiffness of the limbs. This is to be supervised by the Provo Staff. THIS IS NOT BE CLASSED AS CONDITIONING (sic)."*

---

[141] MOD016202
[142] MOD016202
[143] MOD016203
[144] MOD016204
[145] MOD016205-6
[146] MOD016207
[147] MOD016210

14.123 Peebles gave the following explanation for his creation of these documents. In reaction to the death it was obvious to him that the procedures in place within the Battlegroup needed to be looked at. He approached WO1 George Briscoe, who gave him Joint Services Intelligence Organisation (JSIO) F branch documents which had not been provided to him during his handover (JSIO F Branch Introduction to Interrogation and Tactical Questioning – Course Notes). Peebles said that he also spoke to Provost Sgt Smith, Radbourne, Ellis-Davies (in relation to time-scales) and another person at the JFIT, before he drew up the revised policy.[148]

14.124 With regard to tactical questioning, Peebles said that he asked Radbourne what was and was not allowed to maintain the shock of capture, to identify what the Brigade position was in this regard. Peebles said that Radbourne informed him that the Brigade needed to review their position.[149]

14.125 Peebles was asked about the "Recommendations on Battlegroup Internment Procedures" document.[150] He accepted that it was incorrect where it stated that "*Currently all prisoners are inspected on arrival by the RMO*". In fact the position was that the inspections during Keilloh's time as RMO could be undertaken by any member of the medical staff. Peebles attributed this to a simple mistake and not an attempt to put forward a false picture. He explained that he had obtained the information from Payne that there had been "*regular visits to the holding centre at the request of the RP Staff*".[151]

14.126 Peebles said that he wanted to bring clarity to the situation in relation to the issue of who had responsibility for detainees. He agreed that the chain of command had been unclear previously.[152]

14.127 Peebles said that by this time he was raising questions with Brigade along the lines of "*What is permissible and not permissible in terms of the conditioning process?*". He said such concerns had arisen in his mind because he thought it "*...quite possible that he [Baha Mousa] was either asphyxiated by the use of hooding or that he was fatigued or had a heart attack or, as it turned out, something worse, of which conditioning would be a contributor to that factor*".[153]

14.128 These documents drafted by Peebles after the death passed through the usual chain of command within the Battlegroup and would have been seen by the Provost staff, the RSM and the Adjutant amongst others. In the light of this, Peebles was asked whether the production of these documents had been motivated by a desire to cover up the failings that had evidently occurred:

> "*Q. There wasn't any intent to cover up for what might be regarded as the failings of the TDF system in this document, was there?*
>
> *A. I don't think it covers it up. It exposes them and I think it is honest about what the failings were. And I, you know, point no finger of blame in any direction, only that things obviously weren't as good as they should have been.*"[154]

---

[148] Peebles BMI02732-3, paragraphs 84-85
[149] Peebles BMI02733, paragraph 85
[150] MOD016200
[151] Peebles BMI 40/126/23-130/6
[152] Peebles BMI 40/128/22-130/2
[153] Peebles BMI 40/130/7-131/15
[154] Peebles BMI 40/129/20-130/2

14.129 I accept that the reference to all prisoners being inspected on arrival by the RMO was simply a mistake as Peebles asserted. But I find it more surprising, however, that the documents "*1 QLR Internment Procedure (Revised)*"[155] or "*Recommendations on Battlegroup Internment Procedures*"[156] made such limited reference to hooding and conditioning, and no mention whatsoever of stress positions, despite his knowledge of these practices by 1 QLR before and during Op Salerno.

14.130 In oral evidence Peebles said he thought that in one of the two papers he produced he had said there should be no conditioning.[157] In this he was again mistaken. In fact the closest he came to this, at least in the three documents above was in the "Detainee Handling Brief".[158] In that brief he said that every fifteen minutes prisoners were to be taken through limited limb movements. Afterwards he had written "*THIS IS NOT BE CLASSED AS CONDITIONING*" (sic), a significant difference from directing that there was to be no conditioning.

14.131 I have found in paragraphs 14.9 and 14.12, that Peebles failed in his duty to ensure that the internment records for the Detainees properly reflected the complaints made and injuries suffered by the Detainees, that this was not part of a cover up but it was one example of defensiveness that led to a certain playing down of the seriousness of what had occurred.

14.132 I find that, similarly, these documents generated by Peebles after Baha Mousa's death, may have been coloured by a desire on his part, perhaps understandably, to distance himself from sole responsibility for the tragic recent events in the TDF. In saying this, I do not doubt that Peebles had also realised the inadequacy of the previous guidance and was seeking to improve matters.

Brigade Level

14.133 In his the email entitled "TQ and Detention", Fenton had asked Burbridge, the SO3 Ops at 19 Mech Bde, to prepare and issue an standard operating procedure on tactical questioning.[159] As a result, Burbridge produced a "TQ Timeline" dated 18 September 2003.[160] The timeline was as follows:

---

[155] MOD016203
[156] MOD016200
[157] Peebles BMI 40/130/7-18
[158] MOD016210
[159] MOD016114
[160] MOD022299

5. 'A'hr indicates arrival time at the location for TQ.

Ser	Time (a)	Required Activity (b)	Remarks (c)
1	A Hr	Arrival at TQ location Medical Inspection Water made available	A detailed log is initiated. To be conducted by a RMO
2	A + 1 onwards	Water made available hourly	Water to be avail more frequently if required
3	A + 3	Examination by RMO	Record kept.
4	A + 6	Meal provided. Examination by RMO	Record kept
5	A + 9	Examination by RMO	Record kept
6	A + 12	Meal provided.	
7	NLT A + 14	Final Examination by RMO Depart for TIF	BG to inform Bde if this timeline will not or has not been met, with justification.
8	A + 16	Consolidated report to Bde HQ	This must include any complaint made by the detainee during his questioning. It must state whether no complaint has been made.

The timeline was addressed to the Commanding Officers of 19 Mech Bde Battlegroups, including 1 QLR. The document specified the system that should be adhered to, including the following advice:

> "TQ must only take place after an individual has received a medical examination. It should be conducted by qualified personnel only. They must have passed the PH&TQ course run by JSIO [...] TQ should be conducted in a single session".[161]

14.134 Burbridge remembered that the contents of the timeline were discussed with Robinson, the Deputy Chief of Staff (Landon), Fenton, himself and Clifton the legal adviser. According to Burbridge, the purpose of the timeline was to provide clear guidance for the Battlegroups on how long a suspect could be detained before release or internment in the TIF. It was not a document which addressed how detainees should be treated during tactical questioning.[162]

14.135 Burbridge confirmed that it was a fair assumption from his production of this timeline that there was no clear guidance in this regard before the issue of his document.[163]

14.136 In my opinion, Burbridge's evidence on these exchanges again reflected the lack of detailed guidance before Baha Mousa's death and the lack of clarity about which branch held the responsibility for the tactical questioning function. This was further illustrated when Burbridge was asked about the email in which Fenton had exhorted the Brigade to "tighten up what we do" and prepare a standard operation procedure.[164] Burbridge was asked what was the standard operating procedure that he understood might be put in place to be enforced by Brigade. He replied:

> "I don't know, ie at that stage [shortly after the death] I didn't know what the SOP needed to say. The G3 ops officer has responsibility to maintain all the SOPs in the brigade even if they don't sit within G3 ... The task to produce the SOP would come to me. The research needed to conduct the SOP would be the result of my conversation with others."[165]

[161] MOD022299
[162] Burbridge BMI04802, paragraph 85
[163] Burbridge BMI 79/59/17-60/1
[164] MOD016114
[165] Burbridge BMI 79/79/1-80/18

14.137 When asked about the detail appearing in the timeline, for example the instructions that tactical questioning was only to take place after a medical inspection, Burbridge answered that this was information taken on advice from the staff branches and not put forward on his own initiative.[166] Burbridge was not able to remember to whom he had spoken within the Brigade and Divisional headquarters in order to produce his timeline.[167]

14.138 As a result of the death of Baha Mousa, Fenton also instructed Radbourne to produce a report into tactical questioning and prisoner handling procedures.[168] Fenton said that in the absence of a guidance document on prisoner handling and tactical questioning he instructed the intelligence cell to gather information on the issue. Fenton believed that a clarification of procedures was necessary, and Radbourne's document was the instruction issued in response to the death of Baha Mousa, which Fenton approved.[169]

14.139 Radbourne said that Burbridge had put together a timeline, and he had taken it upon himself after the death to highlight ways in which prisoner handling could be conducted to ensure such a thing did not occur again. Radbourne's evidence was that he discussed matters with Burbridge, Fenton, Robinson, and SSgt Davies in order to produce the document.[170]

14.140 In his Inquiry witness statement, Radbourne suggested that the document was devised to reiterate "*best practice*", with the intention to "*set out clearly the procedures for detaining prisoners*".[171] I note, however, that Radbourne had previously characterised this slightly differently in his statement to the SIB, stating that following the death of a detainee in September 2003, he wrote a policy document setting out the procedures to be adopted when handling detainees.[172] In my view, the latter better reflected the reality of the position, namely that there was no pre-existing policy beyond Joint Warfare Publication (JWP) 1-10 and thus this was the first policy document of its kind, not a re-iteration of previous best practice.

14.141 In any event, on 27 September 2003, before the issue of the Divisional standard operating instruction 390, 19 Mech Bde issued the document "*Prisoner Handling and Tactical Questioning Procedures (PHTQ)*" which had been produced by Radbourne.[173]

14.142 This was a statement of policy in relation to "*Prisoner Handling and Tactical Questioning (PHTQ)*" set out in the form of a letter with the following Annexes and References:[174] Annex A, SOI Tactical Questioning of Internees; Annex B, PHTQ Timeline; Annex C, Tactical Questioning Report; Annex D, Prisoner Handling – A Battlegroup Guide; Reference A MND SOI 390; Reference B ITD 9 LOAC; Reference C the Timeline of 18 September 2003; and Reference D the TQ Report HQ 3 Div Force MI. It was addressed to external parties for information (SO2 G2 MND(SE) and J2X MND(SE)) and to internal parties for action: Battlegroup Commanding Officers and Intelligence Officers and for information to the Brigade Chief of Staff and Brigade Operations.

---

[166] Burbridge BMI 79/56/6-58/18
[167] Burbridge BMI 79/81/8-17
[168] Fenton BMI 101/86/22-87/8
[169] Fenton BMI 101/88/19-90/9; Fenton BMI05678, paragraphs 41-42
[170] Radbourne BMI 78/156/7-158/6
[171] Radbourne BMI04154, paragraphs 88-89
[172] Radbourne MOD000694
[173] MOD031235
[174] Ibid.

14.143 Radbourne's letter highlighted particular factors of importance included in the attached annexes and references. He emphasised:[175]

(1) the importance of using qualified personnel for prisoner handling and tactical questioning (Ref A);

(2) that 19 Brigade had endorsed MND SOI 390 (Ref A) (not in fact at this stage issued);

(3) the timelines to be adhered to from detention to movement to TIF or release (Annex B);

(4) the framework to follow for tactical questioning procedures (Annex C); and

(5) that a Senior Non-Commissioned Officer (SNCO) or officer must be put in command of prisoner handling and tactical questioning to ensure it runs to the principles set down.

14.144 In respect of Annex A – *"Instruction for the Handling and Tactical Questioning of Internees"*, the material parts were that:[176]

(1) tactical questioning was only to be carried out by those trained in tactical questioning and/or interrogation by JSIO. Additionally only those who had either carried out tactical questioning operationally or taken part in practical resistance to interrogation training with 4(CAC) company within the past two years;

(2) medics were to certify prisoners fit for detention and questioning before tactical questioning;

(3) permission for tactical questioning must be sought from a higher formation;

(4) the tactical questioning phase was to last for no more than twelve hours, and at the end of the fourteen hour period the prisoner should be released, handed to the police or moved to the TIF;

(5) *"Whilst the guarding and holding of internees is a J/G3 function **it forms an important part of the conditioning process which allows an internee to be susceptible to the approaches of the TQ**"* (emphasis added);

(6) *"Internees are not to be hooded during the TQ process, however the Geneva Convention allows for internees to be blindfolded when moving around a military sensitive area. Likewise internees are not to be held in stress positions. They are to be made to sit or stand depending on the environment or tactical situation."*.

14.145 Radbourne told the Inquiry that the phrase relating to the conditioning process was not his and was *"lifted"* from the draft divisional standard operating instruction 390.[177] There were a number of drafts of standard operating instruction 390 in circulation at that time but this phrase did not appear in the final version of standard operating instruction 390.

14.146 In respect of Annex C – *"Tactical Questioning Report"*, the material parts were these:

---

[175] Ibid.
[176] MOD031237-9
[177] Radbourne BMI 78/161/11-16; Radbourne BMI 78/162/21-163/15

> *"All TQs should be conducted using the neutral/logical approach. No other approach should be used".*
>
> *"NO STRESS POSITIONS, CONDITIONING, PHYSICAL ABUSE, HOODS, OR WHITE NOISE TO BE USED. However, in order to preserve the shock of capture, where possible, detainees are to be kept apart and prevented from communicating with each other. Blindfolds are ONLY to be used when detainee is passing through sensitive areas and must be removed afterwards".*
>
> ...
>
> *"A TQ is exactly what it says. It is a tactical assessment of an individual and should last no longer that [sic] 1 hour. If all the information requested on this form cannot be obtained then leave the relevant spaces blank. No further interrogation is to be carried out."*[178]

14.147 In respect of Annex D – *"Prisoner Handling-A Battlegroup Guide"*, the most relevant part was that:

> *"Prisoners should be made to stand or sit but must not be placed in stress positions. However, they must not be allowed to relax or lie down to continue the shock of capture and conditioning process."*[179]

14.148 This final extract, which might all be interpreted as condoning sleep deprivation, was also, according to Radbourne, *"...a direct lift from the draft SOI..."* being produced by the Division. He frankly agreed that as drafted it looked like an instruction that detainees were not to be allowed to sleep. Unbidden, he went on to say that that would represent an illegal practice. He did not question it at the time, but he accepted, albeit with the qualification of hindsight, that he should have done so.[180] Only a little later in his oral evidence, Radbourne had to accept that in fact the line *"However, they must not be allowed to relax or lie down to continue the shock of capture and conditioning process"* did not appear to be taken from the standard operating instruction 390.[181]

14.149 When he was asked further questions about the sentence set out above, Radbourne's evidence became a little confused. He had previously told the Inquiry in his oral evidence that he thought conditioning included stress positions. It was suggested to Radbourne that this sentence indicated that he knew that at the time such processes were being employed. He denied this. He added that a passage in his document in capital letters stating *"NO STRESS POSITIONS, CONDITIONING, PHYSICAL ABUSE, HOODS, OR WHITE NOISE TO BE USED"* was not an indication that he had become aware such techniques were being and had been used at BG Main.[182]

14.150 It is said on Radbourne's behalf that he should not be criticised for any error or deficiency appearing in this document, and I take this to include the instructions that might appear to condone conditioning or sleep deprivation. He had put out what has been described as a *"feeler"*, or draft version of this report on 25 September 2003. It had been sent to Fenton and to the Battlegroup intelligence officers. It included the phrase which might be interpreted as referring to sleep deprivation, but he had received no feedback telling him to alter or correct this.[183]

---

[178] MOD031244
[179] MOD031246, paragraph 5
[180] Radbourne BMI 78/167/17-168/15
[181] Radbourne BMI 78/169/1-17
[182] Radbourne BMI 78/170/16-172/15
[183] Radbourne BMI 78/210/10-211/13; SUB000438-9, paragraph 655

14.151 Fenton accepted that this document, prepared by Radbourne, went out with his approval.[184] He said that he could not remember what he meant when approving the words that guarding and holding of internees was part of the conditioning process, which caused an internee to be susceptible to the approaches of the tactical questioner. He could not remember what the conditioning process was that he had in mind, other than that it was nothing untoward.[185]

14.152 Fenton accepted that the phrasing in this document referring to the guarding of detainees being "...*an important part of the conditioning process which allows an internee to be susceptible to the approaches of the TQ*" was unfortunate. He said that the process he was referring to would not have contained anything untoward, or the use of any illegal activity. Rather he thought it a reference to keeping detainees apart and maintaining their silence so as to prevent collusion or the concoction of a consistent story.[186] He also rejected the notion that a potential interpretation of the text "*They are to be made to sit or stand depending on the environment or tactical situation*", was that detainees should not be permitted to sleep.[187]

14.153 Robinson, in contrast to Fenton, agreed that the text in Annex D "*Prisoners should be made to stand or sit but must not be placed in stress positions. However, they must not be allowed to relax or lie down to continue the shock of capture and conditioning process*", on a plain and fair reading meant that detainees were not to be allowed to sleep.[188]

14.154 Robinson accepted that Radbourne, after compiling the document "*Prisoner Handling and Tactical Questioning Procedures (PHTQ)*"[189] had discussed it with him. But Robinson said that he "...*had no knowledge of prisoner handling or TQing so I was acting as more of a proof reader than anything else*"; and that it was checked by the legal officers at Brigade and Division level before it was disseminated.[190] Robinson told the SIB that he had also sought advice from the SO1 legal at Chicksands at this time and, although he could not remember the content of the advice, he would have passed it on to Radbourne.[191]

14.155 I regret that I find the explanations of Radbourne, Fenton and Robinson for certain parts of Radbourne's letter on prisoner handling and tactical questioning difficult to understand. I have already pointed to Radbourne's conflicting evidence on the reference in the letter to what would appear to be sleep deprivation and to conditioning. I do not believe he was deliberately trying to mislead the Inquiry. I think it more likely that he had difficulty drafting such an important document under the pressure of time and the tempo of events. But on any view it was in places an unfortunate and sloppy piece of drafting.

14.156 As for Fenton, as I have already indicated, I found him an impressive witness. In my view his fault was in not paying sufficient attention to the detail of Radbourne's letter. Had he read it through more carefully I believe he would have recognised the obvious difficulties in the passages which referred to conditioning.

---

[184] Fenton BMI 101/89/7-90/9
[185] Fenton BMI 101/91/7-92/11
[186] Fenton BMI 101/91/7-92/24
[187] Fenton BMI 101/94/17-95/10
[188] Robinson BMI 80/83/1-9
[189] MOD031235, 27 September 2003
[190] Robinson BMI04318-9, paragraph 47n
[191] Robinson MOD000939

14.157 As for Robinson, I have difficulty in accepting that he read the document acting simply as a proof reader. I found this explanation unconvincing, particularly in the light of the fact that he had approached the JSIO at Chicksands for expert advice, which he had fed into the document. I suspect that Robinson's evidence was an effort to distance himself from the document recognising that some of its content was, even after Baha Mousa's death, inappropriate.

Divisional Level

14.158 On 30 September 2003 Barnett issued "*HQ MND (SE) SOI 390 – Policy for Apprehending, Handling and Processing of Detainees and Internees*".[192] It was produced with references to the Geneva Conventions; MND(SE) ROE Profile – Annex F to MND(SE) Iraq MOU, July 03; HQ MND(SE) FRAGO 005 to MND (SE) OPO03/03; and the CPA Memo No 3 on Criminal Procedures, 18 June 03.

14.159 It also included a range of annexes from A to O. The most relevant annexes were: Annex B "*Guidance on Searching, Apprehension and Treatment of Detainees and Internees;*"[193] Annex G "*Instruction for the Handling and Tactical Questioning of Internees;*"[194] Annex M "*Chain of Command Responsibilities for the Handling of Detainees and Internees,*"[195] and Annex N "*Training Guidance on Evidence Gathering and Handling.*"[196]

14.160 The relevant passages from the main body of the standard operating instructions were as follows. Firstly, it replaced the policy as set out in FRAGO 005.[197] Secondly, in relation to the "Guarding and Holding of detainees/internees", it stated that "*Detained persons must be treated humanely and in accordance with International Law and National Standards, which for the UK is encapsulated in JSP 469 – Codes of Practice for Custody*". Key points stressed in this part of the standard operating instructions were that: minimum force levels of restraint were to be used, handcuffs were to be to the front of the body, and suspects should be handed over at the earliest opportunity to a nominated custody officer.[198]

14.161 Thirdly, it was further specified that "*Within 8 hours of apprehension or as soon as possible thereafter, the BGIRO or appropriate officer must categorise the apprehended individual(s) and provide direction for the onward processing...*",[199] and also "*Apprehended persons are to be transferred to the TIF within 14 hours of capture...*".[200]

---

[192] MOD023104
[193] MOD023112
[194] MOD023123
[195] MOD023130
[196] MOD023132
[197] MOD023104, paragraph 2
[198] MOD023105, paragraph 5
[199] MOD023107, paragraph 15
[200] MOD023107, paragraph 17

14.162 The most relevant passages from the annexes were as follows. In relation to Annex B "Guidance on Searching, Apprehension and Treatment of Detainees and Internees", under the heading "General Principles for Treatment of Individuals", a number of principles were set out. They Included: 5(a) *"Apprehended individuals are to be treated at all times fairly, humanely and with respect for his or her personal dignity"*; 5(c) *"Apprehended individuals are not to be kept in direct sunlight for long periods"*; 5(f) *"Physical and mental torture, corporal punishment, humiliating or degrading treatment, or the threat of such, is prohibited"*: and at 5(g) *"The use of hooding and stress positions are prohibited"*.[201]

14.163 Under the heading "Handover" the following appeared *"The apprehended person must be handed to the IZP or taken to the TIF (in accordance with their status) as soon as possible, and within the times laid down by HQ MND(SE) SOI 390"*.[202]

14.164 At Annex G *"Instruction for the Handling and Tactical Questioning of Internees"*, it was stated that this was only to be carried out by those trained in tactical questioning and interrogation by JSIO, and, additionally, only those who had either carried out tactical questioning operationally or taken part in practical resistance to interrogation training with 4(CAC) company within the past two years.[203]

14.165 Further, the interaction between medics and the tactical questioning process was specified in some detail within Annex G:

> *"TQ can not be undertaken without the internee first being examined by a suitably qualified Medic. This should be at the first <u>practical</u> opportunity and the following must occur:*
>
> *The MO is to sign a fit for detention and questioning form…*
>
> *If any detainee is found to be unfit for detention or questioning then they are to be removed to a safe place until such time as they are fit for questioning."*[204]

14.166 Rules for undertaking tactical questioning were set out. Permission to establish a tactical questioning operation had to be sought from a higher formation (minimum Brigade HQ):

> *"Under normal circumstances no more than two TQ sessions should be required to obtain initial intelligence/information. The second session is to allow confirmation and further exploitation.*
>
> *The period of detention for the <u>entire</u> TQ phase for each internee should last no longer than 12 hours…*
>
> *The internee should be treated in accordance with the Geneva Convention at all times and must not be subjected to any physical punishment."*[205]

---

[201] MOD023113
[202] MOD023113
[203] MOD023123
[204] MOD023123
[205] MOD023124

14.167 Further significant direction appeared in the section headed "*Guarding and Holding of Internees during Tactical Questioning*". There, it was stated that:

> "*Whilst the guarding and holding of internees is a J/G3 function it forms an important part of the conditioning process which allows an internee to be susceptible to the approaches of the TQ.*"[206]
>
> ...
>
> "*Internees are not to be hooded during the TQ process, however the Geneva Convention allows for internees to be blindfolded when in a militarily sensitive area. Such blindfolding should cease as soon as the reason for the blindfolding ceases to exist. No internee shall be held in a militarily sensitive area for the sole purpose of blindfolding. Likewise internees are not to be held in stress positions. They are to be made to sit or stand depending on the environment or tactical situation.*"[207]

---

[206] MOD023124
[207] MOD023125

Chapter 3: Commentary on this Part of the Report

14.168 What is revealed by the evidence in this Part of the Report can in my opinion be simply and shortly summarised. Firstly, it is obvious that until Baha Mousa's death it had not occurred to anyone at any level of the command structure that there was a gap in prisoner handling and tactical questioning policy. This does not explain, nor does it in any way excuse, the events which led to Baha Mousa's death and injuries to the other Detainees. However, it does provide a context within which the events of 14 to 16 September occurred.

14.169 Secondly, following Baha Mousa's death various documents were passed up the chain of command, with some information reaching Ministerial level. It is clear that a number of these documents did not contain a completely accurate account of what had happened in the TDF during 14 to 16 September. I have expressed above my conclusions in relation to them and individual responsibility for the documents. For the most part, from Brigade level upwards, those involved in generating the documents were dependent on information being fed to them by 1 QLR. The higher up the chain of command the more reliant were individuals on information fed to them.

14.170 So far as 1 QLR is concerned in respect of the information passed up to Brigade, I have found that in a number of instances it was incomplete. It is not surprising that a full account of what had happened in the TDF between 14 and 16 September was not provided. Most, if not all, of those intimately involved in what actually happened in the TDF were unwilling or at best extremely reluctant, to disclose what had happened. But I have set out above instances of inaccuracies which ought not to have occurred. However, I have also found that there was no attempt by officers of 1 QLR deliberately to mislead. It is nevertheless very unfortunate that a more complete picture could have been provided and was not.

14.171 Thirdly, following Baha Mousa's death it is clear that units at all levels realised that the gap in prisoner handling and tactical questioning policy had to be filled. The efforts which were made to provide policy and procedures were set in motion very quickly. As can be seen, what was produced was in some instances confused and inappropriate. I have found that in one instance this may have been due to a desire by the author, Peebles, to distance himself from his responsibility for what happened in the TDF (see paragraph 14.132). I have also found in another that the drafting was in places unfortunate and sloppy (Radbourne, paragraph 14.155). But I do not find these instances of confusion and inappropriateness lead to an inference that those involved had a greater knowledge of what happened in the TDF at the time rather than after the event.

14.172 Fourthly, the language of some of the Brigade email correspondence generated after Baha Mousa's death, which urgently inquired into the practices that where being applied at Battlegroup level, tended to suggest that there had been at least to some degree a recognition at Brigade level prior to the death that hooding was being used for more than merely security purposes.

14.173 Fifthly, there are instances where I am critical of witnesses who were involved in all the above processes. However, I do not think it would serve any useful purpose to repeat these criticisms in this commentary.

Part XV

Later Events within the MoD

Chapter 1: Introduction

15.1 In the previous Part of this Report, I have considered events in the weeks immediately after Baha Mousa's death, both in theatre and in reports to Ministers in London. In this Part of the report I turn to consider later developments, policy considerations and statements made by the MoD in the months after Baha Mousa's death.

15.2 As part of the Inquiry's investigation, I heard evidence relating to such matters as:

(1) the exchange of letters in late 2003 between the Chief of Joint Operations, Lt Gen Sir John Reith and both Maj Gen Graeme Lamb (Commander Multi National Division (South East) (MND(SE)) and Maj Gen Andrew Ridgway (Chief of Defence Intelligence) concerning the prohibition of hooding, the legitimate use of sight deprivation and a review of prisoner handling doctrine and training;

(2) statements, answers and assurances given by the MoD and Ministers in relation to hooding, tactical questioning and interrogation in particular when prisoner abuse allegations came to the fore in May 2004; and

(3) a review of the policy in relation to hooding that took place in the second half of 2004.

15.3 I considered it appropriate to include investigation of these issues primarily for three reasons.

15.4 Firstly, the Inquiry was concerned to establish whether statements and assurances made by the MoD (and the preparatory work that went into them) cast light on:

(1) the relevant events in 2003, in particular on the specific abuse of Baha Mousa and the other Detainees; and

(2) the extent to which, and the reasons why, hooding or other of the five techniques may have been used on Op Telic 1 and 2; and

(3) relevant aspects of tactical questioning and interrogation training.

Put shortly, in seeking to discover the truth about why Baha Mousa and the Detainees were treated as they were, it was appropriate to look at relevant statements made after the death.

15.5 Secondly, it was important to follow the chain of command upwards, including all the way to Ministerial level, to consider the extent to which there had been any sanctioning of the use of the five techniques during Op Telic 2. It would not have been appropriate to cut off that side of the Inquiry's investigations shortly after Baha Mousa's death when documents produced after the death may have been relevant to the earlier issues.

15.6   Thirdly, the MoD's own assessment of what had happened and what had gone wrong in the detention of Baha Mousa and the other Detainees was relevant to what recommendations I should make.

15.7   At the same time, I was conscious that the focus of the Inquiry should remain on the matters directly relevant to Baha Mousa's death and thus I sought to ensure that the investigation of statements and assurances made after the death remained proportionate to the aims of the Inquiry.

15.8   The Inquiry's approach was not criticised by the MoD, who provided documentary disclosure and submissions in relation to these aspects of the Inquiry's investigations. Indeed, in its closing submissions, in looking at the provision of information to Ministers, Parliamentarians and others, the MoD acknowledged that there were shortcomings in the information that had been provided, whilst urging that there was no evidence of any wilful intent to mislead:[1]

> **The Information provided to Ministers, Parliamentarians and Others**
>
> 2.   The primary feature of the evidence in this area is that the information provided to Ministers, Parliamentarians and others in relation to hooding, interrogation and the treatment of Baha Mousa and his fellow detainees was in some respects incomplete, misleading or inaccurate. This has properly been acknowledged by those witnesses concerned, but there is no evidence that there was any wilful intent to mislead on the part of those involved and the MOD is strongly of the view that there was no such intent.

15.9   Since this Inquiry was established by the Secretary of State for Defence (the relevant Minister under the Inquiries Act 2005), I pay significant regard to the fact that the MoD took no issue with the breadth of the Inquiry's investigations into statements and assurances made after Baha Mousa's death.

15.10   In contrast to the approach of the MoD, the Treasury Solicitor representing many of the officers and civil servants involved in the Inquiry has questioned the extent to which statements and assurances made after Baha Mousa's death are within my terms of reference. It is suggested that since no post-death assurances and statements materially affected the treatment of the Detainees, the nature of the information circulating within Government and the briefings given to Ministers and others "… are not central to the Inquiry's terms of reference".[2] In relation to assurances "given long after Baha Mousa's death", the Treasury Solicitor goes further and suggests that these fall squarely outside the Inquiry's terms of reference and moreover that it is not within the Inquiry's remit to "…investigate Parliamentary processes".[3] The Treasury Solicitor refers to and relies upon other channels for investigating whether Parliament has been misled, while urging that any such suggestion of misleading statements was not in any event borne out by the evidence.

15.11   To the extent that the Treasury Solicitor's submissions sought to dissuade me from making findings or comments upon post-death statements about Baha Mousa, the treatment of the Detainees, hooding and the five techniques, and tactical questioning and interrogation, I have no hesitation in rejecting that submission.

---

[1] SUB001121
[2] SUB001447, paragraph 463
[3] SUB001448, paragraph 465

15.12 As I have already indicated, these submissions found no support from the MoD, whose Secretary of State commissioned this Inquiry and set the terms of reference. More importantly, for each of the reasons set out in paragraphs 15.4 to 15.6 above, I am satisfied that these issues were plainly within my terms of reference. The Inquiry considered in some detail the statements and assurances made after Baha Mousa's death. Having done so, if those statements reveal no information that further explains his death and the abuse of the other Detainees, yet can be seen to have been misleading or incomplete, it would be surprising if a Statutory Inquiry was prohibited from commenting on such statements. I do not consider that this is the effect of the Inquiries Act 2005. Section 24(1) of the 2005 Act (referred to below as the 2005 Act) includes the discretion to include within my Report:

> *"...anything else that the panel considers to be relevant to the terms of reference (including any recommendations the panel sees fit to make despite not being required to do so by the terms of reference)."*

I find that this discretion clearly extends to commenting upon relevant post-death statements and assurances that addressed either the treatment of Baha Mousa and the other Detainees, hooding and other conditioning techniques, and tactical questioning and interrogation. This is so even though such post-death statements plainly were not causative of the death and may not directly explain the death or the treatment of the other Detainees.

15.13 There is one exception. By Article 9 of the Bill of Rights 1689, "*...freedom of speech and debates or proceedings in Parliament ought not to be impeached or questioned in any court or place out of Parliament*". I accept that as regards statements made in, and answers given to, Parliament by the MoD Ministers, it would be for Parliament and not for this Inquiry to make findings about the propriety and honesty of those statements. However, I do not consider that Article 9 prevents this Inquiry from considering briefing materials and draft answers provided to MoD Ministers. Nor does Article 9 prevent the Inquiry from recording what was said in Parliament, for example about hooding, and referring to the facts as established by this Inquiry as to what had actually occurred. That is so even if the effect of comparing the two is to demonstrate the objective inaccuracy of what was said in Parliament.

15.14 I have referred extensively in this Report to Special Investigation Branch (SIB) statements and evidence given at the Court Martial. I have also referred in the previous Part of this Report to the emails and documents, many of them specifically referring to Baha Mousa, that emerged in the first days and weeks after the death in September 2003. With the exception of those documents, I have formed the view that for the most part the later documents do not in fact cast significant light on the events that led up to Baha Mousa's death and the abuse of the other Detainees. In a number of instances, this is because the explanations given in relation to hooding, tactical questioning and interrogation were not as full or accurate as they should have been. In these circumstances, while I reject the suggestion by the Treasury Solicitor that many of the matters to which I shall refer in this Part of the Report are outside the terms of reference, I do not propose to examine every example of statements and assurances made after the death. I instead refer to the key developments in the chronology and take some illustrative examples of the statements and assurances that were given.

Chapter 2: The Chief of Joint Operations Orders the Cessation of Hooding and Urges a Review of Training and Doctrine

15.15   By October 2003, hooding ought already to have ceased in theatre by virtue of the legal advice given by Lt Col Charles Barnett, and the Divisional order Standard Operating Instruction 390.   However, a higher level prohibition on hooding was nevertheless issued by Reith, the Chief of Joint Operations.

15.16   In the latter half of October 2003, Reith wrote to both the Chief of Defence Intelligence, Ridgway, and to Lamb the GOC of MND(SE).   The letters were drafted with input from both Col Ewan Duncan and Rachel Quick OBE.[4]

15.17   The letters had passages in common but I set them both out in full.[5]

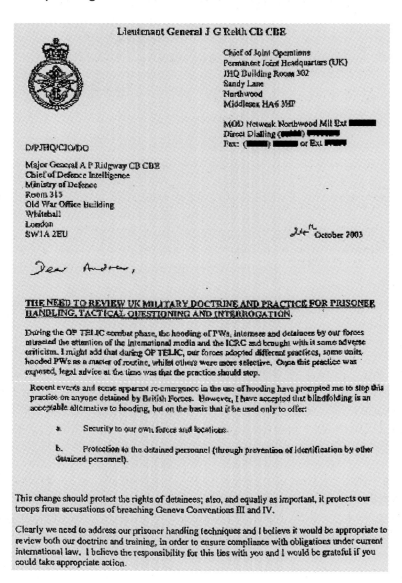

Lieutenant General J G Reith CB CBE

Chief of Joint Operations
Permanent Joint Headquarters (UK)
JHQ Building Room 302
Sandy Lane
Northwood
Middlesex HA6 3HP

MOD Network Northwood Mil Ext ■■■■
Direct Dialling (■■■■) ■■■■■■
Fax: (■■■■) ■■■■ or Ext ■■■■

D/PJHQ/CJO/DO

Major General A P Ridgway CB CBE
Chief of Defence Intelligence
Ministry of Defence
Room 315
Old War Office Building
Whitehall
London
SW1A 2EU

24th October 2003

Dear Andrew,

THE NEED TO REVIEW UK MILITARY DOCTRINE AND PRACTICE FOR PRISONER HANDLING, TACTICAL QUESTIONING AND INTERROGATION.

During the OP TELIC combat phase, the hooding of PWs, internees and detainees by our forces attracted the attention of the international media and the ICRC and brought with it some adverse criticism. I might add that during OP TELIC, our forces adopted different practices, some units hooded PWs as a matter of routine, whilst others were more selective. Once this practice was exposed, legal advice at the time was that the practice should stop.

Recent events and some apparent re-emergence in the use of hooding have prompted me to stop this practice on anyone detained by British Forces. However, I have accepted that blindfolding is an acceptable alternative to hooding, but on the basis that it be used only to offer:

    a.   Security to our own forces and locations.

    b.   Protection to the detained personnel (through prevention of identification by other detained personnel).

This change should protect the rights of detainees; also, and equally as important, it protects our troops from accusations of breaching Geneva Conventions III and IV.

Clearly we need to address our prisoner handling techniques and I believe it would be appropriate to review both our doctrine and training, in order to ensure compliance with obligations under current international law. I believe the responsibility for this lies with you and I would be grateful if you could take appropriate action.

---

[4] MOD053247
[5] MOD022203; MOD020274

Lieutenant General J G Reith CB CBE

Chief of Joint Operations
Permanent Joint Headquarters (UK)
JHQ Building Room 302
Sandy Lane
Northwood
Middlesex HA6 3HP

MOD Network Northwood Mil Ext ▆▆▆▆
Direct Dialling ▆▆▆▆
Fax: ▆▆▆▆ or Ext ▆▆▆

D/PJHQ/CJO/DO

Major General G C M Lamb CMG OBE
Commander MND(SE)
Basra
British Forces Post Office 641   October 2003

CESSATION OF 'HOODING' OF PWs, DETAINEES, AND INTERNEES.

During the OP TELIC combat phase, the hooding of PWs, internees and detainees by UK military attracted the attention of the international media and the ICRC. The adverse comments prompted an examination of long standing standard practices by UK forces in prisoner handling. Subsequently legal advice was for the practice of hooding to stop. Recent events have again focussed attention on the standards and practices employed by our forces when apprehending Iraqi civilians and I believe further clarification is now required.

Following the death in custody of an Iraqi on 15 September 2003, it appears hooding may be a re-emerging procedure. This is to stop and you are to direct all under your command to immediately cease the hooding of persons detained.

Notwithstanding this direction, I am advised that blindfolding is an acceptable alternative and accept this advice on the basis that is used only to offer:

    a.   security to our own forces and locations.

    b.   protection to the detained personnel (through prevention of identification by other detainees).

Thus, you should instruct those under your command that they may blindfold detained personnel in

medical personnel should regularly assess the physical condition of the blindfolded detained personnel. You will understand that this change in practice not only protects the rights of those detained, but also UK forces, who might be accused of breaching Geneva Conventions III and IV.

In light of our experiences during OP TELIC, I feel we need to examine our doctrine and review the training of our forces with regard to PW and detainee handling. The responsibility for both lies with CDI and I have written to him explaining the current situation and asking that he reviews them. I enclose a copy of my letter.

Reith's Letter to Maj Gen Lamb Prohibiting the Use of Hooding

15.18   Maj Gen Lamb told the Inquiry that the letter from Reith would have been discussed with him before it was sent. Maj Gen Lamb emphasised that by October 2003, Standard Operating Instruction 390 had already been issued in theatre and sent to Permanent Joint Headquarters (PJHQ).[6] Thus hooding was already prohibited in theatre by 3 (UK) Div when Reith's letter was sent to him.

15.19   Vivien Rose, one of the senior MoD legal advisers, was involved in providing the legal advice that informed Reith's October 2003 letters. The legal advice stopped short of suggesting that hooding was in all circumstances inappropriate. In her Inquiry witness statement, Rose described the advice in the following terms:[7]

---

[6] Lamb BMI04922, paragraph 39
[7] Rose BMI08042, paragraphs 75-77

75. My and MODLA legal advice, which to the best of my recollection was provided around this time, was that the use of hooding for interrogation purposes would always be unlawful, because it would be contrary to GCIII art 17, but in circumstances which were not concerned with interrogating the prisoner, it was not a breach of the Geneva Conventions to obscure a prisoner's vision temporarily while they were being transported, or in order to prevent that person seeing something sensitive. It might, for instance, be necessary to stop them seeing the identity of a fellow Iraqi in a prison compound where it would otherwise be apparent that that individual was collaborating with UK forces in some way.

76. Our advice was that, where possible, blacked out goggles should be supplied to soldiers for this purpose. I also advised that if a situation arose where it was considered very important to obscure a person's vision and there was no better means, such as goggles or a blindfold, available, it was generally permissible to achieve this by placing a hood over the prisoner's head, although care would have to be taken of the prisoner when hooded, for example to ensure that he had no difficulties breathing because of the hood.

77. My understanding was that the "hoods" used were empty sandbags that were not pulled in or closed in any way below the chin and as such did not make it difficult to breath, provided the prisoner was calm. In all cases I advised that in assessing whether to use a hood in any particular instance it was important to weigh up the degree of discomfort caused to the prisoner against the imperative that they should not be able to see whatever it was that gave rise to the need to blindfold.

15.20 Rose expanded on this explanation in her oral evidence:

"A.   ... it was important to balance the level of discomfort that was being caused to the prisoner against the imperative security needs. My understanding of what hooding involved was that, although it would be uncomfortable to have a hood placed over your head, it didn't restrict the breathing and, therefore, where there was a good reason for it and the prisoner didn't appear to be distressed by it, that that would not cross the line into being unlawful – inhumane or unlawful.

Q.   Did you give any regard to whether there should be, as it were, conditions put upon hooding? You have told us about the prisoner not being distressed.

A.   Yes.

Q.   That would be one factor which would have to be taken into account, do you say?

A.   Yes.

Q.   If he were, it would not be humane to hood him?

A. That's right, because the discomfort would not — the discomfort would outweigh the security needs.

Q. You also took the view that it would be necessary to ensure that the prisoner had no difficulty breathing —

A. Yes.

Q. — with the hood on the head?

A. Yes.

Q. Did you give any consideration, for example, to the length of time over which the hood might be used in this way and remain humane?

A. My understanding was that we were talking about very temporary hooding, while they passed by something on the back of a van or while somebody was being brought through the compound or something like that.

Q. So "very temporary" in your terms —

A. Yes.

Q. — means a matter of a minute or so or minutes, doesn't it?

A. Yes.

Q. We are not talking about hours or days?

A. Yes.

Q. You would regard hours as being inhumane, would you?

A. Well, I would not — I would have thought that there would always be a different way of achieving the goal if what one was talking about was hours, yes.

Q. But your advice was, as you say in paragraph 76 — forgive me, I did not mean to cut over you — your advice, as I understand it, was that it would be generally permissible to achieve this with a hood, all other methods being unavailable?

A. Yes.

Q. That in itself and the circumstances in which a hood may be employed — the conditions that might need to be clearly understood and placed upon the employment of a hood or hoods — would you agree was something that needed to be ironed out so that clear direction was given to those who had to apply it?

A. Yes. My job was to give the advice as to when it was acceptable to hood and there were other people whose job it was to ensure that that was promulgated down to the troops who needed to know it.

Q. You don't say in the statement that you did give any advice on the time, for example, over which it might be appropriate to use a hood, did you?

A. No, but the scenarios that we were considering that were being put to me were the kinds of things that I have mentioned."[8]

15.21 Thus it seems from Rose's evidence that the legal advice in the wake of Baha Mousa's death remained that hooding as an aid to interrogation would always be unlawful, but that hooding for security purposes might be lawful where sight deprivation by other means was not possible, provided appropriate precautions were taken.

---

[8] Rose BMI 93/109/1-111/14

15.22   Martin Hemming was Rose's immediate superior and the MoD legal adviser. He told the Inquiry that Rose may well have spoken to him at this stage, and whether she did or not, he would certainly have agreed with the advice that is recorded as having been given by Rose.[9] Hemming could not recall discussions directly with the Secretary of State about hooding but he did not dispute that, if asked, he would have said that it could be lawful to hood for security purposes provided that the treatment did not cross into being inhumane. Hemming's evidence suggested that he could see circumstances in which hooding could quickly become inhumane but it was not axiomatically so.[10]

15.23   As is apparent from Reith's letter to Maj Gen Lamb, Reith's decision was to go further than the legal advice strictly required and entirely prohibit the use of hoods on those detained by British Forces in Iraq. Reith told the Inquiry that he decided to order the prohibition of all hooding as it had become particularly emotive in light of Baha Mousa's death. He also said that, given the change in the nature of operations, the security reasons for hooding prisoners had for the most part fallen away and sight deprivation for security reasons could be achieved by blindfolding.[11] His evidence therefore suggested that the two main factors he had in mind were the adverse publicity generated by hooding, and the fact that security sight deprivation could be achieved by different means, namely blindfolding or blacked out goggles. Reith's understanding was that hooding for security reasons was still legal but that he personally decided that sight deprivation could be achieved in a better way.[12]

15.24   Reith was not aware of the Heath Statement or the 1972 Directive until his preparations for giving evidence to this Inquiry.[13] Reith's said that he was also not aware of the order given by Maj Gen Robin Brims.[14] It may well be that Reith was mistaken in this latter recollection. Brims said that when he heard that Baha Mousa and the Op Salerno Detainees had been hooded, he remembered his own prohibition on hooding and informed Reith of this. He said that Reith subsequently wrote the letters to Ridgway and Maj Gen Lamb. Brims was by this time his Deputy Chief of Joint Operations at PJHQ.[15]

15.25   In oral evidence Reith made it clear that in respect of the contents of his letters he had relied on information given to him by others. This was so in respect of his references to hooding being a long standing practice, legal advice in theatre that hooding should cease, and that hooding had re-emerged after its prohibition.[16] I note, without personal criticism of Reith, that the comment in his letter that legal advice had been that hooding should stop was not entirely accurate; the National Contingent Command (NCC) Headquarters legal advice had been that hooding for the minimum period necessary for security purposes was lawful.

15.26   It is not impossible that the prohibition on hooding referred to in Reith's letter to Maj Gen Lamb was approved at a higher level than the Chief of Joint Operations. The Secretary of State, the Rt. Hon. Geoffrey Hoon MP, told the Inquiry that he could not

[9] Hemming BMI08479, paragraph 44
[10] Hemming BMI 103/136/21-138/17
[11] Reith BMI08257, paragraph 37
[12] Reith BMI 94/121/11-122/13
[13] Reith BMI 94/89/9-91/9
[14] Reith BMI 94/98/22-99/4
[15] Brims BMI07404, paragraph 77
[16] Reith BMI 94/120/2-121/2; Reith BMI 94/13124-132/21

remember the detail of meetings that led up to the Chief of Joint Operation's order. But Hoon's evidence was that he did recall numerous discussions on the legality of hooding with Reith, the Chief of the General Staff, the Permanent Secretary Kevin Tebbit, and Hemming (the MoD legal adviser).[17] Richard Johnson, at the time the head of the Iraq team in J9 POLOPS at PJHQ, thought that the Chief of Joint Operation's ban was the subject of a Ministerial submission.[18] The submission to the Rt. Hon. Adam Ingram MP, Minister of State for Defence, of 26 September 2003 had referred to PJHQ working on additional guidance and direction that would be provided to theatre in the very near future.[19] However, there does not appear to have been a Ministerial submission directly relating to Reith's October 2003 ban on hooding. Ingram himself could not remember being involved in discussions about hooding around October 2003.[20] I think it more likely than not that the 26 September 2003 submission to Ministers had trailed the fact that consideration was being given to further guidance, but that the Chief of Joint Operation's hooding prohibition in October 2003 was not the subject of a specific further Ministerial submission.

15.27   Whether or not that is so, Reith's direction did not successfully put an end to all use of hooding, even in Iraq. As became apparent when prisoner abuse allegations came to the fore in the Spring of 2004, Reith's direction had not been communicated down to Special Forces on the ground. Special Forces continued to use hoods until May 2004,[21] although I accept that Reith was not aware of this:

> "Q.   Can I just ask you this … the special forces in Iraq, were they part of your chain of command responsibility or were they responsible to somebody else?
>
> A.   Sorry, which forces?
>
> Q.   The special forces in Iraq.
>
> A.   The special forces I had a link to, but they were technically controlled by the Ministry of Defence through the deputy chief of defence staff commitments.
>
> Q.   Were you aware at any time that the cessation order that you had given in October 2003 was not, in fact, something that was complied with by UK special forces until May the next year, 2004?
>
> A.   I was not aware of that.
>
> Q.   Did you become aware of that at some stage?
>
> A.   No, I didn't."[22]

---

[17] Hoon BMI08529, paragraph 24

[18] Richard Johnson BMI06080, paragraph 26

[19] MOD054823. I have addressed this submission in Part XIV of this Report. Although the submission had not been disclosed at the time, Richard Johnson thought this was the submission that he had in mind: BMI 92/155/4-156/14

[20] Ingram BMI08379, paragraph 24

[21] MOD053825; MOD020209; MOD054189

[22] Reith BMI 94/146/6-21

Ridgway's Response to Reith's Letter

15.28 Ridgway responded to Reith's letter of 24 October 2003 on 27 November 2003 in the following terms:[23]

Lieutenant General Sir J G Reith KCB CBE
Chief of Joint Operations
Permanent Joint Headquarters
Northwood
Middlesex
HA6 3HP

27 November 2003

THE NEED TO REVIEW UK MILITARY DOCTRINE AND PRACTICE FOR PRISONER HANDLING, TACTICAL QUESTIONING AND INTERROGATION

Reference:

A.   JWP 1-10 March 2001 Edition.

1. Thank you for your letter[1], in which you highlight your concerns regarding the media impact surrounding poor Prisoner Handling (PH) procedures. I share your concerns and if we are to avoid further adverse allegations against UK Forces in Iraq and other Theatres there is an urgent need to address the situation. Responsibilities in this area are complex. Interrogation and Tactical Questioning (TQ) policy and training are my responsibility. Development of PH Policy on the other hand is the responsibility of DCDS(C)[2]. Management of the Prisoner of War Handling Organisation in Theatre is a J1 (Provost) responsibility, supported by J3 and J4, and therefore appropriately lies with DCDS(Pers).

---

[1]   D/PJHQ/CJO/DO dated 24 Oct 03.
[2]   Prisoner Handling, Survival Evasion Resistance Escape, Combat Recovery and Joint Personnel Recovery Policy was a function of DJW and, following MOD restructuring, now resides within D Strategic Support.

---

23 MOD030341-2

2. The practice of hooding detainees is not, and never has been, taught on any of the TQ or interrogation courses run at Chicksands[3]. It does, however, seem to be an adopted practice by the US, and some UK forces in Theatre may have followed suit. As you point out blindfolding is permitted under the Geneva Convention (GC) for force protection and OPSEC purposes and is accepted under the Law of Armed Conflict (LOAC). I do, however, agree that there is need for better instruction to emphasise the negative IO effects of this activity and that the use of blindfolds should be the exception rather than the rule. My research suggests that, within Joint Forward Interrogation Teams (JFITs), hooding was used to protect interrogators from recognition by terrorist suspects but this practice ceased early during OP TELIC, following medical advice. Darkened sunglasses are now used instead.

b. Whilst the tightening up of both interrogation and TQ training at Chicksands and the procedures within JFITs will have some effect, the majority of alleged incidents seem to have occurred during the arrest and detention of detainees, before they reached the JFIT and entered the formal questioning process. This suggests that arresting units, in the PH role, are not clear on the procedures for the treatment of PW and detainees. To improve this situation the following action is required:

- Reference A requires revision to include clear guidelines on PH procedures for capturing units. - D Strat Support.

- The content and frequency of unit LOAC training should be reviewed. - DGT & E

- Better education of units and individuals prior to operational deployments is needed. - Front Line Commands, following PJHQ direction.

- Departmental responsibilities for the PWHO and PH policy and training need to be reviewed. - DCDS(C).

4. In the meantime, I will ensure that instruction at Chicksands is updated to provide clearer guidance for specialist TQ and Interrogators.

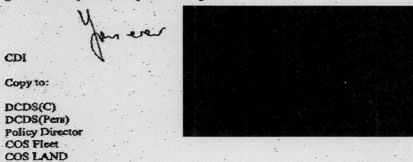

CDI

Copy to:

DCDS(C)
DCDS(Pers)
Policy Director
COS Fleet
COS LAND
COS STC

15.29 Reith stated that he was not aware of the steps which Ridgway took subsequent to his letter of 24 October 2003 and that it was not for him to ensure that Ridgway completed the tasks which he had set. He pointed out that Ridgway's response was copied to the Deputy Chief of the Defence Staff (Commitments) who had responsibility for prisoner handling and that he would have expected the Deputy Chief of the Defence Staff (Commitments) to take forward the request for a review of prisoner handling.[24] Reith did say, however, that he would have discussed the matter with the Deputy Chief of the Defence Staff (Commitments) as he had originally put all the actions for Ridgway in his letter of 24 October 2003, but had then been informed by Ridgway that these were not Ridgway's responsibilities. Reith pointed to the fact that Ridgway's response was copied to those whom Ridgway thought needed to take action. Reith made it clear that it was not his responsibility to take forward training and doctrine matters that were not part of operations, and these had gone for action to the MoD, his superior headquarters.[25]

---

[24] Reith BMI08260, paragraphs 46-47
[25] Reith BMI 94/137/1-139/2; Reith BMI 94/151/10-152/19

15.30 Unsurprisingly, Ridgway's evidence was that on receiving Reith's letter of 24 October 2003, he asked his staff to research the matters Reith had raised. Ridgway said that his response of 27 November 2003 would have reflected the research that had been done. This had included research by staff at the Defence Intelligence and Security Centre (DISC) in response to a request from Ridgway's staff at the DIS (Defence Intelligence Staff).[26]

15.31 Ridgway said that the research that had been undertaken had revealed a degree of confusion about when sight deprivation and hooding could be carried out:

> "Q. You say in paragraph 46...of your statement that as part of this exercise it became clear to you that people were confused as to when sight deprivation and the use of hoods could be employed; is that right?
>
> A. Yes, I think that was certainly true.
>
> Q. How had that message come through to you?
>
> A. I think the research we did into "How is this happening?", one of the potential causes was that – the ability to discriminate between an operational security matter and another matter, another circumstance, was quite difficult, and people perhaps were getting that wrong. But there were a range of other possibilities we found as well, and I think I have mentioned elsewhere that it could be that proximity to other allied forces or crucially whether the training of our tactical questioners was inadequate or flawed in some way. We looked at all of these possibilities and the letter was intended to try and rectify each of these possible causes, contributory causes, to the fact that soldiers were doing things inappropriately in the field."[27]

15.32 As can be seen above, Ridgway's response to Reith had included the comment that "*The practice of hooding detainees is not, and never has been, taught on any of the TQ or interrogation courses run at Chicksands.*"[28] This response echoed information at the time that hooding had not been included in the curriculum for interrogation on Prisoner Handling and Tactical Questioning (PH&TQ) courses.[29] Whilst I have no doubt that Ridgway was in good faith relying on what his staff had been told in their research, I do not accept that this was a fully accurate statement of affairs. In addition to some directly contradictory documents, I have found that the reality was that the teaching on the means to achieve sight deprivation varied from instructor to instructor and that some would have taught that hooding for security purposes was acceptable. In addition, I have found that the courses taught the practice of walking round a blindfolded prisoner to increase the pressure on the prisoner, this practice being contrary to the 1972 Directive. These findings and the detailed evidence supporting them are set out in Part VI of this Report.

15.33 Ridgway's response to Reith also stated that that the practice of hooding at the Joint Field Interrogation Team (JFIT) had ceased following medical advice. Again, I do not blame Ridgway for this. He was plainly relying on what others had told him. However, medical advice was not the reason for hooding being stopped at the JFIT in early April 2003. Here again, inaccuracies had crept in.

15.34 Ridgway's response assured Reith that instruction at Chicksands would be updated to provide clearer guidance for specialist tactical questioners and interrogators.

---

[26] Ridgway BMI08214-5, paragraphs 44-47
[27] Ridgway BMI 100/109/3-23
[28] MOD030342
[29] MOD053857

Ridgway saw the request as being one relating to hooding in the context of tactical questioning and interrogation, and not a request for a wholesale review of training in those areas.[30] Ridgway said that a review was undertaken and the conclusion was that "*...no amendment to the JSIO course was necessary since none of the doctrine and training referred to hooding, but that the ban on hooding needed to be emphasised.*"[31] Ridgway referred in this context to a later email, dated 16 January 2004, which he said showed that the review was indeed carried out:[32]

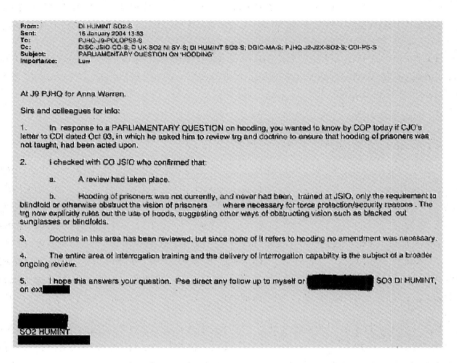

15.35 I accept that as a result of this review, the prohibition on the use of hoods became more clearly emphasised on the tactical questioning and interrogation courses. This was referred to in a later brief for the Secretary of State's attendance before the Intelligence and Security Committee.[33] It is nevertheless of concern that, despite Ridgway rightly calling for this review and for the tightening up of tactical questioning and interrogation training, matters such as the use of blindfolds to increase the pressure on prisoners were not recognised and stopped immediately. The reference in the email shown above to "*Doctrine in this area has been reviewed, but since none of it refers to hooding, no amendment was necessary*", reflects a wholly misplaced confidence in the adequacy of tactical questioning and interrogation doctrine at the time.

15.36 The MoD's Deputy Chief of the Defence Staff (Commitments) at the time was Lt Gen Sir Robert Fry; the post was more commonly known as the Director of Operations. It was to him that Ridgway had suggested that there needed to be a review of departmental responsibilities for the Prisoner of War Handling Organisation, and prisoner handling policy and training. Reith remembered speaking to Fry following Ridgway's response.

---

[30] Ridgway BMI 100/107/15-21
[31] Ridgway BMI08215, paragraph 47
[32] MOD043941
[33] S045 BMI07305, paragraph 44; MOD052685

15.37 Fry was hampered when giving evidence to the Inquiry by not being able to remember exactly what he did in reaction to Ridgway's letter to Reith. He commented that Ridgway's assessment of where responsibilities lay for responding to Reith's request was only Ridgway's opinion, although Fry accepted that the responsibility for prisoner handling policy (at the high level) rested with him. In respect of how the review would have been taken forward, Fry told the Inquiry that:

> "What I would have expected to have happened after that is that a collegiate response would have been developed between myself, the CDI of the day – General Ridgway – the CJO, General Reith, the policy director and also the DCDS personnel, who is also cited in that letter. So unless all of those individuals agreed on a consensual way forward and undertook to fulfil their parts of it, the idea that somehow a single course of action under a single individual was the way in which this would be addressed is, I think, false."[34]

Fry was asked about the potential complexity of the division of responsibilities for prisoner handling:

> "Q. Did it strike you as problematic that there were so many different strands involved with so many different individuals having responsibility without one department or person exercising overall control and responsibility?
>
> A. Well, it strikes me as habitual rather than problematic. It certainly was problematic, but it is not exceptional in circumstances as complex as this for different individuals to be responsible for different areas.
>
> Q. Indeed, at the PJHQ level also, as you set out in your statement, prisoner handling was split between a number of the J branches. You would say again that that was habitual and, while problematic, was a common occurrence?
>
> A. Yes, I think that some things defy easy categorisation. Now the policy for prisoner handling would have been a J1 function, but the actual handling of prisoners on the battlefield would have been a J3 function. That may sound awkward, but to military practitioners it is a well-understood division of responsibility.
>
> Q. But may it be that that division of responsibilities was in part a factor in the speed with which issues which were said to be urgent by General Ridgway were dealt with after Baha Mousa's death?
>
> A. Yes, I think it probably is."[35]

15.38 I shall set out my conclusions in relation to these exchanges at the end of this Part of the Report.

---

[34] Fry BMI 100/21/7-17
[35] Fry BMI 100/38/17-19/15

Chapter 3: Relevant Aspects of the MoD's Response to Prisoner Abuse Allegations from May 2004 Onwards

The context in which the MoD Statements and Assurances on Hooding and Tactical Interrogation Arose in May 2004

15.39 In April and early May 2004, a number of revelations dramatically brought allegations of prisoner abuse, and the practice of hooding, to the forefront of media and political attention. These included the publication of the photographs of abuse by US service personnel at Abu Ghraib; the leaking of the International Committee of the Red Cross's (ICRC) February 2004 report; and particularly in the UK media, the faked photographs of prisoner abuse published by the *Daily Mirror* (see Part III, Chapter 3).

15.40 It is right to recognise the challenging context of the events that followed. I certainly accept that it was difficult for officials who were involved to build up a comprehensive picture as to what had occurred in Iraq, particularly in relation to the policy and practice of hooding. Officials at PJHQ were undoubtedly working under very considerable time pressures with a clamour for information arising from both Parliamentary questions and debates and intense media interest; and at the same time still having to contribute to work on ongoing military operations. The pressures of time were such that checks which might otherwise have been carried out on the accuracy of information were not always practicable in the time limits set for responses.[36]

15.41 In respect of the accuracy of briefings and statements, there were some constraints on what could be said about the particular circumstances of Baha Mousa's death because of a risk of prejudicing the investigation and ultimately any prosecution that took place. However, this should not have prevented an appropriate degree of caution being used when more general statements were being made about policy and practice in Iraq so as to ensure that the statements were not misleading, taking into account what was known about the treatment of the Op Salerno Detainees.

15.42 More relevant was the fact that some officials dealing with the issues at the time were unaware of the background relating to Baha Mousa's case. That does not reflect critically on them personally. But it does suggest that the full significance of the abuse of Baha Mousa and the other Detainees, and particularly the use by 1 QLR of conditioning techniques, had not sufficiently been understood or communicated within PJHQ by this time. It is right to remember that the Court Martial had not yet taken place; still less had the full picture of Baha Mousa's abuse yet emerged. Nevertheless, as I have explored in Part XIV of this Report, significant information about the incident had been reported both at theatre level and to PJHQ and Ministers in the days and weeks shortly after Baha Mousa's death.

---

[36] Kistruck BMI 93/11/5-10

Examples of the Flow of Information in May 2004

15.43 On 10 May 2004, the Secretary of State made a statement to the House of Commons updating Parliament on the abuse allegations. The Secretary of State's statement included that:

> "The second concern raised by the ICRC in relation to the United Kingdom was in respect of the routine hooding of prisoners. That practice had already ceased in UK facilities from last September, and that change had been confirmed publicly."[37]

Questions asked of Hoon, included questions in relation to the use of hoods by British Forces, with reference to the Heath Statement in 1972.[38] Material for this statement had been provided in a submission the previous day.[39]

15.44 Following the Secretary of State's statement to the House on 10 May 2004, his Assistant Private Secretary immediately followed up with a request to both the Chief of Joint Operations and the Chief of Defence Intelligence for urgent information about hooding as an interrogation technique. The Secretary of State wanted to know what policy was in place at the start of Op Telic; when the policy was changed; what new instructions were issued; and what was the current policy. He also wanted to know what the current training policy was on the use of hooding as an interrogation technique. A response was required urgently by the following day.[40]

15.45 Hoon told the Inquiry that it was extremely unusual for a request of this nature to be made directly after giving a statement in the House of Commons. Hoon's evidence was that the request was made because he was not wholly persuaded that he had been fully and properly briefed on the complete picture in relation to hooding. He was also very concerned that the same issues in relation to hooding, the death of Baha Mousa, training and interrogation kept arising. Hoon wanted a single document which set out a comprehensive and accurate statement about the use of hooding.[41]

15.46 On current interrogation training, the Chief of Defence Intelligence's office sought to assure the Secretary of State on 11 May 2004 that the DISC courses explicitly taught that "…the use of hooding is unacceptable as an interrogation technique and potentially harmful to the health of the detainee".[42] The covering minute explained that hoods were used in the resistance to interrogation training of prone to capture personnel and gave reassurance about the guidance for such training.[43]

15.47 Quite a number of those who had been involved in Op Telic 1 and 2 provided information in respect of the Secretary of State's other request for information.

15.48 This was plainly a difficult period with information, often of necessity incomplete, but also in places contradictory, coming in from various sources. At the same time, there were increasing demands for more information both from Parliamentarians and internally within the MoD. Thus, for example, the Rt. Hon. Lord Lester QC was

---

[37] PLT000862
[38] PLT000861
[39] MOD054169
[40] MOD054028
[41] Hoon BMI08532, paragraph 36
[42] MOD052596
[43] MOD052595

to ask a number of questions about the use of hooding;[44] the Chief of the Defence Staff, Lord Walker, raised a series of questions for urgent answer;[45] and the Assistant Chief of the General Staff was pressing for further information, commenting that the Army chain of command appeared unsighted on some matters.[46] Ministers themselves raised queries on the detail as they prepared to answer further questions in Parliament.[47]

15.49 It is not necessary to set out the totality of the information that was provided in the following days. The references set out below, which I stress are only illustrative examples of the information flow at the time, show the slightly confused and sometimes contradictory picture that was communicated.

(1) Had hooding stopped and if so, when?

15.50 Rose indicated in an email dated 12 May 2004 (although the practice of hooding for long periods had ceased) that she thought hooding still took place on initial detention or when moving prisoners from one place to another. She said that there had been what were thought at the time to be good reasons for hooding but it became "… *rather more a matter of practice than it should have done*".[48]

15.51 On the same day, 12 May 2004, it was noted that although Reith's direction on hooding in October 2003 had been passed to the Headquarters of the Directorate of Special Forces, *"For whatever reason, that direction wasn't implemented and up until this morning, S[pecial] F[orces] in Iraq have continued to hood people"*.[49]

15.52 Brims contributed his recollection stating that hooding had attracted the attention of both the international media and the ICRC. The ICRC advice had been that the practices should stop and that "…*other than for particular individual cases, hooding ceased*". He indicated that following Baha Mousa's death, "…*it became apparent that hooding had resumed at some point*". He referred to Reith's review of hooding and Reith's direction that hooding should cease.[50]

15.53 It was also realised at this time that the hooding prohibition had not extended beyond Op Telic in Iraq and an instruction was provided for other theatres.[51]

(2) The circumstances in which hooding had occurred

15.54 One contribution came from S034, who had been the NCC Policy adviser (POLAD) on Op Telic 1. On 11 May 2004, she provided her recollection of prisoner of war issues from Op Telic 1.[52] I have already considered aspects of her memorandum in Chapters 4 and 5 of Part VIII of this Report. S034 reported some of the positives on

---

[44] MOD053675
[45] MOD030343
[46] MOD052875
[47] MOD020209
[48] MOD053670
[49] MOD020209
[50] MOD052867. Brims could not recall writing this document, but it was clearly written by him or on his behalf and is in response to questions posed the previous day by the Assistant Chief of the General Staff (MOD052875); Brims BMI 103/54/19-56/24
[51] Fraser MOD020269; SUB001107, paragraph 13
[52] MOD050815

prisoner handling and the efforts made even at the start of the operation to look after prisoners of war.[53] On the ICRC complaint, S034's account included the following:[54]

> **ICRC Complaint**
>
> 4. ICRC had access to Um Qasr camp and on 1 Apr I was notified by a senior ICRC rep that one of his team intended to make a formal complaint via Geneva of the treatment she had witnessed being meted out to special category prisoners at the camp. The complaint centred on the bagging, cuffing and harsh treatment of those limited numbers of prisoners subject to interrogation on entering the camp. Such prisoners included those suspected of being senior Baath party officials, those on the 'wanted' list, suspected terrorists, and those thought to be responsible for ordering the killing of the two EOD soldiers. And whilst the majority of PWs were compliant, a minority were disruptive and violent (and fights amongst PWs were not uncommon) hence the need for restraining measures. Examples the ICRC gave of harsh treatment included PWs being made to sit in the sun as a punishment for disruptive/violent behaviour, kicking, and use of stress positions. As a result of ICRC's allegations, I recall being told that a very limited number of incidents of abuse (kicking etc) had been uncovered as a result of which the interrogator concerned had been removed from theatre. Air Marshal Burridge acted immediately on ICRC's complaint and gave orders that bagging was to stop forthwith as harsh treatment. The military chain of command was notified of the complaint and closer supervision arranged. (In terms of context, it should perhaps be borne in mind that the war was still very much being fought at this time and 1 Div were on the verge of taking Basra and focusing on the whereabouts of Chemical Ali whilst the US were heavily focused on Baghdad leaving others further down the chain of command to deal with PW issues.) A follow-up meeting with ICRC at Um Qasr was arranged for 6 Apr.

From this account it was plain that the complaints of hooding and other treatment centred on events within the JFIT area of the Theatre Internment Facility (TIF) at Um Qasr.

15.55 Rachel Quick was no longer a PJHQ lawyer at this stage having moved to the MoD. But having spoken to PJHQ J2 (intelligence), in an email dated 12 May 2004 she suggested that hooding was "...*not permitted per se nor trained as an interrogation technique*"; that interrogation teams were trained to use blindfolds; that the "*bad news*" was that there had been some initial confusion in theatre over what type of blindfold was permitted to be used on capture; and that some UK forces in Iraq used sandbags to blindfold some prisoners. She suggested that protecting the identity of HUMINT sources was one reason for blindfolding, as was subduing the prisoner. But she also said that "*It has also been used as a tactic to disorientate the prisoner – it apparently makes them more amenable to interrogation. Although advice was given this method was not permitted, if the intent of the interrogator was to use it as a method of mental cohesion* [sic] *to persuade them to answer questions (this is prohibited under the Geneva Conventions). Once at the detention facility, UK Forces were not permitted to hood/blindfold them*".[55] Quick did indicate that she had not been able to speak to others (Lt Col Nicholas Clapham and Capt Neil Brown) to confirm the content of this email. Nonetheless Quick's email appeared to suggest that one purpose of sight deprivation had been disorientation to make prisoners amenable to interrogation. This was not, of course, an endorsement of this approach from the MoD lawyers who had already advised that hooding for the purposes of disorientation would be unlawful.

15.56 In contrast to the above, proposed lines to take on hooding dated 12 May 2004 had suggested that "*Hooding prisoners would be a temporary measure and would only*

---

[53] S034 72/29/13-25; MOD050815

[54] MOD050816

[55] MOD020213; Quick told the Inquiry that she could not be certain where she had heard this from – it could have been PJHQ J2 intelligence or something picked up from the earlier identified conference but she could not say for certain: Quick BMI 92/33/11-17

be used to achieve safe arrest and transit".[56] This did not fit well with what S034 had said, nor of course with what had previously been reported in respect of the treatment of Baha Mousa and the other Detainees.

15.57 In an email dated 14 May 2004, Brown recounted first hearing of hooding from Lt Col Nicholas Mercer who had been concerned about the use of it particularly at the JFIT, and the large number of prisoners being left hooded for long periods.[57]

(3) How widespread was the use of hooding?

15.58 It was suggested on 12 May 2004 that the practice of hooding was *"... part of the British Forces standard procedure (SOPs). There was therefore no requirement to bring it to Ministers' attention as from very early on in Operation telic the media covered the fact that hooding of Prisoners of War, internees and detainees took place anyway."*[58]

15.59 In his 14 May 2004 email, Brown gave his recollection of the events from Op Telic 1 and expressed surprise *"...that there had been a recurrence of the practice of hooding (for interrogation?) ... I cannot account for what may appear to have been the reappearance of this policy, perhaps because the use of hooding for security/ safety reasons is a common procedure".*[59]

(4) Chicksands training

15.60 In an email forwarded on 11 May 2004, but deriving from information provided by S045 in October 2003, it was stated that:

> *"Hooding is not included in the curriculum on interro or PHTQ courses, although the requirement to prevent a subject from seeing his surroundings on security grounds is taught (and allowed by the Geneva Conventions)... hooding as a means of disorientation is not taught on interro or PHTQ courses, nor was it the purpose of its use on TELIC."*[60]

15.61 S045 stated in an email to Stuart Kistruck on 17 May 2004 that:

> *"...DISC does not, nor did it in the run-up to TELIC, include the use of hoods in any of the PH&TQ or interrogation training it delivered. The potential need to obscure a prisoner's vision to prevent them seeing items could pose a security threat (in accordance with the Geneva Conventions) was acknowledged and the instruction was that this should be achieved by means of a blindfold."*[61]

15.62 Brims said on 13 May 2004 that:

> *"The Defence Intelligence Security centre has never taught the use of hoods as an acceptable interrogation technique and do not train in the use of them as such. There has not been a change in policy."*[62]

---

[56] MOD053649
[57] MOD020218
[58] MOD020211
[59] MOD020218
[60] MOD053857
[61] MOD053852
[62] MOD052868

15.63   In contrast to the above, in his 11 May 2004 email, Brown stated:

> *"Hooding has been SOP in the Army (D Int / Chicksands) throughout and was in place for TELIC as an SOP. In Telic the use of hooding in the JFIT (under-resourced and struggling with numbers) exceeded the guidelines which were for safety/security etc."*[63]

In writing this, Brown told the Inquiry he had in mind that hooding was a standard operating procedure in armed conflict situations for security purposes. He had understood this from discussions he had in theatre, including with intelligence staff. It was routine at the point of capture if the security situation demanded it. Brown said that he had not intended to convey that hooding had been used for purposes other than security, rather that the greater use of hoods was caused by resource problems. Brown said that in the context of the demands in May 2004, his *"wordsmithing"* was not as careful as it should have been in this email.[64] Nevertheless, by referring to *"D Int/Chicksands"* Brown's email would on its face have given the impression that hooding was part of intelligence procedures, even if only for security purposes.

15.64   Two days later in a longer email dated 14 May 2004, Brown wrote:

> *"I have heard that Chicksands have denied teaching hooding and suggested that there may be confusion in the minds of those who have completed the conduct after capture course during which students are hooded. I find this implausible. The people I have spoken to are not stupid. It seems to me more likely that hooding is taught but for actions immediately on capture or for prisoner handling (moving around a facility to be questioned etc) but not as a means of softening up or interrogation. The impression I have is based on informal discussions here in recent weeks but is consistent with the perception I had last year."*[65]

(5) Issues surrounding the Heath Statement and the 1972 Directive

15.65   In an email dated 11 May 2004, Brown said *"My understanding is that the banning of hoods by the Heath govt related to NI/UK."*[66]

15.66   In his 14 May 2004 email, Brown stated:

> *"I took the view that in very clearly defined circumstances (eg as an accepted method of ensuring safety/security immediately after capture) and for short periods the use of hoods would not be unlawful. Without going into any detail I had in mind the direction of the AG that ECHR did not apply (and UK case law in this area was as I understood it ECHR-related), and GC3 was the lex specialis. I determined that this was a proper application of GC3 in what was an armed conflict. That said, the view at 1 Div was that a more conservative approach (a general ban) would not compromise operational effectiveness. That was of course an option available to GOC 1 Div."*[67]

I have addressed both of these emails in more detail in Part VIII of this Report.[68]

---

[63] MOD020204
[64] Brown BMI 75/123/11-126/15; Brown BMI 94/65/7-68/21
[65] MOD020218 and Brown BMI 94/76/15-77/10
[66] MOD020204
[67] MOD020218
[68] See Part VIII paragraphs 8.223-8.234

15.67 In a briefing on 13 May 2004 it was stated by Brig J Mason, Assistant Chief of Staff J1/J4, that PJHQ J9 Legal and Ministry of Defence Legal Advisers (MODLA) "*... are currently engaged on the applicability of the Heath hooding ruling outside of Northern Ireland/UK.*"[69] It is apparent that at this stage, it had not been appreciated that the Heath Statement was not restricted to Great Britain and Northern Ireland.

15.68 It was said later on 17 May 2004 in a briefing from Colin Allkins that "*PJHQ was unaware of the Heath ruling until it was raised in the last two weeks.*"[70]

15.69 With the renewed attention to hooding, it was also recognised at this stage that there was a lack of written guidance relating to sight deprivation. It was noted on 14 May 2004 that "*The Army have not found any reference to the proscription of hooding when handling prisoners of war in their manuals, doctrine and teaching of military law*".[71] While the single paragraph from JSP 383 referring to the use blindfolding (but not any prohibition on hooding) was identified,[72] it was recognised that "*...JWP 1-10 does not contain the words hood, hooding or blindfold, following an electronic search.*"[73]

15.70 On 14 May 2004, the Assistant Chief of the General Staff sent a minute to the Vice Chief of the Defence Staff concerning the fact that "*...relevant Army manuals, doctrine and the teaching of military law make no specific reference to proscribing hooding when handling prisoners of war*":[74]

> ### ADVICE ON THE ISSUE OF HOODING OF PRISONERS
>
> 1. You asked me to provide advice to VCDS on how we should address the fact that relevant Army manuals, doctrine and the teaching of military law make no specific reference to proscribing hooding when handling prisoners of war'. This is obviously a grey area that we will need to address. As this is likely to be a tri-Service issue, and in line with specific direction given by VCDS, I have consulted with the other ACOS' staffs. However, I can still only speak definitively for the Army position. DG T&E, who is the Defence lead on this particular issue, is now working to provide the definitive tri-Service answer.
>
> 2. Notwithstanding the above, there is clearly a requirement to ensure that the emotive issue of hooding is urgently addressed. This should be achieved by ensuring that each of the three Services have clear direction that hooding should not be used for the handling of prisoners. However, in doing so we must also ensure that we do not prejudice military judgement to blindfold prisoners when there is a clear military justification for doing so, such as when it is imperative that prisoners are prevented from seeing sensitive information and there is no alternative means of achieving this effect. Indeed, I am quite clear that this is the reason why hooding occurred in Iraq. There was generally no malign intent but the easiest way to blindfold is to use a sandbag, to which everyone has ready access. The key point is that even under such circumstances hoods should not be used.
>
> 3. Having spoken to DD T&E Pol, there would be merit in running this line past DG T&E. While I am certain that this is the right line to take for all three Services, their views on its appropriateness to the other two Services should be sought. It would mean a short delay in the promulgation of new unequivocal direction but I am assured by PJHQ that no hooding is taking place in any of our operational theatres and thus I believe we can afford a little time to resolve the issue properly.

15.71 On 13 May 2004, in the midst of these exchanges, Ms Arvinder Sambei, Rachel Quick's successor at PJHQ legal, raised for the consideration of Hemming and Rose, the question of whether the hooding issue should be referred to the Attorney-General:

---

[69] MOD020076
[70] MOD020222
[71] MOD052258
[72] MOD023052
[73] MOD020069, 12 May 2004
[74] MOD020067

> "...to provide a clear legal guidance on the following points as the issue causes us some difficulty at an operational level:
>
> 1. Is hooding ... unlawful per se; or
>
> 2. Is it permissible in limited circumstances."[75]

Sambei's email contained her own view of the legal position.

15.72 One response to Ms Sambei's email came from Humphrey Morrison of MODLA. He reiterated the unlawfulness of hooding as an interrogation technique. On security hooding, he commented that hooding against a prisoner's will was prima facie an assault under English law. But he added that there was a difficult question as to whether compelling operational or other circumstances could amount to a defence. He referred to the Chief of Joint Operation's direction in October 2003 and concluded:

> "Given the risk, the alternative of blindfolding and the order of CJO, I do not see how the practice can be legally justified. There might be a separate issue whether an individual who was unaware of the risk, the alternative and the order might have a defence to a charge of assault. It would also be a separate question whether, if a person died as a result of being hooded, the circumstances might amount to an offence of manslaughter."[76]

15.73 The response from Rose to Sambei's query was dated 17 May 2004 and was follows:[77]

> "Thanks Ari,
>
> I would not be in favour of asking the AG at this point.
>
> I understand that the practice has now finally been stopped in Iraq at least so the answer to the question is presumably academic for the period from now on. We do not know where the current public debate about it will end – and we do not want to push the AG into taking a position in the abstract that we and he may then regret in the light of some later claim or allegation.
>
> If we were to seek his advice we would have to be sure that we could provide information about the history of the 1971 advice, what we have been doing in other theatres (AFG, Kosovo etc) and all the circumstances in which we have used hooding in Iraq. I do not think we can devote the resources needed for what would be a substantial exercise at the moment – we are working flat out on related matters and we are also pressing the AG for answers on some operationaly vital things which have been outstanding with him for months. The chances of getting an answer out the AG in anything quicker than months is nil in my view.
>
> We would also need to be clear what we would do in practical and policy terms if the AG gave clear advice that it was illegal but the US and other coalition partners disagreed and wanted to continue using it in some circumstances.
>
> We may have to go down this path if the AG presses us but I do not want to initiate anything from this end.
>
> Vivien

15.74 In her oral evidence, Rose expanded on why she did not agree with approaching the Attorney-General at this stage of events. She gave a number of reasons. She said the issue in relation to hooding had not arisen in other theatres so for that reason there was no need to ask for advice from the Attorney-General. She said the legal view within the MoD was settled and was not causing any operational problems. In fact operationally "they seemed happy to go further than the legal advice required". She felt that in the context of public outrage in respect of treatment of prisoners the Attorney-General might have taken a stricter view than if he was asked to consider the position in different circumstances. There was also the fact that it might take some time for the Attorney-General to give his advice. In any event hooding had already been banned in Iraq.[78]

---

[75] MOD020228-9
[76] MOD053644-5
[77] MOD020228
[78] Rose BMI 93/119/20-124/5

15.75 Her reasons were perhaps most succinctly summarised in the following answer given to Counsel for the Detainees:

> *"I think that what I was saying from my experience of dealing with the Attorney and his secretariat is that there was a risk that, because he was asked in the particular circumstances, he might give a more cautious view than he would give in different circumstances. Whether it accorded with my view or not doesn't matter; I wanted to be sure that if, when we asked him, if we were going to ask him, it should be in a context where cool heads could be brought to bear to the problem without it being looked at in the context that was currently existing. As I say, it's not a question of whether he agrees with me or not or whether it is operationally inconvenient or not, although it would have been operationally inconvenient, but we would have dealt with that. One of the points – and there were other points why I didn't think it was a good idea to refer to it – was the concern that, knowing how he reacted sometimes, he would take a different view than the view he would take in different circumstances."*[79]

15.76 Hemming said that Rose would probably have spoken to him about this issue and that he would have agreed that the Attorney-General should not be consulted at this stage. Hemming's evidence was that hooding having been banned in all theatres, it was by this stage an academic issue. He also considered that the Attorney-General would already have had some knowledge of the hooding issue through briefing by the Army Prosecuting Authority (APA) concerning the facts surrounding Baha Mousa's death; and from seeing the ICRC report of February 2004.[80] A further factor was that if the Attorney-General was to be consulted on this issue, it was supposed to be in good time before the Government was committed to a position, whereas hooding had already been banned. The Attorney-General was also heavily engaged at the time.[81] Hemming would not, however, have agreed with the suggestion from Rose that a reason for not approaching the Attorney-General was the risk that he might be pushed into a position in the abstract which he might then regret in the light of later claims or allegations.[82]

15.77 I can well understand that in combination the factors militating against going to the Attorney-General for an advice on hooding at this stage were very strong. I was, however, left a little uncomfortable that one part of Rose's reasoning was seemingly a concern that in the context of the clamour about hooding, the Attorney-General might take a stricter or more cautious view on hooding than the MoD legal view. I cannot accept there was any risk of the Attorney-General being influenced by such factors. In any event, the omission to obtain an advice did not affect the course of events with which the Inquiry is concerned.

The requests for consolidated internal advice and briefing for cabinet members

15.78 With the continuing pressure to provide further information and detail, two major briefings were sought to clarify the issues relating to hooding.

---

[79] Rose BMI 93/157/6-158/1
[80] Hemming BMI08480, paragraph 46; BMI09044. Hemming was right to suggest that the Attorney-General would already have been briefed by the APA concerning Baha Mousa's death. The JCHR were informed that Lord Goldsmith was provided with a report from the APA on 13 January 2004 and that he saw the ICRC report on 13 May 2004.
[81] Hemming BMI 103/140/17-148/1
[82] Hemming BMI 103/154/5-157/4

15.79 The first request followed a meeting of the full Cabinet on 13 May 2004, in which the Secretary of State was invited to provide a background briefing for other members of the Cabinet.

15.80 The purpose was to *"explain clearly and quickly the United Kingdom's position and the responses we have made to allegations of abuse in Iraq."* The task of bringing together material for this briefing was assigned to Dr Simon Cholerton, who was appointed head of the new Iraq Investigation Team (IIT).[83] The team was formed because of the difficulties encountered in providing clear and timely responses to allegations in Non Governmental Organisation (NGO) reports, and particularly in relation to the *Daily Mirror* photographs.[84]

15.81 The second request was from the Secretary of State who asked for a consolidating briefing to cover:[85]

- *"Heath ruling on interrogation: what was the legal context and previous guidance?* **(plus MOD LA)**

- *Training regime on interrogation/tactical questioning/transit hooding?* **(AG Sec)**

- *Instructions on interrogation/tactical questioning/transit hooding before Op TELIC?*

- *Has any hooding take[n] place during interrogation during Op TELIC, if so on what scale?*

- *What was the scale of hooding during tactical questioning in theatre?*

- *What was the scale of hooding during transit during Op TELIC?*

- *When have human rights organisations brought hooding to the attention of the MOD: dates, nature of concern?*

- *Are we aware of any examples of hooding by UK forces since CJO's instruction not to cease* [sic] *(other than that already raised at reference)?*

- *Of the cases that COs/SIB have been investigating, do any other than that of Baha Mousa involve the use of hooding?* **(AG Sec)**

- *Have we had any complaints from human rights groups about the use of goggles?* **(Anyone?)**

- *In recent years have we used hooding in any other operational theatres?"*

Consolidating briefing for the Secretary of State

15.82 The consolidated briefing for the Secretary of State was provided on 17 May 2004, and signed by Stuart Kistruck, the Deputy Head of the IIT.[86]

15.83 In relation to the Interrogation and PH&TQ courses, the briefing included the following:[87]

---

[83] MOD050825
[84] Cholerton BMI 92/168/14-169/10
[85] MOD052631
[86] MOD054210
[87] MOD054211

> 3. The interrogation course is an additional 5 days of training at the end of the PH&TQ course. It is designed for Service personel who are in an appointment that could require them to conduct interrogation of captured enemy personnel. It teaches individuals how to question captured personnel, in accordance with the Geneva Conventions and the Laws of Armed Conflict, in order to obtain information of potential intelligence interest. The underlying tenet is that a 'broken' PW cannot provide information for the Interrogator to achieve their aim. It identifies the following techniques as totally unacceptable under any and all circumstances, both because they are illegal and they are counter-productive:
>
> > Physical punishment of any sort (beatings etc).
> > The use of any stress position.
> > Intentional sleep deprivation.
> > Withdrawal of food, water or medical help.
> > Degrading treatment (sexual embarrassment, religious taunting etc).
> > The use of 'white noise'.
> > Torture methods such as thumb screws etc
>
> 4. The hooding of prisoners is not taught as part of the annual IDT(A)s, nor is it part of the PH&TQ course which teaches that the hooding of detainees is unacceptable. However, blindfolding or obscuring of a detainee's vision for operational reasons is acceptable if there is clearly justifiable military reason, such as preventing a prisoner from seeing sensitive material, or friendly forces dispositions. It should be noted that there is no prescriptive direction with regard to hooding contained in any of the relevant manuals, doctrine or military law.

15.84   The final sentence from the quotation above correctly recognised the lack of any prescriptive direction regarding hooding. However, having regard to my findings in Part VI of this Report, I find that in stating that hooding was not part of the PH&TQ course and that it taught that the hooding of detainees was unacceptable, the briefing was more reassuring than it ought to have been. That is likely to have been the position by the time this briefing was written. However, before Op Telic was launched, I have found that the teaching on the means of security sight deprivation varied. It was not accurate to state that the course clearly taught that hooding detainees was unacceptable. However, it is obvious that Kistruck was relying here on information that had been provided by the Joint Services Intelligence Organisation (JSIO).[88]

15.85   Kistruck's briefing correctly pointed out in relation to the Chief of Joint Operation's HUMINT Directive, that neither Joint Warfare Publication (JWP) 1-10 nor Allied Joint Publication (AJP) 2.5 explicitly discussed hooding although they did provide that physical or mental torture were not to be used in order to obtain information.[89] Kistruck's briefing then continued as follows:[90]

---

[88] Kistruck BMI 93/14/20-15/17
[89] MOD054212
[90] MOD054212-3

7.   No advice was sought on hooding for arrest or transit and no direction given. PJHQ were not aware of the Heath Ruling until it was raised in the last two weeks. Hooding for the purposes of arrest and transit was normal procedure on operations (as is the case for most Armed Forces in the world). PJHQ do not believe that the use of hoods had not been significantly challenged in practice since PJHQ was established in 1996 and so there was no apparent reason to seek specific advice for Operation TELIC. The hooding of detainees for arrest or transit of detainees was a standard procedure for UK troops prior to TELIC. Hoods were used in Afghanistan and it is likely that they were used in every other operation where individuals were detained. However, as this was standard procedure this would not necessarily have been reported and so records are not immediately available. PJHQ are investigating further but currently have no firm data.

Extent of Hooding

8.   *Interrogations* – We have found no evidence that would suggest that interrogators ignored their training and hooded prisoners at any point during TELIC. Guards at interrogation centres may have used hoods to move prisoners around and we understand that in come cases prisoners may have requested hoods to preserve their own anonymity.

9.   *Tactical Questioning* – Tactical Questioning (TQ) was more widespread than interrogation and all formations have personnel trained in TQ. We do not believe that there were any instances of hooding being used during TQ. This would also have been in contradiction to TQ doctrine as laid out in JWP 1-10 where hooding (or even blindfolding) is considered counterproductive since it prevents direct contact between the questioner and prisoner and inhibits rapport. PJHQ have set in train actions to trawl all units that operated in Iraq to form a definive understanding.

10.   *Arrest/Transit* - Hooding during transit between the point of capture and the detention facility was widespread, as there were very few enclosed vehicles in which detainees could be transported. This was the established norm for UK troops but the extent to which it was used varied from unit to unit. As with TQ PJHQ have initiated a trawl of units but it will take time to collect returns and collate them into a coherent overall picture.

11.   By May 03 Gen Brims had issued direction that 1 Div should cease hooding (despite being given legal advice in theatre that under specific and limited circumstances – those under which UK troops routinely used hooding – it was not unlawful). When 1 Div handed over to 3 Div on 12 July 03 this direction was lost. 3 Div therefore reverted to normal procedure and the practice began again until CJO issued his formal direction in late September 03 that it should cease.

12.   There is no firm evidence that the hooding of prisoners at the PW camp Joint Force Interrogation Team (JFIT) facility, during major combat operations, went beyond the normal use for arrest/transit activity. Anecdotally there may have been problems stemming from the very large numbers of PWs in civilian clothing being held at a facility designed for military prisoners. There were very limited facilities for separating prisoners so it appears hooding was used on prisoners held at the centre. It was concern about this that Gen Brims noted when he visited the JTIF and which prompted him to direct 1 Div to cease the practice. PJHQ are investigating more details on the use of hoods at the JFIT.

Special Forces

13.   The UKSF have not used hooding ███████████ other than in Iraq. This is not representative of a general policy not to hood ███████
████████████████████████████████

Detainees have been hooded throughout this transit period, apart from when they have been subject to tactical questioning and when they are given a medical examination. Sec(HSF)2's submission of 13 May 04 explained why UKSF continued to hood personnel despite CJO's instructions of September 03. From █ May 04 UKSF have used blacked out goggles rather than hoods.

Concerns about Hooding

14.   The ICRC expressed concerns about the duration for which some detainees were being hooded at the JTIF prior to Gen Brims order to cease hooding but although this was early in the conflict we cannot be certain of the date. ████████████████████ ████████████ as to whether the hooding was acceptable on security/safety grounds. It was however, agreed that goggles or blindfolds would be acceptable and serve the same purpose. PJHQ are investigating any documentation, which might exist to support this suggestion. The use of hoods outside of detention centres has not to our knowledge been raised as a concern.

I find that there were three aspects of concern in the hooding section of this consolidated briefing.

15.86 The first is the suggestion that there was no evidence of hooding being used during tactical questioning. While it was correct that there were no reported cases of hooding actually during tactical questioning, the reporting of Baha Mousa's death had shown that hooding had been potentially linked to the tactical questioning process. As I set out in Part XIV of this Report, Ministers had been informed in September that Baha Mousa in 36 hours had spent 23 hours and 40 minutes hooded, and that the hooding had taken place on the advice of one of the tactical questioners. Although this did not expressly link hooding to the tactical questioning process, it ought to have given cause for caution. At least to some of those in PJHQ, the link between the use of hoods on Baha Mousa and the other Detainees and the tactical questioning process may not have been completely clear.[91] But in theatre, the reporting after Baha Mousa's death had included the following: "...*we hood and hand cuff detainees, in order to enhance the shock of capture and improve the level of information extracted from the suspect*"[92] (see Part XIV, Chapter 1). In my view this ought to have alerted PJHQ to the potential link between hooding and tactical questioning. It should have led those in PJHQ to take a far more cautious line on the link between tactical questioning and hooding. The same weakness of failing to link the events surrounding Baha Mousa's death to tactical questioning is evident in a suggested answer to a written Parliamentary Question dated 19 May 2004 from the Rt. Hon. Kevin McNamara MP. The question asked when the Secretary of State "*... was first informed that UK forces in Iraq were practising the banned interrogation technique of hooding prisoners.*" The suggested answer was, "*We are not aware of any incidents in which United Kingdom interrogators are alleged to have used hooding as an interrogation technique*".[93] Ingram, who answered this question in Parliament, told the Inquiry that in hindsight it would have been better if he had been reminded at that stage of the briefing material from the time immediately following Baha Mousa's death.[94]

15.87 The second point of concern is the suggestion that tactical questioning doctrine as laid out in JWP 1-10 suggested that hooding or even blindfolding was counterproductive. I have considered JWP 1-10 in Part V of this Report. The plain fact is that it contained no guidance on sight deprivation whatsoever. I accept that Kistruck was relying on accounts from others of what JWP 1-10 contained, but the briefing was simply inaccurate in this respect.[95]

15.88 The third point of concern arises out of paragraph 12 of Kistruck's briefing. As can be seen from the extract above, the first sentence of paragraph 12 in its final form read "*There is no firm evidence that the hooding of prisoners at the PW camp Joint Force Interrogation Team (JFIT) facility, during major combat operations, went beyond the normal use for arrest/transit activity*".[96] There was a similar passage in the briefing for Cabinet Ministers (see below). I do not overlook that the same paragraph went on to refer to anecdotal evidence of difficulties stemming from the number of prisoners

---

[91] Richard Johnson BMI 92/145/19-146/10. He said that everybody was aware that hooding was a factor with Baha Mousa but at this stage they did not have anything like a clear picture of how this had come about.
[92] MOD030850
[93] MOD050381
[94] Ingram BMI 97/52/1-11
[95] Kistruck BMI 93/24/9-25
[96] MOD054213

and lack of resources. However, I consider that this suggestion that hooding at the JFIT had been in the course of "*arrest/transit activity*" is worrying.

15.89 There was a particular peculiarity about the drafting of this part of Kistruck's consolidated advice. In preparing the advice, Kistruck clearly drew heavily upon a slightly earlier paper by Colin Allkins, a Senior Executive Officer and one of the J9 Policy/Operations officials at PJHQ working on the Iraq desk.[97] But the equivalent paragraph in Allkins' paper included the following:

> "**We do believe** that there was extensive use of hooding during the warfighting phase at the PW camp JFIT facility that went beyond the normal use for arrest/transit activity."[98] [emphasis added]

On the face of the two documents, Kistruck appears to have turned this on its head in asserting that there was "*no firm evidence*" that the use of hooding did go beyond the normal use.

15.90 Kistruck told the Inquiry that he was unaware of the details of the Baha Mousa case at this stage and had not seen the earlier Ministerial submissions from September 2003. He accepted that the change from Allkins' earlier note appeared contradictory. Kistruck said he would not have changed the Allkins wording without good reason. It was possible that it was a typographical error in Allkins' note. He said that he was unaware that the hooding at the JFIT involved hooding after the initial processing while prisoners awaited interrogation. Nor did he know that it had gone on for as long as 24 hours in some cases.[99] Kistruck was pressed about what was in his consolidating advice:

> "Q. Even on the information that you did know, though, that hooding was going on, as you were suggesting here, while awaiting processing at a detention centre, was it not somewhat disingenuous to seek to portray that as being hooding that was still for the purposes of transit?
>
> A. As I recall, it had been explained to me that some of those detainees could have been released imminently and there were force protection reasons until they were actually into the facility. So, in my understanding, it felt as if it was part of the transit process. But I accept that – it could be seen that way. I don't believe it was.
>
> Q. A fuller and more candid explanation – would this be fair – would be to say that the use of hooding had been at arrest, point of capture, during transit to facilities and, on your understanding, while awaiting initial processing?
>
> A. Yes.
>
> Q. Was there any reason why that couldn't have been said in those plain term terms at the time?
>
> A. I don't believe so, no."[100]

15.91 Allkins' evidence was that he had said that the hooding at the JFIT went beyond the normal use for arrest and transit activity because "*Prisoners were remaining hooded for periods of time while they were at the JFIT*" and he agreed that this was

---

[97] MOD020222
[98] MOD020223
[99] Kistruck BMI 93/25/8-30/10
[100] Kistruck BMI 93/30/11-31/6

in contrast to hooding when prisoners were being moved from place to place.[101] Allkins did not know how the opposite came to be stated later in the Cabinet briefing document.[102]

15.92 Dr Simon Cholerton who wrote the Cabinet briefing document (which took the same line on this point) said that he would not have changed the line from the Allkins draft deliberately simply to put the MoD in a better light. He suggested that it was possible that the change arose out of a simple misreading of Allkins' notes. However he thought it most likely that it was an error in Allkins' original note.[103]

15.93 An email subsequent to the issuing of Kistruck's consolidating advice suggests that his line on hooding and transit/arrest may have been queried, and that there had a been a further call to PJHQ to confirm the facts. Kistruck is recorded as arguing that it was justifiable to claim that prisoners were still in the transit/arrest phase until they were processed into a facility:[104]

From: IRAQ-TELICREV 1-S
Sent: Wednesday, May 19, 2004 4:57:53 PM
To: SOFS-APS3-S
Cc: IRAQ-TELICREV3-S
Subject: Hooding and the JFIT
Auto forwarded by a Rule

Ben,

We spoke about hooding and the JFIT. Sarah Seaton had raised concerns about lines on hooding and transit/arrest. You had separately spoken to PJHQ to confirm facts.

There is an element of going round in circles on this. The anecdotal evidence that Colin Allkins had drawn my attention to was the same as Sarah's concern.

Essentially this boiled down to difficulties in processing detainees, they were only kept hooded until they were processed. There are strong military reasons for doing so and I understand that while we cannot lay our hands on actual times the maximum length of time would be for a matter of hours (not days!). I think it would also be justifiable to claim that prisoners were still in the Transit/arrest phase until they were processed into a facility.

I can provide detailed advice but am not sure whether this is necessary the current statement about anecdotal evidence is accurate and appropriate for your note to No 10. I also owe you further advice on the links between hooding and CO/SIB investigations on which I am awaiting some input from AG Sec. One possibility would be to tidy up the details surrounding JFIT at the same time as an answer on SIBs and provide an updated definitive version of my original note. I will also include suggested lines to take.

Are you content with this?

In the mean time I think that the line in the note to cabinet colleagues still stands.

Hooding was used from time to time during operation TELIC in Iraq, for example when transporting prisoners. It has not been used during interrogations and has now been stopped completely.

Stuart Kistruck
Sec(Iraq)

15.94 In relation to this email, Kistruck repeated that he understood that the hooding occurred while prisoners were waiting to be processed into the facility, and that it was justifiable to say that this was hooding in the transit phase.[105]

15.95 I find that this line on hooding at the JFIT, apparently contradicting Allkins' earlier note, arose because first, Kistruck was misinformed about hooding at the JFIT and understood that hooding was only undertaken there while prisoners awaited processing. Secondly, Kistruck took the view that hooding pending processing at a detention centre could be considered as part of the transit phase. Kistruck was not in my view seeking to mislead anyone and his supplementary briefing of 21 May

---

[101] Allkins BMI 90/148/21-149/3
[102] Allkins BMI 90/152/12-154/9
[103] Cholerton BMI 92/174/23-176/6
[104] MOD052626
[105] Kistruck BMI07825, paragraph 24

2004 (considered below) strongly supports that conclusion. Even so, this was not an appropriate line for Kistruck to have taken; it stretched the normal meaning of the words "*transit activity*" and to that extent was inappropriately reassuring.

15.96 I note finally in respect of this consolidated briefing that Kistruck made clear in the final paragraph that the Adjutant General's secretariat had not yet been able to review the SIB cases to identify possible links with hooding. It is right to record this since Kistruck provided a further briefing four days later once this review had taken place which referred to the Baha Mousa case and also gave further details about hooding at the JFIT (see below at paragraph 15.106).

15.97 The substance of this consolidating advice for the Secretary of State was forwarded to No.10 Downing Street on 19 May 2004.[106]

The briefing for Cabinet colleagues

15.98 The briefing for Cabinet Ministers was also sent to No. 10 on 19 May 2004 and circulated to the offices of all Cabinet members.[107] On hooding, the briefing stated:[108]

> **Hooding**
>
> 10.   The practice of hooding has been central to the debate on British handling of prisons. UK Army Doctrine and training states that the hooding of detainees during tactical questioning and interrogation is unacceptable and contrary to the Geneva Conventions and the Laws of Armed Combat. However, blindfolding or obscuring of a detainee's vision for operational reasons during arrest/transit is acceptable if there is a clearly justifiable military reason, such as preventing a prisoner from seeing sensitive material, or friendly forces dispositions, or protecting Iraqis from other Iraqis. It should be noted that there is no prescriptive direction with regard to hooding contained in any of the relevant manuals, doctrine or military law.
>
> 11.   The hooding of detainees for arrest or transit of detainees was a standard procedure for UK troops during operations prior to Iraq, as it is for most armed forces throughout the world. The UK used hoods in Afghanistan. During operations in Iraq hooding during transit between the point of capture and the detention facility was widespread, as there were very few enclosed vehicles in which detainees could be transported. This was the established norm for UK troops but the extent to which it was used varied from unit to unit. There is however, no evidence that hooding was used at any time during tactical questioning or interrogations in Iraq. The Chief of Joint Operations issued formal direction in late September 03 that hooding should cease.
>
> 12.   There is no firm evidence that the hooding of prisoners at the PW camp Joint Force Interrogation Team (JFIT) facility, during major combat operations, went beyond the normal use for arrest/transit activity. Anecdotally there may have been problems stemming from the very large numbers of PWs in civilian clothing being held at a facility designed for military prisoners. There were very limited facilities for separating prisoners so it appears hooding was used on prisoners held at the centre.

---

[106] MOD054177
[107] MOD041663
[108] MOD041666-7

15.99 I note that there were some appropriate and fair comments within this section. The lack of prescriptive direction with regard to hooding was recognised; similarly, the widespread use of hooding.

15.100 However, it is of concern that it was stated that there was no evidence that hooding was used at any time during tactical questioning. Similarly, the suggestion that there was no firm evidence that the hooding at the JFIT went beyond the normal use for arrest/transit activity. Both of these appear to be assertions that were taken from the earlier consolidated advice to the Secretary of State compiled by Kistruck. Cholerton said that it had not occurred to him in the early days of his appointment to the IIT that the allegations associated with Baha Mousa's abuse were in the context of tactical questioning.[109] Cholerton accepted that he probably should have worked out from information that had been presented by Amnesty International and from later information in the Al Skeini proceedings that Baha Mousa and the other Detainees had been hooded whilst in a holding centre. But it was only on seeing later documents that he appreciated they were hooded throughout.[110]

15.101 Late in the drafting process, Rose raised a number of observations about Cholerton's draft briefing. In respect of the hooding section above, she commented, referring to Baha Mousa's case:

> "On **Hooding** is it the case that the person who died from asphyxiation because of the hooding (whose death sparked the order in September 03 to stop all hooding) was not during tactical questioning or interrogations?"[111]

It seems that this did not lead to any change in the draft. Cholerton's response at the time was that:

> "**Hooding** – in the case you are referring to, the individual **did not die due to** asphyxiation he had be [sic] hooded for transit purpose and died later of a heart attack"[112]

15.102 Cholerton's evidence was that he knew very little about the allegations in respect of Baha Mousa.[113] In his oral evidence, Cholerton said that he was confused at the time and did not know that this was a reference to Baha Mousa. He accepted that with hindsight, Rose was right and that he was confused; Cholerton referred to the pressure of the volume of information and the fact that he had only been in the post for six days.[114]

15.103 On interrogation policy, the briefing to members of the Cabinet stated:[115]

[109] Cholerton BMI 92/204/20-205/17
[110] Cholerton BMI 92/207/7-208/10
[111] MOD053390
[112] Rose BMI 93/140/7-24; MOD054181
[113] Cholerton BMI04816, paragraph 40
[114] Cholerton BMI 92/194/14-196/23
[115] MOD041668

Interrogations Policy

16.   It is UK policy that interrogations are carried out well within the terms of the Geneva Convention. UK Military interrogators are trained to a high standard in methods of questioning. The Joint Service Intelligence Organisation's Training Documentation states that the following techniques are expressly and explicitly forbidden:

- Physical punishment of any sort (beatings etc)
- The use of stress privation
- Intentional sleep deprivation
- Withdrawal of food, water or medical help
- Degrading treatment (sexual embarrassment, religious taunting etc)
- The use of 'white noise'
- Torture methods such as thumb screws etc

17.   The underlying tenet is that a 'broken' detainee cannot provide information for the interrogator to achieve his/her aim, so techniques such as those depicted in the Abu Ghraib photographs would in any case by considered counterproductive by UK interrogators. Furthermore, there is a very clear distinction between those responsible for interrogations and those responsible for the stewardship of prisoners.

15.104 Within a section addressing working with the ICRC, the briefing contained the following account of the ICRC's early concerns about the JFIT:[116]

20.   In theatre, ICRC representatives have had full and unfettered access to UK detention facilities from the outset. They visited both the UK's first detention centre in Umm Qasr and then the Joint Force Interrogation Team (JFIT) facility that was part of the US detention facility at Camp Bucca. The ICRC visited the first UK centre in Umm Qasr in March 2003, then the JFIT in April. They also visited the DTDF at Shaibah before it opened in December 2003, then in February and April 2004. (In addition ICRC representatives visited Camp Cropper, where the two UK detainees are held, in October 2003, Jan 2004 and March 2004; we have not seen their reports which were sent to the CPA). Relations with the ICRC have been ▮▮▮▮▮▮▮

21.   During major combat operations ICRC concerns focused on treatment, by military intelligence community, of special category prisoners. The only substantial complaint, made at the beginning of April 2003, concerned treatment an ICRC official witnessed being meted out to special category prisoners. The complaint centred on the bagging, cuffing and harsh treatment of those limited numbers of prisoners subject to interrogation on entering the camp. The matter received immediate attention and the ICRC expressed themselves "satisfied" with the UK response.

22.   As a result of ICRC's allegations, the senior POLAD in theatre recalls being told that a very limited number of incidents of abuse (kicking etc) had been uncovered. The military chain of command was notified of the complaint and closer supervision arranged. ▮▮▮▮▮▮▮

15.105 The briefing mentioned the cases where service personnel had been investigated in relation to the treatment of detainees. In respect of Baha Mousa, it was said:[117]

- **Mr Baha Daoud Salim Musa[1]**. This case has received the most publicity and was the substance behind the 'Mirror' allegations. Mr Musa was detained by 1 QLR during a pre-planned operation. Whilst in detention he died of multiple injuries. Several others arrested with him also sustained injuries. The case is currently with the chain of command. One Junior NCO has been reported for manslaughter. Another SNCO and two soldiers have been reported for assault.

---

[116] MOD041669
[117] MOD041670

Relevant Statements/Correspondence Following the May Briefings

15.106 On 21 May 2004, Kistruck supplemented his consolidated advice to the Secretary of State. A handwritten endorsement on the front page of this submission showed that it was agreed that there was no need for this to be put to Ministers but the information was to be held in case the issue was raised again.[118] In the supplementary advice, Kistruck noted that the earlier advice had not included definitive advice on the possible links between hooding and cases that had been investigated. He updated the picture as follows:[119]

> 2. The majority of the 54 SIB investigations in Iraq relate to shootings or vehicle accidents, but some relate to allegations of abuse during arrest and detention. It was common practice to use hoods while transporting detainees with battle groups until they were transferred to detention centres and so some of the allegations are unavoidably linked to the use of hoods. We are not aware of any allegations of abuse that involve hooding and interrogation. There are potentially links between hooding and the Baha Musa case. There three other cases that involve fatalities, one of which concerns the an individual who was forced to jump into the Shat Al Arab and drowned. In the other two cases (both heart attacks), we have been able to confirm that they had been hooded during their detention but have been unable to be ascertain whether they were hooded at the time of their death.
>
> 3. My minute also identified anecdotal evidence about the use of hoods at the JFIT facility. The details are as follows. The detainees were required to wear hoods until they had been processed into the centre. In some cases we understand that this may have taken some time, however this is understood to have been for a maximum of a matter of hours and not days. The military rationale for obscuring vision was as follows:
>
> • To deny the prisoners the opportunity to observe details of the area they were being held in. Many of the prisoners were suspected terrorists but they were eventually released back into the community. Knowledge of the layout of the facility would have been invaluable should they have wished to attack it in the future.
>
> • The position of the holding area was such that it would have allowed the prisoners to observe the living accommodation inhabited by the interrogators.
>
> 3. I attach a definitive brief on hooding which has been updated to reflect these additional facts and updated defensive lines.
>
> Stuart Kistruck
> Dep Hd IIT

15.107 In fairness to Kistruck I note that this briefing corrected part of the inaccuracies in his earlier briefing of 17 May 2004. Unfortunately, the supplement was not, it seems, actually put before the Secretary of State.

---

[118] MOD054029
[119] MOD054029-30

15.108 The updated defensive lines on hooding to which Kistruck referred were as follows:[120]

DEFENSIVE LINES ON HOODING

- Hooding was used from time to time during Operation TELIC in Iraq, for example when transporting prisoners. It was not used during interrogations and has now been stopped completely.

- UK does not believe it is acceptable to use hoods during interrogation or questioning. Military training makes clear that it is unacceptable.

[If Pressed] There may be some operational circumstances where there is a strong military justification for obscuring detainee's vision. In these instances the UK believes that such action is within the terms of the Geneva Convention.

[If Pressed hard] UK troops in Iraq were directed not to use hoods in Iraq in September 2003.

Additional Q&A if pressed

Why was hooding stopped in September?

Have always accepted that the use of hoods in Iraq was not ideal. A decision was therefore taken to stop their use when the circumstances permitted.

[If Raised] Why did it stop in May and then restart?

1 Div reached a decision in May 2003 that there was no need to use hoods on detainees in transit. This direction was lost during the handover to 3 div on 12 July. However, CJO provided definitive direction in September 03 that the practice was to cease

Do any of the allegations under investigation involve use of hoods?

Not aware of any cases of UK interrogation that is alleged to have involved the use of hoods. Some allegations relate to the detention and transit of prisoners and so it is likely that the individuals involved may have been hooded.

Is hooding currently being used by UK forces anywhere else in the world?

No.

Are there circumstances where you might return to the use of hoods?

There may be occasions when there is a strong military justification for obscuring detainees vision, for example to stop them observing sensitive information. In these cases the UK believes that hooding would be in accordance with the Geneva Conventions.

Special Forces

[If Raised] what about use of hooding after September?
The practice was continued by UK forces conducting the most sensitive detention operations in Iraq

[If pressed] Does the practice continue today?
This is no longer the case

[If pressed for greater detail on these operations]
Not prepared to comment for reasons of operational security

[If pressed] Did there operation involve UKSF
As you will be aware, it is our policy to not normally comment on matters relating to the UKSF

---

[120] MOD054031-2

15.109 There are some obvious points of concern about the accuracy of these defensive lines on hooding. I consider the most serious of these was the suggestion that in response to the question *"Why was hooding stopped in September"*, the answer should be *"Have always accepted that the use of hoods in Iraq was not ideal. A decision was therefore taken to stop their use when the circumstances permitted."* This answer was plainly inaccurate in a number of ways. Although the next answer recognised that the 1 (UK) Div prohibition on hooding had been lost, it was not the case that hooding had been stopped *"when the circumstances permitted"*. The truth was that the death of Baha Mousa had highlighted that hooding was occurring contrary to the earlier prohibition and steps were then taken urgently to reissue the prohibition on hooding. Moreover, the prohibition in May 2003 had not been, as these lines suggested, following a decision that there was no need to use hoods on detainees in transit. It had followed concerns raised by both the ICRC and British officers about the prolonged use of hooding at the JFIT on prisoners awaiting interrogation.

15.110 Cholerton suggested in his Inquiry witness statement that the line that hooding had been stopped *"when conditions on the ground permitted"* was probably adopted to avoid linking the decision to the specific incident of Baha Mousa's death because investigations were still ongoing and it could undermine the judicial process.[121] I appreciate that Cholerton was doing his best to reconstruct why this line had been adopted, but I do not accept that a risk of prejudicing the SIB investigation, even if that was the reason that officials had in mind, justified asserting that hooding was stopped when circumstances permitted. I am quite satisfied that Cholerton was not seeking deliberately to mislead in this line taken by the IIT, but I found his explanation for it unconvincing. In his oral evidence, Cholerton more realistically accepted that a better form of words could have been found. He suggested that in hindsight, they could have had a better line on the reason why hooding was stopped.[122]

15.111 Richard Johnson, by now the Head of the Iraq team in Policy Operations at PJHQ, giving evidence about the same line albeit in a later document in 2004, agreed with Cholerton that there was a reluctance to say very much publicly about the specific circumstances of Baha Mousa's death for fear of prejudicing the investigation. But Richard Johnson accepted that the line given was not a completely frank response and nor did it set out all the information. In response to a question from me, Richard Johnson replied:

> *"A. I think the proposition that that is not a completely candid response and it does not set out all the information, I think that is true."*

His evidence continued:

> *"MR MOSS: Why were fuller answers not, then, being given by your team to explain more candidly, perhaps without direct reference to the court martial or to Baha Mousa's death, the real reasons why hooding had been stopped in theatre?*
>
> *A. I think that the information about the background to the ban on hooding and the background to Mr Mousa's death was being conveyed to ministers in quite some detail. Quite how that formulation of words came to be, I can't recall."*[123]

I reverted to this topic at the end of Richard Johnson's evidence:

---

[121] Cholerton BMI07454-5, paragraphs 2 and 9
[122] Cholerton BMI 92/182/8-17; Cholerton BMI 92/191/21-194/13
[123] Richard Johnson BMI 92/149/1-151/14

> "THE CHAIRMAN: Mr Johnson, I am slightly troubled – more than slightly troubled – by your response to the questions you were asked by Mr Moss about the question and answer given by Lord Bach in the House of Lords on 1 July 2004, which is under MOD050408 and the ones that follow on from it, where I think you very frankly and candidly said that "The practice of hooding was discontinued when there was no longer a military justification for continuing to do so" was, to say the least, not completely accurate.
>
> A. That wasn't quite my intention, Sir. My intention was to say –
>
> THE CHAIRMAN: That is what I understood you to be saying. I'm sorry, I should not have interrupted you. That is what I understood you to mean.
>
> A. I think there were two aspects that may have informed that form of words.
>
> THE CHAIRMAN: Yes.
>
> A. I think one was an attempt to capture what the CJO's thinking was when he gave the order banning hooding and I think the other would have been an attempt to avoid any specific reference to the circumstances of Mr Mousa's death prior to that going to court martial.
>
> THE CHAIRMAN: I can entirely understand the latter, but that would be easier to understand if the person who was drafting the answer and the person who was giving the answer had actually said, "We can't say too much about this for fear of compromising the court martial".
>
> A. I think in a number of other cases that is exactly what was said.
>
> THE CHAIRMAN: Well, the end result is that it does not give a full response to the question, does it?
>
> A. I think that is fair.
>
> THE CHAIRMAN: I wonder how that would be thought proper to have an answer which was not completely accurate in that way?
>
> A. It certainly would not have been any attempt to deliberately mislead. It would have been an attempt, I suspect – as I say I cannot recall – to come up with a formulation of words which would achieve those two things, that reflected the CJO's decision and avoided, you know, anything that might compromise the court martial."[124]

15.112 On 25 May 2004, the Secretary of State replied to a letter from the Rt. Hon. Nicholas Soames MP.[125] Both the draft response and the response actually sent repeated the line that hooding had been stopped when local commanders believed the circumstances permitted. This was, again, an inaccurate explanation of the circumstances in which hooding had come to be prohibited. Essentially the same line had been taken in an earlier letter to Soames from Hoon on 18 May:[126]

---

[124] Richard Johnson BMI 92/157/8-158/25
[125] MOD050968
[126] MOD051010

The policy on hooding is quite straightforward. We regard the use of hoods during interrogation as contrary to the Geneva Conventions. This technique has never been part of the standard operating procedure on Operation TELIC. The Defence Intelligence and Security Centre explicitly teaches interrogators not to use this technique. However there are some circumstances in which hooding prisoners can legitimately be used during their capture to conceal sensitive information such as the disposition of friendly forces. We always recognised that it was desirable to cease the practice as quickly as possible and commanders on the ground judged that we could safely do so by May last year. When these commanders were replaced during a routine roulement in July the direction was lost. However, Chief of Joint Operations then issued a directive in September 2003 that the hooding should stop.

15.113 The draft for the 25 May 2004 response to Soames was provided by Kistruck who had also provided the earlier defensive lines on hooding. Kistruck said that most of the information would have come largely from Allkins but also from other sources.[127] In his second Inquiry witness statement, Kistruck said it was his understanding that Brims had issued an operational directive that hoods were not to be used, and that "...Brims must have taken this decision not to use hoods believing that the operational circumstances permitted it". He thought that the September 2003 decision had just reiterated the earlier decision of Brims once it became clear that the earlier direction had been lost.[128] Kistruck also argued that there were differences of emphasis but no inconsistency between the different explanations given for the cessation of hooding.[129] I found this aspect of his statement was unconvincing. In his oral evidence, Kistruck stated for the first time in relation to this line about the reason for the prohibition on hooding that he was conscious of the need not to prejudice the Baha Mousa investigation. Kistruck told the Inquiry that he was not aware that Brims' reasoning had been that hooding was wrong for the type of operations being undertaken in Iraq, against a background of concerns raised by the ICRC. Nor had Kistruck seen Brims' own note of 13 May 2004.[130]

15.114 Cholerton said that he was involved in providing the advice in relation to the response to Soames but he presumed that the source of the advice was information provided by PJHQ and more widely in consultation with the MoD.[131]

15.115 Hoon was asked by Counsel to the Inquiry about the line taken in the letter to Soames as to why hooding had been stopped:

"Q. You go on to say this: "We always recognised that it was desirable to cease the practice as quickly as possible and commanders on the ground judged that we could safely do so by May last year."

"We always recognised that it was desirable to cease the practice ..." of hooding. Was that right?

---

[127] Kistruck BMI07819, paragraph 6; MOD050970
[128] Kistruck BMI07820, paragraphs 8-10
[129] Kistruck BMI07823, paragraph 21
[130] Kistruck BMI 93/34/23-39/19
[131] Cholerton BMI07457, paragraph 15

> *A. Bearing in mind that this is a year after the events, but certainly that was the Department's view of hooding for purposes of transit of the prisoners, and I think it is wholly consistent with what I have just told the Inquiry in response to your questions.*
>
> *Q. I don't quite understand that, Mr Hoon, if you will forgive me. "We always recognised that it was desirable to cease the practice ..." As I understand your evidence, you were not even aware it was happening until after the death of Baha Mousa.*
>
> *A. I am writing a letter on behalf of the Ministry of Defence as Secretary of State and it is clear from the language that I am using that I am not writing in a personal capacity; I am writing on behalf of the Department and that is why the letter had been sent to me. It is important to distinguish my personal position and my personal knowledge from the responsibilities I had to write on behalf of the Department.*
>
> *Q. Where on behalf of the Department do we see any suggestion that it had always been the Department's view that hooding would cease as soon as possible?*
>
> *A. Because the law, as we have discussed, requires that hooding may only be used for circumstances of security to protect British forces and British information. Clearly, once those security circumstances have come to an end, it would be desirable to cease the practice because thereafter there could not be any lawful jurisdiction for it.*
>
> *Q. If we look, then, at MOD050968. This is another letter to Nicholas Soames, a little later, 25 May now. Again it is signed by you. I appreciate and I certainly do not make the point that you were dealing with the matter personally; you were writing, as it were, on behalf of the Department as the minister. But you say this in the last paragraph: "Local commanders took decisions to cease the hooding of detainees when they believed the circumstances permitted." What was your understanding about that? What was it that had occurred, for example, in April 2003, when General Brims gave his order, the one that it seemed did not have full effect – what was it that happened then, as you understood it, that had changed the circumstances on the ground that hooding was no longer required?*
>
> *A. Bearing in mind that I only learned about this in the period after Baha Mousa's death, but my understanding was that General Brims had seen some prisoners hooded, that he judged that it was no longer necessary for that practice to continue on security grounds and that he ordered that it should stop.*
>
> *Q. That would have been your understanding at the time of writing that letter, would it?*
>
> *A. It was my understanding from September 2003 onwards, so certainly it was still my understanding in 2004, yes."*[132]

15.116 I do not doubt that Hoon believed his response to Soames to be accurate. But with respect to him, his answers suggested that he had not perhaps fully grasped the respects in which his response to this correspondence turned out to have been inaccurate. The evidence to the Inquiry did not support the suggestion that the hooding ban, whether the original verbal ban by Brims in Op Telic 1 or the re-issue of the prohibition in theatre after Baha Mousa's death, was introduced simply because of changed operational conditions on the ground. It was not right to say that it had always been recognised that it was desirable to cease hooding, or that the judgment was made that it was safe to do so in May 2003. I accept that Hoon believed in the truth of the responses which he signed off to Soames at the time. But on this aspect, they were not accurate.

---

[132] Hoon BMI 103/203/18-206/5

15.117 In the context of a draft response to a subsequent Parliamentary Question, Rose raised the concern that it might be disingenuous to claim that there had been a purely operational decision to ban hooding based on changed operational circumstances:[133]

> On 2381 -- I am concerned that it is a little disingenuous to imply that the decision to ban hooding was purely an operational one and had nothing to do with the adverse publicity. What "operational circumstances" changed to allow non-hooding -- maybe the availability of blindfolds ?? I think the answer to the question is the same as with 2329 i.e. we do not accept that there is anything necessarily illegal about using hooding in limited circs. So there was no reason for Ministers to stop it when it was reported on tv.
>
> Vivien

15.118 Despite this perceptive concern by Rose, the previous inaccurate explanation for the cessation of hooding was regrettably perpetuated in later statements:

(1) the response to Amnesty International in June 2004 stated *"In September 2003, however, hooding was no longer considered necessary;"*[134]

(2) answers prepared for questions from a *Guardian* journalist in early June 2004 stated *"The military decision to stop the practice was taken when the circumstances on the ground permitted;"*[135]

(3) suggested answers for supplementary questions for Ingram to respond to an oral Parliamentary Question from the Rt. Hon. Adam Price MP in July 2004 included:

> *"Commanders on the ground judged that we could safely cease using hoods in May last year. However when these Commanders were replaced during a routine roulement in July the direction was lost. In September, when it became clear that this practice had re-emerged, the Chief of Joint Operations issued a Directive to direct that hooding should stop and the Standard Operating Instruction was amended to reflect this change."*[136]

The background note for the Minister included:

> *"We always recognised that it was desirable to cease the practice as quickly as possible and commanders on the ground judged that we could safely do so by May last year";*[137] and

(4) a background note for the Defence Minister Lord Bach in relation to a written Parliamentary Question from Lord Lester (1 July 2004) included the following:[138]

> The use of hoods during interrogation, however, is regarded as contrary to the Geneva Conventions. This technique has never been part of the standard operating procedure on Operation TELIC and the Defence Intelligence and Security Centre explicitly teaches interrogators not to use this technique. We have found no evidence that would suggest that interrogators ignored their training and hooded prisoners during interrogation, nor do we believe that there were any instances of hooding being used during tactical questioning as a technique to extract information.
>
> It was recognised that it was desirable to cease the practice of hooding as soon as there was no longer a military justification for continuing to do so. Chief of Joint Operations issued a directive, dated 30 September 2003, to UK Forces in Iraq, to "immediately cease the hooding of persons detained", although blindfolding in certain circumstances was an acceptable alternative.

---

[133] Rose BMI 93/135/7-137/13; MOD053414
[134] MOD007530-1
[135] MOD050966
[136] MOD050463-4
[137] MOD050468
[138] MOD050411

15.119 The timing of a further answer to a Parliamentary Question was a little confusing. On 12 May 2004, the Rt. Hon. Harry Cohen MP tabled the following question:

> *"To ask the Secretary of State for Defence, pursuant to his oral statement of 10th May on Iraq, whether the routine hooding of prisoners in UK facilities in Iraq was contrary to instructions; on what basis the routine hooding was authorised, and by whom; whether hooding continues of Iraqis by UK forces outside UK facilities; whether hooding by UK forces outside facilities is contrary to instructions; and if he will make a statement."*[139]

15.120 The Secretary of State's answer to this question was not given until 12 October 2004. Consistent with the response drafted by officials, the answer given by Hoon was:

> *"Prisoners held in UK detention facilities in Iraq have not, at any time, been routinely hooded.*
>
> *Hooding was discontinued in Iraq when there was no longer a military justification for continuing the practice. Hooding during arrest and transit is acceptable when there is a strong military reason to do it, for example to offer security to our own forces and locations or to protect the detainee (by preventing identification by other detainees)."*[140]

This answer had been drafted by Allkins. His background note included the following:[141]

> The use of hoods, during interrogation, however, is regarded as contrary to the Geneva Conventions. This technique has never been part of the standard operating procedure on Operation TELIC and the Defence Intelligence and Security Centre explicitly teaches interrogators not to use this technique. We have found no evidence that would suggest that interrogators ignored their training and hooded prisoners during interrogation, nor do we believe that there were any instances of hooding being used during tactical questioning as a technique to extract information.
>
> It was recognised that it was desirable to cease the practice of hooding as soon as there was no longer a military justification for continuing to do so. Chief of Joint Operations issued a directive, dated 30 September 2003, to UK Forces in Iraq, to "immediately cease the hooding of persons detained", although blindfolding in certain circumstances was an acceptable alternative.
>
> **REMEMBER you are accountable for the accuracy and timeliness of the advice you provide. Departmental Instructions on answering PQs can be viewed on the CHOTS public area and on DAWN. Please send to PARLIAMENTARY QUESTIONS.**
>
> | | | | |
> |---|---|---|---|
> | DRAFTED BY | : | C. ALLKINS | TEL: |
> | AUTHORISED BY | : | W. JESSETT | TEL: |
> | GRADE/RANK | : | SCS | |
> | BRANCH | : | PJHQ DCOMDSEC | |

15.121 I note that Allkins could not recall the date on which his background note was drafted. He referred to the fact that 12 October 2004 was merely the official date when the written answer was given. He could not account for the length of time between the tabling of the question in May and the answer given in October.[142]

15.122 Allkins very frankly accepted that the background note did not do justice to the information that had been received about Baha Mousa and his death. Allkins made the point that a considerable volume of briefing material had been sent to Whitehall on this subject. Allkins agreed that the reference to prisoners having

---

[139] MOD050350
[140] MOD050350
[141] MOD050352
[142] Allkins BMI 90/162/6-7; Allkins BMI07352, paragraph 16

not been routinely hooded was not correct. He candidly said of the answer to this Parliamentary Question:

> *"Looking at this now, with my eye on it as a former civil servant, that's an extremely poor piece of work. Almost certainly there is considerable human error involved, almost certainly mine."*[143]

15.123 In Allkins' favour, it should be said that while the answer and background note on any objective view contained inaccurate material, it remained unclear whether he had drafted the material in mid-May when the picture was less clear, or some time later when it may be that some detail had been forgotten. I accept that Allkins was working to a very high and demanding tempo and that like many he relied upon others who were providing information to him.

15.124 In his oral evidence to the Inquiry, Hoon maintained that it was true that prisoners held in UK detention facilities in Iraq had not at any time been routinely hooded.[144] I do not question the honesty of that evidence, still less what was said to Parliament. I do not consider, however, that the former Secretary of State had quite understood what the Inquiry's evidence had shown about the extent to which hooding had occurred in practice at the JFIT early in Op Telic 1, nor the extent of the use of hooding by 1 QLR.

15.125 Allkins' frank acceptance that the line that prisoners had not been routinely hooded was incorrect was accordingly more realistic and more attractive evidence than Hoon's defence of the same statement.

15.126 I set out conclusions on this part of the events at the end of this Part of the Report.

[143] Allkins BMI 90/162/20-166/19
[144] Hoon BMI 103/218/11-221/3

Chapter 4: The 2004 Review of the Policy on Hooding

15.127 In May 2004, the position taken by the MoD was that hooding was not in all circumstances unlawful. Its use had been prohibited in all theatres but the door had been left slightly open as regards the future use of hooding. The MoD statements at this time purposely did not suggest that security hooding would never be used in the future.

15.128 Whether hooding should be retained for limited future use became the subject of a review that was instigated by the Chief of the Defence Staff, Lord Walker on 26 May 2004:[145]

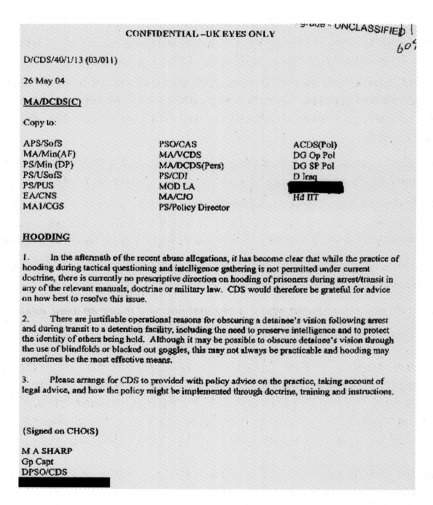

CONFIDENTIAL –UK EYES ONLY

UNCLASSIFIED

D/CDS/40/1/13 (03/011)

26 May 04

MA/DCDS(C)

Copy to:

APS/SofS	PSO/CAS	ACDS(Pol)
MA/Min(AF)	MA/VCDS	DG Op Pol
PS/Min (DP)	MA/DCDS(Pers)	DG SP Pol
PS/USofS	PS/CDI	D Iraq
PS/PUS	MOD LA	
EA/CNS	MA/CJO	Hd IIT
MA1/CGS	PS/Policy Director	

HOODING

1. In the aftermath of the recent abuse allegations, it has become clear that while the practice of hooding during tactical questioning and intelligence gathering is not permitted under current doctrine, there is currently no prescriptive direction on hooding of prisoners during arrest/transit in any of the relevant manuals, doctrine or military law. CDS would therefore be grateful for advice on how best to resolve this issue.

2. There are justifiable operational reasons for obscuring a detainee's vision following arrest and during transit to a detention facility, including the need to preserve intelligence and to protect the identity of others being held. Although it may be possible to obscure detainee's vision through the use of blindfolds or blacked out goggles, this may not always be practicable and hooding may sometimes be the most effective means.

3. Please arrange for CDS to provided with policy advice on the practice, taking account of legal advice, and how the policy might be implemented through doctrine, training and instructions.

{Signed on CHOtS}

M A SHARP
Gp Capt
DPSO/CDS

15.129 On a fair reading of this request, it is clear that it was only the use of hoods for security purposes that was being contemplated. The suggestion being made, subject to the advice to be provided, was that the use of blindfolds or blacked out goggles might not always be practicable and that hooding might sometimes be the most effective means of securing sight deprivation.

---

[145] MOD031356

15.130 Lord Walker told the Inquiry that he no longer had any independent recollection of the detail of this review of policy.[146] Lord Walker's view was that hooding might be the most effective means because it may in some circumstances be the only means available:

> "Q... Did that, General, reflect your view? Do you recall, at the time, that hooding may be under certain circumstances the most effective means?
>
> A. It did.
>
> Q. Why did you hold that view, that hooding might be the most effective means?
>
> A. Because it may have been the only means available in the circumstances at the time.
>
> Q. Is that what it means?
>
> A. Yes, in extremis. I mean, had they had goggles or had they had something else, then they ought to be used. You cannot predict war and you cannot predict where people are going to be found, arrested and handled in all the circumstances.
>
> Q. What I am really putting to you, if you look at paragraph 2 with me – "this may not always be practicable and hooding may sometimes be the most effective means" – you wouldn't say, would you, that if goggles or blindfolds were available, that nonetheless there may be reason for using hoods?
>
> A. No, I think it would have been better – as you can see, it was Martin Sharp who wrote that. I think what I would have put would be sometimes would be the only effective means.
>
> Q. So as with the last witness, Sir Michael Jackson, whose evidence you probably heard, you would go along with him, would you, his view that there may be circumstances where hoods would effectively have to be used and in those circumstances you would condone their use?
>
> A. I have no difficulty with hoods being used to deprive people of vision or the sight of a detainee for that period at capture.
>
> Q. What do you say to those who will say that hooding is per se itself inhumane?
>
> A. They are entitled to their opinion."[147]

15.131 Cholerton lent support to the request for a review of hooding policy, commenting that he was glad that advice was being requested that took account of the operational reality.[148] He told the Inquiry that it would have been easier for senior people to have just announced an outright ban without any work to review whether hooding needed to be retained as a technique in appropriate circumstances.[149]

15.132 The work on this review fell to the Directorate of Joint Commitments initially led by Ms Mandy Hope. Hope sent the following email on 30 June 2004 recording the outcome of the first meeting held to discuss hooding policy:[150]

---

[146] Walker BMI08056, paragraph 19
[147] Walker BMI 100/169/2-170/11
[148] MOD052629
[149] Cholerton BMI 92/199/2-6
[150] MOD020239

From: DJtCts-AD Pol-S
Sent: 30 June 2004 10:30
To: LA2/PA-S
Cc: DjtCts-Pol1-S; PJHQ-J9-LA-S
Subject: Advice on Hooding

Importance: Low

Vivien,

As you know, I held a meeting on Monday to discuss the issue of hooding of prisoners of war during arrest and transit, in order to provide advice to CDS on the requirement and the legal aspects.

We noted CJO's current direction that hooding was not to take place but felt that this was a knee-jerk reaction to recent publicity, albeit probably the right one at the moment.

In brief, the conclusion we came to was that, there is an ongoing requirement to restrict a captive's vision in certain circumstances. We concluded further that we should retain the ability to hood as a capability because there are certain circumstances e.g. a the point of capture in confused and dangerous circumstances, where this might be the only option for UK troops on the ground. In coming to this conclusion we noted, inter alia, that:

in hooding could be legally justified in certain circumstances
that this is not the ideal method
that alternative methods should be used unless genuinely unavailable
that clear, written, guidance should be developed on use of the practice and consequent care of prisoners
and specific reference should be made in annual and pre-deployment training.

We are preparing a draft submission to go to DCDS(C) which will fill in the detail a bit more and which we will circulate to all the appropriate desks including yours of course.
Before we do that however, I would be grateful for an initial reaction to our conclusions. Arvinder was at the meeting but clearly MODLAs views need to be reflected, especially the necessity/desirability of putting this to the AG?

Please could you copy your response to 'all' as Catherine will be taking this forward.

Mandy J Hope
DjtCts AD Pol

15.133 As foreshadowed in the final line of this email, when Hope moved post, the work on hooding policy was taken forwards by one of her staff, Ms Catherine Evans. Catherine Evans was a relatively junior civil servant who I accept was principally pulling together the views of others to formulate a policy recommendation that would ultimately be for the Chief of the Defence Staff to consider.

15.134 By 20 August 2004, a draft submission to the Chief of the Defence Staff and a detailed background paper had been produced by Catherine Evans on which she sought comments from all those involved.[151]

15.135 The recommendations sought the provision of clearer guidance on when restriction of vision was acceptable and by what means; and suggested that blacked out goggles should be the preferred method but retaining the ability to use hooding as a last resort:[152]

---

[151] MOD054195
[152] MOD054196

Recommendations

3.   CDS should:

a.   **Note** the paper at Annex A which provides the background to the options detailed below.

b.   **Note** that, legal, medical and presentational concerns notwithstanding, it remains operationally desirable to restrict temporarily the vision of detainees in particular circumstances.

c.   **Note** that, since CJO's direction in October 2003 that 'hooding' of Prisoner of War (PWs), detainees and internees in all theatres should cease until further advised[1], there remains no consistent policy towards the restriction of vision during arrest and transit, including the use of hoods.

d.   **Agree** that UK Armed Forces should be offered clear guidance (including through doctrine and ROE) on when the restriction of vision is acceptable and by what means.

e.   **Agree** therefore, that work should now proceed to develop doctrine on restricting vision for detainees, focused on providing blacked-out goggles as the preferred method, while retaining the ability to use hooding as a last resort; and to identify logistic considerations and procurement options to achieve this.

15.136 The background section of the submission explained the reasoning behind the desire to retain hooding for use in extreme circumstances where the preferred option of goggles might not be operationally practical:[153]

Background

4.   PSO to CDS noted in May[2] that currently there is no prescriptive direction on the hooding of prisoners during arrest and transit in any of the relevant manuals, doctrine or military law. The lack of a clear policy position came to light during the recent OP TELIC abuse allegations. Since Oct 03, however, hooding of Prisoners of War (PWs), detainees and internees in all theatres when British forces are currently operating has been prohibited by CJO directive. This is largely a reactive measure to public criticism of the practice of hooding, in the absence of any clearly defined policy or doctrinal guidance on the basis of which the MOD could defend its position. Consequently there is a pressing need to formulate a policy towards the practice of restricting vision during arrest and transit, including the use of hooding to achieve this, that addresses the legal, medical and presentational concerns connected to the practice.

5.   Medical concerns over the use of hooding relate to the risk of asphyxiation due to the fact that a detainee's airways are restricted. Although some have sought to argue that, because hooding can be considered inhumane and demeaning treatment, it is in fact illegal, MOD legal advice suggests that the practice remains acceptable under the Geneva Convention if done for security reasons. Nonetheless, they have also indicated that they do not find hooding an acceptable substitute for failing to address the question of resourcing alternative methods to restrict vision. Although no such steps have been taken to date, anecdotal evidence from theatre where troops have improvised to create blacked-out goggles suggests that not only is this an operationally feasible alternative for restricting vision, but may actually be preferable since their use avoids the negative presentational issues connected with hooding. Nonetheless, it is deemed prudent to retain the ability to hood, albeit with clear doctrinal guidance, for use in extreme circumstances where the preferred option may not be operationally practical.

---

[153] MOD054197

15.137 It was recognised that any return to hooding, even if only in extreme circumstances, would necessitate advising Parliament of the change:[154]

> Presentation
>
> 10. Following the Iraq abuse allegations, the practice of hooding has attracted significant interest both in Parliament, the media and amongst human rights organisations. Defence Ministers have advised Parliament on a number of occasions that the practise of hooding PWs, detainees and internees has ceased. Should CDS agree the recommendations, it will be necessary to return to Parliament and advise them of any changes in policy and practice once the consequent work has been completed. The MOD should be prepared for the controversy and potential negative publicity that such an announcement may attract within Parliament, the media and the public at large. To this end, DJtCts will engage with the Iraq Inquiries Team/Sec(Iraq) amongst others, to prepare suitable press lines and briefing material at the appropriate moment.

15.138 Annexed to the background paper was a short assessment of the medical risks associated with hooding:[155]

> **MEDICAL RISKS ASSOCIATED WITH THE PRACTICE OF HOODING**
>
> If the air supply through the nasopharynx is hindered as would be the case if one were to hood an individual, one can expect the induction of a state of asphyxia in that individual, which would if unrelieved cause death. This will then give rise to a state of hypercarbia (increased carbon dioxide level) and hypoxia (reduced oxygen concentration). This will then produce a state of relative hypoxaemia (decreased blood oxygen concentration). In a hot and humid environment this effect would only be heightened. Also, hooding an individual reduces heat loss by up to 30%, thus greatly increasing the chance of heat related illness. The increased levels of stress, both physiological and psychological surrounding these events would further compound matters and hence be an added detriment to most healthy individuals. If one had a past medical history of a respiratory or cardiac disorder then these effects could be more severe.
>
> J S Baidwan
> SO2 J4 Med(B)
> PJHQ

15.139 Appreciating that this was a concise assessment of the medical risks, it is perhaps a little surprising, given the severity of the risk as suggested in this opinion, that the medical risk did not feature more prominently in the recommendations formulated in the draft submission. The background paper did, however, argue that the ability further to quantify these risks scientifically appeared to be limited, and pointed to the lack of an objective evidence base.[156]

15.140 The background paper itself repays reading in full.[157] The requirement for sight deprivation and commentary on the use of hooding were as follows:

---

[154] MOD054197
[155] MOD054208
[156] MOD054201, paragraph 5
[157] MOD054200-209

<u>Requirement</u>

3.   Military advice suggests that the first few hours after a detainee's capture are vital. A soldier is taught that he has a duty to escape and the vast majority of escapes (the figure of 90% has been quoted) occur within the first couple of hours of detention. Once a prisoner has passed through the initial point of tactical questioning conducted at a Unit HQ, the chances of escape rapidly reduce.   When escape is not immediately possible, however, a soldier is taught to gather as much intelligence on the capturing forces as possible. Conversely, in certain circumstances, the capturing forces will wish to preserve the shock of capture. **Consequently, there are justifiable operational reasons for obscuring a detainee's vision during arrest and transit to a detention facility, inter alia, to prevent escape, to prevent attack against the capturing forces, to preserve intelligence, to prevent communication between detainees and to protect the identity of both the detainee and others being held.**

<u>The Use of Hooding</u>

4.   There are a number of methods that can be employed to restrict vision, including the use of blindfolds or blacked out goggles. Prior to OP TELIC it appears that the hooding of detainees for arrest or transit of detainees was a standard procedure for UK troops, in part due to the ready availability of sandbags in theatre and the ease with which these can be used to restrict vision, particularly in hostile circumstances. **There are a number of considerations, nevertheless, that make the practice of hooding unattractive –including the fact that sandbags, the most widely used hood, are not entirely opaque.**

15.141 It is of some concern that the shock of capture was still being discussed in the context of what sight deprivation should be permitted. Catherine Evans said that this would have been derived from points made by those involved in the discussions and consultations.[158] In her oral evidence, she explained that the shock of capture was talked of more as a consequence of sight deprivation and not a justification for it.[159]

15.142 The legal section of the background paper recorded that hooding for security reasons was acceptable in some circumstances under the Geneva Conventions. It was suggested that the legal advice had agreed the need to retain the capability to use hoods in operational circumstances such as the heat of the battlefield where other methods might not be practical. However, there was a legal concern that this should not be seen as licence to return to the use of hooding in Iraq, nor did it justify failing to address the resourcing of other means to restrict vision particularly in more permissive circumstances.[160]

15.143 The background paper was broadly positive about the use of blacked out goggles as an alternative to hooding, but again the shock of capture was mentioned in this context:[161]

---

[158] Catherine Evans BMI07965, paragraph 20
[159] Catherine Evans BMI 91/132/14-134/25
[160] MOD054202, paragraphs 6-7
[161] MOD054203

Suitability of Alternative Methods

9. Certainly, by allowing unimpeded airflow through the breathing passages, blacked-out goggles avoid the risks associated with hooding. The general reaction from theatre to using blacked out-goggles, however, also appears to be positive. Anecdotal evidence would suggest that they are comfortable, easy to fit and effective in obscuring vision and preserving the shock of capture. Importantly, from a presentational point of view, their use does not seem to create the wrong impression with third-party bystanders that hooding may do since they are less likely to be considered demeaning to the detained individual and, therefore, appears to be more acceptable to human rights organisations[3]. Indeed, when given the choice between hoods and blacked-out goggles, UKSF in theatre did not express any real preference between the two. The additional time required to fit goggles was seen as marginal whilst the improved presentational aspects, if anything, made their use more attractive. **Consequently, blacked-out goggles would seem to provide a viable alternative to hoods for restricting vision in the majority of operational circumstances.**

10. Clearly, in those situations where there is an operational requirement to restrict the vision of detainees, it is undesirable that soldiers may have to spend time improvising rather than having an alternative means readily available to them. We need to ensure that the procedure of restricting vision is as straightforward and effortless as possible by providing appropriate resources to troops in theatre by which to achieve this. Consequently, in developing our policy towards hooding, it is important concurrently to consider our policy towards the use of blindfolds/blacked out goggles to ensure that we end up with a consistent and comprehensive approach to restricting vision during arrest and transit.

11. In particular, a decision to establish the use of blacked-out goggles (or equivalent) as the 'best-practice' method of restricting vision will avoid many of the concerns currently connected to the practice of hooding. It will, however, also require further work to investigate the procurement options and logistic considerations for supplying such alternatives to troops in theatre, either for present or future operations. Further advice will be required from Dec(GM)[4] in conjunction with others.

15.144 However, the perceived need to retain hooding in extreme circumstances was explained as follows:[162]

Circumstances Where Hooding May Still Be Required

12. Nevertheless, there are certain operational circumstances such as immediate action in the heat of battle, where using these alternative methods may not always be practical. In such situations, where the need to obscure vision remains, hooding (despite its associated risks) may be the most effective – and safe - means by which to achieve this. **We need to guard against exposing our soldiers to intensified risk by retaining hooding as one of the military options to restrict vision in-extremis circumstances, albeit it with clear guidance over when and how this should be employed to help prevent misuse.**

13. Given that the use of hoods is not the ideal, but should be retained for use in extreme circumstances only, clear parameters need to be defined to ensure that their use is consistent with the spirit of the UK's obligations under international law and care of duty. These may include, but not be restricted to, **the provision that they are for temporary transit and should be replaced by black-out goggles as soon as it is judged operationally feasible to do so; the use of only one hood; forbidding the use of additional tape etc.** The need to assess regularly the detainee's condition and possibly take steps to relieve it if this is operationally practical, should also be stressed.

---

[162] MOD054204

> 14. **Proper written guidance needs to be developed in conjunction with legal advisers and inserted into annual and PDT training syllabus, establishing the use of blacked-out goggles as best practice.** This will help protect both our soldiers and the MOD from future allegations. Legal advice accepts that whilst we cannot guard completely against the risk of the accidents or abuse by a particular individual, nonetheless, we can demonstrate that our policy has been developed with due regard to the law, and that hooding is used appropriately and proportionately where other options are not feasible. In contrast to the OP TELIC abuse allegations, we will be able to point to a clearly defined policy/doctrine and associated guidance/training package to show that the MOD has carefully considered the circumstances in which it may be necessary to resort to the use of hooding and has provided guidance to ensure the human rights/safety of detainees as far as is operationally feasible. Furthermore, comprehensive training should help manage the risks associated with hooding and thus help protect the rights of all involved.[5]
>
> 15. MOD legal advisors are also content with the recommendation that in order to prevent future confusion over whether UK forces are permitted to use hooding within a particular theatre (in accordance with subsequently agreed doctrine), a line should be attached as a note to the relevant detention rule in subsequent Rules of Engagement (ROE) profiles to this effect.

15.145 In her oral evidence, Catherine Evans explained that the key concern was the heat of battle situation. In such circumstances soldiers might be in a fire fight and at the same time trying to secure prisoners. They might have no alternative means of sight deprivation to hand or have run out of goggles or blindfolds. She said in those circumstances hooding should not be ruled out. However, she said that 99 per cent of the time alternative means of hooding should be used. Special Forces had provided reassurance about the practicability of using blacked out goggles on operations.[163]

15.146 A variety of comments were provided on this paper:

(1) Kistruck's comments included questioning whether the paper should point out that hoods were better at protecting the identity of detainees than other methods of sight deprivation. He also said that he did not find the medical advice appended to the paper to be convincing. He further suggested that the paper might add a comment that the use of hoods could be classed as a sensory deprivation technique which could be considered inhumane.[164]

(2) Duncan said "*I do not intend fighting the solution*" but pointed out that the draft did not sufficiently highlight the protection that blindfolding gave to the detained individual.[165]

(3) Capt (RN) Eric Fraser, in the J3 team at PJHQ, pointed out that the direction against hooding for other theatres was only issued on 14 May 2004 and not at the same time as the direction concerning hooding for Op Telic in Iraq.[166]

(4) Intelligence input into the draft from the J2X side of PJHQ stressed that it was necessary to ensure that UK Forces could in appropriate circumstances restrict vision of detainees during arrest and transit. It also suggested that there were occasions when the security of the detainee may be an issue. But it stated that the method of sight deprivation, whether by goggles or blindfolds, did not particularly matter to J2.[167]

---

[163] Catherine Evans BMI 91/148/14-151/5
[164] Kistruck BMI 93/50/21-55/22; MOD054192-3
[165] MOD020268
[166] MOD020269
[167] MOD020271

(5)   A very different contribution was made by Massey, the Assistant Chief of Staff J3 at PJHQ.[168] He was clearly against the whole concept of retaining hooding even *in extremis*:

> From: PJHQ-J3/ACOS-S
> Sent: 31 August 2004 20:30
> To: PJHQ-J9-I A-S; PJHQ-J9-HDPOLOPS1-S
> Cc: PJHQ-J3 DACOS A-S
> Subject: Hooding
>
> Ari
>
> I have just seen Catherine Evans' draft note on hooding (your email of 271312 Aug).
>
> I have serious concerns. There is surely no way that Ministers will (or should even be invited to) contemplate the rehabilitation of this archaic, emotive, baggage-laden practice. One may just as well try to justify the re-introduction of selective torture on the same, highly dubious, grounds of 'operational and force protection reasons'. Forget it. Leave this sort of thing to King Canute.
>
> Far better, in my view, to make a solid case (if we can) for blindfolding, accepting that it may in some circumstances be a little more 'difficult'. But even the latter suggestion hardly bears serious scrutiny. If you get the doctrine, training and equipping right, I fail to see where blindfolds or black goggles would suffer a single disadvantage as compared to hooding.
>
> And for heaven's sake don't get me started on 'the shock of capture' (para 2a). The ECHR will positively drool at the prospect of biting on that one. Good grief.
>
> Regards
>
> Alan
>
> *A M MASSEY*
> Cdre
> ACOS J3
> PJHQ

15.147 The review of hooding was still in progress in November 2004, and was with Fry (the Deputy Chief of the Defence Staff (Commitments)), before submission to the Chief of the Defence Staff.[169] Witnesses struggled to recall what was the final result of the review. Catherine Evans remembered being contacted about it in 2005 after she had moved post. She was informed that the recommendations in the submissions had been reviewed and there was suggestion that it would be clearer and simpler for soldiers to understand if they were told that the only option available for restricting vision was blacked out goggles.[170]

15.148 It is apparent from the evidence which the Inquiry heard in Module 4 (Recommendations), and which I shall examine in Part XVI of this Report, that the MoD did not ultimately adopt the policy of permitted hooding *in extremis*. Rather the use of hoods has continued to be prohibited albeit as a matter of operational policy rather than legal obligation.

15.149 I set out my conclusions about this 2004 review of hooding policy at the end of this Part of the Report.

---

[168] MOD020276
[169] Catherine Evans BMI07962, paragraph 14
[170] Catherine Evans BMI07963, paragraph 15

Chapter 5: Evidence Given to the Joint Committee on Human Rights

15.150 Having regard to what I have said in paragraph 15.13 above, I shall address briefly the evidence the Inquiry received about evidence given to the Parliamentary Joint Committee on Human Rights (JCHR) and concerns raised by the Committee in 2008. I will take these matters in chronological order.

15.151 On 4 June 2004, the JCHR Chairman wrote to Ingram in relation to the ICRC report raising concerns, amongst other matters, relating to the five techniques.[171]

15.152 On 18 June 2004, a draft reply was provided for Ingram by Kistruck.[172] This draft would appear to have been the subject of some revision. Ingram's final response on 25 June 2004 was in the following terms:[173]

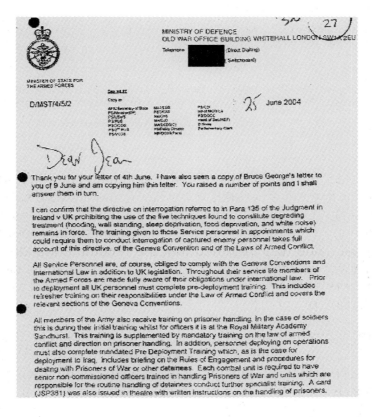

---

[171] MOD050713-4
[172] MOD050957
[173] MOD050702-4

The training of military intelligence officers does not in any respect include the use of any of the methods described in paragraph 25 of the ICRC Report, or indeed any other cruel or degrading treatment, as an interrogation method.

British troops were instructed to stop hooding detainees in September last year, and this remains the case. However, there are some circumstances during initial detention and transit, where for good military reasons, such as to protect sensitive information or to protect the identity of an individual, it is necessary to obscure the vision of detainees'. The UK believes that this is acceptable under the Geneva Conventions but I should make absolutely clear that hooding was only used during the transit of prisoners; it was not used as an interrogation technique.

The Ministry of Defence takes all allegations or suspicions of misconduct or criminal behaviour by UK Armed Forces very seriously. Where it is appropriate, investigations are initiated either on the initiative of the Service Police or after referral by the chain of command. The principal function of the Royal Military Police (RMP) is to enforce the law within the Service community and assist with the maintenance of military discipline. Its powers of arrest are established in the Army Act 1955 and can be exercised anywhere in the world, as Service personnel are subject to English criminal law wherever they are serving. The Special Investigation Branch (SIB) forms part of the RMP and exists to conduct investigations into serious criminal offences committed by or against British Service personnel. The SIB is a fully professional investigative body conforming to Home Office standards and required by statute to follow civilian police force procedures. Statute also requires that the SIB be subject to peer review in the same way as any civilian police force in the UK.

At the conclusion of any RMP investigation a report together with supporting evidence is submitted to the appropriate Commanding Officer and to the Army Legal Services (ALS). ALS then advise the Commanding Officer whether or not there is a *prima facie* case for the purposes of disciplinary action. In serious cases ALS will advise the Commanding Officer on the procedure for referral to a higher authority and then, if appropriate, onto the Army Prosecuting Authority (APA). The APA is statutorily independent of the chain of command and the chain of command is not allowed to seek to influence its case management or decision making processes. In addition to his non-statutory role as head of the ALS, the Director Army Legal Services has a statutory role as the Army Prosecuting Authority for which he is appointed by the Queen. In the exercise of his statutory functions he, too, is entirely independent of the chain of command. As members of professional bodies (the Bar Council or the Law Society), Army prosecutors, who practice in accordance with the

Prosecutors' Code, have an overriding duty to the court to act with independence in the interests of justice. As an additional measure of protection from interference, the APA is answerable to the Attorney General on prosecution issues.

As you would expect, we keep the effectiveness of these procedures under regular review, including the effectiveness of service police investigations. Furthermore, all aspects of our forces disciplinary systems are being considered with a view to modernisation and harmonisation in preparation for a Bill leading to a Tri Service Act, which we hope to introduce in the 2005/06 session.

The Rt Hon Adam Ingram MP

15.153 In his oral evidence to the Inquiry, I asked Ingram about the assertion in this letter that hooding had only been used during the transit of prisoners and was not used as an interrogation technique:

"THE CHAIRMAN: Yes. There, as has been pointed out to you, and in your other references, at the second page of that, in the second paragraph:

"The UK believes that it is acceptable under the Geneva Conventions, but I should make absolutely clear that hooding was only used during the transit of prisoners ..." You are talking there about in the past, presumably.

A. I think so, without reading the whole length again, yes –

THE CHAIRMAN: That's what it seems to be.

> *A. It certainly wouldn't be futuristic because I was addressing their questions which they were raising about the past.*
>
> *THE CHAIRMAN: It goes on: "It was not used as an interrogation technique." Now the real question I need to ask you is this: did that not ring bells in your mind about the Baha Mousa incident?*
>
> *A. I don't recollect whether it did or not. I just don't recollect that.*
>
> *THE CHAIRMAN: If it had, would you not then have appreciated that that was a rather bold statement to make?*
>
> *A. Well, you are asking me to speculate a bit about it and I would then have to consider what other phrase would have been used and there was probably still the police investigation underway at that stage. So it may not have been established at that point that hooding had been used for interrogation in relation to Baha Mousa.*
>
> *THE CHAIRMAN: That is perfectly true, but that's not quite what it says. It says affirmatively "It was not used as an interrogation technique".*
>
> *A. Well, it had not been proved that it had been.*
>
> *THE CHAIRMAN: Sorry?*
>
> *A. It had not been proved that it had been. That could be one interpretation of that at that stage. And I don't know what the outcome of the Baha Mousa trial says specifically on that.*
>
> *THE CHAIRMAN: Yes, well, I mean it seems to be a positive assertion that hooding was not used as an interrogation technique – and I can understand that being made – apart from the Baha Mousa incident about which you have been asked a number of questions.*
>
> *A. Well, with respect, Sir, I don't know whether it is a proven fact that Baha Mousa was subjected to interrogation with hoods on. I don't know what the outcome of that trial concluded or the investigation.*
>
> *THE CHAIRMAN: All right.*
>
> *A. So I think it has to be based upon the fact, was there a fact that that was the case and, if so, then that becomes an erroneous statement."*[174]

15.154 More generally, Ingram's evidence in his Inquiry witness statement was that he would only have approved his letter to the JCHR if it was consistent with what he understood to be the position at the time from briefings and background notes provided to him. Ingram told the Inquiry that he had no reason to think that the content of his letter was incorrect or inaccurate.[175]

15.155 In March 2006, the JCHR took evidence in relation to UK Compliance with the UN Convention Against Torture. In that context Brims gave evidence to the JCHR on 27 March 2006. An MoD briefing pack had been prepared for this session.[176]

15.156 The JCHR issued a report on 26 May 2006[177] (its 19th Report of Session 2005-2006). It referred to the correspondence with Ingram and the oral evidence of Brims:[178]

---

[174] Ingram BMI 97/81/15-83/16
[175] Ingram BMI08385, paragraphs 35-37
[176] MOD050598; MOD050610-1; MOD050647-8
[177] PLT000103
[178] PLT000133

> **Interrogation techniques**
>
> 83. There has been particular controversy over the use of hooding by UK troops in Iraq. Hooding was one of the "five techniques" held by the European Court of Human Rights to amount to inhuman and degrading treatment in breach of Article 3 ECHR, in a landmark decision of 1978, in *Ireland v UK*. The Court held that the techniques employed in interrogations in Northern Ireland, though they did not amount to torture, did amount to inhuman and degrading treatment contrary to Article 3 ECHR. The five techniques were: wall-standing (forcing detainees to remain for long periods in a stress position against a wall); hooding (during interrogations); subjection to continuous loud noise; sleep deprivation; and deprivation of food and drink. The five techniques were never officially authorised in writing but were taught orally at training seminars.
>
> 84. In his letter of 25 June 2004 to the previous Committee, Mr Ingram confirmed that the army directive prohibiting the use of the five techniques, introduced in 1972 following the allegations of ill-treatment in Northern Ireland, remains in force, and stated that it is fully taken into account in training. An internal policy document "Guidance on Interrogation and Tactical Questioning—Support to Operations" states that the five techniques are expressly forbidden, though without specific reference to the *Ireland v UK* case.
>
> 85. In oral evidence to us, Lieutenant General Brims asserted that following allegations made in respect of operations in Iraq "very clear direction" had been given that hooding should not take place, either in interrogation, or elsewhere. It was however permissible to use other means to blindfold prisoners in some circumstances, for example during transfer. Lieutenant General Brims was satisfied that troops on the ground would be aware that the five techniques were prohibited, although they might not be able to state this in terms of the judgment in *Ireland v UK*.

15.157 On 15 July 2008, the JCHR published its 28th report of the 2007-2008 Session, entitled "UN Convention Against Torture: Discrepancies in evidence given to the Committee about the use of prohibited interrogation techniques in Iraq".[179]

15.158 Within that report, the JCHR cited the following aspect of Ingram's letter of 25 June 2004:[180]

> 2. Mr Ingram replied to the Committee in the following terms:
>
> I can confirm that the directive on interrogation referred to in Para 135 of the Judgment in *Ireland v UK* prohibiting the use of the five techniques found to constitute degrading treatment (hooding, wall standing, sleep deprivation, food deprivation, and white noise) remains in force. The training given to those Service personnel in appointments which could require them to conduct interrogation of captured enemy personnel takes full account of this directive, of the Geneva Convention and of the Laws of Armed Conflict.

15.159 The JCHR also cited Brims' evidence to the Committee in 2006 in the following terms:[181]

> 4. In oral evidence, on 27 March 2006, we asked Lieutenant General R. V. Brims CBE DSO, Commander Field Army, about whether he was satisfied troops were fully aware of the prohibition on the use of the five conditioning techniques. Lieutenant General Brims said:
>
> On hooding we have given very clear direction and hooding itself will not take place. It is permissible to blindfold in some other way in certain circumstances but we care not to do that at the moment ... I think if you went and asked most troops, "What are the five things that have been banned?", they would look at you and be unable to communicate to you. If you wrote down these five things, "What is your view on them?", they would say, "You should not do them", if you follow the answer.

---

179 PLT000924
180 PLT000927
181 PLT000928

15.160 The JCHR's July 2008 report then referred to the evidence in the Court Martial of Payne and others, and to the findings of the review by Brig John Aitken. It drew the following conclusions:[182]

Conclusion

13. The evidence presented to the *Payne* court martial, and accepted by the Crown, and the findings of the Aitken report would appear to show that:

- conditioning techniques such as hooding and the use of stress positioning were used by some British troops in Iraq, despite such techniques having been prohibited in 1972;

- the use of hooding and stress positioning by 1 Queen's Lancashire Regiment in 2003 was based on legal advice received from Brigade headquarters;

- the prohibition on the use of conditioning techniques may have been interpreted narrowly, as only applying to interrogation personnel and to operations in Northern Ireland;

- at least until the Baha Mousa case came to light, the prohibition on the use of conditioning techniques was not as clearly articulated to troops in Iraq as it might, and indeed should, have been;

- even as late as January 2008, when the Aitken report was published, the prohibition on the use of conditioning techniques was not clearly articulated to service personnel other than those responsible for interrogation; and

- until 2005, interrogation personnel were trained in proscribed techniques, if only to demonstrate the techniques to which they might be subject if captured.

The JCHR report went on to state:[183]

14. These conclusions call into question the evidence we received from Lieutenant General Brims and which our predecessor Committee received from the Minister for the Armed Forces. Lieutenant General Brims's assertion that ordinary troops would recognise that techniques such as hooding were prohibited is not supported by Brigadier Aitken's findings or the events surrounding the death of Baha Mousa. Nor does Mr Ingram's claim that the training of interrogation personnel took full account of the prohibition on the use of the five conditioning techniques seem consistent with the facts which have now come to light.

15. The evidence we received from Lieutenant General Brims and Mr Ingram formed the basis for the section of our Report on the UN Convention Against Torture dealing with interrogation techniques. It would appear that this evidence was incorrect and that, as a result, we were unable to give a full account to Parliament of the human rights issues relating to the use of such techniques.

16. We have yet to receive an explanation from the Ministry of Defence for the discrepancies between the evidence given to the Joint Committee in 2004 and 2006 on the use of prohibited conditioning techniques and the facts which have emerged from the *Payne* court martial and the Aitken report. The issues relating to the death of Baha Mousa are now the subject of a public inquiry. We recommend that, in response to this Report, the Secretary of State for Defence should confirm we will receive a detailed explanation of the discrepancies between the evidence to the Committee by Mr Ingram in 2004 and Lieutenant General Brims in 2006 and the facts which have subsequently emerged concerning the death of Baha Mousa, as soon as possible after the conclusion of the public inquiry.

---

[182] PLT000930
[183] PLT000931

15.161 In his Inquiry witness statement, Brims defended the account that he gave to the JCHR and asserted in robust terms that the JCHR had wrongly interpreted his evidence.[184] The key point that Brims sought to emphasise was the context in which he told the JCHR that if you wrote down the five techniques and asked most troops what their views of them was, they would say *"You should not do them."* Brims was keen to state that he gave this answer in response to a series of questions that were looking at the then current situation in 2006, not the situation as it had been in 2003. He was therefore talking about the awareness of troops in 2006, not in 2003. Brims added that his statement about the understanding of *"most troops"* could not in any case be construed as a *"clear assurance that conditioning techniques such as hooding and the use of stress positions were not used by the British Army"* as the JCHR had stated.

15.162 It is not for this Inquiry to resolve what might be characterised as the dispute between the JCHR and Ingram/Brims. In the conclusions to this Part of the Report, below, I simply set out references to a number of findings within my own Report as to the relevant facts as I have found them to be.

---

[184] His full account can be found at Brims BMI07404-7, paragraphs 78-84

Chapter 6: Conclusions

Reith's Letters in October 2003

15.163 In October 2003, Reith required Maj Gen Lamb, the GOC 3 (UK) Div, to direct all under his command immediately to cease the hooding of persons detained. Reith permitted blindfolding to be used for force security and protection of the detained person, but only for the minimum period necessary, with checks on the health of those blindfolded.

15.164 In adopting this high level direction, Reith went further than the legal advice he had received. The legal advice remained that hooding for security purposes (but not as an aid to interrogation) could be lawful in some circumstances if better means of sight deprivation were not available, provided that adequate precautions were taken.

15.165 In my opinion, Reith acted responsibly and correctly in taking this course. In fact, within theatre, hooding should already have ceased because of the advice given shortly after Baha Mousa's death and the issue of the Divisional Standard Operating Instruction 390.

15.166 Although Reith's decision was apparently communicated to the chain of command for Special Forces, the direction was not filtered down and Special Forces continued to use hooding in Iraq until May 2004. In addition, the prohibition on hooding applied to Iraq and was not extended to other theatres until May 2004.

15.167 Reith also wrote to the Chief of Defence Intelligence Ridgway on 24 October 2003. He stated that it would be appropriate to review both doctrine and training. Reith suggested that the responsibility for taking this forward lay with Ridgway. In reply, Ridgway noted the complexity of responsibilities in the area. He gave reassurance that hooding had never been taught on any of the tactical questioning and interrogation courses at Chicksands. He agreed that tactical questioning and interrogation training should be tightened up but pointed to the need for action across a range of different areas, copying in those in the MoD whom he considered were responsible.

15.168 Ridgway's reassurance about Chicksands training was given in good faith relying on what he had been told by others. But having regard to my findings in Part VI of this Report, it was not completely justified.

15.169 The prohibition on the use of hoods was probably given greater prominence in Chicksands training as a result of the review of tactical questioning and interrogation training that Ridgway requested following Reith's letter. It did not however lead to changes to some other aspects of this training which were questionable, details of which I have set out in Part VI of this Report.

15.170 Ridgway was entitled to point out that other post holders bore responsibility for other aspects of the prisoner of war handling process. Other than Ridgway's response, I think it likely that the collective response to Reith's request for a review of doctrine and training was both limited and slow. By May 2004, it was still a source of complaint that doctrine in this area was notably lacking. It is likely that this related to the number of different branches that were involved and the complexity of the division of responsibility for prisoner handling matters.

The MoD's Response to Prisoner Abuse Allegations from May 2004 Onwards

15.171 I have set out in Chapter 3 of this Part of the Report examples of the flow of information and the MoD statements and assurances given in May 2004 and beyond, when prisoner abuse issues, including hooding, came to the fore. I have not sought to refer to the account given by every witness on every aspect. In reaching these conclusions I have however considered all of the evidence from relevant witness and the submissions made by the Core Participants. I have reached the following conclusions.

15.172 Firstly, I do not consider it would be fair or appropriate to single out individuals for criticism in relation to the statements that were made in May 2004 and in the months thereafter. In taking this approach, I am mindful that the records in relation to May 2004 are not complete; that witnesses struggled to remember who provided what information; and that a number of civil servants whose names appeared on many of the drafts, in particular Cholerton, Allkins and Kistruck, were relying upon what they were told by others. Had I found proper grounds to conclude that any individual had set out deliberately to mislead, I would not have hesitated to state this was the case. In the event, I do not consider that the evidence went so far as to justify such conclusions against any individual, whether Ministers or civil servants.

15.173 Secondly, I find that there was an unsatisfactory pattern of too many inaccurate assurances and explanations being given within the MoD statements and briefing materials. The worst examples of inaccurate lines that were adopted by the MoD from May 2004 onwards were the following.

(1) Despite the earlier submissions in September 2003 having made clear the duration of Baha Mousa's hooding and having pointed towards a link between the hooding and the tactical questioning process, it was asserted more than once that there was no evidence that hooding was used on Op Telic at any time during tactical questioning. This was only true in the most literal sense of hooding actually during the questioning itself and was prone to be misleading. I recognise that an updating briefing from Kistruck did raise the link between hooding and tactical questioning in Baha Mousa's case. But this did not prevent subsequent statements suggesting that hooding had not been used in the context of tactical questioning/interrogation. Even with only the high level summary that had been provided to Ministers shortly after Baha Mousa's death, the MoD should not have given any assurances that may have been taken to suggest that hooding had not been used in the context of tactical questioning in Op Telic.

(2) The MoD repeatedly suggested that hooding had been stopped "when conditions on the ground permitted" or when it was considered safe to do so. I was not at all convinced by the suggestions that this line was taken because of a fear of prejudicing the investigation into Baha Mousa's death. Even if this had been the concern officials had in mind, it would not have justified an explanation drafted in this form. The assurances and statements given along these lines were simply inaccurate and likely to mislead. They should never have been given in those terms.

(3) It was stated that there was no firm evidence that the hooding of prisoners at the prisoner of war camp JFIT facility, during major combat operations, went beyond the normal use for transit/arrest activity. Other statements sought similarly to suggest that hooding had only been used on capture or for transit. The hooding at the JFIT which I have analysed in detail in Part VIII of this Report could not properly be labelled as transit/arrest activity. The prisoners were awaiting interrogation within the specialist JFIT unit within the TIF often having already had initial processing. This line was inaccurate and likely to mislead. It too should never have been given in those terms.

15.174 Thirdly, I am satisfied that pressures of time, an incomplete picture of information, inconsistencies in the information provided, and the sheer volume of requests made when operational demands were still high, all contributed to such errors being made in the MoD statements.

15.175 Fourthly, notwithstanding this, officials could and should have done more to ensure that statements were consistent both with the totality of the information that had been provided and with other MoD statements that had been issued. In respect of many of the statements that were inaccurate, other MoD statements could be found which gave a better or fuller explanation. This is testament both to a lack of any intention to mislead, but also evidences a failure of the MoD's systems to ensure the greatest possible accuracy of statements and briefings.

15.176 Fifthly, there are lessons to be learned here in how the MoD communicates to Ministers and with outside bodies, even in demanding times of great Parliamentary and media pressure. I do not underestimate the difficulties involved in fielding large numbers of queries against competing demands, with sometimes incomplete information. But by May 2004, it was obvious that mistakes had been made in relation to hooding. It was known that written doctrine had been very scarce, and indeed still was. It was appreciated that Brims' oral ban had been lost. Senior officers had expressed surprise and concern that hooding had re-emerged after Brims' ban. It was also known that hooding had been an Standard Operating Procedure for some units and that the main doctrinal guidance on prisoners of war was silent about sight deprivation. It was known that Baha Mousa and those detained with him had been hooded for long periods with a reported link to the tactical questioning process. It was known, at least by the JSIO, that their own consideration of the written teaching materials showed that they did not refer explicitly to hooding. There were inconsistent accounts of whether or not hooding had been used for disorientation but some suggestions that this had been the case.

15.177 Against this background, it would have been better had the MoD faced more squarely and more openly the mistakes and shortcomings that had already been identified in relation to hooding and tactical questioning. Many of the difficulties stemmed from what I detect was at times something of a corporate approach of taking overly defensive lines in response to difficult questions. As a result, some (but by no means all) elements of the statements, assurances and explanations about hooding and tactical questioning in 2004 were inaccurate, and several of them gave a false sense of reassurance.

The 2004 Review of the Policy on Hooding

15.178 There was concern in some quarters of the MoD that the prohibition on hooding had been something of a "knee-jerk" reaction to adverse publicity, and that while alternative means of sight deprivation were preferable, there might be a need to retain the use of hoods *in extremis*, for security purposes. This became the subject of a policy review instigated by Lord Walker, the Chief of the Defence Staff, in late May 2004. The review was carried out by officials in the Directorate of Joint Commitments, in consultation with the many branches involved.

15.179 The draft recommendations of this review sought the provision of clearer guidance on when restriction of vision was acceptable and by what means. It suggested that blacked out goggles should be the preferred method but the ability to use hooding was retained as a last resort.

15.180 Medical advice was obtained as part of this review. Although brief, it pointed to the risks of asphyxia, hypercarbia and hypoxia, with increased risks in hot and humid environments and compounded by the physiological and psychological stress of being hooded.

15.181 The feedback from Special Forces reported no difficulties on the ground in the use of blacked out goggles rather than hoods.

15.182 In the context of this review, the shock of capture was still referred to in relation to sight deprivation, including a comment that blacked out goggles were effective in preserving the shock of capture. While this appears to have been a reference to a consequence of, rather than a justification for, sight deprivation, it is worrying that the risks of blurring security justification and the shock of capture had not yet been fully understood.

15.183 I do not criticise those who were involved in this review. For the reasons I shall explain in Part XVI of this Report, I disagree with its draft recommendation of retaining hooding *in extremis*.

15.184 Whilst witnesses struggled to remember what became of this review, there is no evidence that the draft recommendation to permit hooding *in extremis* was ever adopted. Such evidence as there is suggested that the thinking changed towards the benefit of giving soldiers on the ground a clear direction that they must use goggles and not hoods.

Evidence Given to the JCHR

15.185 As stated above, it is not for this Inquiry to resolve what I have characterised as the dispute between the JCHR and Brims/Ingram.

15.186 The JCHR's report of 15 July 2008 raised concerns including the use of conditioning techniques in Iraq, the 1 QLR conditioning techniques, the Brigade sanction, training and the articulation to troops of the prohibition on the five techniques. My own findings relevant to these issues are to be found primarily in Parts II, IV, VI, VIII and XIII of this Report, alongside the discussion of recommendations and list of recommendations in Parts XVI and XVII.

15.187 In this Part of the Report I have found that a number of the MoD statements and assurances were inaccurate, and I have sought to consider them alongside the pressures that were current at the time. My analysis of those statements may also help to put Ingram's letter to the JCHR of 26 June 2004 in context. The essence of the comments Ingram made concerning tactical questioning and interrogation training and the use of hooding for transit purposes in that letter were to be found in other MoD statements made in this period. As to the former, I have commented that such statements relied upon what the MoD had been told by the JSIO. As to the latter, I have found that it was inappropriate to characterise the hooding in Op Telic as being for transit/arrest purposes.

15.188 I would only add that on my assessment of the MoD statements, despite their shortcomings, I have found no sufficient evidence to suggest that officials or Ministers (including Ingram) were deliberately seeking to mislead. Earlier in this report I have commended Brims for the action he took in banning hooding. I found him an impressive and compelling witness. But it is not for me to make a determination in respect of the evidence he or Ingrams gave to the JCHR.

Part XVI

Discussion on Recommendations

Chapter 1: Background to Module 4

16.1 In determining early in the Inquiry the issues which I would examine, I specified that in its final Module, the Inquiry would consider what changes had been introduced with a view to examining recommendations for the future.

16.2 This Inquiry was established nearly five years after Baha Mousa's death and the hearings of Module 4 took place some seven years after his death. The changes to policies, doctrine, and training in that period have been significant. Given the circumstances of Baha Mousa's death and other incidents that have taken place, it would be surprising and disappointing if it were otherwise.

16.3 I made clear at the outset of the Module 4 hearings that in making recommendations in this report:

(1) I would need to take into account improvements that had already been made.

(2) I did not want to introduce a raft of bureaucratic regulations.

(3) My aim would be to make simple recommendations, few in number and guided by common sense.

16.4 I remain convinced that it is inappropriate for this Inquiry to make recommendations that are highly prescriptive at the level of fine doctrinal detail. The Armed Forces themselves are best placed to decide upon the wording of policy and doctrine; it is they who must decide what will and what will not work in communicating important messages to service personnel who are to go on operations. My approach will therefore be to concentrate on a restricted number of key points in my recommendations, but giving detailed examples by reference to the current materials, to illustrate why further change is necessary.

16.5 In December 2009 the Inquiry team advised the MoD that it would need to provide witness statements and disclosure to respond to 32 issues identified by the Inquiry. With only minor amendments those issues remained those addressed in the Module 4 oral hearings. They were as follows:

> *"Doctrine and Policy Generally*
>
> *(1) How does MoD's current policy for Captured Personnel of all categories ("CPERS") address sight deprivation, sleep deprivation, stress positions, deprivation of food and water, and subjection to noise?*
>
> *(2) If and to the extent that there may be legitimate grounds for sometimes temporarily depriving CPERS of their sight, does current policy and doctrine adequately ensure that this is kept to the minimum necessary period and in no way harms the health of CPERS?*

(3) To what extent is a prohibition on the use of these five techniques now entrenched in military doctrine? The Inquiry will for example wish to consider why the possible use of hoods was revisited in 2004;

(4) Does the prohibition on the use of the five techniques extend adequately to all those under the control of MOD? The Inquiry will, for example, wish to be assured that Special Forces are now aware of the prohibition on hooding, since there is evidence that Special Forces had continued hooding in Iraq until May 2004. The Inquiry will also wish to be assured that whatever reporting chain differences led to the SF not receiving the hooding prohibition until May 2004 have been identified and would not be repeated in future in respect of orders relating to the proper treatment of CPERS.

(5) What guidance is now given regarding the types of building that can be used as a temporary detention facility on operations? Bearing in mind the operational conditions, to what extent can such guidance extend?

(6) Should the use of the five techniques be specifically criminalised, or is legislation otherwise required?

(7) What provision is made for the review of the doctrine on the handling of CPERS?

Prisoner handling in practice on operations

(8) What is the current practice for the physical handling of CPERS (i) at the point of capture and (ii) in transit to initial detention centres?

(9) At company and battlegroup level, who has what responsibilities for the physical handling of CPERS? How are responsibilities demarcated and communicated?

(10) Within this allocation of responsibilities, what responsibilities towards prisoners do tactical questioners hold, whether or not they are from the detaining battlegroup?

(11) In the context of competing demands on operations, do battlegroups sufficiently prioritise the handling of CPERS and provision of sufficient personnel safely to hold them before CPERS are passed to Brigade or Divisional facilities? Bearing in mind the intensity of operations, how do commanders at battlegroup level ensure that those with key responsibilities for dealing with CPERS are not overburdened with other roles and responsibilities on operations?

(12) Once CPERS are transported to an initial detention centre at company or battlegroup level:

(i) What arrangements are provided for checks on the physical welfare of CPERS?

(ii) To what extent is access to CPERS now limited to those who have a proper need to visit them?

(iii) What arrangements are provided to ensure that CPERS are provided with adequate food and water taking into account the climatic conditions?

(iv) What protections are in place to ensure that tactical questioning does not extend beyond the obtaining of time-sensitive tactical intelligence?

(13) Is there a need, with suitable adaptations for the military context, for a role similar to Custody Sergeants in police custody facilities?

(14) Is there a need for time limits for detention at company and battlegroup level on operations? If so, what should the time limits be or is it impracticable to specify a standard time limit in the military context?

(15) At detention facilities at all levels on operations, what arrangements are now made for record keeping in respect of CPERS including recording those who have access to CPERS and checks on the physical welfare of CPERS?

(16) What provision is now made for medical checks on CPERS and for the recording of such checks and treatment as they are afforded? How are the ethical problems concerning medics "fitting" CPERS for detention and "fitting" CPERS for questioning currently approached? Is the approach appropriate and in the best interests of CPERS?

(17) Within higher formations on operations, is there sufficient clarity as to the responsibilities of different braches in relation to CPERS?

(18) Is adequate provision made for the inspection of detention facilities on operations?

(19) Is there sufficient provision of lawyers qualified and trained to advise on issues relating to CPERS during operations? Are they deployed at appropriate levels within formations and units on operations?

(20) Where deaths, serious injury or injuries suggestive of abuse occur in military custody on operations, is adequate provision made to ensure the retention of evidence and prompt investigation in theatre?

(21) Are sufficient precautions taken to ensure the provision of clear orders about the handling of CPERS on operations and to prevent the loss of orders relevant to CPERS during handovers between units and higher formations on long – running operations?

Defence Intelligence: tactical questioning and interrogation

(22) In relation to the five techniques and in respect of the physical handling of CPERS including aspects such as the use of the "harsh technique", is the current teaching on tactical questioning and interrogation courses adequate in terms of ensuring compliance with the Geneva Conventions and other applicable standards on the treatment of CPERS?

(23) Is suitable provision being made for refresher training of those qualified in tactical questioning and interrogation, including to those in the Reserve Forces?

(24) Is it preferable that TQing should be carried out by a battlegroup's own personnel? If so, are sufficient numbers of military personnel being trained in tactical questioning?

(25) Is there sufficient legal advice and oversight of training in tactical questioning and interogation?

(26) Is tactical questioning and interogation doctrine adequately visible to commanders at company and battlegroup level so that they understand what is permissible and what is prohibited in the physical handling of CPERS during, or as an aid to, tactical questioning of CPERS held by their units or sub-units?

Other Training

(27) To what extent is the proper treatment and handling of CPERS now covered in:

(i) Phase 1 training and subsequent training phases for army recruits and the equivalent RN and RAF training?

(ii) NCO promotion courses?

(iii) Officer training?

(iv) Subsequent Officer promotion courses?

(v) Courses for those designated as Commanding Officers?

(vi) Pre-deployment training?

(vii) Training for Medics who may be deployed on operations?

(28) For the training of Regimental Police / Provost staff and others who may have a leading responsibility for the handling of CPERS at unit level detention facilities on operations,

(a) What training is now provided in relation to safer custody issues with particular reference to the safe use of control and restraint?

(b) What additional training is provided to them in respect of their responsibilities for CPERS during operations?

(29) What precautions are now being taken to ensure that those involved in receiving and providing conduct after capture training do not import techniques taught during such training into UK Armed Forces' own handling of CPERS on operations?

(30) Other than conduct after capture training, are any of the five techniques being used on UK Forces during training? If so, are appropriate precautions in place to prevent their misuse on CPERS during operations. For example, are stress positions being used in PT or as informal punishment during training of UK Armed Forces?

(30A) What steps are taken by the Armed Forces, for example by the provision of training, to inculcate moral courage and moral leadership amongst servicemen?

Record Management

(31) Are sufficient records of operations being kept to ensure that relevant personnel and orders can be traced where subsequent investigations are required. The Inquiry will for example wish to reflect the difficulties encountered in Modules 1-3 in investigating relevant postholders in formations in theatre and at PJHQ, and obtaining copies of some relevant orders and directives.

(32) Are there sufficient measures in place to ensure the safe retention of medical/internment documentation during and after detention?" [1]

16.6　To examine these issues thoroughly was in itself a significant task. Taking into account a number of follow-up queries raised by the Inquiry team, the MoD provided 25 principal witnesses to address these issues. Several provided more than one witness statement and in giving oral evidence, many were accompanied by more junior colleagues with knowledge of specialist areas. Over 600 documents were assessed to be relevant to this part of the Inquiry's work, running to over 11,000 pages. While some redactions were necessary, all the documents relevant to this Module have been made available on the Inquiry's website.

16.7　Independent of the work of this Inquiry, the Army has sought to carry out its own assessments of the progress made in relation to Captured Persons (CPERS) handling. Such assessments have included:

(1)　*"An investigation into Cases of Deliberate Abuse and Unlawful Killing in Iraq in 2003 and 2004"* a report of Brig Aitken dated 25 January 2008;[2]

(2)　1st part assurance: A review of Policy, Training and Conduct for Detainee Handling, February 2010, a report for the Director General Land Warfare;[3]

---

[1] MIV008232-7
[2] MOD041542-62
[3] MIV004106-23

(3) 2nd part assurance: Army Inspectorate Review into the implementation of Policy, Training and Conduct of Detainee Handling, 15 July 2010, a report by the Army Inspector, Brig Purdy OBE.[4]

16.8 I appointed the following experts to assist the Inquiry in examining the adequacy of current policies, doctrine and training:

Lieutenant General (Retired) Sir Philip Trousdell KBE CB. Trousdell has considerable experience of the infantry on operations and in higher command posts. In addition to serving as the General Officer Commanding (GOC) Northern Ireland, earlier in his career he served as Commandant of the Royal Military Academy Sandhurst.

Dame Anne Owers DBE. Owers was for nine years HM Chief Inspector of Prisons. In that role she oversaw HMIP's feasibility study of acting as an independent inspector of military detention facilities on operations, including visits to the UK temporary holding facilities in Afghanistan. Owers assisted the Inquiry with the issues surrounding detention practice on operations.

Professor Brice Dickson and **Professor Sir Adam Roberts KCMG FBA**. Dickson is Professor of International and Comparative Law at Queen's University Belfast and the former Chief Commissioner of the Northern Ireland Human Rights Commission. Roberts is President of the British Academy and Senior Research Fellow in International Relations at Oxford University. I invited Dickson and Roberts to contribute reports from the respective standpoints of International Human Rights Law and International Humanitarian Law/the Law of Armed Conflict (LOAC).

Professor Vivienne Nathanson and **Dr Jason Payne-James**. Nathanson is Director of Professional Activities at the British Medical Association with responsibilities including medical ethics and human rights. Payne-James is a leading forensic physician with extensive experience of forensic medicine including its practice in the police detention setting. I invited them both to contribute reports relating to the policies and practice in relation to the medical care of CPERS.

Mr Jon Collier. Collier is a serving prison officer, serving as a Principal Officer based at the National Tactical Response Group of the National Offender Management Service. He qualifies control and restraint instructors in the Prison Service and delivers advanced control and restraint training as well as having an operational role in relation to interventions in serious incidents. I invited him to provide a report addressing the MoD's training in relation to use of force in the course of military detention.

16.9 Each of these experts dedicated considerable time to studying the relevant current military documents and were of considerable assistance to the Inquiry.

16.10 The Module 4 oral hearings took place over eight sitting days from 5 October to 14 October 2010.[5]

16.11 In the days and weeks leading up to the Module 4 hearings, it became apparent that the process had already had some effect in encouraging further improvements within the Armed Forces. Four examples illustrate this:

---

[4] MIV005225-82
[5] BMI 108-115

(1) Cdr David Pledger's first written statement in relation to the MoD's current training in 'SERE' (Survive, Evade, Resist, Extract) concentrated on the practical resistance to interrogation training provided to selected service personnel.[6] Asked by the Inquiry to expand upon the theoretical training provided to all personnel, and whether it contained warnings against the use of the five techniques by British Forces, Pledger accepted in his second statement that it had become "...*increasingly clear that a suitable warning/caveat is required...*". He assured the Inquiry this would be included in the revision to the SERE DVD when next revised.[7]

(2) Capt Peter Adams, Director of Training at the Defence Intelligence and Security Centre (DISC), provided a second statement to the Inquiry on 1 October, the week before the Module 4 hearings started. He accepted that a handout which had permitted the practice of walking around a blindfolded CPERS to increase the pressure on him had only been changed in September 2010.[8]

(3) Gp Capt Andrew Hall provided the Inquiry with a statement dated 28 July 2010. He stated that pre-deployment training for RAF personnel in categories 1 and 2 (respectively those who remain on main bases and whose duties require periodic deployment outside defensive locations) included a lesson given to a plan containing the prohibited techniques as a Key Learning Point.[9] However, the training materials to which he referred, dated November 2009, did not in fact include any specific reference to the prohibited five techniques.[10] The MoD later disclosed an updated lesson plan dated August 2010 which did contain express reference to the prohibited techniques.[11]

(4) The Inquiry having raised issues concerning the video, Prisoner Handling on Operations, used in annual training, the Operational Law Branch raised a request shortly before the Module 4 hearings that the video should be edited because of a concern that the current version "...*may give rise to an inference that the PW's goggles remain on in order to condition him for the purposes of interrogation, which would be contrary to UK policy and almost certainly illegal*".[12]

16.12 Such examples may, I hope, serve to illustrate the benefit of the Module 4 process which the Inquiry adopted, and in which I recognise the MoD proactively engaged. Without having reached the stage of formal recommendations, the very process of open scrutiny of current policy, doctrine and training has highlighted these and other areas for improvement.

16.13 To its credit, it was apparent that the MoD was intent on making changes without delay once such issues had been identified. I applaud this approach. It would not have been appropriate to await the Inquiry's report before making straightforward improvements.

---

[6] Pledger MIV004818
[7] Pledger MIV008993, paragraph 2
[8] Adams MIV012254, paragraph 8
[9] Hall MIV004810, paragraph 5
[10] MIV003912-31; MIV003932-53
[11] MIV012440
[12] MIV012416

16.14 Where possible I have taken account of such very recent changes, some of them post-dating the Module 4 hearings, both in this Part of the Report and in making my recommendations.

16.15 I received submissions on Module 4 from a number of the Core Participants. Submissions were also received from Redress[13], Human Rights Watch[14] and British Irish Rights Watch[15].

16.16 In the course of this Part of the Report in making my recommendations I have endeavoured to take into account all of these submissions where they fall within my terms of reference. I have adopted and adapted some. Others, I have not felt it necessary to incorporate in my recommendations. But I recognise that my judgment on what is or is not sensible to recommend may not be so infallible that it rules out the wisdom of others. I invite the MoD to look carefully through all of the submissions, in particular those of the Core Participants, with a view to ensuring that any valuable points, not sufficiently recognised by me, are taken into account.

16.17 In this respect I flag up the following which do not feature in my own recommendations but may nevertheless be worthy of consideration:

(1) Submissions on behalf of the Detainees. The Detainees emphasise that doctrine and training instructions should be rationalised in number and content; and that such instructions should always show the date and status of the instructions. I make clear in my recommendations the need for guidance to be clear, concise and simple. The Detainees also recommend that a central review body is established to look at all documents which relate to CPERS. I can see some attraction in this latter suggestion although I am loathe to recommend yet another body to monitor what I regard as something which should be properly and efficiently done in the first place.

(2) Submissions by the Treasury Solicitor on behalf of its clients. Their submissions support to some extent the submission of the Detainees that publications relating to prisoner handling should be reviewed for consistency, clarity and economy of expressions. I add here that the suggestion that service publications should be rigorously examined for "translation" into plain English was a theme which was echoed by many and one which I heartily endorse. The Treasury Solicitor also raised the suggestion that a written check list should form part of any handover and should include matters relating to detention. Whether this is practical is a matter for consideration but bearing in mind the omissions in respect of orders at the handover between 1 UK (Div) and 3 UK (Div) and their subordinate units, it is in my view a suggestion worthy of further consideration.

---

[13] NCP001259-97
[14] NCP001298-306
[15] NCP001307-37

Chapter 2: Policy and Higher Level Doctrine

16.18   At the higher strategic policy level the treatment of CPERS is principally addressed in three MoD policy documents:

(1)   the Secretary of State's "Strategic Detention Policy", March 2010[16];

(2)   the two (now separate) MoD policies on Tactical Questioning[17] and Interrogation[18] both dated 4 October 2004. Late drafts of both these documents were disclosed to the Inquiry the week before the Module 4 hearings; witnesses were able to address them. Before October 2010, there was a Joint Interrogation and Tactical Questioning policy, November 2008 re-issue.[19]

(2a) The Secretary of State's Strategic Detention Policy

16.19   Purdy's report suggests that early in the work of his review, it was noted that there was a lack of an overarching MoD policy statement on the handling of detainees.[20] The first such statement to fill this gap was the policy statement by the Rt. Hon. Bob Ainsworth, then the Secretary of State for Defence, in March 2010.[21]

16.20   The policy statement is wide in ambit, applying whenever UK Forces undertake detention in an operational theatre[22] and to members of the Armed Forces, civilian employees and contractors.[23]   The Secretary of State emphasises the importance which he attaches to the humane treatment of those detained.[24]   The statement continues,

> *"1.3 This is essential to ensure that we uphold our international obligations to promote the legitimacy of an operation internationally and among the British public and to maximise support within the country where operations take place. Failure to do so could prejudice operational success and would be contrary to the values and standards of the Ministry of Defence (MOD) and the Armed Forces. Therefore, policy and operations staffs must address detention as an integral element of an operation from the earliest stages of planning.*
>
> *1.4 The conduct of detention operations is a challenging task, often undertaken in very difficult circumstances. The standards that can be achieved will clearly be dependent on the precise nature of the operational environment, and it is likely that facilities will improve as operations endure, but at all times they must meet our legal obligations. I expect the Armed Forces to strive to maintain the highest standards practicable."*

16.21   As a high level policy document, it is not perhaps surprising that the statement addresses the legal position at a high level of generality. The policy provides:

---

[16] MIV002414-6
[17] MIV012545-76
[18] MIV012577-614
[19] MOD042380-409
[20] MIV005240-1, paragraph 19
[21] MIV002414-6
[22] MIV002414, paragaph 1.2
[23] MIV002414, paragraph 2.1
[24] MIV002414, paragraph 1.2

(1)   that the MoD will comply with *"all applicable domestic (i.e. UK law) and international law"*;[25]

(2)   the MoD and the Armed Forces must *"Ensure that all Detained Persons held by UK Forces are treated humanely at all times, in accordance with applicable host state law, international law and UK law"*;[26] and

(3)   they must *"As a minimum, without prejudice to the legal status of a Detained Person, apply the standards articulated in Common Article 3 to the Geneva Conventions. Where other standards are applicable they must be applied"*.[27]

16.22   There are a number of other strategic principles outlined in the policy. They are that the detention policy framework must be addressed when seeking authority for any given operation: provision of a safe and secure environment for detained persons; record keeping; transfer to other nations' custody; cooperation with the ICRC and procedures for reporting abuse of detained persons.[28]

16.23   These legal and other strategic principles are required to be met by the application of *"appropriate and comprehensive doctrine"* and training, both of which are required to be regularly and comprehensively reviewed.[29]

16.24   The policy then sets out the governance structure. At Ministerial level, the Minister of State is identified as the Ministerial focus for detention issues. The Director General Security Policy is the owner of the policy and the Assistant Chief of Staff of Defence Staff Development, Concepts and Doctrine is made responsible for the provision of doctrine to fulfil the policy. The single service is responsible for training. The Chief of Joint Operations is responsible for ensuring that effective arrangements are in place for ensuring compliance with the policy. The Provost Marshal (Army) who is the Competent Army Authority for Custody and Detention is required to act as the Defence subject matter expert for operational detention on overseas operations. He is responsible for inspection and monitoring UK-run detention facilities in operational theatres.[30]

16.25   Under the heading *"Command and Leadership"*, the policy requires commanders at all levels to carry out their duties in accordance with the policy, to control potential risks and to monitor the effectiveness of detention arrangements. All personnel are required to inform their superiors of detention-related concerns. Commanders and managers are to foster a culture that encourages personnel to take responsibility for achieving the strategic principles of the policy and act in accordance with best practice.[31]

16.26   The Policy Statement is to be reviewed at least every two years.[32]

---

[25] MIV002414, paragraph 2.2
[26] MIV002414, paragraph 3.1(b)
[27] MIV002415, paragraph 3.1(c)
[28] MIV002414-5, paragraph 3.1
[29] MIV002415, paragraph 3.2
[30] MIV002415-6, paragraph 4
[31] MIV002416, paragraph 5
[32] MIV002416, paragraph 6

16.27   As Counsel to the Inquiry observed in opening Module 4 of the Inquiry, the Strategic Detention Policy does not refer in any way to the prohibition on the five techniques.[33]

16.28   At the time the Strategic Detention Policy was settled, Mr Barry Burton was the Head of Legal Policy within the Operations Directorate in the MoD. This was a 1* (Brigadier-equivalent) post with responsibility for detention policy on operations. In his oral evidence to the Inquiry, he explained that it was a conscious decision, not an oversight, that the prohibition on the five techniques was not referred to. The reasoning was explained as follows:

> "I think there is always a balance to be struck between providing strategic direction to an organisation such as the Ministry of Defence and the military that work within it and providing the greatest possible detail of any prohibition or any provision that might be made available to individuals carrying out any particular piece of work. We took the view in constructing the note that was signed by the Secretary of State in March that to place too much detail into that work risked there being omissions that we couldn't foresee. Therefore, recognising that the five techniques would be covered in all of the subordinate material that falls below it, we concluded that it was, in our judgment, at least at the time, not right to include further detail but to stick at the strategic policy level and we invited the Secretary of State to take that approach."[34]

16.29   In contrast, Dickson urged that the Strategic Detention Policy should contain reference both to international human rights law and the prohibition on the five techniques:

> "Q ... One of the aspects that the Inquiry has been grappling with is the fact that this doesn't contain a reference to the prohibition on the five techniques. Did you have a view on that and its omission from this document and whether that makes sense given the strategic nature of it?
>
> A. Yes, I did. More generally I was surprised that there doesn't appear to be reference to international human rights law – that there is reference to international law, but not to international human rights law, and there are prohibitions in it of certain forms of treatment, torture, inhuman and degrading treatment most obviously. It is clear from those international documents that even in times of war, they cannot be derogated from. So I would have thought that some reference to those non-derogable provisions, the right to life, the right not to be tortured, et cetera, should be mentioned even in this very high-level document.
>
> Within that, given the very sensitive nature of the five techniques, the fact that they were at the heart of the interstate case brought by Ireland against the UK in the 1970s, would mean that they too should be specifically referred to.
>
> Q. Yes. Again just, as it were, by way of testing what you are saying and nothing more, the contrary argument that might be mooted against that is this: as soon as one descends into that sort of level of detail, for example referring to the Article 3 ECHR prohibitions and the five techniques as being an example of that and where that comes from international human rights

---

[33] BMI 108/13/14-17
[34] Burton BMI 108/41/4-19

law, questions arise about equally important prohibitions that are not referred to. A specific example of that might be the prohibitions in Article 17 of the Third Geneva Convention on not, for example, insulting or subjecting prisoners to disadvantageous treatment if they refuse to answer questions. So the issue almost becomes "Where do you draw the line?", because as soon as you go to one specific, are you therefore overlooking other provisions, for example of the law of armed conflict, which may in some circumstances give even greater protection than Article 3 of ECHR?

A. Yes, I take that point, and that is partly why I prefaced my previous answer by referring more generally to the prohibitions in international human rights treaties of torture or cruel or inhuman or degrading treatment. One has to draw the line somewhere, I agree. But I repeat that the five techniques have been specifically banned by the UK Government because of their use in Northern Ireland in the 1970s and because they were referred to by Ireland in the interstate case. The statement made by the Prime Minister was made to Parliament I think a month or two after the interstate case was lodged in Strasbourg, way before the European Commission or the European Court adjudicated on the complaint.

Q. Yes.

A. So it was clear that the UK Government wanted to put an end to those practices throughout the army, and given their history and given what we know has happened since, it seems to me wise to include them specifically, perhaps in a footnote, perhaps in a sub-paragraph, but even at this very high-level document I think it makes sense to make mention of this.

Q. So weighing the pros and cons, you would still come down in favour of inclusion of a reference to the prohibition on the five techniques even in this high-level strategic document?

A. Yes, I would, and, you know, we all have in our minds the fallout from the Abu Graib incidents as regards the Americans in Iraq. Armed forces and countries, in fact, are judged by the way they treat detainees in this kind of situation and, therefore, I would have thought it's a matter of high strategic importance to try to ensure that these practices aren't used and therefore they should be referred to in a document like this."[35]

16.30 In his written statement to the Inquiry Trousdell set out arguments for and against the inclusion of the prohibition on the five techniques in the Strategic Detention Policy:

"Given that the prohibition originated with a statement in the House of Commons by the Prime Minister, and was subsequently lost (to a significant extent) in subsequent military doctrine, it might be thought that the opportunity should be taken to restate it under the Secretary of State for Defence's direct authority. However a conventional military expectation might be that, important though the prohibition on the techniques is, it does not sit comfortably within a document that is dealing with high level strategy. Put another way, there are many other important imperatives in, for example, the Geneva Conventions that might warrant inclusion. In my reading of the materials, this strategic policy has been accurately translated at the doctrinal level in JDP1.10..."[36]

16.31 Having heard all the evidence of the MoD's factual witnesses, Trousdell's conclusion in his oral evidence was that *"... given the fact that the banned techniques now appear in every level of documentation, particularly in the training documentation, I think it would be unnecessary for it to appear in the ... strategic level policy"*.[37]

---

[35] Dickson BMI 113/73/25-76/25
[36] Trousdell MIV010051, paragraph 9
[37] Trousdell BMI 115/4/16-20

16.32 In considering the Secretary of State's Strategic Detention Policy I have taken into account the way that the prohibition on the five techniques is now addressed in subordinate doctrine and instructions. From the standpoint of this Inquiry's focus on the prohibition on the five techniques, and the worrying evidence of how it became lost over time, there is undoubtedly an argument for specific reference to the prohibition in the Strategic Detention Policy.

16.33 I am concerned, however, that the wider legal protections for detainees, of which the UK's prohibition on the use of the five techniques is but one part, must be respected. I accept Burton's argument that there is a risk, in a short high level overall strategy document of this kind, in including detailed protection for detainees in just one area. For example, in relation to prisoners of war, Article 17 of the Third Geneva Convention includes the requirement that *"No physical or mental torture, nor any other form of coercion, may be inflicted on prisoners of war to secure from them information of any kind whatever. Prisoners of war who refuse to answer may not be threatened, insulted or exposed to any unpleasant or disadvantageous treatment of any kind"*.[38] In some respects, this protection goes beyond the prohibition on the five techniques, and indeed is likely to give greater protection than Article 3 European Convention of Human Rights (ECHR) / Article 7 International Covenant on Civil and Political Rights (ICCPR), as Dickson himself accepted.[39] As will be evident from my assessment of the subordinate doctrine below, considerable improvements have been made in entrenching the prohibition on the five techniques at the joint doctrine level. Against that background, I consider that there is a disadvantage in focusing at this high strategic level of document on the prohibition on the five techniques. To do so may detract from other legal safeguards for detainees which may require a yet higher level of protection.

(2b) JDP 1-10 AND JDP 1-10.1, JDP 1-10.2, JDP 1-10.3

16.34 As explained in Part V of this Report, at the time of Op Telic 1 and 2, it was a notable omission that the joint doctrine on prisoners of war, Joint Warfare Publication (JWP) 1-10 contained no reference whatsoever to the prohibition on the five techniques.

16.35 The current joint doctrine is, in this respect, markedly different. Joint Doctrine Publication (JDP) 1-10 applies to all CPERS. It is supplemented by supporting publications, properly called Joint Tactics, Techniques and Procedures. These cover 'Prisoners of War' (JDP 1-10.1),[40] 'Internees' (JDP 1-10.2)[41] and 'Detainees' (JDP 1-10.3).[42]

16.36 JDP 1-10 was last published in May 2006 although amendments were issued in April 2008.[43] In advance of the Module 4 hearings, a '2nd edition Study Draft' of a new version of JDP 1-10 and the subordinate publications was disclosed to and published by the Inquiry.[44]

16.37 I shall refer to these as the current JDP 1-10 and new draft JDP 1-10 respectively.

---

[38] MOD016384

[39] Dickson BMI 113/73/25-76/25; Dickson MIV010123, paragraph 104

[40] MOD042410

[41] MOD028709

[42] MOD028787

[43] MOD028624-708

[44] MIV004146-498

16.38 The provisions of the current JDP 1-10 in relation to both "Prohibited Acts" and "Permitted Activities" are very important and it is appropriate that I should set them out in full:[45]

SECTION II – PROHIBITED ACTS

206. UK Armed Forces are required by law to act humanely towards all captured or detained persons. To that end, the law prohibits members of UK Armed Forces from committing certain acts (see paragraph 207). These prohibitions are of universal application. Any individual found offending against these prohibitions can expect to be charged with crimes under Service law or domestic or international criminal law.[5]

207. Acts which are and shall remain prohibited at any time and in any place whatsoever with respect to all classes of captured or detained persons are:

  a.   Violence to the life, health and physical or mental well-being of persons, in particular murder as well as cruel treatment such as torture, mutilation or any form of corporal punishment.

  b.   Collective punishments.[6]

  c.   Taking of hostages.

  d.   Acts of terrorism.

  e.   Outrages upon personal dignity, in particular humiliating and degrading treatment,[7] rape, sexual slavery, enforced prostitution, forced pregnancy, forced sterilization and any other form of sexual violence.

  f.   Slavery[8] and the slave trade in all their forms.

  g.   Pillage.[9]

---

[5] See Chapter 1.

[6] This forbids the inflicting of punishments upon the population on account of the acts of individuals for which the general population cannot be regarded as responsible, for example, the destruction of houses in a village of which the offender is an inhabitant.

[7] Captured or detained persons are not to be photographed, filmed or taped other than for authorised administrative purposes.

[8] Internees and detainees may not be set to work. Enlisted PW may be required to engage in labour having no military character or purpose. NCO PW may be required only to perform supervisory work. Officers may not be required to work, although they may volunteer. Suitable arrangements for payment should be put in place. See JDP 1-10.1, Chapter 2.

[9] To plunder, that is to steal by force. (COD)

2-3   Change 1

---

[45] MOD028649-52

h.   Physical mutilation or medical or scientific experiments of a kind which are neither justified by medical, dental or hospital treatment of the person concerned nor carried out in his or her interest, and which causes death to or seriously endangers the health of that person.

i.   The passing of sentences and the carrying out of executions without previous judgement pronounced by a regularly constituted court, affording all the judicial guarantees which are recognised as indispensable by civilized peoples.

j.   Reprisals.

k.   Threats[10] to commit any of the foregoing acts.

208.   There is a fundamental difference between the *handling* of captured or detained persons and the *questioning and interrogation* of such individuals. Prisoner Handling describes all aspects of dealing with persons who fall into the the hands of UK armed forces during operations. Tactical Questioning is the obtaining of information from captured or detained persons, the value of which would deteriorate or be lost altogether if the questioning was delayed. Interrogation is the systematic longer term questioning of a selected individual by a trained and qualified interrogator.[11] To reflect this distinction, handling and questioning activities are subject to separate doctrine[12] and training. In accordance with extant policy,[13] Tactical Questioning and Interrogation (TQ & I) must only be conducted by specially trained and qualified TQ & I experts, who have been properly authorised to engage in such activity.[14]

209.   Following allegations of inhumane treatment made by individuals detained detained by the police and UK armed forces in Northern Ireland in the early 1970s, the UK government has proscribed the following techniques, which **MUST NEVER** be used as an aid to tactical questioning or interrogation:[15]

a.   **'Stress positions'**. Forcing captured or detained persons to adopt a posture that is intended to cause physical pain and exhaustion;

---

[10] Threatening violence is prohibited.

[11] *MoD Policy on Tactical Questioning and Interrogation: Support to Operations* (DI HUMINT 31 Jan 07).

[12] JDP 1-10 *'Prisoners of War, Internees and Detainees'* deals with the handling of those categories of individual. JDN 3/06 *Human Intelligence* covers tactical questioning and interrogation; JDN 3/06 will be subsumed by JDP 2-10.1 *Human Intelligence* in 2008.

[13] *MoD Policy on Tactical Questioning and Interrogation: Support to Operations* (DI HUMINT 31 Jan 07).

[14] In limited circumstances it will be necessary for an individual to be questioned immediately upon apprehension by troops not qualified in tactical questioning. Such questioning should be confined to establishing an individual's status or eliciting information vital to preserve force protection.

[15] PM Heath Statement to Parliament 2 March 1972 (*Hansard*). The allegations were later heard in the European Court of Human Rights in Ireland v UK (Application 5310/71) in 1978. The Court confirmed that use of the techniques as an aid to interrogation amounted to inhuman and degrading treatment in contravention of the European Convention on Human Rights. The ongoing proscription of the '5 techniques' is currently articulated in MOD policy (see footnote 12 above).

b.   **Hooding.** Putting a bag over a captured or detained person's head and keeping it there, whether as part of the TQ&I process or not;

c.   **Subjection to noise.** Holding a captured or detained person in an area where there is a continuous loud and hissing noise;

d.   **Deprivation of sleep.** Depriving captured or detained persons of sleep;

e.   **Deprivation of food and drink.** Subjecting captured or detained persons to a reduced diet.

SECTION III – PERMITTED ACTIVITIES

210.   Those engaged in the handling of captured or detained persons are to be mindful of their obligation to treat such individuals humanely at all times. However, it is recognised that operational circumstances may necessitate captured or detained persons being held in, or transported between, facilities which by their their temporary nature, crude construction or limited logistic support result in some some discomfort; this might give rise to some environmental noise, interference with with sleep or limited diet. All reasonable steps should be taken to mitigate such conditions and they should never be exploited as part of the TQ&I process. The reason for the activity, and the context in which it is carried out, will be crucial in determining its legitimacy. For example:

a.   **Search positions.** It may be sometimes be necessary to search a captured captured or detained person. This may require the individual to stand against against a wall with limbs spread, albeit only for the purposes of the search and only for so long as the search is conducted.

b.   **Restraint.** Circumstances may require the use of restraining equipment (e.g. 'plasticuffs') specifically issued for such purposes to personnel engaged in handling. For example, restraint may be necessary where an individual is attempting to escape or is assaulting those engaged in handling. The use of force that is reasonably necessary in self-defence is always permitted (see para 205 above).

c.   **Restriction of vision.** In order to maintain operational security, it might in some cases be necessary to obscure the vision of captured or detained persons (e.g. when transiting through or past militarily sensitive sites or activity).[16]

---

[16] Handling or detention facilities should be designed and constructed to be secure and separate from (or screened from) other military activities.

JDP 1-10

Ordinarily, this can easily be achieved by travelling in enclosed vehicles, or vehicles with opaque glass. Where this is not practicable, a captured or detained person may be required to wear blacked out goggles specifically issued for that purpose, but only for the time and extent necessary to preserve operational security. The practice of hooding any captured or detained person is prohibited.

d. **Restriction of hearing.** In order to maintain operational security, it might in some cases be necessary temporarily to restrict the hearing of captured or detained persons. Where it is not practicable to avoid bringing the captured or detained person into close proximity to the operationally sensitive activity, the individual may be required to wear ear defenders specifically issued for that purpose, but only for the time and extent necessary to preserve operational security.

211. The concurrent use of blacked out goggles and ear defenders should only be used in exceptional circumstances, and then only for the time and extent necessary to preserve operational security. Captured or detained persons should never be subject to any other form of sensory deprivation, unless by their own request (e.g. by specifically asking to be concealed under a blanket for fear of being identified by other captured or detained persons). Aids to senses, including spectacles and hearing aids, should never be removed from captured or detained persons. A record should be made of every occasion when sensory deprivation, such as blacked out goggles and/or the application of ear defenders, takes place; this is to include the date/time, a brief explanation of the circumstances and the justification, and this information should be included in the detention record of the person concerned.

212. The examples given above are by no means exhaustive. The handling of captured or detained persons requires common sense, a strong commitment to treating individuals humanely and firm command and leadership.[17] Inhumane treatment must be brought to the attention of the chain of Command immediately. Whenever there is doubt as to whether a particular activity is is appropriate or lawful, advice should always be sought from the Force Provost Marshal and LEGAD.

---

[17] Violation of the obligation to treat captured and detained persons humanely and the Command and individual responsibility to prevent, interrupt and report such violations is addressed in Chapter 3.

2-6   Change 1

16.39   It is, of course, absolutely necessary and appropriate that the prohibition on the five techniques should appear in a clear manner. I commend the broad approach of explaining not just the prohibition but also its background.

16.40   However, in my opinion, there are a number of shortcomings in the way that the prohibition on the five techniques is addressed in the current JDP 1-10.

16.41   Firstly, some of the prohibited techniques could be given better basic definitions that would provide clearer guidance more suited to current operations.

The prohibition on stress positions as addressed in JDP 1-10

16.42 It is neither helpful nor appropriate that in JDP 1-10 the definition of a stress position is conditional on the intention of the person enforcing it. This aspect has not been addressed in the new draft JDP 1-10 which contains essentially the same wording.[46] This difficulty with the current approach risks service personnel putting CPERS into unlawful stress positions but claiming that they did so not *"intending"* to cause physical pain and exhaustion but to enhance security and/or obtain information. Yet there can simply be no excuse for requiring a CPERS to adopt the "ski position" used on Baha Mousa and the other Detainees, whatever the intention. Even much less extreme positions such as requiring CPERS to keep their hands on their heads would become illegitimate if forced to be maintained without respite for such a long period that it became painful. It is also inapt that the current wording uses the phrase *"physical pain and exhaustion"*.[47]

16.43 A number of MoD witnesses accepted that the reliance on intention here was unnecessary and/or inappropriate: see Burton, Capt Rupert Hollins, S004 (although both Hollins and S004 expressed other reservations), and S067.[48] Dickson expressly criticised the reliance on intention in relation to stress positions as it appears in the legal presentation used on the Tactical Questioning and Interrogation (TQ&I) course at the DISC.[49] Trousdell was implicitly critical of the definition.[50]

16.44 A better working definition of stress positions attracted a large degree of support from the Core Participants' legal representatives at the end of the submissions phase on Modules 1-3 of the Inquiry. It was:

> *"Any physical posture which a captured person is deliberately required to maintain will be a stress position if it becomes painful, extremely uncomfortable or exhausting to maintain."*[51]

16.45 In helpful discussions about how stress positions were defined, two of the MoD's factual witnesses did raise concerns about dispensing altogether with *"intention"* within the definition.

16.46 Hollins' concern was to avoid legitimate use of force being stigmatised as criminal:

> *"…I imagine there is going to be some risk if it's just relying on a result clause, rather than an intention, that quite innocent behaviour or behaviour which is incidental to some lawful purpose might end up particularly being stigmatised or criminalised, and I would just want to be certain that soldiers could be clear on that."*[52]

16.47 Similarly, S004 considered that the definition of a stress position may need to allow for the application of "restraint positions" on CPERS who are assaulting their captors or others, and the control and restraint techniques may themselves cause pain,

---

[46] MIV004170-5

[47] MOD028650, paragraph 209(a)

[48] Burton BMI 108/61/7-14; Hollins BMI 108/85/8-88/5; S004 BMI 111/19/4-22/4; S004 BMI 111/107/23-109/24; S067 BMI 108/104/21-105/14

[49] Dickson MIV010119-20, paragraph 98 referring to the slide at MIV003532

[50] Trousdell MIV010052, paragraph 13

[51] BMI 107/105/9-12

[52] Hollins BMI 108/86/17-23

although ultimately he did not appear to consider that this working definition would create any difficulty for the training his team gives at DISC.[53]

16.48 Following this evidence the MoD, through its Counsel Mr David Barr, continued to endorse this definition in the Module 4 hearings but with a caveat:

> "MR BARR: Sir, I can say that the Ministry of Defence continues to endorse the definition which was agreed for discussion purposes at the end of Module 3 in the context of questioning. That is to say as a prohibition as an aid to questioning. However, we see that on its own if it is applied more widely some problems arise –
>
> THE CHAIRMAN: Yes.
>
> MR BARR: – in that legitimate activities such as for example the application of approved control and restraint techniques or the use of force in self-defence, or possibly even voluntary PT for prisoners –
>
> THE CHAIRMAN: I can't actual see any problem with self-defence. That brings you into something completely different, doesn't it? Presumably the ordinary rules or law in criminal cases would apply.
>
> MR BARR: Yes. And what it amounts to is we are saying outside the context of questioning one has to be careful to make clear that the ordinary rules of law will apply to things like control and restraint –
>
> THE CHAIRMAN: Yes.
>
> MR BARR: – self-defence and strenuous voluntary exercise.
>
> THE CHAIRMAN: I follow.
>
> MR BARR: But that was the only qualification that I wanted to make."[54]

16.49 I conclude that a better definition of stress position would be: "*Any physical posture which a captured person is deliberately required to maintain will be a stress position if it becomes painful, extremely uncomfortable or exhausting to maintain*".

16.50 I agree that, depending upon the circumstances in which stress positions are being referred to, it may be appropriate to make clear that this prohibition on stress positions does not affect the right of service personnel to use reasonable force in self-defence or to effect an arrest.

16.51 Depending upon circumstances such reasonable force may include:

(1) the use of control and restraint techniques or other forms of reasonable force to bring a CPERS under physical control either at the point of capture, or to control a CPERS who later attempts to escape or assault others;

(2) (where outnumbered at the point of capture) requiring CPERS to adopt positions such as sitting with their hands on their heads, or sitting on their hands, provided that they are permitted to change position from time to time so that the positions do not become exhausting, extremely uncomfortable or painful to maintain.

16.52 I do not think it appropriate or necessary, as the Detainees submitted, that the definition should include the additional definition of "*a deliberately required position which does not meet this threshold will be a stress position if the intent behind its*

---

[53] S004 BMI 111/19/4-22/4; S004 111/107/23-109/24
[54] BMI 113/174/11-175/11

use is to act as a punishment or an aid to questioning".[55] In my judgment such a definition risks our over-complicating what ought to be a simple and clear definition.

The prohibition on hooding as addressed in JDP 1-10

16.53 As to hooding, the current JDP 1-10 refers to "*Putting a bag over a captured or detained person's head and keeping it there, whether as part of the tactical questioning and interrogation process or not*".[56] The new draft JDP 1-10 uses the terminology "CPERS" and uses the word placing rather than putting but is otherwise unchanged.[57]

16.54 When the Inquiry raised with the MoD factual witnesses the suggestion that the reference to "*keeping*" the bag over a person's head was superfluous, there seemed to be general consensus that this was indeed an unnecessary part of the current guidance.[58] The latest tactical questioning and interrogation policies refer more simply to "*Hooding. Placing a cover over the CPERS head*".[59]

16.55 I conclude that the essence of the guidance on hooding should be that it is prohibited at any time for whatever purpose to place a sandbag or other cover over a CPERS' head.

16.56 In the course of their submissions the MoD and the Detainees put forward competing arguments as to the legality of hooding.

16.57 The MoD submitted that:

(1) "*Hooding as an aid to interrogation during international armed conflict is illegal*";[60]

(2) "*Whether hooding for security purposes is unlawful in international armed conflict is fact sensitive*";[61]

(3) Hooding for security purposes will be lawful if the following conditions are met:

"*[i] The need to hood falls within the IHL principle of military necessity. To meet this principle there must be a genuine security need to hood and the hooding must be confined to the period during which the need subsists.*

[ii] The decision to hood conforms with the IHL principle of proportionality. There would have to be a compelling military objective in the particular circumstances which, when weighed against the consequences for the individual concerned, would not render the use of a hood excessive in relation to the military objective.

[iii] There is no violation of the prohibition on cruelty, degrading treatment and outrages against personal dignity, in particular humiliating or degrading treatment, Art 13 GC3 (PWs), Art 5 GC4 (saboteurs et al), Art 27 GC4 (civilians), Rule 87 CIL or Common Article 3. In this regard it is appropriate to consider cases determined under Art 3 ECHR in relation to the IHL obligation of humanity because: "It is generally understood that the detailed rules found

---

[55] MIV012684, paragraph 15
[56] MOD028651, paragraph 209(b)
[57] MIV004173, paragraph 215(b)
[58] Burton BMI 108/58/18-59/4; Hollins BMI 108/85/1-6; Trousdell MIV010052, paragraph 15
[59] MIV012591
[60] SUB001013, paragraph 84
[61] SUB001013, paragraph 85

in international humanitarian law and human rights law give expression to the meaning of humane treatment"[fn]. In this connection Ocalan and Hurtado (discussed in detail in the Art.3 ECHR section of these submissions) demonstrate that hooding per se is not axiomatically inhuman and that the issue is fact dependent.

[iv] The circumstances are not such as to amount to an insult. It would clearly be unlawful for hooding to be used as a means of insulting the person, in the sense meant in Art 13 GC3 (PWs) or Art 27 GC4 (civilians) or as a means of dishonouring the person in the sense meant in Art 14 GC3 (PWs) or Art 27 GC4/Hague Regulation 46 (civilians), or intimidating him/her contrary to Art 27 GC3 (PWs).

[v] It does not cause physical suffering: see Art 32 GC4 (civilians) or seriously endanger health: see Art 13 GC3 (PWs).

[vi] No other rule of IHL is broken.

[fn] Henckaerts & Doswald-Beck, supra, at p.308."[62]

16.58 However, the MoD emphasised both in its written[63] and oral closing submissions[64] that the legality of hooding was addressed because questions had been asked of witnesses about its legality. MoD's position remained that hooding had been banned as a matter of policy and that nothing in its submissions as to the circumstances in which hooding would be lawful should be understood as an indication of a desire to revisit this policy.

16.59 The Detainees take issue with the MoD's legal analysis. They argue that hooding is *prima facie* illegal. They point to the availability of less oppressive methods of sight deprivation that would not be harmful to health and would render a prisoner less psychologically vulnerable. They point to the importance in this context of the common law of assault and battery as well as proportionality considerations.[65]

16.60 Given the clear and uncompromising message from the MoD that it has banned hooding and has no intention to revisit that ban, I do not consider that it is either necessary or appropriate that I should make findings as to the legality of hooding. Whether hooding might in certain situations be capable of being justified in law is in my opinion likely to be fact sensitive.

16.61 However, given all the evidence this Inquiry has heard, my conclusions about the practice of hooding are as follows. Firstly, hooding prisoners with sandbags carries higher medical risks than the use of blacked-out goggles or blindfolds. The MoD's own medical advice, albeit rather brief, confirmed this in 2004.[66] On this ground alone it would be very hard to justify the practice of hooding CPERS.

16.62 Secondly, sandbags are an inefficient means for security forces to deprive CPERS of their sight. Hessian sandbags are not of a particularly close weave and to some extent prisoners can see through them. On grounds of professionalism and efficiency alone, therefore, the Forces should avoid the use of hoods. While it is true that many soldiers carry hessian sandbags as a standard item of kit, given the relative inefficiency of hessian hoods as a means to deprive CPERS of their

---

[62] SUB001013-5, paragraph 86
[63] SUB001015, paragraph 87
[64] BMI 107/79/1-82/24
[65] SUB002866-71, paragraphs 61-70
[66] MOD054208

sight, it is hardly surprising that many have interpreted their use as being for wider and illegitimate purposes than mere sight deprivation. Where sight deprivation is justified, the Armed Forces should do it by more effective means than by sandbags or hoods of any sort, but never, I hasten to add, by plastic bags, the use of which there was some evidence in the Inquiry.

16.63 Thirdly, there are no real drawbacks to the use of blacked-out goggles. Even Special Forces have found them entirely acceptable on operations.[67]

16.64 Fourthly, in addition to the increased medical risks, by removing sight of the entire face of the CPERS, hooding has a greater dehumanising effect than blindfolds or the use of blacked-out goggles. This is in addition to the increased risk of abuse by sight deprivation generally, that arises because the CPERS is unlikely to be able to identify those involved in mistreatment.

16.65 Fifthly in some countries to which our Armed Forces may be deployed, hooding may also have been used by others as an adjunct to serious mistreatment or torture and thus carry a greater risk of having an adverse psychological effect on CPERS.

16.66 Sixthly, one only needs to consider the MoD's own submissions on the potential legality of hooding in some circumstances, to see that hooding carries a very significant risk of being unlawful in very many situations.

16.67 Seventhly, it is neither practicable nor fair to expect service personnel on the ground to have to make judgments on whether or not to hood, risking unlawful conduct in so doing, when more appropriate means of sight deprivation, where it is justified, can be made available.

16.68 Eighthly, the need to deprive prisoners of their sight on operations in certain limited situations is foreseeable. The MoD must plan to do so in ways that are proportionate to the legitimate security aim. It is now hard to conceive of many situations where hooding could ever be seen as an appropriate and proportionate means of achieving sight deprivation.

16.69 Ninthly, it is regrettable that insufficient thought had been given to the use of sandbags for sight deprivation before 2003/2004. The MoD policy is now clear and hooding is prohibited.

16.70 Tenthly, a return to permitting the use of hoods, even *in extremis*, for sight deprivation would carry very significant legal risks.

16.71 I conclude that for all the reasons set out above, the arguments in favour of a complete prohibition on the use of hoods are overwhelming. Since sight deprivation can be achieved practicably and more effectively by less dehumanising means it is difficult to conceive how a return to the use of hoods could be justified whether militarily, legally or as a matter of policy.

---

[67] MOD054180

Subjection to noise as addressed in JDP 1-10

16.72   The current JDP 1-10 refers to *"Subjection to noise. Holding a captured or detained person in an area where there is a continuous loud and hissing noise"*.[68]

16.73   This definition is, in my view, too narrow and far too closely tailored to the specific technique of playing "white noise". Many types of noise could be applied with the purpose of disorienting CPERS, not just continuous loud and hissing noise.

16.74   To an extent, it seems that the MoD has noticed and moved some way to address this concern. The draft wording in the new draft of JDP 1-10 is *"Holding a CPERS in an area where there is a continuous excessive loud noise"*.[69]

16.75   I consider that this is an improvement but the guidance ought to be wider still. The crux of what should be prohibited is subjecting CPERS to any unnecessary excessive noise. It need not be continuous.

16.76   Additional guidance can and should make clear that operational detention facilities can be inherently noisy places but that steps should be taken to mitigate such conditions.

16.77   There is a further aspect that needs to be addressed in the guidance in relation to noise and that is the use of generators and similar equipment for noise shielding security purposes. It is in some senses a point of detail that need not necessarily appear within the main definition of subjection to noise but it does need to be addressed in JDP 1-10.

16.78   Earlier in this Report I have addressed the use of generators both at the Joint Forward Interrogation Team (JFIT) in late March to early April and near 1 Queen's Lancashire Regiment's (1 QLR) Temporary Detention Facility (TDF). While I have reached very different factual conclusions about why generators were being used at each location, I am concerned that current guidance does not adequately address the appropriateness or otherwise of using generators or similar equipment as noise shields.

16.79   It is understandable that tactical questioners and interrogators should be concerned to ensure that CPERS who are kept in a holding area are not able to hear what is said in an interrogation room or in whatever room, tent or area is being used for tactical questioning. In part this is for the CPERS' own protection in that CPERS who do provide information may be subject to reprisals. I accept that there is a legitimate operational need to prevent CPERS in holding areas from overhearing what is said during questioning.

16.80   In his Module 4 evidence, S004 was quick to assure me that the Interrogation branch does not teach the use of generators as a noise shield, *"Absolutely not, not by us"* was his response. Indeed he stated more generally that noise should not be deliberately increased in the vicinity of CPERS whether for security or other reasons.[70]

16.81   Looking at the current guidance in the current JDP 1-10, there is nothing to make clear that, even if the predominant interest is security rather than as an aid to interrogation, it would be wrong deliberately to increase noise levels in the vicinity

---

[68] MOD028651, paragraph 209(c)
[69] MIV004173, paragraph 215(c)
[70] S004 BMI 111/46/21-47/6

of CPERS. The new draft of JDP 1-10 contains a general reference to taking all reasonable steps to mitigate the discomforts, including continuous loud noise, of temporary holding facilities.[71] However, since the prohibition on subjecting CPERS to "*continuous excessive noise*" is linked to "*…as an aid to tactical questioning and/or interrogation…*"[72] it is far from clear whether deliberate subjection to increased noise as a security measure would be permitted. Moreover, in the current DISC training materials which I address below, precisely the wrong impression may be given by the slide which advises:

> "*Excess Noise: Only if there is a Valid operational reason (security?) but only for the minimum time necessary.*"[73]

16.82 This is part of the legal briefing. It sits unhappily with S004's explanation, which I accept, that he would not himself countenance teaching that noise in the vicinity of CPERS could be deliberately increased, even for security reasons.

16.83 In relation to the guidance provided in JDP 1-10 on subjection to noise I therefore conclude that:

(1) The core of the prohibition should relate to subjecting CPERS to any unnecessary excessive noise.

(2) The guidance can continue to explain that holding facilities may be inherently noisy places but that steps should be taken to mitigate such conditions.

(3) The guidance should include that it is not legitimate deliberately to increase the noise in the vicinity of CPERS even for security purposes. Facilities should be designed, wherever practicable, to avoid holding CPERS where they could overhear others being questioned. Where strictly necessary ear defenders may be used if there is no other practicable means to prevent CPERS overhearing questioning provided this is for the minimum time necessary. But generators or similar loud equipment should not be placed in the vicinity of CPERS as noise shields.

More general considerations in relation to the prohibition on the five techniques as addressed in JDP 1-10

16.84 Purdy commented in his July 2010 report that many soldiers do not understand the meaning of "*proscribed*" and that in the interests of clarity, aide memoires will henceforth describe the techniques as "*prohibited*".[74]

16.85 I fully endorse this approach. For consistency, JDP 1-10 and subordinate doctrine and instruction should use simple language such as banned or prohibited.

16.86 The MoD should also give careful consideration as to whether referring to the techniques as being banned or prohibited "*as an aid to interrogation or tactical questioning*"[75] remains appropriate. The use of hooding is prohibited for all purposes. It is not permissible to deprive prisoners of food or drink at all, and the rationing

---

[71] MIV004173, paragraph 213
[72] MIV004173, paragraph 215
[73] MIV003533
[74] MIV005242, paragraph 22
[75] MIV004173, paragraph 215

of food and water in circumstances where there are shortages of food and water affecting guards and prisoners alike does not in my view constitute "deprivation" at all. If distinguished from the legitimate use of force, searches and control and restraint, "stress positions" should never be used whatever the circumstances or purpose. The techniques would be unlawful if used as a punishment, as well as if used as an aid to tactical questioning and interrogation. I do not consider that this is an area where I should make prescriptive recommendations about how the MoD doctrine is written. But I would urge that further consideration is given to whether the phrase "...*as an aid to interrogation or tactical questioning*" remains an appropriate element of how the five techniques are prohibited.

16.87 In the new draft of JDP 1-10, the prohibition on the five techniques appears within Section IV under the heading "*Tactical Questioning and Interrogation*".[76] This may have been inadvertent but it is in my view wholly inappropriate. The prohibition is an important aspect of doctrine that has direct relevance to *all* personnel involved in CPERS handling and organisation. To place the prohibition in a section addressing tactical questioning and interrogation risks misunderstandings about the scope of the prohibition on the five techniques.

16.88 In the current JDP 1-10, the prohibition on the five techniques appears in the main body of JDP 1-10 but not in the subordinate Joint Tactics, Techniques and Procedures (JTTPs). Appreciating the need to avoid unnecessary duplication, this should be remedied in the next re-drafting of JDP 1-10 and the JTTPs.

16.89 I conclude that:

(1) In the interests of clarity for all, the five techniques should be referred to as being banned or prohibited rather than proscribed;

(2) the MoD should give careful consideration as to whether referring to the five techniques as being prohibited "*as an aid to interrogation*" remains the most effective means of communicating the prohibited techniques;

(3) in JDP 1-10, the prohibition on the five techniques should not appear only within the tactical questioning and interrogation section since it has a wider application and importance; and

(4) the prohibition on the five techniques should be in JTTPs as well as JDP 1-10.

The approach to permitted activities in JDP 1-10

16.90 The MoD Module 4 factual witnesses and the Inquiry's experts alike commended the approach of the doctrine on CPERS giving guidance on what is permitted as much as on what is prohibited. I agree. JDP 1-10 should continue to give guidance on permitted activities. I accept also that if JDP 1-10 is not to be a cumbersome document, such guidance must be succinct; it is neither practicable nor desirable to seek to legislate for every situation service personnel may face on the ground.

16.91 There is, however, scope for further improvements in the messages conveyed in the permitted activities section of JDP 1-10.

---

[76] MIV004172-3

Restriction of vision

16.92 The current guidance is as set out in paragraph 38, above and appears at paragraph 210 of the current JDP 1-10.[77]

16.93 This is a section which has undergone more significant revision and the new draft of JDP 1-10 appears as follows:

> *"213...c. **Restriction of vision**. In order to maintain operational security, it may in some cases be necessary to obscure the vision of CPERS (e.g. when transiting through or past militarily sensitive sites or activity).[22] Ordinarily, this can easily be achieved by travelling in enclosed vehicles, or vehicles with windows covered. Where this is not practicable, CPERS may be required to wear blacked out goggles specifically issued for that purpose, or, if no goggles are available, a blindfold may be improvised. Goggles or blindfolds should only be employed for the time and extent necessary to preserve operational security. The practice of hooding any CPERS is absolutely prohibited.*
>
> *[Footnote][22] This only applies to areas that are genuinely sensitive, e.g. operations rooms, signals offices etc. All efforts should be taken to avoid the need for CPERS to ever be present in or pass through such areas. Handling or detention facilities should be designed and constructed to be secure and separate from (or screened from) other military activities."[78]*

16.94 The substance of this new draft gives welcome emphasis to the fact that, as regards military facilities, it is only sight of *"genuinely sensitive"* parts of facilities that would justify the deprivation of sight of CPERS and then only if it was not practicable to avoid CPERS being taken through such areas.

16.95 However, the evidence in Modules 2 and 3 of this Inquiry shows that it is all too easy for operational security reasons to give rise to the routine use of sight deprivation. Against that background it is unfortunate that the important content of the existing footnote 22 is relegated to a mere footnote.

16.96 During the Module 4 hearings, the Inquiry explored with witnesses five principles in relation to permitted sight deprivation. I consider that the following five principles need to be consistently spelt out in the joint doctrine and subordinate doctrine and instructions:

(1) where practicable the need to deprive CPERS of their sight should be avoided in the first place by common sense steps such as appropriate design and layout of facilities, the planning of operations, choice of routes, and covering up of equipment;

(2) even if it is impracticable to avoid CPERS seeing facilities or equipment in the first place, there must be a *genuine* sensitivity about the facilities or equipment before sight deprivation can be justified;

(3) when sight deprivation does take place it must only be for as long as is strictly necessary;

(4) sight deprivation should not become routine; it must always be capable of being justified by the operational circumstances on the ground; and

---

[77] MOD028651-2
[78] MIV004173-4

(5)   when sight deprivation is used, the fact that it has been used should as soon as practicable be noted in a simple brief record giving the date/time/duration/ circumstances/justification for its use.

I make further comment on aspects of sight deprivation below (see paragraphs 16.267 to 16.273).

Sleep

16.97   I am concerned that neither the current JDP 1-10 nor the new draft JDP 1-10 addresses managing CPERS' sleep in the context of permitted activities. This is a significant omission in my view and was criticised by Trousdell.[79] While the prohibition on sleep deprivation is concisely articulated, the evidence to the Inquiry shows that there can be disagreement as to what "sleep deprivation" means in practice in the early stages of detention.

16.98   The submissions of the Treasury Solicitor in respect of Modules 1 to 3 of the Inquiry urge that the very term "sleep deprivation" is controversial because there are different views of what constitutes sleep deprivation. The submissions criticise any suggestion that preventing someone from sleeping at all amounts to sleep deprivation.[80] Thus the Treasury Solicitor submissions on Modules 1 to 3 appear to contemplate that deliberately keeping CPERS awake in the very early stages of detention does not amount to sleep deprivation.

16.99   This submission only serves to highlight the potential for confusion in this area. For, at least according to existing doctrine, a CPERS can be woken up to be questioned immediately (whether for tactical questioning or interrogation) provided that the policy on sleep patterns and minimum period of rest is respected. However, a CPERS may not deliberately be kept awake at any stage simply on the basis that he may shortly or imminently face questioning. S067 suggested that it is clear from the prohibition on sleep deprivation contained in the tactical questioning policy that it would never be appropriate to deliberately keep a CPERS awake.[81]

16.100   I mean no criticism of S067 in commenting that his hope that the policy on what amounts to sleep deprivation is already clear, is flatly contradicted not only by the mixed evidence to the Inquiry on this aspect, but also the submissions of the legal team representing the majority of military witnesses.

16.101   The current confusion is further illustrated by the inappropriately ambiguous legal presentation given on the tactical questioning and interrogation courses. The slide disclosed to the Inquiry which addresses sleep deprivation states "*Sleep deprivation: Only if there is a Valid operational reason (imminent questioning?) but only for the minimum time necessary [Note – DCDS (IC) Guidance: 8 hrs (4 Hrs Continuous) total]*".[82]

16.102   I conclude that JDP 1-10 needs to make clear that it is not permissible deliberately to keep prisoners awake, even for short periods, merely because they may shortly face tactical questioning or interrogation. CPERS may nevertheless be woken up

---

[79] Trousdell MIV010053, paragraph 20
[80] SUB001276-7, paragraph 83
[81] S067 BMI 108/111/20-113/2
[82] MIV003533

in order to be tactically questioned or interrogated if the questioning is ready to take place and provided that the policy on minimum periods of rest is respected.

Feeding patterns, provision of water

16.103 In his evidence to the Inquiry, Trousdell noted that JDP 1-10 and other doctrinal documents included many references to food and water. However, he commented, that it was only in the previous joint tactical questioning and interrogation policy that detail was provided as to the number and timing of meals and that this level of detail is missing in JDP 1-10 (and for that matter SOI J3-9).[83] While the number and timing of meals for CPERS may obviously be subject to disruption in the early stages of capture, I agree with the concern raised by Trousdell.

16.104 I conclude that JDP 1-10 should give some guidance in relation to the number of daily meals for CPERS and the timing of them. However such guidance will obviously need to take into account the operational realities, particularly close to the point of capture.

Segregation

16.105 Segregation is a practice permitted and indeed required by several of the provisions in JDP 1-10 and the subordinate JTTPs. For example, Annex 1B "*Actions at the Point of Capture*" for Prisoners of War[84] requires that officers and Senior Non-Commissioned Officer (SNCO)s should be segregated from their men and further segregation by rank and appointment should occur as they move through the prisoner handling chain.[85]

16.106 It is entirely appropriate that segregation is addressed in JDP 1-10, not least because the Geneva Conventions require segregation in some circumstances. However JDP 1-10 would benefit from a short simple explanation of how segregation should be effected. The key point here, as regards segregation close to the point of capture, is that if different tents/buildings are not available, and CPERS have to be held in a single room, segregation should be effected by prisoners facing different directions and guards verbally requiring them not to talk to one another. Unless such direction is given, there is a risk that sight deprivation may be used, perhaps for extensive periods, merely on the basis that there is an operational need for segregation. Such reasoning played a direct part in the hooding of Baha Mousa and the other Detainees for such unacceptably long periods. While Col Rufus McNeil was rightly concerned that in-theatre documents should not become overly long, he accepted that further guidance could be given in this area, albeit that he thought it could be accommodated within the general guidance given on sight deprivation.[86]

16.107 While I am clear that it would be wrong to be over prescriptive in this area, I conclude that when dealing with permitted activities, JDP 1-10, in providing guidance on sight deprivation, should make clear that sight deprivation should not be used as a means of segregating CPERS to prevent them communicating with each other.

---

[83] Trousdell MIV010061-3, paragraphs 40-43
[84] JDP 1-10.1 at MOD042422-5
[85] MOD042422, paragraph 1B2(d)
[86] McNeil BMI 109/58/25-61/21

Reservations raised by Professor Dickson in relation to JDP 1-10

16.108 I have considered whether the guidance in relation to sight deprivation should be more restrictive and specify that it may only be used where there is a real and immediate risk to the life of security force personnel or other CPERS.

16.109 In his written report, Dickson expressed reservations as to whether sight deprivation is justifiable:

> "Sight deprivation is almost certain, in and of itself, to be characterised as inhuman or degrading treatment, and therefore a violation of Article 3 of the European Convention on Human Rights and of Article 7 of the International Covenant on Civil and Political Rights, unless it occurs only for a very short time and is for a clearly justifiable reason"[87]

> "... while I can readily accept that the use of "search positions" and "restraint" is easily justifiable, I am much less convinced of the general justifiability of "restriction of vision" and "restriction of hearing". Before being able to approve [the sections in JDP 1-10 that refer to sight and hearing deprivation] I would need to be given examples of situations in which operational security would genuinely be put at risk if such restrictions were not imposed ..."[88]

16.110 In his oral evidence, Dickson was taken to some specific examples from current operations in Afghanistan where the Armed Forces have considered it necessary to apply sight deprivation. Having considered those examples, Dickson was prepared to accept that:

> "...Obviously in Afghanistan, for example, where there might be a real risk of the kind of mortar attack that you described or an attack on a helicopter or information obtained through sight of particular equipment in an army vehicle, for example, there might be a real risk there and there might be an immediate risk in that such an attack may not ensue within the next day or two days or a week or a month but somewhere down the line. I think it's right that under the law as it stands, both nationally and internationally, the words "immediate risk" have to be taken in context. So, yes, those examples you have given me from Colonel McNeil's evidence would, I think, be ones where sight deprivation for the particular duration of the existence of the risk would be justified under international law."[89]

16.111 Having heard McNeil's evidence, while noting his acceptance that more could be done to avoid some instances of sight deprivation, I accept that in current operations there are likely to be some instances where there is an unavoidable need for sight deprivation to take place.

16.112 Accepting on this further evidence that there are some cases where sight deprivation is justified, at least in Afghanistan, Dickson remained of the view that there should be explicit guidance in the doctrine that CPERS can only be deprived of their sight where not to do so would lead to "...a real and imminent risk to the lives of members of the armed forces".[90] Elsewhere in his report, Dickson suggested that "...an international human rights court would doubtless insist on being shown convincing

---

[87] Dickson MIV010094, paragraph 40
[88] Dickson MIV010098, paragraph 49
[89] Dickson BMI 113/86/6-21
[90] Dickson MIV010099, paragraph 49

proof of the existence of rights to life which would be at real and immediate risk if deprivation of sight did not take place".[91]

16.113 The "real and immediate risk" test derives from *Osman v UK (1998) 29 EHRR 245* and is familiar as the test to be applied in asking whether there is a positive obligation on the authorities of a state to take preventive operational measures to protect an individual whose life is at risk from the criminal acts of another individual.

16.114 The question of sight deprivation of CPERS and any threshold of risk that needs to be reached before it can be applied, is a rather different question. I note in passing that Dickson was not able to point to any particular case law that supported the application of the *Osman* test into this rather different context. In *Öcalan v Turkey* (2005) 41 EHRR 5, the European Court of Human Rights (ECtHR) did not find any violation of Article 3 ECHR in the particular circumstances of that case where Mr Öcalan had been blindfolded in an aircraft and hooded for the duration of a road journey. There is no explicit indication in the judgment of the Grand Chamber in that case to suggest that a threshold test of "real and immediate risk" should be applied.

16.115 It may be open to doubt whether "real and immediate risk to the right to life of others" is a test that can easily be applied by the private soldier or Non-Commissioned Officer (NCO) on the ground who has to make a quick decision as to whether or not to apply blacked-out goggles to a CPERS.

16.116 More fundamentally, however, I do not see it as within the proper scope of this Inquiry to rule on a matter of law such as whether the legal test that would be applied by the ECtHR to the use of sight deprivation by security forces would be the "real and immediate risk" test. I make clear that I have not heard full argument on the point.

16.117 No doubt the MoD will need to monitor developments in the Strasbourg and domestic jurisprudence on this aspect carefully to check that their doctrinal guidance properly reflects the obligations owed under Article 3 ECHR.

16.118 At present, I would not go beyond the recommendation that the MoD should ensure that sight deprivation when used is, in the words of the Inernational Committee of the Red Cross (ICRC), "truly justified". I suggest that doctrine and subordinate instruction that encapsulates each of the five principles set out at paragraph 16.96 should assist in ensuring that sight deprivation is limited to that which is truly justified.

16.119 Dickson suggested that in every case of sight deprivation, there should be explicit and recorded justification for the use of sight deprivation.[92] I agree. Both the current and new draft versions of JDP 1-10 contain a requirement that the use of sight deprivation and justification for it be recorded.[93] I consider that consistent emphasis of the five principles outlined above would help to reinforce this message.

16.120 Finally, Dickson suggested that the use of sight deprivation should be authorised by a senior officer either before it starts or as soon as possible thereafter.[94]

---

[91] Dickson MIV010112, paragraph 81
[92] Dickson MIV010095-6, paragraph 43
[93] Current JDP 1-10: MOD028652, paragraph 211; New draft JDP 1-10: MIV004175, paragraph 214
[94] Dickson MIV010095-6, paragraph 43

16.121 This suggestion was put to McNeil:

> "MR MOSS: The second part of the suggestions from Professor Dickson is that there should be approval from a senior officer for the use of sight deprivation. I think in fairness to Professor Dickson, he accepts it may not always be possible in advance, but it should be given afterwards. Is that something which could be done on the ground?
>
> A. Again, I don't think that's practical. We won't have senior officers in places where we quite often believe that our troops will need to make that decision and I don't believe in retrospective endorsements. You either have an endorsement that is required to go ahead or you don't. You can have a check that things have been applied for the right reasons – and we've already referred to that in terms of possibly amending the capture card – but no, I think by and large that is impractical."[95]

16.122 McNeil was a measured and impressive witness. I accept his evidence both that senior officers would not likely be present at the point of capture to give authorisation and that retrospective authorisation in every case would not be practical. For this reason I do not think it sensible to recommend that a senior officer should be required to authorise the use of sight deprivation.

16.123 However, Dickson's underlying concerns in this respect are in my view well founded: there is a risk that the use of sight deprivation may become routine. For that reason I think it important that the guidance on sight deprivation should include a specific warning that its use must not become routine. Later in this Part of the Report I make recommendations in respect of improved CPERS detention records and the introduction of the post of Battlegroup Detention Officer. I believe that both would provide further safeguards against the inappropriate use of sight deprivation.

An additional recommendation for incorporation in JDP 1-10: Telling CPERS why they are being deprived of their sight

16.124 Owers' evidence included a warning about the fear that CPERS may experience when deprived of their sight, particularly when being transported by helicopter. In some countries, including Afghanistan, such feelings may even include a fear of being thrown out of the aircraft and certainly of being taken out of the country.[96]

16.125 Sight deprivation should only be used where truly justified for force protection, operational security or protection of other CPERS. Since disorientation or maintaining the shock of capture should play no part in the consideration of whether or not CPERS should be deprived of their sight, I consider that it would be humane to seek, where practicable, to explain to CPERS why they are being deprived of their sight.

16.126 Col S069 gave evidence to the Inquiry on day 108 as Deputy Assistant Chief of Staff Operational Support for J2 (intelligence matters) at Permanent Joint Headquarters (PJHQ). As the lead on HUMINT matters in the delivery of intelligence capability across the Chief of Joint Operations' area of business, he told the Inquiry that he would have no difficulty with CPERS being told why they were being deprived of their sight:

---

[95] McNeil BMI 109/69/22-70/13
[96] Owers BMI 114/96/22-98/19

> *"Q. But the explanation may at least give some reassurance that it is to be for a short time and the purpose is given as being so that they don't see things which they should not see?*
>
> *A. Yes, there is no problem with communicating that to them.*
>
> *Q. And if that is right, it perhaps should be part of the policy that's set out as an instruction?*
>
> *A. Yes. It can be. There's no reason why it can't be."*[97]

16.127 Similarly, McNeil did not seem to perceive any real difficulty in principle with advising CPERS why they are being deprived of their sight:

> *"Q. ... If it is the case that sight deprivation is no longer being used at all for the purposes of conditioning or maintaining the shock of capture, if that is out of the equation altogether, is there any reason in theatre why those detained should not be told of the reason why goggles are being put on, namely for operational security?*
>
> *A. I think that's probably fair. You need to think if there were any unintended consequences of that, but on the face of it, that seems a fair observation.*
>
> *Q. Is that something that happens at the moment in the sense that interpreters are used to convey that message or that a simple phrase is taught as part of pre-deployment training so that soldiers can convey that message or, again, would that be an area where there might be scope for some improvement?*
>
> *A. Again, if we considered that that made sense, then we could mandate it. We don't currently. So we don't tell people to do that. Some will. Some on the ground will make a judgment that it is a sensible way to calm down a detainee as they transport them and therefore I suspect it happens quite regularly, but I can't say that it's mandated."*[98]

16.128 I do not consider that it is sensible to require that CPERS be told in every case why goggles were being provided as a precondition to sight deprivation being applied. In some cases, lack of interpreters or other issues may make it impracticable.

16.129 Nevertheless, I conclude that JDP 1-10 should indicate that *where practicable* CPERS should be told the reason why sight deprivation is being applied. Together with restricting sight deprivation to those cases where it is truly justified and avoiding the use of hoods in all cases, I consider that this would help to ensure that sight deprivation is not used in such a way as to become inhumane. It has another benefit too: specifically telling CPERS why they are being deprived of their sight should act as some deterrent to those who might otherwise seek to use it for the purpose of disorientation and/or the shock of capture. Where practicable, suitable simple phrases in relation to sight deprivation should be included in mission specific language training. In my view, telling CPERS why blacked-out goggles are being applied can only contribute towards the goal of securing humane treatment.

16.130 In this context, it is encouraging to note that the very latest Detention Standing Orders for admission procedures for detainees apprehended by British Forces in Afghanistan states that part of the admission brief given to detainees now contains an explanation as to why and in what circumstances blacked-out goggles will be

---

[97] S069 BMI 108/131/15-23
[98] McNeil BMI 109/58/2-24

applied.[99] The widespread use of this approach, where practicable, should be encouraged.

Wider Observations on JDP 1-10 beyond the five prohibited techniques

Physical Environment: Checklist guidance for Unit Holding Areas

16.131 Two of the Inquiry's experts, Trousdell and Owers noted that both the current JDP 1-10.1 to JDP 1-10.3 and the new draft of those documents, give far more detailed guidance in relation to the physical structure of collecting points and higher theatre facilities such as prisoner of war camps, than for forward unit holding areas.[100] As both these witnesses realistically recognised, there is a limit to how much useful guidance can be provided for forward unit holding areas as they may vary from the most basic tented accommodation or similar, to various buildings that have been occupied. However, Owers suggested that JDP 1-10 would benefit from a checklist covering both the principles and the practicalities of accommodation for unit holding areas. I agree with this suggestion and note it was actively welcomed by MoD's factual witnesses as being an appropriate improvement.[101]

16.132 I conclude that a simple checklist covering both the principles and the practicalities of accommodation for unit holding areas should be included in JDP 1-10.

Death in Custody: Checklist for Battlegroups, actions on a death in custody

16.133 The latest draft of JDP 1-10 contains a requirement that higher level CPERS holding facilities should have contingency plans that can be used in the event of a death in custody.[102] There is, however, no guidance in relation to action to be taken by a Battlegroup in the event of a death of a CPERS other than in relation to honourable burial and formal reporting arrangements.[103]

16.134 Once again, I am conscious of the need to avoid being overly prescriptive in this area. A death of a CPERS may involve firstly a wide range of circumstances such as death from natural causes, death from a battle wound or death from some form of abuse in custody. Secondly, it may take place in a very wide range of operational circumstances from a death in at or near a dangerous front line battle area, to a death in a cell in a permanent facility well behind the front line. Brig Edward Forster-Knight accepted in his evidence the desirability of such a checklist and indicated that his team was working on such a document.[104]

16.135 I conclude that a simple checklist for actions on a death in custody could and should be incorporated into JDP 1-10. Its aims should include ensuring that after all attempts have been made to preserve the life of the CPERS, *where practicable* the scene of the death and the body if *in situ*, should be preserved pending the arrival of the

---

[99] MIV012772

[100] Trousdell MIV010058, paragraphs 33-34; Owers MIV008892, paragraphs 57-58

[101] McNeil BMI 109/111/21-112/2; Forster-Knight BMI 109/139/11-140/9

[102] MIV004277, paragraph 921(d)

[103] MIV004416, MIV004436-9, MIV004479. At theatre level, the current theatre instruction in SOI J3-9 is limited to the requirement of reporting the circumstances surrounding the death to the Force Provost Marshal and will refer the matter to the SIB: MIV000048. There is a standard operating procedure for actions on first on scene at the higher level temporary holding facilities: MIV012626, MIV012541

[104] Forster-Knight BMI 109/198/2–200/2

Royal Military Police/Special Investigation Branch (RMP)/(SIB). This should include, if practicable, the sealing of the area. Also, where there is a death in custody, particularly one that is sudden or unexplained, prompt checks must be made on the welfare of other prisoners.

16.136 Had such simple measures been taken on the night of Baha Mousa's death, the injuries to the other Detainees would have been identified and treated sooner; it would have been immediately apparent that abuse had taken place and important forensic evidence in relation to his death might well have been preserved.

Complaints

16.137 During Op Herrick it is apparent that detention practice has developed and improved to the extent that on arrival and discharge from detention at the higher level temporary holding facilities, CPERS are asked whether they have any complaints to make.[105]

16.138 This appears to be an area where improved practice on the ground has moved ahead of doctrine. Even the latest draft of JDP 1-10 does not include any provision about proactively asking CPERS whether they have any complaints. The new draft does provide guidance on what to do once a complaint is made,[106] and on informing CPERS on arrival to the higher level detention facility of the method for making a complaint.[107]

16.139 In his evidence to the Inquiry, Forster-Knight was in favour of incorporating the improved practice introduced in Afghanistan into wider doctrine.[108] He was, however, doubtful as to whether the same procedure could be used for detention at Battlegroup level. I agree that in some operational circumstances this would not be practicable but much would depend upon the type of operation. In a post warfighting environment such as that in which 1 QLR were engaged on Op Telic 2, prisoners who were being released by the Battlegroup could well have been asked whether or not they had any complaints.

16.140 I conclude that:

(1) JDP 1-10 should be amended to include the practice whereby on entry to and exit from a theatre level detention facility, CPERS are proactively asked whether or not they have any complaints concerning their treatment. This should not be done in the presence of the capturing soldiers/unit;

(2) JDP 1-10 should also require the Force Provost Marshal for an operation to consider what arrangements for complaints would be most practicable and effective in respect of detention before theatre level facilities; and

(3) when considering complaint mechanisms for individual operations, the MoD should also take into account the value of asking more neutral questions about CPERS' treatment during detention which may help to elicit more information about areas of CPERS' concern about their treatment.[109]

---

[105] McNeil BMI 109/112/7-116/14; Forster-Knight BMI 109/204/14-205/3
[106] MIV004180-1
[107] MIV004274, paragraph 914. There are further provisions within JDP 1-10.1 regarding a PW's right to make complaints at MIV004399, paragraph 224
[108] Forster-Knight BMI 109/209/23-210/12
[109] Owers BMI 114/98/21-100/17

Protection to Whistle blowers

16.141 JDP 1-10 is silent as to the protection that should be afforded to those who raise concerns or complaints in good faith in respect of how other service personnel have treated CPERS. Raising concerns with the chain of command will often be what is expected and encouraged, but it may often be an exceptionally difficult thing to do if the abuser is a fellow member of the unit, and all the more so if it is a more senior member of the unit.

16.142 Paragraph 113 of the new draft of JDP 1-10 makes clear the obligation to report abuse of CPERS through the chain of command.[110] This is developed in the draft chapter 3.[111] However, these sections do not address protection that will be afforded to the "whistle blower" and the only guidance given in respect of complaints about the chain of command is to report them directly to a member of the Service Police.[112] Just as service personnel may very well be reluctant to raise with their own chain of command concern about CPERS handling by fellow members of their own unit, so too are they likely to be very reticent in many cases to report them to the Service Police.

16.143 I conclude that:

(1)   it is right to present the chain of command and the Service Police as the primary and preferred recipients for complaints and reports about mistreatment of CPERS; however

(2)   JDP 1-10 should address the protection to be afforded to those who make such complaints in good faith; and

(3)   consideration should be also be given to:

(a)   suggesting the unit's detention officer as a suitable officer with whom concerns about CPERS handling can be raised [as to the post of Detention Officer, see paragraphs 16.285 to 16.293 below]. The Padre and the Regimental Medical Officer (RMO) could also sensibly be mentioned as appropriate officers to whom such concerns could be raised; and

(b)   other means such as confidential telephone lines via which concerns might be raised.

The complexity, layout and general drafting of JDP 1-10

16.144 Evidence to the Inquiry on the overall style and readability of JDP 1-10 varied considerably. Dickson referred to JDP 1-10 as:

> *"...a very unwieldy document. I have looked at the latest amended version, in the hope that it might represent a radical overhaul of the earlier version, but it does not. In my view there is still plenty of room for the document to be shortened and made more user-friendly."*[113]

In oral evidence, Dickson maintained this line notwithstanding considerations as to the target audience and their expected level of knowledge:

---

[110] MIV004158
[111] MIV004176-82
[112] MIV004180, paragraph 315
[113] Dickson MIV010097, paragraph 47

"A. I can see that you might want to use different language depending upon the intended audience of the document. But even given that these higher level documents, these strategic documents, et cetera, doctrinal documents, are intended to be read by commanders, I must say, even as an academic lawyer of some years, I find them at times pretty impenetrable. I find them hard to navigate. The use of abbreviations was extreme. There was duplication, repetition, which sometimes, I thought, led to ambiguity, if not complete uncertainty, as to the meaning. I just thought they were overly long and complicated and not readily digestible even by the highest commanders.

Q. So even when you take into account different target audiences and acronyms being known by the military to a certain extent, you still found them difficult to navigate and not clearly set out; would that be right?

A. That would be very right, yes.

Q. I think the other aspect of it, perhaps, is this: insofar as there are, for example, both annexes and appendices and particular ways that pages are paginated and so on, which to the uninitiated perhaps is confusing, that it might be said that those all reflect staffing protocols for these sort of staff office documents which are understood and are there for a reason within military documents. Would you have any comment about that as the contrary argument to what you are saying?

A. I can perhaps understand how these documents have come to be as they are and they are the latest iteration of earlier documents which have been amended and updated, but even given all of that, I think – and I am not making this as a lighthearted comment – I think someone with experience of the Plain English Society's work could profitably look at these documents. When I worked for the Human Rights Commission in Northern Ireland, we did put our documents past the Plain English Society in order to ensure that they made sense to the average person in the street.

Q. Yes.

A. Now I realise that the documents we are talking about here are not for the average person in the street, but nevertheless they should be written for the average commander. With respect – I do repeat that I have no first-hand knowledge of how the services work – I would have thought that the average commander, even with a hard copy of these documents – not a copy online – would find them a bit difficult to navigate because annexes that are referred to are many pages ahead or behind of the page in which the reference is made. They sometimes refer, these annexes, to other documents which are never summarised. They may be legal documents, international treaties, which are never summarised. The mere mention of the treaty may mean nothing at all to the person reading the document. So I do think that they could be gone through afresh and rewritten in a much more accessible way."[114]

16.145 By way of example Dickson referred to what he saw as the poor drafting in the current JDP 1-10.3 of the instruction to move CPERS back from the point of detention to the more purpose built theatre level facilities.[115] As with a number of the JTTPs, the text of paragraph 119 of the current JDP 1-10.3 in fact gives less information than the annexed flow diagram. The flow diagram at Annex 1 A of JDP 1-10.3, suggests a time limit for moving CPERS from point of apprehension to the unit holding area of *"As soon as practicable – no longer than 8 hrs"*. There is then a time limit for holding within the unit holding area of a *"maximum of 12 hrs"* with any extended stay required to be authorised by theatre legal staff. That would tend to suggest a maximum time

[114] Dickson BMI 113/70/11-72/17
[115] Dickson MIV010101, paragraph 55; JDP 1-10.3 at MOD028797-9

to transfer to the host nation of twenty hours. But the flow diagram in fact appears to give the total time from apprehension to handover as twelve hours. Moreover, in the operational conditions in Afghanistan these time limits have proved to be, by some considerable margin, unattainable. At the time of the Module 4 hearing the time allowed for transfer from Battlegroup level to the Temporary Holding Facilities (THF) was 36 hours from the point of detention.[116] Detention is authorised for a maximum of 96 hours before release or transfer to the Afghan authorities.[117]

16.146 In contrast to Dickson, Roberts considered JDP 1-10 and its subordinate JTTPs to be "...*impressive publications which spell out the framework of rules governing the treatment of 'captured, interned or detained persons' with clarity*".[118]

16.147 Hollins was the MoD witness with most direct responsibility for JDP 1-10. He accepted the need for simplicity in its drafting.[119] However, he did urge for understanding of the difficulties involved. In particular he referred to the difficulty of knowing whether to repeat material in each of the annexes JDP 1-10.1 to JDP 1-10.3 or bring material forward into the main text of JDP 1-10.[120]

16.148 I bear fully in mind that in addressing certain shortcomings and areas for improvement in JDP 1-10 and other doctrine and guidance, I am recommending that additional guidance be given which of course has the potential to add to the length of the documents.

16.149 I consider that a fair appraisal lies somewhere between the views expressed by respectively by Dickson and Roberts.

16.150 In respect specifically of the current JDP 1-10, I consider that the doctrine is over long in part because there is too much repetition of material in JDP 1-10.1 – JDP 1-10.3 that could more succinctly be included in JDP 1-10 as applying to prisoners of war, internees and detainees alike. I note and endorse the approach in the new draft of JDP 1-10 which has sought to put more information forward into the main body of JDP 1-10 and less material into the subordinate JDP 1-10.1 – JDP 1-10.3. That approach has much to commend it. There are some important differences, including international obligations between the handling of prisoners of war, internees and detainees. However, there is far more that can be expressed as being common to all three categories of CPERS.

16.151 My conclusions are as follows:

(1) Plain English, simplicity of structure and brevity are very important considerations in the drafting of JDP 1-10 and all the subordinate doctrine and instructions regarding CPERS. In revising current doctrine and instructions, Development Concepts and Doctrine Centre (DCDC) and PJHQ should give greater emphasis to these considerations, while allowing for the target audience and complexity of the subject matter.

---

[116] MIV000015, paragraph 26
[117] MIV000005, paragraph 6. This period is extendable beyond 96 hours, exceptionally, with Ministerial approval or on medical/logistical grounds approved at HQ ISAF level: MIV000006, paragraph 7.
[118] Roberts MIV010349, paragraph 79
[119] Hollins BMI 108/92/18-93/10; McNeil 109/117/1-24
[120] Hollins BMI 108/93/11-23

(2) Before its completion, the next draft of JDP 1-10 should be thoroughly assessed to ensure (i) that material is not unnecessarily duplicated and (ii) that the wording and diagrams are clear and readily understandable to the commander who may need to consider and apply aspects of JDP 1-10.

(3) It is particularly important that timescales are stated clearly in JDP 1-10, both in the text and in flow diagrams. JDP 1-10 timescales in relation to detainees and other CPERS should be demanding as this encourages the rapid move of CPERS away from forward detention areas where risks of abuse are greatest. However, the next redraft of JDP 1-10 needs to make clear that the stated timescales should be adhered to whenever possible, but may need to be amended in some theatres. I note that the latest redraft of JDP 1-10 reflects an awareness of this need.[121]

(4) DCDC should review whether its protocols for layout and pagination of joint doctrine really serve the end user. While understanding the need to permit updating and amendments, in my opinion pagination of the kind "2A3-3" is not likely to benefit the commander on the ground who has to navigate, understand and apply the doctrine to forces under his command.

(2c) The Gap in Doctrine below JDP 1-10

16.152 Both the Army Inspector Purdy and Trousdell highlighted what they see as a gap in the current doctrine. At present there is no generic SOI for the handling of CPERS on operations. The doctrine/instruction jumps straight from the high level joint doctrine of JDP 1-10 and its three JTTPs to the theatre-specific SOI J3-9 for operations in Afghanistan.[122]

16.153 The Inquiry was assured that this is something which PJHQ is well aware of and is working to resolve.[123] It is understandable that JDP 1-10 does not and cannot descend to the level of detail that would be found in a theatre-level SOI.

16.154 I conclude that it is important that PJHQ completes its work on a generic SOI for CPERS handling. It should stand as the starting template for CPERS handling on future operations. It should obviously reflect the changes already being contemplated to JDP 1-10, further changes made as a result of this Report, necessary changes in tactical questioning and interrogation policy, and (without being too Iraq or Afghan-focused) the lessons learned from Op Telic and Op Herrick.

(2d) The Tactical Questioning and Interrogation Policies

16.155 The Inquiry's consideration of tactical questioning and interrogation policies was complicated by the fact that Module 4 witnesses addressed the "*2008 Reissue of MoD Policy on Interrogation and Tactical Questioning*".[124] However, the week before the Module 4 hearings, the MoD disclosed late drafts of the 2010 separate tactical questioning policy[125] and interrogation policy.[126] These separate policies were

---

[121] MIV004367, paragraph 209 and footnote 8

[122] Army Inspectorate Review 15 July 2010 at MIV005242, paragraph 27; Trousdell MIV010049-50, paragraph 4

[123] MIV005242, paragraph 27

[124] MOD042380-409

[125] MIV012269-300

[126] MIV012301-39

then finalised during the currency of the Module 4 oral hearings. The final tactical questioning policy is dated 4 October 2010[127] and the final interrogation policy is dated the same day.[128] With some redactions, the Inquiry has been able to publish both documents.

The 2008 Interrogation and Tactical Questioning Policy

16.156 Since the 2008 tactical questioning and interrogation policy has now been replaced. It is not necessary that I should refer in detail to concerns that arise from that earlier policy. There remain concerns about the 2010 policies but they are undoubtedly improvements on the 2008 policy.

16.157 However, as I shall also make clear in dealing with tactical questioning and interrogation training, I have significant concerns that hitherto there has been a systemic failure to scrutinise practices relating to tactical questioning and interrogation with sufficient vigour.

16.158 The 2008 policy is a case in point. It was for nearly two years the high level policy in this area yet its drafting, even on an initial reading, can be seen to be inadequate. Some examples:

(1) the policy was intended to apply to both tactical questioning and interrogation. However, in relation to approaches that may be used, Serials 4 and 5 in the detailed Annex A referred only to "*interrogation approaches*" with no guidance given whatsoever in relation to tactical questioning;[129]

(2) Serial 8 in the same table contained a series of ill-drafted internally inconsistent statements about sight deprivation during an interrogation session, an issue of obvious sensitivity. On one reading of "recommendation a" this permitted sight deprivation during the actual interrogation session, a measure not even permitted during the use of interrogation in depth in Northern Ireland in 1971;[130] and

(3) while the five prohibited techniques were referred to as being "*expressly and explicitly forbidden*", this appeared in the column entitled "*recommendations*".[131]

16.159 I do not overlook other aspects of the 2008 policy which gave a correct emphasis on the importance of humane treatment of CPERS. I am bound to conclude, however, that the 2008 policy gave all the appearances of not having been assessed and reviewed with the thoroughness that would be expected of such a high level policy in such a sensitive area. Trousdell said of the 2008 policy that:

---

[127] MIV012545-76

[128] MIV012577-614

[129] MOD042393

[130] MOD042396. Recommendation '**a**' was that "*During an interrogation session a CPERS can only be deprived of vision/hearing in the following circumstances: (1) For Force Protection. (2) So that they cannot see sensitive locations, eqpt and personnel or overhear sensitive comms …*". Yet recommendation '**b**' was that "*CPERS must not be deprived of vision during either a TQ or interrogation session …*" and then recommendation '**c**' was that "*During an interrogation session only blacked out sunglasses/goggles or purpose made masks and ear defenders are to be used where necessary and proportionate on the basis of a(1) and (2) above…*"

[131] MOD042400

"It is surprising and concerning to see this kind of ambiguity in such an important high level doctrinal publication, especially one dealing with an area that is known to carry high operational risk."[132]

16.160 I endorse that assessment.

The 2010 Tactical Questioning and Interrogation Policies

16.161 As I have indicated, the 2010 policies are undoubtedly improvements on the previous joint interrogation and tactical questioning policy. I note in particular the following specific changes:

(1) The decision to have separate policies on tactical questioning and interrogation is a sensible one, given the different command and control structures for the two activities.

(2) Both policies have given much greater prominence to the prohibited techniques. The definitions used have already taken into account some of the issues raised during the Inquiry. Thus the description of the prohibition on hooding no longer refers to *keeping* a bag on a CPERS head, simply to *"placing a cover over a CPERS head"*.[133]

(3) There is an appropriate qualification to the circumstances in which non-tactical questioning qualified soldiers may ask questions of a CPERS. This section of the policy now makes clear that questioning by unqualified soldiers should only be undertaken of willing CPERS and not to unwilling CPERS, even if the matter relates to direct and immediate force protection issues.[134]

(4) The information in Annex A to each policy is better organised with material that was previously referred to as "recommendations" now correctly specified as *"Instructions"*.[135]

(5) In the tactical questioning policy,

    (a) command oversight is given greater emphasis;[136]

    (b) there is a requirement for each Unit Commanding Officer to receive a technical questioning briefing from the PJHQ J2X;[137]

    (c) a new Battlegroup post of Unit Coordinator of Tactical Questioning (UTQ) is created with responsibility for day to day oversight of technical questioning activity.[138]

16.162 These are all sensible and welcome improvements which I would respectfully endorse. The creation of a Battlegroup post to have oversight of technical questioning matters below Commanding Officer level is, in particular, a means of providing additional assurance with the chain of command and is therefore a welcome innovation.

---

[132] Trousdell MIV010073, paragraph 74
[133] MIV012553, paragraph 24(a); MIV012584, paragraph 24(a)
[134] MIV012550, paragraph 10
[135] MIV012560; MIV012591
[136] MIV012555-6, paragraphs 33-34
[137] MIV012555, paragraph 33
[138] MIV012555, paragraph 33

16.163 However, I remain concerned that in several respects the 2010 policies remain inadequate.

Approaches, in particular the harsh approach

16.164 The interrogation policy contains two Serials in its Annex A which address interrogation approaches.

16.165 For reasons that were, in my view, never adequately explained in the Module 4 evidence, no such guidance on approaches appears at all in the tactical questioning policy. I consider this to be a serious, surprising and worrying omission.

16.166 The MoD is fully aware that there is significant controversy about the harsh questioning approach; firstly on whether it is lawful at all, and secondly if so as to how its proper limits can be adequately defined and enforced. Against that background I find it entirely unacceptable that the tactical questioning policy should be silent as to whether or not the harsh approach is permitted as part of tactical questioning.

16.167 This position is all the more surprising given the emphasis in the 2010 tactical questioning policy as to oversight responsibilities of the UTQ. One is bound to ask how those officers are meant to have command and control of tactical questioning activity if the MoD's policy does not define what approaches are permitted, nor give even basic guidance as to their proper limits. It is not sufficient that they might be covered in an oral briefing from PJHQ staff who may or may not have a clear understanding of what the limits of approaches should be. If the Commanding Officer of a unit had to rely on the tactical questioning policy to inform him whether or not the harsh approach was permitted, he would be left *"flapping in the breeze"* as Trousdell aptly described it in his evidence to the Inquiry.[139]

16.168 S067 was responsible for drafting the 2010 tactical questioning and interrogation policies. During his Module 4 evidence, S067 initially stated that:

> *"A. The harsh technique is no longer taught to tactical questioners and is no longer used in the tactical questioning regime.*
>
> *THE CHAIRMAN: Is not that more sensible then to say "don't use the harsh in TQ'ing"?*
>
> *A. For clarity, sir, that would be a worthwhile addition –*
>
> *THE CHAIRMAN: It would be quite simple to do that, wouldn't it?*
>
> *A. But it is in fact no longer taught or used.*
>
> *THE CHAIRMAN: Yes, but the best thing is to say "Don't use the harsh in TQ".*
>
> *A. Yes, sir."[140]*

S067 then needed to correct himself in this regard when his evidence continued the following day:

---

[139] Trousdell BMI 115/81/5-7
[140] S067 BMI 108/122/1-12

> *"…I would like to take this opportunity to correct something I said yesterday, Sir, which is I stated that I thought the harsh technique was not taught on the tactical questioning course. I have since been corrected by colleagues and told that it is indeed touched upon, the detail of which I'm not exactly aware of, but I would like to take this opportunity to correct what I said yesterday."* [141]

16.169 I make no personal criticism of S067 in this regard. But I consider it to be characteristic of a systemic muddle in respect of tactical questioning and interrogation that the officer with responsibility for producing the draft of tactical questioning policy was not in a position to know whether or not tactical questioners are currently trained in respect of the harsh approach, and that the policy should remain entirely silent on the point.

16.170 It is abundantly clear from the evidence I have heard that tactical questioning and interrogation policy and practice inevitably involves difficult legal and policy judgments about where the line is to be drawn between illegitimate and/or unlawful pressures upon prisoners and legitimate and lawful means of obtaining life saving intelligence.

16.171 Striking this balance is not a new challenge. But it is one with which the tactical questioning and interrogation policies must engage more closely, so as to ensure that there is better guidance to which the Interrogation branch at DISC, Chicksands should then teach. Given the complexities and sensitivities of the issues involved, I would add that the instructing staff at Chicksands are entitled to expect that the tactical questioning and interrogation policies should go into sufficient detail so that they can be clear about where the lines are to be drawn and then teach to that policy.

16.172 As will be apparent from my assessment of current tactical questioning and interrogation training, this failure to give a clear policy lead on whether or not the harsh approach is permitted in tactical questioning has contributed to an entirely unsatisfactory state of affairs on the tactical questioning training course. The harsh approach is currently touched upon in the tactical questioning course but students no longer practice it, even though it remains possible that they might be authorised to use it in future operations.

16.173 It is entirely unsatisfactory that such a recent tactical questioning policy does not address the harsh approach.

16.174 I therefore conclude that urgent consideration must be given to amending the tactical questioning policy to make clear what approaches are and are not authorised for use in tactical questioning. Further, in future all tactical questioning and interrogation policies should descend to greater detail on approaches, as a minimum making clear which approaches are authorised for use in which discipline, tactical questioning or interrogation.

16.175 I turn to consider the substantive issue of whether the harsh approach is appropriate at all.

16.176 In doing so I consider that it is not appropriate for me to appear to make any kind of ruling as the legality of the harsh approach. This is an issue which may arise for

---

[141] S067 BMI 109/26/18-25

consideration in individual litigation and the question of whether particular conduct on any given occasion was lawful or not would be fact sensitive.

16.177 I am, however, clear about the following matters in relation to the harsh approach.

16.178 Firstly, it makes no difference that the harsh approach is now designed to be used only in relation to a certain category of CPERS who do not engage with interrogators. S067 told the Inquiry that the loud version of the harsh approach was constrained by the interrogation policy and

> "...is intended to be used in very specific circumstances discussed with a controller beforehand, specifically, as the policy says, on an uncooperative CPER. This is an individual who is refusing to engage or speak to a – speaking to the interrogator and it is designed specifically to counteract the resistance to interrogation technique whereby the CPER focuses on a spot above the interrogator's head and tries to blot out what they are saying."[142]

16.179 The difficulty with this explanation is that it is precisely the prisoner of war who is refusing to answer questions, who is intended to be protected by Article 17 of the Third Geneva Convention:

> "No physical or mental torture, nor any other form of coercion, may be inflicted on prisoners of war to secure from them information of any kind whatever. Prisoners of war who refuse to answer may not be threatened, insulted or exposed to any unpleasant or disadvantageous treatment of any kind."[143]

16.180 So it can be no defence of the harsh approach that it is only used against uncooperative CPERS.

16.181 Secondly, the harsh approach at the very least comes close to the edge of what is legally permissible in the treatment of CPERS.

16.182 As noted above, under Article 17 of the Third Geneva Convention, prisoners of war who refuse to answer questions must not be *"threatened, insulted or exposed to any unpleasant or disadvantageous treatment of any kind"*.[144] The current interrogation policy rests on a fine distinction in relation to "insults". It states that *"Under no circumstances must the CPERS be threatened or insulted"* and *"A harsh approach must not be used to ridicule the person of the CPERS..."*. But the policy specifically permits the interrogator to *"...deride their military performance or circumstances of capture"*. The sarcastic/cynical version of the harsh *"...is used to ridicule the military performance of a CPERS in the hope that he will respond to defend himself from accusations of incompetence. This approach is not to be used to ridicule the physical person by race, colour, creed, religion or gender"*.[145]

16.183 Thus it would seem that the interrogation policy would permit the interrogator cynically to deride the captured enemy commander as an incompetent and perhaps cowardly

---

[142] S067 BMI 109/16/14-23

[143] MOD016384

[144] MOD016384. I concentrate here on the Third Geneva Convention relative to prisoners of war. However, Article 27 of the Fourth Geneva Convention relative to the protection of Civilian Persons in Time of War, requires that protected persons shall be protected *"...against all acts of violence or threats thereof and against insults and public curiosity"*. Article 31 provides that *"no physical or moral coercion shall be exercised against protected persons, in particular to obtain information from them or from third parties."*: MOD020336

[145] MIV012604, paragraph 5(d)

leader because of the circumstances of the capture of his unit, but this is said not to be an "*insult*" because it derides the commander's performance, and is not an insult to the "*...person of the CPERS*". This is a very fine line.

16.184 As regards the loud version of the harsh approach, this is stated to be limited to "*... short bursts to bring an uncooperative CPERS back into the full realisation of their situation*". The interrogator may "*berate, cajole and deride*" in the manner of a drill sergeant to his drill squad. Guidance is given that "*...it is unlikely to be necessary to use a harsh approach for longer than 2 minutes at any one time. Great care must be exercised if it is used more than once in any one interrogation session as it may become ineffective*".[146] I am concerned that the comparison with a drill sergeant is an inapt and difficult one. The latest information from the MoD, see paragraph 16.206 below, suggests that the MoD now shares this view.

16.185 From earlier training material, the Inquiry is aware that the loud harsh involves invading the personal space of the CPERS and is likely to involve shouting up close to the CPERS' face, although not directly into their ears.

16.186 The interrogation policy would appear to rely here on an assumption that being berated, cajoled or derided by being shouted at close range in the manner of a drill sergeant, but for a relatively short period of time, is neither "*unpleasant*" nor "*disadvantageous treatment*". Again, if justified at all, this is on any view a very fine line.

16.187 The evidence of Dickson and Adams reflected the reservations which they held, from the LOAC and International Human Rights Law viewpoints respectively, as to the harsh approach.

16.188 Dickson commented that International Human Rights Law does not prohibit harsh approaches as such when detainees are being questioned. However, he added, the caveats that such treatment must not produce feelings of fear, anguish or inferiority, nor spill over into sexism, racism or religious slurs, and that the protections granted by the Geneva Conventions may be higher than International Human Rights Law in this area.[147] His report further stated that:

> "*The reference at point (a) to "harsh approaches" is a bit worrying, even though the term is then qualified: it must not amount to intimidation, coercion, unpleasant or disadvantageous treatment, or inhuman or degrading treatment. I would be interested to know what kind of approach would not fall into any of those categories but still be "harsh". The reference at point (b) to drill sergeants' "berating, cajoling and deriding" suggests that "harsh approaches" can take the form of shouts, roars and belittling remarks, yet these would surely be at the very least "unpleasant" and "degrading" forms of behaviour. Likewise, point (c) prohibits insults but allows sarcasm, scolding and derision, which would surely be "unpleasant" (although not, probably, degrading). Drawing a precise line between permissible and impermissible interrogation practices is obviously very difficult, and this serial does make a valiant attempt to do so. But I nevertheless think that it is still somewhat internally inconsistent and that further clarification would be desirable.*"[148]

16.189 In his oral evidence to the Inquiry, Dickson referred to the potential for inconsistency within the 2010 interrogation policy's treatment of the harsh approach between telling

---

[146] MIV012604, paragraph 5(d)(1)
[147] Dickson MIV010122-3, paragraph 104
[148] MIV010111, paragraph 78

interrogators that they must not insult CPERS but that the approach permitted them to ridicule their performance: "...*If ridiculing the military performance of a captured person isn't insulting that person, I don't know what would be*".[149]

16.190 Adams raised significant concerns about the compatibility of the harsh approach with the Geneva Conventions:

> "...*A lot of the harsh approach or what is implied by the harsh approach in these documents is actually going to be quite difficult to square in the clear provisions of the Geneva Conventions. I think it's Article 17 in the Prisoner of War Convention and there is an equivalent article in the Civilians Convention. That's a very small correction to what Professor Dickson said this morning, when he implied it was only prisoners of war who were, as it were, guaranteed respect and so on. That applies also to civilian detainees under Geneva Convention IV. If a category is created, described as "harsh", without clarity as to what it involves, this may, of course, lead some to conclude that "harsh" means "harsh" and anything goes. I think the category of "firm", which is another of the categories that we find in these documents, is admirable. I have no problems at all with that. But I do think that creating a notional category of "harsh" and then failing to provide much content to it is asking for trouble.*
>
> *Q. So – if I don't put words in your mouth. I am sure you won't accept it from me – are you saying that it's difficult to envisage how the harsh approach can be carried through without breaching the Convention, without breaching the law?*
>
> *A. Yes.*"[150]

16.191 Thirdly, the MoD has previously permitted the harsh approach to include practices which are entirely unacceptable and should never have been taught. More than three years after Baha Mousa's death, a statement was prepared for the Court Martial by a Warrant Officer at DISC, Chicksands. Dated 26 October 2006, it exhibited a video clip, recorded in December 2005 which as of October 2006 was being used on courses as "...*an ideal example of how to question/interrogate and stay completely within the guidelines of the law and the instruction given on the relevant courses*".[151]

16.192 A pixellated version of that video was disclosed to the Core Participants and published by the Inquiry. The transcript reveals the "interrogator" on the course to say – in some cases shout – amongst other things, the following to the "CPERS":

> *"What's your first name? WHAT'S YOUR FIRST NAME? What was your mission? COME ON DICKHEAD, WHAT WAS IT? WHAT WAS YOUR MISSION? Do you understand the question? You're a bit simple and fucking Kagan army, are you? Bit simple? You get fucking dropped on your head as a kid, did you?*
>
> *WHAT'S YOUR FUCKING NAME? WHAT IS IT? WHAT UNIT ARE YOU FROM? What's your date of birth? Mm? What is it? Don't you know? Were you fucking hatched? Were you? What's your date of birth? Come on, mong, it's not a difficult question? What is it?*
>
> ...

---

[149] Dickson BMI 113/106/11-13
[150] Adams BMI 113/162/23-163/23
[151] MOD013214

> *Look at me. Fucking look at me. What's your date of birth? Come on. What fucking unit are you from? Don't you know? You the unit fucking rent boy, were you? Is that why you didn't fucking say? Only there for one fucking reason, weren't you? Mm? You and your fucking mates. What was your mission? What was your fucking mission?"*
>
> ...
>
> *Pick up your fucking blindfold. Don't put it on your fucking head. I'll tell you when to put it on your fucking head. Do you FUCKING UNDERSTAND ME? I'll TELL YOU when you DO IT. Right. You go back into the fucking holding facility. And while you're in there, I'm going to give you three questions to fucking think about. Yeah? Only three. That is: what other OPs are there in Alba? Yeah? What's their mission in Alba? Yeah? The third one, last one for you stupid boy, is, how long are they going to stay there? OK? And if you answer those questions, yeah, I'll make sure that you're treated properly here. If you don't answer those questions, you know the Albans are outside, don't you? And you know the Albans are just waiting for you? OK? Of course, I've got no idea what they'd do to you. No idea at all. But I think you do. OK?*
>
> *Put your blindfold on. Put your hands out in front of you, thumbs uppermost. GUARDS!"*[152]

16.193 I emphasise that such questioning would not now be permitted under the 2010 interrogation policy. However, it is symptomatic of the risks the MoD is running in this area by continuing to permit the harsh approach that its own approved ("ideal example") previous teaching in this area contained personal homophobic insults and only thinly veiled threats about what enemy forces might do to the CPERS if he was released having not cooperated.

16.194 It is completely unacceptable that such training was permitted to be given, all the more so when it was being presented as an ideal example of how to interrogate and stay within the law.

16.195 Fourthly, there are strong indications that the utility of the harsh approach is limited. I note that the loud version of the harsh is described in the interrogation policy as being "... *not intended as an information extraction tool*". In contrast, however, the sarcastic/cynical harsh is used in the hope that the CPERS will respond to defend himself from accusations of incompetence.[153]

16.196 A number of witnesses told the Inquiry that the harsh approach was of limited utility at least in some theatres. Of particular note was the evidence of Adams that "*DISC has been advised by theatre that under current operational conditions, the 'harsh' has yielded little and is not therefore used on Op HERRICK*".[154] Similarly S004, currently the Officer Commanding I Branch, told me that:

> *"...The neutral approach is much more – has greater utility in a formed questioning area such as interrogation. And the harsh has limited utility based on the feedback I've received from theatres."*[155]

When asked by me whether the dangers of permitting tactical questioners to use the harsh technique outweighed all benefits, S004 replied:

---

[152] BMI01610-1
[153] MIV012604, paragraph 5(d)
[154] Adams MIV012255-6, paragraph 12
[155] S004 BMI 111/77/20-24

> "S004: I'm not sure it would override all possible benefits because that is a bit hypothetical, but it's not something that we practice them in, therefore they are very unlikely to be using it, because all of our emphasis on the theoretical – the majority of our emphasis on the theoretical and all of our effort on the practical is aimed at the firm logical and the friendly logical because those are proved to be –
>
> THE CHAIRMAN: They are successful.
>
> S004: – most successful. I'm reluctant to say that something doesn't work in a given theatre, sir."[156]

16.197 I take account of the possibility that experience may vary in different theatres of operation. Nevertheless I think it fair to conclude that the evidence, at least to this Inquiry, as to the utility of the harsh approach does not suggest that it is routinely successful in extracting information from CPERS.

16.198 Fifthly, even if lawful, the harsh approach carries an undesirable risk if used for tactical questioning in forward areas. Although tactical questioning would usually only be carried out with the tactical questioner, the CPERS and possibly an interpreter present, use of the harsh approach is likely to be overheard if not witnessed by other members of the Battlegroup. Trousdell commented as follows:

> "While it is beyond my area of expertise to say whether or not the harsh approach may in some cases be legitimate as part of interrogation, I do have a concern that the existence of a harsh technique is a catalyst for misinterpretation by the unqualified. One can imagine talk in theatre such as "I was on a course last month where we were taught how to use a harsh technique on prisoners" which could lead to serious misunderstanding on the part of others. Harsh techniques by TQers close to the front line may trigger undisciplined and forbidden behaviour."[157]

16.199 I have cited above the concern of Adams that if a category is created, described as "harsh", it may lead some to conclude that "harsh" means "harsh" and anything goes. (see paragraph 16.190 above).

16.200 These five factors lead me to the fundamental conclusion that the harsh approach should no longer have a place **in tactical questioning**. In my view even if the harsh approach as currently taught is lawful, its risks if used in forward deployed areas outweigh the benefits of its use. As a matter of policy, MoD should expressly forbid tactical questioners from using what is currently known as the harsh approach. This should be made clear in the tactical questioning policy and in all relevant training materials.

16.201 The Inquiry was principally concerned with tactical questioning rather than interrogation. In relation to the harsh approach in interrogation, I confine my comments and conclusions to the following.

16.202 Firstly, I have reservations about the current use of the drill sergeant analogy to explain the proper limits of the harsh approach in interrogation. While this will be a familiar concept to military students, I am concerned that aspects of some drill sergeants' approach to berate, cajole and deride their drill squad may not be compliant with Article 17 of the Third Geneva Convention if used on CPERS.

---

[156] S004 BMI 111/79/24-80/9
[157] Trousdell MIV010075, paragraph 86

16.203 Secondly, I agree with the reservations expressed by both Trousdell and Adams about the terminology of "harsh" which is prone to be misunderstood.

16.204 Thirdly, I would expect interrogation of CPERS to be carried out by better qualified interrogators than tactical questioners, and in more controlled conditions.

16.205 My conclusions in relation to the harsh approach **in interrogation** are:

(1) the harsh approach even as recently redefined carries high legal risk with clear arguments that its use may be contrary to the Geneva Conventions;

(2) to the extent that the MoD considers that the harsh approach can still lawfully be used in interrogation:

(a) there is a need for very clear guidance to be given within the interrogation policy and in training as to the proper limits of the harsh approach.

(b) I welcome MoD's acceptance that the analogy with a drill sergeant is unhelpful (see below); and

(c) the approach, even if retained for interrogation, should also be given a label which is less apt to be misinterpreted as permitting unlawful, threatening or intimidatory conduct.

(3) in light of the legal and other risks in the use of the harsh approach, specific Ministerial approval should be sought before the harsh approach is approved for use in any operational theatre.

Addendum

16.206 Since the above paragraphs in this section on the harsh approach were drafted, the Inquiry has received a letter from the MoD entitled "Update on the 'Harsh' approach and legal audit of tactical questioning and interrogation practices and training" dated 7 March 2011. The letter explains that the MoD has considered the harsh approach in the light of advice by Counsel and an advice on training. It is appropriate that I set out the relevant passage in full:[158]

> **The 'Harsh' Approach**
>
> The MOD has reached a number of conclusions about the 'harsh' approach, having considered Counsel's advice and having reflected upon the potential importance of Tactical Questioning and Interrogation in operational environments. MOD believes that there is a need to retain elements of the 'harsh' approach in both Interrogation and Tactical Questioning and that by applying strict parameters legal risks can be effectively managed.
>
> It may be helpful to remind the Inquiry, first of all, that the 2010 MOD Interrogation policy defines two types of 'harsh' approach; first the 'Loud Harsh'; and secondly, the 'Cynical/Sarcastic Harsh'. So far as concerns the Loud Harsh, this is intended to be used where there is a need to gain the attention of a person who is being questioned and who is deliberately ignoring the questioner or otherwise not engaging with him. Within clear and stringent parameters the MOD considers that a requirement exists for a questioner to raise his voice or even to shout at a subject if it is necessary to refocus him on the questions being asked. The strict parameters which the MOD considers are necessary properly to control the use of a refocusing approach are:
>
> • The approach should only be used in circumstances where it is necessary and appropriate to refocus a CPERS on the questions which he is being asked.

---

[158] MIV012736-8

- The frequency with which a loud approach is used to refocus the subject of tactical questioning or interrogation should be limited to ████████████████████

- The duration of the approach should be limited so that it lasts a maximum of ████████

- Speech must be coherent and translated.

- The questioner must not shout into the subject's ear.

- There must be no violence or threat of violence.

- There must be no intimidation of any kind.

- The questioning must not seek to frighten or instil fear.

- There must be no threats of any kind, whether express or implied.

- There must be no coercion of any kind.

- The content must not be insulting, humiliating or degrading.

- The captured person's attributes must not be ridiculed (e.g. race, religion or gender).

- The questioner must not touch the captured person.

The MOD believes that the titles "harsh" or "loud harsh" are a misnomer for the above approach and it is considering a more appropriate label. The new label will aim to reflect the purpose of the approach which is to refocus the subject on the questions which he is being asked.

On reflection, the MOD accepts that drawing an analogy between a Tactical Questioner or Interrogator and a drill sergeant is unhelpful and this will be removed from relevant documentation.

So far as concerns the 'Cynical/Sarcastic Harsh', there are occasions during questioning when the use of sarcasm or cynicism can assist either a Tactical Questioner or an Interrogator. Accordingly, it wishes to retain a form of what is currently the sarcastic / cynical element of the 'harsh' approach. Again, a more appropriate name is required because 'harsh' is a misleading description. MOD recognises that this approach must also be the subject of clear and stringent parameters which should include:

- The approach should only be used in circumstances where it is appropriate[1].

- It will be used only for so long as is necessary to have the effect required.

- The content must not be insulting, humiliating or degrading.

- The captured person's attributes must not be ridiculed (e.g. race, religion or gender).

- There must be no intimidation of any kind.

- There must be no threats of any kind, whether express or implied.

- The questioner must not seek to frighten or instil fear.

[1] The approach is known to be a useful tool in questioning persons with certain personality traits, e.g. the self important.

- There must be no coercion of any kind.

- The questioner must not touch the captured person.

It is recognised that particular care needs to be taken to ensure that the use of sarcasm and cynicism do not lead the questioner into insulting a captured person. The former practice of teaching questioners to deride the military performance of a captured person should stop in order to minimise this risk.

At present, the 'harsh' approach is not being used by Tactical Questioners in Afghanistan. However, the MOD wishes to retain the option, if necessary, to use the revised and relabelled elements of the 'harsh' approach described above both in Tactical Questioning and in Interrogation. The MOD does not anticipate that these approaches will be required very often in Tactical Questioning but has good reason not to want to rule them out. It has at least one example of where the use of the harsh approach in a situation in Iraq assisted the rescue of hostages.

It is accepted that a high level of command and control (in the widest sense) as well as carefully designed training will be needed to ensure that Tactical Questioners (and Interrogators) apply the above approaches correctly and that risks are mitigated as far as possible.

Tactical Questioning and Interrogation Policies

As was indicated in the MOD's closing submissions in Module 4 the MOD accepts that its current TQ and Interrogation policies are amenable to improvement. For example, it is recognised that the TQ policy should include a list of permissible techniques and that amongst other things there needs to be revised and expanded guidance about sight deprivation and sleep. Revised policy will also need to incorporate the MOD's latest thinking, set out above, which has resulted from its recent examination of the 'harsh' approach.

Work is in hand to redraft the policies but the MOD wishes to wait until it has the benefit of the Chairman's recommendations before completing the redrafting process.

The MOD has sought to inform itself further by commissioning a detailed independent analysis of the utility of all of Tactical Questioning and Interrogation techniques. This will be led by an independent Chairman from outside of Defence, with a military Colonel as its deputy. The full report is not expected to be complete before the summer.

Training

Training of the 'harsh' approach on the TQ course will be reviewed by the Defence HUMINT Organisation, as the training sponsor, and the redefined approach taught to future TQ students alongside the other approaches (rather than merely 'briefed' as previously). However, because there is currently no requirement to use the redefined approach in TQ in Afghanistan, it will be made clear, including in the Afghanistan TQ directive[2], that it should not to be used in TQ in that theatre. Should existing Tactical Questioners who have not had the appropriate training in the revised version of 'harsh' deploy to a theatre where there is a requirement to use it they will also receive the necessary additional training.

Remedial training will also be provided to interrogators on the revised and redefined approaches.

16.207 It is apparent from this letter that the MoD has given much further thought to the harsh approach for both tactical questioning and interrogation. I welcome this, but in view of the importance of the issues surrounding the harsh, I have not thought it sensible (or necessary) to alter the comments which I have made above on the position before receipt of the letter. Those comments in my view remain valid. However, it is necessary that I add further comments on the MoD's latest position on the harsh.

16.208 I have carefully considered the "strict parameters" necessary properly to control the use of the harsh approach. Obviously, they represent an improvement on the previous position. Nevertheless, I have considerable reservations as to how in practice instructors will be able to demonstrate and teach sarcasm and cynicism that does not lead and amount to insulting the prisoner, and greater reservations on the practicality of ensuring that such training is adhered to. For instance, the parameters for the "loud harsh" prohibit "intimidation" and "coercion" of any kind. This will involve the questioner/interrogator in treading a fine line between what is legitimate and what is intimidation or coercion. It will also involve some subjective judgment by the instructors of the subject of the questioning and interrogation. Much the same can be said of the parameters for the "cynical/sarcastic harsh".

16.209 In my opinion the risks of using the harsh approach, whether "loud" or "cynical/sarcastic" will remain. In the circumstances, although I recognise that the MoD, no doubt for good reason, wishes to retain elements of the harsh approach, my firm conclusion is that its use in the tactical questioning process carries too great a risk. So far as interrogation is concerned I remain sceptical about the practicalities of eliminating the risks to which I have referred. But I recognise that the new parameters are an improvement on the previous position. In an age of the widespread availability of small recording devices (even if prohibited for use by servicemen), there is a significant risk of footage of any the "harsh" approach being recorded and distributed. Even if the harsh approach is amended, it is for consideration whether the potential adverse impact of such footage of interrogation once published is really justified by the advantages perceived to come from the amended harsh approach. I repeat the view expressed in paragraph 205(3) above that before the harsh approach is used in any operational theatre Ministerial approval should be sought.

Sleep

16.210 I have already addressed the need for greater clarity in relation to sleep deprivation and permitted activities in the context of JDP 1-10.

16.211 The policies on tactical questioning and interrogation provide that a CPERS must be permitted a total period of eight hours rest in a 24 hour period of which no less than four hours must be in a continuous block.

16.212 The policies on tactical questioning and interrogation contain the instruction that:

> "b. In order that a CPERS cannot work out what will happen next, the pattern of sleep/rest allowed to the CPERS can be determined by the unit co-ordinator of TQ" / "...by the interrogation controller."[159]

16.213 S067 suggested in his evidence that this was not intended to permit the random waking of CPERS, but rather to ensure that a questioner is able to wake the CPERS to deal with intelligence or information as it arises.[160]

16.214 In his evidence S067 suggested that Counsel to the Inquiry had been the first person to suggest that the current policy could be read as permitting a CPERS to be kept awake pending imminent questioning. He suggested that tactical questioners did not need further guidance in this area.[161]

16.215 I disagree with S067's evidence in these respects. As I have referred to in paragraphs 16.100 to 16.101 above, the submissions on behalf of the majority of military witnesses to this Inquiry reflect the understanding of their clients (or some of them) that keeping CPERS awake in the early stages of custody does not amount to sleep deprivation. The legal briefing slide on the issue at least on one view contemplates the same stating "*Sleep deprivation: Only if there is a Valid operational reason (imminent questioning?) but only for the minimum time necessary...*".[162]

---

[159] MIV012563; MIV012595
[160] S067 BMI 108/111/11-19
[161] S067 BMI 108/113/3-17
[162] MIV003533

16.216 Later in his evidence, in questioning from the Detainees' Counsel, S067 explained that

> "...The intention in this paragraph is that a CPERS should not expect to be sleeping at a certain time – sorry, I'll clarify that. There shouldn't be a routine in place that allows the CPERs to work out that he is going to get some sleep in an hour's time or two hours' time and therefore, if he can just hang on in one piece of questioning or stick to one line of alibi cover story, that, you know, he will realise that if he gets to a certain time then the questioning will finish for that day."[163]

16.217 He went on to accept that in retrospect the meaning of this part of the policy might be expanded in the next revision.[164]

16.218 I conclude as follows:

(1) in line with the clarifications I have recommended in respect of JDP 1-10, the tactical questioning and interrogation policies need to make clear that it is not permissible deliberately to keep prisoners awake, even for short periods, merely because they may shortly face tactical questioning or interrogation;

(2) CPERS may nevertheless be woken up in order to be tactically questioned or interrogated if the questioning is ready to take place provided that the policy on minimum periods of rest is respected; and

(3) both policies should also make clear that the discretion to wake a CPERS for immediate questioning is not to be abused by way of repeated or random waking of the CPERS with a view to disorientation of the CPERS.

Self and system induced pressures

16.219 I am concerned that neither the tactical questioning policy nor the interrogation policy gives sufficiently detailed guidance as to how questioners may seek to use self induced and system induced pressures.

16.220 Both policies refer in their respective Annex A's to a list of self induced pressures, which include fear of death or dying and fear of harsh physical treatment. The instructions column states that tactical questioning/interrogation techniques:

> "...impacting on these pressures must comply with the guidance and constraints detailed in MOD Interrogation Policy, [the respective references for each policy are listed] and Annex B [and the relevant paragraph of annex B is listed]."[165]

16.221 For the interrogation policy, the relevant paragraph of Annex B is paragraph 10 which states:

> "**System Induced Pressures.** In addition to Self Induced pressures stated in Annex A, System Induced Pressures are placed on the CPERS by the fact of their being captured. These effects may be used by the interrogator to identify triggers that may be used in the interrogation process.
>
> System-induced pressures include:
>
> i. Irregular and apparently meaningless system.

---

163 S067 BMI 109/9/24-10/8
164 S067 BMI 109/10/16-21
165 MIV012565; MIV012597

> *ii. The need for constant alertness.*
>
> *iii. Shows of knowledge by interrogators.*
>
> *iv. Prison diet that may be repetitive and bland.*
>
> *v. Unaccustomed discipline for CPERS who hold senior rank or who are mature in age.*
>
> *vi. Confinement.*
>
> *vii. Enforced idleness."*[166]

A near-identical provision appears in the tactical questioning policy, Annex B paragraph 8.[167]

16.222 The main difficulty which I perceive with this approach is that it leaves so much discretion to the I branch at DISC, Chicksands, in what to teach in relation to how tactical questioners and interrogators may seek to exploit the system and self induced pressures. Indeed, during the course of his oral evidence, S004 as Officer Commanding I branch, indicated the area of what does and does not amount to increasing pressures artificially was one where his branch needed advice.[168]

16.223 At the very basic level, there is not even the general guidance within these policies to the effect that tactical questioners and interrogators may not do anything artificially to increase the self induced pressures that a CPERS may feel. This omission is surprising and of concern given that the latest draft of JDP 1-10 contains an explicit warning that *"…under no circumstances are active measures to be taken to increase self-induced pressures; a CPERS is safe in British custody and any attempt to convince a CPERS otherwise will ultimately undermine their exploitation"*.[169]

16.224 Burton, although not a specialist in this area, saw no difficulty with the imperative not to increase self induced pressures artificially being included in the policy. S067, who is a specialist in these matters, also seemed to accept this point:

> *"Q. Can we go on then, please, to serial 7, "Effects of self-induced pressures". There's nothing in this section, is there, as I think there wasn't in the old version, about not prolonging the shock of capture artificially as it were?*
>
> *A. No, sir.*
>
> *Q. Should that be in there?*
>
> *A. Sir, self-induced pressures by their definition are taking place within the head of captured person. We take steps to make sure that they are not enhanced by outlawing any threats of maltreatment that might possibly contribute to those. But we are not in a position to be able to influence what's happening inside a captured person's thoughts.*
>
> *Q. No, but what are you in a position to do, if I may say so, is to ensure that soldiers, if they follow your instruction anyway, do not artificially prolong the shock of capture by any measures.*
>
> *A. No, sir, that is correct."*[170]

---

[166] MIV012606
[167] MIV012572
[168] S004 BMI 111/89/8-90/4
[169] MIV004169, paragraph 205
[170] S067 BMI 108/115/7-25

16.225 S004, who of course commands the branch that teaches the tactical questioning and interrogation courses saw no difficulty with the policies making clear that nothing must be done artificially to increase self induced pressures.[171] As was explored during the Inquiry's evidence, there are difficult lines to be drawn in relation to self induced pressures: if a CPERS expresses a fear of ill treatment, is the questioner bound to give reassurance or merely desist from anything that might reinforce the fear of ill-treatment from British Forces? It is precisely because these are difficult lines that the policy needs to be more detailed in guiding I branch, DISC on what can be taught. Without this there is a real danger of the teaching, and thus practice in the field, overstepping the mark.

16.226 As regards system induced pressures, there are similarly difficult questions concerning what should and should not be permitted. Although I must in fairness emphasise that there are materials that have since been replaced, and searching of prisoners no longer forms any part of the teaching of I branch at all, the initial disclosure of 2008 materials included some inappropriate references in dealing with detailed searches.[172] It is welcome that internal reviews within the MoD have obviously caused references of this kind to be removed.

16.227 While I recognise that no policy can be so prescriptive as to legislate for all eventualities, I conclude that the tactical questioning and interrogation policies must strive to give more detailed guidance on the extent to which tactical questioners and interrogators may seek to exploit self and system induced pressures.

Inspection and audit

16.228 The interrogation policy contains a provision that an inspection audit of interrogation paperwork and processes will be carried out at six monthly intervals in all theatres where interrogation activities are taking place. This is to be carried out by the Commander of the Defence HUMINT Organisation.[173] I consider that the auditing of the interrogation "processes" should include, and should be stated in the policy to require, review of a selection of recordings of interrogations of the inspectors' choosing. Interrogators should know that the recordings of interrogations that they carry out may be inspected in this way.

16.229 There is no equivalent audit and inspection serial in the tactical questioning policy. The policy is now clear that the chain of command for tactical questioning runs to the unit Commanding Officer and actual inspection of tactical questioning at a forward level would clearly be more problematic. Nevertheless, the unit coordinator of tactical questioning who has day to day oversight of such activity is to liaise with the theatre J2X and may seek advice from the theatre J2X. While command responsibility for tactical questioning rests with the Unit Commander, there is therefore a linkage that runs to PJHQ J2X via the theatre J2X.[174] In the Module 4 hearings, the MoD witnesses were not able immediately to answer whether tactical questioning records were the subject of audit in theatre. I am grateful to S067 who looked into this matter on a recent visit to Afghanistan. He established that tactical questioning records were not being audited. This obviously underlines the concern that I raised during the Module 4 hearings. The MoD has promised to rectify this with immediate effect, and the

---

[171] S004 BMI 111/24/1-9
[172] MOD028275; MOD044043
[173] MIV012602
[174] MIV012556, TQ Governance Linkages

Inquiry has been told that the first tactical questioning audit took place in May 2011. The MoD has assured the Inquiry that this will now be rectified in the next redraft of the tactical questioning policy.[175] I conclude that the current tactical questioning policy is inadequate in failing to include a clear and simple auditing procedure. I am reassured by the MoD's candid acceptance of this gap and the interim action it has taken. The MoD are right to accept that this must be addressed in the next version of the tactical questioning policy.

(2e) Specific Criminalisation of the Five Techniques?

16.230 I have considered whether it would be beneficial for specific legislation to be introduced to criminalise the five prohibited techniques. I am satisfied, however, that the prohibition on the five techniques is now firmly re-established in military doctrine. Quite apart from existing criminal offences that are likely to cover use of the five techniques in future, I accept the evidence of Burton that the prohibition can be enforced, including with the sanction of imprisonment, through existing legislation. I note, however, that the mechanism through which the MoD intends to achieve this requires a standing order to be put in place for each operation, prohibiting the use of the five techniques. In the case of Op Herrick, a standing order to this effect was only put in place during the course of the Inquiry's Module 4 hearings, this has since been modified with improved wording relating to how the five techniques are described.[176]

16.231 I conclude that it is important for DCDC to ensure that JDP 1-10 contains the requirement for such standing orders to be put in place for each operation, as Burton has indicated, will be included as a revision. It is then equally important that the Chief of Joint Operations ensures that there is sufficient coordination of CPERS planning that an appropriate standing order is in fact put in place for each operation. The form of standing order should take into account the conclusions I have reached concerning how the prohibited techniques should now be defined.

16.232 I do not think it necessary to create specific legislation to criminalise the use of the five techniques; this can be achieved by different means. Given the extent to which the prohibition on the five techniques has now been entrenched in doctrine, such legislation is not necessary to cater for a possible MoD or government change of policy in respect of the five techniques.

(2f) Medical policy: treatment of captured persons

16.233 In Part VI, Chapter 6 of the Report, I have already referred to significant improvements which have been introduced in this area by the MoD since 2003. In brief, the "*Surgeon General's Policy Letter 01/05*" was published in January 2005.[177] It required, amongst other things, that each detainee be medically examined as soon as reasonably practicable after admission to a detention facility; that he be examined again prior to transfer to another facility and upon release; that written records be kept of such examinations, in accordance with normal medical standards; that the

---

[175] MIV012801; letter from Ms Eloquin to Core Participants dated 24 June 2011

[176] MIV012780, the first such standing order was dated 5 October 2010. MIV012778 the current version is dated 9 March 2011;

[177] MOD004959-70

normal rules of consent to medical care should apply; that medical personnel inspect detention facilities to ensure that they are hygienic and healthy; and that medics avoid involvement in interrogation. I fully endorse all of those requirements.

16.234 By the time of the Module 4 hearings, the policy letter had been updated twice, once in October 2008, and once in September 2009.[178] It is now proposed that the next iteration of the policy be incorporated into JDP 1-10. I agree that this would be sensible. It would have the merit of informing a wider audience of the role and ethical parameters within which military medics work.

16.235 The Module 4 hearings uncovered two particular issues about appropriate medical care for CPERS. The first is an ethical issue: is it ethically sound for a medic to assess whether a CPERS is fit for detention? The second is more important for practical purposes: within what period of time after capture should the MoD policy require that a CPERS is medically screened?

16.236 The first issue is ultimately of little practical consequence. Professor Nathanson contended that it is unethical for a healthcare professional to state that a CPERS is fit for detention or questioning, since that act cannot be seen as protecting the health of the CPERS, which is the medic's ethical duty.[179] By contrast, Dr Payne-James' view was that merely to state that someone is fit for detention is not unethical because it does not actually conflict with the duty to act in the patient's best interests.[180] The MoD made it clear that it shares Nathanson's views, both in submissions,[181] and when Air Commodore Anthony Wilcock, the Head of Medical Strategy and Policy in the Surgeon General's Headquarters, gave evidence on its behalf.[182] In practice, any difficulty arising from the prohibition against stating that someone is fit for detention can be overcome in the following way. The medic may validly advise that someone is not fit for detention or questioning; alternatively, the medic may validly advise that no specific intervention different from the normal process is required. The practical effect of the latter course is the same as stating that someone is fit for detention but, according to Nathanson and Wilcock, the latter course avoids any breach of ethics.[183] Payne-James saw no real difficulty with this approach.[184] Whilst this may be seen as a rather semantic debate, I think it would be prudent for military medics to take this approach, which has no practical disadvantages and which may avoid breaches of ethical duties.

16.237 I therefore conclude that Armed Forces medical personnel can and should be involved in providing advice that a CPERS is not fit for detention or questioning; alternatively, the medic may validly advise that no specific intervention different from the normal process is required in respect of that CPERS. They should not advise that a CPERS is fit for detention or fit for questioning.

16.238 The second issue, as well as being more important, is more difficult. The current Surgeon General's Operational Policy Letter requires a routine medical examination within four hours of capture.[185] However, the Inquiry was told that in practice, in

---

[178] BMI05744-64; MIV002683-702

[179] Nathanson BMI 110/140/12-141/9

[180] Payne-James BMI 114/44/3-18

[181] MIV012648, paragraph 12

[182] Wilcock BMI 110/81/12-89/17

[183] Nathanson BMI 110/141/10-142/25; Wilcock BMI 110/84/1-86/13

[184] Payne-James BMI 114/38/11-39/2; Payne-James BMI 114/44/21-45/25

[185] MIV002688, paragraph 7(i)(1)

Afghanistan, a *"pragmatic interpretation"* is taken of this requirement, setting the deadline as within four hours of arrival at the first formal detention facility.[186] In Afghanistan, CPERS may not arrive at a formal detention facility until 36 hours after capture.[187] The Inquiry was provided with a draft amendment to the Policy Letter, which proposes to formalise this arrangement, and expressly exclude the point of apprehension, Unit Holding Area (UHA) and any collection points from any obligation to conduct a routine medical examination, unless authorities in theatre direct otherwise.[188]

16.239 In my view, this is a retrograde development. I have been assisted by, and I agree with, cogent submissions made on behalf of the Detainees, that prompt and properly recorded medical examinations serve three key purposes:[189]

(1) They help ensure that CPERS receive appropriate medical care;

(2) they help prevent abuse of CPERS. Soldiers who have contact with CPERS will know that injuries will be traceable to a particular period of time; and

(3) they help secure justice and appropriate accountability for misconduct, as well as protecting the innocent from false allegations.

16.240 The medic treating a CPERS should be motivated by the first of these three concerns. From his point of view, the latter two matters are largely incidental. However, from a broader perspective, there is no doubt in my mind that the latter two benefits are important consequences which follow from prompt and recorded medical examinations.

16.241 Of course, I fully accept that in *"forward"* positions, medical expertise and facilities may be in very short supply. The opportunity for medical examinations in certain circumstances may be very limited. Such circumstances will vary considerably. For these reasons, the MoD submits that whether a forward medical screening examination is necessary and should be conducted must remain a decision for the discretion of the commander on the ground. It submits that commanders can be given guidance as to how the exercise this discretion.[190]

16.242 Whilst I recognise there is force in this submission, I consider it to be outweighed by the benefits of prompt, routine medical examinations. I think that the current practice in Afghanistan, where the requirement for an examination may not arise until 40 hours after capture, is unsatisfactory. In my view, save where there are exceptional circumstances, all CPERS should receive a routine medical examination within a short period of their capture. As to what that short period should be, I cannot give a definitive answer, but I consider that some sort of fixed limit is necessary in order to make the rules clear to soldiers on the ground. I alight on the figure of four hours merely because that is the figure which appears in the current version of the Surgeon General's Policy Letter. Of course, where there is no doctor available in a forward location, the examination should simply be conducted by the most qualified medic available. I understand that there should be at least one qualified medic in each forward sub-unit.

---

[186] Wilcock MIV004674, paragraph 5
[187] MIV000015, SOI J3-9, paragraph 26
[188] MIV002702b
[189] MIV012708, paragraph 61
[190] MIV012652, paragraph 32

16.243 There was a related issue as to the timing of medical examinations which arose during the evidence in Module 4, namely, whether it was proper for the policy to require that there be an examination before interrogation. Currently the Surgeon General's Policy Letter does contain such a requirement. However, Wilcock informed the Inquiry that the MoD intends to remove this requirement, because it is considered improper for there to be a *"temporal link"* between medical examination and interrogation; such a link implies that the medic is involved in interrogation, which is ethically unsound. Wilcock added that it would be appropriate for the *"detention authorities"* (i.e. non-medical authorities) to require a medical examination before interrogation; but inappropriate for any *medic* to be subject to such a requirement.[191] Nathanson's initial response to this issue was to say: *"...we think it is better to say that* [the medical examination and interrogation are] *not formally temporally linked, but to instead put the emphasis on performing the examination as early as is possible to ensure that vulnerable people, people who are ill, are identified early and got into the appropriate level of treatment"*.[192] She then accepted that she agreed with Wilcock, that it would be ethically sound if the non-medical authorities were required to ensure that interrogation did not take place unless there had been a medical examination, as long as the medics were not directed that their examination should take place before questioning.[193]

16.244 I am inclined to agree with Nathanson's initial response. In my view, what really matters is that the medical examination takes place as soon as reasonably practicable after arrest. Nonetheless, I can see that it might be prudent to conduct a medical examination, or a further medical examination, as the case may be, before interrogation.[194] In light of the ethical concerns raised by Nathanson and Wilcock about the *"temporal link"*, it would probably be best that the requirement for a medical examination before interrogation is directed to the non-medical staff, and that the medics are simply told to examine as early as reasonably practicable.

16.245 As I have said, good progress has been made in this area since 2003.

16.246 To supplement this progress, I conclude that the following measures should be included within the MoD policy:

(1) all CPERS must undergo a medical examination within four hours of capture, unless there are compelling circumstances making such examination impossible. This examination should be conducted by the most medically qualified individual available;

(2) the CPERS should be examined by a qualified doctor as soon as reasonably practicable (i.e. usually upon transfer to a facility where a doctor is based);

(3) non-medical authorities should be prohibited from allowing interrogation of a CPERS to take place until he or she has been medically examined. Medical staff should not be directed that their examination of the CPERS should take place before interrogation; they should be directed merely to examine as early as reasonably practicable; and

---

[191] Wilcock BMI 110/81/12-83/20
[192] Nathanson BMI 110/149/25-150/5
[193] Nathanson BMI 110/150/6-21
[194] For the avoidance of doubt, I do not think that there should be a requirement for a medical examination prior to tactical questioning (as opposed to interrogation) in all cases, since tactical questioning will often be conducted urgently, immediately after capture.

(4) an electronic or written record of the examination of all CPERS should be made at the time of the examination and preserved.

Chapter 3: Current Theatre Level Instruction and Detention Practice

(3a) Introduction

16.247 In Module 4, I was keen that the Inquiry should consider not just current MoD policy and doctrine for detention, but its operational practice and training for detention as well.

16.248 The overwhelming majority of current operations involving detention occur in Op Herrick in Afghanistan.

16.249 The Inquiry considered the operational context for detention issues in Iraq in 2003 in some considerable detail. But I am very conscious that, in line with my terms of reference and what is proportionate for Module 4, the Inquiry has heard much less evidence about current operations in Afghanistan.

16.250 In these circumstances, while I consider the main theatre instruction for detention in Afghanistan and subordinate aide memoires in this Part of the Report, I have been careful in making recommendations to respect the particular challenges of operations in Afghanistan. I have also kept in mind the limitations of the evidence the Inquiry received in relation to Op Herrick. In a number of places I have made observations which I would invite the MoD to consider, rather than prescriptive recommendations.

(3b) Overview of the current theatre instructions and aide memoires

SOI J3-9

16.251 The standard operating instruction governing stop, search, question and detention operations in Op Herrick is known as SOI J3-9. The Inquiry has been able to publish this standard operating instruction in redacted form.[195]

16.252 At a basic level, it is right to acknowledge the improvements in this standard operating instruction when compared to the written orders that were in place before Baha Mousa's death. Some key examples are as follows:

(1)　SOI J3-9 is an enduring instruction that continues through the rolling deployment of different Battlegroups into Op Herrick. There is a greater continuity of guidance in relation to detention practice and less scope for important detention orders being lost on handovers;

(2)　the prohibition on the five techniques is set out early in the standard operating instruction in paragraph 8 of the introduction[196] and then in more detail in Part 1 paragraph 27 as *"proscribed techniques"*.[197] The prohibition on hooding is set

---

[195] MIV000001-78
[196] MIV000006
[197] MIV000016

out for a third time in dealing with the restriction of vision.[198] All the techniques are referred to again in the detention aide memoire annexed to the standard operating instruction;[199]

(3) reflecting the improved governance arrangements, the Force Provost Marshal has an enhanced role including oversight of the detention facilities in theatre, acting as the subject matter expert for detention and licensing and inspecting Battlegroup level detention facilities;[200]

(4) not only is there a tactical questioning policy in place, but those with oversight of chain of command responsibilities are expressly required to read it;[201]

(5) the standard operating instruction is clear about what method is to be used when sensory deprivation is necessary, namely blacked out goggles, or *in extremis* blindfolds, but these must not cover the mouth or nose;[202]

(6) it is a requirement that a record is made of every occasion when sensory deprivation takes place;[203]

(7) there is a specific prohibition on taking photographs of detainees other than for operational reasons;[204] and

(8) clear emphasis is given to the duty to report abuse.[205]

16.253 In respect of timescales, I have already noted in commenting upon JDP 1-10 that the timescales envisaged at joint doctrine level have not proved to be achievable on the ground in Afghanistan. Rather than a maximum time limit from point of detention to delivery to the host nation, SOI J3-9 allows UK Forces up to 36 hours from point of detention to get the CPERS to one of the two theatre level Temporary Holding Facility (THFs), Kandahar and Bastion. The instruction does, however, encourage CPERS to be moved to the THFs without delay. Detention is authorised for a maximum of 96 hours before release or transfer to the Afghan authorities, subject to certain exceptions.

16.254 Since it is widely recognised that the risks of abuse of CPERS are likely to be highest at the forward deployed areas, it is to some extent of concern that the timescales for CPERS to arrive at the THFs in Afghanistan is as long as 36 hours. However, one has to recognise the particular operational climate and the need for the majority of moves to be by helicopter. I also note that whereas 36 hours is the maximum period, McNeil indicated that in 55% of cases the move is achieved within three hours, and in 95% of cases within 24 hours.[206]

16.255 However, in reviewing SOI J3-9 during the Module 4 process, it was apparent that the headline paragraph addressing timelines, paragraph 26, at one stage wrongly referred to the timescale as being 72 hours.[207] Nor was this an entirely isolated mistake because it was repeated in the legal annex to the Task Force Helmand

---

[198] MIV000017, paragraph 28(d)(3)
[199] MIV000021
[200] MIV000008, paragraph 13(c)
[201] MIV000011, paragraph 6
[202] MIV000017, paragraph 28(d)(3)
[203] MIV000017, paragraph 28(d)(6)
[204] MIV000018, paragraph 28(j)
[205] MIV000019, paragraph 31
[206] McNeil BMI 109/86/16-24
[207] MIV000016, paragraph 26

Operational Order 001-10 of 16 June 2010, with 72 hours again being given as the time limit for transfer to the THF.[208] While I am satisfied that the correct emphasis is being given to moving CPERS up the chain as quickly as possible in difficult operational conditions, it is important that the messages on detention timescales are clear and consistent. Such errors in the leading in-theatre instruction are likely to undermine efficient CPERS handling.

16.256 The accurate and efficient documenting of CPERS' detention is as important as it is difficult to achieve, starting as it must with personnel who may be fighting under the most demanding situations. The more immediately relevant forms and cards in use on Op Herrick include:

(1) The Detainee Capture Card;[209]

(2) Detainee Incident Form;[210]

(3) Detainee Record of Custody;[211] and

(4) Detainee Medical Examination Form.[212]

Tactical Aide Memoire and Individual Aide Memoire

16.257 Information in this main theatre instruction is further cascaded by means of a tactical aide memoire (issued down to NCO level) and individual aide memoire (issued to down to soldier level).

16.258 The tactical aide memoire includes the following guidance to commanders:

> *"Prohibited Techniques. The following techniques must never be used:*
>
> *Stress Positions.*
>
> *Hooding.*
>
> *Subjection to Noise.*
>
> *Deprivation of sleep.*
>
> *Deprivation of food and drink.*
>
> ***Use of Blacked out Goggles.** The use of blacked out goggles is permitted for OPSEC reasons e.g. for moving through a militarily sensitive area – refer to Chain of Command and TFH S02 Legad for advice. If goggles are not available material can be used as a blindfold, but any blindfold used MUST NOT cover the nose or mouth, or restrict breathing in any way. Once the OPSEC reason for applying goggles has passed, the goggles / blindfold MUST be removed.*
>
> *Best Practice Reminders:*
>
> *Plastic cuff to the **front** of the body only.*
>
> *Detainees should not be held in the dark.*
>
> *Detainees should be allowed to pray.*

---

[208] MIV004966, paragraph 31
[209] MIV000035
[210] MIV000037
[211] MIV000053
[212] MIV000059

Females should be kept separate from men, under female supervision.

Same gender to conduct searching. Females should search children.

Juveniles (under 18) must be separated from adults, unless they are part of a family grouping. Where possible family groups should be held together. Where segregation from the family is considered necessary, legal guidance should be sought

Detainees must be protected from the elements and hostilities with PPE (helmet and CBA) issued where necessary/available.

Detainees must be provided food and water adequate for health.

All property is to be removed from the detainee, recorded on a property receipt, bagged and marked so that it is identifiable to the owner. Detainee property must accompany the detainee and be handed over with the detainee at the THF – NB: Items which may appear innocuous to the patrol on the ground may have J2X relevance.

Where 2 or more detainees are suspected of having committed a criminal offence together, they must be segregated from each other in order to avoid contamination of evidence through collusion or threats. Where segregation is not possible, detainees must be closely guarded to prevent conversation/collusion.

Commander's Responsibility. *The commander on the ground is responsible – and accountable – for ensuring that detainees are treated humanely, with dignity and respect for their cultural and religious customs and beliefs. Detainees must not be subjected to conditioning, torture, intimidation, inhumane or degrading treatment. The commander must ensure that checks are conducted regularly on detainees being held to satisfy himself that they are safe and secure, being fed, given water, and protected from the elements and physical danger. By displaying courtesy and respect to detainees – de facto[213] the local population – UK Forces will help create a more favourable operating environment, thereby increasing the chances of operational success (hearts and minds).*

This TAM is for guidance only, and detailed advice can be obtained from TFH Legad or PJHO."[214]

16.259 The Individual Aide Memoire detention section includes the following guidance:

"   ***DETENTION***

*You may detain, if necessary, any person aged 7 and over whom you **reasonably suspect** of being an imperative threat to security, having committed, being in the process of committing, or being about to commit, any criminal offence. Detainees are a category of prisoner distinct from Prisoners of War and internees. Detainees are those individuals who, during operations abroad not amounting to International Armed Conflict, are held by UK Armed Forces because they have committed, or are suspected of committing a criminal offence. Detainees must be treated humanely at all times. They are entitled to respect for their person, honour and convictions and religious practices.*

If you arrest a detainee you must:

- Inform the chain of command immediately and seek to hand your detainee over to the RMP or the MPS at the earliest opportunity.

- Inform the person as follows: "1 am a member of ISAF and I am detaining you for...

---

[213] As an aside, it is undesirable that language such as "de facto" should appear in cards that are cascaded down to this level.
[214] MIV002913-4

- Conduct a person search and complete a **Record of Search (Pers/Veh)**. You are responsible for any confiscated property. This property must be handed over with the detainee.

- Hand an **Apprehension Notice** to the detained person.

- Inform the person of his/her right to have a friend/family member notified, and to where he/ she is being taken.

- Complete a witness statement (attach to the Record of Search).

Detainee Handling **Do**s

- You may use issued plasticuffs or handcuffs to restrain the detainee(s).

Plasticuffed/handcuffed arms should be to the front of the body.

- You may use blacked-out goggles to prevent the detainee from seeing operationally sensitive information. No other form of eye cover is to be used.

- You must segregate juveniles from adults unless they form part of a family group.

- A juvenile is anyone under the age of 18 or who you suspect of being under the age of 18.

- You must provide detainees with food, water and suitable shelter. You are fully responsible for their wellbeing and welfare.

- You must allow detainees to pray.

- You must provide the individual with medical treatment if it is required.

Detainee Handling **4Don't**s

- Do not question the detainee unless you are Tactical Questioning (TQ) course qualified.

- TQ can only be authorised by your CO.

- Do not allow any non-TQ qualified personnel to question the detainee.

- UK personnel must never use the (following) five **prohibited** techniques.

a. **Stress positions.** Forcing captured or detained persons to adopt a posture that is intended to cause physical pain and exhaustion;

b. **Hooding.** Putting a bag over a captured or detained person's head and keeping it there, whether as part of the tactical questioning and interogation process or not;

c. **Subjection to noise.** Holding a captured or detained person in an area where there is a continuous loud and hissing noise;

d. **Deprivation of sleep.** Depriving captured or detained persons of sleep;

e. **Deprivation of food and drink.** Subjecting captured or detained persons to a reduced diet.'[215]

Conclusions in respect of in theatre instructions and aide memoires

16.260 Having regard to the limitations on Op Herrick evidence to which I have referred, I consider is it is appropriate that I should distinguish between:

(1) aspects of the in theatre instructions and aide memoires where I consider improvements must be made; and

(2) issues to which I would simply invite the MoD to give further consideration.

---

[215] MIV003071-2

16.261 I conclude that the current Op Herrick SOI J3-9 and aide memoires ought to include the following further improvements:

(1) the definitions of the prohibited techniques contained in SOI J3-9 should be updated to reflect the conclusions I have already set out in dealing with JDP 1-10. Not all detail can be replicated in aide memoires but the key messages should be;

(2) SOI J3-9 should reflect the greater emphasis that is given in the latest draft of JDP 1-10 to avoiding in the first place, where practicable, circumstances in which sight deprivation may be necessary (this was accepted by McNeil).[216] More generally, it should reflect the five principles which I have set out at paragraph 96. Within reason, these key messages should also feature in the aide memoires. It would be helpful if the instructions could give some clear examples of where sight deprivation would and would not be appropriate;

(3) where practicable CPERS who are subjected to sight deprivation or hearing deprivation should be told the reason for it. If being deprived of their sight for some or part of a journey by road or air, as well as ensuring that the sensory deprivation is kept to the minimum time strictly necessary, CPERS should be told in general terms where they are being taken;

(4) references to the means of sight deprivation need to be consistent. The clearest wording is likely to be "sight deprivation" (rather than blindfolding) "by blacked-out goggles". However permission to use improvised blindfolds, not covering the mouth or nose and only if blacked-out goggles are not available, should be retained as the fall-back position. At the time of the Module 4 hearings, the wording between SOI J3-9, and the two aide memoires is not consistent on this aspect;

(5) timescales for detention are important and need to be clear. Accepting the huge demands of the operation, it is nevertheless unfortunate that in a document as important as SOI J3-9, errors have crept in relating to the principal detention time limits. My expectation is that these will already have been corrected by the time of the publication of this report. If not they should of course be corrected as soon as possible;

(6) while SOI J3-9 requires that a record be kept of every occasion where sight deprivation is used, neither the Detainee Capture Card,[217] nor the Record of Custody forms[218] have spaces or boxes to record this. Service personnel involved with CPERS are more likely to complete the documents correctly if they are simple and include obvious boxes that set out that which should be recorded. The CPERS documents should be as few in number as possible but they require amendment to ensure that those involved in detention are guided more accurately on what to record;

(7) as well as individual custody records, a suitable occurrence book must be maintained at all times whenever CPERS are being held at a unit or sub-unit holding facility; and

(8) in all these matters, recognising that I am recommending the insertion of some further material, there is a paramount need to keep instructions that are cascaded to soldiers on the ground and to junior commanders, clear, concise and simple.

---

[216] McNeil BMI 109/51/20-52/3
[217] MIV000035
[218] MIV000053

16.262 I would also invite the MoD to give consideration to the following matters:

(1) providing detailed guidance within the aide memoires on segregation may go too far, but consideration should be given to the best means of ensuring that service personnel do not resort to sight or hearing deprivation merely as a means of preventing collaboration between CPERS. To permit sensory deprivation in those circumstances risks sensory deprivation of CPERS becoming a matter of routine;

(2) the current in-theatre capture and custody records do not contain any separate section to address the use of force on CPERS. Consideration should be given to whether a separate section for use of force would (a) lead to better record keeping of the use of force and (b) permit more effective interrogation of use of force levels. If, however, the detainee incident form remains the means by which the use of force after the point of capture is recorded, the MoD should ensure that there is simple clear guidance on what types of the use of force require that form to be completed;

(3) selection of guarding/escorting soldiers: It is likely to be impracticable at present to recommend that capturing soldiers, those involved in front-line incidents, should not act as the guards and escorts for CPERS who need to be guarded and taken to the THFs. SOI J3-9 mandates that all personnel involved in the detention should ideally accompany the CPERS to the THF/Temporary Detention Facility (TDF).[219] The MoD should consider how to apply, within the particular operational demands of Op Herrick, the new guidance contained in the latest draft of JDP 1-10 that commanders should:

> "(e)nsure CPERS are kept apart from UK personnel that may have emotional attitudes to CPERS, such as personnel that were close to own force casualties."[220]

(4) McNeil accepted that at forward detention facilities, more could be done in terms of mandating checks on the physical welfare of CPERS.[221] At present, the Tactical Aide Memoire (TAM) gives some guidance to Commanders by stating:

> "The commander must ensure that checks are conducted regularly on detainees being held to satisfy himself that they are safe and secure, being fed, given water, and protected from the elements and physical danger."[222]

The MoD should consider whether timescales and frequency of checks can be specified, though I recognise that much will depend here on the operational situation. At present, however, the Detainee Record of Custody contains space for a record of feeding and water times, but there is no particular section for the welfare checks which the Commander has a duty to ensure are carried out.[223] I am concerned not to impose a recommendation for checks at a frequency that that may be impracticable on the ground but the MoD should consider what further guidance in this area beyond the current TAM is achievable and would provide further assurance without adding unnecessary regulation.

---

[219] MIV000014
[220] MIV004217, paragraph 5D2(g)
[221] McNeil BMI 109/95/3-96/15
[222] MIV002914
[223] MIV000053

(5)   Although the duty to report abuse is clearly set out in SOI J3-9[224] consideration should be given to the following: (i) providing assurance to 'whistle blowers' as to their protection from victimisation; (ii) practical guidance on what UK Forces should do if they see their own colleagues engaged in abuse; (iii) alternative contacts (other than the directly stated requirement to submit a report "to the FPM via the BPO within four hours") that could be used by a soldier who has cause for concern about how a CPERS has been treated. These might include the Detention Officer, the Padre and the RMO.

16.263 In Part XI Chapter 6 I have endorsed the current practice that a single comprehensive order encapsulates the applicable procedures for CPERS, which in the case of Op Herrick is SOI J3-9. In my opinion it is essential that in enduring operations the CPERS procedures are addressed in such an order so as to minimise the risk that orders in relation to CPERS are not lost in the roulement of formations and units. CPERS handling is too important to be the subject of a collection of disparate FRAGOs.

16.264 I therefore conclude that the MoD should continue its recent practice of ensuring that the procedures for CPERS are contained within a single comprehensive order that is kept up-to-date and which can be easily handed over to incoming formations in enduring operations.

Addendum: 6 May 2011 version of SOI J3-9

16.265 As part of the agreed process by which the MoD kept the Inquiry informed of ongoing changes in detention policy and guidance, the MoD has very recently disclosed to the Inquiry the latest in theatre guidance for Op Herrick. This is a 6 May 2011 revision of SOI J3-9.[225]

16.266 Since this was provided in the later stages of the drafting of this Report, I simply make the following brief observations as an addendum to my observations on the version of SOI J3-9 that was considered in the Inquiry's Module 4 hearings:

(1)   **Timescales.** The timescale for transferring prisoners to the THFs has been reduced from 36 to 24 hours.[226] The mistaken reference to the limit being 72 hours[227] has been corrected. These are welcome developments.

(2)   **Definition of the five techniques**.

(a)   At paragraph 33, the latest version of SOI J3-9 introduces the prohibited techniques with the following words:

> *"The 5 techniques listed below must never be used as an aid to tactical questioning or interrogation, as a form of punishment, discriminatory conduct, intimidation, coercion or as wanton ill treatment."*[228] (original emphasis)

I judge that this change is very likely to have been a well-intentioned attempt to ensure that the prohibition on the five techniques is not limited to their use as an aid to interrogation. However, I have serious reservations about guidance

---

[224] MIV000019, paragraph 31
[225] MIV012803
[226] MIV012813
[227] MIV000016, paragraph 26
[228] MIV012823, paragraph 33

which introduces the prohibition on the five techniques in terms that prohibit their use only in a qualified fashion. The five techniques should simply not be used in any circumstances. It would be better, in my opinion, simply to state that the five techniques are prohibited and must never be used. The definition of each of the five prohibited techniques can be so drafted as to exclude from the prohibition conduct which is acceptable, such as the temporary use of certain positions during the search of a prisoner.

(b) Paragraph 33 goes on to define the individual prohibited techniques in the following way:[229]

> a. **The use of any stress position.** Requiring a detainee to adopt a posture with the primary intention of causing physical pain or exhaustion.
>
> b. **Hooding.** Placing a bag over a detainee's head. **Hooding is prohibited in all circumstances.**
>
> c. **Subjection to Noise.** Holding a detainee in an area where there is excessive noise (ie the noise is too loud, persistent or close).
>
> d. **Deprivation of Sleep.** Detainees must receive a minimum of 8 hours of rest and/or sleep per 24 hour period, with an opportunity to sleep for a single period of no less than 4 hours in a continuous block.
>
> e. **Deprivation of Food and Drink.** Subjecting a detainee to a reduced diet.

Some aspects of these definitions have been improved, in particular the definition of the subjection to noise. Others, in my opinion, remain inappropriate such as a stress position being dependent upon the intention of the soldier. I refer here, without repeating, the earlier discussion in this Part of the Report, which addresses the definition of the five techniques in the context of the latest draft of JDP 1-10.[230] The same considerations apply in respect of the standing order prohibiting the use of the five techniques in the handling of detainees now contained in Annex K to Part 1 of the new SOI J3-9.[231]

(3) **Restriction of vision.** There is an improved section on restriction of vision which goes some way to highlighting that the need to obscure prisoners' vision should be avoided in the first place where this is practicable.[232] There remains scope for further improvement in communicating clearly and concisely the five principles about sight deprivation that I have set out at paragraph 16.96.

(4) **Recording the use of sensory deprivation**. The SOI retains the obligation to record every occasion when sensory deprivation takes place. Appropriately, the SOI now states that these details should be passed up the chain of command with the detainee to be examined by the THF staff on arrival, with the Force Provost Marshal (FPM) monitoring adherence to this process.[233] However, it remains the case that neither the Detainee Capture Card[234] nor the Detainee Record of Custody[235] have spaces for soldiers to record this information.

---

[229] MIV012823-4, paragraph 33
[230] MIV004146
[231] MIV012842
[232] MIV012825
[233] MIV012825
[234] MIV012841, Annex J to Part 1
[235] MIV012875-80, Annex D to Part 2

(3c) Relevant aspects of current detention practice in Afghanistan

Sight Deprivation

16.267 SOI J3-9 permits the Armed Forces to deprive prisoners of their sight "...*in situations where it is necessary for OPSEC reasons or Force Protection purposes to protect sensitive information ... As soon as the reason for restricting a detainee's vision has passed, the goggles must be removed*".[236]

16.268 Based on the examples given by McNeil, I have already indicated in dealing with policy and higher level joint doctrine, that there will remain a number of individual cases where it may prove appropriate to use goggles to deprive CPERS of their sight. I accept McNeil's evidence that it is not practicable to give a time limit beyond which CPERS should not be deprived of their sight because it may in some cases be dependent on journey times. Commanders down to Junior NCOs on the ground need to exercise common sense in these matters, inculcated by the overarching need to ensure fair, humane treatment.

16.269 I note however McNeil's acceptance that more could be done to cover up sensitive equipment to negate the need for sight deprivation. [237]

16.270 During the course of Forster-Knight's Module 4 evidence, it became apparent that CPERS had goggles applied for all movements within the two THFs at Kandahar and Bastion. Forster-Knight explained the reasoning for this including that:

> "We are dealing with extremely violent men in the main, many of whom are extremists in the Taliban organisation and many of whom are part of Al Qaeda. These individuals are highly dangerous. They need to be held in a very clearly safe and secure environment. We need to balance their human rights with the human rights of the other detainees and we did have intimidation of detainees in the past.
>
> We do have cases where – and of course we don't know these people particularly well, we don't know their tribal hierarchies, we don't understand necessarily who the leaders are. We also know that the Taliban will been engaged in killing or maiming individuals who support ISAF and I have to make judgments over balancing the human rights of that individual detainee and depriving him of his sight, which in the main is for no more than two minutes at any one time, with being seen by other detainees and maybe being implicated once he has left that detention facility.
>
> I note what your experts say. I note the legal and policy issues surrounding these very difficult situations. But my judgment is that we do have this right because of those extending factors. We do apply these for a very short duration. We also have to think about sensitive equipment and issues within the facilities themselves and we also have to apply simple common sense easy-to-follow practice for our people who are dealing with very difficult situations in Afghanistan and therefore we adopt a common principle throughout our various detention facilities.

---

[236] MIV000017, paragraph 28(d)(3)
[237] McNeil BMI 109/46/15-47/8

> *That really gives you a summary of why we do this, why it is routine, and, as I say, I emphasise this is not a precursor to interrogation because we do it when we are moving them through every stage of the facility and broadly most people are blindfolded in those moves, those sort of circumstances, for no more than about a couple of minutes."*[238]

16.271 As a result of this evidence MoD gave further disclosure including the standard operating procedures for the THFs which show this use of sight deprivation.[239]

16.272 Since this Inquiry is looking at current operations in Afghanistan from the perspective of the principles of operational CPERS handling and current policy and doctrine, I am disinclined to make prescriptive recommendations about judgments being made on the ground at THF level. However, it is obviously a matter of some concern that sight deprivation is being used for all CPERS moves within the THF. But I note also that this is ordinarily for very short periods of time and is achieved by the use of goggles not hoods. It is therefore very different to the kind of sight deprivation applied in the JFIT in the early stages of Op Telic 1 or in 1 QLR's TDF. I note that the very latest disclosure from MoD indicates that it recognises that this issue is a complex one and requires finely balanced judgment. The MoD is committed to the Provost Marshal (Army) (PM(A)) reviewing the routine use of goggles for CPERS movements as part of all future inspections of the THF with the aim of removing it as routine practice as soon as possible.[240]

16.273 The current routine use of blacked-out goggles within the THFs is a matter of concern but it is not a practice in respect of which I should make formal recommendations that second guess the judgment of senior commanders on the ground, in particular the judgment of the PM(A). The PM(A) ought formally to review whether the current practice is strictly necessary and ensure that it is not being used in circumstances that are not clearly justified by operational security and/or CPERS own protection. The routine use of blacked-out goggles for transfers within a holding facility is not desirable even for short periods of time, but I recognise that there may be circumstances where it is necessary.

(3d) Division of responsibilities at Battlegroup level

At Commissioned Officer Level

16.274 As I have explained in Part II Chapter 20 of this Report, a principal concern arising out of the events between 14 to 16 September 2003 at 1 QLR's Battlegroup Main (BG Main) was the lack of clarity as to who had the overall responsibility for the welfare of detainees below the level of Lt Col Jorge Mendonça.

16.275 The starting point in considering the responsibilities for CPERS at Battlegroup level must be that the ultimate responsibility rests with the Commanding Officer. He may delegate tasks relating to CPERS making clear his intent, but he cannot divest himself of responsibility for the CPERS held by his unit. Mission command, as it applies to CPERS handling, means that the Commanding Officer should not delegate to his subordinates the task without informing himself of the nature of the task, how satisfactorily it is being performed, and whether the resources are proving sufficient.

---

[238] Forster-Knight BMI 109/167/14-170/16
[239] MIV012775-6; MIV012771-2; MIV012828
[240] MIV012775

16.276 It follows that no aspect of the latest draft of JDP 1-10, SOI J3-9 nor the recommendations that I make should be interpreted as in any way diluting the responsibility held by the Commanding Officer.

16.277 Nevertheless, one has to recognise the breadth and depth of a Commanding Officer's responsibilities such that it is inevitable that only a relatively small percentage of his time is likely to be devoted to CPERS matters. It is of note that in other areas of key activity such as intelligence and operations, the Battlegroup headquarters has an officer dedicated to that function.

16.278 To some extent, JDP 1-10 does seek to give a clearer delineation of responsibilities for unit level detention. In each of the existing JTTPs, there is a requirement that an officer must be placed in charge of the UHA. Thus the current JDP 1-10.3 provides as follows:

> "1 C2. **Staffing of the Unity Holding Area**. [sic] In addition to basic requirements to prevent escape and injury, Commanders must ensure that guards and UHA staff are aware of their legal requirements under the GC and provide sufficiently trained personnel to meet these requirements. The staffing provisions outlined in JDP I-10.2 'Internees' apply equally to detainees. While detailed requirements will vary depending upon the variables of theatre[fn], it is likely that a UHA will be required to hold both internees and detainees the staffing and infrastructure requirements will increase. Basic requirements include:
>
> **a. Commandant**. An officer must be placed in charge of this facility. That officer is **directly accountable** for its command and control and the detailed custody arrangements for all detainees. He is directly responsible for the safety and security of all detainees under his custody and control. There is no requirement to appoint a separate commander to manage detainees although consideration may be given to appointing an individual to specifically manage detainees owing to the administrative burden of conducting transfers and handovers.
>
> [fn] Unit Commanders must produce detailed UHA Orders in each instance"[241]

16.279 Similar provisions apply for Prisoners of War[242] and Internees.[243] The new draft of JDP 1-10 gives guidance for all UHAs along very similar lines:

> "e. **Staffing of the Unit Holding Area**. In addition to the fundamental requirements to prevent escape and injury, commanders must ensure that guards and UHA staff are aware of their legal obligations under the Geneva Conventions (GCs) and theatre ROE and provide suitably trained personnel to meet these requirements. They are to keep a record of those on duty and that record is to be placed in the unit operational archive. Detailed staffing requirements will depend upon the variables of theatre[fn] but should include as a minimum:
>
> (1) **Officer Commanding**. An officer must be placed in charge of the UHA. That officer is then directly accountable for its command and control and the detailed custody arrangements. He is directly responsible for the safety and security of those under his custody and control.
>
> (2) ...
>
> [fn] Commanders must produce detailed unit holding area orders in each instance."[244]

---

[241] MOD028806

[242] MOD042464

[243] MOD028751

[244] MIV004246-7

16.280 What links the approach in both the current JDP 1-10 and the new draft of the same joint doctrine is the appointment of a specific officer to command and control the detailed custody arrangements which is based upon the existence of a UHA of which that officer becomes the 'commandant'.

16.281 This approach may work perfectly well in some situations. But where I perceive a difficulty in these arrangements is on operations where CPERS are detained, but there is either no UHA, or only a UHA that is running on an intermittent basis.

16.282 This appears often to be the situation that arises in Op Herrick. The 12 April 2010 version of SOI J3-9 referred to the Force Provost Marshal licensing and inspecting Battlegroup detainee holding areas *"once constructed"*.[245] McNeil explained in his first statement how larger scale detention operations might involve the planning and construction of temporary collection points for detainees, which might be Battlegroup Holding Areas or designated collection points known as *"forward triage facilities"*. The latter are, it seems, manned by RMP or Military Provost Staff (MPS).[246] Where Battlegroup Holding Areas are used, Forster-Knight explained that they are run on a day to day basis by the embedded RMP and the officer nominated to be responsible for them is simply the base commander of the forward base where the UHA has been established.[247]

16.283 I do not seek as such to criticise those arrangements since they seem to me to reflect the particular circumstances of Op Herrick.

16.284 However, one difficulty with the current approach is that whereas JDP 1-10 appears to envisage a single readily identifiable officer who would have command and control of CPERS held in a unit level facility, the current arrangements are more *ad hoc*. It seems that for smaller scale detention operations where no UHA is set up, the detention responsibilities simply run with the Officer Commanding the sub-unit involved in the operation. The Commander has a clear command responsibility while the operation is running but would not have any particularly enduring role in relation to CPERS within the Battlegroup separate from his sub-unit command. For larger scale operations where a UHA is established, the Company Commander is likely to be the officer carrying responsibility for the UHA set up within his company location. Again, however, this responsibility would subsist only for so long as CPERS are held by that particular company and would not involve any responsibility across the Battlegroup as a whole.

16.285 I consider that there would be considerable advantages in having a single identifiable officer, a "detention officer", from Battlegroup Headquarters who would have a coordinating and management role for CPERS. This must not dilute the responsibilities of the Commanding Officer. But unlike the Company Commander who is placed, *ad hoc*, as the Officer Commanding a sub-unit level detention facility during a deployment, such a "detention officer" would:

(1) act as a focus on CPERS matters during mission specific training;

(2) have an enduring role during the deployment to assist the Commanding Officer on CPERS matters, to monitor compliance with timescales, compliance with other CPERS standards and record keeping;

---

[245] MIV000008
[246] McNeil MIV005004, paragraph 23
[247] Forster-Knight BMI 109/145/12-146/8

(3)   be a clear point of contact for those at Brigade level who need to liaise with Battlegroups in relation to CPERS and equally be able to obtain information for the Battlegroup on CPERS matters from Brigade and MPS in theatre;

(4)   avoid responsibilities for CPERS "falling between the cracks". The danger is that, below the Commanding Officer, the Adjutant, the Intelligence Officer and the Company Commanders may all carry some responsibilities but there is a lack of a coordinating role both in training and during the deployment; and

(5)   have a role in ensuring that Military Annual Training Test 7 (MATT 7) and other training conducted at Battalion level inculcates the vital messages concerning the correct handling of CPERS.

16.286 Trousdell indicated in his oral evidence the sort of advantage that such a detention officer could bring:

> "…What this means is the commanding officer, who clearly would still be responsible for what happens in his unit, would have somebody to whom he could turn for advice. But it also means that, in planning an operation, he has somebody who has this particular level of expertise to ensure it's written into the operation order, and it also means that the commanding officer could say to the detention officer, "It appears that B Company are likely to take quite a lot of prisoners in the operation that's coming up. Just ring the company's second in command and make sure that they are absolutely in accord with all your teachings".
>
> Of course, if you have this officer, then on all your mission-specific training – indeed maybe all your normal training – it means that you can rehearse, as a commanding officer, the whole structure in your organisation that deals with prisoners, and the detention officer would be perfectly capable of writing some serials into a training exercise that, for instance, rehearses the TQers and that rehearses soldiers in how they should act as guards. So you would up the level of expertise and professionalism in a unit by having somebody like this."[248]

16.287 To fulfil this role, the detention officer would plainly need to be a commissioned officer within Battlegroup Headquarters. Beyond that I would not seek to recommend that the detention officer should be of any particular rank, although clearly the officer must be of sufficient seniority and experience to carry responsibilities for CPERS and to deal with company commanders and others in the Battlegroup. In many cases, it may well be that the Adjutant would be the ideal candidate to be detention officer because of the Adjutant's peace-time responsibilities in respect of disciplinary, legal and detention matters. However, in my opinion, it would not be appropriate to fetter the Commanding Officer by requiring that the Adjutant must carry out the role of detention officer. But clearly the role should not be undertaken by the intelligence officer or the unit coordinator of tactical questioning.

16.288 In regard to resources and expense, I would envisage the detention officer being an existing Battlegroup officer who is given the additional responsibilities of detention officer; it should not require additional manpower within each Battlegroup. In terms of training, the detention officer would need a degree of specialist training, the details of which should be informed by a training needs analysis. It is likely to include some operational detention training at the Military Corrective Training Centre (MCTC), Colchester. However, Forster-Knight made clear that he has already commissioned work on a two week strategic and operational level detention course in the military,

---

[248] Trousdell BMI 115/36/22-37/19

where attendance for those with Battlegroup responsibility for detention may be viable. [249]

16.289 Provided that the detention officer role did not dilute the responsibilities of the Commanding Officer, McNeil did not appear to raise any objection to it.[250] Forster-Knight saw some positive advantage in it.[251] The role was positively advocated by Trousdell and I conclude that it seems the best way of bringing greater clarity and ultimately better assurance in relation to CPERS handling at Battlegroup level. If detention is genuinely to become a core skill for deployed forces, as it must, it is appropriate to recognise this at Battlegroup headquarters level.

16.290 Finally in this context, I should mention also increasing focus on the role of the RMP and the MPS. I consider that aspect in a little more detail below when addressing responsibilities for detention at NCO level. For present purposes it suffices to note that the MPS, as the real specialists in detention within the Army, are in reality very small in number. As at 11 August 2010, Forster-Knight told the Inquiry there were only eleven MPS deployed on operations, due to rise to sixteen. Forster-Knight would wish to see more custody specialists at key stages of the detention process particularly at unit or sub-unit level.[252] That aspiration is an understandable one, and its achievement would I am sure be beneficial.

16.291 At present, it is normal for a single RMP sergeant to join Battlegroup headquarters with more junior RMPs attached to sub-units. MPS are not routinely attached to Battlegroups though they may go forward to run particular detention facilities. Even if, in these constrained financial times, resources are found for an increase in MPS and/or RMP numbers, there is no realistic prospect in the short to medium term that a commissioned RMP or MPS officer could be attached to every Battlegroup headquarters months before deployment and see through the coordination and oversight of CPERS handling during planning, training and then through the deployment itself.

16.292 In short, it is unrealistic to expect that the RMP or MPS could meet a coordinating role at commissioned officer level in each Battlegroup headquarters.

16.293 I would add that I see positive advantage in the detention officer being a member of the Battlegroup and *not* a member of the RMP/MPS. If detention is truly to become a core operational skill, it is important that it is not seen to be the preserve of specialists such as the MPS. The MPS have an extremely important role to play. Under the FPM and ultimately the PM(A), they are subject matter experts in detention and will play key roles in advising, inspecting and, in relation to some detention facilities, actually running them. But the availability of MPS expertise in no way displaces the need for all those deployed who may come into contact with CPERS (or have chain of command responsibility for those that do) to be well versed in the practical aspects of CPERS handling and the standards to be maintained. Even if there were sufficient RMP or MPS personnel available, giving them the coordination and oversight role within a Battlegroup risks re-enforcing the misconception that detention is a specialist, non-core military skill.

---

[249] Forster-Knight BMI 109/149/7-18
[250] McNeil BMI 109/93/10-94/19
[251] Forster-Knight BMI 109/147/15-148/7
[252] Forster-Knight MIV005289, paragraph 20

At NCO Level

16.294 The current JDP 1-10 and latest draft of the new JDP 1-10 make clear the need for Commanders to make use of specialist personnel who may be available at UHA level. Thus the latest draft of JDP 1-10 says this about the Service Police and Unit Custody Staff respectively:

> "812. The UHA is the first point in the CPERS handling chain where service personnel can expect the assistance of the following specialist personnel:
>
> *a. **Service Police**. Service Police will usually be available for the transport and processing of Category 'A' Prisoner of War (PW)[fn1] or other high value CPERS and associated evidence. They will be able to collate evidence linked to a suspect and gather the necessary evidence, initial and subsequent, required to support any criminal proceedings. The written and verbal evidence of the Service personnel involved in the initial apprehension of an individual is critical. If the Service Police are not available within the unit, the use of unit custody staff should be considered in order to ensure the correct handling and documentation of evidence.*
>
> *b. **Unit Custody Staff. Most units will deploy with unit custody staff** trained in the basics of operational custody handling (unit custody staff are trained at the Military Corrective Training Centre (MCTC)). Commanders should ensure that the specialist knowledge of the unit custody staff is used to good effect in the UHA although it should be recognised that the unit custody staff are not a substitute for the MPS.[fn2]*
>
> *[fn1] See JDP 1-10.1, paragraph 108 for categorisation of Prisoners of War (PW).*
>
> *[fn2] The Military Provost Staff (MPS) are the Defence Subject Matter Experts in CPERS handling practice."[253]*

16.295 As Issue 13 the Inquiry posed the question as to whether there is a need, with suitable adaptations for the military context, for a role similar to custody sergeants in police custody facilities.

16.296 Given the military context, the analogy with a police custody sergeant cannot be an exact one. There seemed, however, to be a broad acceptance that it was desirable to have designated staff with a level of custodial expertise to give the day to day supervision of unit level facilities.

16.297 Forster-Knight told the Inquiry that the introduction of custody experts into Battlegroup level locations, with responsibilities similar to those of custody sergeants in a civilian context, would reduce the level of risk still further. [254]

16.298 Trousdell stated that:

> "...The care and administration of detainees requires many separate items to be coordinated. This, to a large extent routine administration, which requires an enduring and sustained attention to detail, will be a task for middle management. Because this appointment will require an acceptance of responsibility and the use of initiative it would be allocated to a senior non-commissioned officer.
>
> In recognising that one person should be responsible for the reception of detainees, for their routine administration whilst in the UHA, and for their correct documentation before despatch to the next holding area, the employment of somebody in a custody sergeant role seems to me to be very necessary. Given that under current policy all soldiers are trained in the

---

[253] MIV004245-6
[254] Forster-Knight MIV005291, paragraph 27

> *handling of detainees and also take part in MATT 6 and 7, there is an increasing depth of knowledge in this area. This expertise should be coupled to the administrative excellence of a senior NCO to perform the role..."* [255]

16.299 There was disagreement, however, as to how the Forces can best achieve this.

16.300 Trousdell envisaged that the *"...administrative excellence of a senior NCO"* would best come from the unit Provost Sergeant with an enhanced set of skills. He thought it unlikely that the Force levels would permit the role to be carried out by a member of the MPS or even the RMP.[256] In his oral evidence he explained that as, for good reason, many Commanding Officers liked to travel with their Regimental Sergeant Majors (RSM), the RSM would often be out on the ground during operations. Accordingly he envisaged the detention officer working closely with the Regimental Provost Sergeant on detention issues, to the extent that the RSM was positively described as not being involved in the CPERS administration, apart from his normal general oversight as RSM.[257] As with the detention officer, Trousdell envisaged that the additional training required for the Provost Sergeant would be limited given that which unit custody staff already receive. Trousdell was in favour of being prescriptive and making it a formal part of the Provost Sergeant's role that he bears the administrative responsibility for CPERS on operations:

> *"A. I think I would be prescriptive about it, and the reason for that is that every job in an infantry battalion has a job description and, next to it, it shows the courses which you are mandated to attend before you take on that appointment or during the early period of your appointment. It seems to me that you would enhance the ability and the standing, perhaps, of the provost sergeant by rewriting his job description in order to cover this area, so I would say he is the man. I think it also – on operations, this is a sergeant who I expect would have the capacity to take this on as his main job."* [258]

16.301 Forster-Knight maintained that ideally *"...we should have more MPS personnel available to be deployed at all levels. MPS under resourcing is now recognised as a problem at the highest levels within the Army".*[259] He explained how RMP or MPS were used to man forward triage facilities in Afghanistan *"... who may temporarily be redeployed at risk from other tasks (e.g. manning the THFs)".* Below the forward triage facilities, the RMP attached to units would be used at Battlegroup level wherever possible, although they are few in number and have a range of other policing duties.[260]

16.302 In his oral evidence, Forster-Knight accepted that there was a capacity issue with the RMP carrying out this function but maintained that they were well suited to the task:

> *"I think the RMP skill-set is particularly suited to this because of their policing skill-set. They are trained to arrest, detain, question. They are trained to secure evidence. They are trained to take biometrics as part of their indigenous police training. But you are absolutely right to say that there is a capacity issue there of the ability of the military police to do this forward detention task and I have been in discussion with the army about this and how we might look to the future of changing that."* [261]

---

[255] Trousdell MIV010060-1, paragraphs 37-38
[256] Trousdell MIV010061, paragraph 38
[257] Trousdell BMI 115/38/25-41/25
[258] Trousdell BMI 115/45/25-46/11
[259] Forster-Knight MIV005291, paragraph 27
[260] Forster-Knight MIV005290, paragraphs 21-22
[261] Forster-Knight BMI 109/141/22-142/6

16.303 Therefore, subject to securing the resources to achieve it, it is clear that Forster-Knight would wish to see MPS who could be deployed forward (and not just RMP) as the ideal longer term solution. When I raised with Forster-Knight the possibility that this might be seen as a form of *"empire-building"*, his response was that others had suggested that to be so, but he relied upon the expertise of the MPS as the custodial experts, drawing the analogy that one would not get a telecoms engineer to fix a car.[262]

16.304 Trousdell's preference for the use of the Provost Sergeant as the key administrative NCO for CPERS detention was put to Forster-Knight during his oral evidence:

> *"Q. Now, pending, if it comes, a resolution of those resource and capacity issues, one of the issues that General Trousdell raises in his report to the Inquiry is whether there isn't a role for the provost sergeant perhaps with enhanced skill-sets, enhanced training, as a single identifiable NCO to carry a coordinating responsibility in this regard. In that sense it might be said that one of the difficulties of having two RMP per sub-unit dealing with it, when they also have other responsibilities, is that absence of a single clearly identifiable NCO who carries the coordinating responsibility at that level of the unit. Would you have any observations about that?*
>
> *A. Sir, I would. General Philip's observations I believe are correct in principle. I believe, however, that things have moved on in the detention business and I believe that personally the regimental provost involvement in detention needs to be subsumed by the MPS and I would advocate a solution where the MPS are pushed forward.*
>
> *We have a choice. We can either take a generic military individual and train them for a few weeks on a detention course or we can take someone who is a specialist in detention and push them forward and see them advising the commanding officer and any officer that he might appoint to be in charge of a unit holding area. My preference, as the defence subject matter expert, is the latter. I see that the MPS should be doing this role.*
>
> *Q. But in terms of the shorter term, are you content, with obviously all the detailed knowledge that you have from visits to theatre and so on, that as the short-term measure that using the RMP and perhaps not the provost sergeant is mitigating the risk in the best way possible?*
>
> *A. Well, mitigation of risk, sir, comes in a number of strands. Since I took over as the provost marshal army, I have sought to approach this from a number of different directions. The first thing is that I have placed a lieutenant colonel in Afghanistan as the force provost marshal, whereas previously the major commanding the provost company was double-hatted.*
>
> *I have also placed an MPS officer in theatre to run alongside the provost marshal to provide that expert advice to the provost marshal and provide a much higher level of supervision in theatre.*
>
> *Q. Yes.*
>
> *A. We are also using the RMP forward to provide that extra governance and assurance and, in the absence of being able to push additional MPS forward at this time, that is, I think, the most appropriate mechanism. But this is also bound with the very clear direction of the force commander that detainees are to be removed from the ground as quickly as possible and brought back to the main detention facilities so that the risk to them is reduced. So I think that the reduction of risk issue is a multi-stranded argument which needs to be looked at in that way and not just one silver bullet, if you like."[263]*

---

[262] Forster-Knight BMI 109/222/17-223/16
[263] Forster-Knight BMI 109/143/4-145/11

16.305 Having considered these remarks, Trousdell still maintained that the use of the Provost Sergeant was preferable to the RMP or MPS given the realities of manpower:

> "A. Well, I understand that my argument in this area – my proposal in this area – was rather elegantly holed below the water line by the provost marshal army when he was sitting in this seat, but I think we just need to revisit that. What he was saying is that he has, in his organisation, the expertise to cover this area and, indeed, we see in the evidence that from the Secretary of State downwards the PMA is now seen as the subject matter expert in this area.
>
> I don't doubt that in Colchester and in members of his Royal Military Police – but not all of them – that they have the expertise to advise in the whole area of CPERS. But I have some concerns about his proposition.
>
> The first one is that the army is not going to get any bigger. Its manpower is absolutely capped. Indeed it may be about to get smaller. So if you need to have more military police or MPS, which he says he requires, that manpower can only come from somewhere else in the army. There has to be a compensating reduction if he increases. So I think he will have a very hard fight on his hands to persuade other areas of the army that they have got surplus manpower, manpower that they don't really require.
>
> So I think that he will have difficulty in bringing his very good plan to fruition. I therefore believe that there is a way of achieving the effect that he wants to create – which is people with a higher standing and expertise in this area – I believe you can create that effect by having a detention officer and having a unit provost sergeant who has also been trained to carry out those activities.
>
> I would underpin that by saying that – very understandably – much of what we have heard in this room is Afghan-centric, and I believe that what is required is for the services to understand the principles that have been exposed in many areas and to strip away the Afghan answer to those principles and to retain the principles so that they can build on those for future operations.
>
> I'm not optimistic that in future operations there will be a surplus of RMP and MPS who have been sitting waiting to join units to be their experts on operations and I find it quite difficult to believe that there will be jobs created for MPS and RMP in non-operational times so that they are available to deploy when they are required. I just don't see that as being an efficient use of military manpower.
>
> So in the much bigger picture, I really do believe that the detention officer and the custody sergeant/unit provost sergeant idea is worth exploring very thoroughly."[264]

Conclusion regarding coordination of CPERS administration at NCO Level

16.306 I understand and sympathise with the Provost Marshal's desire to have the administrative NCO and CPERS detention at Battlegroup level reserved for a member of the MPS. I can also see the advantage of a person with the skill-sets which a RMP NCO would have occupying that post. However, in the current climate, I think it unlikely, probably very unlikely, that the MPS or even RMP population will increase to anything like the level needed to fulfil this additional staffing role. In the

---

264 Trousdell BMI 115/46/20-48/20

circumstances, in my judgment, the more realistic solution is to adopt that advocated by Trousdell.

16.307 I therefore recommend that the Regimental Provost Sergeant is nominated to carry out the dual function of Detention Sergeant and traditional Provost Sergeant's duties. But whether this post is taken by a member of the MPS or the Regimental Provost Sergeant there should be a defined role for the CPERS administration which should be carried out by an SNCO, and a clear written explanation of unit level responsibilities for CPERS before any operation. If responsibilities are changed during an enduring operation this should be recorded. In this way the debacle of the failure properly to identify who was responsible for detainees at 1 QLR should be avoided.

(3e) Inspection and Licensing of Operational Custody Facilities

16.308 I have already alluded to the fact that on Op Herrick, the FPM is tasked with licensing CPERS detention facilities at Battlegroup level.[265] I readily endorse the process by which facilities that are going to be used to detain CPERS at Battlegroup level should be licensed for that purpose by the in-theatre FPM. This is one means by which shortcomings in the physical environment for CPERS, even if only held for relatively short periods, ought to be ameliorated.

16.309 Inspection of operational detention facilities after they have been licensed raises more difficult issues.

Main detention facilities higher up the CPERS chain

16.310 As regards internal inspections, Forster-Knight, as PM(A) with responsibility for the inspection and monitoring of all UK-run detention facilities within operational theatres, personally carries out inspections of the THFs in Afghanistan twice a year. Further inspections are carried out by his SO2 Custodial.

16.311 Forster-Knight exhibited his recent inspection reports which appear to be thorough documents and demonstrate the way in which the PM(A) has perhaps benefited from the recent liaison with HM Inspectorate of Prisons (HMIP).[266]

16.312 Forster-Knight told me in his oral evidence that he makes it his business to look at the interrogation side of affairs. Naturally, he does not review the wider intelligence exploitation process.[267] The only recommendation that I make as regards the internal inspection process for the higher level detention facility is that the PM(A) and those inspecting in his name should be expressly recognised as having the right and duty to inspect CPERS handling throughout the detention process, including during interrogation. At theatre level detention facilities, as regards the physical handling of CPERS, the PM(A)'s inspection remit should not end at the door of the interrogation room, and start again when the CPERS is released back to the custody of the guard staff. I do not overlook the inspection and audit by the Defence HUMINT Organisation now provided for in the 2010 interrogation policy, which is clearly welcome and

---

[265] MIV000008
[266] MIV004090-MIV004105
[267] Forster-Knight BMI 109/172/22-174/7

beneficial. However I consider it appropriate that there is additional assurance that the remit of the PM(A) is expressly recognised to extend to CPERS handling within the interrogation process. In making this recommendation, I have taken into account information which the Inquiry has received in relation to criminal investigations of interrogators' conduct within the interrogation room, an outline of which was made known on terms of confidentiality to the Core Participant teams.

16.313 As regards external inspection, the starting point must be to recognise the benefits of appropriate independent inspection. Both Dickson and Roberts recognised inspection as being a vital safeguard.[268] Internal inspections have a significant role to play but independent inspections are important in identifying the need for systemic improvements and "cultural" alterations to the way CPERS are handled and also in providing a degree of scrutiny and assurance that is open to the public and transparent.

16.314 The ICRC continues to be the international body which in practical terms is most likely to be involved in inspecting UK operational military detention facilities. It remains MoD policy to grant full access to the ICRC. This is an important safeguard but it is not a panacea. The ICRC is committed to working by way of confidential reports to the detaining State. That approach is one that must be fully respected, and has its advantages. But it does mean that its reporting cannot achieve that part in the assurance that comes from transparent public scrutiny.

16.315 Against that background, it is welcome that:

(1) the PM(A) demonstrated in his evidence to the Inquiry a commitment to external validation/inspection by a suitable external body or individuals. Forster-Knight explained that the first route remains external inspection by HMIP;[269] and

(2) the MoD continues to liaise with HMIP over the feasibility of it undertaking the independent inspection role for the main theatre detention facilities.

16.316 Owers is no longer the Chief Inspector of Prisons. The question of HMIP acting as an independent inspector of the main military detention facilities is, the Inquiry was told, an ongoing matter of negotiation between her successor, Mr Nicholas Hardwick, and MoD Ministers.

16.317 It was apparent from Owers' very helpful evidence that if it took up the role as inspector to operational military detention facilities, HMIP would not be able to operate in all respects in the way that it does as the Inspectorate for domestic civilian prisons. These differences include:

(1) the fact that unannounced inspections are not practicable where the facility is a theatre level detention facility in a combat zone;

(2) that interaction with CPERS in such a facility would be very different to the sort of interaction the HMIP inspectors engage in during their domestic work, where a degree of trust between inspectors and prisoners is seen as integral to how the HMIP does business;

(3) that HMIP may not be able to have access to all parts of the detention activity in theatre; and

(4) that HMIP are not expert in interrogation matters.

---

[268] Dickson MIV010083, paragraph 13; Roberts MIV010330, paragraph 40
[269] Forster-Knight BMI 109/180/19-182/18

16.318 Given HMIP's wealth of experience and expertise, I am sure that their appointment in the inspection role for the main operational detention facilities would bring significant benefit. However, HMIP are independent and they must no doubt make up their own minds as to whether the appointment would necessarily involve such significant divergence from their preferred working methods as to be unacceptable to them.

16.319 I would simply encourage that two factors are given the fullest consideration in the ongoing negotiations:

(1) the significant benefit that HMIP involvement in the inspection process would bring; and

(2) the fact that while inspecting operational detention facilities may involve compromises to, and divergence from, HMIP's normal practice, certain practical realities (e.g. inspection only with a warning; CPERS who may very well be distrustful of *any* inspector from the UK; and limitations on visiting some areas in theatre) would apply to any body that undertook the inspection role.

16.320 Were it to be the case that HMIP did not feel able to fulfil the inspection role for the main theatre detention facilities, the MoD should urgently consider other routes to achieving independent inspection/validation of those facilities by the best means that can be achieved short of full HMIP involvement.

Inspection of Forward Detention Facilities

16.321 While the situation will vary from theatre to theatre, very often there are likely to be considerable difficulties with non-military UK inspectors gaining access to detention facilities in forward deployed areas. In the feasibility studies that have taken place in Afghanistan, Owers did not have access to forward detention facilities and it is extremely unlikely, on safety grounds amongst others, that civilian inspectors could go to unit and sub-unit forward bases in Afghanistan.

16.322 The present arrangement in Op Herrick is that the MPS in theatre inspect UHAs. The Officer Commanding the MPS is required to inspect UHAs every two months or sooner if an urgent requirement is noted. [270]

16.323 Under current operational conditions, these internal inspections cannot be without notice because of the need to arrange the security, guarding, transport (by helicopter), feeding and accommodation of the MPS who carry out the inspection. In any event, the Inquiry was told that quite apart from these practical considerations, the inspections are not intended to be unannounced.[271]

16.324 With forward bases that are as dangerous and difficult to access as in Afghanistan, I do not find it surprising that internal inspections are limited in this way. However, I conclude that:

(1) the nature of the internal inspections that can be achieved will probably vary from theatre to theatre;

---

[270] FRAGO dated 15 August 2010, MIV012543
[271] Forster-Knight BMI 109/182/19-183/9

(2) the PM(A) and in-theatre FPM should take account of the in-theatre situation in assessing whether unannounced MPS inspections would be feasible and beneficial. Currently in Op Herrick it is plain that they are not feasible; and

(3) the absence of any mechanism by which higher formations or independent inspectors can inspect UHAs make it all the more important that the detention officer, as part of his advisory and oversight responsibilities, should be able to carry out less formal checks at unit and sub-unit level on CPERS handling including how UHAs are being run and whether proper custody records are being kept. The Commanding Officer should also be visiting UHAs from time to time but part of the benefit of having a designated post of detention officer would be the greater time that officer could dedicate to CPERS matters than the unit commander.

Chapter 4: General Military Training for Handling Captured Persons

(4a) Introduction

16.325 Annual mandatory training in relation to operational law, including proper standards for the treatment of prisoners is addressed within the Army by MATT (Military Annual Training Test) 7. As with other MATTs, MATT 7 is designed to revise and reinforce training and education that should already have been received. All personnel in deployable and deployed units receive the full MATT 7 package of training each year. The material comprises:

(1) a LOAC section of 45 minutes comprising a twenty minute DVD, a powerpoint presentation with different scenarios of twenty minutes and a five minute test;

(2) separate sections on Rules of Engagement, the use of force, judgemental training and investigations; and

(3) on searching and prisoner handling, 40 minutes including a DVD of 25 minutes and PowerPoint presentation of fifteen minutes.

16.326 Within the searching and prisoner handling PowerPoint presentation, the five prohibited techniques are highlighted as one of the *"five key takeaways"* that must be kept in mind at all times, another being humane treatment of all CPERS.

16.327 In expanding upon the key message of the humane treatment of CPERS, the PowerPoint presentation includes this text to be delivered by the trainer:

> *"We have a collective duty to protect and account for all captured personnel at all times. This includes protecting them from hazards of combat and natural hazards, from ill treatment, from humiliation and from public curiosity including the media; this includes not taking photographs of them unless you are required to do so as part of your duties. POW retain their personal protective equipment and PPE will be provided as required for all other CPERS, advice should be sought from MPS in case of any doubt. We treat all captured personnel firmly and fairly at all times as shown in the DVD when the officer starts making a scene when put in the Snatch wagon."*[272]

16.328 The next slide covers the five techniques specifically, stating:

> *"Detention*
>
> *There are the five techniques which are prohibited if used to assist the questioning process:*
>
> *1. Hooding (Sensory Deprivation)*
>
> *2. Stress positions*
>
> *3. Excessive Noise*
>
> *4. Sleep Deprivation*
>
> *5. Food and Water Deprivation."*[273]

---

[272] MIV000883
[273] MIV000883

16.329 The text that accompanies this slide is as follows:

> "Hooding is prohibited, however blacked out goggles and ear defence may be applied where there is a military necessity to prevent captured personnel seeing or hearing information. They must only be applied for the minimum amount of time.
>
> Stress positions are prohibited but captured personnel can be placed in restraint positions purely to exercise control – for example to prevent escape. Where necessary plasticuffs can be applied to the hands in front of the body.
>
> Wherever possible captured personnel must be protected from excessive noise and must not be deprived of food and water or sleep unless there is a valid operational reason for doing so – this could include food and water rationing because of supply limitations.
>
> The prohibited techniques must never be used to prepare captured personnel for questioning."[274]

16.330 Mr Jon Collier commented on the restraint aspects of this in paragraph 37 of his report:

> "As to the slide at MIV000883 (4), the wording "captured personnel can be placed in restraint positions purely to exercise control" is difficult to understand. It seems that individual soldiers receiving this presentation are left to interpret it in their own way – there is no further detail on what form restraint should take. Restraining an individual in certain positions may give rise to a risk of positional asphyxia..."[275]

16.331 On the same part of the MATT 7 guide, there is then a fairly lengthy citation from the Aitken report by way of background information.[276] This gives the background to the prohibition on the five techniques. Slightly worryingly, it includes the passage in the Aitken report that suggests in relation to the 1972 Directive that, "It is likely that, since the direction was specifically limited to the use of the Five Techniques in internal security operations, **its provenance was probably limited to Northern Ireland operations only**; and it is also likely that, since the direction was limited to the use of the Five Techniques as an aid to interrogation, it did not extend outside the intelligence community" (bold added for emphasis). It is not entirely clear what is meant in this context by "provenance" but this section is apt to be misunderstood as perpetuating a misunderstanding that the prohibition did not extend beyond Northern Ireland.

16.332 The background information goes on to cite the Aitken report further:

> "Against this background, we need to be clear about what was and was not an illegal technique. Some aspects of the Five Techniques may not, in themselves, be illegal: it is the circumstances that define their legality. For example, there will be occasions where it will be perfectly reasonable to deprive temporarily a captured person of his sight or hearing (to protect the security of our own troops, or to prevent collusion with other captured personnel, for example). The requirement to search a captured person may quite legitimately involve him being made to stand against a wall with his arms outstretched – technically a 'stress position' if maintained to the point of discomfort. At the point of capture, it may be necessary for soldiers to order their prisoners to adopt uncomfortable positions – if the soldiers are outnumbered, for example, or if those being arrested pose a threat to those detaining them. These may all be lawful actions; but it will be noted that in all these examples there is no

---

[274] MIV000883
[275] Collier MIV010305
[276] MIV000883-4

> *suggestion of using the Techniques as an aid to interrogation. On the other hand, the decision in the Ireland case makes it clear that it is unlawful to require a captured person to maintain a 'stress position' once he is secure in a detention unit, or to hood him, or to subject him to noise, or unnecessarily to prevent him from sleeping, or to deprive him of food and drink, as an aid to I&TQ. The issue is therefore to an extent one of context; and the Army's challenge must be to ensure that as clear a delineation exists as possible to guide all soldiers in what is and is not acceptable practice."*[277]

16.333 The prisoner handling DVD has the advantage of being, in respect of production and appearance, a far more 'gritty' and (in most respects) realistic presentation than the previous LOAC video which was shown to soldiers before Op Telic 1 and 2. In both the outdated nature of the scenarios depicted and the production quality, the previous LOAC video had become, it seems, at risk of being seen as something of a joke when presented annually.

16.334 There are, however, some issues of concern with the 2005 prisoner handling DVD to which I shall return below.

16.335 Also of relevance to the Inquiry is MATT 6, Values and Standards. This emphasises the core values of selfless commitment, respect for others, loyalty, integrity, discipline and courage. Respect for others is explained to be a hallmark of the British Army, including in how it deals with civilians in the execution of duty. Camp Breadbasket is given as an example of breach of the standards leading to discharge from the Army and periods of detention.[278] In addressing courage, moral courage as well as physical courage is explained:

> *"**Moral Courage** is equally important. This is the courage to do what is right even when it may be unpopular, or risk ridicule or danger, and to insist on maintaining the highest standards of decency and behavior at all times and in all circumstances, earning respect and fostering trust. Courage – both physical and moral – creates the strength upon which fighting spirit and success on operations depend. It is a quality needed by every soldier, but it is especially important for those placed in positions of authority, because others will depend on their lead and respond to it."*[279]

16.336 As well as their use in annual tests, MATT 6 and MATT 7 materials are drawn upon in initial training. Officer cadets at Sandhurst are taught the MATT 7 materials but their training goes into greater depth including amongst other things, consideration of JDP 1-10 and the current Op Herrick tactical aide memoire. In Phase 1 training, soldiers receive instruction on the correct handling of CPERS primarily using material from MATT 7. This is linked to the Army's values and standards and MATT 6 material. Revised training in this area is going to provide a theory lesson, a battle lesson in the field to demonstrate practical techniques, and then a battle exercise where students will be required to conduct the procedures themselves and be assessed.[280]

---

[277] MIV000884
[278] MIV001038
[279] MIV001042
[280] Edkins MIV004624-5, paragraphs 11-12

(4b) Consequential changes to how the prohibition on the five techniques are explained in training

16.337 The changes that I have recommended in respect of JDP 1-10 at the start of this Part would obviously give rise to the need for consequential changes in MATT 7, in particular in relation to how the five techniques are defined and explained. By way of example, it is questionable that MATT 7 gives such emphasis to the techniques being prohibited "...*if used to assist the questioning process*", especially in relation to hooding which is prohibited for all purposes. Similarly the reference to CPERS not being deprived of sleep "*unless there is a valid operational reason for doing so*" is apt to be misunderstood.[281] Having considered the observations I have made on JDP 1-10, there will obviously be a need for MATT 7 to be recalibrated to take into account such changes as are made to the joint doctrine.

(4c) The importance of clear and consistent messages in the training delivered

16.338 As will be apparent even from the brief overview set out above, it is plain that there have been marked improvements in the training provided. The main recurring theme which arose for further improvement in the training provided is the need for clarity and consistency in the messages being delivered in training.

16.339 There was evidence in particular of some inconsistency between the different services within the Armed Forces and some outdated materials being used by the Navy and the Royal Air Force (RAF). The RAF training materials seen by the Inquiry contained little reference to the five techniques,[282] and the Navy materials none at all.[283] Materials for the Royal Marines, for example, included anachronistic references to JWP 1-10, which has of course been superseded by JDP 1-10.[284]

16.340 The Inquiry was told that, so far as the Navy is concerned, such shortcomings will soon be addressed by the introduction of a maritime version of MATT 7, known as "*Core Maritime Skills 7*" (*CMS 7*). CMS 7 will teach individuals about the prohibition on the five techniques.[285] That improvement in Navy training is obviously to be welcomed.

(4d) Promotion courses and Commanding Officers' courses

16.341 There is, as one might expect, an extensive range of courses within the Armed Forces for those being promoted to different ranks within the different Services. The MoD

---

[281] MIV000924, see to similar effect the test at question 30
[282] MIV003908-11
[283] Murdoch MIV004658, paragraph 5
[284] MIV002016
[285] Murdoch MIV004667-8, paragraph 20

provided the Inquiry with extensive evidence about these courses.[286] Many of the courses address prisoner handling; many others do not. I do not propose to provide a detailed critique of the large quantity of training materials provided to the Inquiry. My general impressions of those training materials were as follows. Firstly, it is plain that the LOAC is a regular feature in these courses. The Armed Forces obviously take seriously the need for servicemen to be familiar with LOAC. Secondly, however, materials for promotion courses exhibited inconsistency and anachronisms of the type I have already referred to.[287] Such matters, whilst minor in themselves, do suggest that more rigorous review and quality control of course materials is required, possibly with some sort of central overview.

16.342 Of particular interest are courses for those designated as Commanding Officers. Not all Commanding Officers receive specific training beyond that covered during routine continuous professional development training. However, those preparing to command Battlegroups on operations do receive specific guidance on detainee handling.[288] They attend a Battlegroup Commanders' Course at the Land Warfare Centre which includes a briefing from the Operational Law Branch which covers the prohibited techniques, examples of wrongful actions, the requirement to hold offenders to account and some points specific to Op Herrick in Afghanistan. During the planning exercises on the course, students are required to consider detainee operations as part of their "*Mission Analysis*".[289] All of this is patently sensible and I endorse it.

(4e) Moral courage

16.343 As Trousdell observed in his report, "[t]o *stand out against the chain of command or your immediate superiors in a hierarchical organisation like the Army takes immense moral courage*".[290] Moral courage, including the courage to intervene when one's colleagues or superiors are doing wrong, is plainly an important element in avoiding the repetition of events similar to those of 14 to 16 September 2003.

16.344 The Army's "*core values*", which are taught to all soldiers and officers, are relevant in this respect. There are six core values: selfless commitment, respect for others, loyalty, integrity, discipline and courage. Officers and soldiers are taught about these values in MATT 6, entitled "*Values and Standards*".[291] I have already referred briefly to MATT 6 above.

16.345 As to "*courage*", that is defined by the Army both as physical courage, and also as moral courage. The pamphlet "*Values and Standards of the British Army*", which is issued to commanders, defines moral courage in the following terms:

> "...*Moral courage is equally important [as physical courage]. That is the courage to do what is right even when it may be unpopular or to risk ridicule or danger, and to insist on maintaining the highest standards of decency and behaviour at all times. This earns respect and fosters*

---

[286] The evidence appears, in particular, in the witness statements of Bestwick MIV004986, MIV004989; Edkins MIV004622; Gammage MIV005014; Murdoch MIV004657; and the documents referred to in those statements

[287] The Platoon Commanders Battle Course at MIV001851 also refers to the defunct JWP 1-10

[288] Edkins MIV004626-7, paragraph 24

[289] Edkins MIV005649

[290] Trousdell MIV010054, paragraph 23

[291] Edkins MIV008784, paragraph 4

> *trust. Courage – both physical and moral – creates the strength upon which fighting spirit and success on operations depend. It is a quality needed by every soldier, but it is especially important for those placed in positions of authority because others will depend on their lead and respond to it."[292]*

16.346 An equivalent pamphlet for soldiers states:

> *"Courage: doing and saying the right thing – not the easy thing… Moral courage is doing the right thing, not looking the other way when you know or see something is wrong even if it is not a popular thing to do or to say."[293]*

16.347 MATT 6 training is delivered in part by showing a DVD video. This makes two references to the obligation not to look away from or cover up wrongdoing.[294]

16.348 It is obvious to me that it is far from easy to inculcate values through training. To train someone to have moral courage, and specifically to intervene when others are doing wrong, is bound to be difficult. Moral courage is to a large extent an aspect of an individual's character, and there is only so much which training can realistically do to change someone's character. But with that said, it is also obvious that the Army must do what it can to inculcate moral courage, notwithstanding these challenges. From what I have seen of the training which is delivered, it already makes a fair attempt to do so.

16.349 Submissions on behalf of the Detainees make some sensible suggestions as to how this aspect of training may be enhanced.[295] Whilst I am not persuaded that all of their suggestions in this area are sound, I do agree with the following points:

(1) Training in this area could be effectively delivered by the use of discussion and role-play with reference to particular "scenarios". Royal Navy materials showing a participatory approach for students serve as a useful example of this.[296]

(2) Training materials should include reference to occasions when UK troops have breached the LOAC. To a significant extent, they already do: Camp Breadbasket and Baha Mousa are mentioned in MATT 6 and MATT 7 materials.[297] Reference to such occasions will help to avoid any risk of complacency about the conduct of UK Forces.

16.350 Training servicemen to have moral courage is related to the topic of whistleblowing, with which I have already dealt above.

(4f) Conclusions in respect of non-specialist training

16.351 I have reached the following conclusions:

(1) Important lessons have been identified by the MoD already but now need to be applied across the board in training. It is particularly important that:

---

[292] MIV008753, paragraph 10
[293] MIV008219
[294] MIV012452
[295] MIV012728-30, paragraphs 95-99
[296] MIV011545
[297] MIV000747

(a)   CPERS training includes both theoretical and practical training in what Forces personnel can and should do when handling CPERS; and

(b)   CPERS training is woven into the full range of military exercises and training. Such training should be "end to end", not just focused on the planning and the actual combat/public order side of the operation, but including what happens after a CPERS is captured. Thus, practical exercises should not routinely end with the enemy or insurgent being captured, as often appears to have been the case before 2003. Exercises for commanders need to test and train them in CPERS handling issues and problems, including in the command and control of tactical questioning. If training does not include aspects of the CPERS chain, it will not become part of the core military skill. This should be a particular priority for mission specific training.

(2)   There are too many inconsistencies between different training materials. To some extent this may be explained by the recent pace of change and improvements in training materials. But there is now a clear need to review training materials across the Services to ensure that the messages are clear and consistent. The arrangement now agreed whereby the PM(A) will act as a coordinator and validator of prisoner handling training should assist in bringing greater consistency to the training materials.

(3)   The MATT 7 PowerPoint presentation on the five techniques should be amended: to ensure that the definitions of the techniques are consistent with amendments to JDP 1-10; that it is clear that the techniques are not only prohibited as aids to interrogation (in particular hooding is prohibited in all circumstances) and so that the background information section is fully accurate.

(4)   As the MoD has already recognised,[298] the 2005 prisoner handling DVD needs to be amended to avoid misleading messages about sight deprivation in the context of interrogation, and the inappropriate presentation of the interrogation facility. Some steps have already been taken in this regard. Where such training materials touch on specialist areas such as tactical questioning and interrogation, the relevant subject matter experts should be consulted. Other changes are also needed to reflect current best practice. "Bagged and tagged" is an ambiguous phrase which should not be used. In reviewing the DVD, consideration should also be given as to whether:

(a)   the prohibition on the five techniques might be incorporated into the film, although I should underline that it does appear prominently in the MATT 7 package because it is a key aspect of the PowerPoint presentation. Again some steps have already been taken in this regard but it should be considered when the DVD as a whole is reviewed; and

(b)   all of the CPERS handling within the DVD is commensurate with best practice, allowing for the need for realism and that CPERS treatment in military operations may in circumstances need to be firm as well as fair.

---

[298] MIV012416-7. On 24 Sept 2010 a letter to HQ Land Forces from Maj O'Bree of the Operational Law Branch warned that there was a concern that the last seconds of the film "...*may give rise to an inference that the PW's goggles remain on in order to condition him for the purposes of interrogation, which would be contrary to UK policy and almost certainly illegal*". Editing the clip was advised and text was to be inserted advising that goggles need to be removed without delay once clear of an operationally sensitive area. Pending the editing, an instruction is to be given orally to similar effect.

I add that from disclosure provided shortly before finalisation of this report, it appears that the MoD has already made improvements to this DVD. The latest version has deleted the previous inappropriate depiction of the interrogation facility and has inserted text referring to the prohibition on the five techniques, and the limited use of blacked-out goggles. I note however that there remains a reference to the ambiguous phrase "bag and tag". While there needs to be a balance ensuring that the DVD is realistic and engaging, there remain some scenes from the original DVD where it might be questionable whether the tone and approach of the soldiers is fully commensurate with best practice. I would still recommend that it should be thoroughly reviewed.

(5) Greater clarity and guidance needs to be given in relation to the concept of "restraint positions". In my opinion "restraint positions" is not a helpful phrase. In any event, more must be done to give practical guidance to help service personnel distinguish between unlawful stress positions, on the one hand, and the legitimate use of force to effect a search, or an arrest or prevent assault or escape, on the other. Troops need guidance on common sense precautions for preventing assault or escape at the point of capture where arresting UK Forces might be outnumbered. This may include making CPERS sit with hands on their heads or sit on their hands etc., provided that such positions can be changed from time to time so that they do not become painful or extremely uncomfortable.

(6) MATT 7 and mission specific training for CPERS handling should incorporate suitably pitched training on the risks of positional asphyxia/death by struggle against restraint.

(7) MATT 7 training, and its equivalent for the other Services, and mission specific training, is only of use if it is correctly received by all those who may deploy. There needs to be better recording of the take-up of MATT 7 (and equivalent training) to avoid the need to rely upon Reception Staging and Onward Interrogation (RSOI) training in CPERS handling.

(8) Those responsible for designing the mandatory operational law and values and standards training must keep the training relevant and up-to-date both in its content and in the style and means of delivery.

(9) It should be a priority for unit commanders to ensure that operational law training delivered annually is delivered to the highest standards, so as to avoid it becoming stale or routine. Understanding that there are limits to how often the core materials can be updated, I nevertheless encourage the use of different media to keep the materials fresh and up-to-date. I acknowledge, however, that there is a balance to be struck between keeping the materials fresh by offering some variety in what is presented, and always ensuring that the key elements are trained consistently each year.

(10) Phrases such as "calm, neutral and professional" and "firm, fair and efficient" can properly be used as shorthand for those involved in CPERS handling. Maintaining or prolonging the shock of capture is apt to be misunderstood and should not feature in ordinary training. I have addressed separately tactical questioning and interrogation training, and Survive, Evade, Resist and Extract (SERE) training and the terminology used in such training.

Chapter 5: Tactical Questioning and Interrogation Training

16.352 The most recent version of the interrogation branch training materials evidences a significant improvement when contrasted with those materials that survived from the period 2003 to 2004. However, significant further attention needs to be given both to the processes for auditing, managing and controlling the I branch training materials, and the detail of what is taught. In both respects the Module 4 evidence to the Inquiry revealed serious grounds for concern.

(5a) Audit, management and control of Interrogation Branch's Training Materials

16.353 Since 1972 no British Forces should have used sight deprivation, whether blindfolding or hooding, as an aid to interrogation.

16.354 As recently as September 2010, the Interrogation branch at Chicksands was distributing a handout which contained guidance authorising interrogators to conduct a visual scrutiny of blindfolded prisoners when they first arrived in an interrogation room; and to "*increase the pressure*" by moving around the prisoner while still blindfolded:[299]

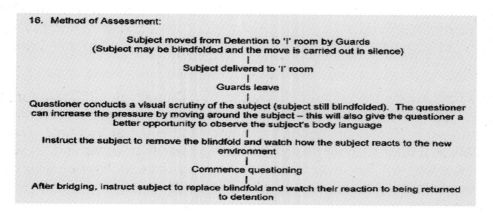

16.355 Thereafter, even the amendment of September 2010 was not done thoroughly so that an inconsistency and ambiguity remained about when the blindfold should be removed:[300]

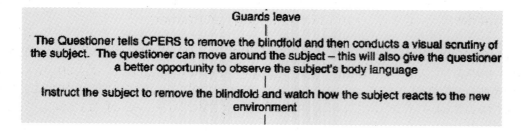

---

[299] MIV000454
[300] MIV010129

16.356 Despite the largely reassuring reports of Aitken and Purdy, the MoD would do well to reflect and act upon the shortcomings that have permitted ongoing training in breach of the prohibition on the five techniques to continue up until September 2010, seven years after Baha Mousa's death.

Auditing of interrogation branch training materials

16.357 The detail of what is taught to interrogators and tactical questioners is very important. Given the fine lines that have to be drawn as to permissible and inappropriate conduct, there is, in my view, no alternative but for DISC to ensure that the detail of what is taught on both courses is audited to ensure that it fully complies with the MoD's legal obligations and the tactical questioning and interrogation policies.

16.358 In considering the Module 4 evidence regarding training at Chicksands, I take into account that Adams, as Director of Training, is several levels above the day to day provision of training. Nevertheless I am bound to observe that I found Adams' first statement to the Inquiry to be unduly optimistic and reassuring about the training provided by the interrogation branch.

16.359 Adams' first statement on 20 August 2010 stated that the teaching on the tactical questioning and interrogation courses was adequate in respect of ensuring compliance with the Geneva Conventions.[301] Yet at that stage the handout advocating increasing pressure on CPERS by moving around them whilst blindfolded was still being provided to students. His first statement suggested that walking around a blindfolded CPERS is no longer taught[302] but his second statement said that the teaching in that regard had only changed in May 2010 and that by human error, the handout was only changed in September 2010.[303]

16.360 Adams relied upon the oversight provided by a Directorate of Operational Capability audit in 2007 which found that DISC was *"highly regulated and compliant with both law and policy"*.[304] The interrogation branch materials at that time clearly included materials that ought to have been questioned and then amended; of which walking round blindfolded CPERS to increase the pressure is only one. The audit in 2007 does not seem to have identified the problematic content within the interrogation branch training materials.

16.361 Adams further relied upon a review carried out on 16 April 2010 by SO1 Legal D Int Corps although there was no written record of that review.[305] Having regard to the many areas for further improvement referred to below, and largely accepted by S004 in oral evidence, one again has to doubt how effective this review was in assessing the real detail of the presentations used in the training.

16.362 In his second statement, Adams indicated that a comprehensive and independent legal audit of current tactical questioning and interrogation training materials was underway. It had been commissioned as part of a continuing process of review in order to provide assurance and identify any residual areas of concern.[306] DISC plan

[301] Adams MIV006124, paragraph 5
[302] Adams MIV006126, paragraph 12
[303] Adams MIV012254, paragraph 8
[304] Adams MIV006134-5, paragraph 45
[305] Adams MIV006134, paragraph 43
[306] Adams MIV012253, paragraph 4

to conduct a formal legal review after the release of the new tactical questioning and interrogation policies and annually thereafter.[307]

16.363 I set out below my conclusions:

(1) tactical questioning and interrogation training requires very difficult judgments to be made on such matters as the proper limits of approaches, what constitutes a threat to a CPERS, and how self-induced and system-induced pressures are approached. (See also the addendum to the Harsh Approach at paragraph 16.206-16.209 above.);

(2) in addition to the provision of tactical questioning and interrogation policies that do more to address the detail of these difficult areas, the auditing of training given by the interrogation branch at Chicksands needs to be more detailed and rigorous than has hitherto been the case;

(3) it is completely unacceptable that as recently as September 2010 interrogation branch handouts were permitting the use of sight deprivation expressly to increase pressure on CPERS;

(4) it is encouraging that detailed and independent legal review has been commissioned by DISC;

(5) the annual legal review of training materials planned by DISC is a necessary step which I commend. It must, however, include a rigorous scrutiny of the detail of the presentations and speaking notes used on the tactical questioning and interrogation course. Previous audits, including of the legal presentations, have not done enough to highlight problem areas; and

(6) a more senior and more independent legal review of the kind now being conducted as a one off *ad hoc* review is required. Such a review should not be necessary on an annual basis but should provide a suitable measure of further assurance if conducted every three years.

Management and control of interrogation branch training materials

16.364 The process by which interrogation branch had to disclose its current training materials to the Inquiry revealed a worrying level of shortcomings.

16.365 I make clear that I accept what S004 told me about the pressures on him and the interrogation branch. Since what was not disclosed to the Inquiry in good time were later documents that were improvements on previous versions, I entirely accept that S004 acted in good faith in the disclosure exercise in which he played a significant part. More generally I found S004 to be an honest and straightforward witness. A capable instructor with much subject matter expertise, I formed the impression that he and his branch are, however, struggling to meet the administrative demands of producing sufficiently audited and managed training materials against the demands of running the courses alongside litigation demands. My concerns relate therefore more to the systemic shortcomings evident from the Module 4 process.

16.366 Without suggesting that any blame attaches to him personally, I record that Adams accepted there had been the following difficulties in the material disclosed to the Inquiry:

---

[307] Adams MIV006137, paragraph 56

(1) PowerPoint presentations were disclosed to the Inquiry without the relevant speaking notes;

(2) when DISC disclosed material to the Inquiry in late May to early June 2010, some of the material disclosed as the current teaching materials had already been superseded and so was not in fact the up-to-date teaching material; and

(3) some of the teaching materials disclosed in May to early June 2010 contained teaching points of concern that were only amended and improved later, and included in further disclosure in late September 2010.

16.367 Concerns about the management of the interrogation branch's teaching materials are not new. One of the issues raised with the Inquiry's Module 3 witnesses was why it was that the tactical questioning and interrogation training materials from the 2002/early 2003 courses had not been retained. Both the Court Martial and this Inquiry had to rely on partial disclosure of those course materials from handouts that students had retained, combined with the course materials from later courses.

16.368 Against that background, it is of particular concern that management of the training materials in the interrogation branch was not such that at a given point the branch could accurately produce the current teaching materials, without confusion as to earlier versions.

16.369 There are further indications of poor document management practice. The PowerPoint presentation dealing with bridging is an important one because it has to address the part of the session where a tactical questioner or interrogator may send the CPERS away pending further questioning, giving the CPERS questions to think about for the next session. It is here that there are difficult judgments to be made about what can be said by way of "encouragement" to make the CPERS answer the questions during the next session. This used to be labelled "Bridge, carrot, stick".

16.370 The latest version of this presentation includes some amendments designed to ensure that the "encouragement" to answer does not lapse into threats. In the third slide, students are advised that they "*May improve impact of this by **stating** what CAN happen if he answers questions to the TQer's satisfaction. Equally, **state** what MAY happened if he does NOT answer questions*" (underlining added for emphasis).[308] This is a subtle but not insignificant change from the previous version which stated "*Improve the impact of this by **implying** what CAN happen if he answers questions to the TQer's satisfaction. Equally, can **imply** what MAY happen if he does NOT answer questions*" (bold added for emphasis).[309] Thus the presentation has been changed to encourage the students to state factually what can or may happen rather than imply what can or may happen because it is felt that the former is less likely to constitute a threat.

16.371 The difficulty is that the earlier version of this slide had been kept within the PowerPoint presentation but as a hidden slide not to be shown to the students. I consider that a recipe for confusion and risks the slide being used again at some later stage. Whilst I am encouraged that S004 assured the Inquiry that hidden slides will not be used in future,[310] it is nevertheless of concern that this was thought a sensible approach in the first place.

---

[308] MIV010385
[309] MIV010386
[310] S004 BMI 111/69/15-25

16.372 I was struck by the candour of S004's evidence in relation to these shortcomings. He told me while short of administrative support, what was really needed was:

> "...a more robust system drilled into the behaviours in the branch would probably assist so that becomes automatic. We have not had that in the past. We are working towards it now and we are taking advice now from Captain Adams as to the best way to have a version control put in place. Subject to that, we have put our own in place."[311]

16.373 In his second statement, Adams explained that the DISC "Course Design Cell" had assumed responsibility for all Chicksands' training materials with the exception of lesson plans, in February 2010. He told the Inquiry that quality control reviews of the lessons plans, to check that they are consistent, coherent and up-to-date would start "... in 2011, upon completion of this year's quality assurance taskings, and to focus DISC's limited quality assurance resource on high value and high volume courses".[312]

16.374 With respect to Adams, this does not go far enough or show the requisite urgency. There is no excuse for courses teaching subject matters as risk-laden as tactical questioning and interrogation to be based on teaching materials that are not systematically managed with proper version control.

16.375 I conclude that:

(1) There has hitherto been a marked inadequacy in the document management and control processes with the interrogation branch and its predecessor branches.

(2) DISC should take immediate remedial action to ensure that:

(a) old versions of interrogation branch teaching materials are retained but archived separately from current, in-use teaching materials;

(b) interrogation branch teaching materials are always dated; and

(c) when legal advice, policy changes, or internal reviews require changes to interrogation branch materials, the changes should be checked for accuracy and made consistently across the body of training materials.

(5b) Remaining areas of concern in interrogation branch teaching

Approaches: the harsh approach

16.376 In addressing the tactical questioning and interrogation policies, I have recommended that the harsh approach should be prohibited for tactical questioning, and that if retained at all for interrogation, it needs clearer policy guidance, a more appropriate name, and should be subject to Ministerial authority before use on operations. These matters have to an extent been addressed in the letter from the MoD to the Inquiry of 7 March 2011 (see the Addendum to the harsh approach at paragraphs 16.206 to 16.209).[313]

---

[311] S004 BMI 111/11/19-25
[312] Adams MIV012252, paragraph 3
[313] MIV012736-9

16.377 Apart from the policy considerations, however, I consider that the training in respect of the harsh technique is currently muddled and poorly thought through.

16.378 The May 2010 disclosure to the Inquiry contained two slide presentations on basic approaches. As produced to the Inquiry, one was used on the tactical questioning course and made no mention of the harsh approach at all.[314] The second was labelled as that used on the interrogation course and had slides that gave headline points on the limits of the harsh approach:

> *"Harsh*
>
> *Can be used in TQ and Interrogation.*
>
> *Does not have to be delivered as a shout!*
>
> *Two main types:*
>
> > *– Sarcastic / Cynical*
>
> *Cynical or Sarcastic Harsh*
>
> *Insult the CPERS professionalism and / or performance.*
>
> *Deride their 'military' skills.*
>
> *Deride their ability to command.*
>
> *Deride their organisation / system / commanders / equipment etc.*
>
> *However*
>
> *DO NOT USE racial, sexual or religious slurs.*
>
> *Loud Harsh*
>
> *Short bursts only (seconds not minutes!).*
>
> *To bring the CPERS back to a full realisation of their situation.*
>
> *Do not ask questions – If you do, don't wait for an answer !!*
>
> *Consider difficulties through a Terp.*
>
> *Consider reliability of information from a 'Harsh'."*[315]

16.379 These two slides have been replaced by a single PowerPoint demonstration that Adams told the Inquiry is used on both the tactical questioning and interrogation courses. The relevant slide states only:

> *"The main Basic Approaches / styles are*
>
> *– Friendly*
>
> *– Firm*
>
> *…….Both with logic!*
>
> *Neutral*
>
> *Harsh."*[316]

---

[314] MIV000393-6
[315] MIV000684-5
[316] MIV010370

The accompanying speaking notes in relation to the harsh and neutral state only:

> *"**The Likelihood of using the next two is minimal – (just talk thro the principals)**
>
> **Harsh** – the one everyone expects to get, but it still has it's uses if it is done well and in line with MoD Policy guidance. – TQ*
>
> ***Neutral** – a vital approach used to gain an assessment of the Prisoner – TQ."*[317]

16.380 Adams told the Inquiry that the "harsh" and "neutral" are covered briefly in the tactical questioning course but are not taught in depth because other approaches are more useful. Whereas on the interrogation course the harsh is taught in depth.[318] S004 told the Inquiry that tactical questioning students are *"… given a theoretical understanding of the harsh and the neutral, but they aren't practised in those because they are not going to use them"*.[319]

16.381 I consider that this approach is an unhappy and inappropriate compromise that leaves the position muddled. In this respect I agree with Dickson who commented:

> *"Well, I just think it's rather curious to make the trainees aware of the existence of these other approaches without actually explaining how they differ from the three approaches which are explained in more detail. Although I think it's right to say that this is done because the expectation is that the trainees in question would never have to resort to harsh or neutral approaches, I think to make them aware of those approaches without actually spelling out what they entail or what consequences might flow from them is rather unfortunate, to say the least."*[320]

16.382 I conclude as follows:

(1) If, contrary to my recommendations, the MoD wishes to permit tactical questioners to use the harsh approach they must be properly trained and practised in it.

(2) It would, however, be far better for tactical questioners to be told in clear terms that it is not an approach they are ever to use.

(3) The current, in my opinion, unfortunate compromise whereby tactical questioners are given an idea of what the harsh approach entails but not trained properly in it risks the improper understanding and use of the harsh approach.

(4) The interrogation branch teaching materials appear to have deleted from the presentation on approaches, those slides which previously set out the limits of the harsh approach. This is self-defeating in that it gives less rather than more guidance to student interrogators in this difficult area. If the MoD elects to retain the harsh approach as approved for use by interrogators DISC should reinstate as a matter of urgency a proper presentation on its limits for student interrogators.

(5) If the harsh approach is retained in any form for either tactical questioners or interrogators, obviously training for it must be addressed afresh in the light of the parameters set out in the MoD's letter of 7 March 2011.

---

[317] MIV010370
[318] Adams MIV012257-8, paragraph 16
[319] S004 BMI 111/78/6-8
[320] Dickson BMI 113/112/23-113/8

Bridging

16.383 The second example of approved "motivation" to give to CPERS in the bridging presentation is this:

> "Example 2. If you answer my questions to my satisfaction you will be held in British custody. While in custody I can guarantee your personal safety and that you will treated in accordance with the GC.
>
> If you do not ..."[321]

16.384 I consider that this should not be used as an approved example of motivation for a CPERS to answer questions at the future questioning session. It is too close to being a threat. Article 17 of the Third Geneva Convention prohibits CPERS who refuse to answer questions from being threatened.

16.385 As to example 1, "If you DO NOT answer my questions to my satisfaction, who is going to look after your wife and children if you are in British custody?" [322] Whether it should or should not be used is less clear-cut. Opinions may differ but I consider it would be unwise to use it.

16.386 Such cases may have already have been considered as part of the MoD's own legal review.

16.387 I conclude that the MoD should give further careful consideration to the examples used in training for bridging between questioning sessions to ensure that they comply with the Geneva Conventions.

Conditioning

16.388 A number of the interrogation branch materials and various job descriptions and training statements still use the term conditioning. Where currently used, the phrase is meant to connote the lawful use of pressures.

16.389 I am pleased to note the evidence of Adams that it is now accepted that this use of the word "conditioning" in this context is "not ideal" and that DISC wishes to disassociate itself from the negative image the use of this word suggests.[323]

16.390 I conclude that "conditioning" should cease to be used as an approved Chicksands or HUMINT term. It is dangerously ambiguous since it can be used to refer to unlawful means of putting pressure on a prisoner as well the intended meaning of the legitimate use of existing pressures. The tactical questioning and interrogation courses should explain that "conditioning" should not be used because of its dangerous ambiguity.

"Maintaining" or "Prolonging" The Shock of Capture

16.391 The shock of capture is in itself an unimpeachable term that accurately describes the emotions felt after capture. However, I have similar reservations about the

---

[321] MIV010389
[322] MIV010388
[323] Adams MIV012256, paragraph 13

terms "maintaining" or "prolonging" the shock of capture as I do about the term "conditioning".

16.392 In saying that steps should be taken to "maintain" or "prolong" the shock of capture, service personnel are prone to the misunderstanding that they are meant to do something positive and unpleasant towards the CPERS. While Trousdell prefaced the comment with an acknowledgement of his relative lack of experience in relation to interrogation, I consider there is much force in his observation that "[f]*rom a common sense point of view to ask a soldier who has been involved in recent combat to prolong, or indeed anything else, the shock of capture is to invite trouble*".[324]

16.393 In fact, the only conduct that DISC expects and encourages service personnel to use so as to maximise the prospect of a CPERS providing information is to move CPERS up the chain as quickly as possible; and to treat CPERS firmly, fairly and efficiently. In the military context, in the early stages of capture, this involves not offering the CPERS comforts (cigarettes and the like) or fraternising with them. The treatment is sometimes described as being coldly efficient but must not entail any use of unjustified force or threat of violence.

16.394 The difficulty in using the phrase "maintain/prolong the shock of capture" as part of the tactical questioner's lexicon, as Trousdell points out, is that unqualified personnel will be prone to misunderstand what is intended.

16.395 I conclude that DISC should:

(1) Consider whether to refrain from using "maintain the shock of capture" and "prolong the shock of capture" even in their own courses.

(2) As a minimum, students on the tactical questioning and interrogation courses should be expressly warned of the dangers of unqualified personnel misunderstanding these phrases. Tactical questioners and interrogators in dealing with capturing or guarding personnel must emphasise swift handling up the CPERS chain and firm, fair and efficient handling not prolonging or maintaining the shock of capture.

Points of detail arising from the interrogation branch material

16.396 I have set out above my conclusions in respect of the more central areas of concern relating to the interrogation branch training materials.

16.397 At Annex 1 to this Part of the Report I have included in list form points of more detail in relation to the latest version of the training materials disclosed to the Inquiry. It is not appropriate that these should form part of my recommendations. It is for those responsible for providing the training material to compile and edit them in the light of my recommendations in this Part of the Report. My comments are provided as guidance only and by way of examples.

Improvements in the interrogation branch training materials

16.398 I have necessarily concentrated in the sections above on areas of residual concern in the interrogation branch training materials.

---

[324] Trousdell MIV010075, paragraph 85

16.399 However, it is right that I should record that these materials have improved very significantly from those from 2002 to 2005 that were available to the Court Martial.

16.400 Dickson stated that he was for the most part impressed with the legal briefing given on both courses commenting that the first part of the presentation forcefully brings home the dangers for all in not adhering to the laws, policies and procedures for CPERS.

16.401 Some of the most recent improvements in the training materials are particularly notable. A new presentation on CPERS handling within the tactical questioning process has been introduced.[325] As well as emphasising the need for firm, fair and efficient handling, it has sections on the risks of positional asphyxia. For the most part, this is an impressive presentation that indicates a renewed emphasis is being given to the importance of the proper treatment of CPERS.

---

[325] MIV010617-42

Chapter 6: Survive, Evade, Resist and Extract (SERE) Training given to UK Service Personnel

16.402 Service personnel receive different levels of SERE, formerly Conduct after Capture (CAC), training depending upon the nature of their roles. The current training was explained in two written statements from Pledger, the Commanding Officer of the Defence SERE Training Organisation (DSTO).

16.403 As regards the resistance training element of SERE, many service personnel will receive only the basic level of training. This comprises theoretical training made up of SERE Level A on a DVD and pre-deployment resistance briefs.

16.404 The Level A DVD is a training film that is part of the required annual training for service personnel but it must also be seen within six months of deploying. The current version was made in 2008 and it is due for review in 2011. I have seen this DVD, although as current training material it has a sensitivity that militates against its disclosure. The pre-deployment brief is a PowerPoint brief given by a trained DSTO instructor.

16.405 In his second statement to the Inquiry, Pledger conceded that at the time of signing his statement, neither the SERE Level A DVD nor the pre-deployment briefs contained a specific warning that the treatment towards captives illustrated in the training material is designed to illustrate conduct that might be adopted by an enemy that does not abide by the Geneva Conventions and in no way reflects how UK or NATO forces should treat CPERS.

16.406 Pledger candidly accepted that it was increasingly clear that such a warning was required in these materials and would be included in the next revisions (2011 for the film and December 2010 for the pre-deployment briefs).[326]

16.407 Practical resistance training is only provided to a more limited group of service personnel, whose roles are such as to place them at greatest risk of capture.

16.408 Practical resistance training has now been physically separated from tactical questioning and interrogation. It is carried out at approved sites that do not include DISC, Chicksands. Further improvements have been made. Involvement in practical resistance training cancels any tactical questioning or interrogation qualification unless the person requalifies. Those who qualify as tactical questioners or interrogators are no longer permitted to practise on practical resistance training courses. All of these are sensible and appropriate improvements in practice that should endure in the future.

16.409 Practical resistance training may include the five prohibited techniques being applied to UK service personnel so that they are better able to deal with such abuse should they suffer it, if taken prisoner by a non-Geneva Conventions compliant enemy. It is not appropriate to publicise further detail as to the extent to which service personnel are exposed to the techniques in such training. None of the Core Participants to this

---

[326] Pledger MIV008992-3, paragraph 2

Inquiry sought to suggest that such training is in itself inappropriate. I accept the need to train selected personnel in this way.

16.410 Sensible precautions must, however, be taken to ensure that no personnel involved in practical resistance training, whether as students or as support staff such as guards, leave the exercises under any misapprehension as to the unacceptability of treating British CPERS in the manner practised in the training.

16.411 To that end warnings are already given in the briefing materials and students must sign a declaration as part of the debrief that includes the following wording:

> *"The treatment of students during this exposure in no way reflects the treatment of captives held by British or NATO Forces. The exposure that you have undertaken is designed to simulate a captive environment that you may experience if held by an enemy who does not abide by the conditions of the Geneva Conventions."*[327]

Similar wording is contained in the debrief given to guards and the exposure briefs used for the training.[328]

16.412 Trousdell was critical of this wording referring to it as a wasted opportunity to drive home a message which would further erect a wall between conduct after capture and prisoner handling as taught in MATT 7. He suggested it important that these paragraphs be rewritten to give much stronger emphasis to the prohibition on the prohibited techniques.[329] I agree. Since resistance training should be the only place where service personnel see the prohibited techniques being used by British personnel I consider it appropriate that the warnings in practical resistance training be improved to include specific reference to the prohibition on the five techniques. To be fair to Pledger, when this matter was raised with him by the Inquiry, he gave full support in his supplementary statement to all levels of resistance training including a specific reminder about the prohibition on the five techniques.[330]

16.413 Having considered all of the evidence in relation to conduct after capture training and the Module 4 evidence relating to SERE training including resistance training, my conclusions are set out below:

(1) Some key improvements have been made to separate further tactical questioning and interrogation training from resistance training. Key changes have been to curtail tactical questioning and interrogation students from practising on resistance training courses; the physical separation of DSTO facilities from DISC Chicksands and the requirement that involvement in resistance training other than the standard annual SERE training or deployment briefings cancels tactical questioning and interrogation qualifications unless and until the person has requalified. There is no suggestion that these improvements are anything other than permanent changes but for the avoidance of doubt I endorse each of them as sensible and appropriate improvements that should endure.

(2) *All* theoretical and practical resistance training must include a warning which explains in terms that the training is to show conduct that can be expected of a non Geneva Conventions compliant enemy and does not reflect the standards

---

[327] MIV006046
[328] MIV006031; MIV006035
[329] Trousdell MIV010071, paragraph 64
[330] Pledger MIV008994, paragraph 5

required of British and NATO forces. Any of this training which uses, illustrates or refers to the use of any of the prohibited techniques should include a specific reminder of the prohibition on the five techniques and a reminder to personnel to abide by their MATT 7 training (or equivalent) in how they treat CPERS.

(3)   When reviewing the current SERE DVD, DSTO should take into account the latest developments in tactical questioning and interrogation policy. DSTO should seek to ensure that, without affecting the realism of the training material, more care is taken to avoid using language in the SERE DVD which is also used (with a different meaning) in tactical questioning and interrogation training. Such ambiguity of terms may be confusing for those receiving the training and should be avoided as far as possible.

(4)   The report of the Army Inspector has already highlighted a concern as to whether adequate safeguards are in place to prevent inappropriate lessons being learned from informal, unit organised, escape and evasion training. Purdy recommended that Headquarters Land Forces should direct that if any "escape and evasion" training is undertaken other than under the auspices of the authorised Defence SERE training centre, this activity may not include any form of conduct after capture or resistance to interrogation training.[331] I emphasise that recommendation and add that evidence in Module 1 of this Inquiry suggests that such informal unit level training has been an enduring problem with occasional examples of such exercises spilling over into resistance interrogation training. The MoD must make all units aware that, not only is DSTO the only body trained to provide resistance to interogation training, but that if any escape and evasion training is carried out it must under no circumstances involve, whether at the point of "capture" or otherwise, the use of any of the prohibited five techniques. Thus, for example, soldiers being trained in survival and evasion skills should at no time be hooded in order to prevent them knowing the location at which they may be taken at the start of the exercise.

---

[331] MIV005250-1, paragraph 49b and recommendation 6

Chapter 7: Regimental Police / Unit Provost Staff Training

16.414 In order for the provost staff of a Battalion to become qualified as unit custody staff, they must attend the All Arms Unit Custody Staff Course (AAUCSC). Not all provost staff do become qualified in this way, apparently because of a lack of course capacity. But if a unit runs custody facilities where their own soldiers may be detained, at least one qualified member of the unit custody staff must be on duty whenever a soldier detainee is in custody. The Inquiry was told that this was due to rise to two members of staff from April 2011.[332] Current doctrine makes clear the need for commanders to ensure that the knowledge of provost staff trained on the unit custody course is used to good effect.[333]

16.415 Since 2006, unlike before Op Telic 1 in 2003, the AAUCSC has contained a specific operational detention phase. It includes teaching on the ethos of humane treatment, categorisation of CPERS, the Geneva Conventions, escorting prisoners on operations, the requirements of a UHA, the use of restraints and the use of force, dealing with a death in captivity, and the role of the ICRC.[334]

16.416 For the most part, I have found the content of this course to be impressive and well organised. Some consequential changes will be needed to take account of the changes that I have suggested at the doctrinal level in particular in relation to stressing the five principles in relation to sight deprivation.

16.417 Unit custody staff are not custodial specialists to anything like the same extent as the MPS. The latter run the MCTC and are trained to a very similar level as Ministry of Justice standards for prison officers. MPS training includes in that regard, the full training that a prison officer would receive in specialist control and restraint techniques, including regular refresher training.

16.418 As I have set out in Part VI of this Report, in the years before Op Telic, the course for provost staff at the MCTC adopted a perhaps unwise compromise in respect of Home Office control and restraint techniques. Students were given a short demonstration of the techniques yet were told that they were not qualified or approved to use them.

16.419 As part of Module 4, I was keen to understand how practice in this area had developed.

16.420 Forster-Knight told the Inquiry in his statement that:

> *"Since Apr 2010 the AAUCSC contains an improved package of control and restraint in a custodial environment which is taken from the UK HM Prison Service approved techniques (and delivered by MPS SNCOs who are HM Prisons Service qualified instructors) and includes teaching in the dangers of positional asphyxiation and associated issues. This is delivered during a two day package of theory lessons and practical exercises. They also receive training*

---

[332] MIV005295, paragraph 34

[333] MOD042426, JDP 1-10.1 for example at paragraph 1C2(b); the latest draft JDP 1-10 at MIV004246, paragraph 812(b)

[334] MIV001191-333; MIV005317-84, these course materials including others taught as part of the teaching on how soldier detainees are treated.

in the use of approved restraints which includes handcuffs and plastic cuffs (the latter are for use on operations only)."[335]

16.421 This written evidence was the cause of some concern both to Owers and to Collier. The latter provided a helpful statement outlining HM Prison Service control and restraint training. The concerns were firstly, as to how prison service approved control and restraint techniques could adequately be taught in a two day package when the prison service equivalent was a one week long course. Secondly, as to what provision was made for refresher training. Thirdly, as to how unit custody staff would be able to use Prison Service control and restraint techniques; many are designed for three people, when there may be only one or two unit custody qualified staff on duty in an operational custody environment.[336]

16.422 This matter was, however, much clarified by the oral evidence of Maj Paul Baker who appeared in a supporting capacity with Forster-Knight:

> "...If I can just sort of set the scene in terms of how we analyse this, we very much regard unit custody facilities and therefore the unit custody staff as being equatable to police custody suites and the Military Corrective Training Centre for the military provost staff equatable to HMP.
>
> Taking that as our starting point we looked – clearly within the MPS and MCTC we are used to the Ministry of Justice full control and restraint course. We looked. We then did research with the Police Training College as to what is delivered to those persons that are working in police custody suites and then we designed the training, taking what we regarded as the relevant elements from the Ministry of Justice C&R course to benchmark it and, we believe, slightly exceed that which is provided to persons working in police custody suites.
>
> So to get down to the specifics, it is mostly personal protection breakaway type techniques, along with de-escalation methods, with a very small element of teamwork bolted on to that, which again is part of the Ministry of Justice training. The reason we allow for that is because within a unit custody facility there is a minimum of one course-trained person on duty at all times in order for them to comply with the terms of the license that we inspect to.
>
> As of April next year, that will rise to two course-trained people on duty at any one time. Therefore, there is sufficient to operate a two-man team. Indeed some custody facilities have far more trained persons on duty at any one time. So we are equipping them with the basics of a standard which they can safely use."[337]

16.423 As to refresher training, Baker went on to explain that as this aspect of the course had only started in April 2010, there had not yet been a need for refresher training but that refresher training would be starting between January to April 2011.[338]

16.424 My conclusions in respect of provost training on the AAUCSC are as follows:

(1) The AAUCSC course materials appear generally well managed and designed. They will need consequential changes accurately to reflect changes in the joint doctrine relating to the prohibition on the five techniques.

---

[335] Forster-Knight MIV005295, paragraph 36
[336] Collier MIV010304-5, paragraphs 33-35; Owers MIV008898, paragraph 79
[337] Baker BMI 109/162/9-163/16
[338] Baker BMI 109/165/5-17

(2)   In relation to breakaway, personal protection and control and restraint techniques taught on the AAUCSC, the position has improved since 2003. The MCTC should continue to monitor that the teaching of such techniques is appropriate having regard to a realistic assessment of the number of unit custody staff who are likely to be on duty (whether in a firm base or on operations). It is important that the refresher training is rolled out and that there is proper take-up and recording of unit custody staff refresher training.

(3)   Assuming that my recommendation that the provost sergeant should double as the detention sergeant is accepted, he or she will need to be fully and properly trained in all prisoner handling practices.

(4)   In reducing the number of firm base unit custody facilities, the MoD should be careful not to erode the unit level operational detention expertise which is provided to a Battlegroup by the attendance of unit provost staff on the AAUCSC unless the equivalent expertise can be provided to each Battlegroup by the MPS.

Chapter 8: Record Keeping

16.425 In dealing with policy and doctrine, with the medical policy and with detention practice on operations, I have already made a number of recommendations in respect of record keeping.

16.426 In this Chapter I address more briefly wider concerns about difficulties which the Inquiry encountered in respect of the Op Telic operational records for 2003.

16.427 It is right to acknowledge that the record keeping challenge for an operation such as Op Telic must be very great indeed, not least during the warfighting stages of the operation. The sheer volume of material on different media, the sequential deployment of formations and units, the different IT systems in use, and the protective marking of materials are just the sort of factors which add to the challenge of keeping a comprehensive record. It would be neither helpful nor practicable to keep all information that is created on operations.

16.428 At the same time, there have been aspects of the record retention of concern to this Inquiry.

(1) While many hundred evidential requests from the Inquiry were met, some concerning omissions were left incapable of being answered. Most notably the MoD was unable to disclose the final version of the Directive governing interrogation and tactical questioning and other HUMINT activity. While drafts of the Directive did survive, this is a striking and inexcusable example of a significant high level document not being retained.

(2) While the Inquiry could effectively establish the members of 1 QLR from the nominal rolls, it was surprisingly difficult to establish the membership of some of the higher formations in the early stages of Op Telic.

(3) Many of the email addresses used refer to the post and not the rank. This may have many benefits for when the post holders change and perhaps for security. But in carrying out an investigation it can make it exceptionally difficult readily to understand which individuals saw what information.

16.429 As regards custody records, Owers made clear in her report that good record keeping is an essential part of safe prisoner management; and it is not just the keeping of proper records, but their use and interrogation in internal audit and external inspections.[339]

16.430 More widely, the retention of proper records is a key part of ensuring that, if allegations are made involving the death or serious injury to a CPERS, an effective investigation can be held.

16.431 A detailed statement on broader record management was provided by Ms Katherine De Bourcier, Head of Corporate Information and Departmental Records Officer in MOD.[340] While noting the generally reassuring audits of current policy in this area, De Bourcier pointed to two factors impacting adversely on actual capability in this area:

---

[339] Owers MIV008887, paragraph 37
[340] De Bourcier MIV004615-21a

> *"The first is a lack of comprehensive effective electronic records systems; the second a shortfall in supporting skills, ways of working, culture and behaviours relating to keeping records."*[341]

16.432 She set out a number of the initiatives that are under way to address these difficulties.[342] Her conclusion was that:

> *"Overall, it is not possible at this stage to provide assurance that there are no longer information gaps in records created on operations. MOD is working to address the areas it identifies as causing the greatest problems, which have been identified in this statement. Through the DII/F programme, and related information management initiatives, it is seeking to deliver a comprehensive approach to solving the current shortfalls, and implement effective information governance. But the scale of MoD as an organisation and existing problems with legacy systems means that delivering this goal is complex and inevitably time consuming. Notwithstanding this, unless a decision is taken to keep every piece of information relating to operations as a record (which in itself would not be good records management practice) and the technical means to do this are put in place, then there will always be a risk that gaps in the record remain."*[343]

16.433 Subsequent to De Bourcier's evidence, the MoD disclosed to the Inquiry its policy on Defence HUMINT data management.[344] It is encouraging to see that policies are being formalised for the maintenance of tactical questioning and interrogation records. Such policies are, however, only effective insofar as they are the subject of auditing to ensure that the records are in practice being first completed and secondly retained. I have set out above at paragraph 16.229, the fact that when the issue was raised in the Inquiry's Module 4 hearings, there was in fact no auditing of tactical questioning records taking place in Afghanistan, although this has since been remedied.

16.434 It is not possible for me to make any sensible specific recommendations on this topic. I am pleased to note De Bourcier's assurance that despite the understandable difficulties involved, ways are being sought to improve the MoD's performance in record keeping. I do not doubt that this task is not an easy one.

---

[341] De Bourcier MIV004617, paragraph 5
[342] De Bourcier MIV004619-20, paragraphs 10-14
[343] De Bourcier MIV004620, paragraph 15
[344] MOD055845-67

Part XVI Annex 1

Detailed Comments Regarding Interrogation Branch Training Materials

1.   In addition to the changes that arise from the conclusions in Chapter 2 (Policy and Higher Level Doctrine) and Chapter 5 (Tactical Questioning and Interrogation training) above, I set out below more detailed comments regarding the latest disclosed version of the interrogation branch training materials.

Legal Presentation[345]

2.   The slide should not use the phrase "*Under **NO** circumstances can any of the techniques be used solely for the purpose of conditioning the detainee*".[346] "Solely" gives the wrong impression and the message about conditioning is ambiguous. The same applies to the slide on stress/restraint positions.[347]

3.   The treatment of restraint positions could be improved.[348] It is not helpful to refer to pain as a side effect of restraint positions.

4.   The slide should not suggest that imminent questioning may be a valid operational reason for sleep deprivation.[349] The references to valid operational reasons in this slide are unduly vague.

CPERS Handling Within the Tactical Questioning Process[350]

5.   This subject presentation would appear a natural and important place to refer to the prohibition on the five techniques but at present only some of the prohibited techniques appear in this presentation.

6.   The speaking notes should not state that "*The inside of the Interrogation facility is a sensitive location*".[351] Whether or not that is the case will depend upon how the facility has been designed and operational circumstances on the ground. This presentation currently risks treating sight deprivation of prisoners taken to an interrogation facility as being a matter of routine. That is the wrong message.

7.   In dealing with segregation of prisoners, the presentation should make clear that segregation should be achieved by means other than sight deprivation.[352]

---

[345] MIV003488-554
[346] MIV003530
[347] MIV003532
[348] MIV003532
[349] MIV003533
[350] MIV010617-42
[351] MIV010637
[352] MIV010626

Basic Approaches[353]

8.   Teaching students that an inducement for cooperation would be to allow the CPERS a change of position risks confusing and undermining the message that stress positions are absolutely forbidden.[354] Forced prolonged standing in one position for a long period such that it became extremely uncomfortable would amount to a stress position. Greater care is required in how the message is presented over these two slides.

Assessment of Prisoners Handout[355]

9.   At paragraph 16, the amendments as to when the blindfold should be removed, have not been made sufficiently thoroughly. The message is unclear.[356]

Assessment of Prisoners Presentation[357]

10.   The slide on Assessment wrongly treats blindfolding of prisoners taken to the interrogation room as a matter of routine.[358]

The Shock of Capture and Pressures on a Prisoner[359]

11.   In providing this presentation, trainers need to be careful not to go beyond the important concept of firm, fair and efficient handling which involves a cold/detached but professional approach. The reference to "*Atmosphere of ruthlessness*" is not appropriate.[360]

12.   The way that "*noisy environment*" including a reference to generators is addressed is sub-optimal, although I note that students are instructed to ask if there is nowhere better to put the prisoners.[361]

Generally

13.   No handout provided to students currently covers all of the five prohibited techniques. The prohibition is sufficiently important to warrant prominent and adequate treatment in a handout that students can take away from the course.

14.   Both JDP 1-10 and SOI J3-9 have moved towards a clear preference for the use of blacked-out goggles with blindfolds only being permitted for sight deprivation where blacked-out goggles are not available. The interrogation branch materials are outdated in not properly reflecting this development in doctrine and instruction in prisoner handling.

[353] MIV010363-82
[354] MIV010368-9
[355] MIV010126-30
[356] MIV010129
[357] MIV010437-60
[358] MIV010455
[359] MIV010546-68
[360] MIV010564
[361] MIV010565

15.   In places the presentations are badly out of date, for example the 2010 version of S004's introductory talk refers to ITD 6 as teaching the LOAC which is two iterations out of date. There is a need for a general check for accuracy that cross references to other policies and materials are up-to-date.

Part XVII

Recommendations

My recommendations are addressed to the MoD and are all contained in the bold type below. Any text which follows each recommendation is for the purpose of guidance and cross reference.

Joint Doctrine Publication 1.10

Recommendation 1

The MoD should retain its current absolute prohibition on the use of hoods on Captured Personnel (CPERS).

The arguments in favour of the complete prohibition are overwhelming. It is difficult to conceive how a return to the use of hoods could be justified whether militarily, legally or as a matter of policy.

Part XVI, paragraphs 16.61 – 16.71

Recommendation 2

Joint Doctrine Publication (JDP) 1-10 should include the requirement for standard orders to be issued for each operation prohibiting the use of the five techniques.

By issuing such standing orders, any service personnel who use the five techniques on CPERS in that operation may be prosecuted for using the five techniques in breach of military standing orders. Accordingly, I accept that there is no need for specific primary legislation to criminalise the use of the five techniques. The form of the standing order should take account of the recommendations I have made in respect of the definition of the five techniques.

Part XVI, paragraphs 16.230 – 16.232

Recommendation 3

The definition of stress positions in JDP 1-10 and elsewhere should be broadened so that it is not dependent upon the intention of the person enforcing the position.

It is not appropriate for me to be prescriptive as to the definition adopted. However, a better definition would be: "*Any physical posture which a captured person is deliberately required to maintain will be a stress position if it becomes painful, extremely uncomfortable or exhausting to maintain*". Depending upon the circumstances in which stress positions are being referred to, it may be appropriate to make clear that this prohibition on stress positions does not affect the right of service personnel to use reasonable force in self defence or to effect an arrest.

Part XVI, paragraphs 16.48 – 16.52

Recommendation 4

The essence of guidance on hooding should be that it is prohibited at any time for whatever purpose to place a sandbag or other cover over a CPERS' head.

Previous guidance referring to "keeping" the bag over a person's head was inappropriate and superfluous. More recent drafting has improved.

Part XVI, paragraphs 16.53 – 16.55

Recommendation 5

The definition of the prohibition on subjecting CPERS to noise should be broadened. It should prohibit subjecting CPERS to any unnecessary excessive noise. Guidance in JDP 1-10 should explain that:

(1) holding facilities may be inherently noisy places, but steps should be taken to mitigate such conditions;

(2) it is not legitimate deliberately to increase the noise in the vicinity of CPERS even for security purposes;

(3) facility design should, where practicable, avoid the risks of CPERS hearing sensitive information including questioning of others;

(4) where strictly necessary, ear defenders may be used to prevent CPERS overhearing sensitive information; and

(5) generators or other loud equipment should not be used as noise shields.

The MoD's current draft guidance is too narrow in defining the prohibition in terms of *continuous* excessive loud noise.

Part XVI, paragraphs 16.72 – 16.83

Recommendation 6

In the interests of clarity for all, the five techniques should be referred to as being banned or prohibited rather than proscribed.

Part XVI, paragraphs 16.84 – 16.85, 16.89

Recommendation 7

The MoD should give careful consideration as to whether referring to the five techniques as being prohibited *"as an aid to interrogation"* remains the most effective means of communicating the prohibited techniques.

Hooding prisoners is prohibited in all circumstances. It is not permissible to deprive prisoners of food and drink at all. Stress positions properly defined should never be used.

Part XVI, paragraphs 16.86, 16.89

Recommendation 8

The prohibition on the five techniques should not appear only within the Tactical Questioning and Interrogation section of JDP 1-10 since it has a wider application and importance.

Part XVI, paragraphs 16.87, 16.89

Recommendation 9

The prohibition on the five techniques should appear in the Joint Tactics, Techniques and Procedures guidance as well as in the main body of JDP 1-10.

Part XVI, paragraphs 16.88 – 16.89

Recommendation 10

Five principles on permitted sight deprivation should be consistently emphasised in JDP 1-10 and subordinate doctrine and instructions:

(1) **where practicable the need to deprive CPERS of their sight should be avoided in the first place by common sense steps such as appropriate design and layout of facilities, the planning of operations, choice of routes, and covering up equipment;**

(2) **even if it is impracticable to avoid CPERS seeing facilities or equipment in the first place, there must be a *genuine* sensitivity about the facilities or equipment before sight deprivation can be justified;**

(3) **when sight deprivation does take place it must only be for as long as is strictly necessary;**

(4) **sight deprivation should not become routine; it must always be capable of being justified by the operational circumstances on the ground; and**

(5) **when sight deprivation is used, the fact that it has been used should as soon as practicable be noted in a simple brief record giving the date/time /duration/circumstances/justification for its use.**

Part XVI, paragraphs 16.92 – 16.96

Recommendation 11

JDP 1-10 should make clear that it is prohibited deliberately to keep prisoners awake, even for short periods, merely because they may shortly face tactical questioning or interrogation. CPERS may nevertheless be woken up in order to be tactically questioned or interrogated if the questioning is ready to take place, provided that the policy on minimum periods of rest is respected.

Part XVI, paragraphs 16.97 – 16.102

Recommendation 12

JDP 1-10 should give some guidance in relation to the number of daily meals for CPERS and the timing of them.

Such guidance will obviously need to take into account the operational realities, particularly close to the point of capture.

Part XVI, paragraphs 16.103, 16.104

Recommendation 13

In dealing with segregation, JDP 1-10 should make clear that sight deprivation should not be used as a means of segregating CPERS to prevent them communicating with each other.

Part XVI, paragraphs 16.105 – 16.107

Recommendation 14

JDP 1-10 should include guidance that where practicable CPERS should be told the reason why sight deprivation is being applied. Suitable simple phrases in relation to sight deprivation should be included in mission specific language training.

Part XVI, paragraphs 16.124 – 16.130

Recommendation 15

JDP 1-10 should include a simple checklist covering both the principles and practicalities of accommodation for unit holding areas.

Part XVI, paragraphs 16.131 – 16.132

Recommendation 16

JDP 1-10 should include a simple checklist for actions on a death in custody. Where there is a death in custody, particularly one that is sudden or unexplained, prompt checks must be made on the welfare of other CPERS.

Without being prescriptive as to its content, the MoD should consider including guidance that where practicable the scene of the death (and the body if *in situ* after medical treatment) should be preserved pending the arrival of the Royal Military Police (RMP)/ Special Investigation Branch (SIB). If practicable the area should be sealed off.

Part XVI, paragraphs 16.133 – 16.136

Recommendation 17

JDP 1-10 should incorporate the requirement that on entry to and exit from a theatre level detention facility, CPERS are proactively asked whether or not they have any complaints concerning their treatment. This should not be done in the presence of the capturing soldiers/unit. JDP 1-10 should require the Force Provost Marshal (FPM) for an operation to consider what arrangements for complaints would be most practicable and effective in respect of detention before theatre level facilities. Consideration should be given to the value of asking more neutral questions about CPERS' treatment during detention which may help to elicit more information about areas of CPERS' concern about their treatment.

Part XVI, paragraphs 16.137 – 16.139

Recommendation 18

JDP 1-10 should address the protection that will be afforded to service personnel who make complaints or allegations in good faith of the mistreatment of CPERS. It should give guidance as to those who can be approached when service personnel have concerns about the treatment of CPERS.

Recognising the primacy of the chain of command and the Service Police, the MoD should consider the benefits of identifying the unit detention officer, the Padre and the Regimental Medical Officer (RMO) as those who can be approached. Consideration should be given to other means such as confidential telephone lines via which concerns might also be raised.

Part XVI, paragraphs 16.141 – 16.143

Recommendation 19

In the current redrafting of JDP 1-10 and in future subordinate doctrine and instructions regarding CPERS:

(1) **plain English, simplicity of structure and brevity should be given greater priority while allowing for the target audience and complexity of the subject matter;**

(2) **the wording should be thoroughly assessed to ensure (a) that material is not unnecessarily duplicated and (b) that the wording and diagrams are clear and readily understandable to the commander who may need to consider and apply the guidance on the ground; and**

(3) **timescales must be stated clearly both in the text and in flow diagrams.**

Timescales in relation to CPERS handling should be demanding as this encourages the rapid move of CPERS away from forward detention areas where risks of abuse are greatest. The next redraft of JDP 1-10 needs to make clear that the stated timescales should be adhered to whenever possible, but may need to be amended in some theatres.

Part XVI, paragraphs 16.144 – 16.151

Recommendation 20

The MoD should ensure that Development Concepts and Doctrine Centre (DCDC) reviews whether its protocols for layout and pagination of joint doctrine really serve the end user.

Part XVI, paragraph 16.151

Generic Standard Operating Instruction For CPERS Handling

Recommendation 21

Permanent Joint Headquarters (PJHQ) should complete work on a generic theatre-level Standard Operating Instruction (SOI) for CPERS handling. This should stand as the starting template for CPERS handling on future operations.

There is currently a gap in the current doctrine below the level of JDP 1-10 and its associated Joint Techniques Tactics and Procedures (JTTP)s. The SOI should reflect the contemplated changes to JDP 1-10, changes introduced as a result of this Report, changes in tactical questioning and interrogation policies, and the lessons learned from Op Telic and Op Herrick.

Part XVI, paragraphs 16.152 – 16.154

Tactical Questioning and Interrogation Policies

Recommendation 22

Urgent consideration must be given to amending the tactical questioning policy to make clear what approaches are and are not authorised for use in tactical questioning. In future all tactical questioning and interrogational policies should descend to greater detail on approaches, as a minimum making clear which approaches are authorised for use in which discipline, tactical questioning or interrogation.

It is entirely unacceptable that no such guidance appears in the tactical questioning policy completed as recently as 2010.

Part XVI, paragraphs 16.165 – 16.174

Recommendation 23

The harsh approach should no longer have a place in <u>tactical questioning</u>. The MoD should forbid tactical questioners from using what is currently known as the harsh approach and this should be made clear in the tactical questioning policy and in all relevant training materials.

The MoD's recent review of the harsh approach is welcome. But even as amended by the proposed new parameters and terminology, the risks of using the harsh approach in tactical questioning will remain and are too great.

Part XVI, paragraphs 16.175 – 16.209

Recommendation 24

To the extent that the MoD considers that the harsh approach can still lawfully be used <u>in interrogation</u>:

(1)   there is a need for very clear guidance to be given within the interrogation policy and in training as to the proper limits of the harsh approach;

(2)   the approach should be given a label which is less apt to be misinterpreted as permitting unlawful, threatening or intimidatory conduct;

(3)   the approach should not include an analogy with a military drill sergeant; and

(4)   in light of the legal and other risks in the use of the harsh approach, specific Ministerial approval should be sought before the harsh approach is approved for use in any operational theatre.

Part XVI, paragraphs 16.175 – 16.209

Recommendation 25

In line with Recommendation 11 above, the tactical questioning and interrogation policies need to make clear that it is not permissible to deliberately keep prisoners awake, even for short periods, merely because they may shortly face tactical questioning or interrogation. CPERS may nevertheless be woken up in order to be tactically questioned or interrogated if the questioning is ready to take place provided that the policy on minimum periods of rest is respected. Both policies should make clear that the discretion to wake a CPERS for immediate questioning is not to be abused by way of repeated or random waking of the CPERS with a view to disorientation.

Part XVI, paragraphs 16.210 – 16.218

Recommendation 26

The tactical questioning and interrogation policies should give more detailed guidance on the extent to which tactical questioners and interrogators may seek to exploit self and system induced pressures.

Part XVI, paragraphs 16.219 – 16.227

Recommendation 27

The interrogation policy should require, as part of the auditing process, a review of a selection of video recordings of interrogations of the inspector's choosing. Interrogators should know that the recordings of their interrogations may be inspected in this way.

Part XVI, paragraph 16.228

Recommendation 28

The tactical questioning policy should be amended to include a clear and simple auditing procedure.

I am reassured by the MoD's candid acceptance of this gap and the interim action it has taken. The MoD is right to accept that this must be addressed in the next version of the tactical questioning policy. Forms used for recording tactical questioning should be designed to capture the information to be audited.

Part XVI, paragraph 16.229

Medical Policy

Recommendation 29

Armed Forces medical personnel can and should be involved in providing advice that a CPERS is not fit for detention or questioning. Alternatively, the medic may validly advise that no specific intervention different from the normal process is required in respect of that CPERS. Medics should not advise that a CPERS is fit for detention or fit for questioning.

Part XVI, paragraphs 16.235 – 16.237

Recommendation 30

The medical policy for CPERS should include the following:

(1)　**CPERS must undergo a medical examination within four hours of capture, unless there are compelling circumstances making such examination impossible. This examination should be conducted by the most medically qualified individual available;**

(2)　**CPERS should be examined by a qualified doctor as soon as reasonably** practicable (i.e. usually upon transfer to a facility where a doctor is based);

(3) the non-medical chain of command should be prohibited from allowing interrogation (as distinguished from tactical questioning) of a CPERS to take place until the CPERS has been medically examined. Medical staff should not be directed that their examination of the CPERS should take place before interrogation; they should be directed merely to examine as early as reasonably practicable; and

(4) an electronic or written record of the examination of all CPERS should be made at the time of the examination and preserved.

The MoD currently proposes to formalise the arrangement whereby the requirement to examine a CPERS within four hours of capture is interpreted to mean within four hours of arrival at the first formal detention facility. I consider this a retrograde development. It must be recognised, however, that there may be operational circumstances where medical examination within four hours of capture is not possible.

Part XVI, paragraphs 16.238 – 16.246

Current Theatre Level Instruction and Detention Practice

Recommendation 31

The definitions of the prohibited techniques contained in SOI J3-9 should be updated to reflect the recommendations I have made above in respect of JDP 1-10.

Not all detail can be replicated in aide memoires but the key messages should be.

Part XVI, paragraphs 16.261(1), 16.266(2)

Recommendation 32

SOI J3-9 should reflect the greater emphasis that is given in the latest draft of JDP 1-10 to avoiding in the first place, where practicable, circumstances in which sight deprivation may be necessary. More generally, it should reflect the five principles in Recommendation 10. Within reason, these key messages should also feature in the aides memoire.

Part XVI, paragraph 16.261(2)

Recommendation 33

Where practicable CPERS who are subjected to sight deprivation or hearing deprivation should be told the reason for it. If being deprived of their sight for some or part of a journey by road or air, as well as ensuring that the sensory deprivation is kept to the minimum time strictly necessary, CPERS should be told in general terms where they are being taken.

Part XVI, paragraph 16.261(3)

Recommendation 34

Theatre level detention instructions and guidance should be reviewed to ensure that references to the means of permissible sight deprivation are consistent.

Without being prescriptive as to the wording that should be used, the clearest wording is likely to be "sight deprivation" (rather than blindfolding) "by blacked-out goggles". However, permission to use improvised blindfolds, not covering the mouth or nose and only if blacked-out goggles are not available, should be retained as a permissible fall-back position.

Part XVI, paragraph 16.261(4)

Recommendation 35

Theatre level detention instructions and guidance should be reviewed to ensure that references to timescales for detention are clear and consistent.

Timescales for detention are an important aspect of managing the risk of abuse. Previous in theatre instructions in Afghanistan have contained unfortunate internal inconsistencies on detention timescales, although work has already been undertaken to correct these.

Part XVI, paragraphs 16.253 – 16.255, 16.261(5)

Recommendation 36

CPERS documents should be as few in number as possible but they require amendment to ensure that those involved in detention are guided more accurately on what to record.

Current CPERS documents have no obvious place for soldiers to record the use of sensory deprivation, even though recording such use is a mandatory requirement.

Part XVI, paragraphs 16.261(6), 16.266(4)

Recommendation 37

A suitable occurrence book must be maintained at all times whenever CPERS are being held at a unit or sub-unit holding facility.

Part XVI, paragraph 16.261(7)

Recommendation 38

The MoD should continue its recent practice of ensuring that theatre level instructions and procedures for CPERS are contained within a single comprehensive order that is kept up to date and which can be easily handed over to incoming formations in enduring operations. It is inappropriate to permit CPERS handling to be governed by a series of fragmentary orders that may be lost or confused in the roulement of formations and units.

Part XI paragraph 11.105

Part XVI, paragraphs 16.263, 16.264

Recommendation 39

The Provost Marshal (Army) (PM(A))should formally review whether the current practice of using blacked out goggles for all movement of CPERS within Temporary Holding Facilities (THF) in Afghanistan is strictly necessary and ensure that it is not being used in circumstances that are not clearly justified by operational security and/or CPERS own protection.

The routine use of blacked out goggles for transfers within a holding facility is not desirable even for short periods of time, but I recognise that there may be circumstances where it is necessary. I am disinclined to make prescriptive recommendations about judgments being made on the ground at THF level in Afghanistan.

Part XVI, paragraphs 16.270 – 16.273

Supplementary Note In Respect of Theatre Level Instruction and Guidance

Recognising that I am recommending the insertion of limited further material in theatre level instructions and guidance there is a paramount need to keep instructions that are cascaded to soldiers on the ground and to junior commanders, clear, concise and simple.

Without making formal recommendations Part XVI, paragraph 16.262 of this Report lists further matters on which I would invite the MoD to give consideration.

Recommendation 40

Each Battlegroup should have a "Detention Officer" being a commissioned officer within Battlegroup Headquarters. The role should encompass coordination and management of CPERS; acting as a focus on CPERS matters during mission specific training; ensuring that Military Annual Training Test (MATT 7) and other training relevant to CPERS inculcates the vital messages about the correct handling of CPERS; assisting the Commanding Officer during operations by monitoring compliance with timescales, record keeping and other CPERS handling standards; acting as a clear point of contact with Brigade on CPERS matters and liaising as necessary with the Military Provost Staff (MPS); ensuring that the responsibility for CPERS does not 'fall between the cracks' of other Battlegroup level officers.

The role must not, however, dilute the responsibility of the Commanding Officer. The role should not be carried out by the intelligence officer or the unit coordinator of tactical questioning. The detention officer would be an existing Battlegroup officer who is given additional responsibilities.

Part XVI, paragraphs 16.274 – 16.293

Recommendation 41

On operations where CPERS may be taken there should be a Senior Non-Commisioned Officer (NCO) who acts as the "Detention Sergeant" who has responsibility for the administrative aspects of CPERS handling. In most cases, it would be appropriate for the Regimental Provost Sergeant to fulfil this role.

I recognise that if MPS numbers are sufficient, members of the MPS would be extremely well qualified to fulfil it. RMP NCOs might also do so.

Part XVI, paragraphs 16.294 – 16.307

Recommendation 42

Before any deployed operation, the Commanding Officer must ensure that there is a clear written explanation of unit level responsibilities for CPERS. If responsibilities are changed during an enduring operation this should be recorded.

Part XVI, paragraph 16.307

Recommendation 43

The PM(A) and those who in his name carry out inspections of the main operational detention facilities should be expressly recognised as having the right and duty to inspect CPERS handling throughout the detention process including during interrogation.

Part XVI, paragraphs 16.310 – 16.312

Recommendation 44

In the ongoing deliberations as to what arrangements should be made for external inspection of main operational detention facilities, the fullest consideration should be given to:

(1) **the significant benefit that Her Majesty's Inspector of Prisons (HMIP) involvement in the inspection process would bring; and**

(2) **the fact that while inspecting operational detention facilities may involve compromises to, and divergence from, HMIP's normal practice, certain practical realities (e.g. inspection only with a warning; CPERS who may very well be distrustful of *any* inspector from the UK; and limitations on visiting some areas in theatre) would apply to anybody that undertook the inspection role.**

Were it to be the case that HMIP did not feel able to fulfil the inspection role for the main theatre detention facilities, the MoD should urgently consider other routes to achieving independent inspection/validation of those facilities by the best means that can be achieved short of full HMIP involvement.

Part XVI, paragraphs 16.313 – 16.320

Recommendation 45

The PM(A) and the in theatre FPM should take account of the in theatre situation in assessing whether any unannounced MPS inspections of forward detention facilities would be feasible and beneficial. The unit detention officer, as part of his advisory and oversight responsibilities, should be able to carry out less formal checks at unit and sub-unit level on CPERS handling including how unit holding areas are being run and whether proper custody records are being kept.

Part XVI, paragraphs 16.321 – 16.324

Recommendation 46

The MoD should consider whether the lessons learned procedures need to be adjusted or supplemented so that the clearer and more urgent lessons and changes to previous practice are fed back far more quickly both to the operational theatre and into the pre-deployment training cycle.

Part VIII, paragraph 8.513

General Training

Recommendation 47

CPERS training should include both theoretical and practical training in what Forces personnel can and should do when handling CPERS.

It is important that training is not limited to prohibitions but conveys good practice, permitted activities and how CPERS handling should be carried out.

Part XVI, paragraphs 16.90, 16.351(1)(a)

Recommendation 48

CPERS training should be woven into the full range of military exercises and training. Such training should be "end to end", not just focused on planning and the actual combat/public order side of the operation, but including what happens after a CPERS is captured. Practical exercises should not routinely end with the enemy or insurgent being captured, as often appears to have been the case before 2003. Exercises for commanders need to test and train them in CPERS handling issues and problems, including in the command and control of tactical questioning. This should be a particular priority for mission specific training.

Part XVI, paragraph 16.351(1)(b)

Recommendation 49

Training materials across the Services need to be reviewed to ensure that the messages about all aspects of CPERS handling are clear and consistent.

The arrangement now agreed whereby the PM(A) will act as a coordinator and validator of prisoner handling training should assist in bringing greater consistency to the training materials. There are currently too many inconsistencies between different training materials. To some extent this may be explained by the recent pace of change and improvements in training materials.

Part XVI, paragraphs 16.337 – 16.340, 16.351(2)

Recommendation 50

The MATT 7 PowerPoint presentation on the five techniques should be amended to ensure that the definitions of the techniques are consistent with amendments to JDP 1-10; that it is clear that the techniques are not only prohibited as aids to interrogation (in particular hooding is prohibited in all circumstances) and so that the background information section is fully accurate.

Part XVI, paragraphs 16.328-332, 16.351(3)

Recommendation 51

The 2005 prisoner handling DVD should be amended to avoid misleading messages about sight deprivation in the context of interrogation, and the inappropriate presentation of the interrogation facility. Where such training materials touch on specialist areas such as tactical questioning and interrogation, the relevant subject matter experts should be consulted. "Bagged and tagged" is an ambiguous phrase which should not be used. In reviewing the DVD, consideration should also be given to:

(1) whether the prohibition on the five techniques might be incorporated into the film; and

(2) whether all of the CPERS handling within the DVD is commensurate with best practice, allowing for the need for realism and that CPERS treatment in military operations may in circumstances need to be firm as well as fair.

From disclosure provided shortly before finalisation of this Report, it appears that the MoD has already made improvements to this DVD but it remains appropriate that it should be thoroughly reviewed.

Part XVI, paragraphs 16.333 - 16.334, 16.351(4)

Recommendation 52

Greater clarity and guidance should be given in training in relation to the concept of "restraint positions". More must be done to give practical guidance to help service personnel distinguish between unlawful stress positions, on the one hand, and the legitimate use of force to effect a search, or an arrest or prevent assault or escape, on the other. They need guidance on common sense precautions for preventing assault or escape at the point of capture where arresting UK Forces might be outnumbered.

In my opinion "restraint positions" is not a helpful phrase. Where outnumbered at the point of capture it may be legitimate to make CPERS sit with hands on their heads or sit on their hands, provided that such positions can be changed from time to time so that they do not become painful or extremely uncomfortable.

Part XVI, paragraphs 16.329 – 16.332, 16.351(5)

Recommendation 53

MATT 7 and mission specific training for CPERS handling should incorporate suitably pitched training on the risks of positional asphyxia/death by struggle against restraint.

Part XVI, paragraphs 16.330, 16.351(6)

Recommendation 54

There needs to be better recording of the take-up of MATT 7 (and equivalent training) to avoid the need to rely upon Reception Staging and Onward Interrogation (RSOI) training in CPERS handling.

MATT 7 training, and its equivalent for the other Services, and mission specific training, is only of use if it is correctly received by all those who may deploy.

Part XVI, paragraph 16.351(7)

Recommendation 55

Those responsible for designing the mandatory operational law and values and standards training must keep the training relevant and up-to-date both in its content and in the style and means of delivery.

Part XVI, paragraph 16.351(8)

Recommendation 56

Unit commanders should ensure that the annual operational law training is delivered to the highest standards, so as to avoid it becoming stale or routine. Different media should be used to keep the materials fresh and up-to-date.

I acknowledge that there is a balance to be struck between keeping the materials fresh by offering some variety in what is presented, and always ensuring that the key elements are trained consistently each year.

Part XVI, paragraph 16.351(9)

Recommendation 57

Training soldiers to maintain or prolong the shock of capture is apt to be misunderstood and should not feature in general training. Phrases such as "calm, neutral and professional" and "firm, fair and efficient" can properly be used as shorthand for those involved in CPERS handling.

Part XVI, paragraph 16.351(10)

Recommendation 58

MATT 6 training should include discussion and role play scenarios relevant to moral courage. Training materials should include reference to occasions when UK troops have breached the Law of Armed Conflict (LOAC) to avoid any risk of complacency about the conduct of UK Forces.

Part XVI, paragraphs 16.343 – 16.350

Tactical questioning and interrogation training

Recommendation 59

Enhanced auditing of tactical questioning and interrogation training should be introduced to ensure that the interrogation branch at Chicksands adequately trains students including in the proper limits of approaches, what constitutes a threat to a CPERS, and how self induced and system induced pressures are approached.

Part XVI, paragraphs 16.357 – 16.363

Recommendation 60

The annual legal review of training materials planned by Defence Intelligence and Security Centre (DISC) is a necessary step which I commend. It must, however, include a rigorous scrutiny of the detail of the presentations and speaking notes used on the tactical questioning and interrogation courses.

Part XVI, paragraph 16.363(5)

Recommendation 61

A more senior and more independent legal review of the kind now being conducted as a one off *ad hoc* review is also required. Such a review should not be necessary on an annual basis but should provide a suitable measure of further assurance if conducted every three years.

Part XVI, paragraph 16.363(6)

Recommendation 62

DISC should take immediate remedial action to ensure that:

(1)   old versions of interrogation branch teaching materials are retained but archived separately from current, in-use teaching materials;

(2)   interrogation branch teaching materials are always dated; and

(3)   when legal advice, policy changes, or internal reviews require changes to interrogation branch materials, the changes are checked for accuracy and made consistently across the body of training materials.

Part XVI, paragraphs 16.364 – 16.375

Recommendation 63

The tactical questioning and interrogation courses must train students adequately in all approaches that they may be required to use operationally. The current compromise whereby tactical questioning students are given an idea of the harsh approach but not trained fully in it should cease. To the extent that MoD may choose to retain the harsh approach (whether for interrogation or tactical questioning) the courses must take particular care to teach the limits of the approach including the new parameters following the MoD's legal review.

As set out in Recommendation 23, above, I recommend that the harsh approach is no longer approved for use by tactical questioners.

Part XVI, paragraphs 16.376 – 16.382

Recommendation 64

The MoD should give further careful consideration to the examples used in training for bridging between questioning sessions to ensure that they comply with the Geneva Conventions.

Part XVI, paragraphs 16.383 – 16.387

Recommendation 65

"Conditioning" should cease to be used as an approved Chicksands or HUMINT term.

The term is dangerously ambiguous since it can be used to refer to unlawful means of putting pressure on a prisoner as well the intended meaning of the legitimate use of existing pressures. The tactical questioning and interrogation course should explain that "conditioning" should not be used because of its dangerous ambiguity.

Part XVI, paragraphs 16.388 – 16.390

Recommendation 66

DISC should give consideration to avoiding the terminology "maintain the shock of capture" and "prolong the shock of capture" even in their own courses. As a minimum, students on the tactical questioning and interrogation courses should be expressly warned of the dangers of unqualified personnel misunderstanding these phrases. Tactical questioners and interrogators, in dealing with capturing or guarding personnel, must emphasise swift handling up the CPERS chain and firm, fair and efficient handling not prolonging or maintaining the shock of capture.

Part XVI, paragraphs 16.391 – 16.395

Supplementary Note In Respect of Tactical Questioning and Interrogation Training

Without forming part of my formal recommendations, Part XVI Annex 1 contains a number of more detailed comments on interrogation branch training materials on which I invite the MoD to give consideration.

Survive, Evade, Resist and Extract Training

Recommendation 67

All theoretical and practical resistance training must include a warning which explains in terms that the training is to show conduct that can be expected of a non-Geneva Conventions compliant enemy and does not reflect the standards required of British and NATO forces. Any of this training which uses, illustrates or refers to the use of any of the prohibited techniques should include a specific reminder of the prohibition on the five techniques and a reminder to personnel to abide by their MATT 7 training (or equivalent) in how they treat CPERS.

Part XVI, paragraphs 16.405 – 16.413

Recommendation 68

When reviewing the current Survive, Evade, Resist and Extract (SERE) DVD, Defence Survival Training Organisation (DSTO) should take into account the latest developments in tactical questioning and interrogation policy. DSTO

should seek to ensure that, without affecting the realism of the training material, more care is taken to avoid using language in the SERE DVD which is also used (with a different meaning) in tactical questioning and interrogation training. Such ambiguity of terms may be confusing for those receiving the training and should be avoided as far as possible.

Part XVI, paragraph 16.413(3)

Recommendation 69

The MoD must make all units aware that, not only is DSTO the only body trained to provide resistance training, but that if any escape and evasion training is carried out it must under no circumstances involve, whether at the point of "capture" or otherwise, the use of any of the prohibited five techniques nor any element of conduct after capture or resistance to interrogation training.

Part XVI, paragraph 16.413(4)

Regimental Police/Unit Provost Staff Training

Recommendation 70

The Military Correction Training Centre (MCTC) should continue to monitor that breakaway, personal protection and control and restraint techniques taught on the All Arms Unit Custody Staff Course (AAUCSC) are appropriate having regard to a realistic assessment of the number of unit custody staff who are likely to be on duty (whether in a firm base or on operations).

Part XVI, paragraphs 16.418 – 16.424

Recommendation 71

Refresher training for unit custody staff in whichever breakaway, personal protection and control and restraint techniques they are taught on the AAUCSC should now be rolled out ensuring that there is proper take up and recording of those who attend it.

Part XVI, paragraphs 16.423 – 16.424

Recommendation 72

Unit Detention Sergeants (see recommendation 41) should be properly trained in CPERS handling practices.

Part XVI, paragraph 16.424(3)

Recommendation 73

In reducing the number of firm base unit custody facilities, the MoD should be careful not to erode the unit level operational detention expertise which is provided to a Battlegroup by the attendance of unit provost staff on the AAUCSC, unless the equivalent expertise can be provided to each Battlegroup by the MPS.

Part XVI, paragraph 16.424(4)

Summary of Findings

1. Baha Mousa was a 26 year old Iraqi. He was a hotel receptionist in Basra and father of two young children. His wife died in February 2003, a month before British Forces took part in Op Telic. Early in the morning of Sunday 14 September 2003, Baha Mousa was arrested following a weapons find on Op Salerno, a series of hotel searches carried out by British Forces in Basra. Along with others, Baha Mousa was taken to the Temporary Detention Facility (TDF) at Battlegroup Main (BG Main), the headquarters of 1 Queen's Lancashire Regiment (QLR). He arrived at the TDF at about 10.40hrs that Sunday morning. He spent the most part of the next 36 hours "hooded" with a hessian sandbag over his head. He was forced to adopt "stress positions", a term used to describe any posture which someone is forced to maintain which becomes painful, extremely uncomfortable or exhausting over time. Both techniques had been banned as aids to interrogation more than 30 years earlier. During his detention, Baha Mousa was subjected to violent and cowardly abuse and assaults by British servicemen whose job it was to guard him and treat him humanely. At about 21.40hrs on 15 September 2003, following a final struggle and further assaults, Baha Mousa stopped breathing. By that time he was in the centre room of the TDF, a small disused toilet, quite unfit as a place to hold a prisoner. All reasonable attempts were made to resuscitate Baha Mousa, to no avail. He was pronounced dead at 22.05hrs. A subsequent post mortem examination of his body found that he had sustained 93 external injuries. Nine other Iraqis were detained with him. All were subject to significant abuse. They all sustained injuries, physical and/or mental, some of them serious. These grave and shameful events were the subject of this Public Inquiry.

The Purpose and Approach of this Summary

2. This Report is a lengthy document and therefore it seems to me appropriate and sensible to provide a Summary which sets out comparatively briefly my findings and conclusions relating to the more significant aspects of the Inquiry. It is not intended to be a substitute for the full Report, still less a Summary of all that I have considered and reviewed. Further, this Summary will not refer to the detailed evidence, whether of witnesses or documentary exhibits, as the full referencing will be found in the relevant Parts of the Report.

3. It follows that important matters may not be referred to here at all or only dealt with in part. This Summary takes a relatively broad approach and an editorial line demanding brevity and for obvious reasons, therefore, I do not repeat all the issues or detail which appear in the main body of the Report. I should make it clear, that if this brevity results in any actual or perceived shade of difference of meaning or emphasis as between the Summary and the full Report, it is the latter which fully and accurately expresses my intended findings and conclusions. Further, I point out that when it comes to criticism of individuals, it is very important that reference is made to the full text of the criticism in the appropriate Part of the Report.

4. Similarly, since the Introduction at Part I of this Report sets out a brief history leading to the setting up of this Inquiry as well as outlining my tasks and my approach to them, I need not repeat the matters there set out.

5. The issues addressed in this Summary need to be understood in the operational context in which they occurred: the tempo of operations; the poor state of the local

civilian infrastructure; a daily threat to life from both civilian unrest and an increasing insurgency; the deaths of fellow service personnel and incessant oppressive heat. In combination these factors made huge demands on soldiers serving in Iraq in 2003 as I detail in Part I Chapter 4 of this Report.

6. In this Summary, I propose to summarise as fairly as I can the events of 14 to 16 September, setting out in general terms my findings and comments on the responsibility of individual members of 1 QLR. I propose also to set out these events in the context of the historical background of the prohibition on the so-called "conditioning techniques", how relevant doctrine and guidance then developed, leading up to the orders and guidance that were in place before Op Telic. I shall also review my findings on teaching and training and its adequacy in respect of prisoner handling and the Law of Armed Conflict (LOAC), touching upon issues relating to those responsible for training and carrying out tactical questioning and interrogation. In addition I shall briefly turn to events in Iraq, and the pre-invasion orders and guidance developed, including in the handover between units and formations between Op Telic 1 and Op Telic 2. I will consider the knowledge and use of conditioning techniques and what has been termed the Brigade sanction. Finally, I shall make reference to the events following the death of Baha Mousa.

7. The order of the matters summarised, with some exceptions, follows the order of the Parts of the main Report.

The Events of 14 to 16 September 2003 (Part II)

The Arrests and Transfer to BG Main and the TDF

8. On 14 September 2003, 1 QLR undertook Op Salerno, an operation seeking to identify and arrest specific individuals suspected of being former regime loyalists (FRLs) involved in terrorist activities in Basra. It involved searches of hotels thought to be harbouring these individuals. One of the hotels searched by 1 QLR was the Hotel Ibn Al Haitham (the Hotel). 1 QLR did not find any of the targeted individuals there, but following the discovery of weaponry and other suspicious items it arrested seven male Iraqi civilians, including Baha Mousa, at the Hotel.

9. The search and arrests were carried out inside the Hotel by a multiple from A Company, 1 QLR with the radio call-sign "G10A". The multiple was commanded by Lt Craig Rodgers and has therefore come to be known as "the Rodgers Multiple".[1] Another multiple under the command of CSgt Christopher Hollender, but on this day commanded by Cpl Kelvin Stacey, provided perimeter security outside the Hotel. The brigadier who commanded 19 Mech Bde, of which 1 QLR was a part, Brig William Moore, was present for at least a part of the operation, observing from the roof of the Hotel. 1 QLR's Commanding Officer, Lt Col Jorge Mendonça, and the soldiers who accompanied him on patrol, known as his TAC group, were in the Hotel's vicinity.

10. These seven Detainees were employed or connected with the Hotel as follows: D001 as a cleaner and part-time guard; D002 as night watchman; D003 as the restaurant manager; D004 with responsibility for the generator; Kifah Matairi as the electrician;

---

[1] The expression "the Rodgers Multiple" has been used as convenient short hand for the Inquiry to describe G10A. Findings relating to individuals within the Rodgers Multiple do not imply findings relating to Craig Rodgers unless that is explicitly stated.

Ahmad Matairi as a co-owner of the Hotel; and Baha Mousa as the night receptionist. C001, the son of another co-owner, D006, was initially present at the Hotel but escaped.

11. The search of the Hotel revealed a number of weapons, ammunition, grenades, other military equipment, money, and fake identification cards. It was after these items were discovered, some of them concealed within a telecommunications shop in the premises and under his control, that C001 fled.

12. The Detainees make allegations of ill-treatment in the foyer and degrading treatment in the toilet at the Hotel, the detail of which I set out in the Report. To a limited extent some soldiers confirmed that there were relatively minor assaults and others that some Detainees were taken to the toilet.

13. In respect of the events at the Hotel, I conclude the following. The nature of the weaponry and military paraphernalia discovered justified the decision to arrest these Detainees. However, I regard it as highly unlikely that the Detainees or any of them were in fact involved in insurgent or terrorist activity.

14. Notwithstanding inconsistencies in the evidence of the Detainees concerning events at the Hotel, I find that there were some low-level assaults on some of the Detainees while they were lying on the floor of the reception area. Further, some of the Detainees, even if not all, were taken to the Hotel toilet area, and it is likely they were taken there in order to humiliate them. I am satisfied that toilet water was flushed over at least some of the Detainees.

15. Although I consider that some of the soldiers must have known about the abuse at the Hotel, and some must have taken part in it, the lack of satisfactory evidence makes it impossible and unfair to identify any particular soldier.

16. The 1 QLR radio logs for that morning reveal that guidance was sought by A Company in relation to the manner in which the Detainees were to be conveyed from the Hotel for tactical questioning. It was directed that the Detainees were not to be hooded and at this stage they were not. At around 10.00hrs, D001, D002, D004, Baha Mousa, Kifah Matairi and Ahmad Matairi were taken by truck to 1 QLR BG Main. They were to remain at BG Main for approximately 48 hours, until they and the other Detainees were transferred to the Theatre Internment Facility (TIF) at Um Qasr, 70 or so kilometres from BG Main.

The Arrest of D006 and D005

17. D006 and D005 are respectively the father and brother of the escaped C001. After the escape, D003 indicated to Lt Michael Crosbie, the A Company Intelligence Officer, that he knew where C001 lived. D003 therefore went with Crosbie to C001's house. A forced entry, known as a "hard knock", was made on the house. I find that this was justified in the circumstances. I find that this violent entry resulted in broken and smashed furniture, but there is insufficient evidence to conclude that there was any physical mistreatment of D005 and D006, who occupied the house, while they were there.

18. D003, D006 and D005 were then taken to Camp Stephen, A Company's base. During this journey I find that an implied threat of physical violence was made to D003 by

Crosbie, and that an unidentified soldier struck D003 with a glancing blow to the face. It is possible that Crosbie did not see this assault.

Events at Camp Stephen

19. D003 remained at Camp Stephen for only a short time before being transferred to BG Main. D005 and D006 were held at Camp Stephen for approximately two hours before being transferred to BG Main. D005 alleged that he was mistreated at Camp Stephen, although the detail of his allegations has varied in different accounts he has given. In respect of these allegations I accept that he was made to remain in a stress position for a lengthy period, but I am unable to make any finding of further abuse here.

The Arrest of Maitham

20. Ahmed Maitham became the tenth Detainee when he was arrested at around 21:00hrs on Sunday night. Soldiers from B Company, 1 QLR, in a multiple led by Sgt Stephen Wilding, noted that the vehicle being driven by Maitham matched the description of a stolen vehicle. They found in the vehicle three AK 47 rifles, a quantity of ammunition, balaclavas and some paperwork. Maitham explained that his vehicle, with him in it, had been hijacked by armed men who had fled, leaving the weapons, after the car was involved in an accident.

21. Maitham was first taken to a local police station, and then to BG Main. Although Maitham has given inconsistent accounts of his treatment during this period and his explanation for the presence of weapons in the vehicle was implausible, I make no finding that he was involved in any insurgent activity. However, I reject the allegation that he made of mistreatment during his transfer to BG Main.

Arrival at the TDF, 1 QLR BG Main

22. D001, D002, D004, Kifah Matairi, Ahmad Matairi and Baha Mousa arrived at BG Main at about 10.40hrs on Sunday 14 September 2003. They were received by Cpl Donald Payne, a member of the Regimental Provost Staff, and taken into an unfurnished building; the TDF. First D003, and then D005 and D006, were brought to the TDF later that Sunday. They were finally joined by Maitham later on Sunday evening.

The detainees' accounts of their treatment

23. With a few exceptions, which I set out in the body of the Report, I found the Detainees' accounts of their treatment at BG Main to be broadly accurate. Omitting for now the aspects which I rejected, or making it clear where I have rejected their evidence, those accounts may be summarised as follows.

24. D001 described being hooded on arrival and soon thereafter being beaten and having his feet kicked into a stress position. He said that this treatment was continuous up to the time of Baha Mousa's death on Monday evening. D001 also referred to the Detainees being arranged in a circle on their knees, and soldiers going around the circle hitting and kicking the Detainees; causing them to emit groans and other noises and thereby playing them like musical instruments. This was undoubtedly a description

of a practice which was labelled by the soldiers who were involved as "the choir". D001 recalled being given water, but only remembered being fed once, at breakfast on the second day.

25. D002 has suffered severe Post Traumatic Stress Disorder (PTSD) as a result of his arrest and detention in the TDF. Despite attempting on two separate occasions to give oral evidence to the Inquiry, it proved to be a very difficult and traumatic experience. I have no doubt that those difficulties were genuine. D002 nevertheless managed to confirm the truth of his Inquiry witness statement. He described having three sacks placed over his head and being forced to maintain a stress position. He was hit and kicked if he dropped his arms. He described being pulled up from the ground by the sandbag ties around his neck, which felt as if he was being strangled. D002 stated that he had been repeatedly hit on the head by the soldier accompanying him to and from his tactical questioning session. CSgt Robert Livesey has admitted to punching D002 twice in the head at this time. D002 also stated that his teeth had been broken when he was punched in the mouth, although no broken teeth were identified during D002's medical examination a week later. He also stated that he was made to run around and dance.

26. D003 also recalled being hooded with first two, then three hoods, and that the beating and ill treatment started immediately and continued throughout the day and night. He was hit if he failed to maintain a stress position and also struck with a metal bar. D003 also said that he had been taunted and insulted, and made to dance.

27. D004 said that he had two hoods placed over his head. He was beaten and kicked and subjected to suffocating holds. The abuse had started very shortly after entering the TDF and it continued throughout the three days. He said he had suffered broken ribs and swollen kidneys, however a contemporaneous medical examination did not record his ribs being broken and the level of injuries he sustained does not match the level of beatings which he alleges.

28. D004 also was made to "dance", and was the subject of photographs in which soldiers posed as if about to punch him.

29. Ahmad Matairi also described having more than one hood put on his head and being kicked and punched throughout his detention. He was suffering from a hernia, and this began to swell. There is no medical evidence to support his evidence that his ribs were broken as he asserted. Nevertheless, for the most part his evidence fits into the spectrum of complaints made by other Detainees.

30. Kifah Matairi sadly died following an unrelated accident in 2005. He had, however, described the treatment he experienced in statements to the Special Investigation Branch (SIB) of the Royal Military Police (RMP), who investigated Baha Mousa's death and in a statement provided for judicial review proceedings. He described being hooded and forced to maintain a stress position involving his arms being held out and his knees being bent at 45 degrees. He was kicked repeatedly to the kidney area, abdomen, ribs and genitals whenever his arms dropped, and he had his eyes gouged.

31. Kifah Matairi also recounted how he had petrol rubbed under his nose, fluid poured over his head and a lighter held to his head with the intention, he thought, of causing him to believe he was about to be set alight.

32. D005, the youngest at eighteen years old, said that he was hooded and beaten. Between his tactical questioning sessions, he was compelled to sit next to a hot and noisy generator. He alleged that he was later placed in the middle room of the TDF and forced to squat with his face directly over the hole in the ground which formed the toilet. D005's account of the physical assaults perpetrated on him was undermined by the lack of discernable injuries recorded in the medical examination conducted soon after being in the TDF. Nevertheless, much of his evidence fits with the evidence of other Detainees.

33. D006 suffered from pre-existing arteriosclerosis. On reception into the TDF his pills were taken for safekeeping by Payne, and he and D005 were put into the left-hand room and hooded. He stated that he was beaten with a torch on the head and back, and kicked. D006 collapsed on Monday morning and was prescribed aspirin and propranolol. Photographs revealed no serious injuries or marks of injuries on his body. While I am sure he believed his evidence to be accurate and truthful, I find that his understandable resentment has caused him to exaggerate the mistreatment and injuries which he suffered. However, I do not doubt that he was the victim of some abuse probably falling short of beatings.

34. Maitham arrived at the TDF later than the other Detainees. He saw other Detainees hooded and in stress positions. He was hooded soon after arrival and was then beaten and kicked. He thought his beatings continued throughout Sunday night, and became intermittent on Monday. He also described a soldier putting fingers into his mouth. Maitham suggested in his second statement to the Inquiry that Sgt Ray Smulski had slapped him during the tactical questioning process, but this was the first time that such an allegation had been made, and Maitham had previously said that he had not been beaten in the tactical questioning room. I find this allegation not proved. That incident aside, and although bearing in mind my findings concerning the lack of credibility in Maithaim's evidence about the circumstances of his arrest, the rest of Maitham's account fits into the general pattern of the evidence of the other Detainees.

35. In each case, I bear in mind the likely disorientation experienced by a Detainee who was hooded for lengthy periods of time and deprived of sleep, and the effect that may have on his ability accurately to remember the length and extent of any ill treatment. Further, I accept that the Detainees may have discussed what occurred among themselves and that there is a possibility of some exaggeration by them. I accept also submissions made on behalf of Core Participants that the beatings and enforcement of stress positions cannot have been incessant.

36. That said, it is clear that there are underlying themes common to the accounts of all the Detainees and in some cases there is strong supporting medical evidence of injuries, both physical and psychiatric.

The Injuries to the Detainees

37. On 21 September 2003, Dr Ian Hill OBE, an accredited Home Office pathologist, conducted an autopsy on the body of Baha Mousa. In a report dated 11 February 2004, Dr Hill provided his findings and also reported on the other Detainees he had physically examined on 22 September. In addition he commented on photographs showing injuries to the Detainees he had not himself physically examined that day.

38. In addition, the psychiatric injuries to the surviving Detainees and the father of Baha Mousa, Col Daoud Mousa, have been assessed and reported upon by a consultant psychiatrist named Dr Mohamed Adib Essali and by a Professor of Epidemiological and Liaison Psychiatry named Professor Simon Wessely.

39. A detailed summary of the findings is found at Part II, Chapter 7 of the Report. On any view, it is plain that serious physical injury was inflicted on a number of these Detainees and that the effect of the attacks was the understandable onset of psychiatric damage or disturbance to most or all of them as well as to Baha Mousa's father.

40. I conclude that the generality of the medical evidence demonstrates beyond doubt that most, if not all, of the Detainees were the victims of serious abuse and mistreatment by soldiers during their detention in the TDF.

Events on the Detainees' Arrival at the TDF: Late Sunday Morning

41. When the Detainees arrived at BG Main, they were processed into the TDF under the supervision of Payne and other soldiers, including Stacey, the acting Commander of the Hollender Multiple.

42. The first six Detainees were placed in the right-hand room, hooded and placed into stress positions. The stress position used at this point is sometimes referred to as the "ski position". It involved the Detainees squatting with their knees bent and their arms held in front of them parallel to the floor. A sandbag, or in some cases two or three sandbags, were placed over each individual's head. When D003 arrived at around 11.51hrs, he was hooded and placed in the right-hand room, and when D005 and D006 arrived they were hooded and placed in the left-hand room. D005 and D006 were later to be joined in this room by Maitham.

43. Payne supervised the reception of the Detainees, put hoods over their heads and placed them in stress positions. On the day he gave his oral evidence to the Inquiry, Payne produced a further witness statement which disclosed that each time he returned to the TDF he had enforced the stress positions with greater force than he had hitherto been prepared to admit. In oral evidence he admitted that he routinely kicked and punched the Detainees each time he returned to the TDF. I am entirely satisfied that the actions of Payne went beyond the mere rigorous enforcement of stress positions and into the realm of assault. While he would not admit that this behaviour by him started before Sunday evening I reject his evidence on this point and find that it started soon after the Detainees' arrival at the TDF.

44.   Stacey assisted Payne in returning the Detainees to their stress positions when they fell over or dropped their arms. I also find that Stacey kicked Detainees' legs back into the stress position.

45.   Pte Johnathan Lee, a member of the Hollender Multiple, admitted punching a Detainee, about 30 minutes after their arrival.

46.   Although I find that it is likely that assaults on the Detainees did start from the moment they were placed in the TDF, it is not possible for me to identify any individual soldiers other than Pte Lee and Payne as responsible for these assaults.

The Fallon and Crowcroft Stag: Sunday Afternoon

47.   Most of the soldiers who delivered the Detainees to BG Main, including Stacey, departed after an uncertain period in the region of one to two hours.

48.   Thereafter, while the Detainees remained in the TDF they were guarded by soldiers either from the Hollender Multiple or from the Rodgers Multiple, who were supervised on an intermittent basis by Payne. Guard duties were divided into periods of time called "stags", consisting of two or three allocated soldiers. The evidence suggests that these stags were not rigidly adhered to and that other members of the relevant Multiple assisted with the guard duty from time to time.

49.   Pte Darren Fallon and Pte Wayne Crowcroft manned the first stag. They were told by Payne to make sure that the Detainees did not speak, and that they be kept awake and in stress positions. I have no doubt that the conduct of Payne in forcefully enforcing the stress positions was the example followed by Fallon and Crowcroft. Both Fallon and Crowcroft denied kicking or punching the Detainees, or seeing anyone else assault them; but they accepted that the Detainees were manhandled into stress positions and kept hooded. As I explain below, I reject their evidence that they neither saw nor participated in assaults.

The Payne Video

50.   The Inquiry has seen a video clip depicting Payne shouting, swearing and manhandling into stress positions six of the hooded Detainees in the right-hand room of the TDF. I find that the video was filmed at around 12.00hrs on Sunday 14 September 2003 and therefore near the start of the Fallon and Crowcroft stag. They must have witnessed this type of behaviour. Further, I suspect they know who took the video but have declined to tell the Inquiry.

Other Incidents during Sunday Afternoon

51.   Lt Douglas Ingram, the 1 QLR A Company Crime Officer, visited the TDF and witnessed a soldier punch a Detainee in the stomach. It is probable that this soldier was either Fallon or Crowcroft. Ingram reported this punch to Maj Michael Peebles, the Battlegroup Internment Review Officer (BGIRO). LCpl Simon Kendrick from the Intelligence Cell of 1 QLR went into the TDF to photograph the Detainees. He noticed slight cuts and bruises on their faces, but did not report this state of affairs further than the photographic record he captured which was passed up the Intelligence Cell

and on to the Joint Forward Interrogation Team (JFIT). Kendrick went into the TDF several times during Sunday, witnessing the Detainees' condition steadily deteriorate as they were forcefully kept in stress positions. This must also have been obvious to Fallon and Crowcroft. In Part II, Chapter 7 there is a table which collates some of the key evidence about the extent to which the Detainees' deteriorating condition would have been visible to those present at the TDF.

52. At one point during Sunday afternoon, Fallon said that one of the Detainees lunged at him, as if making a rugby tackle, in an attempt to escape. Fallon and Crowcroft wrestled with the Detainee and put him face down lying on the floor. It is probable that this Detainee was Baha Mousa. Pte Craig Slicker admitted punching this Detainee in the stomach after being informed that he had tried to escape.

53. Crosbie described to the Inquiry visiting the TDF to check on D005 and D006. I find that it is likely that this occurred late on Sunday afternoon. A guard demonstrated to Crosbie "the choir" by kicking the Detainees on their backs causing them to make some noise such as a cry or groan. Crosbie then left the TDF as he thought what he had seen was distasteful. He assumed the soldier would stop, but he took no action to stop him nor did he report what he had seen. This was a serious and inexcusable breach of duty.

54. Peebles visited the TDF three or four times on Sunday. The third occasion was at around 16.30hrs. This was after he had been told by Brigade that the Detainees were not thought to be "friendlies". He told Crowcroft and Fallon that the Detainees might be connected with the murder of three Royal Military Policemen. This was an ill-judged comment to make to the guards as it ran the obvious risk of causing the guards to seek some retribution for the RMP killings. Final submissions on behalf of the MoD acknowledged that in fact none of the Detainees was implicated by evidence in the death of any British personnel.

55. The Inquiry also heard evidence from Pte Lee that on their return to Camp Stephen after the guard duty, Fallon and Crowcroft had boasted that they had punched and kicked the Detainees. Pte Gareth Hill, another member of the Hollender Multiple, had given similar evidence in a statement to the SIB, although this part of his account had changed by the time that he gave evidence to the Inquiry. Despite their denials I find that Fallon and Crowcroft did boast about assaulting the Detainees.

56. Moreover, I find that in November 2005 Crowcroft also told WO2 Paul Urey words to the effect, "We all kicked him to death". Crowcroft gave a different version of this conversation but I prefer Urey's account of it.

57. I conclude that during the Fallon and Crowcroft stag the Detainees were subjected to brutal assaults. It is possible that other soldiers were also involved, but I find that Fallon and Crowcroft witnessed these assaults and personally participated in them. The conduct displayed in the Payne video probably depicts less serious mistreatment or abuse than that used later by Payne, nevertheless it was an example of conduct towards the Detainees that was bound to affect the behaviour of the guards who saw it. I find that Payne was involved in the punching and kicking of the Detainees when he visited the TDF periodically throughout the Fallon and Crowcroft stag.

The Arrival of the Rodgers Multiple: the "Free for All"

58.   At 18.48hrs on Sunday the Rodgers Multiple left Camp Stephen to travel to BG Main to provide half the Multiple to serve as guards over Sunday night. In the hour that followed their arrival at the TDF, I find that a serious incident of violence against the Detainees took place involving members of the Multiple.

59.   Payne admitted punching the Detainees in the presence of the whole Rodgers Multiple, including Rodgers himself. He also asserted that about ten of the Multiple joined in with violent acts against the Detainees. It is obvious that the allegations made by Payne concerning misconduct by others must be considered with great caution. There is however evidence from some members of the Multiple relating to this violent incident which supports the conclusion that it was not only Payne who was responsible, as does the evidence of the Detainees themselves.

60.   Pte Christopher Allibone saw four or five soldiers punch Detainees. Pte Thomas Appleby said he saw Payne punching them and members of the Multiple shouting and swearing at them but not punching or kicking them. Pte Gareth Aspinall admitted that he had slapped the Detainees on this occasion. Pte Stuart MacKenzie also admitted that he had slapped them around the back of the head to shock them. I remain suspicious that both MacKenzie and Aspinall acted more violently than either was prepared to admit.

61.   Pte Aaron Cooper admitted throwing about ten punches. He said other members of the Multiple were also punching Detainees. He named some of those he said were responsible, including Rodgers, but his evidence on this particular issue was inconsistent and, in my judgment, too weak to be relied upon to identify the individual perpetrators.

62.   I do not accept that those who have admitted some violence during this incident, namely Payne, Pte Cooper, MacKenzie and Aspinall, were the only perpetrators of violence against the Detainees at this time. It is nevertheless not possible to determine with certainty the identity of those others who punched or kicked the Detainees.

63.   The evidence is insufficient for me to find that Rodgers took part in or was present during the course of the violence. However, in my view Rodgers, even were he not present, must have become aware of this incident, which had the characteristics of a "Free for All" affray, at the time or very soon afterwards. As the Multiple Commander, Rodgers bears a significant responsibility for this disgraceful breach of discipline.

Sunday Night from 20.00hrs to 06.00hrs

64.   During this period the Rodgers Multiple provided the guard. They were briefed by Payne to keep the Detainees hooded and in stress positions and to prevent them speaking to each other. The Detainees allege that they remained hooded, handcuffed and in stress positions and that they were beaten by their guards and prevented from sleeping.

65.   In addition, throughout Sunday night SSgt Mark Davies and Smulski carried out tactical questioning of the Detainees.

66. The first stag was conducted by Allibone and Pte Damien Kenny. In evidence, Allibone attempted to minimise what he had done. I strongly suspect that he was engaged in forcefully maintaining the stress positions. Kenny has very little memory of the events in question. I am unable to accept his assertions that no abuse of the Detainees took place and conclude that he must have seen the Detainees being abused, although it may be that he cannot now remember what he saw. There is insufficient evidence to determine whether Kenny took part in the assaults.

67. MacKenzie accepted the Detainees were handled firmly, and admitted that he slapped and hit them. Pte Cooper accepted the Detainees were kept in stress positions. He said that during his stag he began to feel guilty about what he and others had done to the Detainees during the "Free for All", and therefore did not punch them, but accepted he may have tapped them on the back of the neck with moderate force.

68. I accept that during this stag Pte Cooper and MacKenzie dealt with the Detainees less harshly than previously. However, I think it probable that throughout their first stag both MacKenzie and Pte Cooper used significant force to keep the Detainees awake and in stress positions.

69. Appleby admitted that during his stag with Reader between midnight and 02.00hrs, he gave the Detainees a "*tap*" to keep them awake. Reader conceded that he had slapped a Detainee with a hard blow when enforcing a stress position. In an interview with an SIB officer he had indicated that he had used violent actions such as kicking.

70. During Appleby and Reader's stag they were ordered by Smulski to take D005 outside the TDF and shout at him to disorientate him. I accept that the force used on D005 was not such as to cause him any serious or lasting physical injury, but this incident may have contributed, even if in a small way, to the consequent PTSD which I find D005 has suffered.

71. It is probable that Appleby and Reader used more force than they were prepared to admit in evidence and that the forcefulness of their actions when maintaining the stress positions amounted to abusive treatment of the Detainees.

72. At some point during the night time stags, D005 was placed kneeling with his head over the hole of the toilet in the middle room of the TDF. I am unable to determine the soldiers responsible for this. I do not think that this lasted for the whole night, as D005 stated, but whatever the length time, this was a cruel act and a horrible experience.

Monday Morning

73. At around 05.45hrs on Monday morning the remainder of the Rodgers Multiple returned to the vicinity of the TDF. The principal guards on Monday morning were Pte Jonathan Hunt and Pte Paul Stirland, with other members of the Multiple also in and around the TDF during this period.

74. LCpl Adrian Redfearn graphically described the state in which he found the Detainees. They looked as though they had been in a car crash, exhausted, some with visible injuries, and the conditions in the TDF were indescribable. By this time other witnesses had also noticed injuries to the Detainees; such evidence is summarised in the table in Part II, Chapter 7. In contrast to Redfearn, Rodgers only described seeing the Detainees seated on the floor, sweating and moaning. On this point, I prefer the

evidence of Redfearn; I am satisfied that Rodgers' description was both inaccurate and untruthful.

75. A Multiple driver, Cpl John Douglas, gave clear, unequivocal evidence describing the treatment of the Detainees. I find that he was probably referring to a period encompassing the whole stag on Monday morning and possibly the night time stags on Sunday night. He described shouting to keep the Detainees in stress positions. He confirmed that excessive force was used on the Detainees by many members of the Multiple, including punching, kicking and slapping. Douglas himself accepted slapping Detainees in order to enforce stress positions.

76. D005 and D006 were medically treated during Monday morning. D006 was examined by Cpl Steven Winstanley and after consultation with Dr Derek Keilloh, he was given asprin and propranolol. D005 was complaining of breathing difficulties and was also examined by a medic. However, when D005 thought he was going to be given some oxygen, an irritant, possibly fly killer, was sprayed on his nose. I accept that this incident occurred, but I do not find that Cpl Winstanley was responsible for it.

77. Redfearn said that he allowed the Detainees to rest out of the stress positions as often as he could. He had told the SIB that he had ordered their hoods to be removed, for them to be given water and allowed to lie down. I am sceptical about these assertions. He did say, however, that whenever Payne visited he countermanded these instructions. Redfearn denied using force or seeing the guards do so. However, I find that during Monday morning he himself did assault the Detainees.

78. Stirland said he had been told by the night time guards to give the Detainees a slap if they got out of hand. He admitted to slapping one of them around the head when he had managed to get free of his plasticuffs. Stirland denied using any other violence on the Detainees but said that he had seen Payne demonstrate the choir.

79. Fus Lee Richards was also a driver for the Multiple. Although his evidence was confused about dates and times I accept his account of some members of the Multiple striking the Detainees. In my judgment he saw this happen on Monday morning.

80. I find that during Monday morning the TDF was hot and smelt of urine. I accept Douglas' and Richards' evidence that Payne and members of the Rodgers Multiple assaulted the Detainees. With the exception of Redfearn, I find the evidence insufficient to identify the individuals responsible for these assaults. I am satisfied on the balance of probabilities that Redfearn, Pte Hunt and Stirland must have seen soldiers, in addition to Payne, assaulting the Detainees.

81. I think it probable that Pte Hunt knew the identity of some of those who assaulted the Detainees but has chosen not to reveal who they were. Moreover, he ought to have reported what he had seen up the chain of command. Similarly, I do not accept that Stirland has given full and accurate evidence about the state of the TDF or what happened. He too should have reported matters at that time.

82. In the case of Redfearn, I have preferred his evidence to that of Rodgers concerning the state of the Detainees and the conditions in the TDF on Monday morning. However, I prefer Richards' account over Redfearn's denial, that Redfearn did encourage the guards to treat the Detainees roughly and that he himself was involved in assaults on the Detainees during Monday morning.

Monday Afternoon

83. At around 13.00hrs on Monday, most of the Rodgers Multiple went back to Camp Stephen, leaving Aspinall, Pte Peter Bentham and Pte Lee Graham at the TDF to guard the Detainees until around 21.00hrs when the Rodgers Multiple returned.

84. Aspinall saw injuries to the Detainees, but maintained that apart from slapping the Detainees' faces on three or four occasions, he and his two fellow guards did not themselves assault them. He said that Payne aggressively enforced stress positions throughout the afternoon, and demonstrated to others the choir. Aspinall said that he had to leave at about 14.00hrs or 15.00hrs as he could no longer bear to stay in the TDF due to the deteriorating conditions and the violence.

85. Bentham was very reluctant to give a description of what he had witnessed. He accepted that the Detainees were hooded and kept in uncomfortable positions. He stated that during his guard the Detainees were allowed to relax, but that unidentified Non-Commissioned Officers (NCOs) from BG Main told them to keep the Detainees in stress positions. Again with reluctance, he conceded that he had seen Payne demonstrate the choir. Bentham said he did not hit any of the Detainees, nor did any soldiers from his Multiple.

86. Pte Lee Graham, notwithstanding previous detailed written statements, in evidence to the Inquiry claimed he had little recollection of the events in question. However, he confirmed that he was endeavouring to tell the truth when he made his SIB statement. In that statement he had described seeing Payne repeatedly kick the Detainees, and demonstrate the choir. Pte Lee Graham's SIB statement supported much of the Detainees' claims about their treatment during Monday. Pte Lee Graham, himself, admitted slapping Detainees to shock them back into stress positions. His statement also contained an allegation that SSgt Christopher Roberts, of the Commanding Officer's TAC group, entered the TDF and kicked three Detainees (I return to this allegation below).

The GMTV Group's Visit to the TDF on Monday Afternoon

87. Two independent groups of soldiers visited the TDF on Monday afternoon. The first comprised LCpl James Riley, LBdr Richard Betteridge and SAC Scott Hughes, members of a group of soldiers which was escorting a GMTV party visiting BG Main. All three entered the TDF.

88. All three heard shouting coming from the TDF, and saw Payne demonstrate the choir. Hughes went into the TDF twice. His description of what he saw went considerably further than LCpl Riley or Betteridge in describing the actions which occurred. He saw soldiers clicking their fingers and eliciting apparently trained responses from Detainees. He saw Payne karate chopping and pulling up by the eye sockets a Detainee nicknamed "*Granddad*". He also saw a Detainee with his hands and fingers plasticuffed, situated in the middle toilet room of the TDF. This latter Detainee was kicked in the genitals by Payne. I find this, probably, was Baha Mousa. Hughes identified Slicker, Bentham and Payne as soldiers involved in these incidents.

89. In so far as there are differences in degree between the conduct described by Hughes, Betteridge and LCpl Riley, this may be explained by Hughes spending more time in

the TDF and by an element of Betteridge and LCpl Riley playing down what they saw. Where there are material differences, I prefer Hughes' evidence.

90. I conclude that Payne did violently demonstrate the choir, and that he did assault a Detainee nicknamed "*Grandad*" (probably Kifah Matairi). He did so without apparent fear that his conduct might be reported up the chain of command. I find that it is more probable than not that Hughes correctly identified Bentham as having fiercely squeezed water into the mouths of two of the Detainees, and as having slapped two of the Detainees' heads and kicked most the Detainees' feet. I also find that D003 correctly identified Bentham as the guard who kicked him several times in the back and stomach on the second day.

91. Hughes, Betteridge and LCpl Riley ought to have intervened and reported what they had seen. It is some mitigation that Payne was senior in rank to them. Nevertheless, it is possible that if they had reported matters immediately, it might have prevented Baha Mousa's death.

The G5 Visit

92. The second group, known as the "G5" group, was comprised of Capt Chris Good, 1 QLR's Civil and Military Cooperation Officer, there to attend an O Group meeting, Cpl David Schofield, LCpl Dean Liggins and Pte Anthony Riley.

93. Schofield heard cries of distress coming from the TDF, and on entering it saw the Detainees hooded and restrained. A Detainee kneeling in the centre of the room was punched as hard as physically possible in the kidney area. Schofield did not intervene as he thought the soldier punching was of senior rank to him. But he told Good what he had seen, after Good's return from the O Group meeting.

94. Pte Riley heard screaming coming from the TDF. He saw a Detainee in the middle room with a number of injuries to the face. It is probable that this was Baha Mousa. He also saw Detainees hooded, handcuffed and kneeling facing the wall. A Detainee called "*Grandad*" was kneed in the back a number of times by a soldier.

95. Good agreed that Schofield had mentioned screams and shouts, but did not remember what Schofield had told him he had seen. On looking into the TDF himself, Good saw that some of the Detainees were injured but said that this was not unusual as Iraqis involved in crowd disturbances might have been kept in the camp. Good said that later that day he had expressed concerns about what he had seen to the Officer Commanding C Company, Maj Kenyon, but Kenyon had no recollection of such a conversation before Baha Mousa's death.

96. I conclude that the evidence of Schofield and Pte Riley was generally truthful and accurate. Liggins was not impressive as a witness and may also have confused this visit with a separate occasion on which he saw detainees at BG Main. Pte Riley immediately reported what he had seen to Schofield, his immediate superior. Likewise, Schofield reported to Good what he had seen.

97. I find it difficult to reconcile Good's evidence of what he saw with the evidence of Schofield and Pte Riley and others in relation to the condition and treatment of Detainees. In my view Good has sought to minimise the seriousness of what he saw.

In any event, he ought to have acted promptly and reported immediately to a more senior officer at BG Main.

98. The conditions in the TDF and the state of the Detainees deteriorated appreciably over the whole of Monday. The Detainees were kept hooded and forced to remain in stress positions throughout the day. Payne visited the TDF periodically to ensure that stress positions were maintained, and on a number of occasions he demonstrated the choir. Other 1 QLR soldiers, not from the Rodgers Multiple, also visited the TDF and it is possible that some of them also assaulted the Detainees.

Other Visitors to the TDF Before the Death

99. I accept the evidence of the guards that there were a number of other visitors to the TDF during the whole 36 hours who have not been identified, some from 1 QLR and some from other units. Of the identified visitors to the TDF there are some about whom it is uncertain precisely when they visited.

100. LCpl Ali Aktash visited the TDF, probably on Monday morning or early Monday afternoon. I have kept in mind the fact that Aktash admitted previously exaggerating his allegations when speaking to journalists, in particular claims that senior members of 1 QLR knew of and encouraged mistreatment of the Detainees. However, the evidence he gave concerning what he saw of the direct treatment of the Detainees in the TDF supports much of the evidence given by the Detainees and fits the general picture of the way in which the Detainees were treated. Aktash saw some of the Detainees in a stress position, with their arms out, being enforced by the guards and described kicking of the Detainees' hands. He claimed to have seen Payne push his thumb into the eye sockets of a hooded Detainee. Payne did not deny that his fingers went into a Detainee's eye socket but said it was an accident. I do not accept it was an accident.

101. WO2 Joel Huxley was the 1 QLR H Company Quartermaster Sergeant. Pte Daniel Ellis alleged that Huxley was personally involved in violence against the Detainees. Aktash said Huxley later admitted violence. Schofield and Pte Riley described assaults by a soldier who arguably fitted Huxley's description. Ellis was so vague and uncertain that I am unable safely to rely on his evidence. The descriptions of a large, older, soldier punching a Detainee given by Schofield and Pte Riley matched a description of Huxley at the relevant time. I think it very probable that they each saw and were attempting to describe the same man. No formal identification parade has ever taken place, but during his evidence to the Inquiry Schofield was shown a recent picture of Huxley and stated that it was not a picture of the man he saw in the TDF. For that reason it would be unsafe for me to find that the soldier seen by Schofield and Pte Riley punching a Detainee was Huxley. Finally, Aktash said that he had a conversation with Huxley in November 2003 during which Huxley had said he had beaten up one of the Detainees. Huxley denied the conversation. I found Huxley an unimpressive witness, but that was not a basis on which to conclude that he was lying. Although I found Aktash an honest witness I do not find his evidence alone of sufficient weight to base a finding that Huxley did assault the Detainees. Accordingly, I do not find this allegation proved on a balance of probabilities.

102. There is however evidence from, amongst others, Payne, Slicker and Cpl Chris Stout, all of whom worked or were based in and around the 1 QLR stores, that the noise of

Detainees being assaulted could be heard outside the TDF. I find that it is inconceivable that Huxley did not hear such noises when the Detainees were present in the TDF. As a senior NCO he ought to have intervened to prevent what was going on, and report it up the chain of command, but he did not.

103. Additionally, a number of witnesses alleged that SSgt Roberts, the Battlegroup Physical Training Instructor (PTI), was involved in specific violence. SSgt Roberts accepted that he had visited the TDF on Monday. Pte Liam Felton alleged that SSgt Roberts struck a Detainee in a chopping motion and instructed the guards how to inflict pain on the Detainees without leaving marks. Slicker said he saw SSgt Roberts strike a Detainee with karate chops. Aspinall too said that SSgt Roberts had karate chopped a Detainee. Pte Lee Graham told the SIB that he saw SSgt Roberts kicking three of the Detainees, and Pte Lee told the Court Martial that he had seen SSgt Roberts coming out of the TDF effectively admitting he had punched and kicked Detainees.

104. I found Felton to be a wholly unreliable witness and discount entirely his evidence in reaching a conclusion in relation to SSgt Roberts. I do not attach much weight to the evidence given by Pte Lee at the Court Martial. It was vague and in evidence to the Inquiry he was unable to remember the incident at all.

105. Pte Lee Graham's evidence changed over time in order progressively to limit what he admitted knowing. However, his SIB statement of 12 October 2003 contained many details of what happened in the TDF during Monday which are clearly true and supported by the evidence of others. Although there are inconsistencies in Slicker's evidence, I do not consider that they wholly undermine his account. He had the courage to admit to his own shameful assaults on the Detainees. In my view, he may have been truthful when making his allegations against SSgt Roberts. In the same way, I accept Aspinall's allegation as honestly given.

106. SSgt Roberts was an unsatisfactory witness: reluctant, evasive, and attempting to distance himself from what had happened and his part in it. There were inconsistencies between his Inquiry witness statement and his oral evidence. It is also very difficult to accept that, on Monday afternoon, he did not see the dreadful condition of the Detainees and the TDF itself. On an assessment of all the evidence, I find that Roberts karate chopped at least one Detainee and kicked probably three.

107. Sgt Andrew Potter of B Company 1 QLR visited the TDF and saw prisoners being forcibly kept in stress positions. The guards were screaming at them. Potter was disgusted and ordered the guards to cease, but was told they had been ordered by someone of senior rank. Potter raised this issue later that day with Sgt Smith, the Provost Sergeant, who told him it was part of the tactical questioning procedure. Potter was an impressive witness and I accept his evidence as truthful and accurate.

108. Slicker stated that he had seen Rodgers, Redfearn and SSgt Roberts assault the Detainees when they where hooded and standing in the shape of a horseshoe. Those soldiers were punching and striking the Detainees. I have dealt with the allegation against SSgt Roberts above. There are difficulties in reconciling what Slicker said he saw Rodgers and Redfearn do with the timing and with who else Slicker remembered being present. In my view Slicker's account is not of sufficient weight against Rodgers and Redfearn to reach the conclusion that they were involved in the violence described.

109.   Slicker also admitted punching a Detainee in the stomach after he had been told that the Detainee had tried to escape. This Detainee was probably Baha Mousa. Further, on a separate occasion, Slicker assaulted a Detainee by kicking him in the area of the kidney. On 10 November 2005 Slicker was summarily dealt with by his Commanding Officer for the offence of assault relating to his admission of assaulting one of the Detainees.

110.   Father Peter Madden was the padre for 1 QLR. He was unable to remember whether he visited the TDF when the Op Salerno Detainees were there. Stacey stated that Madden had visited the TDF on Sunday morning, and Rodgers said he visited on Monday morning, as did Pte Hunt.   Aspinall said Madden visited the TDF during Monday.

111.   I found Madden to be a poor witness, particularly in relation to inconsistencies as to whether he felt any responsibility for the welfare of detainees kept at BG Main, and whether, before Op Salerno, he had seen detainees being forced to maintain set positions.

112.   I find that Madden did visit the TDF on Monday. Whether this was in the morning or afternoon, it follows from my findings that he must have seen the shocking condition of the Detainees, and the deteriorating state of the TDF. He ought to have intervened immediately, or reported it up the chain of command but, in fact, it seems he did not have the courage to do either.

Tactical Questioning of the Detainees

113.   During the period they were held at the TDF each Detainee was subjected to tactical questioning. One officer and three NCOs were principally involved. They were Peebles, the BGIRO, SSgt Davies and Smulski, the two tactical questioners, and Livesey, the second in command of the 1 QLR Intelligence Cell.

114.   SSgt Davies arrived at BG Main at around 09.30hrs on Sunday. He thought that the hooding of the Detainees was permitted, operationally justified for security purposes, and could disorientate and thereby aid interrogation. He had been trained that stress positions were not permitted and noise was not to be used as an aid to tactical questioning. Sleep disruption, that is waking a prisoner to feed or question him, was permitted and appropriate, but sleep deprivation was not to be used. He had completed his tactical questioner's training only a few months before deployment and had no practical operational experience of tactical questioning before Op Telic 2.

115.   SSgt Davies said he saw no signs of injuries on the Detainees. He said he never saw the Detainees being subjected to any violence; he did not witness the choir; he did not see them in any stress positions; and he saw no measures taken to prevent them from sleeping.

116.   Peebles and Livesey gave evidence that SSgt Davies visited the TDF during Sunday. I find it is probable that SSgt Davies did visit the TDF on more than the one occasion he said he could remember. I think it probable that on his visit later on Sunday evening he must have seen the condition of the Detainees, and at the least, that they were uncomfortable and in distress; but he may not have seen them in stress positions. SSgt Davies ought to have reported what he had seen.

117.   SSgt Davies used the harsh technique of questioning during all the tactical questioning sessions he conducted. The general use of the harsh technique is considered elsewhere in the Report.

118.   SSgt Davies accepted that at one point D005 was placed very close to a large generator, which was loud and hot. SSgt Davies said he gave the instruction for this intending it to be for about five minutes only. I find that Peebles acquiesced in this decision. SSgt Davies explained D005 was sent to the generator so that he could think about his answers in isolation from the other Detainees and be quickly returned for questioning. Peebles, however, said it was part of a "*naughty boy routine*". I am sure that the motive for placing D005 by the generator was to punish him and to pressure him into answering questions. He was left there for a period of about an hour and forty five minutes. This incident represents serious misconduct for which both Peebles and SSgt Davies were responsible.

119.   Smulski arrived at BG Main at around 23.45hrs and sat in on SSgt Davies' tactical questioning session with D002. Smulski had received his tactical questioning training in 1999, but had no practical operational experience of tactical questioning before Op Telic 2. He said that he thought hooding was permitted for security purposes, but did not know whether it was permitted as part of the conditioning process, to aid tactical questioning. He had been taught that stress positions were prohibited. He thought that the use of "*startling or unsettling noise*" was acceptable to maintain the shock of capture.

120.   Smulski agreed that he had given the guard instructions to "*exercise*" the Detainees. In particular, this accords with the evidence of Appleby and Reader that they were told to take D005 out of the TDF to shake him up. Smulski also instructed the guards to use a metal bar to make a noise and keep the Detainees awake. He made two or three visits to the TDF on Monday and saw the Detainees looking agitated. He noticed bruising on the abdomen of one Detainee, but made no inquiry about it and did not report it.

121.   It was Smulski who suggested that Baha Mousa be moved to the middle room after it had been reported that he was removing his plasticuffs and hood.

122.   In my view, at this time Smulski was inadequately prepared for tactical questioning. He had been trained over four years previously and had no practical experience. I accept that he genuinely thought, clearly erroneously, that using noise to keep the Detainees awake was permissible. However, he was wrong to encourage the guards to do this by banging a metal pole. Furthermore, I find that by his visit to the TDF on Monday afternoon and during the course of the tactical questioning, Smulski would have been able to see the distressed condition of the Detainees. He ought to have taken action and reported this.

123.   Both SSgt Davies and Smulski were aware that the Detainees were hooded although neither may have considered that this was solely as an aid to tactical questioning. While I think it possible that SSgt Davies was unaware that the Detainees were in stress positions, I find that Smulski, who made more visits to the TDF than SSgt Davies, did see the Detainees in stress positions.

124.   Peebles agreed that in the TDF the Detainees would have been kept hooded, handcuffed and in stress positions. When he visited the TDF on Sunday afternoon,

he said he did not notice anything abnormal about the Detainees. Early on Monday morning he said he had looked into the TDF and the Detainees were not in stress positions, but were quiet and the conditions unremarkable. Later on Monday morning he again looked into the TDF and saw the Detainees hooded and dishevelled. Peebles did not at any time order the conditioning process to cease, even though he knew that it would have started shortly after the arrival of the Detainees and despite his understanding of when tactical questioning had finished.

125. I find that Peebles must have become aware of the shocking state of the Detainees by Monday. I also suspect that Peebles did know of the physical abuse of the Detainees by Payne and other soldiers. Even if he did not know of that, he must have understood the serious adverse effects of hooding and stress positions in the significant heat for a period of around 36 hours. Peebles ought to have ordered the cessation of hooding and stress positions long before Baha Mousa's death. He also ought to have reported to the Battlegroup second in command, Suss-Francksen, or the Commanding Officer, Mendonça, what he had seen.

126. It is relevant here to record the admission of violent conduct made by Livesey, who acted as a note taker for the tactical questioning sessions, and as escort to some of the Detainees. Livesey punched D002 to the head twice when returning him to the TDF after he had been questioned. It is probable that this blow caused the injury to D002's face identified by Dr Hill. This was an inexcusable serious breach of discipline. Livesey also admitted that he had visited the TDF on two or three occasions on Monday. He saw the Detainees still in stress positions and being roughly handled. Livesey ought to have intervened to stop this conduct or referred it up the chain of command.

The Death of Baha Mousa

127. By about 21.30hrs on Monday, the rest of the Rodgers Multiple returned to BG Main to relieve the afternoon stag. On arrival the vehicles parked outside the TDF. Rodgers went directly to a briefing with Peebles. Aspinall and Pte Lee Graham left the TDF and went to the vehicles. There is no evidence that Pte Hunt, Stirland or Kenny played any part in the final moments of Baha Mousa's life. Similarly, there is no material evidence that Appleby or MacKenzie were significantly involved, although they gave evidence as to what they had seen inside the TDF at the time.

128. From the Multiple, Reader, Pte Cooper, Douglas and Redfearn were inside the TDF. These soldiers in the TDF saw Baha Mousa before the final struggle and agreed that he was standing in the doorway of the centre room or internal corridor. He had removed his hood and, according to some witnesses, had extracted himself from the plasticuffs around his wrists. Accounts of the witnesses to the final struggle thereafter diverge.

129. I have set out in the Report (Part II Chapter 16) detailed evidence of those witnesses who were present in the TDF in the crucial moments before Baha Mousa died. I have also referred in the Report to the evidence of Dr Hill, who carried out a post mortem examination. It was from Dr Hill's findings that Dr Deryk James, a pathologist instructed by the Inquiry, based his conclusions on the cause of death. I also refer to the evidence of other pathologists who gave evidence at the Court Martial and provided statements for the Inquiry but did not give oral evidence to me.

130. So far as the factual issues in relation to the events immediately surrounding Baha Mousa's death are concerned, it is clear that Payne and Pte Cooper were involved in the final struggle.

131. Pte Cooper remembered responding to a shout for help coming from the TDF and going into the middle room and seeing Payne struggling with Baha Mousa. Payne and Pte Cooper got Baha Mousa to the floor, with Payne's knee in Baha Mousa's back and attempted to replace the plasticuffs. Baha Mousa broke free twice and Payne began punching and kicking him, and banging Baha Mousa's head against the wall with his hands. Pte Cooper said the assault lasted around 30 seconds and when it ceased Baha Mousa was no longer moving.

132. Payne's account was that he saw Baha Mousa outside the middle room with his hoods and plasticuffs off. He shouted, and Baha Mousa turned back to face the middle room. Payne put his knee into the small of Baha Mousa's back and put him to the floor. He and Pte Cooper attempted to replace the plasticuffs but Baha Mousa thrashed about and broke free. Payne said the plasticuffs were successfully applied at the second attempt. He made no allegation of violence by Pte Cooper. He stated that Baha Mousa was thrashing about and struck his own head on the wall or floor during the struggle to replace the plasticuffs.

133. Redfearn said that he arrived at the middle room of the TDF to see Baha Mousa face down on the floor with Payne and Pte Cooper on his back, attempting to replace the plasticuffs. Redfearn saw Baha Mousa thrashing about and his head banging the floor and wall. Redfearn denied jumping on Baha Mousa's legs as another witness said he had done. He believed that Payne and Pte Cooper could control what was going on and therefore went into the right-hand room. When he returned Baha Mousa was propped up, motionless, against the wall.

134. The Regimental Medical Officer (RMO), Dr Keilloh, was summoned and immediately gave mouth to mouth resuscitation at the TDF. Baha Mousa was then taken to the Regimental Aid Post (RAP) where CPR was carried out by the entire 1 QLR medical staff. At 22.05hrs Keilloh pronounced Baha Mousa dead.

The Pathologists' Evidence

135. In addition to the post mortem report produced by Dr Hill on 31 September 2003, the Inquiry commissioned a report from James. There is no dispute that Baha Mousa sustained 93 identifiable external injuries, and a number of internal injuries. Dr Hill initially concluded that the cause of death was a combination of strangulation, postural asphyxia and multiple injuries. However, in the light of later, more comprehensive witness evidence, Dr Hill modified his opinion. Ultimately he said that, if the premise that someone was pulling tightly on the hood over Baha Mousa's head was incorrect, then strangulation did not play a part in the death, and the cause of death was positional asphyxia.

136. On the basis of the findings of physical injuries made by Dr Hill and the photographs of the post mortem, James concluded that the cause of death was "'*struggle against restraint*' *in a man exposed to whatever associated causal factors can be demonstrated to have been present*", with the final event being a cardio-respiratory arrest. Dr Hill,

although he preferred the description, *"postural or restraint asphyxia"* to *"struggle against restraint"*, did not dissent from this opinion.

137. At the Court Martial, Professor Christopher Milroy gave an opinion as to the cause of death similar to that of James. He found the death to have been caused by *"a combination of the restraint with associated struggle and the position that he was held in ... together with multiple injuries to the body"*.

Conclusions on the Death of Baha Mousa

138. In reaching my conclusions concerning this final violent struggle, I have kept in mind the fact that witnesses can genuinely differ in their accounts when describing violent events taking place over only a few minutes, and occurring some years ago. Some witnesses have admitted to not being truthful in the past, and some have a reason to try to protect their actions from criticism. I have made allowance for those factors.

139. In summary form my conclusions are as follows. Baha Mousa was not attempting to escape shortly before the final struggle. I accept that from time to time during his detention in the TDF Baha Mousa may have extracted himself from his plasticuffs and removed his hood. However, as I find, his injuries show he was being subjected to sustained assaults and it is not at all surprising that he attempted to free himself from his plasticuffs and remove his hood in order to try to protect himself.

140. On Payne's own evidence, Baha Mousa turned to face back into the middle room of the TDF when Payne shouted at him. By that stage, as the medical evidence tends to show, Baha Mousa was probably exhausted. I reject the suggestion that he intended or was trying to escape or that Payne had any valid reason to think so. I find that Payne acted to punish Baha Mousa for freeing himself from the plasticuffs, his hood, and for leaving the middle room.

141. Notwithstanding that Pte Cooper's credibility had been undermined by previous contradictory statements and that he had an obvious interest in playing down his part in this dreadful incident, I nevertheless accept that Pte Cooper was genuinely endeavouring to do his best to tell the Inquiry the truth about the final struggle. I find that Pte Cooper did no more than exert sufficient force to attempt to put the plasticuffs back on Baha Mousa. After the second attempt to replace the plasticuffs, Pte Cooper took no further part in the struggle. Douglas' account supported a conclusion that in the later stages of the struggle it was Payne alone who assaulted Baha Mousa.

142. I find that Payne lost his temper and continued unlawfully to assault Baha Mousa until it was obvious that he had stopped struggling.

143. So far as the pathologists' evidence is concerned, I accept James' explanation of the cause of death, which is largely supported by Dr Hill and Milroy. I find that there were two main causes of death. Firstly, Baha Mousa had been made vulnerable by a range of factors, namely: lack of food and water, the heat, rhabdomyolysis, acute renal failure, exertion, exhaustion, fear and multiple injuries. Both stress positions, which are a form of exertion, and hooding, which obviously must have increased Baha Mousa's body temperature, contributed to these factors. Secondly, against the background of this vulnerability, the trigger for his death was a violent assault consisting of punches, being thrown across the room and possibly also of kicks. It also involved an unsafe method of restraint, in particular by being held to the ground

in an attempt to re-apply plasticuffs. The combination of both causes was necessary to bring about Baha Mousa's death; neither was alone sufficient to kill him.

Events on the Ground Immediately After Baha Mousa's Death

144. Shortly after the death of Baha Mousa, 19 Mech Bde Headquarters were informed. At about 22.30 an SIB investigation was initiated but only started in practical terms the following day. Before this, perhaps unsurprisingly, conversations occurred between the soldiers concerned relating to what had happened.

145. After the death, some members of the Rodgers Multiple remained in the vicinity of the TDF. Aspinall, Pte Cooper, Allibone and Appleby all gave similar evidence that Payne said to a group of soldiers from the Rodgers Multiple that, *"If anyone asks, we were trying to put his plasticuffs on and he banged his head."*

146. Rodgers was informed of the death by Payne. Rodgers said that he then reported the death to Maj Richard Englefield and then went to the TDF where he was informed by Mendonça that it was an SIB matter and that he should not speak to the soldiers. Nevertheless he did speak to Aspinall, who appeared to be wound up and stressed, and who told him that there had been a struggle and Baha Mousa had banged his head against a wall.

147. Payne's account was that he only discussed the circumstances of Baha Mousa's death immediately after it occurred with Capt Mark Moutarde, and that Reader, Pte Cooper and Redfearn were present. Payne said that he told Moutarde that Baha Mousa had banged his head; that he, Payne, had restrained Baha Mousa, and that he could not believe he was dead. Payne denied that he told members of the Multiple to tell a false story. Redfearn recalled a meeting with Moutarde, and remembered Payne saying that he could not believe Baha Mousa was dead. He formed the impression than Payne was endeavouring to cover his back. Pte Cooper and Reader accepted that the meeting had taken place, and confirmed what Payne had said. Moutarde, however, said he had no recollection of this meeting.

148. I accept the general tenor of the conversation between Payne and members of the Rodgers Multiple as described by Aspinall, Pte Cooper, Allibone and Appleby. I find Payne was seeking to ensure that there was a uniform explanation that Baha Mousa's death was an accident. I have found that there was a conversation between Payne and Moutarde and the gist of what Payne said was that he could not believe Baha Mousa had died. This too was part of an attempt to explain the death as being the result of an accident.

Moutarde's Reporting of the Incident

149. Moutarde could not remember seeing anything untoward in the TDF after Baha Mousa's death. In his evidence up to and including his Inquiry witness statement he had said that he could not remember discussing the death of Baha Mousa with any of the soldiers involved. A document prepared by Moutarde on 15 September 2003 came to light late in the Inquiry's investigation and after Moutarde had produced his statement. Moutarde said that he still had no memory of any discussion with the

soldiers about this incident, but the document made clear that he had obtained their account.

150. The document was a memorandum to Mendonça. It named Payne and Pte Cooper as having been involved in a violent struggle with Baha Mousa and said that Baha Mousa had banged his head. It stated that Baha Mousa was of significant intelligence interest because he was suspected of being involved in the RMP killings. Moutarde asserted that he had been given this information and it was not a fabrication to blacken Baha Mousa's character. (As I have recorded earlier, there was in fact no evidence to substantiate this allegation.)

151. This document for Mendonça must be compared to a document headed "Provisional SINCREP" (a military abbreviation of "serious incident report") from 1 QLR to 19 Mech Bde Headquarters, timed and dated at 23.40hrs on 15 September. It did not name Payne and Pte Cooper as having been involved, nor did it mention the struggle or the banging of Baha Mousa's head. Moutarde told the Inquiry that this SINCREP would have been produced by the Operations Room staff possibly with some input from him.

152. I do not find that Moutarde attempted deliberately to provide Mendonça and the Brigade with a false picture of what happened. However, Moutarde must have known of the conditions in the TDF he encountered after the death, and that information is something which he ought to have communicated up the chain of command.

Other Visitors to the TDF Following Baha Mousa's Death

153. In addition to Moutarde, a number of other soldiers from the Battlegroup or attached to 1 QLR visited the TDF almost immediately following Baha Mousa's death.

154. Possibly the first soldier, other than guards or medical staff, to visit the TDF was Sgt Charles Colley an RMP sergeant attached to 1 QLR. He took no steps to secure the TDF nor any to preserve physical evidence. He said he found the TDF smelt but was not disgusting and said the Detainees looked ruffled. He said that he saw no injuries.

155. Capt Gareth Seeds, the Operations Officer, gave a significantly different description of the TDF. He said the Detainees were still restrained; they were obviously tired, dirty and in pain; and one of the Detainees was in the foetal position on the floor. Seeds was embarrassed, ashamed and disgusted by what he saw. He enlisted the help of Maj Peter Quegan in taking to the toilet a Detainee who was obviously in pain. Although he did not see injuries on the Detainees, it was clear to Seeds that at least some of the Detainees had been beaten. Quegan essentially supported this account.

156. Seeds went to the 1 QLR second in command, Maj Chris Suss-Francksen. Suss-Francksen remembered that Seeds' concern was that the Detainees were still handcuffed, but he did not remember that Seeds had wanted to report the conditions in the TDF.

157. Englefield, the Officer Commanding A Company, accepted that he had been in the vicinity of the TDF on Monday evening before Baha Mousa's death, but asserted that he did not go into the TDF at any time when the Detainees were there.

158. Mendonça, in his Inquiry witness statement, said that after being informed of the death, he went straight to the TDF but did not remember going into the building or seeing the Detainees. In oral evidence he accepted that it was possible that he went into the TDF but he maintained that he did not remember doing so. He was not aware of the conditions as described by Seeds and Quegan.

159. I reached the following conclusions about the events in the immediate aftermath of the death of Baha Mousa.

160. Both Seeds and Quegan were honest witnesses giving accurate descriptions of the conditions in the TDF and the physical state of the Detainees. I preferred their evidence to that of Colley and Suss-Francksen, who I find both substantially underplayed the seriousness of what they must have seen. I find it more probable than not that Moutarde did go into the TDF, and that being the case I do not accept that he can have thought there was nothing amiss. Suss-Francksen and Moutarde (and possibly Colley) should have ensured the surviving Detainees received medical attention and were properly cared for.

161. Apart from Moutarde's memorandum to Mendonça, neither Keilloh, Suss-Francksen, Colley nor Moutarde made a formal report about what they had seen and none of them reported what they must have known regarding mistreatment of at least some of the Detainees. There was a reluctance to accept that 1 QLR had done anything wrong. I do not, however, conclude that there is a basis for finding that officers of 1 QLR sought to cover up Baha Mousa's death or to prevent the circumstances of it from being investigated; plainly the SIB were called upon by 1 QLR to instigate an investigation in the hours after the death.

The Treatment of the Detainees after the Death of Baha Mousa

162. D002 and D004 gave evidence that even after the death of Baha Mousa, they were subjected to physical assaults. Further, D004 stated that trophy photographs were taken on Tuesday morning, showing him being beaten. D002, D003, D004, D005 and Kifah Matairi all alleged that they were made to undertake forced exercises on Tuesday morning, which included being made to "dance like Michael Jackson".

163. It is accepted by some soldiers that a period of exercise of the Detainees occurred before they were transferred to the TIF at Um Qasr. Rodgers, Stirland and Pte Hunt described the Detainees being walked up and down outside the TDF.

164. Cpl Kenneth Simmons, attached to 1 QLR's Motor Transport Platoon, was the driver of the lorry which was to transfer the Detainees from BG Main to Um Qasr. He had been told by soldiers at the TDF that the Detainees had been the subject of "a good kicking". He noticed injuries to the face and body of some of the Detainees. Simmons was instructed to assist in the exercising of the Detainees, by walking them up and down over a distance of approximately twenty metres outside the TDF. The Detainee whom Simmons helped appeared to him to be in a lot of pain

165. Cpl Claire Vogel, an RMP corporal, also visited the TDF on Tuesday morning. She described seeing the Detainees performing aerobics or warm-up type exercises, but

did not think that the smell or heat of the TDF nor the apparent exhaustion of the Detainees was in any way untoward.

166. I conclude that although it is not possible to rule out isolated instances of violence or other abusive behaviour by guards during Monday night, I am of the view that the level and frequency of any violence must have been far less than before his death. Furthermore, although I am unable to identify the individuals responsible, I am of the opinion that some of the soldiers did tell the Detainees to "*dance like Michael Jackson*" and forcibly made them exercise. I accept Simmons' evidence in relation to the state of the TDF and the condition of the Detainees. It follows that Vogel, as an RMP should have taken steps to report what she must have seen of the TDF and of the state of the Detainees.

The Detainees' Arrival at the TIF

167. On arrival at the TIF, Simmons described the Detainees as needing assistance alighting from the lorry, and described a female American officer at the processing centre being furious, and threatening to report the condition of the Detainees. S018, the second in command of the JFIT interrogation facility based within the TIF, was shown injuries to two of the Detainees which resulted in them being evacuated to hospital. As a result he confronted Rodgers about the condition of the Detainees.

1 QLR's Medics

168. At the relevant time there was no formal policy and no standing orders or general instructions within 1 QLR as to the medical care for civilian detainees. This lack of formal process is exemplified by the fact that Keilloh instructed his medical staff that no documentation was required in relation to any medical assessment of a detainee unless some medically adverse finding was made. No records were required when the medical findings were compatible with the detainees remaining at the TDF for up to 48 hours. A system of regular documented examinations of detainees was instituted promptly after Baha Mousa's death.

169. In relation to the general treatment of detainees before Op Salerno, Sgt Ian Goulding, a Regimental Medical Assistant, Class One (RMA1), and LCpl Steven Baxter (also an RMA1) were aware that prisoners were hooded and placed in stress positions as part of a process of conditioning. Pte Steven Paul Winstanley was aware of the use of hooding. Keilloh too was aware of hooding, but had been told that hoods were not applied for more than ten to fifteen minutes at a time, and he did not perceive this to represent a medical problem.

The Medical Treatment of the Op Salerno Detainees

170. Cpl Winstanley, Baxter and Pte Winstanley carried out the initial medical assessment of the Detainees on Sunday. I accept that an examination of the Detainees, apart from D005, D006 and Maitham, did take place, despite only D001 recalling one, and even he said that he was examined only because he was feeling unwell. An explanation for the other Detainees not remembering this is that, alongside their shock and confusion soon after arrest, I find it likely that any examination was cursory. Further, these examinations appear not to have been documented, save possibly for one.

171. Pte Winstanley told the Inquiry that he had attended the TDF again later on Sunday night to examine two Detainees who were refusing to stand up. Pte Winstanley's account was that this visit generated an "FMed 5", which was a type of form used to record medical examinations.

172. Cpl Winstanley examined D006, due to his heart condition, on Monday morning. D006 appeared in distress and therefore Cpl Winstanley consulted with Keilloh. Following this, aspirin and propranolol were prescribed to D006. This incident also resulted in an FMed 5 document.

173. Only two FMed 5 forms survive. The first, dated 14 September 2003 was contended by Pte Winstanley to relate to the visit to the TDF he made on Sunday night, and to refer to an examination of Baha Mousa. It recorded that he had no injuries or previous illnesses. Pte Winstanley states that this was thereafter countersigned by Cpl Winstanley. Cpl Winstanley however maintained that this FMed 5 was completed after the initial routine medical examination earlier on Sunday. Both soldiers denied that this FMed 5 had been made out after Baha Mousa's death in an attempt to show that Baha Mousa had been examined with a finding of no visible injuries.

174. The second FMed 5, relating to Cpl Winstanley's visit to D006 on Monday, does not record the name of the patient and was not disclosed by Cpl Winstanley to the SIB until 22 September 2003, after he had made his first statement on 17 September 2003, in which he made no mention of it.

175. The medics were all involved in the attempted resuscitation of Baha Mousa. Keilloh gave Baha Mousa mouth to mouth resuscitation at the TDF, Baha Mousa was then taken by stretcher to the RAP where CPR was carried out.

176. There were conflicts in the evidence given by members of the medical team in relation to the extent to which injuries had been visible on Baha Mousa's body. Keilloh maintained that apart from a small trace of blood under Baha Mousa's nose, he had not noticed any of the injuries subsequently found on the body. However, Goulding, Sgt Stephen Saxton and Pte Kevin Armstrong noticed bruising; Cpl Winstanley noticed bruising and swelling, and Baxter noticed Baha Mousa had a puffy face and torn skin on the wrists. Thus, Keilloh was the only medic not to observe injuries to Baha Mousa's body.

177. Keilloh spoke to Capt Andrew Le Feuvre at BMH Shaibah Hospital, the doctor who signed Baha Mousa's death certificate, in order to provide details about the death. Neither doctor remembered this conversation although a contemporaneous handwritten note by Le Feuvre indicated that it had occurred. The death certificate recorded that the disease or condition directly leading to death was a cardio-respiratory arrest. While it may have been wrong of Le Feuvre to sign this certificate (as he admitted), even if relying on Keilloh's word, having neither treated Baha Mousa before death nor even seen the body subsequent to death, I have rejected the serious allegation that there was an attempt by either of the doctors to cover up the real cause of death. The available evidence falls far short of substantiating such a suggestion.

178. After the death of Baha Mousa, D004 and Ahmad Matairi were examined by Keilloh. His evidence was that he understood D004 to have been complaining of being kicked once, resulting in pain in the abdomen and renal area of the lower right back. He remembered that Ahmed Matairi was complaining of lower back pain after being

kicked. Keilloh said that he saw no marks on the body of either man and he did not believe their allegations of assault, but he nevertheless prescribed each man pain relief medication and gave them an anti-inflammatory injection.

179. Dr Hill recorded that D004 sustained a variety of mild injuries. Ahmad Matairi was also bruised, and as had been evident to a number of the guards and visitors to the TDF he had a visible hernia. It was Kellioh's evidence that he did not notice these injuries.

180. In the light of all the evidence, I reached the following conclusions in relation to the activities of the medical staff.

181. It is right that I record that in the challenging circumstances of the attempt to resuscitate Baha Mousa it appears that the medical staff did all that they could to preserve his life. However, there are other areas where I find fault with the actions of some of the medical staff.

182. I find that Baxter and Pte Winstanley saw that the Detainees were hooded and in stress positions when they went into the TDF on Sunday 14 September. They ought to have reported this up the chain of command, particularly their medical chain of command, given their medical training and understanding of the effects of the intense heat in Iraq. I find that Cpl Winstanley saw Detainees hooded, and I suspect that he also saw Detainees in stress positions. He too should have reported what he had seen.

183. The circumstances of the creation of the first FMed 5 are suspicious. Neither explanation given is convincing. However, Pte Winstanley and Cpl WInstanley gave differing explanations as to the origin of this document, which is inconsistent with them having agreed to forge the document after the event. I do not find that this is what they attempted to do. Similarly, although I am suspicious of the authenticity of the second FMed 5, there is not sufficient evidence to find that it was dishonestly drawn up after the event by Cpl Winstanley. In this connection however, I find that Cpl Winstanley must have seen the conditions in the TDF on Monday morning when he examined D006. Accepting, as I do, the evidence of Redfearn that the conditions at that time were appalling, I have found that Cpl Winstanley ought to have reported this up the chain of command.

184. Goulding understood what the process of conditioning entailed and knew of the length of the detention of the Detainees. In the light of those factors, as a senior NCO in the medical section, his failure to go to the TDF to inspect the conditions there, either before or after, the death of Baha Mousa, amounted to a failing on his part.

185. Keilloh was the senior medical officer within 1 QLR. He had not received any training or instructions in respect of prisoner handling, in general, or relating to his medical function in the prisoner handling process. I accept that he thought prisoners were only hooded for ten to fifteen minutes, and that he did not know they were put into stress positions.

186. Keilloh rightly conceded that the procedure in place before Baha Mousa's death for examining and recording the results of the examination of detainees was inadequate. He ought to have realised this and changed the position before Baha Mousa's death.

187. I also find that Keilloh was probably aware of the presence of the Detainees as a group in the TDF before Baha Mousa's death. He certainly knew, probably on Monday morning, of D006's heart condition. He knew detainees might be held for up to 48 hours, and knew of the very poor facilities in the TDF and of the effects of the considerable heat.

188. It is difficult to accept that when attempting to resuscitate Baha Mousa, Keilloh did not see signs of mistreatment to his body. Furthermore, in the light of the evidence from other members of the medical staff that after the death, comments were made in the RAP in relation to the injuries to Baha Mousa, I conclude that after this attempt to revive Baha Mousa, Keilloh knew that he had sustained injuries in the TDF. He ought then to have gone to the TDF to check on the condition of the other Detainees.

189. It is also difficult to accept that Keilloh later missed the signs of injuries to D004 and Ahmad Matairi. Even if he did, his response to the complaint of both D004 and Ahmad Matairi was inadequate. He ought to have checked the TDF after the death of Baha Mousa shortly followed by complaints of assault made by two other Detainees.

190. Keilloh's failure to go to the TDF after Baha Mousa's death to examine all of the other Detainees was a serious failing. So was his failure to report what I find he must have known to a more senior officer in the Battlegroup.

191. The findings I have made in respect of the issues concerning the interaction of the 1 QLR medical staff with the Op Salerno Detainees can be properly put in context by recognising that in respect of military medics, there was a lack of training and guidance in respect of prisoner handling and checking detainees, record keeping, and their involvement, if any, in the process of interrogation. These important issues are discussed in Part XVI of the Report.

Were the Events of 14 to 16 September 2003 a "One-off"? (Part III)

192. It has been necessary to consider other incidents in Iraq involving soldiers from 1 QLR, in order to establish whether the events of 14 to 16 September were a single incident with tragic consequences or whether they were indicative of a culture of violence within that Battlegroup. The Inquiry therefore heard evidence in relation to incidents involving the Rodgers Multiple; evidence given by 1 QLR witnesses regarding other isolated incidents; and evidence arising out of newspaper reports of statements given by two unidentified soldiers.

193. A diary kept by MacKenzie purported to record incidents involving the Rodgers Multiple. It indicated that on occasions, Iraqi civilians were treated violently. Mackenzie asserted that the diary entries were generally true and accurate, albeit they contained some assumptions. Some members of the Rodgers Multiple confirmed the type of violence described while some others denied it.

194. Evidence from Richards and Douglas lent some support to the diary entries. Heavily qualified agreement to some aspects of the diary came from Pte Cooper, Allibone and Bentham. Other witnesses from the Rodgers Multiple denied that there was any culture of violence and contradicted the diary entries. However, some independent

support for MacKenzie's account appears in the 1 QLR logs which recorded operations corresponding with entries in the diary.

195. It must clearly be acknowledged that Mackenzie's credibility as a witness was very poor. However, in the light of the supporting evidence from fellow members of the Rodgers Multiple and other contemporaneous sources, I find that the MacKenzie diaries generally give an accurate account of the sort of casual violence in which some members of the Multiple indulged. Moreover I find that Rodgers must have had some awareness of such incidents occurring.

196. The Inquiry also heard evidence from LCpl Graham Jones in relation to three specific incidents of violence, and the general rough treatment towards civilian prisoners, involving members of 1 QLR. Bdr Terence Stokes of S Company also described two incidents of ill disciplined violence against civilian detainees. Furthermore, I also accept that Simmons, the driver, saw hooded detainees on more than one occasion being thrown or kicked out of the back of vehicles while at either of the 1 QLR A or C Company locations.

197. I also briefly considered some other evidence in relation to a 1 QLR C Company operation on 9 September 2003, targeting members of the Garamsche tribe. In accordance with my terms of reference I made it clear during the course of the evidence that the Garamsche incident was of limited relevance to the main issues. However, I find that members of the Garamsche tribe were subjected to physical assaults that day.

198. Although at times racist language was used by soldiers, there is no sufficient evidential basis to suggest that the violence was racially motivated.

199. The evidence in relation to the Garamsche incident and the other specific incidents of violence against detainees does demonstrate that the events of 14 to 16 September cannot be described as a "one off" event. There were other incidents of abuse and mistreatment of Iraqi civilians by soldiers of 1 QLR. However, the evidence does not demonstrate disciplinary failures so widespread as to be regarded as an entrenched culture of violence within 1 QLR.

Broader Issues Raised by the Events of 14 to 16 September 2003

200. The events of 14 to 16 September 2003 raise five areas of broader concern which inform my analysis of the wider context for these events, in Parts III to XV of the Report, and the recommendations I make in Parts XVI and XVII:

(1) the use of conditioning techniques;

(2) loss of discipline and lack of "moral courage";

(3) delay and breach of the fourteen hour limit;

(4) inadequate detention procedures: the TDF, custody records, food and water; and

(5) a failure to supervise and the dispute over who was responsible for the Detainees' welfare.

The Use of Conditioning Techniques

201. In relation to conditioning, I have found that the Op Salerno Detainees were subjected to the process of conditioning from their arrival at the TDF until the time of Baha Mousa's death. They were placed in the "ski" stress position, as can be seen in the Payne video, and later in other kneeling positions or with their arms held out. It is likely that there were some short breaks in the process, when hoods were taken off, and when the guards gave up enforcing stress positions. However, I find it likely that the Detainees were kept in stress positions for the overwhelming majority of the time between their arrival at the TDF and Baha Mousa's death. With the exception of D006 they also remained hooded during most of their time in the TDF.

202. This conditioning process was 1 QLR's standard practice at that time. It was initiated by Payne on arrival of the Detainees, and from at least 16.30hrs on Sunday when he ordered it to start, Peebles knew it was taking place. There was widespread knowledge among members of H Company, at BG Main that the conditioning process was occurring; the Rodgers Multiple were aware of it, most as participants; and I find that SSgt Davies and Smulksi, the tactical questioners, knew of it also, although SSgt Davies may not have been aware that these Detainees were placed in stress positions.

Loss of Discipline and Lack of Moral Courage

203. My findings raise a significant concern about the loss of discipline and lack of moral courage to report abuse within 1 QLR. A large number of soldiers, including senior NCOs, assaulted the Detainees in a facility in the middle of the 1 QLR camp which had no doors, seemingly unconcerned at being caught doing so. Several officers must have been aware of at least some of the abuse. A large number of soldiers, including all those who took part in guard duty, also failed to intervene to stop the abuse or report it up the chain of command.

204. Part II, Chapter 20 contains a table which summarises all findings I make of assaults by named individuals.

Delay and Breach of the Fourteen Hour Rule

205. At the time of the detention of the Op Salerno Detainees, FRAGO 29 as modified by FRAGO 005 mandated that internees be delivered to the TIF within fourteen hours of their arrest or as soon as possible thereafter. In the case of the Op Salerno Detainees, their arrest took place at around 07.00hrs on Sunday and their arrival at the TIF was not until about 14.00hrs on Tuesday, a period of approximately 55 hours.

206. This was not the first occasion on which the fourteen hour rule had been breached by 1 QLR. A number of reasons probably contributed to these delays: a lack of resources to transport or escort internees to the TIF, the two hour journey time to the TIF, delays in obtaining tactical questioners from Brigade, and the erroneous belief that at night the TIF was closed and could not receive internees.

207. As to why the fourteen hour rule was breached in the case of the Op Salerno Detainees, two reasons were put forward by 1 QLR witnesses: firstly, that there was a lack of manpower resources to transfer the Detainees; and secondly, that the Detainees

were not transferred in the late afternoon periods because it was understood that the TIF would shut at night. It is obvious that there was also a third reason, namely the duration of tactical questioning, which did not finish until mid-afternoon on Monday.

208. There was communication between 1 QLR and 19 Mech Bde in relation to the delay. It is likely that Peebles spoke to Maj Bruce Radbourne of the 19 Mech Bde G2 branch, on Sunday, to inform him that the Detainees would be held over the fourteen hour limit as tactical questioning was still taking place. Radbourne ought to have ordered the transfer immediately or referred the matter within Brigade, but he did not do so. On Sunday evening, 1 QLR requested a second tactical questioner from Brigade, resulting in Smulski's attendance. Peebles stated that on Monday morning he informed Maj Russell Clifton, the 19 Mech Bde legal officer, that the fourteen hour limit had been breached; although Clifton agreed there was a conversation, he denied that he was told the fourteen hour limit had already been breached and that tactical questioning was continuing. I prefer Clifton's account. Thereafter, on Monday morning, the Brigade Chief of Staff, Maj Edward Fenton spoke by telephone to either Seeds or Suss-Francksen seeking an explanation for the delay, and was told that there was a lack of resources to transport the Detainees to the TIF. On Monday evening Fenton spoke to Suss-Francksen, who told him that the delay was caused by lack of manpower and vehicles, and that it was too late to deliver the Detainees to the TIF that night. Fenton accepted this explanation and said that the Detainees should be moved early on Tuesday morning.

209. While I have found that 1 QLR genuinely but mistakenly believed they could not transfer detainees to the TIF at night, this does not explain why the Detainees were not transferred during the day on Monday. Although I have some sympathy with the explanation that there was a lack of resources to transfer the Detainees, in my judgment the principal reason for their prolonged detention at BG Main was so that they could be further questioned.

210. Had the fourteen hour rule been complied with then Baha Mousa would have been transferred to the TIF long before Monday night. I find that neither 1 QLR nor 19 Mech Bde were assiduous enough in ensuring the rule was adhered to.

Inadequate Detention Procedures

211. In addition to the deficiencies in the medical inspection of the Detainees, as outlined above, there were other serious shortcomings in the detention procedures used at BG Main.

212. The facilities for holding the Detainees, particularly the TDF, were wholly inadequate. There were no beds or other furniture, and the lack of doors meant there were no restrictions on who could enter. There was no meaningful custody record, or even a log of personnel visiting the TDF. The Detainees were not properly fed whilst at BG Main. I find they were given only a breakfast on Monday morning and on Tuesday morning. They were given water in a cursory, and sometimes demeaning, fashion.

213. It was also a significant error of judgment for the soldiers who had undertaken the arrest at the Hotel to be tasked to guard the Detainees.

The Failure to Supervise and the Dispute over Responsibility

214. These failings occurred against a background of a lack of supervision and meaningful responsibility over the guards at the TDF. Ever since the death of Baha Mousa there has been a sharp debate among Maj Antony Royce, Mendonça, WO1 George Briscoe, Payne, Sgt Smith and Peebles as to where the responsibility lay for the welfare of detainees. In essence, Royce, Mendonça, Briscoe and Payne thought that the BGIRO was responsible (at the time of Op Salerno, this was of course Peebles). Peebles asserted that Briscoe as the Regimental Sergeant Major (RSM), and below him the Regimental Provost staff, were responsible. Sgt Smith, the Provost Sergeant thought both the BGIRO and the RSM had some responsibility.

215. It is clear that the creation of the BGIRO role affected the conventional chain of command for detention at unit level, which ordinarily ran from the Adjutant to the RSM and then the Regimental Provost staff. After the introduction of the BGIRO role, Royce, who had been Peebles' predecessor as BGIRO, drafted a "*1 QLR Internment Procedure*" document dated 9 July 2003, which addressed, amongst other matters, the BGIRO's responsibility for making the internment decision, but it did not state that the responsibility for prisoner handling had shifted from the RSM to the BGIRO. Having taken over the role of BGIRO from Royce, Peebles said that he considered the chain of command in Iraq to be the same as if the Battalion were in the United Kingdom. However, even if Peebles was never explicitly informed of a shift in responsibility, in my judgment, by the time of the events in question he should have appreciated that in practice he was the officer overseeing treatment of detainees at BG Main. He accepted in his own evidence that he had a "*pivotal*" role in dealing with detainees at BG Main.

216. It is vitally important that this lack of clarity in the allocation of responsibility for the prisoner handling process, and for ensuring the welfare of detainees, is not repeated. I address this issue further in Parts XVI and XVII.

Responsibility: The Key Personalities within 1 QLR

217. In relation to some key individuals within 1 QLR, it is appropriate to describe in a little more detail the consequences of the findings I have made in relation to what occurred during 14 to 16 September 2003 at BG Main.

Payne

218. It is clear on any view that Payne played a fundamental role. At the Court Martial Payne pleaded guilty to the offence of a war crime, namely inhuman treatment of a person protected under the provision of the Fourth Geneva Convention. He was sentenced to twelve months' imprisonment and reduced to the ranks. On the day he gave evidence to the Inquiry, Payne accepted that the case put forward by him at the Court Martial was not the whole truth and that the basis of his guilty plea had been false. He conceded that he had used gratuitous violence on the Detainees, including kicks and punches, and also implicated the whole of the Rodgers Multiple, including Rodgers, in acts of violence. I accept Payne's admission that he used gratuitous

violence whenever he returned to the TDF. This accords with the evidence given by the Detainees and some other soldiers. However, where Payne makes allegations against others it has clearly been necessary carefully to consider his motives for doing so.

219. Payne thought hooding and stress positions were a standard operating procedure for dealing with Detainees. In the light of the understanding at 1 QLR that this was a practice sanctioned by Brigade, this understanding was to some extent justified. It was nevertheless not a sanction for those techniques being applied for up to 36 hours or for the force actually used in applying them.

220. I reject the suggestion that Payne's use of gratuitous violence did not occur until the "Free for All" incident on Sunday night (see Part II Chapter 10). The Payne video, taken on Sunday around midday, illustrates the nature of the force Payne used to maintain stress positions. I accept the Detainees' accounts that the violence, including being struck by kicks and punches, started shortly after they were placed in the TDF. I also find that at some point Payne demonstrated an episode of the choir to members of the Rodgers Multiple and himself precipitated the "Free for All" incident. Payne's numerous other visits to the TDF over the 36 hour period were routinely accompanied by violent acts against the Detainees.

221. I have concluded that in the final minutes Payne was involved in a violent assault on Baha Mousa. I find that his conduct on this occasion was a contributory cause of Baha Mousa's death. After the death he sought to persuade others to say that the death was accidental, when, plainly, he knew it was not.

222. I have described Payne's part in the events leading up to Baha Mousa's death as a dreadful catalogue of unjustified and brutal violence on the defenceless Detainees. D005 and D006 have given evidence that Payne was capable of some small acts of kindness. Nevertheless, I am driven to the conclusion that his actions demonstrate him to have been a violent bully. His example was followed by more junior soldiers. He bears a very heavy responsibility for the events in question.

Sgt Smith

223. The Provost Sergeant, Sgt Smith, was frequently unavailable to supervise Payne at the TDF, largely as a result of other duties he was required to fulfil. However, on Sunday evening he became aware that the Op Salerno Detainees were still being questioned, and he approached Peebles about this. I accept Sgt Smith's account that Peebles told him the Detainees would be moved after tactical questioning was completed. When Sgt Smith visited the TDF again on Sunday evening at around 21.45hrs, he ordered the guards to remove the Detainees' handcuffs and hoods, and to allow them to relax out of stress positions. After being tasked on other duties during Monday, he spoke again to Peebles at some time between 16.00hrs and 18.00hrs that day, voicing his concern about the length of time the Detainees had been at the TDF. He was told that the Detainees would be taken to the TIF the following morning.

224. I find it is to Sgt Smith's credit that he made these attempts to raise with a more senior officer, Peebles, the necessity to transfer the Detainees. Nevertheless, by Monday morning Sgt Smith was aware of the length of time the Detainees had been hooded and in stress positions. He ought then, as Provost Sergeant, to have made time to go

to the TDF to supervise Payne. Had he then seen the condition of the Detainees I am confident he would have done something about it.

Briscoe

225. The RSM, Briscoe, after the BGIRO role was introduced, did not have the same level of responsibility for the detainees as Peebles. On balance, I accept Briscoe's account that he did not visit the TDF during the detention of the Op Salerno Detainees, and that he did not know what was going on in the TDF during that period of time.

226. However, in my view, Briscoe ought to have known what was going on. The role of the RSM has been described as being the eyes and ears of the Adjutant and the Commanding Officer. The RSM, in part, is also responsible for the discipline of soldiers and NCOs. Had this function been carried out properly Briscoe should have discovered the abuse of the Detainees being perpetrated in the TDF.

Rodgers

227. Rodgers commanded the Multiple whose members guarded the Op Salerno Detainees for the majority of their detention. Rodgers denied that on any of his visits to the TDF he saw anything untoward. I do not accept that this can be true. By the time of Rodgers' first visit on Sunday evening the Detainees had been hooded and in stress positions for most of the day, and subject to assaults by Payne, Crowcroft and Fallon. By Monday morning, when Rodgers again visited, the conditions were shocking. Rodgers stated that even on Tuesday morning there was nothing he witnessed to cause him to think that the Detainees had been treated inhumanely. Simmons' evidence concerning the same period detailed the overt injuries to some Detainees and the smell of urine in the TDF. I infinitely prefer Simmons' evidence. Accordingly, Rodgers' denial of these aspects of the detention adversely affects his credibility.

228. I strongly suspect that Rodgers was aware of the low-level incidents of violence and abusive treatment of the Detainees by the Multiple at the Hotel. I find that he knew at the time, or very soon after became aware, of what had happened during the "Free for All" on Sunday night. It is not credible that he did not know after his visit on Monday morning that the Detainees had been assaulted throughout the night. As commander of the Multiple he ought to have known, and I find that he did know.

229. It represents a very serious breach of duty that at no time did Rodgers intervene to prevent the treatment that was being meted out to the Detainees, nor did he report what he knew was occurring up the chain of command. If he had taken action when he first knew what was occurring, Baha Mousa would almost certainly have survived. Furthermore, as the Officer Commanding the Rodgers Multiple he must accept responsibility for the serious instances of ill discipline by members of the Multiple.

Englefield

230. Above Rodgers in the chain of command was Englefield, the Officer Commanding A Company, who led the raid on the Hotel. Englefield's account included the recollection that he had visited the TDF, or its immediate vicinity, once on Sunday night, and once

on Monday night. He too asserted that on none of his visits to the TDF did he go into the TDF nor hear or see anything untoward.

231. In some respects Englefield was an unsatisfactory witness whose credibility was undermined by two notable aspects of his evidence. Firstly, he attempted to say that Pte David Fearon had not stolen money from the Hotel; secondly, Englefield had referred in an SIB statement to the use of hoods as a method to *"break"* detainees. During his oral evidence to the Inquiry, initially, but without success, Englefield tried to deny the plain English meaning of this aspect of the account he had given to the SIB.

232. Nevertheless, I am unable to find on the evidence available that Englefield witnessed anything amiss in the TDF on either occasion that he might have been in its vicinity. I am of the view also that Englefield was entitled to believe and accept that the Detainees were at that time the responsibility of the BGIRO and the Provost Staff.

Moutarde

233. As the Adjutant, Moutarde told the Inquiry that his usual practice was to visit the TDF about twice during every 24 hour period. He did not remember doing so in relation to the Op Salerno Detainees, but accepted that he probably would have made at least one visit, possibly more, while they were detained. He was unable to remember any specific detail of what he saw but said he would have seen what he was used to seeing routinely; namely, the type of action seen on the Payne video, but without the swearing.

234. Moutarde accepted it was highly likely that he visited the TDF after the death of Baha Mousa, although again he had no recollection of doing so. If he did so, he must have seen the disgusting conditions as described by Seeds and Quegan. I accept the evidence from members of the Rodgers Multiple that Moutarde was party to a conversation with Payne and others in the vicinity of the TDF after the death. In those circumstances I find it more probable than not that Moutarde did go into the TDF soon after the death.

235. Once he had seen the state of the Detainees and the TDF on Monday evening he ought to have taken immediate action to investigate and to ensure that they were not subjected to any further mistreatment.

Peebles

236. It follows from my findings concerning the allocation to the BGIRO of the responsibility for the welfare of detainees that the acts and omissions of Peebles also played a very central part in the events which occurred during 14 to 16 September 2003. Peebles ought to have known that hooding and stress positions being enforced by guards, in the heat, for a protracted period of time, was a situation fraught with danger. He ought to have known this, even if he considered himself not to be responsible for the welfare of the Detainees. Peebles' failure to order conditioning to cease prolonged the ordeal the Detainees were subjected to and was an unacceptable failure.

237. Furthermore, I also conclude that evidence given about the state of the Detainees and the condition of the TDF, in conjunction with what other soldiers such as Ingram

told Peebles, and Peebles' own evidence describing the timing of his visits, result in the finding that Peebles was aware that the Detainees were also being subjected to serious assaults.

Mendonça

238. As the Commanding Officer of 1 QLR, Mendonça shouldered very considerable responsibilities when leading 1 QLR through the challenging circumstances of the Op Telic 2 tour in Basra. Mendonça was ultimately awarded the Distinguished Service Order (DSO) for his service in Iraq. It is evident that he possessed impressive leadership qualities.

239. During the course of the SIB investigation, the Court Martial and the Inquiry, Mendonça has been the subject of allegations from some soldiers that he was involved in or witnessed acts of violence towards civilians in Iraq. These allegations have all been addressed, and I do not repeat them here.

240. It is possible that soldiers from 1 QLR were involved in some other instances of ill discipline during the tour. However I am not satisfied that the evidence justifies a finding that Mendonça knew that his Battlegroup was prone to incidents of gratuitous violence.

241. Mendonça knew that 1 QLR practised conditioning of detainees. He understood that detainees would be hooded, put into stress positions, which he took to mean positions to prevent relaxation rather than cause pain, and that they would not be allowed to sleep before questioning.

242. The central question is of course, what Mendonça knew about the treatment of the Op Salerno Detainees. Mendonça said that although he knew of their detention, and that he now accepted that during the course of their detention, the Detainees must have been assaulted by members of 1 QLR, he had no knowledge of the abuse and violence against them at the time.

243. Mendonça visited the TDF on Sunday night, at some time after 22.17hrs. His account was that he saw the Detainees seated, quiet and to the best of his recollection, without hoods, not in stress positions and not exhibiting signs of pain or injury. I do not accept the evidence of Rodgers that Mendonça and Briscoe visited the TDF on Monday morning. Both Mendonça and Briscoe deny this, and I prefer their evidence to that of Rodgers. Mendonça also said that he went to the TDF, but could not remember entering the building, soon after Baha Mousa's death. He could give no explanation for not going into the TDF. He stated that he was unaware of the conditions in the TDF at this latter stage of the detention.

244. In general terms Mendonça was an impressive witness. I formed the view that his evidence was given truthfully and in the main accurately. I have reached the following conclusions in relation to him.

245. Mendonça knew that conditioning entailed the hooding of detainees and the use of stress positions. I accept that he believed that if a stress position was used, it was a mild technique designed to prevent detainees from relaxing. I also accept that he delegated to the discretion of the BGIRO the administration of this process and the control over how long it lasted.

246. It is surprising, but not impossible, that Mendonça did not see the Detainees hooded or in stress positions on Sunday night. This visit may have occurred during the short period after Sgt Smith had ordered that the Detainees were not to be hooded, handcuffed or in stress positions. Bearing in mind my assessment of Mendonça's credibility I am not prepared to reject his account that he did not see anything untoward on this visit to the TDF.

247. In relation to the visit to the TDF on Monday night, Mendonça would have known that the Detainees had been held far in excess of the fourteen hour deadline, and that the process of tactical questioning, and therefore conditioning, had been protracted. A Detainee had just died in the custody of his Battlegroup. I find that this situation called for Mendonça to take steps to ensure that the other Detainees came to no harm. If he had seen the conditions in the TDF at that time he would have been able to immediately improve the Detainees' situation.

248. As the Commanding Officer, Mendonça ought to have recognised that a process enforcing hooding and stress positions involved a very serious risk of a detainee being exposed to inhumane treatment, and that the extreme heat compounded this risk. The failure of Mendonça to prevent the use of this type of conditioning process within his Battlegroup, or to even formally raise the matter with the Brigade, is a very significant one.

249. In these circumstances, it was also an error of judgment for Mendonça not to involve himself more closely in the oversight of the prisoner handling process, notwithstanding the other priorities he faced. Further, I think it likely that he fostered a "robust" approach to operations. I accept that Mendonça thought that he made it clear that the robust posture was not to carry over to into the handling of prisoners. However, the risk that such an approach would spill over into the treatment of detainees made the requirement for proper supervision of the guards and oversight of the prisoner handling process all the more necessary.

250. I find that Mendonça can properly be criticised for not inquiring into why the Detainees had not been sent to the TIF by Monday, and for not visiting the TDF himself that day to ensure that the Detainees were in a suitable condition.

251. In respect of the acts of physical violence against the Detainees during 14 to 16 September 2003, I accept that Mendonça was unaware of such conduct. However, the assaults involved at least a number of junior soldiers from more than one multiple, four junior NCOs and two senior NCOs. Payne's conduct alone tends strongly to suggest that he was untroubled about being seen doing what he was doing. I have found that Rodgers, a platoon commander and junior officer, knew what was happening, as did Peebles, a Major. I conclude that Mendonça ought to have known what was happening in the TDF.

252. Next, and in summary form, I shall point up some of the broader headline areas of particular concern which the Inquiry highlighted, and which inform both my analysis of events and the responsibility of individuals as well as my ultimate recommendations.

The Historical Background (Part I)

The Historical Context to 1996

253. On 2 March 1972, the Prime Minister, Rt. Hon. Edward Heath MP, announced in the House of Commons a ban on the five techniques (the Heath Statement). The techniques were hooding, the use of white or background noise, sleep deprivation, wall-standing (a form of stress position) and a limited diet. Despite this ban it appears that the five techniques did not disappear.

254. In the main body of the Report, I have been selective in my references to events before the Heath Statement. I do not consider it necessary or appropriate to make detailed findings on the use of conditioning techniques before that Statement.

255. What is clear is that doctrine and practice had developed separately in relation to interrogation in warfare and interrogation in internal security/counter insurgency operations.

256. In relation to the interrogation in warfare, guidance on interrogation was provided in both the 1951 Regulations for the Application of the 1949 Geneva Conventions and for the Treatment of Prisoners of War and the 1955 Pamphlet "Interrogation in War". While not beyond criticism on aspects such as the Geneva Convention prohibition on threats, the tenor of the guidance for the interrogation of prisoners of war was to make use of the prisoners' bewilderment, asking questions firmly in the form of orders, and maintaining strict discipline. There was no suggestion of the use of the five techniques in the guidance on interrogation in warfare.

257. It was in internal security and counter insurgency operations that the five techniques had come to be used. It is clear that some or all of the five techniques had been in use by the Armed Forces for many years before their use in Northern Ireland. An MoD historical narrative produced in 1971 admitted to their use in Malaya, Kenya, Cyprus, British Cameroons, Swaziland, Brunei, Aden, British Guiana, Borneo-Malaysia and finally, Northern Ireland. Their use over the years resulted in a number of government inquiries. Arising from events in Aden, the Bowen Report of November 1966 made a number of recommendations in relation to interrogation procedures. The operative guidance, the 1965 Directive on Military Interrogation and Internal Security Operations Overseas, was amended as a result. The 1965 Directive made no mention of the five techniques, referring only in general terms to "psychological attack" and "permissible techniques".

258. During the 1971 internment operations in Northern Ireland the five techniques were used. Allegations of mistreatment made by some of the men then arrested led to the establishment of the Compton Inquiry, which reported in November 1971. The report concluded that the five techniques constituted physical mistreatment but not "brutality". The men who had complained of ill-treatment during in-depth interrogation were subsequently to become the subjects of proceedings in the European Court of Human Rights in the Irish State Case in which that Court held the use of the five techniques in these cases amounted to a practice of inhuman and degrading treatment in breach of Article 3 of the European Convention on Human Rights.

259. The Compton Inquiry in a sense pleased no one. The Government of the day, unhappy with its findings, set up the Parker Inquiry to consider whether, and if so in what respects, the procedures then in place for the interrogation of terrorist suspects required amendment. Hooding, wall-standing and the use of noise were understood to carry important security benefits as well as the pressure they brought to bear for the purposes of interrogation. There was an active debate in relation to these techniques then thought by some to assist in obtaining intelligence in the context of terrorism/insurgency, and the extent to which their use should be presented as a security measure.

260. The Majority Report of Lord Parker and Mr Boyd Carpenter concluded that the moral question of whether the five techniques should be utilised depended upon the intensity with which they were applied and the provision of effective safeguards against excessive use. Subject to those safeguards, the Majority saw no reason to rule out the techniques on moral grounds.

261. The Minority Report of Lord Gardiner concluded that the five techniques were illegal in domestic law. He derided the decision to abandon, in colonial type emergency situations, the UK's "...*legal, well-tried and highly successful wartime interrogation methods and replace them with procedures which were secret, illegal, not morally justifiable and alien to the traditions of ... the greatest democracy in the world*".

262. The force of Lord Gardiner's argument and reasoning was recognised by the Government. While the Majority Report was not in terms disavowed, the Government's approach to future operations was more consistent with the Minority Report of Lord Gardiner.

263. Consequently, in the House of Commons on 2 March 1972, the Prime Minister, the Rt. Hon. Edward Heath MP, stated that the five techniques would not be used in future as an aid to interrogation. The Heath Statement was re-enforced in the Irish State Case when on 8 February 1977, the Attorney General stated that the United Kingdom gave an unqualified undertaking that the five techniques would not in any circumstances be reintroduced as an aid to interrogation. The Heath Statement is the real starting point for the Inquiry and I consider in the Report what it was intended to cover, what effect it had, and what consequences flowed from it.

264. An order of 1 March 1972, specific to Northern Ireland, had directed that the five techniques should not be used as an aid to interrogation, but also prohibited all use of hooding.

265. The true scope and extent of the Heath Statement has been a matter of debate. Having considered all of the materials available to the Inquiry I find firstly that the Heath Statement was intended to ban the use of the techniques as an aid to interrogation. I do not consider that it was intended to ban all use of hooding in all military operations, though it is undoubtedly the case that an order to that effect was issued for operations in Northern Ireland. Secondly, I think it most likely that the Heath Statement was intended to apply to operations worldwide. Thirdly, however, it is less clear whether it applied worldwide to all military operations or only worldwide to internal security/ counter insurgency type operations as opposed to warfare/international conflict. The point may be largely academic. The MoD recognised in 1972 that the five techniques would already be prohibited and unlawful in warfare by reason of the Geneva Conventions.

266. Following the Heath Statement, the 1965 Directive was revised. The 1972 Directive was formulated in two parts. Part I contained the main principles and was capable of being published. Part II gave more detailed instructions and was not intended to be published. After further debate about its extent, the 1972 Directive was limited to internal security operations. In making the decision, the discussions within the MoD again demonstrate that it was then recognised that the five techniques would be unlawful if used in warfare.

267. Part I of the 1972 Directive contained the specific prohibition on the use of the five techniques. In contrast to the Heath Statement, it was not in terms specifically limited to the use of the techniques as an aid to interrogation. Moreover the prohibition in Part I referred to blindfolds as well as hoods. However, I am clear that it can properly be inferred that sight deprivation was banned only as an aid to interrogation. The whole Directive was addressing interrogation by the Armed Forces in internal security operations. Part I of the 1972 Directive remained in force up to 2003.

268. Part II of the 1972 Directive was issued within the MoD with the intention that it was to be observed in all future training on interrogation in internal security operations, and was to be reflected in all interrogation training instructions. Part II included guidance on the methods and approaches that were permissible in interrogation.

269. There was a contemporaneous rationale for limiting the 1972 Directive to internal security operations and for it being issued using the mechanism of two separate parts with cross references. However, I conclude that these features can now be seen to have contributed over time to the loss of MoD corporate knowledge about the prohibition and its extent. It perpetuated the divide between doctrine on interrogation and prisoner handling doctrine in warfare and in internal security operations.

270. With hindsight, themes can be extracted from how matters developed after 1972:

(1) there was a failure to introduce any amendment to the doctrine on interrogation in wartime to mirror the specific prohibition on the five techniques that applied to internal security operations;

(2) the separate treatment of interrogation in warfare and interrogation in internal security/counter insurgency operations was perpetuated;

(3) the level of written guidance on interrogation, while often noted to be outdated, gradually degraded and became less specific; and

(4) guidance on prisoner handling did not adequately address sight deprivation.

271. The first of these failures is particularly regrettable because the undesirable difference between warfare and internal security interrogation doctrine was specifically noticed not long after the events of 1972. It was meant to be, and should have been, rectified. The point arose from SAS operations in Oman in 1973. There is no doubt that it was recognised as a concern at this time that the 1972 Directive and its constraints did not apply to warfare, and that doctrine in respect of interrogation in warfare was very outdated. Consequently, in September 1973, the Vice Chief of the General Staff directed the Intelligence Centre, Ashford to draft updated Joint Service guidance on interrogation in war. In doing so he required that close regard should be paid to the 1972 Directive including its constraints and principles. Such guidance, in the form of Joint Service Publication (JSP) 120(6) was finalised in June 1979, replacing the 1955 Pamphlet. Its production had taken almost six years, a reprehensible delay. Moreover,

although it set out sound principles in relation to the treatment of prisoners of war derived from the Geneva Conventions, JSP 120(6) did not contain any reference to the prohibition on the five techniques. I find that this document ought to have so referred. To that extent, the drafting of JSP 120(6) failed to meet the original instructions of the Vice Chief of the General Staff.

272. JSP 120(6) nevertheless did contain a short section on sight deprivation, permitting prisoners to be blindfolded where necessary for operational security. It also reiterated the Geneva Convention requirement for humane treatment of prisoners. But the instruction in JSP 120(6) on sight deprivation for operational security did not endure later changes. JSP 120(6) also reflected the gradual decline in the level of detail provided on interrogation methods. The 1955 Pamphlet had given guidance on all aspects of interrogation of prisoners of war. JSP 120(6) was stated merely to provide guidance for those who were not trained interrogators.

273. As regards guidance for prisoner of war handling, rather than interrogation, JSP 391 "Instructions for the Handling of Prisoners of War" was issued in 1990. It replaced the 1951 Regulations. Like JSP 120(6), JSP 391 contained much sound guidance on the principles of humane treatment of prisoners of war and reflected the prohibitions on violence, intimidation and insults. But it did not refer to the prohibition on the five techniques and it contained no guidance whatsoever on sight deprivation. Such guidance would have been obtained from JSP 391 only if the reader had followed an oblique cross reference to JSP 120(6).

274. These shortcomings contributed to the situation that no Op Telic Order, nor any readily accessible MoD doctrine at the time of Baha Mousa's death in 2003, referred to the prohibition on the five techniques. As the MoD concede, the five techniques should have been banned as an aid to interrogation in all situations and in all operations, wherever they took place. With respect to the gradual loss of the doctrine, the situation was only to get worse in years 1996 to 2003.

1996 to Early 2003

275. A review of interrogation policy took place in 1996 to 1997. In the course of this review, both parts of the 1972 Directive, JSP 120(6), the Compton and Parker Reports and the most relevant Articles of the Geneva Convention were all correctly identified as extant doctrine. As had been the case in 1972 to 1973, it was explicitly recognised that the use of the five techniques in interrogation in warfare would be unlawful, being in breach of the Geneva Conventions. It was also recognised that Part 1 of the 1972 Directive was narrow in its remit, applying only to internal security operations.

276. On 21 July 1997 the revised policy for interrogation and related activities was issued, having been agreed at Ministerial level. This revised policy:

(1) contained the strategic imperative that interrogation methods during all operations should comply with the Geneva Conventions and international and domestic law;

(2) cancelled Part II of the 1972 Directive (which had only applied to internal security operations); and

(3)   required that the procedures to be used by UK interrogators in an operational theatre should be governed by a detailed directive that incorporated current legal advice and was issued on behalf of the UK Joint Commander.

277.   In short summary, the effect was that for internal security operations, Part I of the 1972 Directive (and its prohibition on the five techniques) remained in place. But now, for all military operations across the whole conflict spectrum, a detailed directive had to be issued to govern the procedures to be used by UK interrogators.

278.   While it is true that the changes introduced to interrogation policy in 1997 made clear that compliance with the Geneva Conventions and international and domestic law was required, this 1996/1997 review was another regrettable missed opportunity to have made clear in the doctrine that the prohibition on the five techniques applied as much to international conflict/warfare as in internal conflict situations. I have no doubt that those who drafted the 1997 Policy understood that to be the position, and would have expected the prohibition on the five techniques to be contained in any operation specific detailed directive.

279.   Meanwhile the gradual degradation in the level of detailed guidance within interrogation doctrine continued.   JSP 120(6) became obsolete. The precise date when this occurred cannot be ascertained. But it is clear that it was superseded by Joint Warfare Publication (JWP) 2-00 "Intelligence Support to Joint Operations", first promulgated in 1999. While JSP 120(6) had been far less specific than the 1955 Pamphlet on interrogation methods, JWP 2-00 was now yet more general in nature. It concentrated on the intelligence cycle and architecture. It did not deal with interrogation and tactical questioning. Such references as there were to interrogation were incidental. In contrast to JSP 120(6), JWP 2-00 included no guidance at all on sight deprivation.

280.   Thus, the position had been reached whereby the only doctrinal guidance available in relation to the interrogation of prisoners of war was from NATO Standardisation Agreements, the 1997 Policy guidelines, both at a high or very high level of generality, and a further requirement for a detailed directive to be produced to govern procedures in any operational theatre.

281.   It is a matter of great regret that by this time the UK had no adequate written doctrine for interrogating prisoners of war. The MoD creditably conceded as much in its closing submissions. But is it is not as though this gap in doctrine went unnoticed at the time.

282.   In 1999, S040 was a Naval Lt Cmdr (the equivalent of a Major in the Army) and the Officer Commanding the Reserves Wing and a Reserves Unit at the Joint Services Interrogation Organisation (JSIO). He had noted the absence of interrogation doctrine and the consequent difficulty of training and exercising the reserve companies. S040's Commanding Officer accordingly tasked him to conduct a review.

283.   S040 was relatively new in post. He canvassed widely to gather the existing doctrine. S040 then sought input from the Army Legal Service (ALS) about interrogation. This request referred to the Geneva Conventions, NATO STANAGs 2044 and 2033, JSP 391, JSP 120(6) and JWP 1-10, but, significantly, the request did not refer to the Heath Statement, the 1972 Directive or the 1997 Policy. As the JSIO review progressed, those omissions were not rectified, and an ignorance of what those texts provided coloured the review's debate. This is representative, not of any failing on S040's part, but the wider MoD corporate loss of understanding of what doctrine was applicable.

284. On the positive side, the JSIO review did identify a need for direction and clear policy. Both capability and doctrinal shortcomings were identified. When S040's paper was put up for consideration in May 2000, the Commanding Officer of the JSIO noted that the issues requiring clarification were complex and warned that this was traditionally a charter for procrastination. That was all too prophetic. No further policy or doctrine on tactical questioning or interrogation was drafted between 2 May 2000 and Baha Mousa's death in September 2003.

285. While S040's paper was gradually taken forward by others, the emphasis shifted significantly towards the capability issues, rather than focusing on both doctrinal shortcomings and capability issues. By mid 2002, the review was still stating that that there was no MoD endorsed doctrine for interrogation. But by now this was clearly a secondary concern. By early 2003 the concerns about the lack of doctrine appear to have been lost altogether, the review now stating that there was adequate doctrine, in JWP 1-10, but that the UK had not invested in the means to deliver it. Eventually the paper and the capability issues on interrogation were subsumed into a wider review of human intelligence capabilities that was then ongoing but was not completed until after Baha Mousa's death.

286. It is baffling that by early 2003 the review paper had come to suggest that there was adequate interrogation doctrine. No further interrogation doctrine had been published since the earlier versions of the review had suggested that there was no MoD endorsed doctrine for interrogation. Nearly three years after drafting his initial paper correctly identifying doctrinal shortcomings, S040 was preparing to mobilise to Iraq where he was to command the JFIT. On 1 March 2003, weeks before the ground offensive, he wrote a lessons learned memorandum commenting that the JFIT had no interrogation doctrine on which to build its function and recommending, "*Interrogation doctrine must be promulgated without delay*".

287. So much for interrogation doctrine and guidance. As to prisoner handling doctrine, in March 2001 JSP 391 was replaced by JWP 1-10 "Prisoners of War Handling". This was the main prisoner of war handling doctrine in place during Op Telic in 2003.

288. JWP 1-10 expressly recorded that it was not a detailed guide to the interrogation of prisoners of war. It did address tactical questioning, albeit fairly briefly, including the prohibition on physical or mental pressure or other forms of coercion to induce prisoners of war to answer questions. Whilst clearly reiterating the need for humane treatment of prisoners, JWP 1-10 contained no reference to the prohibition on the five techniques. Like its predecessor publication, JWP 1-10 did not give any guidance whatsoever on sight deprivation.

289. JWP 1-10 was a detailed and lengthy publication. It should have addressed both sight deprivation and the prohibition on the five techniques. I am satisfied that both omissions were wrong and brought about unfortunate consequences on the front line. A significant body of evidence discloses that during Op Telic it was plainly not evident to experienced officers and NCOs that stress positions and hooding were wrong. Specific reference to the five techniques, and hooding in particular, with guidance on the use and mechanics of sight deprivation of prisoners, was a necessary constituent of adequate written military doctrine at this time.

290. By the time of Op Telic, a late draft of JSP 383 "The Manual of the Law of Armed Conflict" (finally published in 2004) was in circulation and available to some MoD and

Army legal advisers. It briefly addressed the subject of interrogation and stressed the importance of treating prisoners humanely. It warned that no physical or mental torture or any other form of coercion may be used to obtain information. Importantly, it also mentioned that blindfolding and segregation may be necessary in the interests of security, restraint or to prevent collaboration before interrogation, but that those measures must be truly justified and be for as short a period as possible. This guidance mirrored guidance produced by the International Committee of the Red Cross (ICRC). I reject the argument advanced by the MoD that this guidance was very clear about the method to be used. Without more, a reference to blindfolding would have been understood by many soldiers to permit the use of hoods as a form of blindfolding. The manual did not refer to the prohibition on the five techniques being designed as a manual on LOAC rather than on human rights law.

291. It appears to be the case that, aside from Part 1 of the 1972 Directive, this part of JSP 383 was the only place within all of the available policy and doctrine publications in 2003 where sight deprivation was addressed in any way. I note, however, that JSP 383 was a manual, then only in draft form, and primarily for military lawyers. It was not readily accessible operational guidance for commanders on the ground.

292. Taking a step back, it can be seen that at the time of Op Telic there was no proper MoD endorsed doctrine on interrogation of prisoners of war that was generally available. Knowledge of Part I of the 1972 Directive on internal security operations as a policy document containing the prohibition on the five techniques had largely been lost, and the prohibition was not contained in JWP 1-10. Despite JWP 1-10 status as the lead publication on the handling of prisoners of war, it also made no mention of sight deprivation.

293. This position had developed over decades and was the product not only of failings but also of missed opportunities. In those circumstances, although I make comments about the role played by some individuals at certain times, it is fair and appropriate to conclude that the position outlined above was as a result of a corporate failure by the MoD.

294. I do not lose sight of the fact that although doctrinal shortcomings may have contributed to the use of a process of unlawful conditioning being adopted by 1 QLR, it cannot excuse or mitigate the kicking, punching and beating of Baha Mousa which was a direct and proximate cause of his death, or the treatment meted out to his fellow Detainees.

Teaching and training (Part VI)

295. The training in relation to various functions carried out by the Armed Forces was of considerable relevance to the Inquiry's investigation of the course of events during Op Telic 1 and Op Telic 2.

LOAC, Prisoner Handling training and Counter Insurgency Training

296. Two aspects of the training for the infantry soldier on the ground were of particular interest; the training in the LOAC and prisoner handling exercises conducted at unit level.

297. All soldiers undergo training in LOAC. At the relevant time leading up to Op Telic, it was mandated by Army Individual Training Directive 6 that all personnel were to receive one 40 minute period of training in LOAC annually. Such training was substantially based on the pamphlet, "The Soldier's Guide to the Law of Armed Conflict". Although the guide clearly emphasised the principle of the humane treatment of prisoners, it did not mention the prohibition on the five techniques or give any detailed guidance on prisoner handling and the treatment of civilian detainees.

298. A significant number of soldiers giving evidence to the Inquiry recalled that the LOAC training sessions also involved the presentation of a video in relation to LOAC. The video that most witnesses remembered seeing was the 1986 video "The Law of Armed Conflict". The video was based on a conventional cold-war scenario. It addressed the legitimacy of targets, recognising protective emblems, the white flag and protecting non-combatants. But it did not address civilian detainees nor did it refer to the prohibition on the five techniques.

299. A second video, "Handling prisoners of war" went into more detail. But the Inquiry received very little evidence to suggest that regular soldiers ever saw this second video. Unlike the first video, it did briefly cover sight deprivation stating that prisoners should only be blindfolded if moved through sensitive military locations. It did not include any express mention of the prohibition on the five techniques. Its content was probably largely academic because it appears to have had a very limited circulation.

300. At Sandhurst, officers would receive more training than the annual training requirement for all personnel. But this was still training at a level of broad generality and there is no indication that it covered the prohibition on the five techniques.

301. In general terms, although certainly not exclusively, the soldiers' evidence about the LOAC training gave the impression that it had become formulaic and outdated, that the age and style of the video training undermined the seriousness of the content, and that, insofar as the training may have consisted of a mere showing of a video, it was somewhat perfunctory.

302. I accept that the basic message that violence towards prisoners was forbidden was asserted in LOAC training. The Inquiry heard a significant amount of evidence to illustrate that soldiers knew there was a clear duty to treat prisoners humanely. The difficulty is that what amounts to inhumane treatment may not always be clear. Military opinion varied on whether hooding was humane treatment, and some did not consider all use of stress positions to be inhumane.

303. In relation to prisoner handling exercises, a number of soldiers deployed on Op Telic 1 and 2 told the Inquiry that they had witnessed the hooding of those playing prisoners and/or had been hooded themselves during exercises. I accept that these exercises were mainly attempting to train in the procedures at the point of capture, at which hooding was seemingly utilised for security purposes. However, such exercises ran the risk that soldiers might have been misled about what was acceptable in relation to the restriction of sight further up the prisoner handling chain. Most often, where prisoner handling was part of a military exercise, it stopped at the point of capture. For the most part, handling further up the prisoner handling chain tended not to be practised on exercises.

304. Later in their careers, some officers would probably have been taught about the prohibition on the five techniques. Between 1977 and 1996 the Army Staff Course (ASC) included a Counter Insurgency (COIN) element and the teaching of this module included reference to the Parker Report. The Parker Report was required reading for this course from 1977 to 1996, and the various handbooks issued for the course, at least between 1989 and 1996, contained the history of the use of the five techniques in Northern Ireland, the Parker Report, the Heath Statement and the 1972 Directive. Mendonça, Commanding Officer of 1 QLR throughout the relevant events, attended this training course in 1995, as did at various other times a number of senior officers who deployed during Op Telic 1 or 2. The training records indicate that in 1995, the year Mendonça attended, the course would also have included a syndicate discussion on the use of force which included viewing a video which explained and included discussion on the history of the prohibition on the five techniques.

305. As he was to tell me in evidence, by 2003 Mendonça had forgotten these elements of the course. He was not alone in failing to remember this aspect of training. Some 29 other witnesses to the Inquiry attended the ASC course. Of those only three gave evidence indicating that they specifically remembered being taught about the prohibition on the five techniques on the ASC. Accordingly, I conclude that regrettably the teaching did not succeed in instilling lasting knowledge of the prohibition in all officers who attended the course.

Provost Staff Training

306. Detention of soldiers at battalion level is dealt with by soldiers appointed as Regimental Police (RP), also known as Provost Staff. They are not the same, nor as thoroughly trained, as the Military Provost Staff (MPS). To equip them to detain soldiers within their own battalion base, at least one RP from each unit must have completed the Regimental Police Course (RPC).

307. Unsurprisingly, the RP's familiarity with detention matters meant that on Op Telic they would often be used for prisoner of war, detainee and internee handling. That was certainly the case in 1 QLR.

308. The RPC was a week long course. It obviously included the principle of using minimum force on prisoners, as well as how to escort prisoners and the use of restraints. However, the course focused on the detention of British soldiers. It did not include any teaching in relation to prisoner of war handling, or the handling of civilian detainees on operations outside the UK. It did not include the prohibition on the use of the five techniques. Neither did it include formal instruction in control and restraint techniques. However, a "general interest" demonstration of control and restraint techniques was a feature of the course. During this demonstration, RP staff had the opportunity to try out physical holds and locks, even though they would remain unqualified to apply them in practice. The Inquiry heard evidence that in this informal demonstration, students would be warned about the risks of positional asphyxia in prisoners subject to restraint.

309. The lack of training relating to detention on operations and the informal glimpse of control and restraint techniques are areas of concern in relation to the RPC course. I consider the lack of any training in relation to detention of captured persons on operations to have been a deficiency in the RP training. At the very least RP should

have been taught that the same basic standards of treatment should have been applied to detention on operations as in the detention of British soldiers. Further they should have been told this should apply to all categories of prisoner, whether prisoners of war or suspected insurgents, terrorists or criminals.

310. The identified insufficiencies in the RPC training programme were not, in my opinion, a causative factor in the treatment of the Op Salerno Detainees. Payne, the former Provost Sergeant of 1 QLR, restrained Baha Mousa during the fatal struggle partly by putting his knee into Baha Mousa's back. There is no sufficient evidence to support a finding that in doing so he was incorrectly applying a technique he had been taught on the RPC.

JSIO Tactical Questioning and Interrogation Training

311. The Inquiry considered in depth the training given to tactical questioners and interrogators by the JSIO. Most seriously, it has been necessary to investigate whether tactical questioners might have been expressly taught to use the five prohibited techniques, or any of them, by their instructors. Students and instructors gave evidence and I have considered all the relevant surviving teaching materials.

312. The starting point is that for the historical reasons already analysed, there was an absence of policy or doctrine to which the JSIO could teach. However, I am confident that the JSIO courses taught that prisoners must be treated humanely. Relevant aspects of the Geneva Conventions and LOAC were referred to, although their full implications may not have been well understood. Students were taught to maintain a firm, fair and efficient prisoner handling process in part to help to maintain the shock of capture.

313. As regards the written training materials, I conclude that it is very likely that by 2002 to 2003, these did not include any specific reference to the prohibition on the five techniques. Some individual instructors who were familiar with the background may well have included reference to the prohibition on the five techniques in their own teaching on the courses. Nevertheless, I am sure that insufficient emphasis was given to the prohibition on the five techniques in the JSIO teaching.

314. While the specific prohibition on the five techniques was not sufficiently taught, during elements of the course it is likely that instructors referred to prohibitions on some of the individual techniques, in particular stress positions. It is likely that the courses taught the prohibition on sleep deprivation, but this was subject to different approaches on the part of instructors in relation to keeping prisoners awake pending initial tactical questioning soon after capture.

315. As to sight deprivation, the surviving written training materials suggest that the teaching was that prisoners should be deprived of their sight for security reasons, using a blindfold. The prohibition on using hoods or blindfolds as an aid to interrogation was not specified within the written materials. It was stated, inappropriately, that the pressure on a blindfolded prisoner could be increased by walking around the blindfolded prisoner when he first arrived in the interrogation room, before the blindfold was removed. This was teaching the use of sight deprivation as an aid to interrogation contrary to the Heath Statement, and the 1972 Directive. This should not have been taught. It may

have weakened the message that sight deprivation as an aid to interrogation was prohibited.

316.   I am satisfied students were taught that sight deprivation for security purposes was acceptable and that sight deprivation actually during questioning was prohibited and counter productive. For the most part, I consider that the message conveyed was that sight deprivation *as an aid to interrogation* was prohibited. However, the teaching imparted the message that the deprivation of sight for security reasons had an incidental benefit of maintaining the shock of capture. This too risked undermining the message that sight deprivation as an aid to interrogation was prohibited. I find it likely that blindfolds were what were usually used on the course as the means of depriving the sight of those playing the part of prisoners. However, hoods were possibly used on some occasions. I find that teaching on what means could be used for security sight deprivation in an operational theatre most likely varied from instructor to instructor. This part of the teaching was particularly prone to different interpretation depending on the particular instructor. Students were at risk of coming away from the courses with an unclear understanding of the proper limits and purposes of sight deprivation.

317.   It is clear that in some aspects the teaching was unacceptable. As I have indicated, teaching students to walk around a blindfolded prisoner to increase the pressure before the blindfold was removed was wrong. The teaching of the harsh approach included direct insults and permitted racist and homophobic verbal abuse. Application of the harsh technique in an angry manner risked being a form of intimidation to coerce a prisoner, and the technique also included the use of indirect threats to instil fear.

318.   I find that some senior instructors, the heads of the branch and their immediate chain of command, might all have done more to ensure that not teaching the basics of the five techniques was made clear and to ensure compliance with the requirements of Article 17 of the Third Geneva Convention. Nevertheless, I attribute the main fault for the inclusion of inappropriate training and/or exclusion of appropriate material to a systemic failure over a number of years. As dealt with in detail in this Report, and touched on elsewhere in this Summary, central features of this systemic failure were a wholesale lack of MoD doctrine in interrogation under which JSIO could formulate its training, and the lack of proper accessible legal advice and legal assessment of JSIO training.

319.   1 QLR did not have any trained tactical questioners. But the JSIO did run a shortened course before Op Telic 2 on 10 June 2003 which was attended by some members of 1 QLR, including Payne. I accept that this training made it clear that it did not qualify any attendees to conduct tactical questioning, and that blindfolds would have been used on the course to demonstrate sight deprivation rather than hoods. However, I am not convinced that the teaching would have made clear that blindfolds were preferred to hoods as the means to achieve sight deprivation on operations. I accept the training covered the maintenance of the shock of capture. However, I reject the suggestion made by Payne that sleep deprivation, specifically as an aid to interrogation, was encouraged on the course. It is possible, however, that those attending may have been told that it was acceptable to keep prisoners awake during the very early hours of detention pending imminent tactical questioning.

Conduct After Capture training

320. Conduct After Capture (CAC) training prepares British service personnel for the event of them being captured. I do not doubt that it is necessary for all, and that more intense practical training in CAC is necessary for those prone to capture.

321. Most service personnel received only theoretical annual and pre-deployment training (PDT) in CAC. While this training was classroom based and theoretical, more express warnings should have been included in the theoretical training.

322. Practical CAC training, in which a variety of the five techniques might actually be used on British soldiers to prepare them better to deal with being captured, was given only to a minority of personnel who were prone to capture. Such training consistently contained a warning by way of a briefing to all those involved in the training that procedures would be used on the course that would simulate what a non Geneva Convention compliant enemy might do. This warning would have been better if it had also included a specific reminder about the prohibition on the five techniques. Perhaps more significantly, the MoD has rightly accepted that the use of recently trained interrogators to take part in practical CAC exercises was an imprudent practice. I find it did run a real risk of contamination.

323. There was evidence that unauthorised and informal CAC type training exercises were from time to time run at unit and sub-unit level. Where this might have occurred, I view it as highly unlikely that appropriate warnings were consistently issued about the techniques being used. There is anecdotal evidence that such training has been a repeated problem. It must cease.

Medical Staff Training

324. The final category of relevant specialist training is that given in relation to the medical care of detainees. Two aspects of this training are of particular interest. Firstly, the extent of the ethical duty to avoid involvement in interrogation, and secondly what instructions existed concerning the practical procedures for the medical treatment of detainees.

325. Historically, in relation to the situation in Northern Ireland in the early 1970s, the MoD had in place a detailed policy as to the medical care of detainees. However, by 2003 this had regrettably been lost and there was no MoD or Armed Forces' policy dealing specifically with the provision of medical care to detainees. This was a serious lapse.

326. Significantly, the result of this lack of policy was that RMOs deployed on Operation Telic 2, including Keilloh who was in direct contact with Baha Mousa and the other Op Salerno Detainees, were provided with no specific guidance as to how to deal with prisoners.

PDT

327. The most current training received by those soldiers in Iraq during Op Telic 1 and 2 was their PDT. Some PDT is provided by the Operational Training Advisory Group (OPTAG). Other training is designed and conducted by the Battlegroup itself, or as

part of training offered by higher formations. PDT is honed and improved the longer operations endure. It can be truncated and far less developed at the start of a major operation.

328. There were significant pressures on PDT, in particular for Op Telic 1, but also for Op Telic 2. As regards prisoner handling, the training must also be assessed taking into account the doctrinal shortcomings I have already identified. Those shortcomings were not the fault of those providing training immediately prior to deployment on Op Telic.

329. For Op Telic 1, the OPTAG contribution to PDT was in the form of a CD package containing PowerPoint presentations. The subjects addressed included CAC and a briefing on prisoner of war handling. The latter aimed to confirm what soldiers should already have known from their annual LOAC training. It included appropriate references to humane treatment, and the prohibitions on violence and coercion to obtain information from prisoners. But it was silent on sight deprivation and did not mention the prohibition on the five techniques. Since, by 2003, the prohibition on the five techniques had substantially disappeared from the doctrine and guidance on interrogation and tactical questioning, it is not fair to criticise those who created the Op Telic 1 CD package for this omission.

330. Additionally, in relation to Op Telic 1, once in theatre but before the ground force invasion, the 1 (UK) Div Legal branch led LOAC training and the MPS led a 40 minute prisoner handling session, both aimed at combat troops. For those troops able to attend the latter sessions, it is likely they were advised not to put sandbags over prisoners' heads. The inclusion of this instruction arose from the particular experience of the Officer who led the MPS training. Since at least parts of the infantry appeared to have received the message from exercises and elsewhere that hooding was a routine practice for prisoner of war handling, it is very unlikely that a single in-theatre briefing would have been sufficient to eradicate that understanding. Self evidently, these MPS sessions were not sufficient to prevent the practice of hooding prisoners during Op Telic 1.

331. I recognise that the training period for Op Telic 2 was also less than ideal. 1 QLR were still carrying out duties on Op Fresco covering the fire-fighters' strike. This was outside the MoD's control. Additionally, 1 QLR did not receive a formal warning order for deployment until May 2003. This resulted in 1 QLR not receiving priority treatment for their training needs. Due to the deployment of many of the F branch JSIO instructors on Op Telic 1, 1 QLR did not manage to have any of its personnel trained in tactical questioning before deployment.

332. The OPTAG training for Op Telic 2 consisted of fuller training than a simple CD package. But even for Op Telic 2, the OPTAG training was adversely affected by the lack of time and resources. It was not possible to complete the full cycle by which OPTAG would normally check that their training had been fully received and understood.

333. Three elements of the OPTAG training were of particular interest to the Inquiry. Firstly, as part of the All Ranks briefing, a presentation on "Legal Powers" was given by Lt Col Charles Barnett the 3 (UK) Div Commander Legal. This briefing conveyed the message that soldiers were not to humiliate or harm prisoners. Barnett did not think that this briefing addressed the ban on hooding which had been introduced in Iraq during Op Telic 1. This recollection conflicted with that of Royce of 1 QLR, an important Inquiry

witness, who attended the lecture. He thought that this presentation had specified that detainees (as opposed to prisoners of war) could not be hooded. In my view, both witnesses were honestly seeking to recall what was said. The explanation is probably that Royce gleaned his knowledge of the hooding ban from some part of the training, but not from Barnett in the course of this specific lecture. It would have been better if Barnett had included the hooding ban in his presentation but it was not a culpable omission taking into account the ground he had to cover.

334. Secondly, one of the "Train the Trainer" packages was in "Patrol Skills and Public Order". This addressed prisoner handling at or near the point of capture and contained some instruction on arrest and detention techniques, including "control positions". These were described as prisoners kneeling back on their crossed calves with hands behind their head, for a limited period of time, and not "full" stress positions. However, explicit warnings that control positions could only go so far were probably not given.

335. Thirdly, some members of 1 QLR gave evidence that the OPTAG training had included the hooding of prisoners for security purposes. I do not accept that the OPTAG "Train the Trainer" packages positively advocated hooding. Unfortunately, it is however also likely that the OPTAG training did not include any clear guidance that hooding had been prohibited in theatre during Op Telic 1.

336. There was a clear need for more precise and detailed training in relation to sight deprivation. I do not single out the OPTAG trainers for criticism in failing to provide this in the context of the short notice, curtailed training and importantly, the inadequate doctrine at this time in 2003.

337. 1 QLR also instigated an "in-house" training programme. The Inquiry heard evidence that this too was hindered by lack of time, resources, and a clear indication of 1 QLR's intended role on deployment. As part of training, 1 QLR soldiers carried out public order/internal security type exercises at the Whinney Hill facility, Catterick. There is a significant body of evidence that hooding was used at least during some exercises as part of this training. There are a number of reasons forming the context in which this occurred: hooding had been taught on previous prisoner handling exercises, including promotion courses at Brecon; some 1 QLR soldiers had seen 1 Black Watch (BW) hood prisoners during the 1 QLR recce in early May 2003; the primary available doctrine JWP 1-10 did not mention hooding; and OPTAG training had not included the Op Telic 1 hooding ban.

338. The inclusion of hooding as a method of sight deprivation in 1 QLR training occurred after hooding had been banned in theatre during Op Telic 1, so it was clearly inappropriate. Responsibility for this does not lie with those individuals who delivered PDT within 1 QLR. The fact hooding was included in the 1 QLR training reflects the wider lack of any clear or detailed training or policy on sight deprivation.

Early Theatre-specific Orders on Prisoner Handling and the HUMINT Directive for Op Telic 1 (Part VII)

339. In assessing the early directives and orders for Op Telic, it is necessary to remember the application of the doctrine of "mission command" which guides how the Army operates. The principle of mission command means that higher level directives and orders are not to be expected to include detailed instruction in how to achieve the desired outcome. Instead, a clear intention is to be stated, with an explanation of what effect is to be created. The mode is one of setting out what is to be achieved and why, not dictating fine detail of how to do it. However, a commander will also have a duty of oversight in relation to directives and orders issued. Just as importantly, the commander still has responsibility for the outcome. Tasks can be delegated but not responsibility.

340. The high level directives for the Op Telic campaign addressed prisoner handling and interrogation and tactical questioning (the latter usually under "HUMINT" instructions) in the following manner.

341. Before the launch of Op Telic, there was a cascade of high level Directives which included some guidance in relation to prisoners of war. The Chief of the Defence Staff, Admiral the Lord Boyce, issued the CDS's Execute Directive to Lt Gen Sir John Reith, the Chief of Joint Operations at Permanent Joint Headquarters (PJHQ). In turn, Reith issued a Mission Directive to Air Marshal Brian Burridge, the National Contingent Commander. Reference to prisoners of war in these Directives was at a high level of generality largely referring to, and relying upon, JWP 1-10.

342. Burridge issued his own Directive to the commanders of the three Services and other recipients such as the Joint Force Logistics Commander. This made explicit the obligation to ensure that all those involved in prisoner of war and detainee handling had an understanding of and complied with the Geneva Conventions, the LOAC and the provisions of JWP 1-10.

343. Maj Gen Robin Brims of 1 (UK) Div also issued Directives, in addition to operational orders. I acknowledge that Brims issued impressive guidance, communicating very clearly his intent and the critical importance of maintaining discipline.

344. There was greater specific detail in relation to the prisoner handling process included in the operation orders, including the following.

345. The main operation order covering the early stages of the war was the 1 (UK) Div Base OpO 001/03; which contained two annexes directly relevant to prisoner handling: a Legal Annex including the injunction that enemy prisoners of war were to be treated in accordance with the LOAC and any further policy issued by UK National Contingent Command (NCC), and an Annex comprising 1 (UK) Div's "Enemy Prisoner of War Standard Operating Instruction", emphasising the principle of humane treatment, the parameters of the Geneva Conventions and more detail on prisoner handling. The Divisional Order was reflected in, and cascaded by, Brigade level orders including 7 Armd Bde's Operation Order dated 6 March 2003.

346. 1 (UK) Div's Divisional Support Group issued DSG FRAGO 29 concerning prisoner of war handling. Once again this was a document which emphasised the importance of prisoners of war being handled in accordance with the Geneva Convention and made reference to the JWP 1-10. But as a predominantly logistics order, no other information was provided on the physical aspects of prisoner handling.

347. An aide memoire on LOAC was also issued to all personnel, which included specific rules in respect of prisoners of war and civilians and reiterated the message of humane treatment.

348. On the basis of the material disclosed to the Inquiry, the following conclusions are appropriate.

349. I find that there was a clear message imparted to all soldiers about the importance of the humane treatment of prisoners of war and compliance with the Geneva Conventions and LOAC. In the higher level Directives, reference to and reliance upon JWP 1-10 and the Third Geneva Convention was not an unreasonable approach.

350. Moving towards the more tactical level, the instructions naturally became more detailed. Yet none of the Divisional or Brigade orders addressed hooding or gave guidance on sight deprivation or the prohibition on the five techniques. For the most part, the approach remained either to refer to JWP 1-10 or to précis the advice contained within it, which was, as we have seen, silent on both the five techniques and sight deprivation. Thus as a result, on the ground, the guidance given to soldiers and junior commanders was inadequate. To answer the question of whether prisoners of war could be deprived of their sight, and if so by what means and for what purposes, units deployed on Op Telic 1 would have had to rely on their previous training.

351. However, having reached this conclusion, I do not think it proper or appropriate to blame individual Division and Brigade level staff officers for this shortcoming. Commanders issuing orders addressing amongst many other things prisoners of war handling were entitled to rely on JWP 1-10. The MoD is corporately responsible for the fact that the guidance in JWP 1-10 was itself inadequate. I am satisfied that the historic failures to maintain adequate prisoner of war handling and interrogation doctrine led directly to inadequate prisoner of war handling guidance being issued in the lead-up to the warfighting phase of Op Telic 1.

352. As can be seen, the authorisation for interrogation and tactical questioning to be undertaken and directions in respect of those procedures were required to be contained in a detailed directive as mandated by the 1997 Policy for Interrogation and Related Activities. Reith, the Chief of Joint Operations, did issue a HUMINT Directive for Op Telic.

353. The version of the Directive seen by the Inquiry was dated 27 February 2003. I find that it was only a draft of the Directive. It is a concern that MoD did not retain the final version of such a significant document.

354. The Directive did not include any reference to the prohibition on the five techniques or specify the actual methods and approaches that were permitted to be used in interrogation or tactical questioning. This arose because the key officers involved in drafting the Directive were not aware of the Heath Statement, nor were they even aware of the more recent 1997 Policy.

355. The MoD rightly conceded that the HUMINT Directive did not meet the terms of the 1997 Policy. Its content was indeed inadequate. In my view this unacceptable position is not the fault of the individuals involved in drafting the HUMINT Directive. Rather, it is a consequence of the systemic failure within the MoD which allowed knowledge of the Heath Statement, the 1972 Directive, and even the current interrogation policy from 1997, to have effectively become lost.

356. As I have concluded in Part VII of this Report, to this extent, the MoD did not have a grasp on, or adequate understanding of, its own interrogation policy. Whilst repeating that the omissions in the Directive cannot excuse the attacks perpetrated on Baha Mousa and the other Detainees, the absence of a clear statement in the Directive that the five techniques were prohibited as aids to interrogation may have contributed to the failure to prevent their use.

357. On 25 February 2003 a submission was put to the Secretary of State for Defence, the Rt. Hon. Geoffrey Hoon MP. It sought approval for HUMINT operations, including interrogation and tactical questioning, in support of UK forces deployed on Op Telic. He, in turn sought the approval of the Foreign Secretary of the day, the Rt. Hon. Jack Straw MP. Both Ministers gave the recommended approval for HUMINT operations.

358. On 14 March 2003, a minute to the Secretary of State invited him to note the arrangements that had been made for handling prisoners of war. Hoon's response duly noted these arrangements and in particular that they were designed to ensure that the UK met its legal obligations.

359. I do not think it appropriate to criticise these two submissions to Ministers nor their response. It is not realistic to expect that the doctrinal shortcomings in relation to the five techniques and guidance on sight deprivation should have been apparent to those directly involved in these two submissions.

Early Hooding and Concerns about Prisoner Handling at the JFIT March / April 2003 (Part VIII)

360. In the first few weeks of the warfighting phase of Op Telic, it is clear that UK forces used hoods on prisoners at the JFIT. The ICRC and various British officers raised concerns about this practice, which led to the banning of the use of hoods in theatre.

361. The JFIT was a self-contained compound within the prisoner of war facility at Um Qasr. This facility changed names a number of times. By the time of Baha Mousa's death it was known as the TIF. For ease of reference and consistency, I shall refer to it as the TIF, although in relation to the early hooding events, it held prisoners of war not internees.

362. The TIF was run by the UK's Prisoner of War Handling Organisation under the command of Col S009. The JFIT staff ran the interrogation of suspected high value prisoners. The JFIT was commanded early in Op Telic 1 by Lt Cdr S040. His Operations Officer was Capt S014. S040 reported direct to the 1 (UK) Div J2X, Maj S002, who had responsibility for HUMINT matters at Divisional level. S009 also reported to Division but he did not control the activities of the JFIT. Thus there were separate chains of command for the JFIT and the Prisoner of War Handling Organisation.

363. The controversy over the use of hoods at the JFIT arose during the warfighting phase of Op Telic. That context needs to be understood. The camp had to be constructed almost from scratch. Resources were few. Fighting was still going on nearby. The facility was sometimes targeted. Initially conditions and facilities were difficult for the military staff and prisoners alike. The JFIT compound, once constructed, was intended to deal with 30 prisoners but on occasions had to deal with considerably more.

364. Shortly after the arrival of the JFIT at the TIF, S009 saw prisoners within the JFIT compound, kneeling on their haunches in the sun, cuffed to the rear and hooded with plastic sandbags. S009 assumed the positions they were in to be stress positions, although he had not seen positions used other than prisoners kneeling on their haunches. He did not know how long the prisoners had been kept hooded. When he raised his concerns directly with those in command at the JFIT, he was told that the methods being used were known and approved of by 1 (UK) Div.

365. At the request of S009, Col Christopher Vernon, the Chief Media Operations 1 (UK) Div, visited the TIF. This was probably around 27 or 28 March 2003. He too witnessed a number of prisoners hooded, handcuffed to the rear and kneeling with their posteriors resting on their heels in what could be considered stress positions.   Some were kneeling in this way but others were sitting.

366. Brims visited the TIF and witnessed a single hooded prisoner being moved under escort. This was on 28 March 2003. Brims was concerned that hooding did not fit the type of operation in which UK forces were involved. He resolved to review the practice.

367. Lt Col Nicholas Mercer, 1 (UK) Div's legal adviser, raised strong concerns. Over 28 and 29 March 2003 Mercer visited the Prisoner of War Handling Organisation and on one occasion saw a large group of prisoners hooded, handcuffed to the rear and kneeling in the sand. He noted a generator running outside an interrogation tent. He wrote a memo to Brims expressing his concern that this treatment violated the Geneva Convention. I accept the general tenor of Mercer's evidence as to what he witnessed.

368. S014, the Operations Officer of the JFIT, explained that padded masks were initially used for sight deprivation, but the supply of these quickly ran out and sandbags as hoods were used as an alternative from early on in the JFIT's operations. Sometimes these hoods were folded up to give a double layer of covering to the eyes away from the prisoner's mouths. S014 stated that the hooding was for security reasons. However, I find that the maintenance of the shock of capture was also understood by him to be a side benefit of the use of hoods. S014 denied that stress positions were used. Prisoners were however not permitted to sleep before their initial interrogation.

369. S040 also said that sight deprivation had been applied for the purposes of security. After the blindfolds had run out, the use of sandbags for this purpose was a naturally occurring process. S040 accepted that sometimes more than one hood was used, and that some sandbags made of synthetic fibres were used. He accepted that in some cases, prisoners may in total have been hooded for longer than 24 hours.

370. S002, as J2X for 1 (UK) Div, had responsibility for matters across the whole HUMINT spectrum but I accept that tactical questioning and interrogation would have been only a small part of this responsibility. He witnessed prisoners hooded at the JFIT. He

understood that prisoners might be hooded for security reasons for up to 24 hours, but told the Inquiry that he believed that the hoods would be taken off intermittently for fifteen to twenty minutes every two hours or so. He recalled that S014 had indicated before the warfighting phase that hooding would carry benefits which included preserving the shock of capture. He was also aware that when prisoners were brought to the JFIT they were not allowed to sleep before being tactically questioned or interrogated.

371. S002 also became aware, through concerns raised by the ICRC, of the practice of double hooding and the use of synthetic fibre hoods at the JFIT. Angered by this, he flew to the JFIT and intervened to prevent it. I accept that he did so. But S002's evidence was problematic. He told the Court Martial that he was not aware of the use of plastic hoods despite his Inquiry evidence that this practice had made him sufficiently concerned to fly straight to the TIF.

372. The MoD has conceded, appropriately, that some of the practices applied during the early days of the JFIT were of concern. I find that some aspects of prisoner handling at the JFIT were inappropriate and unacceptable. This included hooding for unduly lengthy periods; the use in some instances of double hooding, and plastic weave sacks; prisoners kept for lengthy periods in the sun, and prisoners being prevented from sleeping prior to initial interrogation. Greater effort and improvisation could have reduced the need to deprive prisoners of their sight.

373. On the available evidence, I conclude that there was no policy of holding prisoners in stress positions at the JFIT. The noise from generators was used to prevent interrogation sessions from being overheard, but this was more a case of a security precaution in a poorly resourced facility in the early stages of the war than the use of a coercive conditioning technique. It did not however meet current best practice.

374. S040 and S014 bear responsibility for these aspects of prisoner handling at the JFIT. Both men considered security as the primary reason to justify the deprivation of sight of prisoners at the JFIT. However, for S014 I find that the desirability of maintaining the shock of capture was part of the reasoning for the continued use of hooding. S002 deserves some credit for the action he took to stop double hooding and the use of plastic weave sandbags. He gave impetus to improving resources so as to minimise the need for sight deprivation. In other respects, however, he shared in the errors of judgment of S014 and S040 in permitting prolonged hooding and keeping prisoners awake. The errors of judgment of these officers are however to be judged in the context of genuine security concerns about the layout of the JFIT, the lack of proper doctrine providing guidance about sight deprivation, the tempo and demands of their operations at the time and the lack of resources preventing the use of other means of sight deprivation such as purpose made blindfolds.

375. Mercer was opposed to the hooding of prisoners in all circumstances and considered it unlawful. A range of staff officer lawyers took contrary views and supported hooding, but only for security purposes and with constraints. There was thus a disagreement amongst the lawyers in theatre. I have made different findings concerning certain of the legal officers involved. Ultimately, I find that the only fair criticism that can be made of the legal officers is that in most cases they did too little to find out precisely what was happening at the JFIT before giving advice.

The Ban on Hooding

376. The concerns of those officers who had seen hooding and did not agree with it led to the hooding issue being raised at the level of the higher formations in theatre.

377. In addition to raising his concerns with the JFIT on the ground and inviting Vernon to visit, S009 contacted the ICRC about his concerns.

378. Brims consulted his staff at 1(UK) Div on the matter. A series of meetings and discussions at Divisional level regarding hooding started on 28 or 29 March, and Brims' ban on hooding was made some days later.

379. After seeing hooded prisoners at the TIF on 29 March 2003, Mercer wrote to Brims setting out his concerns. Mercer also spoke to S002. S002 drafted a memorandum replying to Mercer which defended the practice of hooding for security purposes and also acknowledged the practice of not allowing prisoners to sleep during the early stages of their detention at the JFIT. S002's reply was representative of a strongly defensive line presented in response to Mercer's concerns.

380. Since Mercer and S002 could not agree, by 1 April 2003 at latest, Mercer had referred the issue of hooding to the NCC Headquarters. It seems that by this stage the majority view within 1 (UK) Div favoured a ban on hooding even if NCC Headquarters did not agree with the legal advice given by Mercer. S002 was however still arguing that the JFIT should be permitted to continue hooding.

381. Concurrently with these steps, the ICRC visited the TIF and saw hooding being employed at the JFIT. On 1 April 2003 the ICRC informed the NCC policy advisor (POLAD) S034 that it intended to make a formal complaint about the UK's treatment of prisoners, one particular concern being in relation to the hooding of prisoners at the JFIT. An ICRC report dated February 2004 addressing allegations, amongst other things, of hooding and inappropriate conduct at the TIF, was leaked and thus, uncommonly, was in the public domain before the instigation of this Inquiry.

382. As a result of the emerging concerns about the use of hooding through the various avenues described above, both Burridge, the NCC Commander, and Brims, the General Officer Commanding (GOC) 1 (UK) Div, issued bans on hooding in theatre by verbal orders made between 1 and 3 April. In outline these bans arose as follows.

383. It is probable that S002 became aware of the ICRC concerns including in relation to double hooding and the use of synthetic plastic weave hoods on 31 March or 1 April 2003 and immediately went to the TIF to investigate. I accept that S002 stopped both these practices. It is possible that S002 also issued his own direct order to cease hooding altogether at the JFIT, but there is insufficient evidence to determine this with an appropriate level of certainty.

384. Having been contacted by the ICRC, S034 raised the issued of hooding with Burridge. I am sure that Burridge directed that hooding was to stop. He understood that there was a legal grey area in relation to hooding for security purposes but that in most circumstances it would be inhumane; and that furthermore it was a practice in conflict with the intended impression the UK forces wanted to convey to the Iraqi people. Burridge accepted that, whilst there was no requirement for it, it would clearly have been desirable for the order to have been in writing.

385. Brims ordered that hooding was to cease for all purposes, with the caveat that exceptions might be possible on application to 1 (UK) Div for permission. The decision was probably made and the order given some time between 1 April and 3 April 2003. This oral order was communicated by Divisional conference call by either the Chief of Staff, Col Patrick Marriott or Maj Justin Maciejewski the SO2 G3 Operations.

386. A meeting with a delegation from the ICRC then took place at the TIF on 6 April 2003. I find that the position put to the ICRC was that sight deprivation for security purposes for the limited period necessary was lawful but that a decision had been taken to stop hooding, and that this reflected the seriousness with which the complaints by the ICRC were taken. The legality of hooding for security purposes was defended by the NCC Headquarters, despite the orders from Burridge and Brims that hooding should cease. Mercer was understandably frustrated at being prevented from expressing his view at this meeting that hooding for security purposes was unlawful and that any type of sight deprivation was wrong. However, S034 was not acting improperly in preventing Mercer from arguing an inconsistent legal view from that expressed by the NCC Headquarters.

387. Before turning to the difficulties over how the hooding ban was implemented and communicated, I record that a number of officers deserve credit for raising concerns or being involved in the decision to ban hooding. Those officers were Burridge, Brims, Marriott, Vernon, Mercer and S009. In my opinion, their approach to the use of hooding was appropriate.

388. In broad terms, there were two difficulties in communications that followed the orders of Burridge and Brims. As to Burridge's order, some senior staff officers at the NCC Headquarters were clearly not aware that Burridge had ordered that hooding should cease. Some in 1 (UK) Div wrongly understood the NCC Headquarters position to be that hooding was not regarded as unlawful but that 1 (UK) Div was free to issue its own order. In fact, I accept that the NCC Headquarters decision as articulated by Burridge was that hooding should cease. This particular confusion was not of any substantial causative significance given that 1 (UK) Div did in fact decide to stop hooding.

389. As to Brims' ban, it is apparent that regrettably, the reception of his order was patchy. Significantly, neither the Brigade Commander of 7 Armd Bde, Brig Graham Binns nor his Chief of Staff, Maj Christopher Parker, were aware of Brims' order banning hooding. That meant, in turn, that the oral order banning hooding did not reach 1 Black Watch (BW), who were later to hand over to 1 QLR. Plainly, and with the benefit of hindsight, it would have been better had Brims' order been followed up by a written order issued by his Chief of Staff, Marriott. However, at this time the Division was coping with the massive demands of the warfighting operation. The communication of Brims' hooding ban is therefore something in respect of which 1 (UK) Div, and Marriot, could have performed better, rather than being a matter that is deserving of personal criticism.

390. Despite the bans, some hooding of prisoners continued during Op Telic 1. The Inquiry identified several examples.

   (1) For a period hooding continued within the JFIT even after Brims' order. This was justified on the basis of security while moving prisoners around the compound pending the arrival of alternative means to deprive prisoners of their sight. In

Part VIII of this Report, I am critical of S014 and to a lesser extent S040 for their role in this.

(2) Prisoners were also continuing to arrive at the JFIT hooded. To some extent at least this was reported up the chain of command.

(3) There is no factual dispute that 1 BW continued to hood some prisoners into May 2003. It would appear that two of the deaths in 1 BW custody involved detainees who had been hooded. Those deaths are not within my terms of reference but the limited evidence I received in relation to them did not suggest that hooding had contributed to the deaths.

(4) On 5 April 2003, ITN News broadcast footage of a British arrest operation that had taken place the previous day. This showed prisoners hooded. It is possible that this operation took place only a day after Brims had banned hooding. Even so it ought to have registered as a sign that the order may not have been successfully communicated.

(5) A coalition force operation took place on 11 April 2003 in which the RAF Regiment transported hooded prisoners by Chinook helicopter. One of the prisoners died. A report of the incident referred to the fact that the prisoners had been hooded.

391. In addition, an Amnesty International report dated 29 May 2003, addressed allegations of abuses in custody. Many abuses more serious than hooding were alleged. However, a perceptive and astute reading of the report might have picked up on a pattern of allegations of hooding after Brims' ban.

392. These several examples demonstrate repeated missed opportunities to recognise that hooding was continuing and then rectify what ought to have been appreciated was the poor communication of the hooding ban.

393. The legal and wider debate about the use of hooding continued even after Brims' ban. The Inquiry considered the extent to which the use of hooding was "staffed up" for an authoritative decision.

394. I find that more could have been done by some of the lawyers involved to ensure that the legal issue regarding hooding received further consideration. However, given the pressures of the warfighting operation at the time and the fact that an order had been issued prohibiting the use of hooding, I do not criticise any of them as having fallen below acceptable standards of conduct or performance.

395. On the intelligence side, I find that the controversy in theatre about the use of hooding had caused staff officers in the NCC Headquarters to notice that doctrine in relation to interrogation, including the use of hooding, was scarce. The HUMINT officer in theatre at this time was Lt Col Ewan Duncan. I accept that Duncan raised these issues with PJHQ. It was not seen by them as a priority task. The intelligence branch at PJHQ might have reacted more proactively. But again, it is relevant that an order had already been issued in theatre banning the use of hooding. The middle of a warfighting operation was not the time to be writing doctrine. Again, the key issue was the historical failure to have in place adequate tactical questioning and interrogation doctrine.

396. Between March 2003 (when the concerns in relation to hooding at the JFIT arose) and the death of Baha Mousa, the records of Ministerial correspondence show that on a number of occasions those at the highest level of the MoD were required to provide

information in relation to the policy on hooding. Some correspondence was plainly inaccurate where it purported to assure the addressee that the ICRC had expressed themselves content with the treatment of prisoners. Similarly, some gave an incorrect impression in relation to the duration and frequency of the use of hoods. In places the objective effect of the information was misleading. The MoD bears a corporate responsibility for the fact that inaccurate answers relating to hooding were sent out in the name of the Minister of State.

The later Development of Orders through Op Telic 1 (Part IX)

397. The orders and instructions issued by 1 (UK) Div, and below that, by 7 Armd Bde, were either directly handed over to incoming formations at the start of Op Telic 2 or laid the foundations for the system of prisoner handling that was adopted and developed during Op Telic 2.

398. FRAGO 56 of 24 March 2003 was issued during the warfighting phase but looked ahead to how the stabilisation part of operations would be run. It identified arrest and detention as part of the law and order functions of 1 (UK) Div, together with a power to intern civilians. For arrests, it specified that as soon as practicable after an arrest, the arrested person should be transferred to the local police or handed over to the service police (the RMP). For internment, individuals who were deemed a security risk were to be handed over to the RMP or taken to an RMP station as soon as practicable. As soon as possible thereafter, and within 24 hours, the arrested person was to be handed over to what was planned as a Detention and Internee Management Unit.

399. FRAGO 79 of 3 April 2003 was drafted by Mercer and provided guidance on the power to stop, search and detain. In respect of detention, it required that prisoners be handed over to the RMP as soon as practicable and in any event within six hours. A 1 RMP FRAGO dated 9 April 2003 supplemented FRAGO 79 setting out the RMP responsibilities. Within 24 hours of being presented to the RMP Custody Senior NCO the arrested individual was either to be released or transported to the TIF.

400. Following a number of deaths in custody and the ICRC having received complaints about the handling of detainees, renewed guidance on the detention of civilians was issued by 1 (UK) Div's Daily Miscellaneous FRAGO 152, dated 20 May 2003. This was reproduced at Brigade level by 7 Armd Bde FRAGO 63 of 21 May 2003.

401. The FRAGO 152 guidance drafted by Mercer reiterated the requirement to hand detained persons to the RMP as quickly as possible and in any event within six hours (with an expectation that prisoners would be handed over within one hour, except by those units in remote locations). It also contained a clear warning that prisoners must be protected from violence and threats of violence and that breach of this would probably lead to disciplinary action.

402. Of particular significance, FRAGO 152 appears to have been the only written order before Baha Mousa's death which referred to a prohibition on hooding prisoners, directing that, "*under no circumstances should their faces be covered as this might impair breathing*". Although this injunction could have been phrased in more unequivocal terms, the wording was designed to prevent soldiers adopting forms of sight deprivation other than sandbags that might impair breathing. Mercer believed

that Brims' ban on hoods had already been communicated in theatre and FRAGO 152 was intended to be further guidance. Any proper reading of FRAGO 152 should have led the reader to conclude that hooding was indeed banned. It is to Mercer's credit that he ensured this order was issued, and I conclude that it would not be fair to criticise Mercer for failing to make the hooding ban clearer or more prominent in FRAGO 152.

403. FRAGO 163 (and its Brigade equivalent, FRAGO 70), were issued on 30 May 2003, and provided for the handover of prisoners to the RMP within one to two hours, save in exceptional circumstances. Delivery to the TIF was to be within six hours of arrest when practicable. This order also expressly instructed, that under no circumstances were suspects to be "interrogated" before being processed by the TIF.

404. Mercer confirmed to the Inquiry that these provisions within FRAGO 163 were included as safeguards to minimise the risk of prisoner abuse. He also confirmed that notwithstanding use of the word "interrogated" in the final language of FRAGO 163, his intention had been to ensure that the only questioning of prisoners by UK forces, whether tactical questioning or interrogation, should take place at the TIF. There was, therefore, an undesirable ambiguity in this instruction. I attach only limited criticism to Mercer in this regard. In very many respects he showed singular dedication to the highest practicable standards of prisoner handling.

405. A substantial change in the command structure for the Op Telic campaign was set out in OPO 005/003 of 8 June 2003. It established the new Multi National Division (South East) (MND(SE)), reflecting withdrawal of the NCC Headquarters and the extension of 1 (UK) Division's area of operation into four provinces in southern Iraq. This order also included an Annex setting out law and order and internment procedures which were to be adopted with immediate effect. Of note, it now became the SO2 Detention's responsibility to make the initial decision whether or not a prisoner should be interned.

406. The most significant changes to the processes for handling internees were however brought about by FRAGO 29, which came into effect on 5 July 2003, just before the start of Op Telic 2 and the handover from 1 (UK) Div to 3 (UK) Div.

407. The following key changes to internment procedures were instituted by FRAGO 29. Firstly, the G2 branch (Intelligence) assumed overall control of the internment process from the SO2 Detention. Secondly, responsibility for the assessment of prisoners detained by Battlegroups transferred from the RMP to the new Battlegroup post of BGIRO. Thirdly, Battlegroups no longer had to hand detainees over to the RMP within one to two hours, with the RMP having to deliver to the TIF within six hours. There was no handover to the RMP and the Battlegroups themselves had a new limit of fourteen hours from arrest to delivery to the TIF. Thus the period for which detainees could be held by Battlegroups was significantly extended.

408. There had been a significant reduction in the number of RMP troops in theatre by the end of Op Telic 1. This was a real factor in the changes brought in by FRAGO 29. I accept that it might to some degree have also been thought that the BGIRO would be more suitable as a decision maker in relation to threats to security than the RMP. The introduction of the BGIRO role was also in part to remedy the delay in intelligence from internees being fed back from the JFIT to the Battlegroups.

409. Evidently, the geographical distances in question and the sometimes hazardous operational context were factors behind extending the timescale for delivery of detainees to the TIF from a maximum of six hours to fourteen hours. Furthermore, at the time of the issue of FRAGO 29, it is likely that the TIF was in fact closed to the reception of new prisoners during night hours. As I note in the Report, the position changed at some stage before Op Salerno.

410. Notwithstanding these possible benefits in the changed regime, I find that there were significant risks associated with the introduction of FRAGO 29. The evidence reflected a degree of confusion as to which branch was in overall control of the processing of internees. There was risk in putting the G2 branch in overall charge in that G2 staff had a vested interest in exploiting detainees for intelligence gathering. The FRAGO 29 system required the BGIRO to gather enough information to determine whether an individual posed a threat to force security. This too ran the identifiable risk that questioning at Battlegroup level might go beyond the gaining of immediate tactical information and extend towards full-scale interrogation. Moreover, the ambiguity of FRAGO 163 prohibiting "interrogation" rather than tactical questioning and interrogation before the TIF, was now compounded by the absence of any instruction at all on tactical questioning and/or interrogation in FRAGO 29.

411. I formed the impression that there was a disinclination to accept responsibility for the strategic direction that had been implemented by FRAGO 29. Communication about the order was inadequate within 1 (UK) Div. Legal staff were consulted only late and then did not question the order to the extent that might have been expected. Within the Divisional headquarters, staff officers held widely differing views as to what questioning could take place before the TIF. The level of consultation within the Division had not served to draw out these conflicts of view. Had it done so, the order could and should have given clear guidance. Instead FRAGO 29 was silent on tactical questioning and whether it was permitted prior to the TIF.

412. Although it is of course easier in hindsight to identify the disadvantages of the approach mandated by FRAGO 29, I conclude that at the time more consideration should have been given to the changes the order was intended to bring about and the identifiable attendant risks. Such consideration may not have changed the overall approach of FRAGO 29 but it might have led to better guidance being issued.

Handover of Prisoner Handling Orders between Op Telic 1 and Op Telic 2 (Part X)

413. The Op Telic 1 formations and units handed over in theatre to their Op Telic 2 counterparts. The handovers were staggered so as to provide continuity and avoid all level of commands changing at the same time. At Battlegroup level, 1 BW handed over to 1 QLR on 27 June 2003. 7 Armd Bde handed over to 19 Mech Bde on 4 July 2003. Then finally 1 (UK) Div handed over to 3 (UK) Div on 12 July 2003.

414. If the Op Telic 1 hooding ban had been effectively disseminated, and the handovers at all levels were thorough and efficient, all the Op Telic 2 units and formations ought to have known that it was prohibited for UK forces to hood prisoners in Iraq. This did not happen and I find that the practice of the hooding of detainees continued during the early part of Op Telic 2, not just by 1 QLR, but by also by other units.

Battlegroup Level

415. A number of witnesses from the 1 BW Battlegroup gave evidence to the Inquiry concerning the use of hooding by 1 BW and the process and content of the recce visit and handover with 1 QLR.

416. It is very clear from this evidence that 1 BW did hood some of their detainees during their tour. But the vast majority of 1 BW witnesses did not see or know of stress positions being used by the Battlegroup.

417. Sgt John Gallacher was 1 BW's Provost Sergeant. Gallacher's evidence was significantly different from most other 1 BW witnesses. Gallacher's evidence was that he had attended the JSIO PH&TQ course early in 2003. His mistaken but genuine understanding after completing this training was that stress positions and hooding were appropriate methods for conditioning high value intelligence prisoners. He returned to 1 BW and briefed the Brigade on the use of hooding. In that briefing his evidence was that he also mentioned stress positions, although in the context that British soldiers might be put in stress positions if captured.

418. Once in theatre, Gallacher said that he hooded and put in stress positions those prisoners brought into 1 BW custody who were deemed to be of high intelligence value. He would put them in stress positions but would not kick or punch them or subject them to any similar treatment. He said the stress positions would be used for 20 to 30 minutes but had only been used on five to ten detainees. I accept that Gallacher's evidence in this regard was honest and accurate. His use of stress positions was limited to very few detainees and I find that other 1 BW personnel did not know what Gallacher was doing. Gallacher should have realised that the techniques might be inhumane. His responsibility for using the techniques is less than it might have been, given that I accept that he genuinely believed he was permitted to use them. It is a matter of concern that the Chicksands PH&TQ course had left him with that mistaken impression.

419. A recce visit to 1 BW was conducted by 1 QLR during 7 to 10 May 2003. Brims' oral ban on hooding had not reached 7 Armd Bde or 1 BW and FRAGO 152 had not yet been issued. As a result, 1 BW were still hooding prisoners at this time. This in turn meant that several members of 1 QLR's recce party saw 1 BW hooding prisoners. 1 QLR's Commanding Officer, Mendonça, as well as Maj John Lighten, Capt Michael Elliott and Royce all saw prisoners hooded by 1 BW. They did not see prisoners in stress positions. Royce recalled that it was explained to him on the recce that the hooding and handcuffing of prisoners was a standard procedure and that it had been sanctioned by 7 Armd Bde.

420. On 20 May 2003, as described above, FRAGO 152 had stated that "*Under no circumstances should their faces be covered as this might impair breathing*". The corresponding FRAGO from 7 Armd Bde to its sub-units was FRAGO 63. It attached the same Annex and wording. On its face, the order suggests that it was sent amongst others to 1 BW and, for information, to 19 Mech Bde.

421. The evidence as to whether FRAGO 63 actually reached 1 BW was not all one way. On the balance of the evidence, I am satisfied that FRAGO 63 was sent to and received by 1 BW. Most of the 1 BW witnesses who remembered seeing FRAGO 152

or FRAGO 63 said that they believed that the part of the Annex set out above was an order banning hooding.

422. FRAGO 63 ought to have put a stop to the use of hoods by all 1 BW sub-units by the time of the handover to 1 QLR. Some 1 BW sub-units indeed appear to have ceased hooding as a result of this order. But I find that FRAGO 63 did not put a stop to hooding throughout the 1 BW Battlegroup. The Commanding Officer of 1 BW, Lt Col Mike Riddell-Webster, and the RSM, WO1 David Bruce, must bear some responsibility for the failure to ensure FRAGO 63 was implemented throughout the Battlegroup.

423. Since FRAGO 63 had not stopped all hooding by 1 BW, when they handed over to 1 QLR, some members of 1 QLR saw 1 BW hooding prisoners, as had also occurred at the recce. A number of 1 QLR witnesses said that they adopted the procedure of hooding prisoners because they had seen it in use by 1 BW.

424. The Inquiry considered whether a copy of FRAGO 63 was given to 1 QLR as part of the handover from 1 BW. The operations officers at the time were Capt Nicolas Ord (1 BW) and Elliott (1 QLR). Ord believed that all the operative orders would have been handed over to 1 QLR and these ought to have included FRAGO 63. He went through the orders one by one with Elliott. Elliott took issue with the suggestion that he received a copy of FRAGO 63. He understood hooding to be a standard procedure and would have remembered an order prohibiting its use. There was insufficient evidence satisfactorily to resolve this dispute. It is possible that FRAGO 63 was not in the set of orders handed over to 1 QLR, perhaps because subsequent orders had addressed the internment process. Alternatively it may be that FRAGO 63 was in the orders given to Elliot and that he did not alight on that part of the order which prohibited covering prisoners' faces. In these circumstances it is not fair to criticise either officer.

425. There is no evidence to suggest that members of 1 QLR were aware of the use made by Gallacher of stress positions. I have considered carefully the application of this finding in the case of Sgt Smith and Payne to whom Gallacher would personally have handed over. However, Payne, particularly, would have a strong motive for suggesting he learnt of stress positions from Gallacher, yet he stated that he did not.

426. To complete the picture, I also heard evidence from a limited number of members of other Battlegroups deployed on Op Telic 2 at the same time as 1 QLR. 1 QLR was by no means the only Op Telic 2 Battlegroup to use hooding. But the evidence, albeit from a small number, was that hooding was a method already applied by their units rather than directly adopted from the Op Telic 1 units they had relieved.

Brigade Level

427. 19 Mech Bde assumed responsibility for Basra from 7 Armd Bde on 4 July 2003. Even before the stage of the handover from 7 Armd Bde to 19 Mech Bde, the prohibition on hooding ought to have reached 19 Mech Bde because FRAGO 63 was copied to 19 Mech Bde for information. As the Chief of Staff for 19 Mech Bde, Maj Hugh Eaton would have been responsible for the orders sent for information to 19 Mech Bde during Op Telic 1, including FRAGO 63 which contained the prohibition on covering prisoners' faces. He had no recollection of seeing FRAGO 63 and said that he had doubts as to whether it was in fact received by 19 Mech Bde. There were significant problems with data and correspondence to and from theatre. Nevertheless, Eaton

also admitted that it was possible that the content of FRAGO 63 was simply missed as a point which needed to be made subject of an instruction to 19 Mech Bde troops. There is doubt as to whether FRAGO 63 was received by 19 Mech Bde, but if it was, it is highly regrettable that it engendered no further action.

428. Moving on to the Brigade handover, there was evidence from 7 Armd Bde witnesses that FRAGO 152 would have been handed over in paper and electronic form, and some suggestion that the orders for prisoner handling would have been discussed as well.

429. There was an initial conflict of evidence between Brig Adrian Bradshaw the Commander of 7 Armd Bde, who had stated that all existing FRAGOs would have been handed over, and that prisoner handling issues would have been discussed; and Moore, the Commanding Officer of 19 Mech Bde who was not aware of any ban on hooding and did not remember prisoner handling issues being raised. Bradshaw accepted the possibility that the issue might not in fact have been commented upon.

430. At Chief of Staff level, Parker of 7 Armd Bde maintained that FRAGO 152 would have been handed over in paper and electronic form, although he himself did not remember referring to FRAGO 152 during the handover. Parker was not aware of any oral order prohibiting hooding before FRAGO 152. His counterpart at 19 Mech Bde, Eaton stated that the relevant orders were not discussed with him.

431. By the time of the handover, it seems that for many Brigade officers neither prisoner handling nor hooding appeared to be particularly high profile issues. As a result, prisoner handling may have been seen as relatively low priority in the handover process.

432. The evidence suggested that 19 Mech Bde would not usually reissue 7 Armd Bde FRAGOs which had already been issued to Battlegroups. The expectation was that Battlegroups on the ground would pass on all relevant information to their successor Battlegroups.

433. The Brigade level handover process left many of the key 19 Mech Bde witnesses unaware that hooding had been prohibited. The Brigade Commander Moore, the Chief of Staff Eaton and Deputy Chief of Staff Maj Jim Landon, and a number of the senior staff officers within the intelligence operations and plans branches fell into this category. Others, most notably Clifton the 19 Mech Bde legal adviser, did know of the prohibition on hooding. Overall, however, the handover process left an unsatisfactorily high number of Brigade officers unaware of the prohibition on hooding.

Divisional Level

434. At Divisional level the handover from 1 (UK) Div to 3 (UK) Div occurred between 10 to 12 July 2003. Whilst the prohibition on hooding and/or FRAGO 152 was handed over at least to some of the incoming officers, the prohibition on hooding was not by any means universally understood within 1 (UK) Div and nor was the issue of prisoner handling accorded any special priority as a subject for handover.

435. The GOC 1 (UK) Div at the time of the handover was Maj Gen Peter Wall. He knew of Burridge's order banning hooding but not that of Brims. Wall did not raise the matter with his 3 (UK) Div counterpart, Maj Gen Graeme Lamb. At the level of Divisional

Commander it is perhaps not surprising that this level of detail was not covered. Maj Gen Lamb was not aware that hooding was prohibited.

436. At the Divisional Chief of Staff level, Marriott of 1 (UK) Div appears to have informally mentioned to Col Richard Barrons of 3 (UK) Div that hooding was banned, although Barrons said he did not see the written order FRAGO 152 during the handover. I have concluded that although the prohibition on hooding was mentioned to Barrons, it was not unreasonable in the circumstances that he took no further action such as re-issuing an order prohibiting hooding or ensuring by other means that the incoming 3 (UK) Div forces were definitely aware of it. It was not raised as a particular concern to him, and it was not unreasonable for him to believe that this prohibition would have been handed over "horizontally" from Brigade to Brigade and Battlegroup to Battlegroup, as well as from relevant 1 (UK) Div staff officers to the staff officers within 3 (UK) Div.

437. The Deputy Chief of Staff of 3 (UK) Div, Col Barry Le Grys did not remember seeing FRAGO 152 or any other order relating to hooding during the handover to him.

438. Lt Col Robert Le Fevre, the 3 (UK) Div Senior Intelligence Officer did not remember being made aware of either FRAGO 152 or any other order prohibiting the hooding of prisoners. On the HUMINT side of the J2 branch, S002, the SO2 J2X for 1 (UK) Div conducted a direct handover with S015, the SO2 J2X for 3 (UK) Div. Although the evidence was not consistent as to the information passing between S002 and S015 during their handover, S015's understanding regardless of what was said at the handover, was that hooding was not permitted.

439. In the Legal branch there was clearly a full handover of the relevant issues and orders including Brims' oral order and FRAGO 152. This is unsurprising as it was Mercer who was handing over to Barnett. There was a difference in the evidence of Mercer and Barnett as to the emphasis that was put on the concerns held by Mercer in relation to prisoner handling. I think that it is more likely that it was raised with Barnett as one of a number of areas of concern rather than as the most important legal issue in theatre.

440. Viewed as a whole, the evidence of the handover at Divisional level suggested that the topic of prisoner handling was for the most part not given a high priority by the Divisional Commanders and their Chiefs of Staff. I view this as unsurprising given the breadth of their responsibilities. Within the individual branches of the Division, a number of staff officers accepted that the prohibition on hooding ought to have been handed over during the transition between Op Telic 1 and 2, but thought that the responsibility for doing so rested with a different branch in the headquarters or even with a different formation. No one single branch appears to have regarded it as its responsibility to lead in matters of prisoner handling and detention. It was a recurring feature of the evidence the Inquiry heard concerning the handover between Op Telic 1 and 2 that officers in close hierarchical, and sometimes physical, proximity seem to have emerged from the handover period with inconsistent and sometimes conflicting knowledge in respect of the prohibition on hooding. Some within 3 (UK) Div clearly did know of the prohibition on hooding. But while not perhaps as serious as the position at Brigade, knowledge of the ban was still patchy.

441. It is both an exaggeration and an over-simplification to suggest, as some have done, that the prohibition on hooding was lost in the handovers between Op Telic 1 and

Op Telic 2. Knowledge of the ban on hooding was not as widespread as it should have been even before the handovers. It is certainly right, however, that the level of knowledge of the ban on hooding diminished as a result of inadequacies in the handovers at every level. This effect was most pronounced at Battlegroup level but it extended to higher formations as well. A key lesson to emerge from such difficulties is that instructions in relation to internment, detention and prisoner handling are too important to be governed by a lengthy series of fragmentary orders which are all too prone to be lost and cause ambiguities of interpretation. The far better approach is to have a single enduring standard operating instruction governing the procedures. Such an instruction can be amended as necessary, but it should be a single reference document that all ranks know to consult.

The Development of Prisoner Handling Orders during Op Telic 2 (Part XI)

442. Just after the start of Op Telic 2, on 13 July 2003, 19 Mech Bde issued FRAGO 85. It included an arrest procedures card, intended to outline correct arrest procedures and the process for interning a person. This card had been issued down to the level of patrol commanders.

443. The card stated that suspects were to be treated humanely and with respect, and the guidance required suspects to be handed to the BGIRO within two hours of apprehension. Neither the card nor the accompanying guidance further addressed the physical aspects of prisoner handling. They did not refer to the prohibition on hooding.

444. Clifton explained that the prohibition on hooding was not referred to on the card as he thought that it was already sufficiently understood in theatre, having been banned during Op Telic 1. He also thought that the over-arching command that prisoners ought to be treated humanely should have sufficed.

445. It would have been better if the arrest procedures card had included the prohibition on hooding, but I do not think it would be fair to criticise Clifton for this omission. The card referred to the need to treat prisoners humanely. It warned of disciplinary action. It was issued very early in Op Telic 2 and did not follow the same detailed staffing consideration as did the later Divisional FRAGO 005. It was contemplated at the time that further guidance would be issued by Division.

446. Towards the end of Op Telic 1, Mercer had prepared a separate draft card intended to go to all soldiers, and not just to junior commanders. This had not been issued before the handover to 3 (UK) Div. Mercer's draft had included specific guidance against the use of both hooding and stress positions.

447. In the early stages of Op Telic 2, the Legal branch of 3 (UK) Div, after some uncertainty, correctly identified that the issuing of a soldier's card similar to Mercer's draft was a task that needed to be completed. But it was deferred pending the Divisional guidance that was being prepared. Barnett stated that he did not view the issuing of a soldier's card as being a particularly urgent matter, partly because the arrest procedures card had already been issued, and also because previous guidance had been issued in the legal annexes to the Concept of Operation Orders; in the Soldier's guide to the LOAC; the aide memoires on LOAC, in FRAGO 152, and in soldiers' training.

448. However, no such soldiers' card was issued before the death of Baha Mousa. The decision to defer issuing the soldiers' card until the guidance in FRAGO 005 had been issued was not unreasonable. But Barnett and his legal team were responsible for the failure to issue such a card once that guidance had been issued. I bear in mind that all soldiers had, however, received clear instruction to treat prisoners humanely.

449. Further instructions in relation to the Rules of Engagement and Legal issues were included as Annex M to the MND(SE) CONOPS 03/03 Order of 30 August 2003. Although the guidance on detainees and internees within the legal annex was at a fairly high level of generality, it included reference to treating prisoners of war humanely and protecting them from physical and mental harm. The order indicated that further guidance on the handling of detainees and internees was to be promulgated separately. This was a reference to FRAGO 005.

450. FRAGO 005 "Policy for Apprehending, Handling and Processing of Detainees and Internees" was issued on 3 September 2003. It replaced 1 (UK) Div's FRAGO 29 of 26 June 2003 as the main order on internment procedures. It was therefore the policy operative at the time of the detention and abuse of Baha Mousa and the other Detainees.

451. FRAGO 005 retained the BGIRO system of assessment at Battlegroup level. It qualified the previously absolute fourteen hour deadline for delivery of detainees to the TIF, now specifying that this should be done within fourteen hours, "or as soon as possible thereafter". Importantly, FRAGO 005 did not include any reference to the prohibition on hooding, nor to other aspects of the physical handling of prisoners, nor to tactical questioning, and did not include guidance to be issued down to frontline soldier level in the form of a soldier's card.

452. Barnett stated that the original intention had been to include more detail on tactical questioning and custodial procedures in FRAGO 005, but that he had decided not to after consultation with the various staff branches. Their rationale had been that the procedures had already been specifically trained and that each unit had on their strength individuals trained in these specialist areas. Therefore it was not thought appropriate to put further guidance into FRAGO 005 when there were already procedures in place.

453. Barnett did not include a prohibition on hooding because he did not at that time think it was an issue. He thought that soldiers were aware that hooding had been banned. Evidence of other staff officers revealed the general perception that hooding was not an issue of any particular prominence at this stage.

454. FRAGO 005 was issued in the name of the Divisional Chief of Staff, Barrons. He too did not think that the issue of hooding or prisoner handling was particularly prominent at the time. He also argued, which I accept, that FRAGO 005 was MND(SE) guidance, multi national in scope, and any prohibition on hooding would have had to have been cleared with other troop contributing nations.

455. However, these reasons do not completely justify or explain the absence of any reference to the prohibition on hooding in the consolidating guidance in FRAGO 005. In my view, the process of consolidating guidance should have led to the prohibition being included in FRAGO 005. This was an unfortunate omission and an error of judgment for which Barnett must take some responsibility.

456. It would also have been better if FRAGO 005 had contained further guidance on detention and tactical questioning principles. However, I find that Barnett was advised against the inclusion of this type of information by Le Fevre and Lt Col Robert Warren, the Provost Marshal of MND(SE) for Op Telic 2. I find that their advice to Barnett was too reassuring in the light of the limited guidance available at the time. However, it was not unreasonable for Barnett to have followed their advice.

457. Unfortunately, in the sequence of orders during Op Telic 2, from the Divisional handover right through to Baha Mousa's death, it is striking that none referred in any way to the prohibition on hooding or stress positions. Had they done so it is doubtful that the 1 QLR process of conditioning would have developed or continued in the way that it did.

458. As with the shortcomings in handovers, this reinforces the need for the MoD to avoid in future the situation whereby prisoner handling becomes governed by scattered fragmentary orders. As well as improved training and doctrine, prisoner handling calls for a clear and appropriately detailed written standard operating instruction that is maintained through the roulement of formations and units in enduring operations.

Knowledge of the Ban and Knowledge of the Use of Hooding (Part XII)

459. The Inquiry examined the extent to which soldiers and officers on Op Telic 2 knew that hooding was occurring. It also examined the extent to which they knew of the prohibition on hooding whether from the handovers they received or from prior knowledge of the Heath Statement, from Op Telic 1 oral orders, or, from 1 (UK) Div's FRAGO 152 or 7 Armd Bde's FRAGO 63. I have already addressed the handovers, above, and in Part X of the Report.

460. Witnesses broadly fell into three groups in this regard: (1) those who had no knowledge of the ban on hooding and were also unaware of the practice of hooding; (2) those who did know of the ban on hooding but did not know it was occurring on operations; and (3) those who did not know of a ban on hooding but were aware of the practice being used to one extent or another.

461. The Inquiry has also carefully considered the evidence of those soldiers of whom it might be said that they occupy a further category: those who both knew of the existence of a ban on hooding but also became aware that hoods were used in practice during Op Telic 2 and therefore had a duty to intervene and to report the practice.

462. The evidence did not reveal any significant pattern of those who knew that hooding was occurring and condoned it despite knowing of the prohibition on hooding.

463. For those witnesses ignorant of the practice of hooding occurring during Op Telic 2, it has also been important to assess whether they ought to have known, to have inquired, or to have been on notice of the practice due to the language appearing in some operation orders. Similarly, of those who were ignorant of the ban on hooding, ought the practice itself to have aroused their concern?

Divisional Level

464. Maj Gen Lamb, the GOC, knew of the Heath Statement. He understood that sight deprivation for a short period of time on security grounds was acceptable. Hoods were not ideal for this but could be used if necessary and if care was taken. Maj Gen Lamb had no direct knowledge of hooding prior to Baha Mousa's death. Le Grys, the Deputy Chief of Staff, did not know of the prohibition on hooding and did not know that hooding was occurring. Barrons, the Chief of Staff, did know of the ban on hooding, but stated that he was not aware of the use of hooding or blindfolding. I accept therefore that the highest level of command at 3 (UK) Division did not know that hooding was occurring. It is of concern that the practice of hooding was not reported up the chain of command to the most senior Divisional level.

465. Quite a number of other officers in the individual staff branches at Divisional level fell into the category of those who did not know that hooding had been banned and were also not aware that it was occurring in theatre.

466. Barnett and Capt Sian Ellis-Davies in the Divisional legal team were exceptions to this general pattern. They both knew that hooding had been prohibited. A significant conflict of evidence emerged in relation to an assertion from S017, the Officer Commanding the JFIT on Op Telic 2, that prisoners were being delivered wearing hoods to the JFIT by the arresting units, and that she had reported this to Le Fevre, S015, Barnett, and Ellis-Davies. On the balance of probabilities I accept that Barnett and Ellis-Davies did not know before Baha Mousa's death that hooding was occurring by virtue of being told by S017 that prisoners were arriving at the JFIT hooded. I find that S017 did raise this issue with her superior, S015. However, S015 did not treat this matter with the level of concern and priority that it deserved. He ought to have done more in respect of S017's concerns.

467. A pattern that emerged in the evidence, although not universal, was that the legal staff tended to be aware that hooding was prohibited but not aware that it was occurring. Whereas intelligence staff tended to have some awareness that hoods were being used but were not aware that it had been specifically prohibited. Amongst those who were aware of the prohibition of hooding, there was a misplaced confidence that this was widely known by others.

468. A range of factors contributed to the preponderance of Divisional level witnesses who had not been aware that hooding was occurring: prisoner handling was at most one of several responsibilities they held; they tended not to see individual Battlegroup level orders; many were physically isolated from detention operations on the ground, and other than S017's reporting, hooding was not raised as a matter of concern.

Brigade Level

469. The majority of officers from 19 Mech Bde who gave evidence to the Inquiry, apart from Clifton, did not know of a prohibition on the use of hooding. Moore (the Brigade Commander), the Chiefs of Staff Eaton and Fenton, and their deputy Landon, Capt Charles Burbridge and Capt Oliver King (SO3 G3 Operations), Maj Rupert Steptoe (SO2 Plans), Capt Miles Mitchell (SO3 Plans), and those in the Intelligence branch, Maj Mark Robinson (SO3 G2), Radbourne and WO2 Rhoderick Paterson, were all unaware of the prohibition on hooding.

470. Of these, a number such as Moore, Eaton and Landon, told the Inquiry, and I accept, that they did not know that hooding was occurring. However at Brigade level there was much more extensive knowledge of the actual practice of hooding than was the case at Division. As noted above, those in the Intelligence branch, or involved in the tactical questioning process, in this instance including Robinson, Radbourne, and Paterson tended to know that hoods were being used as a method of sight deprivation. In the G3 operations branch, Capt Oliver King was aware that sandbags were used to hood, and Burbridge saw prisoners wearing hoods on one occasion.

471. The Inquiry also investigated the extent to which staff at Brigade understood that hoods and conditioning were used by virtue of Battlegroup level FRAGOs. Brigade was copied into FRAGOs for Op Quebec, Op Quintessential, and Op Lightning, all operations run by 19 Mech Bde units and containing various concerning references to "bagging and tagging", "bag out of sight once in vans" and "conditioning".

472. Those Brigade level witnesses who were unaware of the ban on hooding but who were aware of the use of hooding included a number who appreciated that hooding was being used in part to maintain the shock of capture. These included Radbourne, whose roles included acting as a tactical questioner, and Robinson the SO3 Intelligence Officer. Robinson was an important witness in respect of the Brigade sanction of hooding. He eventually, after some reluctance, accepted that his understanding at the time was that hooding to maintain the shock of capture would have been appropriate. In the case of the Burbridge, the SO3 operations officer at Brigade, he told the Inquiry that he was not aware before Baha Mousa's death that hooding was used as part of the conditioning process. But there are grounds for suspecting that he may have had some such knowledge.

473. It is extremely unfortunate that none of those within Moore's Brigade headquarters who knew hooding was occurring, raised it as a concern for consideration, and that individual orders referring to hooding and conditioning did not lead to more questions being asked. For the most part, the reason for the former appears to have been that those who were aware of the use of hooding were not aware that it had been subject to a prohibition in theatre, nor did their training lead them to question the practice. References to hooding and conditioning in individual Battlegroup operation orders copied to Brigade were badly missed opportunities to notice, and put a stop to, inappropriate use of hooding and conditioning. I accept, however, that the ambiguous nature of the term conditioning, which was sometimes used to denote the lawful use of post-capture pressures on prisoners, is some mitigation for this omission.

Battlegroup Level

474. In addition to 1 QLR, it is clear that other Op Telic 2 Battlegroups used hooding. Although this was not the focus of the Inquiry's investigations, the evidence suggests that 1 The King's Regiment (Kings) and probably to a slightly lesser extent 1 King's Own Scottish Borderers (KOSB) and 40 Regt RA did use hooding in the early part of Op Telic 2. In the case of 1 Kings, it is likely that hooding was stopped before Baha Mousa's death, following an internal Battlegroup decision. The timing in relation to this is, however, uncertain.

The Brigade Sanction (Part XIII)

475. At the time of Op Salerno and the events of 14 to 16 September 2003, 1 QLR were employing as a standard procedure the process of "conditioning" some detainees before tactical questioning, a process including the use of hoods to deprive prisoners of their sight and stress positions. One of the most contentious issues the Inquiry has had to determine is the extent to which, if at all, the use of these techniques had been sanctioned by 19 Mech Bde.

476. After the promulgation of FRAGO 29, Royce became the first BGIRO of 1 QLR, and was operating as such by early July 2003. I accept that initially Royce understood the hooding of detainees to be prohibited and that he genuinely remembered this information formed part of his PDT (although there remains some real doubt about Royce's claim that he was specifically taught this in a lecture given by Barnett). I also accept that Royce, during either the recce visit or formal handover from 1 BW, saw a prisoner hooded and handcuffed, and was informed that hooding a detainee on capture was a standard operating procedure.

477. Royce's account in evidence to the Inquiry was that early in the tour, as a result of the inconsistent information he had received, he queried the use of hooding with Robinson and was told that it was permissible. About two weeks later, before the first arrest operation undertaken by 1 QLR he talked to Robinson about what the Battlegroup should do to maintain the shock of capture and conditioning of detainees before the arrival of tactical questioners. Robinson's answer was that hooding and stress positions were permitted techniques to be used as part of the conditioning process. Royce suggested that this conversation was also witnessed by a member of the Field HUMINT Team. This witness to an important conversation had not been mentioned previously by Royce. The Inquiry made extensive efforts to trace this individual. Four witnesses were identified as being possible candidates or possibly able to assist identify the individual in question. Three of those were traced and each denied they were the person involved as Royce suggested. The fourth could not be traced.

478. Royce said that subsequently he spoke to Clifton about being required to keep detainees in hoods and stress positions to maintain the shock of capture, and approval for this process was also given by Clifton. Thereafter, Royce spoke to the Commanding Officer of 1 QLR, Mendonça about stress positions, hooding and the conditioning process. Mendonça himself did remember that Royce clarified at a 1 QLR Group meeting that hooding had been sanctioned by Brigade.

479. The detail in Royce's account of the Brigade sanction had developed over time. He did not refer to conditioning, hooding, stress positions or the Brigade sanction in the first statement he made to the SIB in 2004, although the questions asked of him were narrow in scope. In 2005, in his second statement to the SIB, Royce referred to having a passing conversation with Robinson and then with Clifton, in which hooding was approved as a technique. Royce did not mention receiving approval for stress techniques in this statement. The prosecution at the Court Martial did not regard Royce as a witness upon whom it could rely, however he was called as a witness by the Judge Advocate, gave evidence and was cross examined. Aside from the lack of any reference to the presence of a Field HUMINT Team officer, Royce's evidence at the Court Martial on this issue was consistent with his evidence to the Inquiry.

480. Robinson had no recollection of any such discussion. He accepted the possibility such a conversation might have taken place but denied that he would ever have given a sanction for the use of stress positions.

481. Clifton denied such a discussion with Robinson had taken place, and emphatically denied that he would have advised hooding might take place or that he had sanctioned conditioning.

482. Robinson's evidence essentially was that he could not remember a conversation of the type described by Royce, but accepted that he could not definitively deny it occurred. He conceded that at the time in question he would have said that hooding for security reasons and for aiding conditioning was permissible. However, he maintained that if he had been asked about stress positions he would have said they were prohibited.

483. Clifton's account was that he clearly understood that hooding had been banned as a result of a discussion with Mercer during the handover between 1 (UK) Div and 3 (UK) Div. As a result of a conversation with Robinson he also knew that a process of conditioning using certain techniques to maintain the shock of capture was applied to detainees prior to tactical questioning. He did not know and had not considered that the use of stress positions might be one of these techniques.

484. Further, Clifton categorically denied that the conversation as described by Royce actually took place. He said that as he knew of the ban on hooding he would certainly not have sanctioned the use of hoods. His evidence to the Inquiry was that he would not have told Royce that the use of stress positions was permitted.

485. There was some inconsistency in relation to stress positions between Clifton's Inquiry evidence and evidence he had given previously in the context of the Court Martial. He had previously stated that, while not remembering any such conversation, he might at the time have answered that there were certain situations when the use of stress positions would be acceptable but that without knowing the full details of the situation he would not be able to advise on their use, or that the use of stress positions was more the province of trained tactical questioning experts in theatre.

486. Despite the sharp contrasts in their accounts I do not believe that Royce, Robinson or Clifton deliberately sought to mislead the Inquiry. They each attempted to explain brief conversations that took place six years ago and occurred during an intensely busy period. All three men had given previous statements, to the SIB and in evidence at the Court Martial. There were some inconsistencies between these statements. When attempting to explain these inconsistencies Royce, Robinson and Clifton have sought to rationalise what has been said on previous occasions.

487. There is also some evidence from others within 1 QLR which might be viewed as tending to lend support to the claim that there was a Brigade sanction. For example, Mendonça had been told by Royce that the process of conditioning was sanctioned by Brigade. Maj Paul Davis, the Officer Commanding A Company 1 QLR, remembered Royce raising the issue of hooding at a 1 QLR O Group meeting and stating that the issue of whether it was permitted was under discussion. Capt Alan Sweeney the 1 QLR Signals Officer understood Brigade to have sanctioned hoods and stress positions to Royce. Moutarde, the Adjutant gave evidence to similar effect, also stating that he understood there to be a specific direction from Brigade approving hooding. Sgt Ian Topping, the Mortar Platoon Commander in S Company 1 QLR described having

seen detainees hooded when at the Brigade headquarters location. To some extent Topping's evidence was supported by Pte Mark Andrew, a member of his platoon. Sgt Smith and Payne both stated that tactical questioners gave orders as to how detainees were to be treated. Payne believed hooding and stress positions had been cleared by Brigade.

488. In addition, the Inquiry also heard a limited amount of evidence that other Battlegroups under 19 Mech Bde also used sandbags to hood detainees, in some cases with an apparent understanding that it helped maintain the shock of capture. Furthermore, soldiers who operated as tactical questioners for Brigade, such as SSgt Davies, Smulski, Radbourne and Sgt Michael Porter, thought hooding to be permissible and some applied the practice of hooding themselves. These two features also form part of the relevant factual background against which a consideration of the conflict of evidence between Royce, Robinson and Clifton needs to take place.

489. In reaching a conclusion on the issue of the Brigade sanction I have borne in mind the following significant factors. Many individuals within 19 Mech Bde appear to have been ignorant of the Op Telic 1 prohibitions on hooding. The totality of the evidence suggests that tactical questioners during Op Telic 2 did advise Battlegroup soldiers to keep detainees hooded, but there is very little evidence that stress positions were used or permitted. There is support from individuals within 1 QLR for Royce's account that at a 1 QLR O Group he communicated his belief that the practice of hooding was approved at 19 Mech Bde level. I also take into consideration the fact that separate witnesses to the same conversation can genuinely misunderstand or be at cross-purposes with each other. That fact together with the effect of the passage of time and how it tempers what people believed they heard or said, goes some way to explain the differences in recollection between Royce, Robinson and Clifton.

490. I have found that Royce was not mistaken in his assertion that conversations with Robinson and Clifton took place. I am not persuaded that Royce fabricated the fact that these conversations took place. Other 1 QLR personnel to varying degrees support the fact that Royce communicated his understanding about the conditioning process, hooding and stress positions, after discussing these issues at Brigade level. He communicated the fact that the Brigade had authorised a conditioning process to the Mendonça, even if the detail of the process was not fully explained.

491. In his evidence concerning the purpose for which hooding was applied, Robinson was not an impressive witness. But to his credit, Robinson accepted the possibility that he may have spoken to Royce about conditioning and I find that he did. Given what Robinson said he believed at the time, I find that Robinson told Royce that detainees should be hooded. On balance, although I am less confident of this point, I also accept Royce's assertion that Robinson also approved the use of stress positions. It is more likely than not that Robinson did so as at the time he believed conditioning as an aid to tactical questioning was permissible and that it involved some form of restraint procedure. I accept the possibility that in the context of what was described by Royce as a passing conversation, this may not have seemed significant to Robinson.

492. I also accept that Royce at some subsequent point had a conversation with Clifton. The content of such a conversation is difficult to determine. I find it difficult to accept, that having been directly informed by Mercer of the ban on hooding, Clifton then approved the use of hoods. Conversely, Clifton had previously given evidence suggesting that his state of mind at this time meant that, if asked, he would have

answered that there were certain situations when the use of stress positions would be acceptable. I ultimately find that Clifton did not say or give the impression that hooding was permissible, but that if he did give advice on stress positions, he was likely to have said that they were permissible in some circumstances, if approved by a subject matter expert (SME).

493. I have found that Royce genuinely believed he had received assurance from Brigade through Robinson and Clifton that the use of hooding and stress positions before questioning was permissible. It cannot be ruled out that this belief was the product of a genuine misunderstanding between the three officers. It is likely the conversations were of short duration, concentrating more upon the term "conditioning" rather than the specifics of hooding and stress positions.

494. However, I do not find that a genuine belief in this type of assurance amounted to a formal sanction by 19 Mech Bde of the use of hooding or stress positions. These were passing conversations. Moreover, Royce correctly thought this issue important, which is why he approached Brigade officers in the first instance. I find that Royce would have been well advised to have obtained written confirmation of what he regarded as a Brigade sanction.

495. Furthermore, this level of assurance could not and did not absolve 1 QLR from ensuring that detainees in their care were treated humanely and in accordance with the Geneva Conventions. Nor do these findings absolve Royce from all further responsibility for what happened in the TDF between 14 and 16 September 2003. During his tenure as BGIRO, I accept he carefully supervised those prisoners subjected to conditioning. However, the whole process of hooding detainees and placing them in stress positions was unacceptable. Royce should have recognised this and should have recognised the risk of young soldiers using violence to impose stress positions. At the very least he should have alerted his successor, Peebles, to these dangers.

Events Immediately after Baha Mousa's Death (Part XIV)

496. The Inquiry examined the reporting soon after Baha Mousa's death to discover what light it might cast on the events and to assess whether they were sufficient, accurate and timely.

497. It is clear that the SIB was contacted by the 1 QLR's Adjutant, Moutarde, later on the same night as Baha Mousa's death. The SIB personnel in fact arrived to begin their investigations the following day.

498. A serious incident report, or SINCREP was sent by 1 QLR to 19 Mech Bde. Moutarde had some input into the information contained in this report. The content of this report differed from the 1 QLR internal memo, entitled "Brief on Sudden Death of Internee" that had been sent to Mendonça. The description of a graphic struggle having occurred and the names of those some of those soldiers who played a part in the struggle with Baha Mousa: Payne, Pte Cooper, Redfearn, were absent from the SINCREP. The differences between these two documents are suspicious but there is insufficient evidence to conclude that Moutarde intended to provide misleading information to Brigade.

499. Peebles was responsible for the documents sent with the other Op Salerno Detainees to the TIF. He omitted to include information in these documents in relation to the medical conditions of, or treatment received by, the Detainees. In this regard I find that Peebles failed in his duty to ensure that the internment records for the Detainees properly reflected the complaints made and injuries suffered by the Detainees during the period in which they were in 1 QLR custody.

500. Suss-Francksen, 1 QLR's second in command, wrote a memorandum to Fenton as Brigade Chief of Staff arising out of the dispute at the TIF between Rodgers and S018 when the Detainees were delivered there. I find that in so doing, Suss-Francksen sought to counter any emerging criticism of 1 QLR. On balance, I find this memo to have been an attempt, ill judged in hindsight, to manage the reputation of 1 QLR in the eyes of the Brigade, rather than an attempt to mislead the investigations.

501. As stated, the SIB was properly informed of the death in order to begin the necessary investigation. However, there was an element of defensiveness within 1 QLR as illustrated by the actions of Suss-Francksen, Peebles and Moutarde. I find that individually each of these officers could have done more properly to communicate to senior levels the seriousness of the events that had occurred.

502. The death of Baha Mousa was also reported to the highest levels of Brigade and Division within a very short period. Both formation commanders were aware of the incident, at the latest, by early morning on Tuesday 16 September 2003.

503. It is apparent from the evidence which has emerged, notably email correspondence between staff officers at Brigade and Divisional level, that the level of tactical questioning resources was identified as a cause of the delay in transferring the Detainees to the TIF. It is also evident that it was rapidly understood that there needed to be a review of the tactical questioning procedure.

504. At Brigade level, on 16 September 2003, Fenton issued directions to the Legal and Intelligence branches of 19 Mech Bde to comment on the tactical questioning procedure and legal obligations. He also instructed the operations branch to be prepared to issue a Brigade standard operating procedure.

505. Two emails studied by the Inquiry were also relevant insofar as they revealed that there had been some knowledge, at Brigade level and before the death of Baha Mousa, of the use of hooding as part of the tactical questioning process, and not merely confined to security purposes.

506. In his email to other members of the Brigade directing that there be a review of procedures, Fenton had asked whether keeping detainees handcuffed and hooded was still allowed. He then followed this question by stating that he understood "... the need to maintain the 'pressure' in order to get a better product, but I feel we are going to have to work hard to justify this in future". I accept however that Fenton did not know of the use of hooding and stress positions before Baha Mousa's death.

507. Burbridge, the SO3 Ops at 19 Mech Bde, sent an email to Division and to colleagues in Brigade, providing details in relation to the treatment of the Detainees. He said that there was a requirement to hood as part of the tactical questioning, conditioning and disorientation process. I suspect that despite saying that he was not aware before Baha Mousa's death that hooding was used as part of the conditioning process, Burbridge may have had some such knowledge.

508. The death of Baha Mousa was also communicated promptly up to Ministerial level via PJHQ submissions. As part of this information, some of the detail of the reported circumstances of the detention of Baha Mousa was explained, such as the length of the period he was hooded, and the fact that he had persistently tried to escape from his handcuffs and hoods. Regrettably, it is now apparent that some of the information provided to Ministers in this initial report, in particular the suggestion that Baha Mousa repeatedly tried to escape, was not accurate. I have no doubt, however, that it recorded information that was being provided from theatre.

509. At Divisional level, Barnett, the Divisional legal adviser, sent an email on 17 September 2003, which made it clear that hooding for all purposes must immediately cease. He also directed that the Divisional Intelligence and Operations branches should prepare a Divisional standard operating instruction for both tactical questioning and guarding at Battlegroup and Brigade level. Having made some criticism of Barnett in relation to the content of FRAGO 005, it is right to note the clear and appropriate lead he gave following Baha Mousa's death in this email. I find that by 18 September 2003, there was a clear recognition that Divisional level guidance was required, and the Intelligence branch had taken the lead in creating these new instructions.

510. By 18 September 2003, as a result of the information gathered by 19 Mech Bde, Fenton produced a Brigade level report headed *Death in Detention*, to his Commander, Moore. It provided information including a chronology in relation to Baha Mousa's death. The detail for this chronology was provided by 1 QLR, and some of it was inaccurate. There was a notable omission in the report in that Fenton did not include his own telephone conversation with Suss-Francksen on Monday evening of the detention, concerning the reasons 1 QLR had not complied with the fourteen hour time limit.

511. On 18 September 2003, further information was provided to Ministers concerning the death. It was for information rather than seeking a decision. Ministers were told that it appeared hooding had taken place on the advice of one of the tactical questioners. They were told there was no documentation in theatre covering tactical questioning procedures but this was being reviewed urgently. The Minister of State, the Rt. Hon. Adam Ingram MP, expressed surprise that there were no such policies but noted the assurance that the shortcomings were being addressed.

512. From 19 to 20 September 2003 up to 30 September 2003 the new Divisional order Standard Operating Instruction 390 was being drafted. It was intended to be in two parts, one dealing with tactical questioning and the other dealing with detention. Email correspondence within Division during the draft stage revealed that it was understood at the time that such instruction should already have been in place.

513. The totality of the evidence demonstrates that this absence of proper instruction was immediately obvious at every level of the Op Telic 2 hierarchy after the death of Baha Mousa. In response, at 1 QLR, Peebles reviewed the Battlegroup's practices; at Brigade level a new standard operating procedure was directed to be drawn up; and at Divisional level it was recognised that an standard operating instruction was needed.

514. The changes in practice and procedure in theatre that were then put in place after the death were as follows.

515. At 1 QLR, Peebles drafted "Recommendations for 1 QLR Internment Procedures" dated 18 September 2003. It addressed the facilities used for holding detainees and the need for routine medical monitoring. It recommended that permission be sought for using blacked out goggles, that tactical questioning cease until a clearly defined policy was issued, and it recommended the reinstatement of the responsibility of the RP chain of command for the guarding of detainees.

516. Peebles also drew up a revised "1 QLR Internment Procedure", the document previously introduced by Royce. Captured persons were to be brought to BG Main as soon as possible and in any event within two hours of arrest. They were to be seen by the BGIRO and RMO, and had to be delivered to the TIF within fourteen hours. It was specified that there must be a medical inspection on arrival and at least three times within the fourteen hours of detention. Peebles also drafted a "Prisoner Handling Brief".

517. It is very surprising that these documents made such limited reference to the techniques of hooding and conditioning and no mention at all of stress positions, despite Peebles' knowledge of these practices by 1 QLR before and during Op Salerno. The content of the documents produced by Peebles in the aftermath of the death of Baha Mousa may have been intended in part to help to distance him from sole responsibility for the recent events. I accept, however, that he also recognised by this stage the inadequacy of the previously issued guidance.

518. At Brigade level, Fenton instructed Radbourne to produce a report into tactical questioning and prisoner handling procedures. As a result, on 27 September 2003, 19 Mech Bde issued a document entitled "Prisoner Handling and Tactical Questioning Procedures" which had been produced by Radbourne. This document, comprising a letter and annexes, provided guidance and set out instructions for the handling and tactical questioning of internees. Some but not all of it was drawn from the Divisional standard operating instruction that was in preparation.

519. Some of the guidance was perfectly appropriate. But other passages within this document referred to the guarding process as an important part of the conditioning process, and appeared to condone sleep deprivation as a method of continuing the shock of capture and conditioning process. The drafting, circulation and final approval of this text involved not only Radbourne, but also Fenton and Robinson. It is of concern that it was not recognised that some of the content of this document was inappropriate. The explanations for the more concerning aspects of its content were not convincing.

520. At Divisional level, Standard Operation Instructions 390 the "Policy for Apprehending, Handling and Treatment of Detainees and Internees", was issued by Barnett on 30 September 2003. It set out detailed requirements for the medical supervision of detainees, and directed that permission was to be sought from at least Brigade level to establish a tactical questioning operation. It specifically prohibited hooding and stress positions.

521. Thus, it can clearly be seen that before the death of Baha Mousa, the gap in prisoner handling and tactical questioning policy had not been addressed. Very soon after the death, each level of the hierarchy in theatre moved to close this gap. But there still remained some lack of clarity about the techniques that might be permitted within a process of conditioning.

Later Events Within The MoD (Part XV)

522. From the significant amount of evidence disclosed both to the Court Martial and to the Inquiry, this Report refers to the key developments within the MoD in the chronology after the death of Baha Mousa. I have focused on some illustrative examples of the statements and assurances that were given in relation to hooding and the other prohibited techniques and on the key developments in policy.

523. In October 2003, Reith, the Chief of Joint Operations reinforced the ban on hooding in letters to the Chief of Defence Intelligence, Maj Gen Andrew Ridgway, and to Maj Gen Lamb the GOC MND(SE).

524. In the letter to Maj Gen Lamb, it was directed that hooding was to stop and that Reith had been advised that blindfolding was an acceptable alternative means of sight deprivation and that he had accepted this advice. Blindfolds were only to be used for security purposes or to protect the detainee by preventing identification by other detainees. Additionally it was specified that blindfolds were only to be used for the minimum period necessary and with regular medical assessments. By the time this letter was sent, Standard Operating Instruction 390 had been issued in theatre, already prohibiting the practice of hooding.

525. The legal advice provided to Reith at this time was that hooding as an aid to interrogation would always be unlawful, but that hooding for security purposes might be lawful where sight deprivation by other means was not possible, provided appropriate precautions were taken. It can be seen that Reith, nevertheless, took the decision totally prohibit hooding in Iraq. I find this to have been a correct and responsible course to have taken.

526. In Reith's letter to Ridgway, in addition to the above direction on hooding and guidance on the use of blindfolds, Reith identified the need to review the doctrine and training in relation to prisoner handling techniques in order to ensure their legality. He sought to designate this task to Ridgway. Ridgway's reply to Maj Gen Lamb on 27 November 2003 highlighted the fact that the responsibilities in this area were complex and he suggested by whom appropriate action should be taken. Ridgway assured Reith that hooding had never been taught on any of the tactical questioning or interrogation courses at Chicksands. The letter also referred to hooding at the JFIT having been stopped due to medical advice. I accept Ridgway included this information in good faith. Objectively, however, these aspects were not wholly accurate.

527. Ridgway instituted a JSIO review relating to hooding in the context of tactical questioning and interrogation. This was not a wholesale review of all training in tactical questioning and interrogation. The prohibition on the use of hoods became somewhat more clearly emphasised on the training courses as a result. However, despite this review I find that the tactical questioning and interrogation doctrine remained inadequate. To take but one example, it was inadequate in the continuing guidance advocating walking around a blindfolded prisoner to increase the pressure before the blindfold was removed for questioning.

528. Ridgway was entitled to point out that the action required in respect of Reith's request for a review lay with a number of other departments. However, I find that the collective response to Reith's request for a review of doctrine and training was limited and slow. By 2004, there were still complaints that doctrine in this area was notably lacking.

529. The Inquiry has identified an unsatisfactory pattern of inaccurate assurances and explanations given within the MoD statements and Ministerial briefing materials. In particular, in the light of evidence available at the time, the MoD should not have made the positive suggestion that hooding had not been used in the context of tactical questioning during Op Telic 1 and 2. There was no justification at all for the suggestion that hooding had been stopped *when conditions on the ground permitted*". Further statements suggesting that hooding at the JFIT had not gone beyond the normal use for arrest/transit were also inaccurate and prone to mislead.

530. There are no proper grounds to conclude that any individual sought deliberately to mislead in providing this information and I do not seek to single out individuals for criticism. However, it is fair to say that officials could and should have done more to ensure the accuracy of these statements. The existence of other statements also given by the MoD which were fuller and more accurate is testament to a lack of intention to mislead. But this also points to a failure in the MoD's systems for ensuring the greatest possible accuracy of its public statements. I accept that the understandably incomplete picture transmitted from theatre, some inconsistencies in the information which was provided to those outside theatre, and the high number of requests for information which had to be met while other operational demands were extremely high, are likely to have been contributory factors to the inaccuracies in statements that were made. However, I detect that there was at times a corporate tendency towards an overly defensive line in response to difficult questions. It would have been better had the MoD faced more squarely and more openly the mistakes and shortcomings that had already been identified in relation to hooding and tactical questioning.

531. By May 2004 the hooding of prisoners had been prohibited in all theatres of operations. However, it had not been expressly determined that hoods would never be used in the future for security and transit purposes. A review into whether or not the use hoods for limited purposes was a policy that should be retained was then instigated by the Chief of the Defence Staff, Lord Walker. A draft submission and detailed background paper had been produced by August 2004.

532. It recommended that despite legal, medical and presentational concerns, it remained operationally desirable to restrict temporarily the vision of detainees in particular circumstances. It was also recommended that UK Armed Forces should be provided with clear guidance on when the restriction of vision was acceptable and by what means. It suggested that blacked out goggles should be the preferred method, but that an ability to use hoods as a last resort should be retained. It was recognised that this course of action would require Parliament to be advised of the change in policy and practice, and that it may be controversial and attract negative publicity.

533. That recommendation, permitting hooding *in extremis*, was not ultimately adopted by the MoD and, accordingly, the use of hoods has continued to be prohibited albeit as a matter of operational policy rather than legal obligation.

Recommendations (Part XVII)

534. Arising out of the Inquiry's investigation, I have made 73 recommendations. These follow what I believe was an open and beneficial examination of current policy and practice during the Inquiry's Module 4 hearings. Current practice and the background to my recommendations are discussed in Part XVI of this Report. The recommendations themselves are listed in Part XVII.